MARKE....G

MARKETING

an introduction

#MKTG4E

Rosalind Masterson
Nichola Phillips
David Pickton

Los Angeles | London | New Delhi
Singapore | Washington DC | Melbourne

Los Angeles | London | New Delhi
Singapore | Washington DC | Melbourne

SAGE Publications Ltd
1 Oliver's Yard
55 City Road
London EC1Y 1SP

SAGE Publications Inc.
2455 Teller Road
Thousand Oaks, California 91320

SAGE Publications India Pvt Ltd
B 1/I 1 Mohan Cooperative Industrial Area
Mathura Road
New Delhi 110 044

SAGE Publications Asia-Pacific Pte Ltd
3 Church Street
#10-04 Samsung Hub
Singapore 049483

Editor: Matthew Waters
Development editor: Sarah Turpie
Production editor: Sarah Cooke
Assistant editor, digital: Chloe Statham
Marketing manager: Alison Borg
Cover design: Francis Kenney
Typeset by: C&M Digitals (P) Ltd, Chennai, India
Printed in the UK by Bell & Bain Ltd, Glasgow

Library of Congress Control Number: 2017930845

British Library Cataloguing in Publication data

A catalogue record for this book is available from the British Library

ISBN 978-1-47397-584-2
ISBN 978-1-47397-585-9 (pbk)
ISBN 978-1-52642-632-1 (pbk & interactive ebk) (IEB)

At SAGE we take sustainability seriously. Most of our products are printed in the UK using FSC papers and boards. When we print overseas we ensure sustainable papers are used as measured by the PREPS grading system. We undertake an annual audit to monitor our sustainability.

CONTENTS

PART ONE: THIS IS MARKETING

1

MARKETING TODAY

2

THE MARKETING ENVIRONMENT

PART TWO: MAKING SENSE OF MARKETS

3

BUYER BEHAVIOUR

4

MARKET SEGMENTATION, TARGETING AND POSITIONING

5

MARKETING RESEARCH

PART THREE: THE MARKETING MIX

6

PRODUCT

7

SERVICE PRODUCTS

8

PROMOTION (MARKETING COMMUNICATIONS)

9

PLACE

10

PRICE

PART FOUR: MANAGING MARKETING

11

BUILDING BRANDS: USING THE MARKETING MIX

12

MARKETING PLANNING

FOR LECTURERS

A selection of tried and tested teaching resources have been honed and developed to accompany this text and support your course. Visit https://edge.sagepub.com/masterson4e to set up or use your instructor login to access:

- Editable and adaptable PowerPoint slides to integrate into your teaching

- A tutor's manual providing ideas and inspiration for seminars and tutorials, and guidance on how you might use the features in the book in your own teaching

- A selection of Testbank questions to use with your students

ABOUT THE AUTHORS

ROSALIND MASTERSON was a Principal Lecturer at De Montfort University until 2013. She has taught extensively, and has been subject and programme leader, at both undergraduate and postgraduate levels. This book came about as part of an extensive redesign of the university's core first-year undergraduate module: *Principles of Marketing*. She has taught, and been an external examiner, at a number of universities during an academic career spanning twenty years.

Rosalind's commercial experience includes sales and marketing positions within IBM and marketing management for an IT consultancy. She ran her own marketing consultancy and freelance copywriting business for ten years.

Rosalind is a Chartered Institute of Marketing Chartered Marketer, a Member of the Academy of Marketing and a Fellow of the Higher Education Academy.

NICHOLA PHILLIPS is a Senior Lecturer in the Department of Strategic Management and Marketing at De Montfort University. She has developed and taught a range of marketing modules at undergraduate and postgraduate levels. Her research interests centre on digital and transitional identities and online consumer socialisation processes.

An experienced public relations consultant, Nichola has co-ordinated successful campaigns for major consumer brands including Britvic, Johnson & Johnson, Kellogg's, Ladbrokes and Microsoft' MSN network of Internet sites and services, for whom she also acted as Interim PR Manager for Europe, Middle East and Africa. Nichola has a first class degree in Experimental Psychology from the University of Oxford, a Postgraduate Certificate in Higher Education from De Montfort University and is a Fellow of the Higher Education Academy.

DAVID PICKTON is Associate Director, Strategic Partnerships, Visiting Academic, University of Birmingham and Honorary Academic Fellow at De Montfort University having been founding member of its academic Marketing Department and its Head. He has been a visiting lecturer and external examiner at over 20 universities in the UK and internationally.

He is an Editorial Board member of the *Journal of Marketing Communications, Innovative Marketing Journal and Marketing Intelligence and Planning*, and, previously, on the *Journal of Brand Management* and *Corporate Communications: An International Journal*. He has written numerous articles and contributed to various academic texts.

His commercial experience includes marketing management positions on both the client and agency sides of industry, directorship of his own business consultancy and providing executive marketing and management training.

His professional affiliations have included Membership of the Academy of Marketing and Fellowships of the Chartered Institute of Marketing, the Royal Society of Arts and the Higher Education Academy.

ACKNOWLEDGEMENTS

The authors would like to extend their warmest thanks to the contributors to previous editions of this book:

Tony Garry

Len Tiu Wright

Kit Jackson

Phil Garton

Lynn Stainsby

Chris Vaughan-Jones

Tracy Harwood

WHY LECTURERS CHOOSE IT

AN EXCELLENT INTRODUCTION TO ALL THE KEY ASPECTS OF MARKETING. THE NEW EDITION ADDRESSES MANY OF THE LATEST TRENDS AND INCORPORATES A RICH VARIETY OF REAL—LIFE EXAMPLES TO REALLY ENGAGE THE STUDENT

Mohammed Hanif—Patel,
Senior Lecturer, De Montfort University

WHY STUDENTS *LOVE IT*

An engaging and intuitive book to guide students through the marketing world. Not only does it present key principles in a clear way, but it provides examples to improve knowledge acquisition as well. The succinctness of this book made exam revision much easier.

**GOSIA WARWASZYNSKA,
FIRST YEAR STUDENT
INTERNATIONAL MARKETING
& BUSINESS WITH MANDARIN**

This book is easy to read and revise from due to the use of colour and images. It also usefully guides you to wider reading around topics, through the research focus boxes which can help you with essays!

**ELENA STEVENS,
FIRST YEAR STUDENT
ADVERTISING AND MARKETING
COMMUNICATIONS**

YOUR GUIDE to

GET TO KNOW YOUR FOCUS BOXES

Look out for them in every chapter, colour coded according to key marketing themes

digital   **ethical**   **b2b**   **global**   **research**

EXPLORES
DIGITAL INNOVATIONS,
SOCIAL MEDIA
MARKETING
AND ONLINE CAMPAIGNS

digital focus

ILLUSTRATES THE
IMPORTANCE OF
SUSTAINABILITY AND
ETHICAL PRACTICES TO
MARKETING TODAY

ethical focus

LOOKS AT
MARKETING EXAMPLES
FROM AROUND THE
WORLD AND
ACROSS CULTURES

global focus

using THIS BOOK

WHAT KIND OF READER ARE YOU?

DIGITAL

See inside front cover for instructions on how to access your FREE Interactive eBook

PRINT

Open the book, enjoy the feel and hold of your print copy and start reading

NOT SURE?

Take our quiz to find out: **https://edge.sagepub.com/ masterson4e/student- resources/reader-type**

HIGHLIGHTS KEY EXAMPLES FROM A MAJOR AREA OF EMPLOYMENT IN MARKETING, BUSINESS-TO- BUSINESS (B2B)

b2b focus

CLASSIC ARTICLES AND CUTTING EDGE RESEARCH SUMMARISED TO HELP YOU EXPAND YOUR KNOWLEDGE AROUND KEY TOPICS FOR ASSIGNMENTS AND EXAMS

research focus

MINI CASES

AT THE END OF <u>EVERY</u> CHAPTER SHOW YOU HOW IT ALL COMES TOGETHER IN REAL LIFE.

TURN THE PAGE TO FIND THE FULL LIST OF FOCUS BOXES

digital focus

ethical focus

b2b focus

global focus

research focus

PUBLISHER'S ACKNOWLEDGEMENTS

We are very grateful to everyone who has granted kind permission to reproduce their material in this book.

LECTURER REVIEWERS

We would also like to extend our warmest thanks to the following individuals for their invaluable feedback on the previous edition and the draft material for this book:

Michael Bane, National College of Ireland (NCI)

Riccardo Benzo, Birkbeck College, University of London

Graham Harrison, University of Sussex

Orla Higgins, NUI Galway

Joe Liddiatt, University of the West of England

Charlotte Lystor, University of Winchester

Ben Marder, University of Edinburgh

Judy Taft, Nottingham Trent University

Jason Turner, Abertay University

Nicola Williams-Burnett, Cardiff Metropolitan University

STUDENT CONSULTANTS

A special thank you to the following students for providing invaluable feedback on the text:

Danielle Aitken

Arlynn Baer

Beth Barnett

Georgia Blood

Ananda Buraityte

Matthew Burdett

Olivia-Hope Butler

Mundip Chaggar

Abby Cotter

Elizabeth Epton

Emma Hogland

Kristine Ljoner

Amro Mahmoud

Abdullah Okaroh

Carolyn Singleton

Elena Stevens

Daria Szotek

Malgorzata Warwaszynska

Holly Wright

WHAT THIS PART IS ABOUT

The term 'marketing' comes literally from market: a place where traders go to sell and customers come to buy. Sellers have always tried to show their products to advantage, and buyers have always looked for good value. This has not changed. However, marketing has come a long way since the days when traders travelled around the market towns with their goods packed in a wagon.

The first part of this book looks back at marketing history to show where the marketing discipline has come from in order to shed light on its strengths and limitations. It explains why marketing is more important today than it was in earlier times. It looks at how marketing has evolved into such a sophisticated business discipline and also briefly considers the key aspects of modern marketing.

All business organisations, and most non-commercial organisations too, are built around six main business functions: marketing, finance, operations (or manufacturing), human resources (HR), Research and Development (R&D) and Information Systems (IS) or Information Technology (IT). Marketers must work with their colleagues from other disciplines in order to make the best use of the resources available. However, no organisation exists in isolation. It has to interact with other organisations and with individuals. Successful marketing depends upon a thorough understanding of the context in which the organisation is operating. Good marketers will be prepared for changes in their world and so they are constantly scanning their marketing environment and making changes to their plans.

PART ONE

THIS IS MARKETING

MARKETING TODAY

MARKETING CHALLENGES

At the start of each chapter in this book, you will find several challenges. They are there to help you see the significance of the chapter you are about to read. *You aren't expected to know how to deal with the challenges now*; just bear them in mind as you read the chapter and see what you can find that helps.

Degree to job: IBM

- You tell friends who are studying sciences that you are doing a marketing course. One says, 'You're studying advertising, what fun.' Is he right? Is marketing just another name for advertising?

- You are the marketing manager for a large university. Funds are always short. A local bar owner has offered the university Registry a substantial amount of money for its list of student names and mobile numbers so that he can text them with a very tempting offer to visit the bar. The Registry wants your advice.

- You are an assistant manager in an electronics store. The shop is in a quite poor area and business is slow. You have a lot of set top boxes that are getting harder to sell now that all new TVs are digital and able to receive free channels anyway. The manager has offered the sales staff bonuses for every set top box sold. Other salespeople are selling them but they are telling customers that the boxes are needed to receive digital channels on new TVs – and you know this is not true. What will you do?

- Winston Smith installs CCTV systems for a living. He is self-employed and all his jobs are one-offs. Today he's very annoyed because he's just seen someone else adding to one of his systems. The customer was pleased with the work Winston did but couldn't remember his name, so he got someone else in when the system needed enlarging. How could Winston have got that job himself?

INTRODUCTION

A market is a place where things are bought and sold. It is often defined as a place where buyers and sellers meet.

Marketers are the sellers. They set out their stalls, displaying goods to their best advantage, and then try to attract buyers. Of course, modern marketing is rather more complex than a street market, but it is still about attracting customers, serving them well, competing with others and making a **profit** (usually). Marketing is a customer-focused discipline centred on

profit

the difference between what something costs to make and the price for which it is sold

an exchange between two (or more) parties. That exchange is at the centre of marketing activity and is usually of products for money. Good marketing brings about fair exchanges where both sides feel that they have got good value.

In this chapter, marketing is introduced through a brief look at how it evolved to become what it is today. We will consider current marketing issues and where marketing might be tomorrow.

Some organisations see themselves as marketing companies, while others see themselves as primarily manufacturers, or as financially excellent, or perhaps as innovators. They may have different strategic orientations (strategic orientations are explained fully below) but all businesses need customers, ideally loyal ones. The importance of cultivating and managing customer relationships will also be introduced here.

Towards the end of this chapter, there are overviews of some of the key developments in modern marketing.

WHAT IS MARKETING?

The two most commonly quoted definitions of marketing come from the Chartered Institute of Marketing (CIM) and the American Marketing Association (AMA).

The first definition of marketing is:

> The management process which identifies, anticipates and satisfies customer requirements efficiently and profitably. (Chartered Institute of Marketing, n.d.)

This definition stresses the need for management action to understand what customers really want from products. A product must meet customer needs physically (e.g. it should work), psychologically (e.g. they should feel good about owning it), financially (e.g. they should be able to afford it) and timewise (e.g. it should not take too long to actually get it). For the company, this may involve considerable market research and analysis.

Take a moment to think about what people really want from a pair of shoes. Clearly, they need to fit and they need to be affordable, but what else? They may also need to be comfortable, although how comfortable will depend on whether they are high-fashion shoes or walking boots or something in between. It is unlikely that customers will be prepared to travel too far to buy a pair of shoes; they need to be easily purchased. As a final act before purchase, customers usually walk up and down in the shop, look in the mirror, see if the shoes suit them. Do they feel right? Do they look good? Do they make the wearer *feel* good? With today's plethora of choice, this may be the most important consideration.

The second definition of marketing is:

> Marketing is the activity, set of institutions, and processes for creating, communicating, delivering, and exchanging offerings that have value for customers, clients, partners, and society at large. (American Marketing Association, 2013)

Traditional markets are the origin of the term 'marketing'.

© Dave Pickton

The AMA's definition looks for balance between the needs of the firm, the needs of the **customer** and the needs of other **stakeholders**. There are a number of ways in which marketing can create value, most obviously through good products and prices, but also through good service, convenience and any number of imaginative other ways. The AMA's previous definition (2004) referred to 'the organisation and its stakeholders', however, the new one makes more specific reference to 'society at large' and therefore embraces **societal marketing** for the first time.

(The **coloured** words can be found in the glossary at the back of the book.)

customer

a buyer of a product or service

stakeholders

individuals or groups who are involved in, or affected by, the organisation's actions and/or performance

---

research focus: classic concept

Kotler, P. and Levy, S. (1969) 'Broadening the scope of marketing', *Journal of Marketing***, 33 (Jan): 10–15.**
This article argued against focusing marketing too narrowly and asserted that organisations of all types undertake marketing activities. As the authors conclude, 'no organisation can avoid marketing. The choice is whether to do it well or poorly'.

MIXED TERMINOLOGY: CONCEPT, PHILOSOPHY OR FUNCTION?

Marketing can be viewed in many different ways. It is:

- a function
- a department
- a discipline
- a concept
- a philosophy
- an orientation.

societal marketing

meeting customers' needs and wants in a way that enhances the long-term well-being of consumers and the society in which they live

First, let's distinguish between the marketing 'function' and the marketing 'department'. Function is a wider concept. It embraces all marketing activity within the organisation – whether or not it is carried out by members of the marketing department. The department is a defined part of the organisation in which specialist marketers work. They report to marketing managers and directors who lead the department. The distinction is important because, in a truly market-orientated organisation (see below for an explanation of **market orientation**), everyone will think marketing and, at least some of the time, carry out marketing-related activities.

For example, reception staff could be said to play a key role in the maintenance of a company's image and the building of relationships with customers; they do not report to the marketing manager, and are not part of marketing staff, but they do perform a marketing function as part of their job. See Exhibit 1.1 for the most common marketing activities

market orientation

provision of customer value determines an organisation's direction

Marketing research and analysis – *where and who we are now*
Market research – who are our customers and what do they want?
Competitive research – who are our competitors and what do they do?
What is our position in the market? (market share, customer views)
Organisational research – what are we good at? (organisational strengths)
What are we bad at? (organisational weaknesses)
What have we done that worked well in the past? (e.g. promotions)
Are we risk takers?
Objective setting – *where and who we want to be*
Targets – e.g. market share, profits, sales, brand image, brand awareness, numbers of sales outlets, locations where products are available (at home and abroad), new product launches, product updates, customer satisfaction levels ...
Marketing tasks – *how we are going to make it happen*
Planning – selecting and scheduling marketing tasks
Staff – suitably selecting and training
Budgets – allocating to activities
Promotion – advertising, PR, sales promotions, sales force support, direct marketing, packaging, website, social media, etc.
Sales – finding new customers, getting repeat business
Pricing – setting prices, discounts, credit terms, etc.
Distribution – stock holding, packaging, shipping, order handling, etc.
Product management – development, dropping old products, standardisation, adaptation to suit different customers, etc.
Branding – visual design, brand strategy, brand identity
Market entry – selling in new markets (directly or through a third party)
Customer service – complaints handling, after-sales service, warranties and guarantees
Customer management – customer database, events/actions designed to build relationships
Collecting feedback and controlling activities – *how we will keep track of things*
Objectives – have they been achieved? Are they likely to be achieved?
Customer feedback – complaints, compliments, recommendations, repeat buys, satisfaction surveys
Checklists and deadlines – have things happened on time?
Market position – are we doing better/worse than our competitors?

EXHIBIT 1.1 Marketing activities

The 'discipline' of marketing is of primary interest to students and their tutors. Discipline means 'field of study' (Allen, 2000). Organisations are more likely to consider marketing as a function or a department.

Academic researchers are more concerned with the marketing 'concept', marketing 'philosophy' and market 'orientation' though the distinction between these terms is sometimes unclear. They are used differently within different texts and journal articles. Sometimes they are even used interchangeably with no real distinction drawn between the terms. These differences in definition are less important than the principles behind marketing – and are not something to be too concerned about at this stage. Just be aware that such terms are often substituted for each other, without there being any great significance to the way they are used.

'Market orientation' is another term that gets thrown into this mix. An organisation's strategic orientation provides 'the guiding principles that influence a firm's marketing and strategy making activities' (Noble et al., 2002: 25) and so determines how it will interact with its marketplace. Orientation literally means the way a person, or organisation, faces. Market-orientated firms, then, look to markets and markets are made up of buyers and sellers, so a truly market-orientated organisation ought to be both customer and competition facing. (Strategic orientations are covered in more detail below.)

For the purposes of this textbook, the terms 'marketing concept' and 'marketing philosophy' will be used in a similar way. 'Market orientation' will be used to describe those firms that have embraced the marketing philosophy (or concept) and use it to inform all their activities and strategies. So a true market orientation requires marketing actions, not just thoughts or intentions.

ACTIVITY

What does BOGOF stand for?
If you don't know, look it up in the glossary at the back of the book. (All terms in **coloured text** can be found in the glossary and terms are also defined in the margins.)

WHAT MARKETING IS NOT

The world, even the business world, has some erroneous ideas about what marketing is. It is worth being aware of these (it may save some confusion) as it is important to be clear that marketing is not just selling, **advertising**, **promotion** or **marketing communications**. Let's take selling first. Although the idea of selling pre-dates that of marketing, many marketers would claim that selling is a part of marketing, an important part. The underlying aim of most marketing activity is to make sales. However, this could be said to be the underlying aim of most business activities. After all, where is the profit without sales? The clear importance of commercial organisations making sales has led to a counter-movement where sales is held to be a discrete function worthy of a sales director on the board – though this may be a consequence of a more limited view of the nature of marketing.

Peter Drucker, a world-renowned marketer, once famously said: 'The aim of marketing is to make selling superfluous'. Companies should know their customers so well that they only make products that the customers actively want and then a hard sell is unnecessary.

advertising
a persuasive communication paid for by an identifiable source and addressed to the whole of a **target audience** without personal identification

marketing communications
another name for **promotion**; communication designed and implemented to persuade others to do, think or feel something

So selling is a part of marketing, but not all of it. In fact, it would be more accurate to say that selling is a part of marketing communications or promotion (these are alternative terms for the same thing), and that marketing communications is part of marketing. Marketing communications (promotion) will be covered in more depth in Chapter 8. It is a collective term for all the activities that an organisation undertakes to promote its products to its customers. Such activities may include holding **press conferences**, designing appealing packaging, making promotional offers such as prize draws and BOGOFs, supporting websites, sponsoring sports teams and advertising, which means that advertising is only part of marketing communications, which in turn is part of marketing. Clearly, there must be more to marketing than just advertising. So what is included in marketing besides promotional activities?

press conference

a meeting at which journalists are briefed

market research

the systematic gathering, recording and analysing of customer and other market-related data

global focus: the hard sell

It may seem obvious that there are more subtle and effective ways to persuade someone to buy than the hard sell technique, but it depends. In many countries, and some situations, a hard sell is needed. It may even be part of the local culture. If you have ever been a tourist anywhere, but particularly in a less-developed country, then you will almost certainly have been subjected to a hard sell. Trinkets, local crafts, postcards, boat tickets, even accommodation, are thrust at tourists as soon as they arrive anywhere. Many sales are made (and many are later regretted by the new owner of a stuffed donkey or undrinkable local liqueur).

Holiday souvenirs are typical one-off transactions.

© S. Borisov/Shutterstock

brand

used to differentiate between similar products by means of a set of visual cues (e.g. logos) that represent the brand's attributes and associations (e.g. history)

competitive advantage

something about an organisation or its products that is perceived as being better than rival offerings

One of the biggest areas of marketing is **market research** (see Chapter 5). Research is vital in understanding customer needs, buyer behaviour (see Chapter 3) and how to design goods and services to meet those needs. Without new product development (see Chapter 6) a company will die. Marketing is also concerned with getting the right products to the right place at the right time, and so distribution (place) is key (see Chapter 9). Those products also need to be at the right price (Chapter 10) or they will not sell.

Although marketing definitions tend to be centred on customers, marketing is also about understanding your competitors (competitive intelligence) and devising strategies to beat them. Strong branding is a commonly used competitive strategy. Think of the sportswear market; it has some of the strongest, most valuable **brands** – Nike, Adidas, Reebok, Sergio Tachini, Umbro, Head. There are many of them but some are stronger than others and therefore have a **competitive advantage** over their rivals. Yet how much is there to choose in terms of quality, value for money, even style, between Nike shorts and those made by Adidas?

Marketing, then, encompasses a large number of business activities (see Exhibit 1.1).

BEFORE MARKETING

In a subsistence economy, such as the poorest in the world today, there is very little trade. Only when people have a surplus of goods do they swap them with other people for different things. So if farmers have an abundance of apples, say, they may go to market and try to trade them for something else. If they only have enough to feed their own families, there will be no apples left over for others to buy. So markets, and marketing, are only found where the economy has developed beyond these very early stages.

In Europe, before industrialisation, the emphasis was on making enough goods to supply people's needs, not on persuading them to buy them. There is no need to be persuasive when there are not enough shoes, soap or sugar to go round anyway. There was a time when goods were produced in small quantities, sold locally and farmers or craftspeople sold everything they made. There were enough local buyers and no need for the expense, and risk, of travelling to find more custom. So marketing is a relatively new discipline.

Those markets were **supply-led**, not **demand-driven**. That is, the challenge lay in producing enough to meet customers' needs rather than in persuading customers to choose your products. However, as factories opened and towns developed, there were more goods available and the city workers became more reliant on buying things from others to meet their needs. They did not have land on which to grow their own vegetables or keep animals. They needed to buy food with the wages they earned. Farms became larger and so produced surpluses that could be sold at market. Smaller farmers sold their surplus food to intermediaries, who would take it to market for them, where it would be sold alongside other products from other parts of the country, or even overseas.

This represented a major change in the way that goods were sold. Sellers no longer had direct contact with their buyers; there were agents and shopkeepers in between. This had two effects: first, it meant that they were not as aware of customers' requirements, relying as they did upon these intermediaries, and, second, it meant that customers no longer knew their suppliers – they only knew the shopkeepers or stallholders.

So the smarter producers made conscious efforts to find out what customers wanted – i.e. they began to conduct rudimentary market research (largely through those same intermediaries). Some also badged their products so that customers could recognise them. These makers' marks were an early form of branding.

The factories brought with them an even more significant change. Their new mass-production techniques meant that there was a greater supply of products and that they were cheaper. Initially, the focus was still on finding more efficient ways to produce larger quantities as people queued up to buy all these new cheap products. There was more than enough demand to keep the early factories going. However, technology continued to improve and the volume of products available grew until there was no longer a shortage but a surfeit of almost everything. Today's suppliers cannot rely on people to buy everything they produce. They have to compete for customers. In such a situation, they need good marketing skills.

There are still a few supply-led markets though. Some modern products are in short supply just by their nature (e.g. precious stones or antiques), others by design (e.g. limited-edition prints or collectibles). Have you ever struggled to buy a festival or football match ticket? Perhaps you have even paid more than the face value? These are modern-day, supply-led markets.

supply-led

when shortages of goods mean that suppliers can dictate terms of business

demand-driven

when a surplus, or potential surplus, of products to be sold gives the buyers more power than the sellers

THE EVOLUTION OF MARKETING

Before mass production, value for money, pleasant service, a shop sign, a maker's mark and a reputation built by word of mouth were enough to keep a business afloat. Modern marketing is clearly more complex than that, although those early good-business principles are still valid today. More sophisticated marketing techniques were originally developed for the everyday, high-volume products of the new mass-production techniques: washing powder, toothpaste, shoe polish, soap, foodstuffs, etc. They were easier to make and so there were more companies making them. At the same time, transport improved. There were roads, railways and canals available to ship goods to other parts of the country. Consumers had lots of choice and competition became an issue.

These mass-produced products acquired **brand names**, had posters and **press advertisements**, were sold on special offer, and were adjusted to suit customer tastes and to be better than rival products. Manufacturers clearly could not sell such large volumes to so many customers directly and so the intermediaries, the shopkeepers and **wholesalers** became more significant. They were persuaded to stock products (and perhaps not to stock rivals' products), to display them more prominently, to recommend them to customers. So a number of factors led to the birth of marketing, the main ones being:

brand name

the product's, or product line's, given name

press advertisements

adverts placed in printed media such as newspapers and magazines

wholesaler

a reseller, buying products in bulk to sell on to other businesses in smaller quantities

- breakthroughs in production technology
- advances in the technology for transporting goods (particularly railways)
- social changes such as the move away from the countryside and into towns
- increased competition.

marketing environment

the forces and organisations that impact on an organisation's marketing activities

These forces still drive marketing today. Technological advances (such as cloud computing, sophisticated data analysis and the popularity of social media and mobile technologies) still have the power to change the way we sell goods and services. Air freight has made it possible to have fresh foods from around the world. It means we can have tropical fruits in northern Europe all year round. The changing age profile of our population means more products are developed for, and aimed at, older age groups. In many parts of the world, people are leaving rural areas and heading for the towns to find work. They have to buy food that they might previously have grown for themselves. They need housing and transport, etc. Competition now is global; it is no longer limited to rivals based in the same town, or even the same country. European Union (EU) companies compete fiercely with each other across the region – and across the world. The wealth of Europe attracts American, Canadian, Japanese, Chinese, African and Asian competitors. Almost all countries across the world are home to at least some internationally competitive companies.

Marketing had to evolve to cope with the increased supply of goods from mass production techniques.

© Gemenacom/Shutterstock

You will learn more about how these forces shape marketing – and indeed our world – in later chapters, particularly Chapter 2 which looks at the **marketing environment**. 'Global focus' boxes throughout the text provide further insights into the nature of global competition.

DEMAND AND SUPPLY

The concepts of **demand** and **supply** are fundamental in business – and in marketing. The word 'demand' causes some confusion. It is being used here in its economic sense, i.e. it means what people will buy, not just what they would like if only they could afford it, find it, etc.

Today, most markets are demand-driven. This means that the amount of goods made available for sale is dependent upon the customers and how much they will buy. In a supply-led market, the amount of goods available would depend on how much could be produced.

In a supply-led market, the most successful companies will be those that are the most efficient producers. Everything they can make will be bought. However, in a demand-driven market, companies have to compete for custom, hence the modern-day importance of marketing. It is the job of marketers to stimulate demand, to provide the goods and services that people want, and to persuade them to buy.

Ideally, demand should equal supply exactly. At this point firms maximise sales without having anything left over. The point where the supply curve and the demand curve cross (see Exhibit 1.2) is called the equilibrium point. At this price, customers will want to buy just exactly the amount that suppliers want to sell. Take the example of a book publisher. The easiest way to make sure that all its books are sold would be to produce fewer books than demanded. However, this would mean that some customers will be unable to get copies and the publishing firm will miss out on potential sales and so make less profit. It would be in its interest to print more books.

demand

quantity of goods that customers buy at a certain price, i.e. sales

supply

quantity of goods that sellers are prepared to put on the market at a certain price

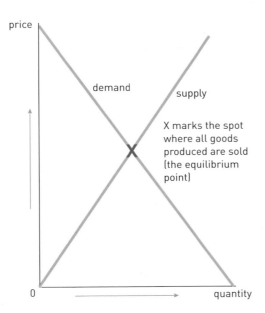

EXHIBIT 1.2 Demand and supply

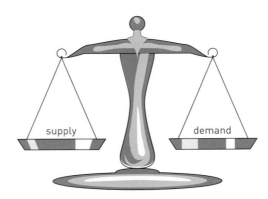

EXHIBIT 1.3 Equilibrium

EXCHANGES

exchange

when two parties swap items perceived to be of approximately equal value

It is often said that marketing is about managing the **exchange** process. If you exchange something, you part with something of value (e.g. a product or an idea) in return for something else of value. The 'something else of value' is, of course, usually money, though it could be another product.

Clearly, there must be two parties to an exchange: the seller and the buyer. Each wants to exchange something for something else that they value more. So the car that the customer is buying must be a car that he or she wants more than the money he or she will part with in order to obtain it, and the car dealer would rather have the money than the car standing on the forecourt. This may sound obvious, but it is a concept worth remembering as you move on to more complex marketing ideas. This valued exchange is at the heart of marketing. If we cannot offer customers goods and services that are worth more to them than whatever they have to give up to obtain them, then we will not sell much.

Good marketing will create and maintain mutually beneficial exchange relationships. They may be very short-term relationships, if the sale is a one-off, or ongoing ones if a company is looking for repeat business. To be sure of repeat business, a company needs to make its customers loyal and loyalty should, of course, be a two-way street. The company needs to be consistent in its good treatment of its customers if it wants the same in return.

Customers give up more than just money. They give up time: the time taken to check out the other options, to test drive other cars, for example. They put in effort that could have been expended doing something else. They have to weigh up the pros and cons of each possible car in order to make their decision. Sometimes customers will pay more for something just because it is less hassle, or quicker, or safer, or for any number of other good reasons. For example, train tickets are cheaper if booked in advance, but it is often just not convenient to book ahead. Many products can be bought more cheaply on the Internet, but not everyone trusts Internet sales. Vegetables are usually much cheaper when bought from a market stall than from supermarkets, but still you see lots of people with supermarket carrier bags full of them.

Customers take a risk when they hand over their money for a product. The product may not do the job it is being bought for, or may not work at all. It may go out of fashion. It may not suit them or other people may not like it. A good salesperson recognises this and tries to reassure customers that the risk is minimal and worth taking.

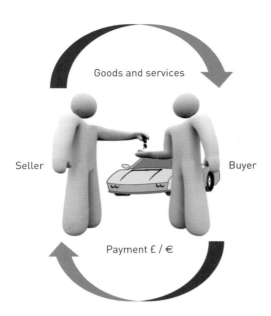

EXHIBIT 1.4 An exchange of value

MARKETS

A **market** is a place where buyers and sellers meet. The term is often made more complex, but it is worth hanging on to that simple definition.

There are lots of different markets (e.g. consumer markets, industrial markets, **b2b** markets, overseas markets). These are broad groups of buyers and sellers, and they can be narrowed down into smaller groupings such as product type (e.g. **white goods** market) or customer type (e.g. youth market) or a combination (e.g. children's clothing market). Often, when people refer to 'markets' they are using the term interchangeably with 'customers'. However, a market needs sellers too and so any thorough study of a market should also include the seller – and its competitors. Exhibit 1.5 provides a framework for categorising markets.

market
a composite of individuals or organisations that have a willingness and ability to purchase products; a market can consist of single or multiple segments

b2b (business-to-business)
business dealings with another business as opposed to a consumer

white goods
large electrical appliances for domestic use, e.g. fridges, washing machines (traditionally coloured white)

Market	Typical purchase descriptions	Purchase
Business-to-consumer (b2c) markets	Personal purchases	E.g. household weekly shop
Industrial markets	Things that will be used in the making of other things	E.g. glass to go into headlights for cars, cooling fluids for machinery
business-to-business (b2b) markets	Things for use in the course of another business	E.g. delivery vans
Not-for-profit markets	Purchases and marketing activities by charities, government organisations, trades unions, clubs and associations, etc.	E.g. as other organisations

(Continued)

EXHIBIT 1.5 (Continued)

Market	Typical purchase descriptions	Purchase
Government markets	Purchases by central government, local government, health services, schools, public libraries, armed forces, police, etc.	E.g. office supplies
Reseller markets	Goods to be sold on, e.g. by retailers, wholesalers, distributors, dealers, etc.	E.g. anything found for sale in a shop
Overseas markets	All above categories – but in other countries or outside the home country's trading bloc (e.g. the EU)	Could be anything at all
Internal markets	Other divisions, subsidiaries or employees of the organisation itself	E.g. own product sales (usually at discounted prices), services provided by one division for another in the same organisation

EXHIBIT 1.5 Market classifications

STRATEGIC ORIENTATIONS

Different organisations take different approaches when it comes to achieving their objectives. Almost all (the successful ones anyway) will have a strategy to guide their future actions but there are many ways to achieve success. The strategies themselves, and the thinking behind them, vary. If an organisation has embraced a marketing philosophy, then the needs and wants of its customers, coupled with a recognition of what competitors offer them, will be the driving force behind its thinking. That organisation will be market-orientated.

However, 'market' is not the only strategic orientation an organisation could adopt. Exhibit 1.6 shows some of the other options.

Orientation	Focuses on	Typical objectives
Production	Production efficiency	Higher profits through reduced costs
Product	Product quality and features	Increased sales through product improvements
Sales	Sales techniques and advertising	Sales volume – often short-term
Customer	Customers' needs	Increased long-term sales through customer loyalty, positive image
Marketing	Customers' needs and competitors' strategies	Long-term profits through good customer relations and a sustainable competitive advantage
Cooperative	Workers' needs	Long-term job security, good working conditions
Financial	Financial ratios and other measures	Return on investment (ROI), higher share prices and dividend payments
Societal	Society's well-being	Environmental regeneration, community welfare

EXHIBIT 1.6 Strategic orientations

Many textbooks ascribe these orientation strategies to specific eras, usually making production the earliest and market the most recent. However, there are still organisations that are product, or production, -orientated, even though market orientation is widely accepted as better in terms of business performance.

Cooperative and financial orientations are beyond the scope of this book. The next section goes into detail about the other, more marketing-related orientations. Production is included as it often appears in marketing texts, though it is out of favour with modern-day management thinkers. Societal orientation is included because of its links with **corporate social responsibility (CSR)** and positive **corporate image**.

PRODUCTION ORIENTATION: PUTTING THE FACTORY FIRST

Firms that have a **production orientation** focus on production efficiency. They try to make their products and services as quickly as possible and at the lowest possible cost. A production-orientated firm will take great pride in its production facilities, which may well be state of the art.

Such firms place great emphasis on **economies of scale** and so are likely to be large-scale producers. It is usually most cost-effective to produce a large amount of a product because it makes it worthwhile to have the largest, fastest machinery or specialist tools, gains bulk **discounts** on component parts, and enables workers to concentrate on certain tasks and so become expert in them. This efficiency often comes at the cost of **product range**. If a firm is making a huge quantity of one product, then it cannot also make others. In fact, it is in the interest of such a firm to offer its customers a limited product choice. The most famous example of a production orientation is the original Ford car, the Model T, of which Henry Ford is alleged to have said, 'They can have any colour they like, so long as it's black'. This lack of consideration for customer requirements means that a production orientation is not in keeping with the marketing philosophy. However, today, technological developments are making it possible to achieve production efficiency and lower production costs without the need to go into large mass-production quantities.

PRODUCT ORIENTATION: PUTTING THE PRODUCT FIRST

Firms with a product orientation are concerned with making the best possible product. They put great effort into product development and improvements, adding new features, expanding ranges, improving quality, etc. Their view was nicely summed up by the nineteenth-century American philosopher and poet Ralph Waldo Emerson, who asserted that if someone can build a better mousetrap than anyone else can, the world will beat a path to their door. This is often used as an indictment of marketing communications – showing it to be unnecessary. However, there are a number of flaws in this product-orientated view, not least that the world can only beat that path to your door if it knows about the mousetrap and where to get one. So communication in some form is required. If you build a better mousetrap, chances are that someone will steal your idea – or build an even better one, or make a cheaper one. Technology moves on and it is hard to keep ahead of the competition even with ground-breaking new ideas. Also, sometimes the mice just get smarter.

corporate social responsibility (CSR)

'the responsibility of enterprises for their impacts on society' (European Commission, 2011)

corporate image

audiences' perception of an organisation

production orientation

the philosophy of an organisation that focuses on production rather than marketing

economies of scale

unit costs fall as larger quantities are produced; a cost advantage associated with large organisations

discount

a deduction from the price

product range

the products sold by a particular company or, more commonly, brand

research focus: classic concept

Levitt, T. (1960) 'Marketing myopia', *Harvard Business Review*, **38 (Jul/Aug): 45–56.**

Levitt, T. (1975) 'Marketing myopia: a retrospective commentary', *Harvard Business Review*, **Sept/Aug: 1–14.**
The first of these two articles is one of the most widely read and quoted articles in marketing. In it, Levitt argued that companies needed to define the nature of their business in a wide sense if they were to best highlight the competitive forces that surrounded them and avoid demise. He warned about the dangers of marketing short-sightedness. In the second article, written some 15 years later, he revisits the issues and considers the use and misuse that has been made of marketing myopia, describing its many interpretations and hypothesising about its success.

In his famous article 'Marketing myopia', Levitt (1960) stated that product-orientated industries inevitably died. The example he used was that of the North American railways, which believed themselves to be in the railroad business and were therefore surprised when they lost all their customers to airlines. They had not appreciated that they were all in the transport market.

Product-orientated firms believe that, if they provide a good quality product at a reasonable price, then people will buy it without much further effort on the firm's part. This concentration on product improvement has its advantages. For example, it may well produce ground-breaking new products. Many technology companies are product-orientated; they produce new computers, machinery, gadgets and gizmos, believing that other people will be as caught up in the invention and its cleverness as its designers are.

Sometimes this works. Vacuum cleaner manufacturer Dyson is a modern example of a successful product-orientated firm. People find it hard to imagine products or services that do not currently exist. Someone – often someone with technical expertise – has to come up with the ideas before they can run them past potential customers to check their likely popularity. Imagine a world without televisions. Would you have come up with such an idea? How about recorded music? These are only twentieth-century inventions. Before that, if you wanted to hear music, you had to learn to play an instrument, or befriend others who could. If you had only ever known communication over distance by letter, would you have asked for a mobile phone? (See Chapter 6 for more on product innovation.)

Of course there are some basic needs that we know we want fulfilled, even without imagining new technology. For example, we want cures for a number of diseases, from cancer and HIV through to the common cold. We want to be able to get to places faster and more reliably. Many of us want to be slimmer. Often, it is more useful to ask people what they want to be able to do, what desires they have, rather than what new products they would like.

Technological breakthrough products, then, usually require a leap of imagination, and faith, on the part of their providers. Most of these products fail in the marketplace. The ones that do succeed tap into a real customer need, either a pre-existing one that was being met less well (or not at all) previously, or a need not previously recognised (e.g. to be able to talk on the phone, hands-free of course, while driving a car).

Other situations where product orientation may be effective are when there is little effective competition or a shortage of that type of product – for example, where a company has a patent, as Dyson had on its 'cyclonic' cleaner technology, or a monopoly, as many train operators have in their designated areas or under the terms of their franchises. Product-orientated companies that do not have these advantages may need to do some very hard selling.

SALES ORIENTATION: SAYING THAT THE CUSTOMER COMES FIRST

Firms that are sales-orientated spend a lot on sales training, sales aids and support materials (brochures, presentations, etc.). They do a lot of **sales promotion** (short-term special offers such as 'buy one get one free', coupons, competitions) and often use hard-sell advertising ('amazing special offer', 'this week only', 'never before available to the public', etc.). They are likely to have a large salesforce that may be quite pushy. Such firms seem to believe that customers will not want to buy their products unless they are pushed into doing so. They are trying to overcome customers' reluctance to buy. Double-glazing firms and timeshare sellers are often sales-orientated.

The emphasis here is on the seller's need to shift stock or to make the targets, rather than on customers' needs. However, as part of the heavy sales drive, the salespeople may pay lip-service to marketing – perhaps by calling salespeople something different, e.g. 'new business executives', and by taking an interest in the customer's requirements (so they can sell them other products). This may really just be part of their sales technique, a way of generating rapport with a **prospect**. Sales-orientated firms are far more interested in their own needs than those of their customers and their salespeople often have high quotas of products to sell with the prospect of large commissions if they succeed. So the success of a sales-orientated firm depends largely upon the skill of its salesforce.

Sales-orientated companies are stuck in the old transaction exchange way of thinking (see above). Pushing a customer to buy something that they may not really want or need, and may later regret, is no way to build a relationship.

CUSTOMER ORIENTATION: ACTUALLY PUTTING THE CUSTOMER FIRST

Many writers do not distinguish between customer orientation and market orientation – but there is a key difference. A market is made up of buyers and sellers so, within this text anyway, a market orientation will be taken to include serious consideration of the competition.

A customer orientation is held by most to be essential to long-term success. How strange, then, that so few organisations are customer-orientated. Many pay lip-service to the idea but fail to gear their systems to satisfying customers, focusing too much on the needs of the organisation itself instead.

An organisation has a number of types of customer. A company that focuses on end customers, without considering trade customers, may find that its products are not actually available to consumers (trade customers include **retailers**, wholesalers, distributors, and import and export agents).

The move to a true customer orientation is not easy and takes a long time. Organisations typically experience considerable resistance from individual departments and employees.

---

sales orientation
strategic view that focuses on short-term sales

sales promotion
short-term special offers and other added-value activities, e.g. two for the price of one

prospect
prospective (i.e. possible future) customer

retailer
a sales outlet that deals with end customers, e.g. a shop

Any organisational change has to be managed carefully to ensure that it is accepted and works, but turning an organisation around, so that all its processes are geared towards the customer, can be particularly gruelling and may cause major conflict. An organisation's orientation is a feature of its culture. Organisational culture can loosely be described as 'the way we do things around here'. The procedures an organisation follows are evidence of its culture. The culture may be formal (as in many banks) or informal (as in many software companies). It may be traditional (like John Lewis) or contemporary (like, say, Virgin Radio). The tone of it is often set by the chief executive or founder and their lead influences the behaviour of all members of the organisation – all successful members that is.

An organisation's culture is possibly the hardest thing about it to change. It can be a source of great strength but, if it is too rigid, it can hold an organisation back and prevent it from moving with the times (as happened with IBM in the late 1980s). Changing an organisation's culture is rather like asking you to become another nationality – and to behave appropriately, forgetting all of your original beliefs and behavioural patterns. You would have to learn to like different food, support a different football team (possibly a whole new sport), maybe wear different clothes, talk another language, etc. Very few firms have yet managed to adopt a true customer orientation that permeates their whole organisation. Do not underestimate the obstacles in their way.

MARKET ORIENTATION: PUTTING THE CUSTOMER FIRST, WHILE WATCHING THE COMPETITION

A true market orientation requires a focus on both customers and competitors. Marketing is about providing products and services that meet customers' needs, but it is also important to do that better than your competitors. Many marketers believe that there is a third, vital, component of a true market orientation, and this is coordination between the different functions of the business. Kohli et al. (1993: 467) defined market orientation as:

> organisation-wide generation of market intelligence pertaining to current and future needs of customers, dissemination of intelligence horizontally and vertically within the organisation, and organisation-wide action or responsiveness to market intelligence.

Much recent evidence suggests that organisations that are market-orientated enjoy better overall performance than those with other orientations and marketing practitioners see clear-cut benefits from the adoption of this orientation. This is in no small part due to these organisations' emphasis on marketing research. They use their superior market information to find new marketing opportunities in advance of the competition.

Market-orientated organisations take marketing research seriously. Research is essential to an understanding of customers and their needs. It may not be formal marketing research; many smaller companies are able to maintain personal contact with their customers, which is by far the best way to get to know them. Larger companies have to find more cost-effective ways to understand their much larger customer base. These may include customer satisfaction surveys, websites, **loyalty schemes**, owners' clubs, helplines and customer service desks.

Market-orientated firms take a long-term view of their markets and the products and brands they develop to serve them. Not for them the quick fix that will make this year's sales targets at the expense of next year's – that's a tactic more likely to be employed by a

loyalty schemes

ways in which companies try to retain customers and encourage repeat purchases, often accomplished by awarding points (e.g. Tesco Clubcard, Air Miles)

sales-orientated company. For example, if you were an industrial machinery salesperson with a quota of sales to make before the year end, achievement of which would gain you a large bonus, then you would want a customer to order sooner rather than later. However, suppose the customer said they could only afford the smaller machine this year, but if you wait until their next financial year they would buy the larger, newer model. Might you offer them discounts and other incentives to order early so that you get your bonus and your company makes its targets (and makes you a hero)? Then, next year, when the new, improved model comes out, how welcome is that customer going to make you? Will they buy any more from you? Probably not.

The advantages of a market orientation are:

Customer centricity

- better understanding of customer needs and wants
- better customer relations
- a better reputation in the marketplace
- more new customers
- more repeat purchases
- improved customer loyalty
- more motivated staff
- a competitive edge.

customer loyalty

a mutually supportive, long-term relationship between customer and supplier, which results in customers making multiple repeat purchases

However, the other orientations should not all be dismissed out of hand – they may work for specific organisations in particular circumstances (Noble et al., 2002). Technology companies, such as Apple Inc., can become market leaders through their product focus while others, such as The Body Shop, are successful thanks to their societal marketing orientation (see below).

research focus

Kaur, G. and Sharma, R.D. (2009) 'Voyage of marketing thought from a barter system to a customer centric one', *Marketing Intelligence and Planning*, 27 (5): 567–614.
   This article charts the developments that have taken place in marketing thinking and provides an extensive review of much of the relevant literature.

SOCIETAL MARKETING ORIENTATION: PUTTING CONSUMERS AND THEIR SOCIETY FIRST

Societal marketing involves meeting customers' needs and wants in a way that enhances the long-term well-being of **consumers** and the society in which they live. Some of the products and services on sale today (e.g. cigarettes) are known to be bad for consumers. Some are damaging to our environment (e.g. petrol), either in use or in production (e.g. power plants). Organisations that adopt a societal marketing orientation recognise the wider implications and responsibilities of marketing and take them into account when formulating strategies.

consumer

the individual end-user of a product or service

For example, they may design packaging that is minimal, made from recycled materials and biodegradable. Their product design may take into account how the product can be disposed of at the end of its life. Their advertising will encourage responsible product use, for example, they would not encourage children to over-indulge in high-sugar treats. The Co-operative Bank's mission statement commits it to being 'a responsible member of society by promoting an environment where the needs of local communities can be met now and in the future' (Co-operative Bank, n.d.).

Cynics would say that societal marketing is just another marketing ploy: responding to a current trend. Societally-orientated companies may be motivated by enlightened self-interest or they may have a genuine desire to do good. Consumers are beginning to choose organic foods and other green products, and these are proving lucrative niche markets as customers seem prepared to pay a little more for them (not too much more, though).

research focus: classic concept

Kohli, A.K. and Jaworski, B. (1990) 'Market orientation: the construct, research propositions and managerial implications', *Journal of Marketing*, 54 (April): 1–18.

Narver, J. and Slater, S. (1990) 'The effect of a market orientation on business profitability', *Journal of Marketing*, 54 (Oct): 20–35.

Both of these pairs of authors are the early researchers of market orientation. Each has taken a slightly different perspective to the elements which best characterise market orientation and that may be used in its evaluation. Much of the work that has followed, both by these authors and others, has taken its directions from these early works.

FOCUSING ON CUSTOMERS

'The customer is king!'

This is a rather sexist and hackneyed phrase, but it has a serious point: companies cannot exist without customers. It would therefore seem to make sense to design the company around the customer, gearing everything to serve the customer better to ensure a positive customer experience. This focus on the customer is at the heart of good marketing and is one of the hallmarks of a market or customer orientation (see above).

It is important that employees recognise that they are there to meet customers' needs and wants rather than their own. It is no good a delivery person standing on the door-step and saying, 'But this is the best time for me to deliver' if it is not a good time for the customer.

It is equally important that investors recognise that without the customer there is no company. A few years ago, Gerald Ratner was widely reported as saying that his firm's products were of poor quality and not what he would buy. The firm's reputation was irreparably damaged, customers quickly turned elsewhere and the company's share price plummeted.

ethical focus: know when to stop

Diageo (the company that makes Guinness and Smirnoff vodka) ran an unusual ad campaign. Titled 'Know when to stop', the TV campaign encouraged people to drink less. Diageo claimed it was part of its corporate social responsibility programme.

The drinks industry has been heavily criticised in recent years for not doing enough to tackle problems caused by alcohol, particularly drink-driving and under-age, excessive drinking. Anti-drinking charities welcomed the campaign as a step in the right direction but pointed out that it didn't amount to much when set against the £200 million (€280 million) or so that is spent each year on alcohol advertising in the UK.

Whose responsibility do you think it is to promote sensible drinking – if anyone's?

CUSTOMERS OR CONSUMERS?

There is a distinction between customers and consumers, both of whom are vital to business success. A customer is someone who buys the firm's products. However, they may not actually use the products themselves. The eventual user of the product is called the consumer.

Consumers are important influencers on **purchase decisions**, even if they do not make the actual decision on what to buy (see Chapter 3 for more on this). For example, children's toys, particularly those designed for young children, are usually bought by other members of their family or by friends. They are the customers but the child is the actual consumer. Most perfume is bought as a gift, usually from a man to a woman. So while perfume consumers are clearly predominantly female, perfumiers' customers are mainly men. A person may be a customer but not a consumer, or a consumer but not a customer, or both consumer and customer.

ACTIVITY

Think about paper. Who buys it? What for? How many different types of customers and consumers can you list? What do they want from paper?

purchase decision
the selection of the preferred product to buy

MARKETING'S CHANGING EMPHASIS

In its short history, marketing has moved its focus from the immediate sale to the preservation of future sales. Good marketing practice today involves thinking beyond the one-off sale. It means longer-term planning and that makes it a more complex process to manage.

TRANSACTIONAL MARKETING

There is still a place for the one-off sale that is sometimes referred to as **transactional marketing**. Here there is no intention to continue a relationship. Both parties are satisfied by that one sale and they go their separate ways. A **transactional exchange** is likely to be appropriate where the product is a basic commodity, such as salt, or an occasional purchase, such as a house. Alternatively, the circumstances of the exchange may dictate that it be transactional. For example, the buyer may just be passing through, a visitor to the area. The seller may only have one thing to sell, perhaps a private car or furniture that is no longer wanted, or they may be winding a business down.

transactional marketing
focuses on the immediate sale

transactional exchange
a one-off sale or a sale that is conducted as if it were a one-off

b2b focus: Dave the decorator

Dave the decorator has a thriving business. He is booked up at least six months in advance. He doesn't need to advertise as word of mouth brings in all the business he needs. Many of his customers are regulars, so impressed by his work that they wouldn't dream of employing anyone else, and most certainly wouldn't do the decorating themselves.

Dave has a lot of experience in interior decorating and so has become an expert on which paints and papers look best in which situations and which last longest. People ask Dave for his opinion on their proposed colour schemes and for his recommendation on types of paint.

Currently, Dave favours an eggshell finish rather than gloss for woodwork. He thinks it looks smarter and says it doesn't fade as quickly. He dislikes ceiling paper and thinks some of the supposedly better wallpapers are overpriced.

People say you can tell Dave's work, not just by the quality of the finish, but by the trademark eggshell woodwork, the plain ceilings and the brand of paper.

So, from Dulux, Crown or any wallpaper manufacturer's point of view, who is the key customer here – consumer or trade?

RELATIONSHIP MARKETING

relationship marketing

a long-term approach that nurtures customers, employees and business partners

Relationship marketing is a long-term approach, typically involving multiple transactions between buyers and sellers. When it was first proposed, relationship marketing was a revolutionary idea that turned sales and marketing on their heads. No longer were end-of-year sales figures the prime measure of success, companies wanted to look ahead to next year and the year after that. Could they count on repeat business from this year's customers?

The other new and exciting thing about relationship marketing was that these long-term relationships were to be built not just with customers, but with all members of the supply chain, both upwards and downwards. The key to maximising long-term profitability was seen to lie not just with loyal customers, but also in ongoing relationships with suppliers. Keeping the same suppliers not only makes for more pleasant, comfortable working relationships, it also saves the time and risk involved in finding new ones. It can have more direct benefits as well. A supplier who is secure and has a good working relationship with the buyers is more likely to be flexible and to try harder.

Although the term 'relationship marketing' can be traced back to Berry (1983), the importance of building long-term customer relationships really became apparent from some ground-breaking studies in the 1990s. Researchers found that retaining customers for just a little longer increased a company's profitability significantly and also that it was much cheaper to hold on to existing customers than to find new ones. Loyal customers may prove a company's best form of promotion: they tell their friends about their good experiences with the company and so word of mouth spreads. Who would you be more likely to believe when they recommend a product – a friend or the company's salesperson?

brand community

a group of people, usually consumers, formed on the basis of their shared admiration for a particular branded product or range of products, e.g. the BMW owners' group

Loyal customers can also become brand fans and actively seek out opportunities to engage with the brand and other fans to share and fuel their passion. Perhaps the best example of a thriving **brand community** surrounds the iconic motorcycle brand, Harley Davidson. Alongside the official Harley Owners Group, the company website features videos celebrating diverse community cultures including Harlistas (Latino Harley owners), the Iron Elite (African American riders) and military and veteran riders.

Harlistas film trailer

research focus

Payne, A. and Frow, P. (2005) 'A strategic framework for customer relationship management', *Journal of Marketing*, 69 (4): 167–76.
In this article, the authors develop a conceptual framework for customer relationship management (CRM) that helps broaden the understanding of CRM and its role in enhancing customer value and, as a result, shareholder value. The authors explore definitional aspects of CRM, and they identify three alternative perspectives of CRM.

RETAINING VALUABLE CUSTOMERS

Long-standing, regular customers can be valuable assets. They buy more products, tell their friends good things about the company (word-of-mouth advertising), are less time-consuming (because they already know how to handle orders with the company and they trust its products) and less likely to be put off by a price increase. It costs approximately five times more to attract a new customer than it does to keep an existing one happy. **Customer relationship management (CRM)** has evolved in response to this need to retain customers and increase their value to the company.

There is a school of thought that takes CRM as a set of technological tools that capture customer information and enable an organisation to use it to market its products more effectively: 'the application of technology to learning more about each customer and being able to respond to them one-to-one' (Kotler, 2003: 34). This is really just a sophisticated form of **database marketing**. It enables a company to **cross-sell** (i.e. sell existing customers additional, different products) and **up-sell** (i.e. sell customers a more expensive version of the product) but customer relationship management is more than just technologically enhanced customer service. It is the use of procedures and management techniques that enhance the customer's experience of the organisation, build loyalty and contribute to long-term profitability. It is about attracting and keeping the right customers. Technology is an enabler and not a main driver – if you have a poor value proposition you are not going to gain or keep too many customers (Woodcock et al., 2000).

It is as important to be skilled in ending relationships as it is to be able to maintain them. A customer will end a relationship that no longer has value. The organisation must be prepared to be similarly ruthless. Some customers, particularly long-standing ones, can in fact cost the firm money.

It is often said that 20% of a firm's customers generate 80% of its profits (the Pareto principle). The other 80% of customers only account for 20% of profits and so may not justify the time and money spent on servicing their needs. This is not a hard-and-fast rule, of course; for

customer relationship management
attracting and keeping the right customers

database marketing
the use of computerised information used for targeted marketing activities

cross-selling
persuading a customer to buy

up-selling
persuading a customer to trade up to a more expensive product

The new loyalty

marketing mix
(see 4Ps, 7Ps) the basics of marketing plan implementation, usually product, promotion, place and price, sometimes with the addition of packaging; the services marketing mix also includes people, physical evidence and process

4Ps
a mnemonic (memory aid) for the marketing mix: product, promotion, place, price

promotion
another name for marketing communications (one of the 4Ps); communication designed and implemented to persuade others to do, think or feel something

price
how much each product is sold for

place
one of the elements of the marketing mix, concerned with distribution, delivery, supply chain management

7Ps
a mnemonic (memory aid) for the services marketing mix: product, promotion, place, price, process, people, physical evidence

physical evidence
the tangible aspects of a service, e.g. a bus ticket, shampoo (at the hairdressers); one of the 7Ps of services marketing

example, new customers take up a lot more time than older ones who know the ropes, but a firm must still have new customers if it wants to grow and thrive. They may well turn into profitable customers in time.

If the relationship is good enough, then some of those regulars may become loyal or even brand ambassadors, i.e. people who feel strongly enough about the brand to recommend it highly, and frequently, and without even being asked. Exhibit 1.7 illustrates these different stages.

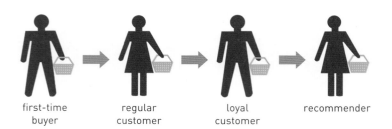

first-time buyer   regular customer   loyal customer   recommender

EXHIBIT 1.7 Customer loyalty

True loyalty is an emotional attachment. Not all regular customers are loyal, and a strong brand is not enough to create loyalty on its own (although it helps). For example, customers may buy products regularly just because they are cheap or convenient, and when something else becomes available, either more cheaply or more conveniently, then they may switch. Someone who usually buys milk from their local petrol station is unlikely to be a loyal customer, just a rather disorganised person who runs out of milk a lot. They could be lured away quite easily by another, more convenient, retail outlet.

See Chapter 11 for more detail on branding.

INTRODUCING THE MARKETING MIX

One of the most enduring, and popular, concepts in marketing is the **marketing mix**. The mix is the basic marketing toolkit that marketers use to implement their marketing plans. It is most commonly known as the **4Ps**: product, **promotion**, **price** and **place**.

This 4Ps mnemonic was first proposed by Jerome E. McCarthy in 1960 and, despite some criticism over the years, it is still taught in universities and used in practice today. However, with the increasing dominance of service products, and the importance of the service elements of physical products, the preferred framework today is the **7Ps**, first popularised by Bernard Booms and Mary Jo Bitner in 1981. The 7Ps add **physical evidence**, **people** and **process** to the original 4Ps.

The 4Ps (or 7Ps) sound deceptively simple but each P covers a range of marketing ideas and theories. A product is so much more than the item you buy. The product that is offered to customers includes its packaging, its brand and its supporting services, and the decision to buy it may have more to do with those things than with the make-up of the item itself. Promotion (or marketing communications) is so much more than just advertising which is, in any case, considerably more subtle than simply saying 'buy this'. Place is about getting the right products to the right people at the right time and about making it easier for customers to buy the products. Without a price, a product is a gift. Set the wrong price (either too high or too low) and products may not sell at all.

Decisions about the 4Ps should not be made in isolation. The Ps need to fit with each other. An exclusive product, such as a designer suit or a Bang and Olufsen stereo, commands a high price, is sold in upmarket shops, or delivered to your door in a smart van, and should be high quality. An everyday product, such as shampoo or cat litter, should do its job reliably, be inexpensive and be widely available. If just one of the Ps is out of sync, then the whole of the product offering will be devalued.

Each of the 4Ps has its own chapter in this book while the additional 3Ps that make it up to 7Ps are covered in Chapter 7. Chapter 11 then brings them all back together to demonstrate how they can be used to build brands.

MARKETING TODAY AND TOMORROW

Looking ahead, what is happening in the world of marketing? This section considers what is changing in the way marketing is carried out. Most of these things are interrelated; each supporting and encouraging other changes. Some are external influences on marketing, such as the major developments in technology. Some are to do with the ways in which people's behaviour and lifestyles are changing as they respond to these developments. Marketers have at least to react to these changes; at best they are proactive in seeking out and taking advantage of new marketing opportunities.

MARKETING IN THE INTERNET AGE

The Internet is becoming the town square for the global village of tomorrow. (Bill Gates, founder, Microsoft)

The Internet has had a significant impact on our lifestyles and on the way that many companies market their products. Firms are harnessing the power of the web to make themselves more competitive and reduce costs. Some organisations, e.g. Amazon, eBay and Google, *only* do business online, while most follow a more flexible business model that incorporates both online and offline customer contacts – so-called clicks and mortar operations. According to e-commerce analysts emarketer.com, online retail sales (not including travel, restaurant or event tickets) are expected to reach $2,0498 trillion in 2017, accounting for 9.9% of total retail spending worldwide rising to 18.7% of total retail spending by 2019. The Asia-Pacific region, largely thanks to China, is expected to remain the world's largest retail e-commerce market where growth is being driven by expanding middle classes and greater mobile and Internet penetration (emarketer, 2016).

Consumer confidence in online transactions has increased due to improved financial security for payments, which also cuts the costs of fraud. In addition more sophisticated web-based management and analysis of customer data helps retailers to serve their customers better with more personalised and timely offers and joined-up customer service across multiple channels and devices.

The Internet has made international marketing a realistic aim for all sizes of business in all sorts of markets. It is hard for a small, offline retailer to compete with larger companies

people
one of the elements of the marketing mix, concerned with distribution, delivery, supply chain management

process
one of the 7Ps of the services marketing mix; the way in which a service is provided

but the Internet is a great equaliser. Compared to a chain of high street stores, a website is relatively cheap to design and many of the most popular online social networking services offer 'plug and play' options to buy and sell products from within social media and mobile applications – for example, Pinterest's buyable product pins. This changes the fundamental nature of competition in many markets, enabling many smaller niche and boutique businesses to rapidly establish themselves and even thrive alongside larger, multinational brands. London-based online fashion start-up *Finery* is one example, recording £5 million sales in its very first year of business. It has even attracted the attention of the UK's leading high street department store John Lewis that has announced plans to sell *Finery* products from Spring 2016 (Hounslea, 2016).

While some firms look to the Internet to reach and serve customers more efficiently, others are finding and exploiting new opportunities by creating Internet platforms that enable buyers and sellers (and lenders and borrowers) to interact directly. The company then charges a commission on each transaction. Amazon marketplace, AirBnB and Uber are internationally successful examples of a phenomenon that has become known as *Uberisation*. Other sites like **www.bigbarn.co.uk** are cutting out business intermediaries (e.g. high street shops) and allowing both farmers and individuals to trade directly with consumers. Its stated mission is to 'reconnect consumers with their local producers, direct, or through local retailers, and encourage local trade. Giving farmers a better deal and consumers fresher, cheaper, accountable food' (BigBarn, 2012).

'The Internet of Things' is an interconnected ecosystem of smart devices which may sound like science fiction but is fast becoming an everyday reality. From mobile phones to coffee makers, washing machines, and a whole host of wearable devices, consumers are spoilt for choice of **innovative products** and services: a plant pot that texts when it needs watering, a dog collar that tracks and reports its wearers' activity, heating and lights that can be controlled by phone and even an alarm clock that automatically sets itself early in response to traffic or weather conditions on its owner's usual route to work are just some examples.

innovative product

a really new product, possibly a technological or medical breakthrough

CONVERSATIONS AND CONNECTIVITY IN THE MARKETPLACE

Of course, Internet marketing is not just about e-tailing or digital products and services. Rapid advancements in digital media and mobile technologies have opened up a world of marketing communications opportunities for brands to engage consumers (more detail in Chapter 9). Earlier in this chapter the traditional marketplace was used to illustrate the fundamental principle of the marketing exchange. But even hundreds of years ago, people came to market to *share* as well as buy. The medieval marketplace would have been a very noisy place as people travelled from miles around to meet up with friends, to exchange news and gossip, to keep up with the latest trends and for entertainment. There may have been music and games, stallholders would have been shouting and calling out about their offers, there would certainly have been hundreds of conversations (both between buyers and sellers and between customers and other customers). In many ways new advances in technology, and particularly social media and the mobile devices that keep us connected 24/7, are making it possible for brands to recreate these immersive experiences and encourage conversations that lead to greater customer involvement and advocacy (see p. 28, digital focus: the art of Nowness).

Even relatively recently, it was media owners (e.g. television companies, newspapers, cinemas) who controlled all the significant means of communication, but that is no longer true. Social media facilitates and amplifies peer-to-peer (p2p) communications which have radically altered the way most organisations approach marketing and promotion. Whereas even a decade ago, relationships between the company and the customer or the company and the media would take priority, now customers are communicating with other customers *about* brands and the balance of power has shifted.

research focus

Lemon, K.N. and Verhoef, P.C. (2016) 'Understanding customer experience throughout the customer journey', *Journal of Marketing*, **80 (6): 69–96.**
Customers now interact with firms through numerous touch points and multiple channels and touch points. This paper provides a comprehensive review of research in the area of customer experience and identifies critical areas for future research as customer journeys become ever more complex.

The Internet and social media empower customers to take more control in the relationships they have with brands. Contemporary consumers have ready access to information and can easily compare products and prices. Expert advice is only a click of a mouse away. It is important that marketers understand these evolving decision-making networks (see Chapter 3 for decision-making). In the age of social media, one consumer's disappointing experience is very easily shared with millions and a negative review can be a big blow to business.

In a world so heavily influenced by peer-to-peer connections, marketing communications cannot be a monologue. Marketers need to hold conversations with their customers and consumers and to integrate their brands into people's lives. Modern marketers want to understand and plan the **customer journey** in relation to all customer **touch points** with the company and its brands. There is a focus on the customer experience and how the relationship between customer and company or brand develops over time. It is about understanding each and every point of contact, actual and potential, and weaving these understandings together.

Socialnomics

customer journey

a customer's experience of the brand, incorporating all the customer's brand-related interactions and emotions; this journey can be mapped as an aid to planning

touchpoints

all a customer, user or consumer's contacts or interactions with a brand including communications and actual use

digital focus: the art of Nowness

Luxury brand Louis Vuitton's global multimedia platform *Nowness* was originally launched in 2010 as an online magazine. *Nowness* doesn't sell things – it's more like an upmarket magazine but without the advertising. Its focus is on video storytelling but it is active across all major social media platforms. *Nowness* has its own independent editorial voice, receives contributions from celebrities, rising stars and the world's foremost designers, creatives and thinkers, and has become an essential daily resource for creative creatures around the globe. *Nowness* content is free to view although users are encouraged to register so that they can personalise their content experience by 'loving' videos, photos and articles. Capturing this data allows *Nowness* to send registered users personalised

(Continued)

(Continued)

recommendations. Members can also view one another's 'loves' while checking out new content from their favourite contributors. It is hard to tell the site is branded or even associated with the LVMH (Louis Vuitton Moet Hennessy) Group, but if you're in the know (with regards to luxury brands high culture and fashion), then you'll know ... and that's the point. Instead of selling its products, *Nowness* enables people to buy in to the brand's reason for being and feel part of an elite global community. LMVH has created a unique online creative content hub that is as rich and luxurious as its products (and customers). Its users, both existing and aspiring LMVH customers share and spread the brands' luxury message far and wide. There is no need for anything as obvious as an ad.

Sources: Bunz (2010); www.nowness.com (n.d.)

Progressive organisations are not only finding new ways to get promotional messages *to* customers, they are also reaping the rewards of collaborating more closely *with* customers: creating and nurturing vibrant online communities, using customer feedback to identify new trends and getting customers actively involved in the process of designing and developing new products and even supporting other customers.

Ted Talks: the voices of Twitter

Customer service and research should be the departments that first adopt Twitter in an organisation. Every brand should be listening when its customers talk, and every brand should be proactively engaged in resolving customer problems wherever they find them, and there are many to be found on Twitter. (Faris Yakob, Chief Technology Strategist McCann Erickson)

research focus

Jeon, S., Sung, T.K. and Dong, H.L. (2011) 'Web 2.0 business models and value creation', *International Journal of Information and Decision Sciences*, 3 (1): 70–84.
Includes discussion of: crowdsourcing, social networking, mashup, product customisation and open market models.

MARKETING AUTOMATION

Digital technologies enable some very sophisticated ways of capturing and analysing data that can be used to manage customer and prospect interactions and support. As the number of channels through which customers and companies can communicate and transact has exploded, marketers have found new ways to track all of this traffic. Many marketing processes are becoming increasingly automated with software tools and technology enabled processes that support planning, budgeting, targeting, database management and analysis, creative campaign execution, lead management and reporting (Biegel, 2009).

Many marketers see automation as a critical technology in its own right and adoption of marketing technology (often abbreviated to martech) is on the rise. In order to take advantage of these new opportunities, marketing departments are developing new organisational structures and there is growing demand for specialist skills in IT, web development, marketing operations, applications, and data management and analysis.

The international nature of the Internet has made it possible to locate call centres anywhere in the world. Operating out of countries such as India, where wages are lower than they are in Western nations, has huge cost-saving potential but is unpopular with many customers. Automated call handling is an even cheaper alternative, but that is even less popular. As companies have tried to drive down costs in search of higher profits, both ideas have become widely used, but at what price for customer relationships? How personal is an email sent to *Firstname* Phillips or a response to a Twitter complaint obviously 'written' by a robot (see also digital focus: the chatbots are coming)

Some companies are now returning to a more old-fashioned idea of service. The HSBC subsidiary bank First Direct boasts that customers always get through to a real person. For First Direct, this is a key competitive difference from other banking services, although it should be noted that they have no branches so their customers do not actually receive personal, face-to-face service.

digital focus: the chatbots are coming

With so many ways for brands and customers to connect, is it any wonder that firms are looking for new techniques to deal with the increasing volume of customer queries? We all know how frustrating it can be to ring up a helpline only to be faced with an automated answering service. Perhaps you've turned to social media channels for support or to vent your frustration only to receive a senseless (or even insensitive) auto-generated reply? The human touch really does go a long way in dealing with difficult customers, but robots have their place too. Voice activated assistants like Apple's *Siri* have become standard on smartphones and around 50% of us make regular use of them. The name Siri is even starting to appear in lists of most popular baby names! Now a number of brands are experimenting with chatbot shopping assistants within the most popular social media platforms such as Facebook. The chatbots act as a personal guides from discovery to purchase – an approach that's become known as conversational commerce.

Kayak's chatbot travel assistant

If early results are anything to go by the bots are here to stay. British tabloid newspaper *The Sun* used Facebook to provide personalised updates to football fans during the critical transfer window. These were highly effective at increasing readership of its online sports coverage. Iconic British fashion brand Burberry used a chatbot to provide individual guides to their collection in the run up to London Fashion Week. Burberry's 2016 London Fashion Week collection was the first to be entirely shoppable and was also streamed via Facebook Live. Chief Executive Officer, Christopher Bailey, explained: 'The changes we are making will allow us to build a closer connection between the experience that we create with our runway shows and the moment when people can physically explore the collections for themselves'.

Toothpaste brand, Signal, is using an interactive animated story to help kids learn how to brush their teeth properly. *Little Brush, Big Brush* is delivered by Facebook Messenger in 21 episodes: It uses a chatbot to customise the story around the child who has to complete regular brushing challenges to help the family in the story find their way home. The Royal Bank of Scotland (RBS) has a virtual online assistant called Luvo to deal with a range of day-to-day customer concerns online. While assistant bots like Luvo are designed to be as humanoid as possible, their real strength lies in their access to data. Luvo has the bank's entire customer database at its fingertips and can even learn from previous customer enquiries.

Will customer service lose the human touch? While some experts predict thousands of customer service jobs could be lost, bots could also be used to ensure human representatives always have the most relevant data at their fingertips making the whole experience smoother for everyone concerned. If bots can take care of the most monotonous and repetitive tasks, then human staff can focus on helping customers with more complex needs. Who knows what the future will bring, but it certainly looks like bots are here to stay.

Sources: Arthur (2016); Farey-Jones (2016); Murgia (2016); Southern (2016)

SOCIAL CHANGE

Social change is one of marketing's key emerging themes, according to the Chartered Institute of Marketing. In part, this is due to the changing demographic profiles of the population. People are living longer and choosing to use their discretionary income in different ways. Targeting the grey market, i.e. the over 50s, is relatively new to marketers who have courted the youth market for decades but, for a number of product areas, these 'baby-boomers' are important markets with substantial buying power.

**Millennials
(Pew Research Centre)**

The markets within both developed and developing economies are also experiencing new behaviours in the younger populations of Generation X (those who succeeded the baby-boomers, born around the 1960s to 1980s) and Generation Y (those succeeding Generation X, born around the late 1980s to early 2000, also referred to as Millennials). These generations (and the ones that follow) will become increasingly important for marketers; by 2020 they will comprise 50% of the global workforce (Mobolade, 2016). The term digital native is sometimes used to describe people who have grown up with technologies that were unthought-of when their parents were young but are now taken for granted as part of everyday life. Emojis and txt speak have become part of the language and increasingly the technology itself (devices, software and infrastructure) is simply the means by which people interface with the world. Developments in digital and social media and mobile devices have transformed the way people communicate, the way they meet new people, socialise generally and even what is considered socially acceptable – or not.

Digital Natives have grown up in a technological world

Source: Anze Bizjan/Shutterstock.com

The World Advertising Research Centre (WARC) offers the following best practice recommendations for marketing to Millennials (Mobolade, 2016):

- Marketers should try to communicate a more meaningful underlying purpose to their brand or business: Millennials believe they can make a difference to the world around them and are drawn to authentic brands that share these values.

- Marketers need to leverage digital content and social media effectively.

- Marketers can reward millennial consumers with access to unique experiences. This generation can be very loyal (perhaps even more so than previous generations) but brand commitment is earned, not bought with points or schemes.

- Marketers should develop products and brands that reflect a diverse, multicultural society.

INFORMATION OVERLOAD

It may be good to talk but as the costs of reaching people have fallen, thanks largely to digital communication technologies, it seems everyone wants to talk to as many people as possible. This desire to communicate is not limited to marketers. Organisations and individuals are sending and receiving more messages than ever before. The average Internet user has 5.54 social media accounts each (Mander, 2015); individuals' lives and views have never been more publically and frequently shared.

One consequence of this is that individuals are exposed to many more messages than they can possibly deal with. Is it any surprise that many feel overwhelmed and are becoming increasingly negative towards advertising messages in particular (Benedictus, 2007). Consumers have to block out the majority of this bombardment in their own self-defence and that presents an additional challenge to marketers who have to find ways to cut through the clutter and be heard. The IAB (Internet Advertising Bureau, 2016) estimates that 22% of UK adults online are currently using ad blocking software and that figure's rising fast. Marketers have responded to this difficulty in getting heard in a number of ways. Some try to get closer to their customers, either through strategic use of CRM or through integrating their brands into consumers' lifestyles. Others look for more original media to convey their marketing messages. Anything that is capable of carrying a message to an audience can be construed as a marketing communications medium and so marketers have lots to choose from and vie with each other to dream up unique media (Pickton and Broderick, 2004). Advertising messages have been written on bus tickets, on the edge of steps, on web pages, in the sky, on the sides of buildings (by laser), and on people's heads, cars and houses. New developments in augmented reality enable more creative and location specific promotional content to appear in the world when viewed through smartphones, just as Pokemon appear in the popular app, Pokemon Go. The Lonely Planet travel guide series has used Layar (www.layar.com) to combine GPS data with information about hotel vacancies and prices to provide tourists with a panoramic view (through their smartphone screens) of the available accommodation options that surround them, wherever they are.

MARKETING METRICS

In the past marketing has been accused of not proving its worth. As a management discipline it has suffered from an unwillingness or inability to analyse and evaluate its effectiveness and efficiency. Marketing metrics is about measuring marketing performance and using the information to improve its management. In today's increasingly cost-conscious and efficiency-driven businesses, it is important for marketers to know how to use marketing analytics to justify marketing expenditure. 'Soft metrics' such as brand awareness, consumer opinions, page impressions, likes, shares and search rankings need to be joined with 'hard metrics' such as distribution, penetration, sales, returns and profits. Quantitative measures need to be used alongside qualitative measures. With more and more channels and touchpoints, it isn't always straightforward to understand which marketing activities are delivering the best **return on investment**. Digital technologies have made many kinds of data much easier to collect, e.g. customer transaction data and customers' specific use of web content. However, analysing and using such data to improve marketing decisions requires specialist skills. Increasingly, the most important question is not what *can* be measured but what *should* be measured to provide actionable insight. It is always important to ensure marketing metrics are closely aligned with **objectives**.

return on investment (ROI)
profit expressed as a percentage of the capital invested

objective
a goal or target

ethical focus: stealth marketing

Have you heard the buzz? Did you recognise it or did you think that stranger who so kindly recommended a drink, a club or a place to eat was on the level? Perhaps they were, but then again they may have been part of a buzz marketing campaign.

(Continued)

(Continued)

Buzz marketing is a variant of word-of-mouth marketing but sometimes, instead of friends and relatives recommending products to you, people are paid to do it. They seem like one of the crowd but they have infiltrated it deliberately in order to sell products.

For example, when a Premiership football club launched a text message service, it was struggling to persuade fans to sign up. They advertised the service in programmes and on the website, and employed a troop of attractive young women to hand out leaflets on match days, but still fans were resistant to parting with 25p a message to find out the latest club news. So the club decided it was time to hire professionals in the form of a local marketing agency.

'We got a group of 14 or 16 actors, who were all football fans', explained Graham Goodkind, founder and chairman of the Sneeze Marketing Agency. 'And they went round bars and clubs around the ground, in groups of two, saying that one of their mates had been sacked from work because he kept on getting these text messages and talking to everyone about it, and his boss had had enough and given him the boot. So they were going round with this petition trying to get his job back – kind of a vaguely plausible story.'

'And then the actors would pull out of their pocket some crumpled-up leaflet, which was for the text subscription service. They'd have a mobile phone in their pocket, and they'd show them how it worked. "What's the harm in that?" they'd say. And they could have these conversations with lots of people – that was the beauty of it. Two people could spend maybe 20 minutes or half an hour in each pub, working the whole pub. We did it at two home games and reckon we got about 4,000 people on the petition in total.'

Subscriptions to the club's texting service soared – though the petitions went straight in the bin.

In the USA, marketers have been paying people to spread marketing messages by word of mouth for some years. A little known sausage brand became much better known after a holiday weekend when hundreds of people arrived at barbecues with packets of sausages and enthusiasm for their low fat recipe. They were invited guests at the parties, but paid agents for the sausages.

Stealth marketing is often criticised as unethical, although its professional proponents usually stop short of breaking any laws. The buzz marketers themselves defend it as a necessary tactic to reach increasingly cynical and media-literate consumers in these over-communicated times. They also say that there are few, if any, complaints. But then if the marketing is stealthy enough, people just don't realise that it's marketing at all.

Sources: Benedictus (2007); Walker (2004)

CONSUMERISM

consumerism

the belief that increasing consumption is economically desirable

consumerist

someone who believes in consumerism

In the Western world, we have more material wealth, more stuff, than any society has ever had before. The amassing of goods is seen as a sign of success. Expensive, desirable possessions confer status. **Consumerists** believe that it is economically desirable to consume (i.e. eat, drink, use) more and more. Modern production techniques mean that we have more than enough of everything. Every day, Western businesses and households throw away millions of excess goods. In the meantime, there are parts of the world that are so poor that they are short of basic necessities: food, water, clothing, shelter. This disparity provokes envy and conflict, yet still, even where governments have the will to do so, it is difficult to even things out.

With this surplus of goods, the power has shifted to consumers. Today, most producers of goods and services are more reliant on their customers than the other way around. A customer can usually go to another supplier but, for the supplier, a replacement customer is harder to find. This would suggest that customers have the upper hand but this is not always true. Large customers, which are usually big companies, can indeed dictate terms to their suppliers. UK supermarkets have such dominance in the food market that they can demand low prices, specially packed products and frequent (often several times a day) deliveries. However, it is harder for an individual consumer to make demands on a large corporation. Even with the current levels of competition for customers, just one customer among thousands is not so significant a loss.

As a consequence, just as workers formed trade unions in the early twentieth century, consumers in the latter half of that century got together and formed pressure groups. The power of numbers can make large corporations listen. Organisations such as the Consumers' Association have significant influence. The media can make an impression too – even the largest of multinationals wants to protect its reputation. Most newspapers have consumer advice columns and are prepared to take on any size of organisation, as are television programmes such as the BBC's *Watchdog*.

research focus

Carrington, M.J., Zwick, D. and Neville, G. (2016) 'The ideology of the ethical consumption gap', *Marketing Theory***, 16: 21–38.**

This conceptual paper explores ethical consumption with a focus on the gap between consumers' attitudes and intentions and their actual behaviour. The authors argue that the ethical consumer is an ideological figure and that the notion of an attitude–behaviour gap is a source of consumer guilt and may paradoxically preserve rather than challenge underlying capitalist structures.

ETHICAL CONSUMPTION

Many of today's consumers share concerns over sustainability and the future of the planet. Citizens and their governments are worried about environmental issues such as energy consumption, waste and pollution. The rise of eco-concern directly challenges the assumption that greater consumption (i.e. we should eat more, drink more, use more) is economically and ethically desirable. For many, marketing is one of the villains here but, actually, responsible marketing has a great part to play in helping the environmental cause.

Companies are more keenly aware of their corporate social responsibilities. While responsible business benefits society, CSR activities also create opportunities to gain added marketing and competitive advantage. There are brands whose values are built on sound environmental principles. For example, Ecover uses natural, sustainable resources for both ingredients and packaging and does less harm to the environment. One brand of toilet paper advertises the fact that for every tree used in its manufacture, three more trees are planted.

Increasing numbers of brands display their Fairtrade credentials proudly on their packaging – and increasing numbers of consumers look for that distinctive logo when choosing products. The Fairtrade mark declares that the producer is an ethical company which actively supports sustainability and fairness to suppliers from less developed countries.

Asda launches
'Wonky Veg' boxes

logo
a graphical device
associated with an
organisation

research focus

Kaur, G. and Sharma, R.D. (2009) 'Voyage of marketing thought from a barter system to a customer centric one', *Marketing Intelligence and Planning***, 27 (5): 567–614.**

This article charts the developments that have taken place in marketing thinking and provides an extensive review of much of the relevant literature.

SUMMARY

This chapter has been an introduction to the marketing concept and its development as well as to this textbook. We have looked at what marketing is, and what it is not. Marketing has been defined and the modern marketing concept explained. The origins of marketing should be helpful in understanding how the discipline has developed and why.

An organisation's strategic orientation has a huge influence on how, and what, decisions it makes. Some organisations put their products at their heart; others focus on customers. Those with a market orientation put their customers first, while keeping a close eye on the competition, but this does not mean that firms must be market-orientated in order to do any marketing at all. Almost all organisations, even those that are clearly production-orientated, must do some marketing in order to survive.

Some basic economics, notably the theory of demand and supply, has been considered. Economic theory is highly relevant to marketing and informs much of what marketing managers do. Marketing is based on the idea of an exchange of equal value – usually an exchange of products for money, but rarely for money alone. Customers give up their time and the opportunity to buy other things when they buy something. They also take risks. The product may not work, it may not be good value, others may think them foolish for buying it, it may not suit them after all. Marketing can help reassure customers and reduce their perceptions of the risks inherent in a product purchase.

Customer relationship management is a key concept in modern marketing and this chapter introduced it through the concept of relationship marketing. Relationship marketing takes a long-term view of both customers and suppliers. This contrasts with transactional marketing, which sees sales as one-off events.

This book has been carefully designed to help those new to marketing as a subject. As well as the questions and case studies that you would expect to find in a textbook of this type, we have included challenges, activities and focus boxes. The focus themes are key marketing issues and they, along with the focus boxes you will see throughout the text, should help build a bridge from your academic studies to the marketing practitioner's world – and your future marketing career.

CHALLENGES REVIEWED

Now that you have finished reading the chapter, look back at the challenges you were set at the beginning. Do you have a clearer idea of what's involved?

HINTS

- See 'definitions' and 'what marketing is not'.

- Good marketers always act ethically; also, check the Data Protection Act 1998.

- This is an ethical challenge: is it right to sell outdated technology? Would it be taking advantage of a vulnerable group? What would be a better strategy?

- Customer retention and CRM, database marketing; if he had kept in touch, then his customers would have known how to find him; also, a simple sticker on the cameras might have helped!

READING AROUND

JOURNAL ARTICLES

Cluley, R. (2016) 'The depiction of marketing and marketers in the news media', *European Journal of Marketing*, 50 (5/6): 752–69.

Hanna, R., Rohm, A. and Crittenden, V.L. (2011) 'We're all connected: the power of the social media ecosystem', *Business Horizons*, 54 (3): 265–73.

McDonald, M. (2009) 'The future of marketing: brightest star in the firmament, or a fading meteor? Some hypotheses and a research agenda', *Journal of Marketing Management*, 25 (5/6): 431–50.

BOOKS AND BOOK CHAPTERS

Baker, M. (ed.) (2008) 'One more time: what is marketing?', in *The Marketing Book* (6th edn). Oxford: Butterworth Heinemann/Chartered Institute of Marketing, pp. 3–18.

Davis, E., Bannatyne, D., Meaden, D., Jones, P., Farleigh, R., Paphitis, T. and Caan, J. (2007) *Dragons' Den: Success, from Pitch to Profit*. London: Collins.

Doyle, P. (2002) *Marketing Management and Strategy*. Harlow: FT/Prentice Hall.

Qualman, E. (2010) *Socialnomics: How Social Media Transforms the Way We Live and Do Business*. Hoboken, NJ: John Wiley & Sons.

ONLINE RESOURCES

Dutton, W.H. and Blank, G. (2013) *Cultures on the Internet: The Internet in Britain*. Oxford: Oxford Internet Institute. Available at: **http://oxis.oii.ox.ac.uk/wp-content/uploads/2014/11/OxIS-2013.pdf** (accessed 06/02/17).

JOURNALS

European Journal of Marketing

Journal of Interactive Marketing

Journal of Marketing

Journal of Marketing Management

Journal of Marketing Research

MAGAZINES

The Drum

The Marketer (Chartered Institute of Marketing magazine)

Marketing Week

(Most libraries will have these magazines – possibly online – ask your librarian.)

WEBSITES

econsultancy.com

mashable.com

www.smartinsights.com

www.oii.ox.ac.uk – a multidisciplinary Internet institute based in the University of Oxford devoted to the study of the impact of the Internet on society.

www.pewinternet.org – the Pew Internet and American life research project.

TEST YOURSELF

1   Define a market. (See p. 3)

2   Is marketing an alternative term for advertising? (See p. 8)

3   What is another term for marketing communications? (See p. 8)

4   Why is marketing less important when there is a shortage of goods? (See p. 9)

5   Why is it desirable for a product's demand and supply to be in equilibrium? (See p. 11)

6   Why is value such an important part of an exchange? (See p. 12)

7   List five advantages of a market orientation. (See p. 19)

8   What is relationship marketing? (See p. 22)

9   What are the four focus themes that run through this book? (See the Introduction)

REVISION TOOLS

Want to test yourself even more? Review what you have learnt by visiting
https://study.sagepub.com/masterson4e

- Practise for exams with **multiple choice questions**
- Revise key terms with **interactive flashcards**

MINI CASE STUDY: LIVERPOOL RELAUNCHED

Read the questions, then the case material, and then answer the questions.

QUESTIONS

1   What problems did Liverpool face in attracting tourists? (Use the information in the case study, but you may also want to look up Liverpool, and rival cities, on the Internet.)

2   How could good marketing help to overcome these problems?

3   Write a short piece (approx. 200 words) on Liverpool for inclusion in a tourist guide. You should identify different aspects of the city that will appeal to different types of visitor.

4   How could relationship marketing help Liverpool to attract more visitors?

In its heyday, as England's busiest port, Liverpool saw the launching of many fine ships but, with those glory days long gone, the city was in need of a relaunch itself.

For years Liverpool had suffered from jokes and abuse and for being more famous for its sense of humour than its work ethic. TV programmes such as *Bread*, *Brookside* and *The Fast Show* built a picture of Liverpool as a city of lazy benefit fraudsters and chancers. As a result, most tourists, shoppers and business travellers avoided it, fearing for their wallets and their safety. Yet locals always claimed that the northern city's poor image was invented by London-based media and that the truth was very different.

Liverpool's waterfront.

© The Merseyside Partnership

A golden opportunity to put things right came in 2008 when Liverpool became the European Capital of Culture. Over £2 billion was invested in the city to fund such ambitious plans as reinventing rundown Paradise Street as a suitable venue for a variety of entertainments, including street theatre and music. The rejuvenation of Liverpool was one of Europe's biggest regeneration projects. The impressive waterfront and the city's fabulous architecture were cleaned up and shown off. New facilities were provided. New hotels were built. This was Liverpool's chance to show the world what a great place it really was.

Liverpool has always had a lot to boast about. As well as writers such as Beryl Bainbridge, Willy Russell, Alan Bleasdale, Catherine Cookson and Roger McGough, Liverpool has produced many pop-cultural icons. More artists with number-one hits were born in Liverpool than in any other British city. Its most famous sons are, of course, The Beatles. These symbols of the 1960s first played at The Cavern Club – now redeveloped as a Beatles museum. The National Trust now owns John Lennon's childhood home (a gift from his widow, Yoko Ono-Lennon) and has opened it to public view. Liverpool Football Club has been one of the country's premier clubs for decades. Comedians as diverse as Ken Dodd, Jimmy Tarbuck and Lily Savage all hail from the city. Cilla Black started her days (as Priscilla White) singing in Liverpool, and more recent music exports include Echo and the Bunnymen, Atomic Kitten, Space, The Lightning Seeds, The Coral and Cast.

Unusually for a city, Liverpool has been abroad itself. Its wealth of architectural styles and the grandeur of its buildings have made it an ideal film double for a number of European cities, including Moscow, Dublin, Paris and, most surprisingly, Venice. The most dramatic aspect of Liverpool has always been best viewed from the Mersey. It is, of course, the UNESCO listed waterfront with its 'three graces': the Royal Liver Building, the Cunard Building and the Port of Liverpool Building, which together form one of the world's most well-recognised skylines. Liverpool's docks were once among the busiest anywhere and the Albert Dock remains so, though now it is home to thriving bars, restaurants and shops, upmarket apartments and the Tate art gallery rather than ocean-going ships.

Even with all these advantages, if the city was to make it on to every tourist's must-see list, it had a lot of image rebuilding to do. A spokesperson for the City Council said, 'People just haven't been listening. Unemployment is reducing and it is one of the safest cities in the country. Liverpool has art galleries, shopping centres and trendy bars. We are also close to becoming the film capital of Britain with the number of films shot here. I don't see why it should be a problem marketing ourselves to the UK and abroad'.

Liverpool was a smash hit as Capital of Culture in 2008 and has managed to build on that success. It has been named in the top three UK city break destinations for the second successive year by readers of travel bible, *Condé Nast Traveller Magazine*, and was recently voted the best loved of Britain's non-capital cities.

Sources: BBCi (n.d.); Liverpool City Council (n.d.); Liverpool 08 (n.d.); Singh (2003); Visit Liverpool (n.d.)

REFERENCES

Allen, R. (ed.) (2000) *New Penguin English Dictionary*. Harmondsworth: Penguin.

American Marketing Association (2013) 'Definition of marketing'. Available at: **www.ama.org/AboutAMA/Pages/Definition-of-Marketing.aspx** (accessed 23/10/16).

Arthur, R. (2016) 'Burberry is also experimenting with chatbots', *Forbes*, 17 September. Available at: **www.forbes.com/sites/rachelarthur/2016/09/17/burberry-is-also-experimenting-with-chatbots-for-london-fashion-week/#7e67eab9639b** (accessed 07/11/16).

BBCi (n.d.) Capital of Culture (web page). Available at: **www.bbc.co.uk/capitalofculture** (accessed 10/08/03).

Benedictus, L. (2007) 'Psst! Have you heard?', *The Guardian*, 30 January Available at: **www.theguardian.com/media/2007/jan/30/advertising.marketingandpr** (accessed 03/02/17).

Berry, L.L. (1983) 'Relationship marketing', in L.L. Berry, G. Shostack and G. Upah (eds), *Emerging Perspectives on Services Marketing*. Salt Lake City, UT: American Marketing Association.

Biegel, B. (2009) 'The current view and outlook for the future of marketing automation', *Journal of Direct, Data and Digital Marketing Practice*, 10 (3): 201–13.

BigBarn (2012) 'Discover real local food'. Available at: **www.bigbarn.co.uk/aboutus** (accessed 20/05/13).

Booms, B.H. and Bitner, M.J. (1981) 'Marketing strategies and organisation structures for service firms', in J. Donnelly and W.R. George (eds), *Marketing of Services*, American Marketing Association, pp. 51–67.

Bunz, M. (2010) 'LMH launches luxury online magazine Nowness', *The Guardian Online*, 26 February. Available at: **www.theguardian.com/media/pda/2010/feb/26/lvmh-luxury-online-magazine-nowness** (accessed 07/11/16).

Carrington, M.J., Zwick, D. and Neville, B. (2016) 'The ideology of the ethical consumption gap', *Marketing Theory*, 16: 21–38.

Chartered Institute of Marketing (CIM) (n.d.) *Marketing Glossary*. London: Chartered Institute of Marketing. Available at: **www.cim.co.uk/cim/ser/html/infQuiGlo.cfm ?letter=M** (accessed 11/06/07).

Co-operative Bank (n.d.) *Social Responsibility*. Available at: **www.co-operative.coop/corporate/ethics-and-sustainability/sustainability-report/social-responsibility/** (accessed 17/02/14).

emarketer (2016) 'Worldwide retail ecommerce sales: emarketer's updated estimates and forecast through 2019'. Available at: **www.emarketer.com/public_media/docs/eMarketer_eTailWest2016_Worldwide_ECommerce_Report.pdf** (accessed 06/03/17).

European Commission (2011) 'Enterprise and industry, corporate social responsibility'. Available at: **http://ec.europa.eu/enterprise/policies/sustainable-business/corporate-social-responsibility/index_en.htm** (accessed 03/08/13).

Farey-Jones, D. (2016) 'Unilever employs Facebook chatbot to teach kids to brush teeth', *PR Week*, 20 October. Available at: **www.prweek.com/article/1412945/unilever-employs-facebook-chatbot-teach-kids-brush-teeth** (accessed 07/11/16).

Hounslea, T. (2016) 'Finery records £5m sales in first year', *Drapers*, 8 February. Available at: **www.drapersonline.com/news/finery-records-5m-sales-in-first-year/7004616. article** (accessed 07/11/16).

IAB (Internet Advertising Bureau) (2016) 'IAB UK reveals latest ad blocking behaviour'. Available at: **www.iabuk.net/about/press/archive/iab-uk-reveals-latest-ad-blocking-behaviour** (accessed 07/11/16).

Jeon, S., Sung, T.K. and Dong, H.L. (2011) 'Web 2.0 business models and value creation', *International Journal of Information and Decision Sciences*, 3 (1): 70–84.

Kaur, G. and Sharma, R.D. (2009) 'Voyage of marketing thought from a barter system to a customer centric one', *Marketing Intelligence and Planning*, 27 (5): 567–614.

Kohli, A.K. and Jaworski, B. (1990) 'Market orientation: the construct, research propositions and managerial implications', *Journal of Marketing*, 54 (April): 1–18.

Kohli, A.K., Jaworski, B.J. and Kumar, A. (1993) 'MARKOR: a measure of market orientation', *Journal of Marketing Research*, November: 467–77.

Kotler, P. (2003) *Marketing Insights from A to Z*. New York: John Wiley & Sons.

Kotler, P. and Levy, S. (1969) 'Broadening the scope of marketing', *Journal of Marketing*, 33 (Jan): 10–15.

Lemon, K.T. and Verhoef, P.C. (2016) 'Understanding customer experience throughout the customer journey', *Journal of Marketing*, 80 (6): 69–96.

Levitt, T. (1960) 'Marketing myopia', *Harvard Business Review*, 38 (Jul/Aug): 45–56.

Levitt, T. (1975) 'Marketing myopia: a retrospective commentary', *Harvard Business Review*, Sept/Aug: 1–14.

Liverpool 08 (n.d.) *2008 Highlights*. The Liverpool Culture Company. Available at: **www.liverpool08.com** (accessed 17/02/14).

Liverpool City Council (n.d.) *Liverpool, European Capital of Culture*. Available at: **www.liverpool.gov.uk** (accessed 10/08/03).

Mander, J. (2015) 'Internet users have average of 5.54 social media accounts', *globalwebindex*, 23 January. Available at: **www.globalwebindex.net/blog/internet-users-have-average-of-5-social-media-accounts** (accessed 07/11/16).

McCarthy, J.F. (1960) *Basic Marketing: A Managerial Approach*. Homewood, IL: Richard D. Irwin.

Mobolade, O. (2016) 'How to market effectively to Millennials', *WARC*, May. Available at: **www.iab-switzerland.ch/wp-content/uploads/2016/06/millwardbrown_article_how-to-market-effectively-to-millennials.pdf** (accessed 07/11/16).

Murgia, M. (2016) 'Robots will replace customer service agents: thank god for that', *The Telegraph Online*, 15 April. Available at: **www.telegraph.co.uk/technology/2016/04/15/robots-will-replace-customer-service-agents--thank-god-for-that/** (accessed 07/11/16).

Narver, J. and Slater, S. (1990) 'The effect of a market orientation on business profitability', *Journal of Marketing*, 54 (Oct): 20–35.

Noble, C.H., Sinha, R.K. and Kumar, A. (2002) 'Market orientation and alternative strategic orientations: a longitudinal assessment of performance implications', *Journal of Marketing*, 66 (4): 25–39.

Nowness.com (n.d.) 'About us'. Available at: **www.nowness.com/about** (accessed 16/11/16).

Payne, A. and Frow, P. (2005) 'A strategic framework for customer relationship management', *Journal of Marketing*, 69 (4): 167–76.

Pickton, D. and Broderick, A. (2004) *Integrated Marketing Communications* (2nd edn). Harlow: FT/Prentice Hall.

Singh, S. (2003) 'Can Liverpool set the record straight?', *Marketing Week*, 12 June.

Southern, L. (2016) 'The Sun's Facebook chatbot drove nearly half of users back to its site', *digiday.com*, 14 September. Available at: **http://digiday.com/publishers/suns-football-chat-bot-drove-nearly-half-users-back-site/** (accessed 07/11/16).

Visit Liverpool (n.d.) 'Liverpool Tourist Information'. Available at: **www.visitliverpool.com** (accessed 05/12/09).

Walker, R. (2004) 'The hidden (in plain sight) persuaders', *New York Times*, 5 December. Available at: **www.nytimes.com/2004/12/05/magazine/the-hidden-in-plain-sight-persuaders.html** (accessed 03/02/17).

Woodcock, N., Starkey, M. and Stone, M. (2000) *The Customer Management Scorecard: A Strategic Framework for Benchmarking Performance Against Best Practice*. London: Business Intelligence.

PART ONE   THIS IS MARKETING

PART TWO   MAKING SENSE OF MARKETS

PART THREE   THE MARKETING MIX

PART FOUR   MANAGING MARKETING

THE MARKETING ENVIRONMENT

MARKETING ENVIRONMENT CHALLENGES

The following are illustrations of the types of decision that marketers have to take or issues they face. *You aren't expected to know how to deal with the challenges now*; just bear them in mind as you read the chapter and see what you can find that helps.

Degree to job: Adobe

- You work in the marketing department of a multinational which has a large investment in East Africa. Your company often considers pulling out. Can you devise a system for monitoring the often volatile situation there?

- You are the manager of a small chain of cafés. Business has been a bit slower this year than it was last, but you are better off than many of your competitors, some of whom have gone out of business. Do you know why that happened to them? Are you in danger too?

- You work for an oil company and Greenpeace protesters are currently camped outside the refinery. They are protesting over a proposed new pipeline and no one at the oil company seems surprised that they are there. In fact, the counter-arguments were prepared in advance and the **press release** has gone to all the newspapers. Greenpeace kept its intentions a secret, so how was this possible?

press release
publicity material sent to editors and journalists

- You work in banking and a colleague has just come up with a new service idea that has got the whole bank talking and will probably get him a promotion. It takes advantage of a technology not previously used in banking. Why didn't you come up with that idea?

INTRODUCTION

The word 'environment' has come to be associated with conservation; with the green movement. However, that is not the sense in which the word is used in this chapter. The *New Penguin English Dictionary* (Allen, 2000) defines environment as 'the circumstances, objects, or conditions by which somebody or something is surrounded', and this is closer to the way the term is used in marketing.

Organisations do not operate in isolation. They have to take account of other organisations and individuals in their plans and in their day-to-day dealings. They operate within a specific marketing environment which is changing all the time. Managers always need to be aware of what is going on in the world around them. They have to identify trends within their organisation's environment and make plans. To do this, they will need good information gained from sound marketing research (see Chapter 5). They will need to have a clear idea of exactly who their market is both currently and potentially (see Chapter 4) and what potential their product has. They need to have a solid understanding of their customers, the ways in which they use products, how they relate to brands, and how they choose what to buy (see Chapter 3). If a company is to be successful, then it is vital that it understands its competitive environment well. Without up-to-date knowledge of what competitors are doing, and of how well that is working, how can a company make its own marketing plans? All this information feeds into product development, the setting of prices, the design of distribution networks and choice of retailers, the creation of promotional campaigns and the development of a distinctive, desirable brand.

This chapter will consider the nature of the marketing environment and explain how to monitor changes within it. There are a number of frameworks available to help with the organisation of this environmental information and this chapter will introduce the PRESTCOM analysis tool (see below for an explanation). The analysis of an organisation's current situation forms the basis for strategic planning and we will touch on that – though it is covered in more depth in Chapter 12. Another analysis tool used here is one of the best known in management: the SWOT analysis (see below).

MARKET DYNAMICS

MARKET LEADER OR MARKET LED?

Some companies are said to be **market led**, others to be market leaders. Strictly, the market leader is the company that sells the most. It is important to be clear which market you are referring to when talking of a market leader. Cadbury's may well be the market leader in chocolate in the UK but not in the USA, where it is more likely to be Hershey's, or in any other European country, each of which has its own favourites.

The term 'market leader' is often used more loosely, however, to refer to a firm that leads the way in a market. This may be in terms of setting prices, releasing innovative products, devising new forms of promotion, moving into different market segments, or any number of other ways of starting an industry trend. Such leaders are not necessarily large organisations. Often the recognised market leader is a smaller firm that is more innovative (e.g. Dyson and its vacuum cleaners), or has more expertise (e.g. some specialised consultancy and accountancy firms), or has exceptional talent (e.g. fashion designers such as Dolce and Gabbana).

If a company takes its lead from other firms within its market, it is called a **market follower**. Market followers watch competitors closely and learn from their successful ideas and strategies. This does not mean that they produce only me-too designs or campaigns, only that they wait for more radical ideas to be tested by others first and cash in on their research experience. This strategy is not limited to new inventions, for example some fashion chains send people out to other stores to see what they have on display and what seems to be selling before placing their own orders for stock.

market led

companies take their lead from competitors and copy their successful ideas and strategies (they are also called market followers), i.e. they are more cautious and wait for more radical ideas to be tested by others first

market followers

take their lead from competitors and copy their successful ideas and strategies (see also market led)

A company that has ambitious growth plans and aspires to be market leader is called a **market challenger** and is likely to attract a more severe reaction from the current market leader.

Followers are, by definition, second (or third, fourth, etc.) into a new market and therefore do not usually get the benefit of **first mover advantage**. Often, the first significant company to move into a market becomes the leader. It can be hard to dislodge as it is the brand people know, the one they tried first and presumably liked – or there would be no market.

Coca-Cola was the first company to make a cola drink and it still outsells all others in most countries. Amazon was the first company to sell books online with a view to making a large business of it, and it had the resources and skills to make that dream a reality. All these firms have first mover advantage.

However, being first into the market does not guarantee success as many IT and Internet companies have found. Sometimes the first in is a very small company which is unable to exploit the market to the full, or which may make mistakes, thus letting another, larger or more able company steal the high ground. Peter Doyle (2006) lists the four most common mistakes made by market pioneers, i.e. the first in:

- marketing mistakes, e.g. misjudging who will want to buy the product and so targeting it at the wrong market segment
- product mistakes, e.g. technical or design flaws and limitations that challengers can exploit
- first-generation technology, e.g. market challengers can incorporate the very latest technology into their products, perhaps leaving the pioneer behind
- resource limitations, e.g. the pioneer may be a smaller company whose resources are therefore limited and who can be outgunned by a larger challenger.

The first company bears the brunt of the risks and so may fail where later companies succeed. If it is successful, it is likely to attract the attention of larger competitors. A highly praised Internet browser called Netscape pre-dates Microsoft Internet Explorer, Mozilla Firefox and Google Chrome. Which one do you use? Market leaders are constantly challenged by the other firms who wish to supplant them. These market challengers employ a number of strategies, and adopt a number of positions, in order to achieve their goal of market leadership. Some challengers are small, but they can be very large. PepsiCo is a market challenger, constantly harrying Coca-Cola and trying to steal some of Coke's **market share**. Most market leaders are large, although it is possible to be a small market leader. It depends on how large your market is. Niche brands sell into small, well-defined **market segments** so it is common to find a small brand leading the way. For example, Bentley by no means lead the car market, but they are one of the leaders of the prestige car market.

It is easier to challenge a market leader in the early stages of a market's development before the leader has built significant economies of scale which bring their costs down and make it very hard for others to compete on price. Apple's iTunes does have viable competition but despite the efforts of services like Amazon and Spotify, Apple still dominates the market.

market challenger

a company that is trying to take over the market leader position

first mover advantage

the first significant company to move into a market often becomes the market leader and can be hard to dislodge from that position

Addicted to risk

market share

a firm's sales expressed as a percentage of the total sales of that type of product in the defined market

market segment

a group of buyers and users/consumers who share similar characteristics and who are distinct from the rest of the market for a product

research focus: classic concept

Oxenfeldt, A.R. and Moore, W.L. (1978) 'Customer or competitor: which guideline for marketing', *Management Review*, Aug: 43–8.
Many commentators have emphasised the importance of recognising the significance of competitors as well as customers to effective marketing. Many naïve views have been developed about marketing by placing too much emphasis on the importance of customers alone. Even though customers are clearly important, there are other factors that have to be balanced for marketing to be carried out well. This is an early article which highlights the need for companies to tune into the competition and balance this with a customer-orientated approach.

ASSET-LED MARKETING

asset-led marketing

basing marketing strategy on the organisation's strengths rather than on customer needs and wants

Not all organisations are marketing focused, so they cannot be said to be either led by the market or driven by it. For example, some companies are said to be **asset-led**. These companies concentrate on doing what they already have the resources and skills to do, rather than looking for market opportunities and adapting to fit them. The asset in question might be equipment, people, contacts, a distribution network, shops – almost anything. In the UK, many shoe repairers also cut keys or take in dry cleaning. They have suitable shop premises to do this. Their shops are major assets to be exploited. Many universities rent out rooms in their halls of residence to tourists in the summer months, using an asset that would otherwise stand empty. Theatres, museums and art galleries rent out their foyers for upmarket parties. Did any of these organisations conduct research to discover people's needs and then design their offerings to fit? No, they realised they had spare space and came up with something profitable to do with it.

Leicester City Football Club making full use of its assets.

Picture courtesy of Leicester City Football Club

It is not just spare space that can be exploited profitably. IBM realised it had hundreds of highly trained management and computing personnel whose skills could be offered to clients as consultants. Many years ago, when textile production was dying in the UK, the factory owners realised that the same machines could be used to knit tea bags.

So, is it best to build your strategy around what your customers want, or around the assets you already have? This is an occasion where companies look for the best of both worlds. The ideal is to meet your customers' needs while making the best possible use of all your assets.

Sometimes circumstances allow you to be more proactive about this, e.g. when moving or building new premises. When Leicester City Football Club had its new stadium built, for instance, it incorporated private rooms of various sizes into the design so that it could develop its business of hiring out space for meetings, lunches and other functions.

SUPPLIERS AND DISTRIBUTION PARTNERS

An important feature of market dynamics is the way in which products actually get to customers. Most businesses use intermediaries to help with product distribution. These intermediaries are the links between producers and their customers and consumers. Transport companies such as FedEx, UPS, Parcelforce, DPD, DHL, TNT, Eddie Stobart, Norbert Dentressangle physically deliver goods to customers on behalf of producers. Agents, wholesalers and retailers may also be part of the **distribution channel**. Some markets have developed their own particular **supply chains**. The distribution of pharmaceuticals, especially prescription drugs, is heavily controlled: usually customers have to visit licensed pharmacists to obtain them. New cars are typically sold through **franchised** dealerships dedicated to specific car manufacturers. By contrast, fast-moving consumer goods (**FMCG**) such as groceries and cleaning products are sold through extensive distribution channels so that customers can buy them almost anytime, anywhere. Chapter 9 describes distribution in detail.

STAKEHOLDERS

There are a large number of individuals and groups within a company's environments that have an interest in the company and its activities. These are its stakeholders. Freeman (1984) defined stakeholders as 'any group or individual who can affect or is affected by the achievement of an organisation's activities'. All organisations have a large number of stakeholder groups and they will be different for each one.

> **distribution channel**
> a chain of organisations through which products pass on their way to a target market

> **supply chain**
> the network of businesses and organisations involved in distributing goods and services to their final destination

> **franchise**
> a form of licence; the **franchisee** pays for the rights to run a business that has already been successful elsewhere, in a new territory and benefits from the expertise of the original owners (**franchisors**)

b2b focus: going shopping

Have you ever bought Coke from Coca-Cola, toothpaste from Colgate, shampoo from L'Oréal, a camera from Canon, a printer from HP, or a mobile phone from Nokia? The answer is most likely 'no', even if you have bought these products before. These are all manufacturing companies and they use different channels of distribution. As end customers, we buy these products from retailers such as Tesco, Carrefour, C&A, Wal-Mart or Amazon, who buy directly from manufacturers. Or we may go to smaller retailers who buy from wholesalers who in turn buy from the manufacturers, sometimes through agents. So even though Coca-Cola, PepsiCo, Proctor and Gamble and Unilever are among the world's biggest consumer goods companies, we have never bought anything from them – at least not directly!

Why do you think that is?

Typically, stakeholder groups include:

- customers (who buy goods and services)
- consumers (who use the goods and services – for further discussion of the distinction between customers and consumers, see Chapter 1)
- influencers, i.e. journalists, analysts, bloggers and vloggers whose opinions are valued by customers and consumers
- employees, including directors
- pensioners, i.e. ex-employees who receive their pension income from the firm
- suppliers of goods and services, e.g. advertising agencies, raw materials providers
- distributors, e.g. wholesalers, retailers, **agents**
- government (local and central)

> **FMCG (fast-moving consumer goods)**
> low-value items that are bought regularly (the shelves empty quickly), e.g. toothpaste

> **agent**
> represents other businesses and sells products on their behalf; does not usually hold stock or take ownership of the goods, just takes orders and is paid a commission

- local community, from whom customers, employees and pressure group members (e.g. local residents' organisations) may be drawn
- shareholders, who own the company
- pressure groups, e.g. trade unions, consumer groups
- bankers, who may have lent the company money
- other investors, e.g. venture capitalists
- professional bodies, e.g. the Chartered Institute of Marketing.

audience
readers, listeners and/or viewers

public relations (PR)
planned activities designed to build good relationships and enhance an organisation's or an individual's reputation

These groupings are very like the potential **audiences** that **PR** people sometimes refer to as publics.

Stakeholder groups will want different things from the firm, and often their objectives for the firm conflict. For example, customers usually want the best quality but at the lowest possible price. Shareholders, on the other hand, will want the company to make high profits so that their dividends are higher and their shares are worth more. Pressure groups such as Greenpeace will want the company to spend money on protecting the environment and will consider any resulting increase in prices, or decrease in profits, as perfectly acceptable. Trade unions may want higher wages and better working conditions. This will, again, push up the company's costs and so it may have to raise its prices (which the customers will not like) or cut its profits (which the shareholders will not like). Setting objectives, developing strategies and managing situations in a way that resolves the conflicts between these differing stakeholder groups are key management tasks that can use up much time and effort.

research focus

Finlay-Robinson, D. (2008) 'What's in it for me? The fundamental importance of stakeholder evaluation', *Journal of Management Development*, 28 (4): 380–8.

The paper presents an overview of the relevance and value of stakeholder analysis and provides a list of key factors for consideration when carrying this out.

Vallaster, C. and von Wallpach, S. (2013) 'An online discursive inquiry into the social dynamics of multi-stakeholder brand meaning co-creation', *Journal of Business Research*, 66 (9): 1505–15.

In 2005 a major airline catering company Gate Gourmet fired 667 of its staff, prompting a sympathy strike at British Airways that grounded flights for a whole day. This paper reports on an in-depth study of online content, comment and interactions involving a variety of stakeholders, all with very different expectations of the brand. The authors stress that in the age of social media, the definition of brand meaning is no longer *controlled* by brand owners and that effective brand management requires pro-active engagement in multi-stakeholder networks both on and offline.

The idea of a firm having a responsibility towards its stakeholders is relatively new in management thinking. Previously, a company's prime duty was thought to be to its shareholders, or owners, alone. This led to many organisations' main objective being short-term profit maximisation, which was often not in its best interests in the longer term. Current managerial thinking takes account of other stakeholder groups when setting the organisation's direction. Just how far to take this has become a moral question that has prompted significant debate.

ENVIRONMENTAL INFORMATION

Organisations build up information on what is happening in the world around them so that they are better able to deal with any threats to their business or to take advantage of any new opportunities before their competitors do.

A firm's environment is commonly split into two parts: its **external environment** and its **internal environment**. Things that happen in the external environment are largely outside the firm's control and so are referred to as **uncontrollables** (or 'uncontrollable variables'), e.g. wars, crop failures, a change of government, new technology. The internal environment ought to be more easily controlled and so occurrences within it are often referred to as **controllables** (or 'controllable variables'), e.g. skill levels of employees, available finance, product range.

Environmental information is used in two main ways:

1   As input to the planning process
2   As part of ongoing analysis of marketing opportunities and threats (**environmental scanning**).

INPUT TO THE PLANNING PROCESS

Particularly during the planning process, it is useful for a firm to have a framework in which to place its environmental data. It can then assess the data's impact and what to do about it. For example, a firm would want to identify its key competitors and investigate their strategies; it is then in a position to develop counter-strategies if necessary. It would want to know about the lives of its customers, so that it could develop products and services to meet their needs.

Planners do not stop at just identifying relevant trends or competitors. They take the environmental data, feed it into a **situation analysis** and so arrive at a fuller understanding of the organisation's current situation on which they can build their plans.

ENVIRONMENTAL SCANNING

Wise organisations continuously scan their environments so that they can keep up with changes and are ready to deal with market developments, be they good or bad. This is an ongoing research exercise. The collected data helps build a better picture of their world. Perhaps they will find that a new law or regulation is being proposed and that it will affect their interests adversely. Take, for example, the proposals by various government organisations to increase taxes on 4 × 4 vehicles, the so-called 'gas guzzlers'. These are highly profitable products for many car companies and so they have been **lobbying** to get the proposals scrapped or watered down, while at the same time taking account of a likely fall in sales (or a total ban) when making their plans. Some firms have research departments, or employ outside research consultants, to scan their environment. However, most do this on a more ad hoc basis.

Some managers rely on personal contacts for their environmental knowledge, possibly because it can be difficult to get hard facts on external environmental trends (economics, for example, has never been an exact science). These personal sources are supplemented by, or cross-checked in, newspapers, magazines, trade journals and other secondary sources (for sources of **secondary data**, see Chapter 5). The approach that academic commentators

external environment
organisations and influences that are not under the organisation's control, e.g. government, competitors, legislation

internal environment
the organisation itself, its functions, departments and resources

uncontrollables
events, issues, trends, etc. within the external environment that are outside the firm's control

controllables
events, issues, trends, etc. within the internal environment

environmental scanning
monitoring the forces that influence the organisation in order to identify changes that may affect performance

situation analysis
an investigation into an organisation's or brand's current circumstances to identify significant influencing factors and trends; the most common framework used is SWOT (Strengths, Weaknesses, Opportunities, Threats)

lobbying
a means of influencing those with power, particularly politicians and legislators

secondary data
data previously collected for other purposes that can be used in the current research task

recommend, however, is to analyse the external environment as a team, i.e. to consult a range of employees from senior managers to the most junior staff. This way the firm benefits from a wide range of viewpoints and is more likely to identify key things that will affect it in the future (Mercer, 1995).

social media listening
monitoring social media conversations around specific words, phrases and hashtags

Cisco social media listening centre

PEST
an acronym for the macro-environment (part of an organisation's external environment): political, economic, social, technological

Increasingly firms are investing in social media monitoring (also known as **social media listening**) to help them identify and assess what is being said about individuals and organisations on the Internet. Effective social media listening is particularly important for firms that rely heavily on word-of-mouth referrals to generate business. Social media analytics software helps managers sift through the online chatter to identify nuggets of valuable data including customer comments and opinions of products, brands and businesses. Effective social media listening can help firms identify the most important customer concerns, track breaking news stories and gain insight into emerging market trends and opportunities.

How do managers decide what is, and what is not, relevant?

Taken to its extreme, the whole world and everything in it can be considered as having an impact upon the organisation – particularly if it is a very large organisation such as Nestlé or Unilever. Clearly it is not practical to study absolutely everything and so the management team must initially decide what sorts of things to include – a number of models have been developed to help them do this: e.g. **PEST**, SLEPT, PRESTCOM. Brownlie (2000) proposed the process for environmental scanning seen in Exhibit 2.1.

monitor	✓ trends, issues and events ✓ develop a list of relevant sources to check regularly
identify	✓ factors (trends, issues, events, etc.) that are significant to the organisation ✓ set, and regularly review, criteria to determine what is likely to be significant and what is not
evaluate	✓ the impact of the identified factors upon the organisation's operation in its current markets
forecast	✓ what is likely to happen next? ✓ examine future threats and opportunities presented by the identified and evaluated factors
assess	✓ the impact of those threats and opportunities on the firm's medium- and long-term strategies

EXHIBIT 2.1 Environmental scanning process

Unfortunately in the hectic world of business, sometimes pressing matters take precedence over long-term thinking. Many organisations have come unstuck by not looking beyond the requirements of current decision-making. The firm's most immediate operating environment (customers, suppliers, distributors, etc.) is likely to change rapidly and to receive more management attention than its wider environment (Brownlie, 2000). For example, sales of red meat have been falling for some time. There have, of course, been a number of health scares associated with the eating of meat (high cholesterol, BSE, foot and mouth disease, excess growth hormones, etc.). It would be easy for farmers to blame their troubles on these scare stories. At the same time, however, many people are eating more chicken or fish, rather than red meat, for more general health reasons and, in many countries, significant numbers of people are becoming vegetarian. These people are unlikely to return to their meat-eating habits when the latest scare dies down.

SOURCES OF ENVIRONMENTAL INFORMATION

- companies' own records (these may not be accessible to outsiders)
- market research reports: these may be specially commissioned, or more general reports can be bought from organisations such as Euromonitor, Mintel and Keynote
- newspapers (archives available online) and magazines; news stories should be triangulated, i.e. checked with at least two other independent sources
- trade magazines and newsletters, e.g. *The Grocer, Computer Weekly* documentaries: again these should be checked
- government reports and statistics; usually available online, e.g. **www.europa.eu** for the European Union
- trade organisations, e.g. the European Association of Aerospace Industries or the Chartered Institute of Marketing
- international bodies and committees, e.g. OECD (Organisation for Economic Cooperation and Development) who publish comparative statistics on many topics for most countries or the WTO (World Trade Organisation)
- trade unions, e.g. Unison, Britain's Trades Union Congress (TUC) or France's Confédération Générale du Travail (General Confederation of Labour or CGT)
- company websites; information from here should be checked – remember that these are really company **publicity**
- customer and consumer online communities and discussion forums
- news organisation websites, e.g. Reuters or the BBC
- consultancy firms: some of these publish reports that can be accessed freely, e.g. KPMG, PWC, McKinsey and Co.

publicity

the stimulation of demand for goods or services by generating news about them in the mass media

MARKETING ENVIRONMENT MODELS

The data that an organisation collects through its environmental research must be analysed. This process involves sorting the data, categorising it and then looking for trends, changes in trends, patterns, dangers and opportunities. There are a number of models of the marketing environment that an organisation can use to help it to analyse environmental data. Relevant factors are put into one or another of the categories within each model. These models are known by their acronyms (the words that are created by the letters that make up the model).

Probably the best-known environmental model is PESTEL

Political

Economic

Social

Technological.

ENVIRONMENTAL

LEGAL

macro-environment

the broad, external influences that affect all organisations in a market, e.g. the political situation in a country

micro-environment

comprises an organisation's competitors, distributors, suppliers and its own internal resources

Common variants are STEP, SLEPT and PESTEL. The L in the last two acronyms stands for legal. The extra E in PESTEL can be environmental or ecological. All of these models are ways of looking at a firm's external environment. The macro-environment is the term favoured by economists and refers to the broadest external environment in which a firm operates.

Many textbooks ignore these environmental acronyms, which might suggest that PEST and its variants have had their day. However, they are a useful *aide-mémoire*. Perhaps their current lack of favour can be attributed to the fact that most omit so much that is important (e.g. the micro-environment), along with a tendency to follow them too slavishly rather than use them as prompts. There is no need to invent things in order to fill every box. If there is nothing of significance happening in one of the categories, then it should be passed over. The important thing is to have thought everything through.

It is important not to get muddled over this term 'environment'. It is commonly used to refer to nature or green issues but that is not what it means here. Green issues are highly relevant in a firm's planning of course, but they present a bit of a problem as to where they should be placed within the model. Should the natural environment even have its own heading in an environmental analysis? Does it fit well under some, or all, of the other headings? Certainly there are political aspects to environmentalism, especially when lobbyists such as Greenpeace, Friends of the Earth or (perhaps at the other end of the political spectrum) the Countryside Alliance are involved (the Countryside Alliance is an organisation that campaigns to preserve certain traditional aspects of British country life, such as hunting). Regulation is relevant in terms of laws and codes governing issues such as pollution or recycling. The using, or spoiling, of irreplaceable natural resources has economic implications. Social attitudes towards green issues are changing. Technology has the power to harm or heal the natural world. Being seen to be greener than rival firms can give a company a valuable competitive edge – there is a significant minority of customers who choose environmentally friendly products.

The natural environment underpins all the other marketing environment categories.

© Dave Pickton

The natural environment affects an organisation in numerous ways. Whether this means it should be treated separately or within the context of other forces is a choice the analyst must make. It will probably depend upon the nature of the organisation, its products and the rest of its operating environment. In this book green issues will be considered where they are relevant within other categories. In this way, their important influence can be considered more seriously and widely. PEST, and its variants, only cover *part* of the organisation's external environment. Marketers must consider all of the external environment and the internal environment as well. The more immediate environment is what economists refer to as the micro-environment. It comprises competitors, distributors, suppliers and the organisation's own internal resources.

The macro-environment refers to broad influences that affect all organisations in a market, whereas the micro-environment contains influences specific to the nature of the business, its suppliers, marketing intermediaries, customers and competitors.

So PEST does not give the whole picture: it only covers the macro-environment. In order to complete the picture, Wright and Pickton (cited in Pickton and Broderick, 2001) proposed a more comprehensive, environmental model: PRESTCOM. PRESTCOM provides a framework for the analysis of both the macro- and micro-environments (see Exhibit 2.2).

PRESTCOM

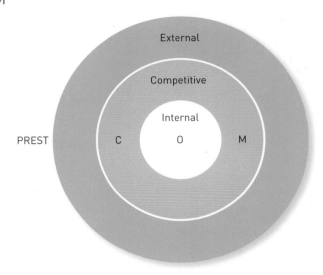

EXHIBIT 2.2 PRESTCOM

PRESTCOM is an acronym that stands for:

Political

Regulatory

Economic

Social

Technological

Competitive

Organisational

Market.

Over the following pages, each of these categories will be considered in turn. As examples of what to include under each PRESTCOM heading, at the end of each section there will be a couple of factors or trends taken from an analysis of Cadbury in 2012. This is not a *complete* PRESTCOM for Cadbury, just an illustration of how to do the analysis.

THE MACRO-ENVIRONMENT

The macro-environment, which is external to the organisation, is represented graphically in Exhibit 2.3.

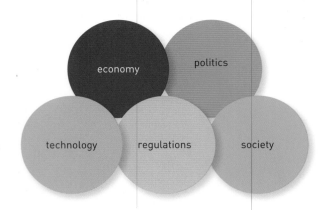

EXHIBIT 2.3 The macro-environment

THE POLITICAL ENVIRONMENT

Players in the political environment include:

- government – i.e. domestic government bodies (central, regional and local, and government-appointed committees), supranational government bodies (e.g. the EU) and foreign governments
- government departments, e.g. Department for Education (UK), Directorate General for Competition (EU)
- industry bodies and watchdog committees, e.g. OFCOM (UK), European Food Safety Authority, European Data Protection Supervisor (EU)
- special interest and pressure groups – i.e. political organisations that exist to further a cause (e.g. Friends of the Earth) or the interests of a particular group of people (e.g. trade unions)
- political parties.

Demonstrations are a common form of political protest.

Source: Eric Crama/Shutterstock.com

These groups affect an organisation and its operations in a number of ways. The philosophy of the government in power sets the business climate. Government policy has a direct effect on the way in which businesses are allowed to operate. For example, some governments are characterised as interventionist and others as non-interventionist. The interventionists are far more likely to interfere in the running of businesses, for good or for bad.

Things to look for in the political environment include:

- the political orientation of the government, e.g. left wing or right wing? Democratic or authoritarian?
- the stability of the political situation – how likely is it to change and how radically? Examples of radical change include coups or war; a less radical change might be an election or a passing on of power such as happened in North Korea when Kim Jong-il appointed his son Kim Jong-un to replace him as Supreme Leader
- existing and proposed government policies, e.g. commitment to austerity measures to reduce debt, reducing people's reliance on state benefits, encouraging home ownership, support (or non-support) for same-sex marriage, attitudes to environmental conservation
- specific business-related attitudes and policies (the attitude may help you to predict new policy), e.g. grants for small business start-ups, links with trade unions, attitudes towards foreign investment, e.g. China has strict controls on foreign firms
- import and export restrictions
- membership of a **trading bloc**, e.g. the European Union
- views on the operation of the market (e.g. are they pro a free market, where the laws of supply and demand dictate product availability and prices, or likely to intervene to influence supply or prices?)
- the government's own commercial dealings; governments have huge spending power but many have at some point followed a policy of giving their own country's suppliers preference when placing their orders
- the relationship between governments, e.g. some Middle Eastern governments are unwilling to allow trade with the West.

trading bloc

a group of countries that work together to promote trade with each other and present a common front to outside nations, e.g. the European Union (EU), NAFTA (North American Free Trade Association)

In the US in 2015, President Obama was a 'lame duck' president, i.e. a president coming to the end of his term and so more likely to take unpopular decisions because he could not stand for re-election anyway.

In Greece in 2012 there was a lot of political unrest as the Greeks took to the streets to oppose the austerity measures imposed by the EU as the price of an economic bail-out. In France also, the people revolted against the constraints of debt reduction policies and elected a new president.

The Syrian civil war has displaced millions of people who have sought sanctuary in Europe. They place huge stress on European infrastructures (e.g. housing, social security, policing) and have even brought about fundamental changes in the way the EU operates, most notably in the Schengen area where some previously open borders now have border controls. It is a humanitarian disaster which also adversely

Border controls mean Swedes and Danes have to carry passports to go to work or to shop on the other side of the Oresund Bridge.

Source: iStock.com/ultrakreativ

affects businesses as they try to move goods between counties and workforces who are used to travelling between countries with ease.

This is clearly an important time to be keeping up with political events and assessing the possible impact of future policy changes.

ethical focus: nationalisation

Sometimes governments, usually when they're in financial trouble, look covetously at privately owned businesses. They may take a greater share of the business's profits by increasing taxes, or they may try to seize the business for themselves. Nationalisation is when a government takes over a business, or part of a business, often without consultation or adequate compensation.

In early 2016, the Zimbabwe government refused to renew foreign companies' diamond mining licences, declaring that in future all diamonds would belong to Zimbabwe. Zimbabwe's president, Robert Mugabe, claimed that foreign mining companies, such as Chinese-run Anjin Investments, were robbing Zimbabwe of its wealth: this despite the fact that all mining companies had to be partly owned by his government. He denied that this was part of a nation-alisation programme but the mines were closed and within a couple of months there were law suits and counter suits in the High Court as companies tried to gain access to the mines to retrieve their equipment and diamonds.

There had been rumours of diamond mine nationalisation since 2007 when diamonds were discovered in Marange. Opportunistic prospectors were forcibly removed and as many as 25,000 arrested as the government claimed the new mine.

The motivation for nationalisation is not always purely financial, the political philosophy of the government is relevant here. An interventionist government is more likely to believe that strategically important industries and basic services, e.g. railways, ports, communications networks, arms manufacturers and food producers, should be publicly owned. In contrast, a non-interventionist government might scale down all of these things, and even privatise publicly owned industries. In the 1980s and 1990s, the UK Conservative government broke up many of the state-owned monopolies and sold off some giant companies including: British Gas, British Rail, British Steel, British Airways, British Petroleum (BP), Jaguar and Rolls-Royce. Left-wing, or socialist, governments tend to be more interventionist than right-wing governments and more likely to favour public sector ownership. Generally speaking, communist governments exert the most control of all.

Think about your own country's government, is it left wing or right wing? Can you imagine a forced nationalisation programme today? Can you think of any government-owned assets that might be privatised?

Sources: BBC News (2007, 2016); Dzirutwe et al. (2016)

Source: Bloomberg/Bloomberg/Getty Images

Cadbury: example of political factors

- The rise in obesity, especially childhood obesity, has given rise to significant anti-sugar lobbies in Western countries and governments, industry bodies and food manufacturers are beginning to respond. For example, most foods now have clearer labelling showing their nutritional content and, in particular, how much sugar they contain.

- The UK government's call to action on obesity encouraged food producers to sign up to the calorie reduction pledge (Department of Health, 2012). FDF (Food and Drink Federation) members pledged in 2014 to place a 250kCal cap on single-serve confectionery, including chocolate. As a result, some products have been reformulated and some bars have become smaller (Mintel, 2015).

THE REGULATORY ENVIRONMENT

The actions that an organisation can take are constrained by the rules imposed upon it and by the duties it owes to other organisations or individuals. These rules and duties may be formalised as laws (e.g. the Human Rights Act 1998) or as codes of practice (e.g. those governing what is, and what is not, acceptable in advertising) or they may be merely accepted behaviour (e.g. an advertising agency not handling competing clients). For marketers, the regulations and codes of practice set by professional and industry bodies can be just as significant as laws. It is important to know, for example, what is permitted when making price offers, setting competition rules, offering sales promotions, making advertising claims, designing packaging, commenting on competing brands, etc. All of these things, and more, will need to follow professional codes of practice.

Laws and regulations vary from country to country. There are very few laws that span borders and, contrary to popular belief, there is no international body of law or international court that covers all trading agreements between companies. Increasingly, there are supranational laws and bodies within trading blocs, e.g. the European Union, but in the main, individual countries' laws still apply and so it is vital that companies from different countries agree which country's rules should apply to a contract at the outset. This variety of laws in countries is one of the things that makes international marketing additionally complicated. Take sales promotion laws as an example: some countries, for example Germany, restrict the value of competition prizes to ensure there isn't too strong a temptation to enter; others, such as Belgium and Denmark, have no such restrictions (DLA Piper, 2014).

Although the parties to the contract can choose which country's law applies to an international contract, they cannot opt out of another country's laws and regulations concerning the product itself and its sale within that country. It is important to understand the laws and business regulations of any country with which you hope to trade. Ignorance is rarely a defence in law and unwary companies who assume that judicial systems and laws in all countries are the same are likely to earn themselves hefty fines – or even find their employees imprisoned.

Things to look for in the regulatory environment include:

- new laws and regulations
- changes in laws or regulations: either in content or punishments
- new legal institutions or other bodies, e.g. courts, advisory committees, tribunals
- changes in the way regulations are administered, e.g. a move away from the UK Financial Services Authority (FSA).

Laws are developed by governments, or the judiciary, and usually take a long time to come into force. This gives organisations (or at least those that have identified the proposed laws through their environmental scanning) an opportunity to try to influence the content of laws during their development. This activity is called lobbying.

Lobbying is a means of influencing politicians. It is often employed by pressure or interest groups (e.g. trade associations) rather than by individual firms. The tobacco industry and farmers both have strong lobbies in many EU countries. Trained lobbyists identify the key members of committees that are debating the proposed changes in law and put

global focus: The European Union

The European Union (EU) is the largest economy in the world and home to approximately 500 million consumers. It is the top trading partner for 80 countries – as a comparison, the US is top trading partner for just over 20 countries. The EU is also the world's largest trading bloc with a common tariff, i.e. all EU member countries charge the same amount of duty on goods imported from outside the EU. This prevents other countries from shipping goods into a country with lower taxes and then taking advantage of the lack of barriers within the EU to move the goods on.

In 2016, there were 28 member states in the EU (pending the outcome of Brexit). The dates in brackets show when the country joined:

tariffs
import taxes charged by governments

duty
an import tax charged by the government

Austria (1995)

Belgium (founding member, 1957)

Bulgaria (2007)

Croatia (2013)

Cyprus (2004)

Czech Republic (2004)

Denmark (1973)

Estonia (2004)

Finland (1995)

France (founding member, 1957)

Germany (founding member, 1957)

Greece (1981)

Hungary (2004)

Ireland (1973)

Italy (founding member, 1957)

Latvia (2004)

Lithuania (2004)

Luxembourg (founding member, 1957)

Malta (2004)

Netherlands (founding member, 1957)

Poland (2004)

Portugal (1986)

Romania (2007)

Slovakia (2004)

Slovenia (2004)

Spain (1986)

Sweden (1995)

United Kingdom (1973)

European Union Parliament Building.

© European Commission, 2012b

The following are candidate countries who have started, or will soon start, accession negotiations:

Iceland

Macedonia

Montenegro

Serbia

Turkey

Sources: European Parliament (2016); European Commission (n.d.)

their arguments to them. They hope to persuade the committees to make favourable changes or to drop any harmful proposals altogether. In Britain, the tobacco lobby has been particularly effective: even when it had been agreed that cigarette companies should no longer be allowed to sponsor sports, it managed to get motor racing and snooker exempted. More recently, alcohol producers lobbied to try and prevent stricter rules on the advertising of alcoholic drinks being imposed, and the UK TV industry successfully lobbied advertising regulators and the UK government to get **product placement** rules relaxed. In 2012, banks came under increasing pressure from proposed legislation such as the potential financial transaction tax. In response, Barclays decided to appoint an EU-level Public Affairs agency to complement its recent appointment of Cicero in the UK and lobby on its behalf.

product placement

arranging for products to be seen, or referred to, in entertainment media, e.g. during TV or radio programmes, films, plays, video games

Cadbury: example of regulatory factors

- EU regulations specify the permitted ingredients in chocolate and cocoa products intended for human consumption, including the maximum permitted vegetable fat of 5% (EUR-Lex, 2014); this has had more impact on UK brands, which traditionally have lower cocoa levels, than it has had on their European rivals.

- UK regulations prohibit schools from providing chocolate or other sugary snacks in school (Department for Education, 2012).

THE ECONOMIC ENVIRONMENT

The E in PRESTCOM refers to the macro-economic environment – *not* to the internal costs of firms. All firms are affected by changes in their macro-economic environment. The macro-economic environment is what is commonly referred to in newspapers as 'the economy'. It is made up of all the buying and selling that goes on in a country (the national economy) or in the world (the global economy). Economic trends today are increasingly global rather than affecting a country in isolation, and this makes it harder for countries to manage their own economies. Most Western governments publish data on economic trends, as do professional organisations such as the Chartered Institute of Marketing (CIM) and international bodies such as the Organisation for Economic Cooperation and Development (OECD).

Things to look for in the economic environment include:

- stage in the **trade cycle**, e.g. **boom** or **recession**?

   o Booms are the good times, characterised by high consumer spending and business profits, and low unemployment. Unfortunately, this increase in demand for goods and services may lead to shortages and so to raised prices (**inflation**) and the need to import more while exporting less (balance of payments deficit).

   o A recession is likely to follow. Consumers cannot afford the high prices and so demand falls. Businesses find they have surplus capacity and cut back, so unemployment rises, and consumers have even less money to spend. It is a vicious circle (see Exhibit 2.4). Traditionally, food retailers do comparatively well in hard times, but those who sell luxuries suffer.

trade cycle

patterns of economic activity consisting of boom, downturn (recession), slump (depression), upturn (recovery); also known as the 'business cycle'

boom

when an economy experiences a rapid rise in spending, often accompanied by higher prices and raised investment levels

recession

when an economy experiences reducing sales and investment; if this continues, it may go into a depression

inflation

when the prices of goods rise without a matching (or greater) increase in their actual value

- Rates of inflation: these have a big impact on companies' costs – and therefore also their prices. In recent years, some countries have experienced zero inflation (e.g. the UK in early 2015), even deflation (where general price levels decrease). This is a problem because people put off purchases and so economic activity falls.
- Unemployment figures: again this helps work out the potential market, and also indicates what kind of products (luxury or basic) might do well.
- Household disposable income figures and trends: these indicate whether or not people are likely to be able to afford a product.
- Availability of credit: both consumer and business. European austerity measures have restricted consumer and business borrowing, making it harder for them to spend; clearly this has a massive knock-on effect on sales – especially of non-essential items.
- The country's approach to **social costs**: how much might your company have to contribute?
- Business taxes, e.g. VAT (purchase tax) which affects prices and corporation tax (on a company's profits).
- Import tariffs: firms that trade internationally have to take account of **import duties** (taxes) and other import barriers when devising their marketing plans.
- Membership of trading blocs, e.g. EU, NAFTA, ASEAN. There are no import tariffs for EU countries trading with each other.

social costs

the costs incurred by society generally as a result of business processes or decisions, e.g. the clearing up of pollution, the provision of transport infrastructure

import duties

taxes paid when goods are brought into a country from outside

Most firms will hold off new product launches during a recession and it is almost certainly not the time to launch the latest luxury model. It may, however, prove a good time to launch cut-down, budget versions of products, e.g. the no-frills version of a mass-market car or super-economy class on an airline. Prices are likely to need careful monitoring and may need to be changed more often than in better economic times. It is important to remember the negative implications of reducing prices though. For example, a low price may be associated with lower quality (see Chapter 10). Also, consumers get used to falling prices and special offers and may delay buying products in the hope that they will become cheaper. This makes demand fall further and adds to the problem.

Just as some companies are said to be recession-proof, so are some individuals (i.e. the very rich). Businesses that target wealthy consumers, e.g. top designers such as Christian Dior

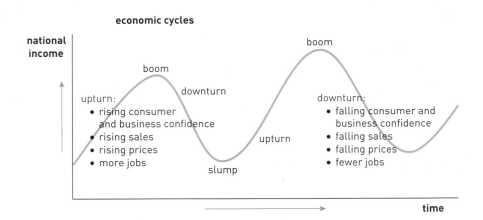

EXHIBIT 2.4 The trade cycle

and luxury goods makers such as Rolex, are less likely to suffer significant drops in sales because of downward shifts in the world economy. Income distribution is as important as average income. In some countries (e.g. Saudi Arabia) a small proportion of the population controls the bulk of the country's considerable wealth.

A firm that understands the economic environment in which it operates is far better placed to take advantage of changes in income and spending. Even a recession can be turned to competitive advantage by well-informed and talented marketers.

research focus

Woodall, T. (2012) 'Driven to excess? Linking calling, character and the (mis)behaviour of marketers', *Journal of Marketing Theory*, 12 (2): 173–91.

The author has identified the need for a new approach to marketing that takes account of wide reaching changes in the marketing environment, notably: recession, increased emphasis on business ethics and shifting social agendas.

Available at: **http://mtq.sagepub.com/content/12/2/173.full.pdf +html**

THE SOCIAL ENVIRONMENT

The social environment encompasses trends and changes in society, i.e. things that are happening to people. Next to the technological environment, this is the area that has perhaps seen the most changes over the last fifty years. Populations have exploded in some parts of the world (notably China and India), while declining in others (notably the Western nations). This has put a massive strain on the resources of some countries, while the richer nations try to close their doors to a potential flood of immigrants.

Cadbury: example of economic factors

- Many Western countries are considering ways to improve the healthiness of food products, for example, the UK government is introducing a sugar tax on soft drinks, especially fizzy drinks. Although the tax is initially only on drinks containing very high sugar levels, clearly chocolate manufacturers would want to monitor the situation to assess the likelihood of the tax being extended to other products.

- Ongoing recession/low growth rates have resulted in generally lower disposable incomes: less money to spend on luxuries such as chocolate. However, chocolate is possibly recession-proof, i.e. in hard times, consumers spend more on low-price luxuries such as chocolate and overall European sales, although sluggish, are not falling (KPMG, 2012).

Things to look for in the social environment include:

- population figures
- age profiles, e.g. many Western nations have ageing populations while in some African countries, where life expectancy is relatively low, the bulk of the population is under 35

- gender balance; ratio of men to women
- lifestyle changes, e.g. a move to urban living, an increase in leisure time, ways in which people spend their time, how people interact (e.g. through online social networking)
- cultural differences, e.g. changes in how children are brought up, changes in men's and women's roles
- religions.

Cadbury: example of social factors

- Over half (53%) of the UK population are either overweight or obese, despite increased understanding of the health risks associated with this (Mintel, 2012).
- UK sales of Fairtrade chocolate confectionery grew from £18 million in 2005 to £343 million in 2010 (Fairtrade Foundation, 2011), reflecting the population's increased concern over the ethics of what they buy; 43% of chocolate products launched in the UK in 2014 carried an ethical or environmental claim, up from 26% in 2012 (Mintel, 2015).

The way we live our lives is changing all the time and products, and marketers, must keep up. It is not so long ago that most women were housewives. Now, in the UK, women account for nearly 50% of the workforce though they are far more likely than men to work part time (Close the Gap, 2016). Scandinavian countries (and New Zealand) have the highest rates of female employment but still, across the globe, women tend to earn less than men (PricewaterhouseCoopers, 2016), however they do still make more of the day-to-day household expenditure decisions. In the past, marketers could just target all women's products and household items at housewives. It is not so easy now. They have to address a variety of different types of women, with different lifestyles and different requirements. The result of this has been a boom in **convenience goods**, such as cleaning wipes and ready meals. It has also led a retail revolution as shoppers seek convenience through home delivery services, mail order, Internet shopping and personal shoppers.

convenience goods

products that customers buy frequently and think little about

digital focus: made for sharing

Do you What's App, Wanelo or YikYak or how about Kik or Bebo? The increasing reach, accessibility and functionality of social networking sites and apps, combined with the very human impulse to connect and share, means social media is as popular as ever. While Facebook leads worldwide with more than 1.5 billion users (adding around half a million new users every single day) the explosion of smartphone use and ownership has seen mobile chat apps like What's App rapidly outpace PC based social networks.

Platforms vary considerably: in their purpose and function, membership and even in their personalities. They have many different styles and forms of communication from the 140 characters of hypertext on Twitter to the aesthetic focus of Instagram. Just as social media help us to express ourselves and connect with each other in new and exciting ways, they also *empower* us as consumers: helping us to make purchase decisions, giving us a voice and more of a say in the products and brands that marketers develop.

Those businesses and brands willing to embrace social media (and with it a certain lack of control over what people say about their brands) are finding creative new ways to forge closer and stronger connections with consumers. Marketers who ignore the social and market impact of these technologies run the risk of becoming famous for all the wrong reasons.

THE TECHNOLOGICAL ENVIRONMENT

In the last two centuries, technology has changed at an unprecedented rate. In the developed nations, people have moved from a way of life based on agriculture, to industry with its mass production, and on to jobs in a microprocessor-based service economy. The most developed countries (MDCs) are now becoming post-industrial information- and communication-based societies.

Rates of technological advancement vary across the world. It would be expected that the MDCs would have all the latest technology while less developed countries (LDCs) lagged behind – and this is generally speaking true. However, international marketers must be careful about making assumptions about countries' readiness to accept types of goods based on their level of economic development alone. It is not uncommon to see colour televisions and satellite dishes in basic homes in poorer countries. Such luxuries can be status symbols that people are prepared to go without basics in order to obtain. There is also the phenomenon of technology skipping, where a developing country misses a whole generation of technology and jumps in at the next level. For example, in parts of Africa mobile phones are common while there are no landlines – the distances are too great to make it viable to install telephone wires. Never make assumptions about other countries – always check.

What to look for in the technological environment:

- new types of technology, especially information technology (IT) or computers but also production technology
- changes in transport, e.g. high-speed train lines
- changes in communications technologies, e.g. the increased presence of large digital screens in shopping centres
- convergence of technologies, e.g. that of computers and telecommunications to produce smartphones
- increased availability of existing technologies, e.g. of high-speed communications networks (e.g. broadband) or of digital television
- new software, especially where there are changes in lifestyle, e.g. social media networking, personal web pages and blogs
- green technologies, e.g. electric cars, solar panels, better recycling facilities.

3D printed house

Cloud computing lets firms share computing resources via the Internet, making new technology more accessible and affordable. Amazon recognised early on that it could generate **revenue** by renting out its excess computing capacity and today Amazon Web Services is the world's most comprehensive and widely used cloud platform. Cloud computing

revenue (sales revenue)
the income a firm receives from the sale of goods and services

IBM: smarter commerce

works by offloading some of the hard work done by local hardware and software, onto bigger, better, faster systems based elsewhere and accessed over the Internet, usually in a very seamless way. This can be a big help for businesses as instead of having to invest in all the hardware, software and infrastructure they require in-house (for example, to host and manage marketing databases) they can pay for the computing power they need, as and when they need it. Typically this reduces up-front costs and makes it easier to scale requirements up or down. Many of the most popular on-the-go consumer software services are only possible because of cloud computing. For example, you can access web-based email clients like Google's Gmail service wherever you are as long as you have an Internet connection. Apple's iCloud lets you upload photos from an iPhone and download them onto a MacBook, or upload music from a MacBook to download and play on an iPod Nano. When you type words into a search engine like Google, most of the hard work that is done to process your query and sift through and serve up relevant results is done by computers located in Dublin, California or Beijing: most users don't know and probably don't care, but they are directly benefitting from the flexibility and convenience that services based 'in the cloud' provide.

digital focus: How Old Robot

How old do I look? It can be an awkward question to ask, and an even harder one to answer so perhaps it's no surprise that Microsoft's How Old Robot application was such a runaway success. It is an excellent example of the flexibility and scalability of software applications built in the cloud. Initially the How Old Robot application was built for a developers' conference to demonstrate Microsoft's pioneering research in facial recognition technology and machine learning. The 'robot' was trained using photographic images of men and women of various ages and learned to use facial characteristics to estimate a person's age from a photograph uploaded by the user. Despite attempts to keep the demo under wraps prior to the conference, news leaked out and the app went viral on social media; How Old Robot gained 25,000 new users within the first three hours. The test site was quickly shut down but after the conference, when the site had been re-written for a non-geek audience with social sharing buttons, and a hashtag, the application was ready for launch. Within a week How Old Robot had 50 million users. People shared when How Old Robot was right although there were even more shares of when it was wrong. They enjoyed trying to trick the robot with photographs of drawings and even ancient Egyptian mummies! It took Facebook two and a half years to achieve the same number of users as How Old Robot did on its first day, making it difficult, if not impossible, to predict such a rapid increase in demand. The app could have been expected to crash, or at least to slow up frustratingly, but thanks to cloud computing capacity could be increased quickly and easily, and just as readily scaled down when the initial hype was past.

It is not just businesses that are affected by changes in technology: consumers' lives would be radically different if technology had not progressed at the pace it has. Houses would be colder and a lot less convenient. The kitchen would be a very different place in which to cook. Hygiene standards would be lower as hot water would be a more complicated treat. There would be fewer home offices if the recent advances in communications and personal computing had not happened.

research focus

Järvinen, J., Tollinen, A., Karjaluoto, H. and Jayawardhena, C. (2012) 'Digital and social media marketing usage in b2b industrial section', *Marketing Management Journal*, 22 (2): 102–17.
   This paper presents an overview of the usage, measurement practices and barriers surrounding digital marketing in the era of social media. It also provides a useful summary of other studies in the b2b sector.

Technological change has far-reaching effects. Its impact can be felt right across the external environment. Technology, and the ability to innovate, are key determinants of competitiveness.

Many external factors could reasonably be placed in several of the PRESTCOM categories. For example, there are overlaps between the technological environment and the social environment. Think, for example, of the different views on the use of mobile phones in public, or noisy personal stereos. There are still recycling resisters and climate change deniers but many have changed the way they live to try and conserve the earth.

ACTIVITY

Look around your room. Are there any items in it that wouldn't have existed twenty years ago? What about ten years ago? And of the things that did exist, would you have been likely to own them?

There is increasing concern about the way we have exploited the planet on which we live. Any responsible analysis must take into account the impact that a firm's marketing will have on the world around us – the Earth is rich in resources but these are not limitless. There is a growing trend towards only harvesting things that can be replaced or regrown. Wooden and paper goods proudly declare it if they are made from sustainable sources. Organic food has become big business in the UK, where consumers are worried about pesticides and genetically modified (GM) products.

research focus

Siamagka, N.T., Christodoulides, G., Michaelidou, N. and Valvi, A. (2015) 'Determinants of social media adoption by B2B organizations', *Industrial Marketing Management*, 51: 89–99.
   This paper focuses on the factors that determine social media adoption by b2b organisations drawing on a key conceptual model, the technology acceptance model (Davis et al., 1989) that is well introduced in the paper. It provides a good overview of the potential benefits of social media for b2b organisations and the barriers that still remain for some, including consideration of reputational risks and legal issues, lack of staff knowledge/training, senior managers' lack of support, and reluctance to lose control of the brand.

The technological environment has to be watched very carefully. Most environmental changes happen quite slowly, over a considerable period of time, but a technological breakthrough can change an organisation's prospects overnight. Long-established businesses often lose their market leadership to younger rivals with better technology.

niche market

a market segment that
can be treated as a target
market; a small, well-defined
market, often part of a larger
market

Swiss watches used to be reckoned to be the best in the world, until the Japanese put
microprocessors in theirs. IBM, once the undisputed leader in almost all forms of computing, lost out to Microsoft's more user-friendly Windows operating system. Cars and planes
harmed the railway industry and vinyl has become a **niche market** thanks to the invention of
CDs, which have in turn lost out to downloads, iPods and other multimedia devices. How
will music be sold in the future?

Cadbury: example of technological factors

- Scientists are searching for healthier versions of chocolate and there have been a number of successes
  in this area, along with product innovations such as bubbly chocolate which is pumped with air and crispy
  chocolate bars made with puffed rice.

- Advances in packaging improve the shelf life of the bars and the ability of the chocolate to withstand heat.
  Mondelez introduced new packaging that is easier to re-seal which it is hoped will have the effect of encouraging people to eat less at one sitting (Brooks, 2012).

Porter's Five Forces

THE COMPETITIVE ENVIRONMENT

The competitive environment (see Exhibit 2.5) is part of the external environment. This section looks at types of competition and key factors to include in an environmental analysis.
For more advanced competitive analysis tools, e.g. Porter's 5 forces, see Chapter 12.

competitors
- direct
- close
- substitute
- indirect

EXHIBIT 2.5 The competitive environment

Some industries are more competitive than others. For example, the rivalry between UK
supermarkets is high, with frequent price undercutting and heavy promotional activity.
Some firms are arch-rivals. Often these companies are vying for each other's market
share – perhaps to take over as the market leader. PepsiCo and Coca-Cola, for instance,
compete fiercely, as do Nike and Adidas. Other companies may opt for **coopetition**, i.e. they
cooperate, most commonly in research and new product development, up to a point.
The finishing touches on the Citroen C1, the Toyota Aygo and the Peugeot 107 may be
different but these city cars are all basically the same (Top Gear, n.d.).

coopetition

when competitors cooperate
with each other for mutual
benefit, e.g. by sharing
research costs

consumer panel

a primary research technique
that seeks the views,
attitudes, behaviour or
buying habits of a group of
consumers

Another example, this time from the market research world, is that of AC Nielsen and
Symphony IRI, both internationally renowned market research companies, especially in
the field of consumer packaged goods (CPG) marketing. Despite a history of bitter rivalry
and long-running court battles over anti-competitive practices, the companies formed a
coopetition alliance in order to develop, recruit and retain a shared **consumer panel**. They
shared the panel members but not the data. Each company uses the panel to collect their
own data on household purchases and use.

The first thing to work out is: who are the competition? Competitive products can be cat-egorised as: direct, close, substitute or indirect.

- *Direct competition*: A direct competitor offers a product that is similar to the company's own. For example, Heineken is a direct competitor to Carlsberg, just as Coca-Cola is to Pepsi.

- *Close competition*: A close competitor offers a similar product – one that satisfies the same need. Other soft drinks, such as Tango, can be said to be close competitors of Coca-Cola and Pepsi. Close competition might be said to extend to any drink, in fact.

- *Substitute competition*: These are products that are different from the company's own, but might be bought instead. Again, they satisfy the same or similar needs. An ice cream is a substitute product for a chocolate bar – either can be eaten as a sweet snack.

- *Indirect competition*: This is competition in its widest sense. People have limited amounts of money to spend and so all products compete for that spending ability. A woman may go out to buy a jacket but then see an irresistible pair of shoes. If she does not have the money for both, the jacket and shoes are in competition.

© iStockphoto.com/Jeurgen Bosse   © iStockphoto.com/Wouter van Caspel

© Eurostar ID brand library

Substitutes for a cross-channel trip: plane, ferry and Eurostar.

Firms analyse the competitive environment to see how they compare with rivals, and to try to understand their competitors' strategies – what they are doing now and what they intend to do in the future. This is essential if the firm is to develop counter-strategies and maintain, or improve, its market position.

research focus: classic concept

Slater, S. and Narver, J. (1994) 'Does competitive environment moderate the market orientation-performance relationship?', *Journal of Marketing*, **58 (Jan): 46–55.**

These authors have been instrumental in maintaining a research interest on issues related to market orientation. In this paper, they address issues pertaining to the effect of competitive environment on the adoption of orientation.

Things to look for in the competitive environment include:

- the main competitors
- the relative strengths of competitors, e.g. in terms of resources or control of the distribution channel
- who is the market leader?
- how the companies or brands compete, e.g. on price or through product differentiation
- the ferocity of the competition; frequent price wars or very high marketing spends suggest high levels of competition
- the nature of competitive products – are they direct, indirect, close or substitute (see above)? – and the relative strengths of those products
- the structure of the industry, e.g. is it dominated by one or two large companies or brands or are there lots of small ones (a **fragmented industry**)?
- competitors' action and intentions.

fragmented industry

one in which there are a lot of players, few of whom have any significant power

Despite the ever-growing internationalisation of business, a company entering a new market is likely to find itself facing at least some new competitors. For example, Coca-Cola and Pepsi lead the market in most countries across the globe, except in India. In India, the favoured cola drink is Thums Up. Coca-Cola found it unusually hard to compete against Thums Up and Pepsi at the same time. The strategy they eventually settled on was to buy the Thums Up company. Now, according to India's *Economic Times* (Bhushan, 2016) new Indian competitors, such as Gujarat's Hajoori & Sons, Alwar-based Jayanti Beverages and Delhi's City Cola, are making inroads into the fizzy drinks market and stealing significant market share from Coke and Pepsi.

Cadbury: example of competitive factors

- Cadburys Dairy Milk remains the UK's bestselling brand but parent company Mondelez takes second place to Mars in the world market (International Cocoa Organization, 2016). There are a number of successful niche players, notably in high-end products, e.g. Hotel Chocolat; in ethical products, e.g. Montezuma's; and in healthier products, e.g. Tasty Little Numbers.
- The Indian market, where Mondelez (formerly Cadbury India) are also market leaders with a 55% market share, has become increasingly competitive due to numerous new product launches and brand extensions (Euromonitor, 2016).

THE ORGANISATIONAL ENVIRONMENT (THE INTERNAL ENVIRONMENT)

The organisational heading in the PRESTCOM analysis is the only one that concerns internal factors, i.e. things that are particular to the company in question. This includes the organisation's structure as well as its assets (people and their skills, money, brands, buildings and machinery, etc.).

There are six basic functions within a business (see Exhibit 2.6), of which marketing is one. It is important that these functions work well together and support each other. This requires good communication between staff and a culture that encourages interaction and mutual support. If all functions display a **customer orientation** (see Chapter 1), then this harmony will be easier to achieve. One of the key things that the company wishes to achieve from this cooperation is a consistent image.

customer orientation

the whole organisation is focused on the satisfaction of its customers' needs

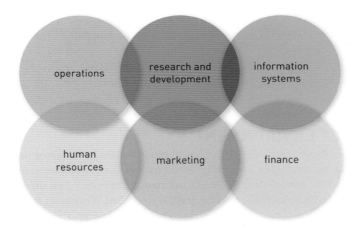

EXHIBIT 2.6 The internal environment

In analysing an organisation's internal resources, the analyst is looking for sources of advantage and disadvantage. For the purposes of marketing planning, these should be of relevance to the marketing function (although that does not mean that they will always be contained within the marketing department).

Things to look for in the organisational environment include:

- key products and brands
- the quality of personnel, e.g. do they have the best engineers?
- staff turnover; do they keep their key staff?
- the state of the company's finances and the size of budgets
- production facilities, e.g. are they the most advanced in the industry? Are they out of date?
- comparative costs; which will affect prices and profits

- strength of the company's balance sheet; are they secure? Can they afford to invest?
- reputation
- suitability of premises, e.g. is the shop attractive?
- strength of the research and development (R&D) department
- IT systems: are they up to date? Leading edge? Unique?
- facilities, e.g. do they own factories or contract out to others? Do they have their own shops?
- location of outlets
- access to transport.

Cadbury: example of organisational factors

- Cadbury is a well-established UK brand now owned by Mondelez (whose parent company is the US food giant Kraft). The new ownership has increased the company resources potentially available to the Cadbury brand.
- Cadbury has a strong corporate brand name in the UK and across the world, as well as a wide range of well-known, popular branded products. Some, e.g. Dairy Milk, are Fairtrade products.

THE MARKET ENVIRONMENT

The market environment is part of the external environment. In modern marketing terms, the word 'market' is most often used to refer to customers or consumers. Increasingly, the recipients of goods or services are referred to as customers even when they are not paying, as in the case of charities and other **not-for-profit organisations**. This is an attempt to improve the effectiveness of organisations by focusing their attention on the people they exist to serve (see the section on customer orientation in Chapter 1).

not-for-profit organisations

organisations whose primary goal is something other than profit, e.g. government, charities, clubs, pressure groups

Markets can be classified according to the customers within them. The major customer groups are described below:

- individuals, i.e. consumer markets: where private individuals buy goods for their own use, or perhaps to give to someone else. For some purchases, a distinction can be made between customers (who pay for products) and consumers (who use the products). For example, children's clothes are bought by adults (customers) but worn by children (consumers) – both groups are important.
- businesses, which may be either industrial or b2b (business-to-business):
  - Industrial buyers use the products they buy as an ingredient, or component, in the making of something else (e.g. Peugeot buying tyres to fit on to new cars) or to contribute directly to the manufacturing process (e.g. oil for machinery). Those tyres could, of course, have been bought by an individual to replace the worn-out tyres on their own car, and that would be a consumer purchase and come from a different source (and be almost certainly more expensive).

- o Organisations also need general supplies, office stationery, etc., which they use rather than make something with it. The sale of such goods is a b2b market.

- government/public sector – governments are extremely large customers, spending millions on goods and services annually.

- resellers, i.e. those who sell on the products they buy to someone else, such as wholesalers, distributors, dealers, franchisees (see Chapter 9).

- overseas markets, i.e. all the above, but in other countries.

EXHIBIT 2.7 Markets

Things to look for in the market environment include:

- who the customers, consumers, users are; develop customer profiles

- how purchase decisions are made

- what the key influences are on purchase choices

- how brand loyal customers are

- motivations to buy

- how much typical customers spend, and how often

- size of the market for the products in question; in terms of **sales volume** and **sales value**

- customers' media habits, e.g. do they read newspapers? Which ones? How much time do they spend surfing? Do they have smartphones, iPads, etc.?

- customer attitudes to the products, the company, other relevant factors, e.g. green issues.

sales volume
the quantity of goods sold, expressed in units, e.g. 2 million apples

sales value
the revenue derived from items sold

Cadbury: example of market factors

- The number of mentions that Cadbury Dairy Milk gets on social media is falling. There were fewer conversations about Cadbury adverts and mentions unrelated to advertising also fell. Green & Black's has fewer Facebook fans than other brands, but is more active on Twitter thanks to competitions and other engagement strategies. (Mintel, 2015).

- The European and North American chocolate market is seasonal with peaks at Easter and Christmas. Chocolate, especially luxury chocolate, is increasingly given as a gift (Mintel, 2012).

THE INTERNATIONAL MARKETING ENVIRONMENT

The PRESTCOM model can be adapted for use in international situations, along with the addition of three Cs:

Political	**O**rganisational
Regulatory	**M**arket
Economic	+
Social	**C**urrency
Technological	**C**ulture
Competitive	**C**ountry

The international marketing environment is very much more complex than the domestic one – not least because no two countries are alike and researchers therefore need to conduct PRESTCOM analyses for each and every country in which the company trades (see Exhibit 2.8).

research focus: classic concept

Kotler, P., Gregor, W. and Rogers, W. (1977) 'The marketing audit comes of age', *Sloan Management Review*, 18 (2): 25–43.

Key areas of marketing are identified and put together in a comprehensive 'audit'. The audit forms an essential part of the analysis process that will eventually form the basis of marketing plans.

THE THREE CS
Country

A country's history and geography should be taken into account when designing and implementing plans.

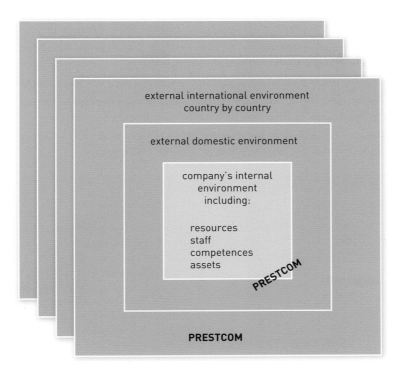

EXHIBIT 2.8 International environments

Things to look for include:

- the relationship between countries; Britain has very good relations with a number of its ex-colonies (many of which belong to the Commonwealth), but not with all, e.g. Zimbabwe; for a number of years the USA and Iran have had no relationship at all but that began to change in 2015 when sanctions against Iran were lifted in exchange for guarantees about their nuclear weapons programme

- geography and climate can affect a country's suitability for certain products and the ease, or otherwise, with which they can be distributed; some countries are remote and inaccessible, e.g. Tibet, which is politically inaccessible as well as being surrounded by the Himalayan mountains

- infrastructure, e.g. transport links, business agencies, distributors; e.g. many land-locked African countries have roads that are too rough to carry trucks of goods safely to their destinations.

Marketing in emerging markets

Currency
Most countries have their own currency and products will normally have to be sold in that currency.

Things to look for include:

- the ease of currency exchange; at the most extreme, some currencies are unconvertible, i.e. cannot be changed into another currency
- exchange rates; prices and the stability of the currency; a currency that varies wildly is risky
- how easy, or difficult, it is to take currency out of the country; normally, firms want to take at least some of their profits back to their home countries
- the possibility of trading in another country's currency, ideally to your own; failing that, something that is easier to manage, e.g. the US dollar.

global focus: Marmite-gate

In 2016 the UK voted to leave the European Union. Soon afterwards the pound fell by as much as 28% when valued against the US dollar and the Euro. There was much speculation about how well the public, and the politicians, understood the implications of leaving the EU but one story captured the British public's imagination and illustrated some of the potential economic perils of Brexit. Unilever wanted to increase the price of the much loved (or hated – depending on your taste) savoury spread Marmite (and other products) by 10% to compensate for its increased costs.

Vegemite ✓
@Vegemite

@Bovril **This is our moment.**

13/10/2016, 07:44

One of many parody tweets at the time and not a genuine post from either company

Cost increases are usually passed on to customers if at all possible. Tesco, often berated for its treatment of suppliers, surprisingly turned consumer champion by refusing to pay. The country went wild – especially via social media #marmitegate #marmageddon #marmexit. Jars of Marmite were offered on eBay for extortionate prices (though there is no evidence that any sold).

Unilever's point was that the fall in the value of the pound made products and ingredients for products more expensive to import. This is of course true where they had to pay euros or any other currency for the products as one pound bought less foreign currency than it did before. Holidaymakers found this to their cost when trying to change pounds into euros before travelling abroad.

While UK importers and holidaymakers lost out from the lowered exchange rate, exporters and tourists coming to the UK gained. The UK tourist industry could hope for a double boost from Brits who could no longer afford to travel abroad and foreign visitors who found the UK was suddenly much more affordable.

Tesco and Unilever reportedly compromised on the cost of Marmite and there was no immediate price hike. Marmite is actually made in Burton on Trent in central England and uses locally sourced ingredients so it's unclear why that particular product should need a price rise – unless it was a clever **publicity stunt** of course.

Brexit: risks and opportunities

publicity stunt

an event designed to capture the attention of the media or other publics

National culture (Geert Hofstede)

Culture

Culture is a key contributor to the kind of person that you are and it is not solely determined by where you were born or who your parents are. As well as ethnic or geographic cultures, there are youth cultures, organisational cultures and religious cultures.

The *Oxford Dictionary of English* (2005) defines culture as 'the ideas, customs, and social behaviour of a particular people or society'. An understanding of a person's cultural background helps marketers to anticipate their responses to products and to tailor campaigns to appeal to them.

International marketers are primarily concerned with the culture shared by the people of a specific country, but it is important to remember that even within a country there are going to be a variety of cultures. Just take a walk down London's Oxford Street and see if you think all the people there share the same cultural background – well, perhaps they are all part of a consumer culture at least.

Things to look for include:

- language
- beliefs
- attitudes
- customs
- superstitions
- uses for products
- the way the people of a country live.

When language lets us down, we often try sign language, or gestures instead, but there is no more a universal understanding of gestures than there is of words. In many countries it is extremely rude to point, whereas in others it is just a normal way to indicate something. On the Indian subcontinent, people shake their head for yes and nod for no; in Europe, it is the other way around. The holding up of the index and middle fingers (or even just the middle finger) is very rude in the UK, but a sign that is not readily understood elsewhere. It can make it quite dangerous for foreigners to count on their fingers in Britain. Even in the UK, it makes a huge difference if you hold the hand the other way, palm out, as the two fingers then symbolise peace. And, if we go back to the end of the Second World War, when British Prime Minister Winston Churchill first used the gesture, he was not being rude – his two fingers symbolised victory.

ACTIVITY

Visit a place that is popular with foreign tourists. How do the people there differ from each other? How do you know that they are from different countries? Can you tell (without actually asking them) where they are from?

Winston Churchill's V for Victory.

Source: Reg Speller/Hulton Archive/Getty Images

ACTIVITY

These cultural differences make the world a more interesting place but are a minefield for unwary international marketers.

SITUATION ANALYSIS

It is very hard (and usually spectacularly unsuccessful) to plan a route ahead without an understanding of the starting point. Take the example of a journey to London. The travel agent is going to need to know the journey's starting point before they can possibly recommend a method of travel. It makes a big difference whether the traveller is currently in Paris, New York or Leicester.

Similarly, a company needs to know where it stands at the moment before it can make plans to improve its position. Acquisition of another chain might well be a suitable way for a large chain of stores with a dominant market position to grow, but a smaller chain, with fewer resources, is unlikely to be able to do this.

An analysis of the current situation is the starting point for most plans. It tells a firm where it is now.

The basic planning process looks like this:

Where are we now?

(situation analysis)

↓

Where do we want to be?

(objectives)

↓

How will we get there?

(the plan)

↓

Are we on the right route?

and

How will we know when we've arrived?

(evaluation and control)

There are a number of techniques and models that the organisation can use to analyse its situation, the most widely used of which is a SWOT analysis. This analysis is based on organising environmental data gleaned from a PRESTCOM environmental analysis.

MONOPOLY = single supplier controls the market
Duopoly = two suppliers control the market between them
Oligopoly = few suppliers control the market
Perfect competition = anyone has perfect knowledge and no one buyers or seller can influence the market
Monopolistic competition = one company has a strong influence but there are others that still enter the market

SWOT

A SWOT analysis is a general management tool rather than being peculiar to marketing. However, it is widely used as a basis for marketing planning. Selected **environmental variables** from the PRESTCOM analysis (see page 78) are placed under one of the four SWOT headings:

Strengths   internal, i.e. under the organisation's control, e.g. well-developed brand

Weaknesses   internal, i.e. under the organisation's control, e.g. small budget

Opportunities   external, i.e. not under the organisation's control, e.g. favourable fashion trend

Threats   external, i.e. not under the organisation's control, e.g. unfavourable fashion trend

SWOT analysis
a situational analysis tool that assesses the organisation's strengths and weaknesses (internal) and opportunities and threats (external)

environmental variables
factors within an organisation's environment that may change, i.e. PRESTCOM elements

Strengths and weaknesses are internal factors, while opportunities and threats are external. So, only organisational factors go into strengths or weaknesses; the rest of the PRESTCOM analysis is external and so feeds into opportunities or threats.

A strength is something that the firm has, or something that it does, that is better than its competitors. For example, a stronger brand name would be a strength.

A weakness is the opposite of a strength: something that the firm has (or does not have) or does that is worse than the competition. For example, an outdated product range would be a weakness.

Threats and opportunities are part of the external environment and therefore an organisation will have far less (if any) control over them.

A threat is something that is going on in the firm's external environment that is likely to cause it problems. The drinks industry is threatened by proposed regulations that will make it much more difficult to promote alcohol.

An opportunity is the opposite of a threat: it is something that is going on in the external environment that is likely to be good for the organisation. For example, an upturn in the economy is an opportunity for many firms.

Opportunities have deliberately been left until last as they seem to be the cause of much student confusion. It is important to realise that the word 'opportunity' is being used in a very particular way here: *an opportunity is not an action.* It is not something that the firm could do. It is just something good that is happening outside that the firm might be able to take advantage of – somehow.

Further examples of possible opportunities are:

- the election of a government that is pro-foreign trade in one of the firm's export markets
- the relaxation of rules governing what can and what cannot be sponsored

ACTIVITY

Pick a company that is in the news. What has been going on in its environment that has helped put it there?

ACTIVITY

Pick one of the following organisations (or choose your own) and make a list of relevant PRESTCOM trends, issues, events (i.e. environmental variables). Then categorise them under the SWOT headings. Choose from:

Microsoft

Virgin

Gap

The Eiffel Tower

Vodafone.

When you've completed the exercise, check the following points:

- Do all your strengths/weaknesses come from the 'organisation' heading? Are they all particular to the firm and (mainly) its responsibility?

- Do all your opportunities/threats come from the external environment (the other PRESTCOM headings)? Do they all affect other companies too?

- Are any of your opportunities actions or things the company can do? If so, then they are strategies or tactics, *not* opportunities!

- Does the same factor appear under more than one SWOT heading? If so, think about this in more detail. For example, if interest rates appear as opportunities and threats, it may be that low interest rates could be an opportunity and high interest rates a threat.

- low interest rates
- a baby boom
- new technology such as 4G (or its successor)
- a competitor going out of business
- a new store opening locally.

Not all of these opportunities will apply to all organisations. For example, the last one (the new local store) may only be an opportunity to local suppliers who may be able to sell more. To other retailers, it is more likely to be a threat. How the suppliers go about persuading the store to stock their products comes further along in the planning process. The SWOT analysis just identifies that an opportunity exists.

A comprehensive SWOT analysis would take account of all elements of PRESTCOM; however, a SWOT analysis should be concise, covering key factors only. Strengths and weaknesses should focus on competitive advantages or disadvantages. Opportunities and threats should be significant to the organisation.

Ranking

SWOT analysis does not stop at listing the relevant variables under their correct headings – that is just the start. The next task is to rank the variables in order of their importance to the company.

Matching

The really interesting bit of the SWOT analysis comes during a process called matching. The firm looks for opportunities that play to its strengths (that match them). If there is an opportunity that matches a strength, then these will be key to the company, and objectives and strategies will be built upon them. For example, AOL merged with Time Warner and so gained access to its cable pipes. This coincided with increased interest from customers in broadband services (such cable pipes are needed to deliver broadband). The pipes were an AOL strength, while broadband presented the company with an opportunity. The two matched. The exploitation of this opportunity became a key part of its marketing strategy.

It is also important to watch out for threats that prey upon weaknesses. These are significant threats, and action needs to be taken to reduce their effect. Let's take the example of AOL again. AOL grew into one of the biggest Internet service providers

(ISPs) by offering a standard, suits everyone, style of service. As the Internet market matured, people wanted different types of product, e.g. home users wanted something simpler and with more support. AOL did not have this. The standardised service was a weakness that was unfavourably matched by the market's new demand for different types of service.

SUMMARY

No organisation exists in isolation. What is happening in and around it largely determines its ability to succeed in achieving its goals. Monitoring changes in the environment helps a company to spot key opportunities and threats, and forms the basis for sound marketing planning. Some firms do have formal processes for the collection of environmental data but many gather their information in a more ad hoc manner, relying on the judgement and contacts of managers.

There are a number of acronyms that can be used as frameworks for the analysis of the external environment. The one proposed here is PRESTCOM, which encompasses not just the macro-environment, but the competitive and internal environments as well.

The key environments to be monitored are: political, regulatory (or legal), economic, social, natural, technological, competitive, the organisation itself (internal), distribution and customers (market). When an organisation is trading internationally, it will have to assess these environments in its home country and in all the others in which it trades.

For many firms, the technological environment is a key determinant of competitive edge. Technological change may speed economic growth; provide a means for innovation; alter the way people work, spend their leisure time and even how they think. It can also make an organisation more efficient. Often, technologies, such as production and transport, have an impact upon the natural environment that may need to be watched out for.

Environmental data can be input into a situation analysis using a framework such as SWOT. This categorises and prioritises the information, and so identifies the key opportunities and threats that the organisation should address. That situation analysis then becomes the base upon which the organisation's marketing plans are built.

CHALLENGES REVIEWED

Now that you have finished reading the chapter, look back at the challenges you were set at the beginning. Do you have a clearer idea of what's involved?

HINTS

- Think about PRESTCOM and environmental scanning.

- Again, think about environmental scanning and SWOT and whether the failure of some cafés presents your business with an opportunity.

- This company should have been monitoring groups like Greenpeace, and could therefore have predicted such action and put contingency plans in place.

- There are any number of reasons why you might not have been as creative as your colleague, but one of them may be that you were not keeping up with relevant changes in the technological environment.

READING AROUND

Most of these suggested readings are aimed at understanding the environment in which marketers currently operate rather than gaining a deeper understanding of marketing theory or analysis tools.

MAGAZINE ARTICLES

Cadwalldr, C. (2012) 'Satellites in the shed? TEDGlobal announces the new DIY revolution', *The Observer*, 1 July. Available at: **www.theguardian.com/technology/2012/jul/01/build-satellite-shed-new-diy-revolution** (accessed 15/04/20) – possible social and technological futures.

Knowles, D. (2016) 'Business in Africa 1.2 billion opportunities', Special Report, *The Economist*, 16 April.

BOOKS AND BOOK CHAPTERS

Harvard Business School (2006) 'Competitor analysis', in *Marketer's Toolkit: The 10 Strategies You Need to Succeed*, Harvard Business Essentials series. Boston: Harvard Business School Publishing Corporation, Chapter 3.

Klein, N. (2015) *This Changes Everything: Capitalism vs the Climate*. London: Penguin.

Monbiot, G. (2016) *How Did We Get Into This Mess?* London: Verso Books.

Usiner, J.C. and Lee, J.A. (2005) *Marketing Across Cultures* (4th edn). Harlow: FT Prentice Hall.

Worthington, I. and Britton, C. (2014) *The Business Environment* (7th edn). Harlow: Prentice Hall.

MAGAZINES

The Economist

New Statesman

Time

The Week

ONLINE RESOURCES

CPG Grey (2013) 'The European Union explained'. Available at: **www.youtube.com/watch?v=O37yJBFRrfg** (accessed 16/04/16).

Ted Talks:

Piff, P. (2013) 'Does money make you mean?' Available at: **www.ted.com/talks/paul_piff_does_money_make_you_mean#t-306023** (accessed 15/04/16).

TED playlist (9 talks), 'Understanding world economics'. Available at: **www.ted.com/play lists/272/understanding_world_economics** (accessed 15/04/16).

WEBSITES

www.cia.gov/library/publications/the -world-factbook/ – the Central Intelligence Agency's (CIA) view of the world.

www.europa.eu – statistics and other information on the European Union.

www.oecd.org – the Organisation for Economic Cooperation and Development – good source for global trends.

www.oxygen.mintel.com – consumer and market insights; you will need a subscription to view full Mintel reports or your university may well have one.

www.statistics.gov.uk – check out the latest UK social trends.

www.wto.org – the World Trade Organisation's website.

TEST YOURSELF

1   Define marketing environment. (See p. 43)

2   What are uncontrollables? (See p. 49)

3   What are the two ways in which environmental information is used? (See p. 49)

4   How is environmental data gathered? (See p. 49 and 51)

5   What does PRESTCOM stand for? (See p. 53)

6   Name three ways in which the political environment can impact upon a firm's marketing operations. (See p. 55)

7   List four characteristics of a downturn that would adversely affect a firm's ability to sell its goods. Why is that? (See p. 60)

8   What are social costs? Why do some people think that companies should account for them? (See p. 60)

9   Under which PRESTCOM heading would you place changes in a country's transport infrastructure, e.g. new high speed rail links? (See p. 63)

10   List and describe four types of competition. (See p. 66)

11   What are the six main internal functions of a business? (See p. 69)

12   What is an opportunity within a SWOT analysis? What is the key difference between opportunities and threats, and strengths and weaknesses in a SWOT analysis? (See p. 77).

REVISION TOOLS

Want to test yourself even more? Review what you have learnt by visiting
https://study.sagepub.com/masterson4e

- Practise for exams with **multiple choice questions**
- Revise key terms with **interactive flashcards**

MINI CASE STUDY: A BRIGHTER WORLD?

Read the questions, then the case material, and then answer the questions.

QUESTIONS

1   Using the information in the case as a starting point, but also other sources such as Euromonitor, Mintel and Keynote, do a PRESTCOM analysis for an electricity company of your choice (e.g. eon, EDF, Ovo).

2   Now do a SWOT analysis for the same company.

3   Summarise the three changes in the marketing environment which you think are most significant for your chosen electricity company. Why are these more important than the other trends or issues that you have identified in your SWOT analysis? *The answer to this question should be written out fully – **not** in bullet points.*

We take it for granted. Press a switch and the light comes on. Feeling cold? Turn up the heating or switch on the fan heater. Hungry? Microwave something quick while the oven warms up. Electricity is such an important part of twenty-first-century life – it's almost impossible to think what we would do without it. Homes would be colder and darker but, even worse, trains would stop, petrol pumps wouldn't work, factories would grind to a halt, there would be fewer things in the shops which would be open less. We just aren't geared up to live without electricity though our great grandparents would have considered it a marvel and a luxury and coped very well without it.

Clean, cheap, plentiful and environmentally friendly power is one of the most sought after prizes of our age. Most of the world's electricity still comes from coal-powered plants. Add in gas- and oil-based generators and these old fashioned generators account for nearly 70% of all the electricity supplied. Coal is polluting and it won't last. Gas comes through international pipelines, which can be used to hold countries to ransom. Most of western Europe is largely dependent on Russia for its gas, which has caused some worrying political posturing. Unfortunately oil is often found in areas subject to political turmoil and its price has been artificially inflated by price collusion for many years, most notably through OPEC (Organisation of the Oil Exporting Countries) which prevents competition between members, effectively fixing prices. Nuclear power is a source of public concern, even more so after the accident at Japan's Fukushima power station in 2011, and it seems impossible to decommission plants safely within our lifetimes. Wind power is weak, solar power involves unsightly panels, hydroelectric power shows promise but requires careful site selection and major investment.

Recently, however, technological breakthroughs, and consumer willingness to take on energy producing projects in their own homes, have brought hopes of a solution and may even break the stranglehold that the big energy companies have on both consumers and businesses. A controversial new process, 'fracking', has revived the US oil industry, though many other countries have resisted that temptation amid safety fears. Fracking is said to cause earth tremors and may release carcinogenic chemicals into water supplies.

Energy customers had some good news in 2015: there was a dramatic fall in worldwide energy prices – although UK domestic customers complained that this was not reflected in their bills. The price reduction was the result of an increase in oil supply, surprisingly reliable production levels in places such as Iraq and Libya, and the determination of Saudi Arabia and its Gulf allies to maintain volume market share even at the cost of sales revenue.

Unfortunately this price reduction may not be all good news. There are concerns that these cheaper prices will take the pressure off governments to find long-term solutions to the energy problem and take attention away from renewables such as wind, water and solar power. Already the UK government has stopped many of its subsidies for solar panels while across the world governments still spend hundreds of billions of dollars subsidising fossil fuels.

Sources: BBC News (2015); Lucas (2015), Shift Project (n.d.)

REFERENCES

Allen, R. (ed.) (2000) *New Penguin English Dictionary*. Harmondsworth: Penguin.

BBC News (2007) 'Mugabe "plans diamond mine grab"', 21 February. Available at: **http://news.bbc.co.uk/1/hi/business/6382443.stm** (accessed 14/03/16).

BBC News (2015) 'What is fracking and why is it controversial?', 16 February. Available at: **www.bbc.co.uk/news/uk-14432401** (accessed 14/04/16).

BBC News (2016) 'Zimbabwe's Robert Mugabe: foreign companies "stole diamonds"', 4 March. Available at: **www.bbc.co.uk/news/world-africa-35720912** (accessed 14/03/16).

Bhushan, R. (2016) 'Small local brands with deeper reach & lower price give Pepsi, Coke a run for their fizz', *The Economic Times*. Available at: **http://articles.economictimes.indiatimes.com/2015-07-01/news/64004543_1_hajoori-sons-pepsico-india-coca-cola-india** (accessed 14/01/16).

Brooks, J. (2012) '£6m Kraft pack will make Dairy Milk re-sealable', *Packaging News*, 3 January.

Brownlie, D. (2000) 'Environmental scanning', in M.J. Baker (ed.), *The Marketing Book* (4th edn). London: Butterworth Heinemann, pp. 81–107.

Close the Gap (2016) 'Statistics: the pay gap'. Available at: **www.closethegap.org.uk/content/gap-statistics/** (accessed 04/04/16).

Davis, F.D., Bagozzi, R.P. and Warshaw, P.R. (1989) 'User acceptance of computer technology: a comparison of two theoretical models', *Management Science*, 35 (8): 982–1003.

Department for Education (2012) 'Departmental advice for school food in England: food-based standards for school food other than lunch'. Available at: **www.education.gov.uk/aboutdfe/advice/f00197541/departmental -advice-for-school-food-in-england/food-based-standards-for-school-food-other-than-lunch** (accessed 19/06/12).

Department of Health (2012) 'Calorie reduction pledge delivery plans published'. Available at: **https://responsibilitydeal.dh.gov.uk/f4-delivery-plans-published/** (accessed 17/02/14).

DLA Piper (2014) 'Prize promotions across the world'. Available at: **www.dlapiper.com/~/media/Files/Insights/Publications/2014/03/Prize_Promotions_of_the_World_Handbook_booklet_V12.pdf** (accessed 14/01/16).

Doyle, P. (2006) *Marketing Management and Strategy* (4th edn). Harlow: FT Prentice Hall.

Dzirutwe, M., Nickel, R. and Rocha, E. (2016) 'Zimbabwe's Mugabe says government will take over all diamond operations', *Reuters*, 4 March. Available at: **http://uk.reuters.com/article/uk-zimbabwe-diamonds-idUKKCN0W52J5** (accessed 14/03/16).

EUR-Lex (2014) 'Summaries of EU legislation: cocoa and chocolate', 20 May. Available at: **http://europa.eu/legislation_summaries/consumers/product_labelling_and_packaging/l21122b_en.htm** (accessed 04/04/16).

Euromonitor (2016) *Chocolate Confectionery in India*, December. Available at: **www.euromonitor.com/chocolate-confectionery-in-india/report** (accessed 06/02/17).

European Commission (n.d.) 'EU position in world trade'. Available at: **http://ec.europa.eu/trade/policy/eu-position-in-world-trade/** (accessed 04/04/2016).

European Parliament (2016) '40 years of EU enlargement'. Available at: **www.europarl.europa.eu/external/html/euenlargement/default_en.htm** (accessed 13/01/16).

Fairtrade Foundation (2011) 'Fairtrade and cocoa: commodity briefing'. Available at: **www. fairtrade.org.uk/includes/documents/cm_docs/2011/C/Cocoa%20Briefing%20FINAL% 208Sept11.pdf** (accessed 17/02/14).

Finlay-Robinson, D. (2008) 'What's in it for me? The fundamental importance of stakeholder evaluation', *Journal of Management Development*, 28 (4): 380–8.

Freeman, R. (1984) *Strategic Management: A Stakeholder Approach*. London: Pitman.

International Cocoa Organization (2016) 'Who are the main manufacturers of chocolate in the world?', 28 January. Available at: **www.icco.org/about-cocoa/chocolate-industry. html** (accessed 04/04/16).

Järvinen, J., Tollinen, A., Karjaluoto, H. and Jayawardhena, C. (2012) 'Digital and social media marketing usage in b2b industrial section', *Marketing Management Journal*, 22 (2): 102–17.

Kotler, P., Gregor, W. and Rogers, W. (1977) 'The marketing audit comes of age', *Sloan Management Review*, 18 (2): 25–43.

KPMG (2012) 'Consumer markets: the chocolate of tomorrow'. Available at: **www.kpmg. com/UK/en/IssuesAndInsights/ArticlesPublications/Documents/PDF/Market%20 Sector/Retail_and_Consumer_Goods/chocolate-of-tomorrow.pdf** (accessed 17/02/14).

Lucas, E. (2015) 'Let there be light', *The Economist*, 17 January. Available at: **www. economist.com/news/special-report/21639014-thanks-better-technology-and-improved- efficiency-energy-becoming-cleaner-and-more** (accessed 14/04/16).

Mercer, D. (1995) 'Simpler scenarios', *Management Decision*, 33 (4): 32–40.

Mintel (2012) *Chocolate Confectionery – 2012 – UK*. London: Mintel.

Mintel (2015) *Chocolate Confectionery – 2015 – UK*. London: Mintel.

Oxenfeldt, A.R. and Moore, W.L. (1978) 'Customer or competitor: which guideline for marketing?', *Management Review*, Aug: 43–8.

Oxford Dictionary of English (2005) Oxford: Oxford University Press.

Pickton, D. and Broderick, A. (2001) *Integrated Marketing Communications*. Harlow: FT Prentice Hall.

PricewaterhouseCoopers (2016) 'Women in work index'. Available at **www.pwc.co.uk/services/ economics-policy/insights/women-in-work-index-2016.html** (accessed 04/04/16).

Shift Project Data Portal (n.d.) 'Breakdown of electricity generation by energy source'. Available at: **www.tsp-data-portal.org/Breakdown-of-Electricity-Generation-by-Energy- Source#tspQvChart** (accessed 14/04/16).

Siamagka, N.T., Christodoulides, G., Michaelidou, N. and Valvi, A. (2015) 'Determinants of social media adoption by B2B organizations', *Industrial Marketing Management*, 51: 89–99.

Slater, S. and Narver, J. (1994) 'Does competitive environment moderate the market orientation-performance relationship?', *Journal of Marketing*, 58 (Jan): 46–55.

Top Gear (n.d.) 'Car review: Citroen C1'. Available at: **www.topgear.com/car-reviews/ citroen/c1** (accessed 14/01/16).

Vallaster, C. and von Wallpach, S. (2013) 'An online discursive inquiry into the social dynamics of multi-stakeholder brand meaning co-creation', *Journal of Business Research*, 66 (9): 1505–15.

Woodall, T. (2012) 'Driven to excess? Linking calling, character and the (mis)behaviour of marketers', *Journal of Marketing Theory*, 12 (2): 173–91.

Successful marketing depends upon a thorough understanding of customers and consumers, their worlds and their needs. Consequently, marketers spend much time, effort and money on research and analysis. They draw on other social science disciplines to shed further light on their customers' behaviour: economics, psychology and sociology in particular. Such in-depth market understanding confers a valuable competitive advantage.

WHAT THIS PART IS ABOUT

Part Two goes behind the scenes and looks at the forces that shape an organisation's marketing activities.

PART TWO

MAKING SENSE OF MARKETS

BUYER BEHAVIOUR

BUYER BEHAVIOUR CHALLENGES

The following are illustrations of the types of decision that marketers have to take or issues they face. *You aren't expected to know how to deal with the challenges now*; just bear them in mind as you read the chapter and see what you can find that helps.

Degree to job: The Station Agency

- You have developed a brand new product that is a technological breakthrough: a communications implant. A computer chip inside the person's ear is voice-controlled and transmits music, phone calls and other sounds: rather like an internal iPhone. A screen on a wrist strap is optional. It's your job to persuade people to try it. Which types of people are most likely to be the first to use such a product and how would you persuade them to do so?

- You are the product development manager for a small, local brewery. You are hoping to develop a new type of beer that will appeal to people who currently rarely, if ever, drink beer. The marketing director has asked you to identify what influences people when they are deciding whether or not to try a new drink. What sorts of things will you consider?

- You are attempting to sell a computer system to a large government department. You have to give a presentation to the end-users of the computer system, the head of department, the IT manager and an accountant. What criteria do you think they will use to assess the suitability of your computer? Who else should you target within the organisation and who do you think has the most influence?

end-user

the person who actually uses the product or service; this is not always the customer, e.g. a computer may be bought by a company's purchasing officer for use by the marketing manager (the end-user)

- *The Apprentice* is a BBC television programme in which young business people compete for the opportunity to be Lord Sugar's business partner in a new enterprise. In one episode, the teams were asked to sell expensive lollipops at a zoo. One contestant's approach was to hand a lollipop to a small child, ask if the child liked it/wanted it – and then charge the parents. What do you think of that idea?

INTRODUCTION

There are a number of well-known sayings about customers, e.g. 'The customer is king' and 'The customer is always right', and it should hardly come as a surprise that marketers invest a great deal of money and effort into finding out about their customers. A company that understands its customers well is far more likely to bring successful products to the market than one that operates on false assumptions.

In Part I the difference between consumers (users) and customers (buyers) was explained. It is important to appreciate the difference. Sometimes customers and consumers are different people, perhaps because a customer buys something for other people to use. Sometimes they are the same. However, it is popular convention when considering buyer behaviour to use these terms interchangeably, which does help distinguish between organisational markets and consumer markets. Following this convention, for the purposes of this chapter, 'customer' and 'consumer' will be used interchangeably unless otherwise specified.

The first part of this chapter focuses on consumers as individuals within a market. It explores how consumers purchase products: how they decide what to buy, and the various stages they may go through in reaching that purchase decision. The chapter goes on to examine what influences them, considering both internal factors (such as their personality or their motivation for buying the product) and external factors (such as friends and family).

Many purchases are made by organisations rather than individuals. The way organisations make decisions is considerably more complex, not least because there are likely to be a number of people involved. The second part of the chapter will look at organisational buying behaviour.

THE CONSUMER DECISION-MAKING PROCESS

Marketers spend large amounts of time and money on attempting to find out how consumers respond to different elements of the marketing mix. There have been many attempts to portray these responses through the creation of consumer models of buyer behaviour. These aim to provide frameworks for explaining the stages that consumers pass through in their decisions on whether or not to purchase a product or service.

consumer models
representations of consumer buying behaviour, usually as diagrams

Engel, Blackwell and Miniard's (2006) model (see Exhibit 3.1) is a well-known example.

Exhibit 3.1 shows the key stages that a consumer passes through in deciding whether or not to buy a product. It is probably most relevant to new or difficult purchases but the model is useful as an aid to understanding all purchases because it shows all the factors facing a consumer when deciding what to buy – even if the digital environment enables us to move rapidly from need recognition to purchase in a few clicks of the mouse. The next part of this chapter will look at these stages in more detail.

NEED/PROBLEM RECOGNITION

The decision to buy something begins with a potential customer recognising that they have a problem or an unfulfilled need. This person realises that there is a difference between their current (or actual) state and their desired state (see Exhibit 3.2). In other words, they want something. The trigger for this need may be an internal factor, such as being hungry or thirsty and therefore needing food or drink, or it may come from an external source, such as a suggestion from a friend (e.g. 'let's have a drink'), an advert or the display in a shop window.

Weather & shopping behaviour

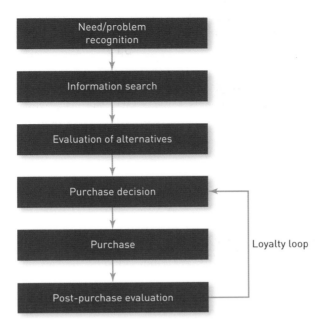

EXHIBIT 3.1 The buyer decision process

Source: adapted from Engel et al. (2006)

In this model, and in most other need or problem recognition models, the problem does not have to be serious or life-threatening. For example, imagine you are watching TV and an advert for crisps appears. This may stimulate a desire for a snack even though you are not hungry. There is no serious problem here, you are not even really hungry, but there is a discrepancy between your actual state (snack-less) and your desired state (eating crisps). You have recognised a problem that could be solved by a packet of crisps.

stimulus

something that provokes a reaction, activity, interest or enthusiasm

Sometimes the stimulus of a need or problem and its answer are more subtle. The stimulus may well come from inside, perhaps being based on a feeling. For example, some people eat ice cream when they are miserable. The trigger is feeling miserable, the need is to feel better and the ice cream is the means – but clearly something else is happening in their heads between the recognition that they were feeling low, and the decision to make themselves feel better by buying something. Then yet another thought pattern kicked in, which made the decision on what to consume to solve the problem. These decisions are much harder to understand, and to predict, than the simple 'I am thirsty so I will drink' type.

Sweets at a supermarket checkout are designed to be external triggers to stimulate impulse purchases.

© Dave Pickton

If marketers understand consumers' needs, it is more likely that they will be able to offer goods or services that will

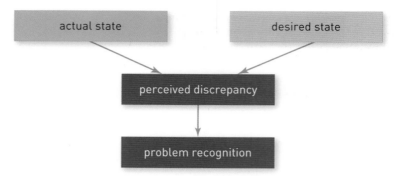

EXHIBIT 3.2 The process of problem recognition

Source: Wilkie (1990)

satisfy those needs. Clearly it would also help if the marketer understood what was likely to generate and influence those needs. Then they could develop an appropriate marketing mix for the customer.

INFORMATION SEARCH

Once consumers have recognised that they have a need, or a problem, they look for information on how to fix it. This is the information search stage of the decision-making process. The required information may be found internally or externally.

information search

identifying the various ways a need or problem can be satisfied

An internal search involves accessing memory and using previous experience. So, for example, if the consumer had felt the need to clean the kitchen sink before, and a particular brand of cleaner had worked well then and so solved the problem, they might buy it again. However, if no satisfactory solution is found within the consumer's memory, then they may have to look for new information elsewhere. External sources of information include, but are not limited to:

- personal sources, such as family and friends
- social networks and online forums
- commercial sources, such as shop assistants, websites and adverts (interestingly, someone who is considering buying, for example, a new laptop PC, tends to notice laptops and adverts for laptops when they might never have registered them before)
- third-party reports, such as magazine comments, newspaper editorials, watchdog reports, blogs, reviews or web pages.

awareness set

a number of products or brands that may satisfy a customer/consumer need or solve a problem

evoked set

the products or brands from which a person will make their purchase choice

The result of this searching, both internal and external, will be that the consumer is aware of a number of different possible solutions to the problem. This list of products may be quite long and is called their awareness set, i.e. all the products/brands that they know of that are possibilities. The rest of the decision-making process is all about cutting that list down until just one product remains – and is bought. Gathering information about the strengths and weaknesses of different products will help turn an awareness set into a more manageable list of serious possibilities (an evoked set).

A common objective of advertising is to make consumers aware of products (i.e. to get them in a consumer's awareness set) and to provide consumers with the information they need to make a decision or at least to progress the product to their evoked set. Marketers need to know where the consumers within their target market look for information: newspapers, websites, magazines, Facebook, retailer sites, Google search, etc., and the relative importance of these sources to the consumers. They can then help consumers to make their purchase decision by making sure that the necessary information is easily available.

EVALUATION OF ALTERNATIVES

Once a consumer has discounted the non-starters in their awareness set, e.g. those products that are too expensive, or not available or just really not their style, they start assessing the remaining evoked set of products to see which will work best, i.e. they evaluate the alternatives. An evoked set is a small subset of the consumer's awareness set, which in turn is likely to be only a small part of the total number of alternatives on offer (Howard and Sheth, 1969). Evoked sets differ from consumer to consumer and over time for the same consumer but marketers need to get their products within these sets if they want to make a sale.

The consumer examines the benefits that can be derived from each product's features and considers how well they are likely to satisfy the need (or solve the problem). For example, a drink with a high sugar content (a product feature) has the benefit of providing quick energy and tasting good. The downside is, of course, potentially rotten teeth and excess weight. Different consumers will attach different degrees of importance to different attributes of the product, e.g. a person's view of the high sugar content may depend upon their propensity to put on weight. 'Salient attributes' are those that the consumer associates with the product and considers to be important.

It is important to realise that the products in a consumer's evoked set may not be the same kinds of products or even be seen as direct competitors by their suppliers. For example, a consumer who wants to relax with a drink may have wine and tea in that same set of possibilities.

Sometimes, consumers may reduce their evoked set to a tighter shortlist which they will test further; they might test drive a few cars for example, or ask for references from a couple of lawyers. This final shortlist is referred to as a consideration, or purchase consideration set (see Exhibit 3.3).

The way consumers evaluate products varies from person to person and according to the specific buying situation. They narrow down the possibilities by assessing the products' distinguishing features against their choice criteria (i.e. the things the product must have

ACTIVITY

Choose a product from those below and write out a list of all the brands you have heard of, i.e. build up your own awareness set for that product:

  football boots

  holiday companies

  mascara

  PCs

  tennis racquets

  razors.

Now cut the list down to the brands you would consider buying (your evoked set). What were your choice criteria?

target market

a group of buyers and consumers who share common needs/wants or characteristics, and on whom the organisation focuses

direct competitor

a product that is similar to the company's own or the company that sells it. For example, Heineken is a direct competitor to Carlsberg, just as Coca-Cola is to Pepsi

purchase consideration set

the mental shortlist of products or brands from which a person will make their final purchase choice

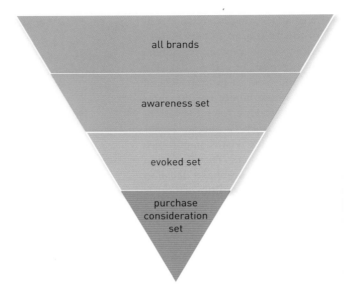

EXHIBIT 3.3 Moving towards the purchase consideration set

Source: adapted from Wilkie (1990)

Ted Talks:
paradox of choice

if it is to solve their problem). They are likely to use a variety of both formal and informal criteria in making their final choice. Typical choice criteria include: price, reliability, service, quality, environmental friendliness, speed of delivery, fashion, status and image (see Exhibit 3.4). Once they have evaluated the alternatives, the buyer should be ready to decide what to buy – if anything.

PURCHASE DECISION

The next stage for consumers is to rank the products in their evoked sets in order of preference (according to their choice criteria). They are then ready to make a purchase decision, i.e. to select their preferred product or brand. Purchase decisions are made in many different places and the surroundings can be an important influence on the decision. For example, buyers may be in a shop, on the Internet, at an exhibition or on the telephone. There are, however, a number of influences that are likely to affect consumers' purchase decisions wherever they are (see Exhibit 3.5).

There are a large number of different influences on purchase decision. For example, purchase intentions are often influenced by the attitudes of other people: friends, family, partners, etc. Think of a young teenager going shopping for new clothes with parents. The parents may consider price and reliability to be more important criteria than the teenager's status or self-image. Unexpected situational factors may interfere with the purchase decision, e.g. a particular product size or colour may be sold out and so the consumer is forced to re-evaluate. These influences are considered in more depth later in the chapter.

Criteria	Includes
Performance related	Reliability
	Quality
	Longevity
	Specification
	Style
	Comfort
	Taste
Financial	Actual price
	Price of extras
	Value for money
	Credit terms
	Running costs
	Depreciation
Social	Status
	Reputation
	Perceived image
	Social acceptability
Personal	Self-image
	Level of risk
	Ethics
	Emotional appeal

EXHIBIT 3.4 Criteria for evaluating alternatives

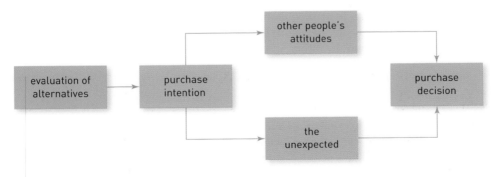

EXHIBIT 3.5 From evaluation of alternatives to purchase decision

PURCHASE

Making the decision to buy a particular product is one thing; actually buying it is another. How many times have you gone out with the express intention of buying one thing, only to change your mind in the shop and buy something else? People rarely come out of supermarkets with just the things that were on the list. Marketers continue to try and influence potential customers right up to the point where the purchase is made – and sometimes beyond. Point-of-sale materials and sales promotions (e.g. special offers) are favourite ways to try and change a person's mind.

point-of-sale (POS)
the place where a product or service is bought

POST-PURCHASE EVALUATION

The post-purchase stage of the decision-making process is particularly important to marketers as it determines whether or not the consumer will purchase the product again and how they will influence other people in terms of purchasing the product. According to Smith and Taylor (2004), consumers tell up to 11 people of a bad experience but only three or four of a good one. This word of mouth is extremely important to organisations, which try and harness its positive power as effective advertising. Unfortunately, it is even more difficult to counteract bad word of mouth than it is to encourage the good. (See Chapter 8 for more on word of mouth.)

word of mouth
individuals passing on information, experiences or promotional messages to each other; see also viral marketing

Consumers evaluate the product they have purchased in terms of what was promised (e.g. in the adverts or by sales assistants in shops) before they purchased it, and how it actually performs. There are three common outcomes of this:

- disappointment – the consumer is unlikely to repurchase the product
- satisfaction
- delight – the consumer is likely to repurchase the product, will talk favourably to others about the product, and will pay less attention to competing brands when watching adverts (and will not feel the need to try them).

Sometimes, when a consumer has invested a lot of time, effort and money into the purchase decision, or when there are many similar alternatives available, they may experience feelings of doubt about whether they have made the right decision. For example, friends may question their decision: 'How much did you pay for that? I could have got you it for half the price'. Based on the work originally conducted by Leon Festinger (1957) on cognitive dissonance, in marketing this is called post-purchase dissonance and means that a customer is psychologically uncomfortable with their purchase. Consumers attempt to reduce this feeling of doubt by either:

cognitive dissonance
when a person is troubled by conflicting thoughts; in marketing this is commonly with regard to a purchase decision: a customer may be unsure whether they made the right decision

- ignoring information that undermines their choice
- paying more attention to information that supports their choice.

post-purchase dissonance
when a consumer is psychologically uncomfortable about a purchase

So marketers' jobs do not end when a customer makes a purchase. They need to reinforce that purchase decision in order to reduce any cognitive (or post-purchase) dissonance and to stimulate positive word of mouth and encourage repeat purchases. Marketers can minimise post-purchase dissonance by setting expectations correctly before the purchase and providing reassurance afterwards. Some of the ways they do this are by:

- ensuring salespeople and other means of promotion (e.g. advertising) do not exaggerate the product features (over-promise)

- allowing consumers to sample or test the goods prior to purchase so that they know what to expect from the product

- helping customers in the early stages of product use, e.g. with installation, training, etc.

- providing reassurance through advertising, good public relations and community building (e.g. owners' clubs)

- offering excellent after-sales support, advice lines, websites, etc.

Clearly, the appropriateness of these techniques depends upon the category of product. Firms are unlikely to offer much in the way of after-sales service for small items like chocolate bars – nor do consumers need it. This sort of service is traditionally offered for larger items, with higher levels of involvement (see below), such as computers, phones and cars.

ACTIVITY

Have you ever bought something and, afterwards, wondered if you have done the right thing? Think back to a time when this has happened. How did it make you feel? What did you do about it? Did you still look around the shops for the same item or go online to search? Did you discuss your purchase with your friends? Did they agree with you? What if they did not? If you found something that might have been better, what did you tell yourself?

According to research on post-purchase dissonance, we are quite good at finding ways to convince ourselves that we made the right original choice. Did you convince yourself? Did anything the company did help?

level of involvement

the extent to which the purchase is important to the purchaser

digital focus: decision-making in the digital age

Has the way we buy things changed in our digital age? Apparently it has. Of course we make lots of purchases online, but technology has also had quite an impact on the other stages of purchase decision-making.

The Internet provides us with so much information that it can be hard to sift and assess it all to decide which brands should be placed in our purchase consideration sets. Online media, especially social media, has prompted consumers to expect more help from brands. It's no longer enough to provide information, or even entertainment, through advertising, brands must also engage in conversations with consumers.

Many consumers have mental pictures of relevant markets. They may even be expert in the relative merits of different tablets, airlines or fashion designers. They use additional information and advice found online to confirm or revise their ideas. Information may be received passively, e.g. through brand-initiated communications such as emails or texts, or may be sought actively, e.g. through search engines or review sites.

Brand conversations can be helpful at any stage of the decision-making process so brand communicators have to be flexible both in what they communicate and in how they do it. Reassure a consumer who is ready to buy a phone. Show them that other people are happy with that phone. There's no point in giving them pages of information on its features all over again. Demonstrate how an online newspaper works to the person who doesn't know whether they want to read one at all. This is more likely to move them on to the next stage of the process than a comparison of the different papers available.

(Continued)

THE LOYALTY LOOP

Depending on the extent to which a customer perceives their expectations to have been met or exceeded by their purchase, the active evaluation stage may be bypassed altogether on subsequent purchase occasions. Management consultancy firm McKinsey's Customer Decision Journey is depicted as a continuous cycle, with committed customers taking a shortcut back to purchase via a loyalty loop (Court et al., n.d.). McKinsey stress, however, that not all loyalty is equal in today's competitive markets. Passive loyalists might stick with a brand out of laziness, confusion or simply a lack of time to consider alternatives but they are not truly committed and may be more readily persuaded to switch. Active loyalists on the other hand not only stick with a brand but are also actively engaged. They are more likely to recommend a product or brand to others and resist competitor attempts to interrupt the loyalty loop.

TYPES OF BUYING DECISIONS

The consumer decision-making model should not be taken as an absolute, infallible process showing all the stages that consumers pass through every time they buy something. It is probably an oversimplification of the thought processes involved in many complex purchasing decisions. There will also be occasions when stages of the process are missed out or they may be worked through in a different order. A major factor affecting the flow and the formality of the decision-making process is the situation in which the purchase is being made. There are three main types of buying situation:

- routine problem-solving
- limited problem-solving
- extended problem-solving.

'Routine problem-solving' is where a consumer buys a product on a regular basis and there is no lengthy decision-making process. Packets of crisps and bars of chocolate are routine purchases. There is very little financial (or any other) risk associated with the purchase of these products and so the consumer does not usually think too much about them.

With 'limited problem-solving', the product is purchased less frequently and is likely to be more expensive and expected to last longer. Typical examples of limited problem-solving products are electrical products such as TVs. These types of product usually involve more deliberate decision-making.

Infrequently purchased expensive items, such as houses and cars, call for 'extended problem-solving'. It is important to the consumer to make the right choice and so they spend time searching for relevant information and evaluating alternatives. Consumers normally have a high level of involvement in these purchases.

LEVELS OF INVOLVEMENT

Some purchases are more important than others. This may be because they are expensive items, or risky or perhaps life-changing. Certain products help to define their owners and there is therefore a strong emotional involvement in the product. The consumer's level of involvement in a purchase decision has a direct bearing on how much time

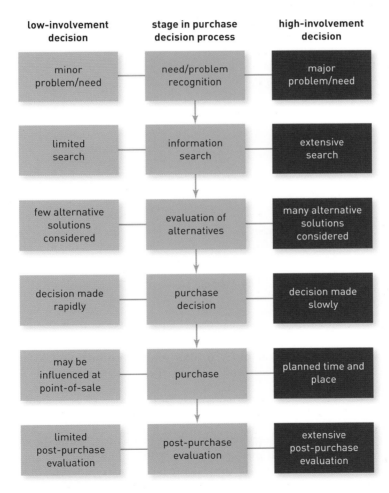

EXHIBIT 3.6 Purchase decision stages and levels of involvement

and effort they put into making the decision as to what to buy, where and how. If a purchase is important to the buyer (e.g. a new car) then they will think harder about and take more time over it, i.e. they are more likely to follow a lengthier, more complex decision-making process. However, when the purchase is of little importance or is a routine purchase (e.g. a sandwich), consumers will often use short-cuts, or choice tactics, to reduce the time and effort they expend in their decision-making process (see Exhibit 3.6).

Both factual and emotional considerations add to the level of involvement a consumer has with a purchase decision. Facts such as cost and the role the product will play in the consumer's life are clearly important and may vary from consumer to consumer, even for the same product group. For example, someone buying a bag for occasional use in carrying papers will invest less money and time than someone who is buying a briefcase that they intend to use every day for work. Emotional involvement with a decision is just as important while being less easy to predict or control. Research suggests there are four factors that affect a consumer's level of involvement with a product purchase (see Exhibit 3.7):

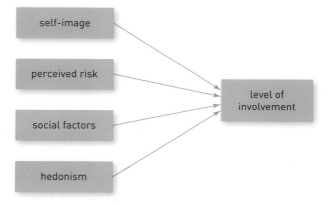

EXHIBIT 3.7 Factors affecting level of involvement

Source: Laurent and Kapferer (1985)

1   *Self-image*: where the consumer thinks that a product will affect the way they see themselves (e.g. cars and clothes), then involvement levels are likely to be higher.

2   *Perceived risk*: where the consumer thinks there are risks in making a wrong choice. This may be financial risk because the product is expensive, physical risk if the product is potentially dangerous, functional risk if there is a worry that the product may not work properly, social risk if there are concerns about how others might react to the purchase, or psychological risk if there is the possibility of a wrong decision or one that might make the consumer feel stupid in some way. If risk levels are high, then levels of involvement are likely to be high as well.

3   *Social factors*: where the consumer thinks that a purchase may affect their social acceptability to others or cause them embarrassment (e.g. being seen in the right [or wrong] nightclub), then involvement levels are likely to be higher.

4   *Hedonism*: where the consumer thinks that the purchase may be capable of delivering a high degree of pleasure (e.g. a holiday), then involvement levels are likely to be higher.

The buying situation and the consumer's level of involvement (see above) both affect their purchase behaviour. Another key influence on how people go about deciding what to buy is how different the competing products are perceived to be. Four major types of buyer behaviour can be seen in Exhibit 3.8.

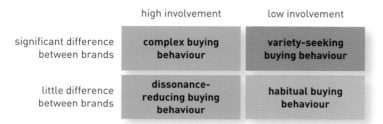

EXHIBIT 3.8 Four types of buyer behaviour

Source: based on Assael (1987)

1   *Complex buying behaviour*: consumers who are making complex decisions usu-ally want to learn (covered later in the chapter) a great deal about the product they are buying as they move through the decision-making process. From this learning develop beliefs, and then attitudes, about the product type before making a decision to purchase. These consumers have a high level of involvement with the product decision and perceive significant differences between brands. The purchase of a laptop or tablet would usually prompt complex buying behaviour.

2   *Dissonance-reducing buying behaviour*: if the consumer thinks there is little difference between brands, they put less effort into collecting brand information and may just shop around. Having seen what is readily available, and checked prices, availability, delivery, etc., they are able to make a decision to purchase relatively quickly. These consumers do have a high level of involvement with the product, but think all brands are similar. It is called dissonance-reducing behaviour because the brand comparisons are intended to reduce the chance of post-purchase dissonance resulting from regret-ting a purchase when a better deal or product is spotted later. The purchase of airline tickets might well fall into this category.

3   *Variety-seeking buying behaviour*: sometimes it is good to have a change, to try something different. There are certain product categories where people are known to buy a differ-ent thing next time deliberately, e.g. sandwiches or restaurants. Marketers often attempt to encourage variety seekers to switch to their product through lower prices and sales promotion (e.g. a meal deal). These consumers have relatively low levels of involvement with the product but do perceive brands to be quite different from each other. Many low-value personal products, like shampoo or shower gel, prompt variety-seeking behaviour.

belief

how or what a person thinks about something, usually based on knowledge, opinion or faith

attitude

describes a person's consistently favourable or unfavourable evaluation, feelings and tendencies towards an object or idea

ACTIVITY

4　*Habitual buying behaviour*: some purchases are routine or always on the shopping list. Consumers spend very little time thinking about these – they just drop them into the supermarket trolley. Marketers try to make this easy for them by dominating shelf space in supermarkets. This way they can encourage repeat purchases and avoid substitution (i.e. consumers buying alternatives) because their product is not to hand. These consumers have a low level of involvement and perceive little difference between brands. Low-value food products like bread and eggs usually fall into this category.

An understanding of the consumer's level of involvement with their products helps marketers to serve their customers better. Consumers will be actively searching for lots of information about high-involvement products and marketers need to provide it in a format that these consumers can find easily and study at their own pace (e.g. web pages, newspapers, magazine adverts).

When selecting low-involvement products, consumers are often passive in their information search. They do not actively search for information so marketers attempt to create, and increase, awareness of their product and to reinforce its positive attributes. Television is often used to advertise low-involvement products because of the opportunity this provides for repetition and reinforcement, and because of the large amount of people who, potentially, will see the advert (think about how many people watch the most popular series, e.g. *Game of Thrones*).

INFLUENCES ON CONSUMER BUYER BEHAVIOUR

Having already looked at the consumer decision process, and the different types of consumer buying decision, the next section of this chapter will consider the internal and external factors that may influence these decisions.

INTERNAL INFLUENCES ON CONSUMER BEHAVIOUR

Although markets can be broken down into distinct groups (or segments – see Chapter 4) of customers who are alike in many ways, these groups are clearly made up of individuals with their own, unique characteristics, but what kind of characteristics are relevant and how do they affect individuals' buying behaviour?

Personality and the self-concept

The term personality describes a person's distinguishing psychological characteristics, which lead them to respond to situations in particular ways. Personality consists of all

high-involvement products

purchases that customers expend time and effort on, usually high cost or high risk, e.g. cars, holidays, wedding dresses

low-involvement products

products that customers spend little time or effort in choosing, often low cost, low risk or regular purchases, e.g. toothpaste, washing-up liquid, jam

personality

a person's distinguishing psychological characteristics that lead them to respond in particular ways

the features, behaviours and experience that make individuals unique and distinctive. It is often described in terms of personality traits, such as dominant, sociable, introvert or extrovert.

Personality is often related to self-image or the concept of self, one of the fundamentals of which is that a person's possessions (e.g. clothes, books, CDs) reflect and express their identity. The term 'symbolic consumption' refers to consumers' tendency to focus on the symbolic meanings that products and brand communicate to others – as much as the tangible, physical characteristics of material objects. For example, new acquaintances commonly check out each other's music collections or books in order to form an opinion of that individual.

Many products and brands appeal to consumers on the basis of their perceived fit with consumers' own self-image or because they are associated with aspirational ideas of who they would like to be (the ideal self). An individual may make use of a variety of brands to express different aspects of their identity, for example a man dressed in Rocawear is a different type of man from one in Hollister.

Millenial identity

digital focus: do you like it?

How many likes is enough to make a social media post worthwhile? Is that carefully shot video of your darling puppy being menaced by a lemon a failure if you get only one or two – or does it depend *who* it was that liked it? Do you have a plan of action to maximise your likes or are you happy to leave it to chance?

Most brands have at least a Facebook page and most also have strategies to capture as many likes as they can and translate likes into purchases. But for brands, some likes are more valuable than others. Brands want to be liked by the right sort of people so that others are reassured this is the right brand for them.

We are heavily influenced by our friends, after all we chose them as friends, and feel encouraged by their liking of a brand that we are unsure about. However, we all have some 'Facebook friends' who we don't really think are our type of people. We may not be so keen to find ourselves grouped with them on the list of a brand's followers.

Our self-image is bound up in the brands we buy so it's important to choose wisely. The type of people who like a brand can be a good clue as to whether this is a brand that says the right things about us. Do they look like/ sound like our type of people? Even more importantly perhaps, are they the type of people we aspire to be? If they are, then we may decide that we need that brand of shoes or racquet, we need to go to that restaurant or try that drink. We need it desperately or we won't be accepted, won't belong. It seems that the secret to being popular, on or offline, is to be liked by all the right people.

Perception

Two people seeing the same advertisement may react to it differently because they perceive the situation differently. Even the same individual may perceive the same advertisement differently at different times. Imagine how you would react to an advert for a snack when you are hungry and compare that to when you have just eaten.

Perception is the process by which people select, organise and interpret sensory stimulation (sounds, visions, smells, touch) into a meaningful picture of the world. There are three main processes that lead to the formation of individual perceptions:

advertisement
see advertising

perception
the process by which people select, organise and interpret sensory stimulation (sounds, visions, smell, touch) into a meaningful picture of the world

- selective attention
- selective distortion
- selective retention.

Selective attention is the process by which stimuli are assessed and non-meaningful stimuli, or those that are inconsistent with our beliefs or experiences, are screened out. This has major implications from a marketing perspective. People are exposed to a massive number of advertisements every day but very few of these advertisements catch the individual's attention; the rest are screened out. Marketers use various techniques (such as colours, sounds, contrasting backgrounds and foregrounds) to ensure their advertisements get attention.

Selective distortion occurs when consumers distort or change the information they receive to suit their beliefs and attitudes. One of the many challenges that marketers face when communicating with audiences is to understand how this selective distortion is likely to work and then either avoid it or make use of it so that their message gets through as intended. This careful presentation of the message is called information framing. For example, in most of Europe blue is associated with cool and red with hot. Many bottled waters use blue to indicate their cooling ability while chilli-flavoured snacks usually favour red packaging or writing.

Consumers remember only a small number of the many messages they see and hear. This is called selective retention. People tend to remember messages that support their existing beliefs and attitudes better than those that do not. For example, the message 'dieting makes you fat' is more likely to be remembered, and acted on, by those who hate dieting than by those who are in favour of it.

Perception and memory are closely associated with learning.

Learning

Learning describes changes in an individual's behaviour that arise from their experiences. Marketers are keen for consumers to learn from promotion so that they know which product to buy and why. Learning can take place in a number of ways (see Exhibit 3.9).

Classical conditioning

Classical conditioning uses an established relationship between a stimulus and a response to that stimulus to evoke or teach people to have the same response to a different stimulus. The most famous example is that of Pavlov's dogs. Pavlov, who was a renowned nineteenth-century psychologist, rang a bell at the dogs' mealtimes. The dogs learnt to associate the bell (the stimulus) with food and their response was to salivate. After a while, they always salivated on hearing the bell – even if no food was forthcoming. Clearly the application of classical conditioning in marketing is more sophisticated than it was for Pavlov's dogs. Marketers may put a stimulus alongside their brand in order to create an association and so build brand awareness. For example, music is often used in advertising. If the association is strong enough, as many jingles are, then just hearing that tune will bring the brand to mind.

---

selective attention

the process by which stimuli are assessed and non-meaningful stimuli, or those that are inconsistent with our beliefs or experiences, are screened out

selective distortion

occurs when consumers distort or change the information they receive to suit their beliefs and attitude

information framing

the ways in which information is presented to people to ensure selective distortion does, or does not, happen

selective retention

the way consumers retain only a small number of messages in their memory

learning

changes in an individual's behaviour arising from their experiences

classical conditioning

the process of using an established relationship between a stimulus and a response, which can then be used to evoke the same response

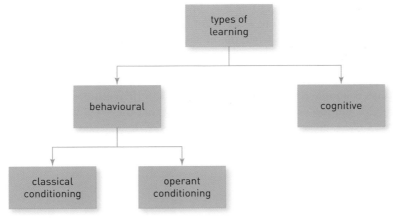

EXHIBIT 3.9 Types of learning

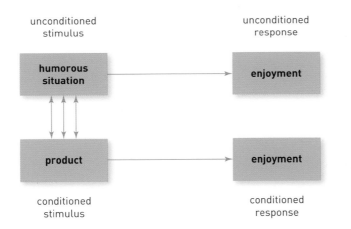

EXHIBIT 3.10 The classical conditioning approach to influencing product attitudes

Operant or instrumental conditioning

Operant conditioning (also known as instrumental conditioning) also requires a link between a stimulus and a response. However, with operant conditioning, the correct response receives a reward (positive reinforcement) while an incorrect response may receive punishment (negative reinforcement). Think about house-training a puppy – this is usually done through operant conditioning. The learning may be too complex to be an absolute; i.e. the stimulus that results in the highest reward is the stimulus that is learnt. Marketers will try to increase the likelihood of the right response, e.g. buy a product regularly, through positive reinforcement such as special offers for regular customers.

While classical conditioning is useful in explaining how consumers may learn simple kinds of behaviour, operant conditioning is much more useful in determining more complex, goal-desired behaviour. The learned behaviour results from expectations of the rewards

operant conditioning (instrumental conditioning)

learning a behaviour that produces a positive outcome (reward) or avoids a negative one (or penalties) that may be received or have been received through previous experiences. Through operant conditioning, an association is made between a behaviour and a consequence of that behaviour, even when the initial stimulus is no longer present.

For example, if the *Financial Times* (FT) sells its paper to students for 20p instead of 85p, it is hoping that they will buy it because it is so cheap (desired response) and then because it has desirable properties (i.e. may help with their studies), the students find it useful (positive reinforcement) and the likelihood that they will buy it again increases (see Exhibit 3.11), even without the initial stimulus of the discount.

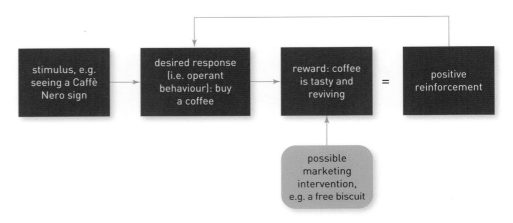

EXHIBIT 3.11 Operant conditioning over time

Cognitive learning

Both classical and operant conditioning are forms of behavioural learning involving stimuli and responses; cognitive learning, however, involves the complex mental processing of information. The cognitive learning approach sees people as problem solvers who actively look for information that will help them. The previous section on the consumer decision process presumes that at least some cognitive learning takes place. Creativity and insight are important if this way of learning is to be successful (Solomon et al., 2010). There are a number of types of cognitive learning including rote learning, where two concepts are associated with each other through repetition without conditioning (e.g. slogans with products), and vicarious learning, which involves learning from others, i.e. without direct experience or reward, e.g. finding out about products through word of mouth.

Motivation and values

Motivation involves a complex relationship between needs, drives and goals. A motive is a need that is sufficiently pressing that the person is driven to seek satisfaction of that need. According to Maslow, these needs can be placed in a hierarchy in terms of their relative importance (see Exhibit 3.12).

cognitive learning

active learning using complex mental processing of information

Influencing behaviour

Ted Talks:
why we do what we do

EXHIBIT 3.12 Maslow's hierarchy of needs

Source: based on Maslow (1943)

An individual will try to satisfy the most important needs of survival first (the bottom row). When these needs are met, they will stop being motivators and the individual will then try to satisfy the next most important need, i.e. the one at the next level up in the hierarchy. For example, an individual who is starving will have no interest in anything else until their hunger is satisfied. Someone in danger of dying of thirst will drink from a dirty pool – and only later worry about whether that was a safe thing to do. Once a person has satisfied their basic physical and safety needs, then, and only then, will they look for the company of others. Human beings are social creatures and so socialising with others is important – but not as important as staying alive. Not satisfied with having friends, a decent social life, romance, people next look for esteem, for the approval and even admiration of others. Typically we do this through our work, or our wealth, but certain products also fulfil this need. Sports cars are not bought just because their drivers want to break speed limits; they are objects of desire and provoke envy in others. They enhance the status of the driver. The final level, self-actualisation, is the hardest to reach. It involves the fulfilment of dreams and ambitions. This is a general model of motivation. It was not created with marketing in mind and Maslow did not envisage its use as a marketing tool. However, many modern ads have dream fulfilment at their heart, positioning their product as the answer to prayers – and not always with tongue in cheek. Many car (and holiday) ads appear to fall into this category.

There are a number of criticisms of this model. First, it is important to remember that it was not developed for marketing. It is useful for marketers in that it helps categorise products by the kind of need they are trying to fulfil and stimulates further thought on how these products should therefore be positioned and advertised; however, any attempt to apply it too rigorously to a marketing situation is likely to raise more questions than it answers. Second, it is difficult to work out the extent to which one need needs to be fulfilled before someone is ready to move on to the next level, and also to measure that level of fulfilment in an individual (Schiffman et al., 2008). Third, the model can also be criticised as being reflective of certain Western cultures only. Other cultures may not be as materialistic or individualistic and may therefore have different priorities (Solomon et al., 2010), for example raising the relative importance of social needs.

It is clearly important that marketers should understand the motives that drive consumers to purchase products. Those motives determine how consumers choose products and such knowledge enables marketers to design product offerings that have the best chance of being chosen. Consumer motives can also be used to group potential customers together and so to segment markets (see Chapter 4). As an example, consider the purchase of a mobile phone: while some people's primary motive may be practicality, others may consider it an important tool for socialising or a status symbol. The phone's advertising would need to take this into account.

segment
the process of dividing a market into groups

---

research focus

Hyllegard, K.H., Yan, R-N., Paff Ogle, J. and Attmann, J. (2010) 'The influence of gender, social cause, charitable support, and message appeal on Gen Y's responses to cause-related marketing', *Journal of Marketing Management,* **27** (1–2): 100–23.

This study examined the influence of gender, type of social cause, amount of charitable support, and message appeal on Gen Y consumers' attitudes and purchase intentions towards an apparel brand in the context of **cause-related marketing.**

Attitudes and beliefs

FairTrade:
ethical consumers

Attitudes and beliefs are acquired through the experience of doing things and the resultant learning process. A belief is a thought that a person holds about something, usually based on knowledge, opinion or faith. Beliefs are important to marketers because beliefs about certain products or brands may affect a consumer's choice criteria. Attitudes are important because they have strong links to behaviour – although consumers sometimes do the opposite of what their attitude suggests they might, e.g. someone who believes strongly in healthy, organically grown food might still buy a cheaper version of a product.

An attitude describes a person's consistently favourable or unfavourable evaluation, feelings and tendencies towards an object or idea. From a marketing perspective, this attitude may be directed at a product or brand (i.e. the object) and thus will be reflected in their behaviour (i.e. whether they purchase the product or not). Attitudes can be discovered by asking the person how they feel about the brand.

Williams (1981) suggests that attitude comprises three components: cognitive, affective and conative. The cognitive attitude relates to beliefs about a product; the affective attitude relates to positive and negative feelings associated with the product; the conative attitude is the link with behaviour (i.e. attitude X is likely to lead to behaviour Y). It is this link between attitude and behaviour that is of prime interest to the marketer, e.g. how a positive attitude towards a product can be translated into a purchase decision, or how someone with a negative attitude can be prevented from taking undesired actions such as posting a poor review. One of the most common advertising objectives is to create favourable attitudes, just as a common aim of customer service representatives is to prevent the consequences of negative attitudes, e.g. by offering something extra or free to compensate for something that went wrong.

research focus

Laran, J. and Tsiros, M. (2013) 'An investigation of the effectiveness of uncertainty in marketing promotions involving free gifts', *Journal of Marketing*, 77 (2): 112–23.

This paper examines the effects of not being sure what the free gift will be on the cognitive, conative and affective aspects of consumer decision-making.

EXTERNAL INFLUENCES ON CONSUMER BEHAVIOUR

The previous section looked at how the consumer decision process might be influenced by internal factors; this section will consider some of the many external influences on this process.

Culture

Culture manifests itself through such things as customs, art, language, literature, music, beliefs and religion. As children grow up, their society provides them with a framework within which they are able to develop acceptable beliefs, value systems and cultural norms (see Exhibit 3.13).

culture

the set of basic values, perceptions, wants and behaviour learnt by a member of society from family and other institutions

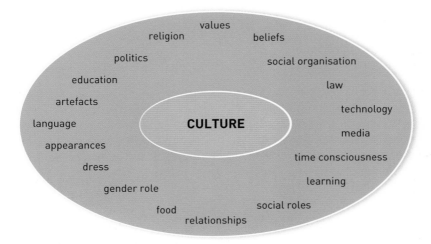

EXHIBIT 3.13 Elements of culture

Within any culture, there will be subcultures. A subculture is a group of people with shared value systems based on common life experiences and situations. These shared value systems may come from ethnic origin, geographic areas, life stage, lifestyle or religion. Subcultures often form very important market segments (see Chapter 4). For example, MTV has a global format that appeals to youth culture across the world.

global focus: high- and low-context cultures

high-context culture

one where communication must be interpreted according to the situation; much of the message is in the context rather than being explicitly expressed in the words

low-context culture

the information to be communicated is put into words explicitly; there is little need to take account of the surrounding circumstances

The noted anthropologist Edward Hall is responsible for the introduction of the concepts of **high-context** and **low-context cultures** into the study of international exchanges. In a high-context culture, such as Japan, it is important to take account of the situation in which something is said. The words alone may not convey the true meaning of the speaker. It is difficult for most Northern Europeans to decode this, but it is important to be aware that 'first we must do x' or 'I'll let you know next week' might well actually mean 'no', depending on the circumstances in which it is said, who is saying it and where they come from. On the other hand, a North American (low context) will have no compunction in saying 'no' if they do not want to make the deal, and will see that as commendable honesty and straight-dealing rather than as shocking discourtesy. The use of language in extreme low- and high-context cultures can be as different as its use in technical manuals and in poetry: the first tries to make the meaning as clear as possible through words alone; the second works on a number of different levels and requires interpretation by someone familiar with the poetic form.

The following are usually considered low-context cultures:

USA	Austria
Canada	Scandinavian countries
Germany	Australia
Switzerland	New Zealand.

The following are considered to be high-context:

Latin American countries

Middle Eastern countries

Japan.

The British are the source of some confusion, especially to Americans, who assume a greater similarity between these two peoples than there really is. (There is an old saying: two peoples divided by a common language.) Britain fits into the middle of the high-/low-context spectrum thanks to the British tendency towards understatement and euphemism, as well as the demands of courtesy which make some statements too bold.

Another country that causes problems in categorisation is France (Usunier and Lee, 2009). The French language has long been considered the ideal diplomatic language because it can be precise or vague according to the speaker's wish.

Reference groups

Reference groups are groups of people to which an individual belongs or wants to belong. These groups may be formal or informal, e.g. sports clubs, professional bodies such as the Chartered Institute of Marketing (CIM) or the gang that goes for a drink after work on Fridays.

These reference groups can have a significant influence on consumer behaviour. They can be classified into three main types:

1 **Membership groups** are groups that an individual already belongs to and therefore have a direct influence on their behaviour.

2 **Aspirant (aspirational) groups** are those groups to which an individual would like to belong; they identify with them but there is no face-to-face contact, e.g. an amateur footballer may aspire to be part of a professional club.

3 **Disassociative groups** are groups to which the individual does not want to belong or be seen to belong. For example, an upmarket shopper may not wish to be part of a discount club no matter how good the deals are.

reference groups
the groups to which an individual belongs or aspires to belong

membership groups
groups an individual already belongs to and which therefore have a direct influence on his or her behaviour, e.g. students belong to a class

aspirant (aspirational) groups
to which an individual would like to belong, e.g. a professional football team or a particular club

disassociative groups
groups to which the individual does not want to belong or be seen to belong, e.g. an upmarket shopper may not wish to be seen in a discount store

These people almost certainly share certain personality traits and belong to a particular reference group.

Source: Oli Scarff/Getty Images News/Getty Images

A football team would be an aspirant group for many athletes.

Source: Paul Ellis/AFP/Getty Images

Reference groups may influence consumers in at least three ways:

1 They expose the consumer to new behaviours and lifestyles.

2 They may influence the consumer's self-concept (e.g. they want to be accepted and fit in with a particular group).

3 They may create pressures to conform to the group norms that affect product or brand choice.

Exhibit 3.14 shows how group influence may affect brand choice for four types of product.

ACTIVITY

Think about the people you know and the things you do regularly. What reference groups do you belong to? How do they influence you as a consumer – or how do you influence the other members of the group?

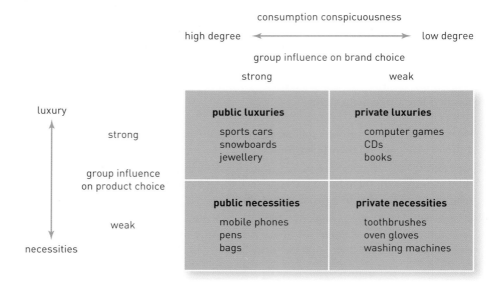

EXHIBIT 3.14 Group influence on brand choices

Source: Bearden and Etzel (1982). By permission of Oxford University Press

research focus

Wei, Y. and Yu, C. (2012) 'How do reference groups influence self-brand connections among Chinese consumers? Implications for advertising', *Journal of Advertising*, 31 (2): 39–53.
 The reference groups considered in this paper include both in-groups (membership groups) and out-groups (aspirational, dissociative and neutral groups).

conspicuous purchase

a product or service that is likely to stand out, perhaps because it has unusual or high status or will be consumed in public

How important a reference group is to a consumer will vary depending on the nature of the product. It tends to be most important for **conspicuous purchases**. A product is conspicuous if:

- it is exclusive and therefore noticeable; many designer brands will fall into this product category (e.g. Rolex, Lacoste)
- it is consumed in the public domain and other consumers may see it, e.g. drinking a particular brand of bottled beer in a nightclub.

global focus: Harley riders

A Harley-Davidson is perhaps the most distinctive motorcycle in the world – and it inspires extreme devotion. If you own a Harley, you are a member of an elite club and this is a feeling the company recognises and fosters.
 Visit its website (**www.harley-davidson.com**) or one of its other international sites, and see how it builds that community feeling. There is welcoming information and tips for new riders. You can post photos

and so build up an online photo album of you, your friends and, of course, your bikes. You can join HOG (the Harley Owners Group) and so get access to special information and invitations to join in at special events. This brand community of Harley owners, and would-be owners, is a privileged, membership group that transcends nationalities.

Social networking

Not all consumers use social networking sites but many do and usage is growing. In 2014, 74% of online adults used social networking sites – 71% being Facebook users (Pew Research Centre, 2016).

Social network interaction can have a powerful influence on consumer behaviour. It works in a number of ways:

- each network or group that a person belongs to is a membership reference group (see above) and as such the opinions of the group are respected and members will try to conform.

- comments and reviews on the site can be an instantaneous form of word of mouth.

- brands may have their own pages; members of these pages (who may only have to 'like' the page to join) are in effect a brand community, i.e. a group united around a brand with which they have a strong relationship. They may feel ownership of the brand and will be motivated to protect it and to convert others to it.

Consumers play different roles within social networking sites. Some are far more active and involved than others and it is these people who are likely to have the stronger influence over consumer behaviour. Research done by Forrester Research categorised Internet users according to their social networking behaviour. The seven categories of social media user range from 'creator' to 'spectator' and finally 'inactive'. 'Creators' actually create online content for spectators to read. In between, there are 'conversationalists' who do things like update their status in Facebook regularly or tweet, 'critics' who write reviews and post comments on other people's blogs etc., 'collectors' who may add tags or vote, and 'joiners' who maintain their profile on one or more sites but do little else (Li and Bernoff, 2011). These classes of networkers are placed on a ladder with the most active being the highest up. These opinion leaders and opinion formers are valuable allies and great potential brand ambassadors.

opinion leaders
individuals who are often asked by people they know for advice or information

opinion formers
individuals with specialist skills or expertise who have influence over others, often through the media

brand ambassador
someone who is passionate and knowledgeable about a brand and recommends it to others; this may be an employee, a celebrity endorser or a customer acting independently

Family

Family members are a strong influence on a consumer's behaviour over their whole lifetime, i.e. not just during the time they live in the family home. Family influence can be divided into one of two categories: family orientation influence and family procreation influence.

Family orientation influence is the influence parents exert over their children, even when there is no longer any interaction. This may be at a general level in terms of values and attitudes towards product types (e.g. whether you view a car as a status symbol or as a functional product to get you from A to B), or at a more specific level (e.g. continuing to purchase the same brand of coffee as your parents did).

Family procreation influence consists of the more direct influences on daily buying behaviour that family members exert upon one another. This is continually evolving with changing social conditions and working patterns. For example, the increase in the number of working mothers has meant the rise of latchkey kids – i.e. children who arrive home from school before their parents arrive home from work and who prepare a snack or tea for themselves. Such consumers have particular requirements for food products, e.g. ease of preparation.

research focus

Lawlor, M.-A. and Prothero, A. (2011) 'Pester power: a battle of wills between children and their parents', *Journal of Marketing Management,* **27 (5–6): 561–81.**
   The authors investigate children's views on pester power in contrast to other research that has concentrated on parental perspectives.

ethical focus: bait apps – the hidden cost of free games

Take a look at the top grossing (profit-making) apps available on the App Store and you might notice something suspicious. The biggest money spinners are typically free of charge, the catch is a whole range of in-app purchases that can cost many times more than premium video games – $100 for a barrel of 'Smurfberries' anyone? While in-app purchases may not be compulsory, 'bait' apps are so-called because they offer just enough game enjoyment to hook players but are designed in such a way as to present minimal opportunities for progress without an additional spend – to unlock extended gameplay, special powers or virtual game currency, for example. If not outright deception then there are certainly ethical questions around advertising such a game for free in the first place. When many such apps are orientated towards children, is it really responsible to induce those who use them to spend money that they may not even appreciate is real? Can a five year old really be expected to understand that their hi-score achievements are thanks to their parents' credit card, not superior game-playing skills? Apple has faced legal challenges for making it too easy for kids to buy add-ons. In February 2013 Apple agreed to pay up to $100 million compensation to parents in the US whose children had run up huge bills using highly addictive apps.
   Whose responsibility do you think it is to ensure that apps are marketed fairly?
   Sources: Martinson (2013); Technopedia (n.d.)

CONSUMER BUYING ROLES

Within groups such as families, or flatmates or clubs, many purchase decisions are made by the group, not just one individual. Consumers fulfil different roles in making purchase decisions and these roles can change depending upon what is being purchased. For example, parents may pay for their children's clothes but leave it to them to decide what to buy, whereas the children may pay for their own sweets but within rules set by their parents.

The roles that individuals play in a decision include: influencer, customer and consumer. An influencer may make suggestions, offer advice or an opinion. Children are frequently influencers within a family although it may be someone from outside the group who exerts influence: a friend, or a salesperson perhaps. A customer is the person who actually buys the products or the person who has the final say. In a family group, this is often one or both parents. The consumer actually uses or eats the product. For example, the whole family would consume a Disneyland, Paris experience.

ACTIVITY

Using the example of a Friday night out, who carries out the roles of influencer, customer and consumer?

research focus: classic concept

Kotler, P. (1965) 'Behavioural models for analyzing buyers', *Journal of Marketing*, **29 (4): 37–45.**
   Kotler offers five approaches/models for analysing and understanding buyer behaviour from Marshellian economics to Veblen social constructs (Veblen originated the term 'conspicuous consumption' so beloved of marketers) and organisational buying behaviour.

THE CONSUMER DECISION PROCESS FOR NEW PRODUCTS

The sale of new products presents special challenges to the marketer. Consumers may view new products as riskier than tried and tested alternatives. They may not properly understand what they are for or how to use them. They may not see a need for them. This section will explore how consumers approach the purchase of new products.

A new product may be defined as a good, service or idea that is perceived by potential customers as being new (see Chapter 6 for more on new products). Consumers have to go through a number of mental processes (see Exhibit 3.15) when deciding whether to buy a new product.

- *Awareness*: the consumer becomes aware of the product but does not have any information about it.

- *Interest*: the consumer actively seeks information about the new product if they think it may be of use to them.

- *Evaluation*: the consumer decides whether or not they should try the new product.

- *Trial*: the consumer tries the new product on a small scale to judge its value.

- *Adoption*: the consumer decides to make full and regular use of the new product

- *Advocacy*: the consumer recommends the product through positive word of mouth.

Marketers need to plan how they can aid potential consumers to move through the various steps by, for example, providing information or having a trial or testing plan.

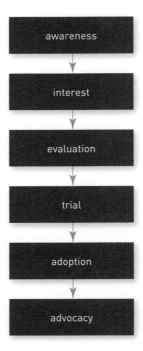

EXHIBIT 3.15 The stages of consumer readiness

INDIVIDUAL DIFFERENCES AND NEW PRODUCTS

Individuals differ in their attitudes to new products generally: some are excited by the idea of something new, others are a little scared. Consumers' willingness to try new products also varies according to the nature of the specific new product. For example, while some people may love to try new food or have the latest fashions, they may not be so willing to buy the latest version of Microsoft Windows or book a space shuttle flight. Rogers (1976) classified consumers into a number of product adoption categories (see Exhibit 3.16):

Consumption & sustainability

early adopters
are amongst the first to try new products, following on from the innovators

late majority
a substantial group of purchasers of a specific product who wait until the product has been well tried out by others before purchase

laggards
the last people to buy a new product, only purchasing when most other people already have it

- Innovators (2.5%) are consumption pioneers who are prepared to try new ideas.
- Early adopters (13.5%) are often opinion leaders within their reference groups. Opinion leaders are those individuals who have special skills, knowledge, personality or other characteristics, and exert influence on others (e.g. DJs).
- The early majority (34%) are quite adventurous in their decision-making and, as a result, adopt new ideas before the average person.
- The late majority (34%) are more sceptical. They adopt new products only after most have tried them.
- Laggards (16%) are conservative and suspicious of change. They adopt a new product only when it has become something of a tradition in itself.

Marketers research and identify the characteristics of the various groups and tailor their marketing mix and, in particular, their advertising messages accordingly.

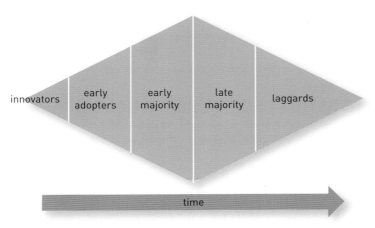

EXHIBIT 3.16 Product adoption categories

Source: based on Rogers (2003)

research focus: classic concept

Rogers, E.M. (1976) 'New product adoption and diffusion', *Journal of Consumer Behaviour*, 2: 290–301.
   Rogers is the recognised proponent of this important marketing concept and model that is sometimes referred to as innovation diffusion and which has widespread application in marketing practice.

The models looked at so far relate to consumer purchases. The next section will look at the way organisations purchase products.

ORGANISATIONAL PURCHASES

Purchases made in the business-to-business (b2b) market are usually larger than the business-to-consumer (b2c) market. When a consumer buys a car, that b2c transaction is only the final stage of a number of b2b purchases that make up the supply chain involved in producing and distributing cars (see Chapter 9 for more on the supply chain). What is more, consumers usually buy cars one at a time. A business may buy hundreds for its company car fleet. Business customers tend to place much bigger orders.

b2c (business-to-consumer)

business dealings with consumers

This section of the chapter looks at organisational customers and how their buying decisions are made, who is involved and what criteria they use.

As well as many of the things that consumers purchase, organisations purchase a diverse and complex range of goods and services. These include:

- utility services (such as water, electricity and broadband)
- raw materials (such as steel, cotton and chemicals)
- component parts (such as chips, switches and valves)

- capital items (such as buildings and machines)
- MRO goods (i.e. maintenance, repair and operations goods such as cleaning materials and tools)
- professional services (such as legal and financial advice).

CHARACTERISTICS OF ORGANISATIONAL MARKETS

There are many similarities between business markets and consumer markets but there are also a number of key differences between these two types of market. They typically differ in terms of:

- market structure
- nature of demand
- complexity of the buying process.

MARKET STRUCTURE

It is important to establish how many customers there are in a consumer market. That is the first step towards estimating potential sales. This is also key in b2b or industrial markets but it is crucial to understand how big and how influential those customers are.

INDUSTRIAL CONCENTRATION

In b2b markets, there are normally fewer buyers but they are far larger in terms of purchasing power. Compare the selling of computers to the consumer market with selling dedicated computer systems to car manufacturers. There are fewer customers but they are more easily identifiable and they buy more.

GEOGRAPHICAL CONCENTRATION

Some industries have a strong geographical concentration. This may have arisen due to the availability of resources (e.g. steel manufacturing in Sheffield), because of political incentives (e.g. EU grants) or for historical reasons (e.g. financial services in London).

NATURE OF DEMAND

Remembering that demand in this sense means actual sales, b2b demand for products can be more complex than consumer demand. The demand for b2b products is: derived, often joint, usually relatively inelastic and may fluctuate considerably. Each of these ideas is briefly explained below.

Derived demand

All business demand is derived demand, i.e. demand that ultimately comes from (or is derived from) the demand for the final product. The demand for steel panels is derived from the demand for cars, which ultimately depends on how many the end consumer wants to buy.

Joint demand

Joint demand is demand that is linked with the sales of other organisational products. So, the demand for tyres has a strong link to the demand for cars.

Inelastic demand

Some b2b sales are not very price sensitive. Businesses do of course want to save money and will shop around for the best deal, but if the purchase is a relatively trivial one, a price rise will not affect overall sales very much. If the sales of a product are largely unaffected by price changes, especially in the short run, demand is referred to as price inelastic. For example, the tyres on a jumbo jet's wheels are one small component of the overall cost of the finished product. A rise in the price of tyres will not affect the overall demand for jumbo jets. (See Chapter 10 for a fuller explanation of inelasticity of demand.)

Fluctuating demand

Demand for goods and services tends to fluctuate more rapidly in b2b markets. This is at least partly because it is derived demand and even joint demand (see above) and so subject to a range of market forces. When a firm has a large order, it wants products to help satisfy it. When business is slow, there is no need to buy in as much.

THE COMPLEXITY OF THE ORGANISATIONAL BUYING PROCESS

The purchasing habits of organisations are rather different from those of individuals. Typically, businesses:

- buy in larger quantities

- negotiate harder on delivery terms

- expect reduced prices for bulk buying

- may require tailored products

- are harder to please

- have more people involved in making the decision to buy

- have longer, more complex decision-making processes.

Businesses buy in larger quantities because they are buying goods and services for more people. An individual may buy one or two ballpoint pens; a company would need several boxes just so that each employee can have one. If the goods they are buying are actually for use in their production process (e.g. Birds Eye buying rice as an ingredient for its ready meals) or for selling on (as shops do), then they will have to buy enough for all their customers.

If a consumer orders something, such as a new shirt or a new computer add-on, then usually they want it to arrive quickly, just because they cannot wait to wear it or plug it in. Businesses have a more pressing need to know that their orders will arrive on time. A company's whole production process may well depend on having sufficient rice to make its paella, or there may be just one time slot, say a national holiday, when it can install its new computer hardware without too much disruption. So businesses tend to insist on particular delivery times and, if their orders are large enough, suppliers will comply.

---

inelasticity
little response to changes in the marketing variable being measured (commonly price, advertising, competitive products, income); the percentage change in demand is less than the percentage change in price (or other variable), so if price rises, sales rise

Organisations are well aware that they are more valuable customers than individual purchasers. Often they expect something in return. They may settle for superior customer service, or they may insist on a discount as an incentive to place a large order.

Some business customers will ask for their own version of a supplier's products. For example, Hotpoint make a cooker for ao.com and there is a Lego Ferrari available exclusively from John Lewis. These special editions provide retailers with a competitive advantage as they offer a model that other stores do not have. Businesses may want cars in the company colours or pens with their name on. They may want the rice they buy to be of uniform size so that they can be sure it will all cook through when they cook it in a large batch. It would not usually be worth the supplier's while to customise its products for an individual customer, but for a large organisation? That is a different matter.

The business buying process tends to be more formal and often involves professional purchasers who adopt sophisticated purchasing systems. Very often, organisations will have policies and guidelines (e.g. a purchasing policy) as to whether purchasing should be centralised or decentralised, and from a single supplier (single sourcing) or a number of suppliers (multiple sourcing). All these policies have advantages and disadvantages.

ORGANISATIONAL BUYING SITUATIONS

There are three main types of organisational buying situation. These may be viewed on a continuum ranging from a straight re-buy, through modified re-buy, to new task at the other end of the scale (see Exhibit 3.17).

straight re-buy

where the buyer routinely reorders a product or service without any change to the order whatsoever; it may even be an automatic process

modified re-buy

the buyer wants to modify an element of the re-buy, e.g. change colour, size, price or delivery time

new task

when someone buys a product for the first time

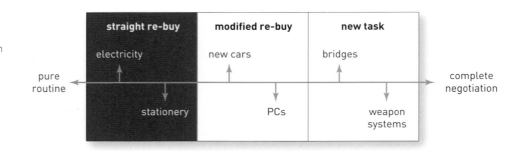

EXHIBIT 3.17 Types of organisational buying situations

Source: adapted from Enis (1980)

- A straight re-buy is where the buyer routinely reorders a product without any change to the order whatsoever. There may even be an automatic reordering system. Straight re-buys are usually low risk, frequently purchased and inexpensive items (e.g. stationery or paint).

- A modified re-buy is where the buyer wants something to be slightly different from the previous purchase. This may be the product specification (such as colour, size or technical specification) or the price or the terms (such as delivery time).

- A new task is a first-time purchase. This is the most complex category of purchase with the most involved, and sometimes lengthy, decision-making process. This is often something that is infrequently purchased or is high risk, e.g. expensive products such as computer systems, or it may be that the organisation is trying a new supplier or has introduced something new to its business, e.g. a lighting manufacturer who has introduced a new range of energy-saving lights.

THE BUYING CENTRE

In any sizeable organisation, there are likely to be a number of people involved in any purchase. The buying centre is not an actual department or formal group, it is a way of looking at all the people who participate in a business buying decision process and assessing their roles and information needs. Buying centres vary depending on the nature of the purchase and of the organisation.

Individuals within a buying centre fulfil one or more of the following roles. These roles may be formal, i.e. part of their jobs, or informal, i.e. they have volunteered or been asked to look into a purchase on a one-off basis. Typical roles within the organisational buying centre (or decision-making unit) are outlined below:

- *Initiators*: people who first identify the need for the product and communicate it to the others, e.g. a dissatisfied canteen customer who complains that there are no healthy choices on the menu.
- *Users*: members of the organisation who will actually use the purchase, e.g. administrators using computers.
- *Influencers*: individuals whose opinions may contribute to the final choice of purchase. Their influence may be related to their expertise (e.g. an IT specialist) or it could be of a more informal and/or personal nature.
- *Buyers*: the individuals who actually make the purchase, or select and approve suppliers, and negotiate the terms of the purchase. In larger organisations there will be a professional buying department.
- *Deciders*: individuals (e.g. the boss) who have formal or informal powers to select or approve suppliers.
- *Financiers*: the individual or department who holds the budget which will fund the purchase.
- *Gatekeepers*: individuals who have some control over the flow of information into the organisation. These may include buyers, technical personnel (e.g. IT experts) or receptionists.

THE ORGANISATIONAL BUYING PROCESS

Individuals within the organisational buying process have their own personal agendas, motives and dynamics. It is important to remember that they are individuals and that each must be understood and treated as such. Organisations do not make decisions – people do. The organisational buying process is longer and more complex than the consumer one (see Exhibit 3.18).

buying centre

comprises all the individuals that participate in the business buying decision process

decision-making unit (DMU)

all the individuals who participate in and influence the customer's purchase decision

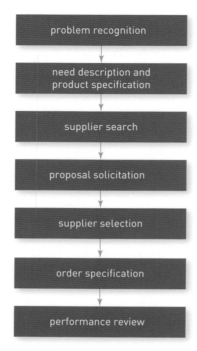

EXHIBIT 3.18 The organisational buying process

Source: based on Kotler et al. (2012)

Kotler et al. (2012) identified seven stages in the organisational buying process. This lengthy and complex process is more representative of the way organisations go about making large or significant purchases. A routine order for paperclips, or the booking of train travel for an employee, will be much quicker and more straightforward. However, the initial decision of which stationery supplier to use for paperclips may well have gone through all these stages.

Many business customers visit trade exhibitions to find new products or suppliers.

Source: iStock.com/pcruciatti

PROBLEM RECOGNITION

An individual, or group, within an organisation identifies a problem that may be solved by acquiring a specific good or service. This may be an entirely routine operation, such as reordering stationery, or a much more complex operation, such as purchasing a capital item (e.g. a fork-lift truck).

For example, if an organisation is to launch a new product, then to do so it may need new manufacturing systems or new component parts for it. External factors that influence the choice of product and supplier may be trade press, exhibitions or sales representatives.

GENERAL NEED DESCRIPTION AND PRODUCT SPECIFICATION

Having identified that they have a need, the organisation needs to think it through and describe it in a way that will help to find the right solutions. This description includes the general characteristics and qualities of the required product in terms of what it has to do, e.g. the manufacturing equipment must be capable of making six varieties of cake, all the same size but with different ingredients, and must be ready to start production within the year.

An organisation will specify the attributes that a product should have. This is very different from the situation in consumer markets, where much of the enjoyment of shopping is not knowing exactly what is required, but seeing what is available. The product specification will often incorporate aspects such as colour, material quality, performance levels and its compatibility with other components. This may require external assistance from, for example, consultants if the product is of a technical nature.

b2b focus: developing a relationship

In recent years, much emphasis has been placed on the importance of buyer–seller relationships and how these may be a source of competitive advantage. The emphasis is on long-term, collaborative relationships between a small number of suppliers and customers. Building trust between organisations is essential to maintaining such relationships and this takes time:

- *pre-relationship stage*: this stage involves the buyer evaluating potential new suppliers
- *early stage*: potential suppliers are in contact with buyers to negotiate trial deliveries
- *development stage*: deliveries of the product increase as trust and understanding develop between the buyer and the seller
- *long-term stage*: the buyer and seller are mutually dependent
- *final stage*: the relationship has become institutionalised.

Decisions need to be made as to the level of relational development required, since it is clearly a waste of valuable resources to invest in unwanted or unprofitable relationships. Technical support, increased access to expertise, better service levels and risk reduction are some of the benefits to the two organisations that need to be considered.

Source: Ford (1980)

SUPPLIER SEARCH

The buyer organisation then searches for the best vendor (selling organisation) to supply the product to the specification requested. This may be done using trade directories, brochures kept on file, exhibitions, Internet searches or through recommendations (or word of mouth).

PROPOSAL SOLICITATION

The next stage is for the organisation's specialist buyer to invite suitable prospective suppliers to submit proposals. These proposals may range from catalogues to formal presentations and substantial written proposals, dependent upon the value and importance of the potential order.

SUPPLIER SELECTION AND COMMITMENT

The buying organisation then reviews the proposals from the prospective vendors and, based on pre-specified criteria, selects one. The selection criteria usually revolve around attributes such as delivery times, product quality, prices, and possibly even honest corporate behaviour. Companies have, historically, used a number of suppliers as this enables them to obtain price concessions. However, increasingly, companies are working more closely with a smaller number of suppliers and, as a result, expect preferential treatment.

ORDER SPECIFICATION

The buyers finalise the order in terms of product specification, quantities, delivery times, price, etc., and forward it to the supplying organisation(s).

PERFORMANCE REVIEW

The final stage is performance review. The buying organisation assesses the performance of the supplying organisation and its products, and decides whether to use them as a supplier in the future.

ORGANISATIONAL PURCHASE CRITERIA

Organisational purchase criteria are usually much more rational, functional and objective than consumer criteria. Criteria such as price, conformity to product specification, quality, reliability and customer service levels, and continuity of supply are likely to be used. However, organisations are composed of individuals who have their own personal goals and motives. Therefore, more intangible, or implicit, criteria may also be important. Such criteria may include preferential treatment, which in turn may lead to useful professional relationships between individuals within, and between, organisations.

research focus: classic concept

Webster, F.E. and Wind, Y. (1972) 'A general model for understanding organizational buying behaviour', *Journal of Marketing*, 36 (Apr): 12–19.

Sheth, J.N. (1973) 'A model of industrial buyer behaviour', *Journal of Marketing*, 37 (Oct): 50–6.

Both of these articles focus on organisational buying behaviour in contrast to consumer market behaviour. The significant factors that influence the eventual buying decision are explored.

SUMMARY

Markets are made up of individual people and organisations. In consumer markets (b2c), these people vary enormously in terms of gender, age, income, education, personality, perceptions, attitudes and many other factors. Marketers need to understand the processes that consumers go through when making purchase decisions: the stages they go through and the criteria they may use. These decisions are influenced by internal factors, such as motivation, attitude and perception, as well as external factors such as family, friends and culture.

Organisational (b2b) buying is more complex than b2c buying. Organisations vary in terms of size, culture, purchasing policy and many other factors. Organisational buying tends to be much more objective and rational than consumer decision-making, to the extent that it may be over-bureaucratic. It is important for marketers to understand the processes that businesses go through and who is involved in purchase decisions.

Before developing a marketing strategy, all these factors must be understood and taken into account. Without this understanding, the marketing organisation is unlikely to exert as much influence as it might have during its customers' decision-making processes.

CHALLENGES REVIEWED

Now that you have finished reading the chapter, look back at the challenges you were set at the beginning. Do you have a clearer idea of what's involved?

HINTS

- Product adoption categories – characteristics of innovators.

- Influences on consumer buying behaviour.

- Organisational decision-making unit (buying centre) and organisational buying process.

- Thinking about the roles the child and its parents play in the purchase process, what reaction would you expect from the parents whose roles have been usurped? What is the likely impact on future business? Is the sales technique used ethical?

READING AROUND
JOURNAL ARTICLES

Belk, R. (1988) 'Possessions and the extended self', *Journal of Consumer Research*, 15 (2): 139–68.

Jayawardhena, C., Morrell, K. and Stride, C. (2016) 'Ethical consumption behaviours in supermarket shoppers: determinants and marketing implications', *Journal of Marketing Management*, 32 (7–8): 777–805.

Maslow, A. (1943) 'A theory of human motivation', *Psychological Review*, 50 (4): 370–96.

Torres, N. (2016) 'Ethical shoppers don't inspire us – they bug us', *Harvard Business Review*, April. Available at: https://hbr.org/2016/04/ethical-shoppers-dont-inspire-us-they-bug-us (accessed 12/04/16).

MAGAZINE ARTICLES

Mattin, D. (2015) 'Post-demographic consumerism', *Admap*, July/August. London: WARC.

Strong, C. (2015) 'Consumer decision-making: implications of time-pressured consumers', *Admap*, June. London: WARC.

BOOKS

Hanna, N., Wozniak, R. and Hanna, M. (2009) *Consumer Behaviour: An Applied Approach*. Dubuque, IA: Kendall Hunt Publishing Co.

Quart, A. (2003) *Branded: The Buying and Selling of Teenagers*. London: Arrow.

JOURNALS

Advances in Consumer Research

Journal of Consumer Research

MAGAZINES

Ethical Consumer (Ethical Consumer Research Association)

Which? (The Consumer Association)

WEBSITES

www.acrwebsite.org – the Association of Consumer Research, which has an interesting section for marketers.

www.mckinsey.com – management consultants McKinsey & Co have a wealth of resources online e.g. an excellent article on the customer loyalty loop.

TEST YOURSELF

1 What are the main stages of the consumer decision-making process? (See p. 91)

2 List the three main types of buying situation and the types of product that might be included in each of them. (See p. 98)

3 What are the four main types of consumer buyer behaviour? (See p. 101)

4 What are the major internal influences on consumer buying behaviour? (See pp. 102–109)

5 What are the main types of learning process? (See pp. 105–106)

6 Name the stages of Maslow's hierarchy of needs. (See p. 107)

7 What is the difference between an attitude and a belief? (See p. 108)

8 List the key roles in the organisational buying centre. (See p. 121)

9 What are the main categories in the consumer product adoption model? (See p. 117)

10 What are the main organisational buying situations? (See p. 120)

11 What are the main characteristics of organisational markets? (See pp. 118–119)

12 What are the main stages of the organisational buying process? (See p. 122)

REVISION TOOLS

Want to test yourself even more? Review what you have learnt by visiting
https://study.sagepub.com/masterson4e

- Practise for exams with **multiple choice questions**
- Revise key terms with **interactive flashcards**

MINI CASE STUDY: GETTING THERE

Read the questions, then the case material, and then answer the questions.

QUESTIONS

1   Identify all the people involved in the two purchase decisions outlined in the case study: Duncan's Paris journeys and the couple's holiday plans. Comment on these people's roles and information needs. Explain and justify your answer.

2   What factors, internal and external, are likely to influence Duncan's decision about Paris? How?

3   Apply the decision-making framework to Annie and Duncan's holiday decision, picking relevant information out of the case and adding to it from your own knowledge (e.g. of information sources) if you can. What is likely to influence the outcome of each stage? How can marketing techniques assist the couple in their decision-making?

Technological breakthroughs in transport have had an even more dramatic impact on the way we live our lives than those in communication. Mass air travel is perhaps the biggest contributor to the changes, opening up possibilities that were impractical, or at least extremely time-consuming, in the past. Before the advent of commercial airlines, a trip from Europe to South Africa or Australia took months.

Boarding the Eurostar.

© Eurostar ID Brand Library

For some time, the emphasis in our hectic and stressed-out world has been on getting from A to B as quickly as possible. Travellers have tended to favour the plane and the car as the speediest modes of transport. Cars were also preferred to public transport as they were considered more comfortable, more convenient and of higher status. The late Baroness Thatcher, formerly Margaret Thatcher, the UK Prime Minister, famously remarked in a 1986 government debate: 'A man who, beyond the age of 26, finds himself on a bus can count himself as a failure', yet today governments are encouraging the use of public transport rather than cars while environmental pressure groups advocate trains and boats rather than planes. Whether or not such green policies will prevail, will depend upon consumer attitudes and behaviour.

(Continued)

(Continued)

Many people are switching from plane to train in order to reduce their carbon dioxide emissions. Eurostar's Business Premier class, which has a 10-minute check-in facility and a work-friendly environment on board, has become increasingly popular with busy executives. In 2009, Eurostar's daily ticket sales were approximately £1.85m and rising, the growth coming mainly from business travel.

Richard Brown, Chief Executive of Eurostar, commented: 'The growth in traveller numbers clearly indicates that concerns about the environmental impact of short-haul air travel, combined with the worsening experience of flying, are prompting more people to look for a greener and easier way of travelling to the Continent'.

Eurostar is leading the way in an image change for train travel generally. Its excellent punctuality record, has been a key factor in changing attitudes towards train travel.

The service has got even better since the terminus at St Pancras opened. Passengers are whisked from London to Paris in just 2 hours 15 minutes and London to Brussels in only 1 hour 51 minutes. When compared to the time it takes just to get to the departure gate at a UK airport (upwards of two hours), the train looks even more attractive.

Duncan Scott travels from London to Paris on business at least once a week. He has always taken a taxi to Heathrow airport (a journey of about 10 miles) and then flown from there. At Charles de Gaulle airport, he gets another taxi to his destination in Paris. However, his friends are starting to harass him about his carbon footprint – some seriously, some light-heartedly. His girlfriend, Annie, has done the research and found that he could walk to his local tube station, catch a tube to Kings Cross Railway Station, stroll through the smart shops and cafes of St Pancras International and from there take the Eurostar to Paris Nord in the heart of the French capital. Then he could take the Metro, though it would mean two changes and would take about three-quarters of an hour, or he could take a taxi which would be quicker. Annie thinks he should take the Metro but Duncan dislikes being underground and is worried about getting lost.

He is also concerned that the train may actually cost more and that his firm will be reluctant to pay for it. The travel department, who book everything, are notoriously inflexible and cost-conscious. However, he is playing golf with his boss and the Finance Director soon and has promised Annie that he will raise the issue. He hasn't dared tell her about the Finance Director's attitude to trains. According to him, train travel is for other people. He flies, drives his Bentley or is driven by someone else – usually someone wearing a peaked cap.

As well as trying to reorganise Duncan's travel arrangements, Annie is worried about Duncan who seems stressed and in need of a good holiday (they haven't had one for nearly a year). She can only take one week off work so they need to spend as little time travelling as possible so that they have enough time at their destination. Duncan thinks they should fly but is leaving the decision to Annie. She is worried about what her friends will say if she flies, given the fuss she has been making about Duncan flying to Paris. One of her friends, Irene, is a travel agent and she is trying to find suitable ferries and trains for them to get to their first-choice destination, Austria, where they had planned to hike. So far it is not looking hopeful. Irene has suggested they go to France or Holland instead. There is the possibility of hiring a barge in Holland, which really appeals to Duncan. Annie would prefer horse riding in the Camargue, although her mother is absolutely against it, claiming that it is far too dangerous. She suspects that they will end up cycling somewhere as a compromise and she is content with that – as long as they don't have to fly.

Travel decisions have been dominating Annie and Duncan's lives. Their flat is liberally scattered with brochures, the PC seems to be permanently linked to travel sites like Tripadvisor and last minute.com and they get at least six automated messages a day from travel companies. When Duncan gets home from a long day, made longer by a security alert at Heathrow, he finds Annie excitedly waving two tickets to Amsterdam (ferry and train). Her mother has decided to treat them to a Dutch canal trip.

Source: Eurostar (2007)

REFERENCES

Assael, H. (1987) *Consumer Behaviour and Marketing Action* (6th edn). Boston, MA: Kent Publishing Co.

Bearden, O. and Etzel, M. (1982) 'Reference group influence on product and purchase decisions', *Journal of Consumer Research*, 9 (2): 183–94.

Court, D., Elzinga, D., Mulder, S. and Vetvik, O.J. (n.d.) 'The consumer decision journey', McKinsey & Company. Available at: www.mckinsey.com/business-functions/marketing-and-sales/our-insights/the-consumer-decision-journey (accessed 14/04/16).

Engel, J., Blackwell, R. and Miniard, P. (2006) *Consumer Behaviour* (9th edn). Fort Worth, TX: The Dryden Press.

Enis, B.M. (1980) *Marketing Principles* (3rd edn). Santa Monica, CA: Goodyear.

Eurostar (2007) 'Press release: Eurostar revenues rise as travellers go for high speed rail'. Available at: www.eurostar.com/uk-en/about-eurostar/press-office/press-releases/2007?page=2 (accessed 17/02/14).

Festinger, L. (1957) *A Theory of Cognitive Dissonance*. Stanford: Stanford University Press.

Ford, D. (1980) 'The development of buyer-seller relationships in industrial markets', *European Journal of Marketing*, 14 (516): 339–54.

Howard, J.A. and Sheth, J.N. (1969) *Theory of Buyer Behavior*. New York: John Wiley & Sons.

Hyllegard, K.H., Yan, R-N., Paff Ogle, J. and Attmann, J. (2010) 'The influence of gender, social cause, charitable support, and message appeal on Gen Y's responses to cause-related marketing', *Journal of Marketing Management*, 27 (1–2): 100–23.

Kotler, P. (1965) 'Behavioural models for analyzing buyers', *Journal of Marketing*, 29 (4): 37–45.

Kotler, P., Keller, K.L., Brady, M., Goodman, M. and Hansen, T. (2012) *Marketing Management* (2nd edn). Harlow: Pearson.

Laran, J. and Tsiros, M. (2013) 'An investigation of the effectiveness of uncertainty in marketing promotions involving free gifts', *Journal of Marketing*, 77 (2): 112–23.

Laurent, G. and Kapferer, J. (1985) 'Measuring consumer involvement profiles', *Journal of Marketing Research*, 22 (Feb): 41–53.

Lawlor, M.-A. and Prothero, A. (2011) 'Pester power: a battle of wills between children and their parents', *Journal of Marketing Management*, 27 (5–6): 561–81.

Li, C. and Bernoff, J. (2011) *Groundswell: Winning in a World Transformed by Social Technologies*. Boston, MA: Harvard Business Review Press.

Martinson, J. (2013) 'Apple's in-app game charges: how my kids ran up huge bills', *The Guardian*. Available at: www.theguardian.com/technology/shortcuts/2013/mar/26/apples-in-app-game-charges-kids-bills (accessed 01/04/16).

Maslow, A.H. (1943) 'A theory of human motivation', *Psychological Review*, 50 (4): 370–96.

Pew Research Centre (2016) 'Social networking fact sheet'. Available at: www.pewinternet.org/fact-sheets/social-networking-fact-sheet/ (accessed 12/04/16).

Powers, T., Advincula, D., Austin, M.S. and Graiko, S. (2012) 'Digital and social media in the purchase-decision process: a special report from the Advertising Research Foundation', *Journal of Advertising Research*, 52 (4): 479–89.

Rogers, E.M. (1976) 'New product adoption and diffusion', *Journal of Consumer Behaviour*, 2: 290–301.

Rogers, E.M. (2003) *Diffusion of Innovations* (5th edn). New York: The Free Press.

Schiffman, L.G., Kanuk, L.L. and Hansen, H. (2008) *Consumer Behaviour: A European Outlook*. Harlow: FT/Prentice Hall.

Sheth, J.N. (1973) 'A model of industrial buyer behaviour', *Journal of Marketing*, 37 (Oct): 50–6.

Smith, P.R. and Taylor, J. (2004) *Marketing Communications: An Integrated Approach* (4th edn). London: Kogan Page.

Solomon, M.R., Bamossy, G., Askegaard, S. and Hogg, M.K. (2010) *Consumer Behaviour: A European Perspective* (4th edn). Harlow: Pearson Education.

Technopedia (n.d.) 'bait apps'. Available at: www.techopedia.com/definition/28550/bait-apps (accessed 01/04/16).

Usunier, J.-C. and Lee, J.A. (2009) *Marketing Across Cultures*. Harlow: FT/Prentice Hall.

Webster, F.E. and Wind, Y. (1972) 'A general model for understanding organizational buying behaviour', *Journal of Marketing*, 36 (Apr): 12–19.

Wei, Y. and Yu, C. (2012) 'How do reference groups influence self-brand connections among Chinese consumers? Implications for advertising', *Journal of Advertising*, 31 (2): 39–53.

Wilkie, W. (1990) *Consumer Behavior*. New York: John Wiley & Sons.

Williams, K.C. (1981) *Behavioural Aspects of Marketing*. London: Heinemann Professional Publishing.

MARKET SEGMENTATION, TARGETING AND POSITIONING

MARKET SEGMENTATION CHALLENGES

The following are illustrations of the types of decisions that marketers have to take about market segmentation. *You aren't expected to know how to deal with the challenges now*; just bear them in mind as you read the chapter and see what you can find that helps.

- You have just joined the marketing department of a car company. Your managing director has asked your advice about the launch of a sports car. The company has invested a lot in the product's development and so the sales targets are high. Should you aim to attract as broad a cross-section of customers as possible or focus your marketing efforts on specific types of customer?

- You are the marketing director of a loss-making brewery. You need to develop new products to revitalise the business. How will you choose what type of beer to sell and to whom?

- You are a marketing manager for a firm of solicitors. Research has indicated that your firm is operating in a marketplace where people see little difference between rival solicitors' services. How could you make your firm stand out from the crowd?

- You work in a travel agency. Recently published market research has shown that there are many different types of holidaymaker. What criteria will you use to identify and describe these different people?

Ben Voyer on
segmentation

INTRODUCTION

Marketers are interested in satisfying the wants and needs of customers and consumers but not everybody wants the same things. This poses a problem for marketers. Marketing the same goods or services to everybody is unlikely to be successful but providing something unique for each individual will be too expensive. There has to be a compromise, and fortunately there is. Marketers can take advantage of the fact that some people share similar wants and needs. These people can be grouped according to their similarities. Market segmentation is about breaking up a market into sections (segments) so that marketing effort can be focused better towards particular segments. This is efficient and effective marketing.

market segmentation
the process of dividing a total market into subgroups (segments) such that each segment consists of buyers and users who share similar characteristics but are different from those in other segments

Segmenting a market requires accurate information on customers and potential customers and this information is found through market research (see Chapter 5). It is important to understand which buyer characteristics (see Chapter 3) are significant in the purchase of the product in question. For example, it is quite common to split markets into male and female, but this is not likely to be the best way to do it if you are selling print cartridges or butter.

There are different ways of segmenting a market and the approach taken will depend on the nature of the market and the way in which a company wishes to deal with it. The way a company segments a b2b market will be different from the way a company segments a consumer market.

Breaking a market into segments is just the beginning of the segmentation, targeting and positioning (STP) process; having identified different groups (segments), decisions have to be made about which groups to target – and how many. This is referred to as **target marketing** (or simply targeting). These decisions lie at the very heart of marketing decision-making as they affect the full range of marketing activities. In choosing targets, marketers have to consider competing brands and present their own brands in such a way as to reduce unnecessary direct competition. This is called brand, or competitive, **positioning**.

This chapter emphasises the need to determine which markets are attractive, and explores different approaches to the important STP process of segmentation, targeting and positioning.

MARKET ATTRACTIVENESS

Some markets will be more attractive to a company than others: perhaps more profitable, easier to sell to or less competitive. One of the most fundamental aspects of marketing is choosing which markets to focus on. The decision is based on an assessment of:

- market opportunity – to identify what is possible
- competitive advantage – to determine the degree of challenge

- the objectives of the organisation – can this market help deliver what the organisation wants to achieve?

These assessments are essential inputs to an organisation's marketing strategy. How many market opportunities are selected will depend on the thinking of top management and the objectives of the firm. Some firms want to be innovators and will be keen to search out new opportunities; some will be followers and quickly imitate the leaders (see Chapter 2). Others will be risk averse and will therefore be slow to make changes. Ironically, this strategy may actually be riskier because they are failing to move with the times.

These shoppers may all be part of a consumer market but their needs and wants are likely to vary significantly.

Source: iStock.com/william87

To stand the best chance of achieving marketing success, a thorough understanding of the market is absolutely necessary. It is unusual for an organisation to attempt to capture an entire market. It is more likely to target one or more segments of that market: usually those segments that seem to offer the best chance of high profits. Not-for-profit organisations also use segmentation and targeting techniques in order to make more effective use of their resources and increase their chances of achieving their objectives (e.g. fundraising or client/patient service).

market attractiveness

an assessment of how desirable a particular market or market segment is to an organisation

WHAT ARE MARKETS?

Markets are people. Or, more accurately, a market consists of individuals or organisations that have a willingness and ability to purchase products. A market can consist of a single segment or multiple segments. Even though markets are often described in terms of products, such as the 'drinks market', 'car market' or 'market for nuclear power stations', it is important that marketers never forget that markets are really composed of people.

Markets comprise customers (more commonly called 'buyers' in a b2b market) and consumers (or 'users') but will also include other groups as well, such as sellers and competitors (see Chapter 1). Successful segmentation, targeting and positioning is dependent on an in-depth understanding all these groups (actual and potential).

There are dangers associated with focusing *solely* on customers. First, not all customers are the same or want the same things. A product that is ideal for one customer may be no good at all for another (think about films or clothes). Second, customers are not necessarily consumers. The users of goods and services may not be the actual customers (buyers). For example, toys are often bought by parents but used by their children. Who should the toy be designed for? Who should the advertising be aimed at? Similarly, some products, e.g. boxes of chocolate, jewellery, perfume, are often bought as gifts. The customer is buying the product with someone else in mind.

Industrial goods and services are almost never bought by the people who will actually use them. Organisations have buying departments to make the purchases that the business needs.

Members of a supply chain, such as agents, wholesalers and retailers, buy things to sell on. They may be the first link in a chain of buyers but they are not usually the eventual consumers.

So yes, customers are important, but so are the final consumers or users of the products. Marketers need to address the needs of them all.

WHY SEGMENT AND TARGET MARKETS?

One of the most profound realisations to strike any marketer is that there is a great diversity among customers. (Louden and Della Bitta, 1993: 30)

mass marketing

delivering the same marketing programme to everybody without making any significant distinction between them

Mass marketing, i.e. selling the same thing in the same way to everyone, is primarily a twentieth-century idea. It relies on large numbers of customers/consumers sharing sufficiently similar needs and wants. This is not the approach in the vast majority of today's markets any more than it was in the distant past. Up until the early 1900s, most goods were produced to meet the needs of specific customers, but as populations and demand grew, this became inefficient. Henry Ford, founder of the Ford Motor Company,

Ted Talks:
the tribes we lead

is frequently attributed with developing and popularising the concept and the technology of mass-production. He standardised his production techniques and his products to achieve economies of scale (though there is now some doubt over whether he actually said, 'you can have it any colour you want so long as it's black'). Production costs per unit were significantly reduced allowing Ford to charge lower prices for cars but the cars had to be very similar in design. This mass-production strategy therefore led inevitably to the mass-marketing strategy of one product (the Model T), in one colour (black), at one price ($360) to the entire market.

In times of scarce supply, customers will make do with whatever is available. In many countries today, there is an over-supply of many products. Those markets are demand-driven, rather than supply-led (see Chapter 1). As a consequence, markets are fragmenting and moving away from mass marketing to more targeted approaches. Under such circumstances, trying to apply mass-marketing techniques, offering a single product and single marketing programme across the total market, while achieving economies of scale, runs the risk that few customers will be adequately satisfied (Dibb and Simkin, 1996). In contrast to mass marketing, some now talk of mass customisation to refer to the way in which, even in very large markets, organisations are being challenged to tailor their product offerings almost to meet individual needs. Once again, technology is being harnessed to provide solutions.

mass-customisation

tailoring product offerings almost to meet individual needs

Potential customers/consumers want different things which creates opportunities for marketers to develop different markets and submarkets *and* to develop different marketing programmes for each. People's requirements are so numerous and diverse that it would be impossible for any single organisation to satisfy everybody. This creates competitive opportunity and the potential for competitive advantage.

digital focus: getting to know your target market

Simple marketing research and analysis, coupled with a basic understanding of market segmentation and targeting principles, can result in more effective marketing.

Many organisations regularly collect and store valuable customer information in databases. Many also fail to make the best use of that information which can reveal valuable insights into customers and potential customers – or students.

Further Education (FE) colleges are on tight budgets and so it is tempting for them to use a uniform marketing communications approach which treats all potential students the same. Clever use of the information they already have in their database could help them to target students more precisely.

The first step is to purge the database, removing duplicate entries, gone-aways and incomplete records. It is vitally important that data is clean and current.

The next step is to decide on a segmentation approach. For an FE college, which runs trade and vocational courses, GCSEs and A levels, it might be effective to segment by demographic and lifestyle characteristics. At one college, an analysis of the database showed that students on trade courses tended to be in their late teens or early twenties, of average affluence, unmarried with one or two children, usually working in craft or trade occupations and with practical activities such as DIY and home computing or computer gaming as hobbies. GCSE or A-level students were usually younger, living at home, single with no children, working part-time in unskilled jobs with music, dancing, reading and gaming as hobbies. Website information can now be tailored to each profile, making it easier for potential students to find the right courses and the other information they need.

Wouldn't it be good if the college knew where these people lived? By subscribing to a geo-demographic data-provider such as Mosaic or Acorn, they can at least find which areas, even which streets, their best prospects are likely to live in. The demographic profiles can be matched to local postcode areas. Targeted mailings, showing the right kind of courses, could then be sent to potential students.

Think about the advantages this brings to the college – and also to their students.

Market segmentation is the splitting of a market into smaller groups (segments) so that marketers can better direct or focus their efforts. Segmentation can be defined as: 'the process of dividing a total market into subgroups (segments) such that each segment consists of buyers and users who share similar characteristics but are different from those in other segments'.

Ideally, from the marketing point of view, a segment would be those people who share the same buying behaviour and practices in *every* respect, but this is not realistic. Instead, marketers use a variety of techniques to find groups of people who are similar enough in the ways that count. It is possible, therefore, to segment a market (i.e. the customers/consumers for a product) according to age, where people live, their interests and lifestyles, their media habits: anything that is relevant to the product being sold. In business-to-business (b2b) marketing, organisations may be segmented according to their location, industry grouping, etc. These segmentation approaches, or **segmentation variables**, are an indication of similarities between customers. A fuller description of the variables used as bases for segmentation follows after the next section which discusses the main factors that make for a good segment to target.

segmentation variables

the characteristics used to divide a market into distinct groups (segments) and to differentiate between members of those groups, e.g. income, education, gender

CRITERIA FOR DETERMINING GOOD MARKET SEGMENTS

There is a wealth of information available to marketers to help them segment markets but not all market characteristics are relevant to the purchase decision. It is important to make sure that the segments chosen are the best ones, not just the easiest ones to use. Usable market segments should be:

- *Measurable*: marketers need to know how many potential customers are in each segment. If it is not measurable, a segment cannot be assessed for its size and profit potential.

- *Homogeneous* (similar) within the segment: the customers/consumers in a market segment should be as similar as possible in their likely responses to marketing mix variables.

- *Heterogeneous* (different) between segments: the customers/consumers in different segments should be as different as possible in their likely responses to marketing mix variables. The less overlap there is between segments, the better.

- *Substantial*: the segment should be big enough to be profitable (or of meeting the objectives of the organisation if they are something other than profit. (See Chapter 12 for more on objectives.)

- *Accessible*: segments need to be reached and served effectively, not only in terms of delivery of product but also in terms of communication with the members of the segment. This can often be a problem. It may not be possible, for instance, to arrange new, or rearrange existing, distribution systems cost-efficiently to reach a chosen segment (Dibb and Simkin, 1996), for example, if the factory is in Central England and the new target is in Tasmania or if the identified target is ex-gamblers with retired racehorses – how could they be identified or communicated with?

- *Operational*: the segmentation approach adopted should be useful in designing *specific* marketing mixes for each segment. If the same approach is used for multiple segments, what was the point? The stability of the segment in the short, medium or long term is also important.

All these things should be used to evaluate whether or not a segment is suitable for targeting. Dibb and Wensley (2002) make the point that there are other important considerations to ensure a market segmentation analysis leads to effective marketing action:

- the commitment and involvement of senior managers within the organisation
- the readiness of the company to respond to market change
- inter-functional/departmental coordination
- the need for well-designed planning.

In practice, companies only have limited and imperfect information and resources and it is not always possible to meet all of the criteria above. Marketers have to keep refining their segmentation bases to make them the best that they can be.

SEGMENTATION APPROACHES

Nivea case study

There are many ways to segment a market. Segmentation variables can be used singly, but it is often more useful to use them in combination. Variables used singly would still represent a fairly indiscriminate market, while, used collectively, a more clearly defined segment emerges. Exhibit 4.1 shows how this works.

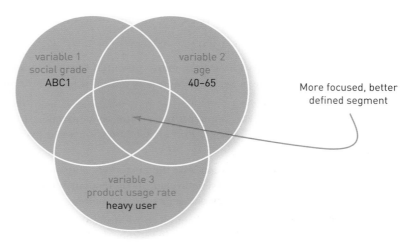

variable 1
social grade
ABC1

variable 2
age
40–65

More focused, better
defined segment

variable 3
product usage rate
heavy user

EXHIBIT 4.1 Using multiple segmentation variables

Exhibit 4.2 is a summary of the different approaches to segmentation in consumer markets. Each approach is described in greater detail in the sections below. Segmentation approaches in business markets will be considered later in Exhibit 4.7.

Consumer (b2c) markets	Examples of variables
• **Geographic segmentation**	Country, region, city, urban–rural
• **Demographic segmentation**	Age, gender, family size, life stage e.g. family life cycle (FLC), religion, race, nationality, education, ethnic group, income, socio-economic grouping: A, B, C1, C2, D, E
• **Geo-demographic segmentation**	House type and house location (e.g. ACORN, MOSAIC)
• **Psychographic segmentation**	Lifestyles, values, motives, personalities, e.g. VALS
• **Mediagraphic segmentation**	Media habits (i.e. TV viewing, papers read, social media sites, etc.)
• **Behavioural segmentation bases:**	
purchase occasion	Day-to-day purchase, special occasion
benefits sought	Value for money, service, status, quality, brand image
usage rate	Heavy, medium, light user
user status	None, ex, potential, first time, regular user
readiness stage	Unaware, aware, informed, interested, desirous, intending to buy, bought, used
attitude to product	Enthusiastic, uninterested, positive, negative
involvement	Low involvement, high involvement (see Chapter 3 for more details)
adopter type	Innovator, early adopter, early majority, late majority, laggard
loyalty status	Total, strong, medium, light, none

mediagraphic segmentation

markets segmented by reading and viewing habits

EXHIBIT 4.2 The main variables used as bases to segment markets

SEGMENTATION IN CONSUMER MARKETS
GEOGRAPHIC AND DEMOGRAPHIC SEGMENTATION

Geographic segmentation and demographic segmentation are probably the most popular forms of segmentation. Geographic segmentation groups customers according to their location, e.g. their neighbourhood, town, country or continent, Demographic segmentation uses population characteristics such as gender, occupation, income, age, etc. (see Exhibit 4.2) – any personal characteristic relevant to the product in question may be used. For a manufacturer or retailer of shoes, size of feet would be relevant; or size of waist for a clothing manufacturer.

geographic segmentation

markets segmented by countries, regions and areas

demographic segmentation

markets segmented by population characteristics such as age, gender, occupation and income

Clothing retailers Long Tall Sally and High and Mighty use size to segment and target the women's and men's market respectively by focusing on larger sizes only. These segmentation variables are relatively easy to measure as there is a wealth of information readily available from both government and commercial sources.

global focus: the world is getting smaller

The world is getting smaller, or so it seems, thanks to improvements in transportation and telecommunications technologies. Writer Marshall McLuhan invented the term 'global village' to describe this process and how it means that information can travel around the globe almost instantly. International trade is increasing as trade barriers are lifted. Through websites, email and mobile communications, and greatly improved physical distribution operators, even the smallest company can attract and satisfy international customers.

Operating in international markets is not without its problems, though. Many things vary from country to country. A thorough segmentation analysis of one country may have no value at all in a different one. There are around 195 countries in the world and they each have their own unique cultures, subcultures, languages, customs, ethics, beliefs, religions and demographic patterns. As if those differences were not enough to complicate the segmentation process, the quantity and quality of relevant information varies significantly from country to country making the data collection itself complex.

geo-demographic segmentation

markets are segmented by a combination of geographic and demographic approaches using house location and house type

National Readership Survey: lifestyle data

GEO-DEMOGRAPHIC SEGMENTATION

Geo-demographic segmentation is a popular method for segmenting consumer markets. It combines aspects of both geographic and demographic data (hence its name). The assumption is that the area and the sort of house people live in say something about the sort of people they are and, importantly for the marketer, the sorts of things they do, buy and use. In contrast, social grading attempts to relate the type of person and the things they do with their occupations (and income).

Acorn (A Classification Of Residential Neighbourhoods) is a UK system that uses the government household census data and specifically focuses on where people live and what types of house they live in. Using sophisticated statistical techniques, Acorn splits the population into groups according to two variables: house location and house type. Mosaic offers both a UK and a global segmentation analysis (see Exhibit 4.3 for groupings). Geo-demographic segmentation systems are available in most developed nations.

Group	Approx. % population	Approx. % households	Description	Examples of types within each group
A	4.3	3.5	Alpha territory	A01 Global power brokers
				A02 Voices of authority
B	9.5	8.2	Professional rewards	B06 Yesterday's captains
				B10 Parish guardians
C	4.8	4.4	Rural solitude	C11 Squires among locals
				C13 Modern agribusiness

Group	Approx. % population	Approx. % households	Description	Examples of types within each group
D	9.2	8.75	Small town diversity	D17 Jacks of all trades
				D 18 Hardworking families
E	3.4	4.3	Active retirement	E20 Golden retirement
				E23 Balcony downsizers
F	13.2	11.2	Suburban mindsets	F26 Mid-market families
				F27 Shop floor affluence
G	5.3	5.8	Careers and kids	G30 Soccer dads and mums
				G32 Childcare years
H	4.0	5.9	New homemakers	H34 Buy-to-let territory
				H36 Foot on the ladder
I	10.6	8.7	Ex-council community	I 38 Settled ex-tenants
				I41 Stressed borrowers
J	4.5	5.1	Claimant cultures	J42 Worn-out workers
				J43 Streetwise kids
K	4.3	5.2	Upper floor living	K48 Multicultural towers
				K49 Rehoused migrants
L	4.0	6.0	Elderly needs	L50 Pensioners in blocks
				L53 Low-spending elders
M	7.4	7.4	Industrial heritage	M54 Clocking off
				M55 Backyard regeneration
N	6.5	7.0	Terraced melting pot	N60 Back-to-back basics
				N61 Asian identities
O	8.8	8.5	Liberal opinions	O63 Urban cool
				O67 Study buddies

EXHIBIT 4.3 Mosaic geo-demographics (the categories have been updated to a 2016 version, the details for which can be found on Experian's website at www.experian.co.uk/marketing-services/products/mosaic-uk.html)

Source: based on Mosaic UK (as at May 2012). MOSAIC is a registered trademark of Experian Ltd

Geo-demographic groupings have been extensively cross-referenced with other shopping and behaviour databases. In the case of Mosaic, these include the Target Group Index (TGI) and BARB data (see also Chapter 5) so that the actual buying and media habits of these groups are known. Geo-demographic systems that are offered for commercial purposes, such as Acorn and Mosaic, are updated frequently so the categories and details do change.

family life cycle

a form of market
segmentation based on the
recognition that we pass
through a series of quite
distinct phases in our lives

FAMILY/HOUSEHOLD LIFE CYCLE SEGMENTATION

Family life cycle segmentation is based on the recognition that a person passes through a series of quite distinct phases in their life, each typified by a different set of circumstances, and within each they display some very different behaviour. Each stage is associated with different needs, social behaviour and purchasing patterns; a family with young children, for example, has very different needs from those of an older couple with no children. Wells and Gubar (1966) initially defined nine life cycle stages (see below) which are still widely used today – although they no longer accurately represent a typical modern life cycle.

Stages in the family life cycle (adapted from the overview of the life cycle in Wells and Gubar (1996))

Bachelor	Young, single
New partners	Young couple, no children
Full Nest I	Young couple with dependent children
Full Nest II	Older couple with dependent children
Full Nest III	Older couple with dependent children, financial position improving
Empty Nest I	Older couple, no children at home
Empty Nest II	Older couple, no children at home, retired
Solitary Survivor I	Still working, income good but likely to sell home
Solitary Survivor II	Older single people

Today, the traditional nuclear family (of 2 parents and 2.4 children) is no longer the norm, and it is far less common for individuals to flow predictably from one stage to another. In 2015, 7.7 million people in UK households lived alone, of which 4.1 million were aged 16 to 64 (Office for National Statistics, 2015). High property prices mean many children remain with their parents into their 20s and early 30s, multi-family households are more common and unrelated adults are increasingly co-habiting or co-owning properties well beyond their student years.

Information about typical household composition and life stage data is a key component of postcode segmentation systems such as Acorn and Mosaic (see above); however, there have also been attempts to update the family life cycle model to make it more reflective of the diversity of modern households: for example Du and Kamakura's model shown in Exhibit 4.4. The diagram shows the most typical states and paths that US households followed from 1968 to 2001. The percentages (reflected in the size of the arrows) indicate how many households made the transition from one stage to another.

More recent research adopts a life *course* perspective. Instead of a focus on discrete life *stage* categories (assumed to be rather stable states – which they often are not), the aim is to increase understanding of consumers' main role trajectories over time providing a basis for marketing decision-making beyond segmentation. The life course approach weaves together both age-related developments (such as work and family pathways) with analysis of short-term life transitions (such as leaving school or divorce) to achieve a deeper understanding of the impact on consumption patterns. Understanding consumers' experiences of key life events such as the arrival of children or divorce, and how they adapt to changes in their

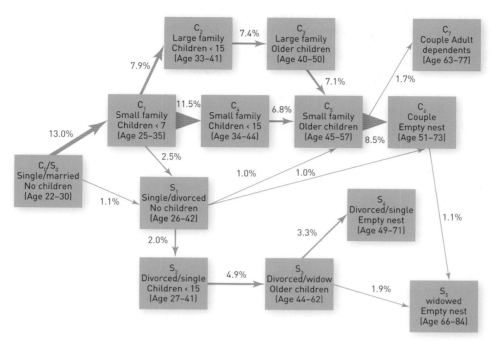

EXHIBIT 4.4 Household life cycles and lifestyles in the United States

Source: Du and Kamakura (2006) Reprinted with permission from *Journal of Marketing Research*, published by the American Marketing Association, Rex Y. Du and Wagner A. Kamakura (2006), 'Household Life Cycles and Lifestyles in the United States', *Journal of Marketing Research*, 43(1): 126.

circumstances, is vital for implementing successful targeting and positioning strategies and an important foundation for building long-term consumer relationships.

SOCIAL GRADING

Groups of occupations (usually of the chief income earner in the household) can be used to segment markets according to social grading. In the UK, the best-known groupings are: A, B, C1, C2, D and E. Exhibit 4.5 shows these groupings and how the UK population has

social grading

segmentation by occupation of head of household; the typical classifications used are A, B, C1, C2, D and E groups

Occupational Groups		Percentage of population 2015
A	Higher managerial, administrative and professional	4
B	Intermediate managerial, administrative and professional	23
C1	Supervisory, clerical and junior managerial, administrative and professional	27
C2	Skilled manual workers	22
D	Semi-skilled and unskilled manual workers	16
E	State pensioners, casual and lowest grade workers, unemployed with state benefits only	9

EXHIBIT 4.5 Social grading

Source: NRS Print: 'NBS January–December 2015' © Copyright National Readership Survey

changed over time, with a greater proportion representing the higher earning professional groups (ABs) and a lower proportion in the C2, D and E categories.

These socio-economic groupings are sometimes inaccurately referred to as social classes. Social class is a related and overlapping concept but has wider connotations than just the occupational measure that is used in social grading.

Social grading is used widely in market research and in the collection of government statistics. This data relates social grades to buying behaviour, disposable and discretionary income, media habits, hobbies and interests – all the sorts of things that marketers need to know. Unfortunately, social grading is not very good at determining discrete segments that are homogeneous within the group and heterogeneous between the groups (see 'Criteria for determining good market segments' on p. 137), which is an important aspect of market segmentation. The information may be fairly easy to find, but it is limited in its usefulness. Despite this, it remains popular but it is advisable to combine demographic variables to make a more focused market segment, as shown in Exhibit 4.1.

To summarise, the thinking behind demographic segmentation is that age, life stage, income or occupation, etc. are factors that will tend to affect buying and usage behaviour. For example, a wealthy lawyer will shop for clothing very differently from a student. A 20-year-old male will exhibit different purchase and use behaviour from a 50-year-old female.

PSYCHOGRAPHIC SEGMENTATION

psychographic segmentation

using lifestyles, values, personalities and/or psychological characteristics to split up markets

Demographic segmentation can help identify markets which have the means and opportunity to buy – psychographic segmentation provides a more detailed understanding of buyers and users, e.g. in terms of motivations, lifestyles, values. It can be used alongside other approaches, such as demographic segmentation.

VALS™ is a popular consumer classification model which uses a combination of psychology, demographics and lifestyles to help marketers understand and target their best customers. Through the use of a survey and proprietary algorithm, VALS™ segments individuals age 18 and older into eight consumer groups. Two dimensions organise the eight groups: primary motivations (the horizontal dimension) and resources (the vertical dimension). Exhibit 4.6 shows the eight types.

CONSUMER SEGMENT DESCRIPTIONS

- Innovators are confident enough to experiment; to try, fail, and try again.
- Thinkers are the old guard, with "ought" and "should" benchmarks for social conduct.
- Believers adhere to right and wrong for a good life.
- Achievers have a me-first, my-family-first attitude.
- Strivers are the centre of street culture; they live in the moment.
- Experiencers want to stand out. They are first in, first out of trend adoption.
- Makers protect what they think they own; they may be perceived as anti-intellectual.
- Survivors are the quiet rank and file. Risk averse they take comfort in the familiar.

US VALS™ Framework

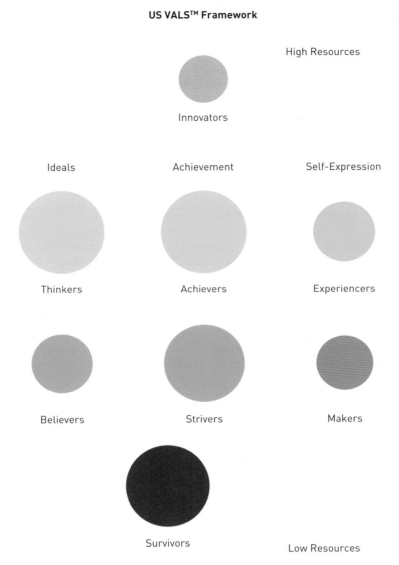

High Resources

Innovators

Ideals   Achievement   Self-Expression

Thinkers   Achievers   Experiencers

Believers   Strivers   Makers

Survivors   Low Resources

PRIMARY MOTIVATION

The concept of primary motivation represents the underlying drivers of consumer attitudes and behaviours. Consumers who are primarily motivated by ideals are guided by knowledge and principles. Consumers who are primarily motivated by achievement look for products and services of personal benefit that convey success. Consumers who are primarily motivated by self-expression desire social or physical activity to make an impact.

RESOURCES

VALS survey

Energy, self-confidence, intellectualism, novelty seeking, innovativeness, impulsiveness, leadership and vanity among others, play a critical role in people's tendency to consume goods and services. These psychological traits, in conjunction with key demographics such as income and education, determine an individual's resources. The level of their resources determines a person's ability to act on their primary motivation.

More details of the VALS™ models can be found at **www.strategicbusinessinsights.com/vals**.

BEHAVIOURAL SEGMENTATION

behavioural segmentation

dividing a market into subgroups (segments) of customers/users according to how they buy, use and feel about products

Behavioural segmentation groups customers and consumers according to how they buy, use and feel about products.

The growth of out-of-town and edge-of-town supermarkets and shopping malls has changed shopping behaviour. As most shoppers travel by car, it has been possible to increase the size of bulk packaging of such items as soap powders as they only have to be transported to the car park. In contrast, social changes, such as the increasing numbers of working mothers and the growth in single households, have resulted in increased sales of pre-packaged meals for one that can be prepared quickly in the microwave.

Behavioural segmentation can be based on very different variables some of which are market specific, some more generally applicable, for example, the chocolate market could be segmented into individual consumption, sharing and gift purchases – this would not be a good way to segment the market for medicines. Typical behavioural segmentation variables include:

- loyalty status
- frequency of purchase
- rate of consumption
- user status
- attitudes towards the product
- benefits sought
- purchase occasion: what the customer is buying the product for – general use or a special occasion such as a party

Loyalty status is increasingly used as a segmentation variable. As the value of maintaining loyal customers has become more widely recognised, degrees of loyalty have become more relevant to marketers.

Frequency of purchase and *rate of consumption* are also common bases for segmentation. For example, airlines distinguish frequent flyers, such as business travellers, from more occasional holidaymakers who might travel only once or twice a year.

User status refers to regularity of use (e.g. non-user, occasional user or regular user) and usage rate varies from light usage through to heavy usage. User status may appear to have similarities with loyalty status but there is more to loyalty than just regular use (see Chapter 1). Clearly companies target non-users in order to get them to buy their brands; however, sometimes they target occasional users in an effort to make them buy the product more regularly, or heavy users in the hope that they will buy even more – or persuade friends to buy. Marketers pay attention to both the loyalty and user/usage status of their customers. As the importance of longer-term customer relationships has become more widely recognised, the concept of customer lifetime value has gained more attention. Customers who buy frequently and/or in large quantities will contribute more to profits than occasional purchasers, and are therefore worth cultivating. The use of customer databases allows organisations to maintain vast amounts of data on their customers' purchasing habits and segment different customer groups accordingly.

Attitudes towards the product and benefits sought: how consumers feel about a product and the benefits they seek from its ownership and use are also useful ways of distinguishing between them. The key benefit for some might simply be a low price, for others, ease of use. In the toothpaste market, there are numerous products aimed at different benefit groups. Sensodyne is for sensitive teeth. Pearl Drops is for tooth whitening. Eucryl is for smokers. Most toothpaste brands have developed sub-brands to appeal to users seeking different benefits: tartar and plaque control, fresh breath, reduced cavities, whiter teeth, etc. Each relevant benefit describes a substantial market segment and provides a great market opportunity.

customer lifetime value

a calculation of the long-term worth of a customer using estimates of expected purchases

diffusion of innovations (product adoption) model

categorises product buyers/users according to their take-up rate of new products

research focus: classic concept

Haley, R.I. (1968) 'Benefit segmentation: a decision-oriented research tool', *Journal of Marketing,* **32 (Jul): 30–5.**
Haley introduced the concept of segmenting on the basis of the benefits offered by the brand.

Purchase occasion is an important factor that often influences buyers' attitudes towards products and their perceptions of value. Wedding cakes, dress and hairdressing services for example are often priced at a premium but customers may well expect (and demand) higher quality and service levels for once-in-a-lifetime purchases.

Markets may also be segmented by using Rogers' (2003) diffusion of innovations model (see Chapter 3). Researchers have found that people are fairly consistently adventurous, or not so adventurous, in their purchase and consumption behaviours. These findings have been linked to particular personality and behavioural tendencies. As new products to the market are launched, they appeal to innovators who are quick to respond to novel ideas. Over

ACTIVITY

Visit a supermarket and choose a category of heavily branded products such as soap, detergents or toiletries. Take a close look at the different brands and their packaging, and identify what benefits each is trying to emphasise. Think about the different ways the competing products are trying to be positioned in terms of the similarities and differences in the benefits they claim to offer. Can you identify the sort of different demographic, behavioural or psychological characteristics they appeal to?

time these products are adopted by each of the adopter categories in turn until those new products become dated and really only appeal to the laggards, who are the slowest to accept new ideas and change. Therefore, it is possible to modify marketing activities to best appeal to each of the groups in turn as the product is first launched, becomes accepted in the marketplace and, eventually, declines in popularity.

research focus

Bruning, E.R., Hu, M.Y. and Hao, W. (2009) 'Cross-national segmentation: an application to the NAFTA airline passenger market', *European Journal of Marketing,* **43 (11/12): 1498–522.**
The authors propose an approach to international segmentation that identifies meaningful cross-national consumer segments focused on airline passengers.

SEGMENTATION IN BUSINESS MARKETS

Segmentation principles apply in just the same way to business markets, i.e. when businesses are selling to other organisations rather than to consumers. Although marketing is most commonly associated with consumer markets (b2c) and even more particularly with fast-moving consumer goods (FMCG) markets, a great deal of marketing is b2b. B2b markets underpin consumer markets as manufacturers rarely sell direct to consumers; instead they sell to wholesalers or retailers or other supply chain intermediaries (see Chapter 9). Take Coca-Cola or Unilever, for example: they rarely, if ever, have dealings with consumers; their goods are instead sold in shops. They do, however, invest a lot of money in advertising to consumers of course, and so are still interested in consumer market segmentation and targeting.

B2b market segmentation often uses similar approaches to those for consumer markets, but there are some additional ones – for example, the type of business or industry they are in, and size of business (see Exhibit 4.7).

Market segmentation in b2b

Business-to-business (b2b) markets	Examples of variables
Macrosegmentation variables	
• Geographic location	country, region, city, urban–rural, industrial estate
• Type of organisation	manufacturer, service, government, local authority, private, local, international
• Industry grouping/ business sector	standard industrial classification (SIC), e.g. textiles, computing, telecommunications, etc.
• Customer size	large, medium, small, key customer

Microsegmentation variables	
• User status	non-user, ex, potential, first time, regular user
• Trade category	agent, wholesaler, retailer, producer
• Benefits sought	economy, quality, service
• Loyalty status	total, strong, medium, light, none
• Readiness stage	unaware, aware, informed, interested, desirous, intending to buy/bought/used
• Adopter type	innovator, early adopter, early majority, late majority, laggard
• Purchasing practices	centralised, decentralised, tendering
• Buy class	straight rebuy, modified rebuy, new task (see Chapter 3)

EXHIBIT 4.7 Segmentation approaches in business markets

In b2b markets, the segmentation variables can be grouped into macro-segmentation variables and micro-segmentation variables (as shown in Exhibit 4.7). As with segmentation in consumer markets, a well-maintained and comprehensive database will make the job much easier and more cost-effective.

Segmentation variables are rarely used singly and there are a number of ways to combine them. Shapiro and Bonoma (1984) proposed a detailed, nested approach in which they identified five general segmentation bases arranged in a nested hierarchy. The process of segmentation should work from the more general outer area (macro-segmentation) towards the more specific inner area (micro-segmentation), probing deeper as it goes (see Exhibit 4.8).

1   *Demographic variables* are used to give a broad description of the business segments based on such variables as location (which Shapiro and Bonoma included as a demographic, rather than geographic, variable), size of business, type of business and business sector (e.g. SIC code; for details see below).

2   *Operating variables* enable a more precise identification of existing and potential customers within demographic categories. User status and technologies applied might be considered here.

3   *Purchasing approach* looks at customers' purchasing practices (e.g. centralised or decentralised purchasing). It also includes purchasing policies and buying criteria, and the nature of the buyer/seller relationship.

4   *Situational factors* consider the tactical role of the purchasing situation, requiring a more detailed knowledge of the individual buyer, others involved and the specific buying situation. This might include potential order size, urgency of order and any particular requirements.

5   *Personal characteristics* relate to the people who make the purchasing decisions. Different customers may display different attitudes to risk and different levels of loyalty to suppliers.

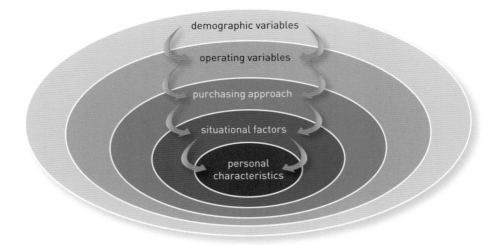

EXHIBIT 4.8 The nested approach to b2b segmentation

research focus: classic concept

Shapiro, B.P. and Bonoma, T.V. (1984) 'How to segment industrial markets', *Harvard Business Review*, May–Jun: 104–10.

　　The difficulty of segmenting industrial markets has dissuaded companies from trying despite the benefits derived from so doing. This article explores the ways of segmenting industrial markets and proposes a nested hierarchy approach.

SIC (Standard Industrial Classification)

system of classifying products by allocating numbers (codes) to every product category, industry or business sector

There is a great deal of information on b2b markets and their segmentation, for example, the SIC (Standard Industrial Classification), which governments use to categorise companies. The SIC system allocates unique numbers to every industry or business sector. The first digit, or couple of digits, indicate the broad industry area. The succeeding digits provide greater detail and are more specific about individual products or product groupings. Exhibit 4.9 shows example details of UK SICs. Other countries and Trade Areas use similar systems, for example there is the North American Industry Classification System (NAICS), Russia has OKVED (which does not translate), the EU has NACE (Nomenclature statistique des Activités Économiques dans la Communauté Européenne) and the UN has ISIC (International Standard Industry Codes). All of these systems adopt similar principles.

TARGET MARKETING

Target marketing involves making decisions about which part of the market an organisation wishes to focus on. It follows on from market segmentation, during which process the total potential market is subdivided according to its characteristics. Targeting is then the choice of which single segment or group of segments the organisation wishes to select. A target market, therefore, would actually be better described as a target submarket or target segment.

UK SIC code	Description
0	Agriculture, forestry, fishing
1	Energy and water-supply industries
2	Extraction of minerals and ores (excluding fuels), manufacture of metals, mineral products and chemicals
3	Manufacture of metal goods, engineering, vehicles
4	Other manufacturing industries
5	Construction
6	Distribution, hotels/catering, repairs
7	Transport and communication
8	Banking, finance, insurance, business services, leasing
9	Other services

EXHIBIT 4.9 Standard Industrial Classifications (SICs)

EVALUATING A SEGMENT FOR TARGETING

Before selecting a market to target, the organisation must undertake a full environmental analysis (see Chapter 2) using a suitable framework such as PRESTCOM and a situation analysis (usually a SWOT). The analysis will take account of its own resources and capabilities, its objectives, its strengths and weaknesses – and also those of its competitors. Armed with all this information, the organisation is well placed to make a sound targeting decision.

PRESTCOM

an acronym for the marketing environment: political, regulatory, economic, social, technological, competitive, organisational, market

research focus

Quinn, L., Dibb, S., Simkin, L., Canhoto, A. and Analogbei, M. (2016) 'Troubled waters: the transformation of marketing in a digital world', *European Journal of Marketing*, **50 (12): 2103–33.**

This paper investigates how strategic target market selection decisions are shaped, challenged and driven in response to the rapidly evolving technological landscape. The findings reveal that the evolving digital landscape has precipitated a sense of crisis for marketers, and the role of marketing within the firm. This extends beyond simply remedying a skills gap and is triggering a transformation that has repercussions for the future of marketing and its practice.

A segment may make an attractive target if it exhibits some, or preferably all, of the following characteristics:

Segmentation: a tutorial

- has sufficient current and potential sales and profits
- has the potential for sufficient future growth
- is not over-competitive
- does not have excessive barriers or costs to entry or exit
- has some relatively unsatisfied needs that the company can serve particularly well.

ethical focus: leave our kids alone!

Should companies be allowed to target children with advertising for their products? Should marketing activity be allowed in schools? The answers to these questions depend on who you ask. Many big companies, e.g. soft drinks manufacturers, argue that children are their main consumers and so yes, of course, there should be adverts aimed at them and heavily branded vending machines in schools. The National Union of Teachers estimated that advertisers spend over £300 million per year advertising to children in UK classrooms. Companies want to catch consumers young and build the relationships that may keep them loyal to the brand throughout their lives.

Specialist agencies, such as TenNine, exist to reach this highly desirable market. TenNine is a media agency specialising in 'ethically responsible messaging' targeted at young people. Their clients include: Nike, Adidas, Orange, Tesco and Unilever. So they also say yes, targeting children is OK, but many parents would say no.

The parents' argument is that advertising uses sophisticated techniques to play on our emotions, our insecurities, our need to be respected, our need to be loved – techniques that are just too powerful, and potentially harmful, to be let loose on kids. TenNine's counter-argument is that they display relevant and responsible messages and help large companies to support the school curriculum by providing equipment and product samples.

This curriculum support might include distributing Revlon perfume samples to pupils as support for PSHE (personal, social, health and economic) and, even more puzzlingly, PE (physical education) classes. Many school sports teams proudly display a sponsor's logo on their kit while drinks vending machines are splashed with logos and can even talk about the products they sell. Cadbury's withdrew their offer of free sports equipment when the Food Commission revealed that pupils would have to eat 5,440 chocolate bars, containing 33 kg of fat and nearly 1.25 million calories, to qualify for a free set of volleyball posts.

In the UK, advertisements for food high in fat, sugar or salt cannot be broadcast during children's television programmes. But they can be fired at children from UK websites – and these foods may well be on the lunch menu at school.

What do you think? Should marketing be allowed into schools?

Sources: Clark (2004); Monbiot (2013)

This is really about helping a company to focus its marketing efforts towards those customers (targets) that it believes will give it greatest success. Customers from outside the target market are not necessarily ignored but they will not be the focus of attention. As a result, companies may miss some potential customers but, using their limited resources (resources, e.g. staff, money, facilities, are always limited), they will have directed their efforts in ways that seem likely to be most effective. Wise marketers recognise that trying to appeal to *everyone* may well have the effect of not appealing successfully to *anyone*.

research focus

Romaniuk, J. (2012) 'Five steps to smarter targeting', *Journal of Advertising Research*, **52 (3): 288–90.**
The author offers five ways to make your targeting smarter, such as making your target market definitions evidence-based and including as many people as possible in your target market group.

TARGETING STRATEGIES

Once the chosen market has been analysed and the attractiveness of the various segments in that market determined, the organisation has to decide which segments to target. Exhibit 4.10 illustrates different targeting strategies.

targeting strategies

used to select a single target market or a group of target markets

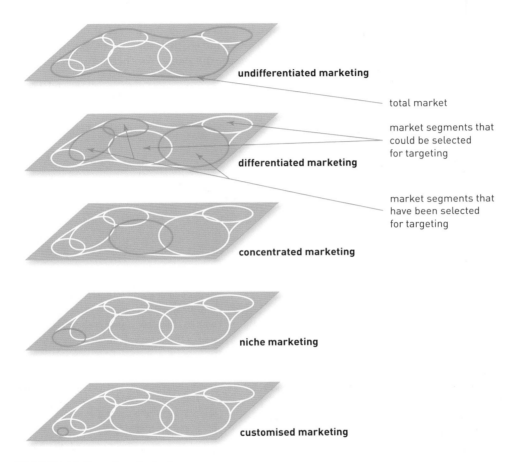

undifferentiated marketing

total market

market segments that could be selected for targeting

differentiated marketing

market segments that have been selected for targeting

concentrated marketing

niche marketing

customised marketing

EXHIBIT 4.10 Targeting strategies

UNDIFFERENTIATED MARKETING

If the market is believed to be composed of customers/consumers whose needs and wants from the product being offered are fundamentally the same, i.e. there is no basic difference between them, an undifferentiated marketing strategy may be employed. This is really mass marketing: one marketing programme for all customers. Although this may result in lower costs, it is very difficult to satisfy all customers/consumers with the same product or marketing mix. An organisation using undifferentiated marketing may also be providing an excellent opportunity for its competitors to capture sales by appealing to the desires

undifferentiated marketing

where the market is believed to be composed of customers/consumers whose needs and wants from the product are fundamentally the same

of specific market segments. For example, if a company only sold blue jeans, it would be giving away all the potential customers for other coloured jeans, or if it only advertised on television, it would be missing a large part of the youth market who do not often watch TV. Few, if any, products are marketed like this. Usually, some form of differentiation takes place, even if only on a small scale. Products such as the original Coca-Cola and Pepsi are reasonable examples of undifferentiated marketing, although it should be recognised that some modifications are made to the marketing mix, and even the product's recipe, in different countries. Both companies have also recognised the potential of segmenting their markets by benefits sought within the market and so, by selling Diet Coke in the USA and the UK (Coca-Cola Light in most other countries), Coke Zero, Diet Pepsi, Pepsi Max, caffeine-free, etc., they become differentiated marketers instead.

b2b focus: the gnome experiment

Some segments are harder to target than others. This is particularly true in b2b marketing where segments are likely to be small, spread out and not well served by any one media channel. Many good products fail because they just aren't well known enough.

THE GNOME EXPERIMENT FOR KERN

Kern and Sohn make scales, balances and weights for schools and laboratories. Their products are technically excellent, delivering highly accurate measurements. However, their market was commoditised. To customers, a scale was a scale – they expected all scales to be accurate and

didn't see any advantage to any particular brand. Kern and Sohn's challenge was to raise awareness of their brand and of the technical superiority of their products – within a clearly defined, narrow market segment: schools and laboratories.

The solution proposed by the Ogilvy agency was the 'world's first mass-participation global gravity experiment'. How better to appeal to the world's scientists? The agency enlisted the scientific community's help to test the following

The well-travelled gnome looks a bit chilly at the South Pole.

hypothesis: 'If Earth was a perfect sphere of uniform density, then gravity would be consistent. But it's not, which means gravity varies wherever you go. So can we chart those discrepancies using just a basic-range Kern scale?'

Ogilvy produced a chip-proof garden gnome and, through a combination of social media, blogs, company websites and traditional media, invited scientists and existing customers across the world to weigh the gnome and send it on. The gnome travelled in his own suitcase, carefully protected and accompanied by a basic Kern scale calibrated to the gravity of his hometown in Germany. His temporary hosts recorded his local weight online before re-packing him.

hypothesis
a proposition put forward for testing

Social media segmentation

The gnome travelled to 152 countries generating 1,445 new sales leads, 65% of which were from the two key target markets: schools (45%) and laboratory-based scientists (25%). He returned home in May 2013 and is now retired – but you can watch the film of his travels on YouTube: www.youtube.com/watch?v=XVxEVMvwCvM.
Sources: Kern (2013); Ogilvy Public Relations (2013)

There can be advantages to following an undifferentiated strategy. Lindgren and Shimp (1996) pointed out that an undifferentiated marketing strategy can enable an organisation to build and maintain a specific image with customers/consumers, minimise its production costs, achieve greater efficiencies and be able to offer its products at competitive prices (or otherwise achieve higher profit margins). They cite three instances, in general, when a mass, or undifferentiated, marketing strategy is most appropriate:

1   When the market is so small that it is unprofitable to market to just a portion of it.

2   When heavy users are the only relevant target because they make up a large proportion of the market.

3   When the brand dominates the market and appeals to all segments of that market, thus making segmentation unnecessary.

DIFFERENTIATED MARKETING

Differentiated marketing recognises differences between market segments and selects two or more target markets to receive different marketing programmes. The Ford Motor Company is a good example of an organisation that uses a differentiated target marketing strategy effectively. By developing a range of models, from the Ka to the Galaxy, it is able to meet the needs of a wide range of people. These models also differ in price, are promoted differently and may even be sold in different areas. Most large organisations have adopted the principles of differentiated marketing, although the specific approaches they have adopted vary (see Chapter 11, on branding strategies). Even the Coca-Cola Company, as an organisation, has adopted a differentiated approach to its total business. It has a number of other drinks brands as well as Coke, e.g. Sprite, PowerAde, Minute Maid, Fanta and Lift.

CONCENTRATED MARKETING

Concentrated marketing targets a single market segment. If that market segment is relatively small, well defined and very focused, it is called a niche market. In the car market, this might be the buyers of luxury sports cars (e.g. Aston Martin or Maserati) or green consumers who would want electric cars. Customised marketing goes a stage further and makes a product offering for just one individual. In consumer markets, this may be for one-off products that are hand-built to a customer's specification. Tailors will custom-make suits or bridal gowns. Architects will design and build a new house to a client's exact specifications. This degree of targeting is more frequently found in b2b markets, especially for large-value orders such as a factory, an engineering project or the organising of a special event on behalf of a company.

Targeting strategies can therefore be seen as a continuum of strategies ranging from the very broad to the very narrow (see Exhibit 4.11).

differentiated marketing
differences between market segments are recognised and two or more target markets are selected, each receiving a different marketing programme

concentrated marketing
where only one market segment is chosen for targeting

niche market
a market segment that can be treated as a target market; a small, well-defined market, often part of a larger market

customised marketing
producing one-off products/ services to match a specific customer's requirements, e.g. a made-to-measure suit or the organisation of a product launch party

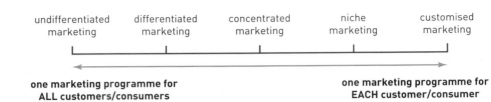

undifferentiated marketing — differentiated marketing — concentrated marketing — niche marketing — customised marketing

one marketing programme for ALL customers/consumers ⟷ **one marketing programme for EACH customer/consumer**

EXHIBIT 4.11 Continuum of targeting strategies

Designed for one particular customer.

Source: StanRohrer/E+/Getty Images

POSITIONING

The process of positioning follows naturally from the targeting decision and forms a direct link between the target marketing strategy and marketing programmes. When the organisation has selected its target markets, but before it develops marketing plans and programmes, it needs to ensure that it fully understands customer/consumer perceptions of the competing brands. A detailed analysis of the target market(s) can show not only how the other offerings are perceived, but also where the organisation's own brand might fit. Customer perceptions are typically a consequence of their previous knowledge and experience of the brands themselves *and* of the companies that own them. Apple, for example, creates close links between itself as a company and its brands (e.g. iPhone, iPod, iPad). See Chapter 11 for more about branding.

Positioning causes some confusion. There are two aspects to it. The process of positioning a product in the market involves the firm making decisions about the marketing mix – the design of the product, where it will be sold, what the packaging looks like and how it will be promoted.

Consumers form a view of the product based on these marketing mix (and other) cues. The product is therefore positioned in their minds – they may see it as reliable but boring, or expensive but high-status. This can be plotted on a perceptual map (see below).

product portfolio

all a company's or strategic business unit's products

Positioning is about how people see a brand, what they think of it in comparison to its competition. It is about the place a brand is perceived to occupy in the minds of the target market relative to other competing brands. It has been referred to as a battle for the hearts and minds of customers/consumers. Companies usually have a number of brands, i.e. a **product (or brand) portfolio** (see Chapters 6 and 11) and may well have more than one version of a product within their portfolio, e.g. Thomas Cook offer lots of different holidays for customers to choose between. When deciding whether or not to offer a new holiday for sale, they will want to make sure it adds something new to the portfolio. If it is just going to take sales away from an existing product, what would be the point? If the new holiday product is for a different, or underserved, part of the market, then it is far more likely to add to profits. Alternatively, it could be aimed at an existing market segment, but positioned differently so that it attracts new customers.

For example, if a holiday company already had enough hotel rooms in Mallorca to satisfy all their customers, there would be no point in contracting for more unless they would attract *extra* customers. Say they have sufficient hotels suitable for families, they do not need any more, but perhaps a hotel that did not cater for children would attract people without children. These people would be a new target market segment.

Alternatively, it might be worth taking on another family hotel if families would perceive it as significantly different from the existing holiday offerings, perhaps as a watersports centre rather than a beach hotel, or as more suited to children under five while the other hotels were better for older children, or as a place for parents who want some peace but with the reassurance that their children are safe and happy and being well looked after by someone else. Then the hotel would be positioned differently. Families would see it differently and others might book.

ACTIVITY

Visit the websites of major car companies and look at their product portfolios. Who do you think these different cars are aimed at (their target market)? How do they compare to each other, and to other manufacturers' competing cars, in terms of image?

Exhibit 4.12 shows how the VW/Audi Group (VAG), which makes the Skoda, Seat, Volkswagen and Audi brands, have differentiated these brand families through careful positioning so that they do not compete directly with each other. VAG refer to these as product platform developments. In Exhibit 4.12, the brands are compared with each other on the basis of price and cost-leadership/differentiation but the process of creating brand differentiation and distinctiveness (and, thereby, positioning the brand in the marketplace) involves many more marketing dimensions and heavy reliance on marketing communications to create specific brand images. Before VAG acquired ownership of Skoda, it had a very poor image. VAG changed that image through improved design and quality and an excellent advertising campaign. The result has been that Skoda is now accepted as a credible brand that competes well with many other mid-range vehicles. It has certainly captured market share from competitors and has won industry awards in the process.

brand image
people's perception of the brand

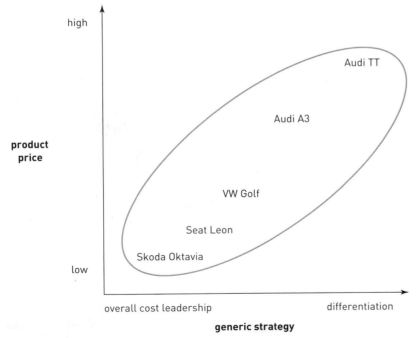

EXHIBIT 4.12 **VAG brand differentiation**

ACTIVITY

PERCEPTUAL MAPS

There are a number of different techniques marketers can use to help ascertain their own customer/consumer perceptions relative to competing bands. These perceptions are often represented on a perceptual map, sometimes called a brand map, position map or space map. Two important perceptual mapping techniques will be outlined here. They are Multi-attribute Attitude Mapping (MAM) and Multidimensional Scaling (MDS). Both forms of analysis can be presented pictorially, which makes the comparison between brand perceptions very straightforward.

digital focus: Facebook friend or LinkedIn contact?

There are thousands of social networking sites on the Internet, many of them designed to appeal to specific market segments. Facebook, YouTube and Twitter are among the best known sites. They have a broad appeal; anyone can join from anywhere in the world – young and old, affluent and poor, men and women, introverts and extroverts, conversationalists and spectators.

Some other sites are more specifically orientated towards certain groups or types of people. They are following a **niche** targeting strategy. LinkedIn is a network for professionals and businesspeople. It is positioned as the site for business-networking, career progression and job seeking. Originally restricted to over 18s, the site reduced its age limit to 13 in 2013 in a bid to attract more student users.

Mumsnet's target membership is clear from its **strap line**: 'by parents for parents' (though it's possibly not the best name to appeal to fathers). Gapyear helps gap year students and backpackers to stay in touch, ask for help and advice, and meet other travellers. Buzfeed aims to provide the hottest social content for users of all kinds of social networks but its editors create and curate content with one particular user-group type, the 'bored at work network' firmly in mind. Tinder revolutionised online dating for singles (and non-singles) with its MobileFirst application that enables users to swipe right to accept or left to reject potential suitors. Bebo used to be a serious rival to Facebook. Its latest incarnation is an online messenger app where users express their creative flair through cartoon chat avatars animated by thousands of hashtags and use an online whiteboard to send drawings to each other. Bebo's target audience is implicit in the slogan, 'probably not for boring people!'.

How many social networking sites are you on? If you use more than one – why do you? Who are your sites and services targeting and how are they positioned?

strap line
a subheading in a press article or advertisement

brand map
diagram of competing brand positions resulting from the perceptual mapping process; also called perceptual maps, position maps and space maps

Multi-attribute Attitude Mapping (MAM)

The first stage of a MAM exercise is to determine the key features or attributes of products in a group – for cars these might include fuel consumption, style, comfort, etc. People are asked to assess competing brands against these attributes by indicating how important each attribute is (from high to low) and how each brand is rated for each attribute (from high to low). The attributes may be given a score out of 10. It is important to ensure that only members of the target market(s) are asked for their perceptions. The views of the general population are not relevant to this analysis. The findings might then be presented as shown in Exhibit 4.13. The horizontal lines indicate how important each of the six identified attributes are perceived to be, and the relative position of brands A, B, C, D and E is shown against each of these attributes. Also shown is what is deemed to be the ideal position according to the respondents. This is identified as brand 'I'.

Using this map, the company can compare its brands to its competitor brands and also to the ideal position, i.e. the target market's perfect version of the product. Brand C, for example, is near the ideal position regarding price, while brand A is close to the ideal position regarding low running costs. None of the brands appears to be close to the ideal regarding style and comfort, although brand C greatly exceeds the expected ideal for performance.

The MAM approach has a number of advantages. For instance, if a number of people are involved in a purchase, they may hold different views about the importance of specific attributes because of their own interests or perspectives. Different views can be individually identified, rather than being aggregated into the total data, and a Multi-attribute Attitude Map produced for each. Rothschild (1987: 89) quotes an industrial market example to illustrate this:

> The most important attributes for the engineer are related to the technical specifications of the product, while the purchasing agent is most concerned with price issues. In such a case the firm can develop a technical ad for engineers and deliver it in *Engineering Digest*, while developing a price/value ad for purchasing agents that can be delivered in *Purchasing Agents Weekly*.

MAM is a useful tool in analysing and determining positioning. It is easy to implement; it identifies which attributes are important to customers/consumers; it identifies how competitors are perceived in relation to each other and to an ideal; and it provides further insight into positioning strategies for different customers/consumers within the target market. This understanding of the different perceptions of product attributes can help in identifying benefit segments (i.e. target markets identified using the segmentation

position map

graphical representation of brand positions resulting from the perceptual mapping process; also called a brand map, perceptual map or space map

perceptual map

results from the perceptual mapping process and shows brands' relative positions (also called a brand map, position map or space map)

perceptual mapping

the process of visually representing target-market perceptions of competing brands in relation to each other

Multi-attribute Attitude Mapping (MAM)

a form of perceptual mapping comparing a product's key features (according to their importance to target customers) with features offered by competitive brands

Multidimensional Scaling (MDS)

a form of perceptual mapping that establishes similarities and differences between competing brands

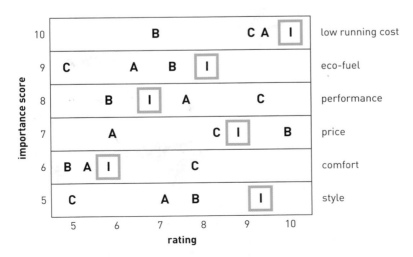

EXHIBIT 4.13 Possible Multi-attribute Attitude Map for a compact car

variable benefits sought – see the earlier section on segmentation), which may then be specifically catered for by launching new products, changing marketing programmes and repositioning just for them.

Multidimensional Scaling (MDS)

Multidimensional Scaling is a popular approach to visualising brand positions. For example, eight competing brands of soap are compared by asking members of the target market to consider the brands in groups of three. This is known as a triadic comparison and is a technique that is used because it is easier for respondents to compare such groups rather than try to consider all the brands together in one go. The respondents simply have to say which two of the three are most similar or, in other words, which they feel

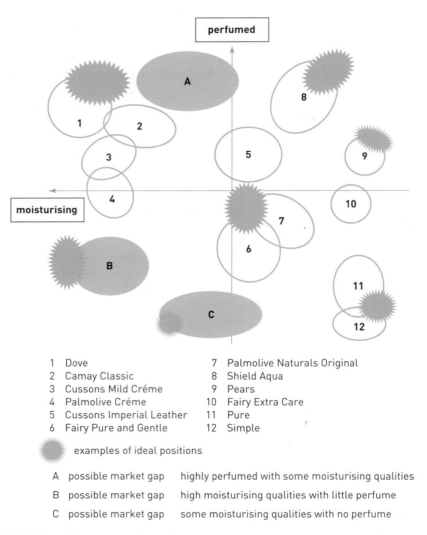

1	Dove	7	Palmolive Naturals Original
2	Camay Classic	8	Shield Aqua
3	Cussons Mild Créme	9	Pears
4	Palmolive Créme	10	Fairy Extra Care
5	Cussons Imperial Leather	11	Pure
6	Fairy Pure and Gentle	12	Simple

examples of ideal positions

A possible market gap   highly perfumed with some moisturising qualities

B possible market gap   high moisturising qualities with little perfume

C possible market gap   some moisturising qualities with no perfume

EXHIBIT 4.14 A possible perceptual map for soaps

is the odd one out. The respondents do not have to work out why they feel this, it is enough that they can choose. All combinations of three brands are assessed in this way and a picture is developed of how similar or dissimilar the brands are to each other. These relative positions are analysed by a computer multidimensional scaling program, which takes into account all the responses and plots the brands' aggregate positions on a chart. The resulting map (see Exhibit 4.14) shows how close the brands are to, or how far away from, each other (hence the reason why these maps are sometimes referred to as space maps).

The map at this early stage would not have any axes. The researcher uses their own judgement on the major underlying reasons for the respondents' perceptions, and then adds the axes. In Exhibit 4.14, the differentiating attributes appear to be the perfuming and moisturising qualities of the soaps.

Respondents are asked about their ideal product and their responses are plotted on the map. As might be anticipated, there is rarely a single ideal product. The result will be a range of ideal positions according to the different preferences expressed. These preferences will tend to cluster, however, into a similar area, as shown by the circles in Exhibit 4.14. The larger the size of circle, the more people have expressed that ideal preference. The positioning of competing brands helps to assess how close the competition is and also shows possible market opportunities by identifying ideal positions and market gaps. Such market opportunities can be exploited by launching a new brand or by **repositioning** an existing brand. Repositioning may also be an appropriate strategy where two brands appear to be too close together. (Repositioning is considered a little later in this chapter.)

repositioning
involves moving existing perceptions to new perceptions relative to competing brands

POSITIONING STRATEGIES

There are a number of different ways in which a brand can be positioned against its competition.

- *Positioning on attributes/product features*: e.g. Head & Shoulders shampoo eliminates dandruff while Ecover products help save the planet.

- *Positioning by price/quality*: e.g. ASDA promotes 'ASDA price' while Tesco promotes 'Every little helps'.

- *Positioning for specific usage occasions*: e.g. there are retailers who specialise in wedding clothes – for guests as well as the bride and groom – and cosmetics companies make travel-sized versions of products.

- *Positioning on benefits or needs*: e.g. Comfort fabric conditioner claims to reduce the need for ironing, Coca-Cola Lite has fewer calories and so helps slimming.

- *Positioning by the product user*: e.g. Shoe brand Kurt Geiger has a more affordable range, Miss KG, aimed at younger women. STA Travel's services are designed for students.

- *Positioning against another brand or with respect to a competitor or competitors*: e.g.

ACTIVITY

Choose a number of different hotel chains (such as Oberoi, Travelodge, Best Western, Hilton, Sheraton, Holiday Inn, Radisson, Hotel Du Vin) and consider how they each try to position themselves within the market. What evidence of this positioning can you identify?

Discount supermarkets Lidl and Aldi directly encourage comparison of their products and those of higher-priced competitors (like brands only cheaper).

- *Positioning in another product class, rather than showing a direct comparison against another brand*: e.g. the 'I Can't Believe It's Not Butter' brand is a spread that clearly compares itself to butter even though it is not.

REPOSITIONING

Repositioning is the marketing process of moving a brand from its current position to a new one, relative to competing brands. It may be actual or perceptual. Actual repositioning involves changing the product to better meet customer needs, e.g. reducing the number of additives in a food product or improving the efficiency of a car engine. Often repositioning is just a correction, or a change, in the way a product is perceived. The product itself is not changed, but a marketing campaign changes what people think of it. So it might be seen as trendier, or healthier, or superior to competitors.

Repositioning may be a good response to competitor activity or other changes in the marketplace. It may involve relatively minor shifts in perception or moving into totally new market segments. A product can be repositioned by changing any element of the marketing mix, for example by changing the product itself to better meet customer needs, e.g. reducing the number of additives in a food product or improving the efficiency of a car engine.

McDonald's has been trying to reposition itself as a healthier fast food brand.

© Dave Pickton

Under VW's ownership Skoda has achieved great success. It is barely conceivable that less than ten years ago Skoda was the butt of jokes, e.g. 'How do you double the value of a Skoda? Fill up the tank'. There were so many jokes that there is even a website devoted to them (skoda-jokes.blogspot.co.uk/)

Johnson & Johnson's Baby brand used to be specifically positioned for baby/infant use. To widen the market, the company successfully repositioned it as an adult, gentle, pure toiletries brand. It achieved this without sacrificing its original position and now maintains two quite distinct positions within the market. This is difficult to do and rarely works.

Ecover, who make environmentally-friendly cleaning products, were losing sales but successfully repositioned from 'a brand for hippies' to a mainstream brand. This also increased their share of the green market by 7%, suggesting that the repositioning had not alienated their core customers (Davidson, 2012).

THE FIVE-STAGE PROCESS FROM MARKET SEGMENTATION TO POSITIONING

There is an identifiable, step-by-step process by which companies can move from an initial understanding of their total market through to a determination of their own brand positions. Exhibit 4.15 shows the full five-stage process.

There is a logical progression from one stage to another. The total potential market is analysed and market segments are identified. Through an understanding of the market segments, the market attractiveness of each can be determined and one or more segments can be targeted. Further analysis can reveal the perceptions of the potential customers and consumers in the target(s), and so the relative positions of competing products (brands) can be assessed. The complete analysis can then be used as a foundation for selecting appropriate marketing strategies and tactics, leading to the implementation of specific marketing activities and actions.

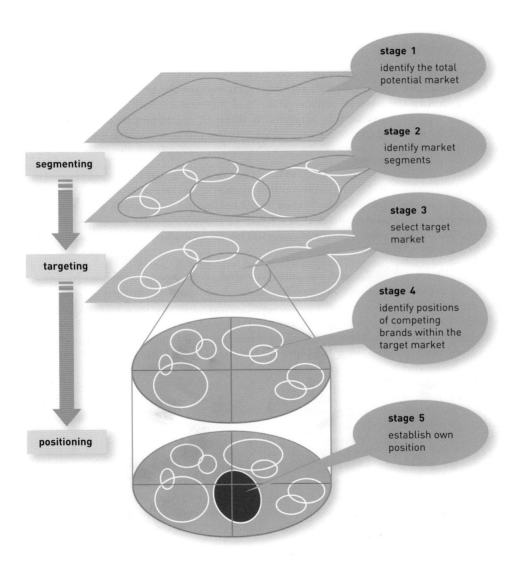

EXHIBIT 4.15 Stages in the market segmentation, targeting and positioning process

SUMMARY

Market selection is one of the most fundamental aspects of marketing. Available market opportunities are matched against a company's objectives, its resources and its assessment of its general business environment to find the ones most likely to bring the organisation success.

Whether they are b2c or b2b, markets consist of customers and consumers, but no single company can fulfil the needs of all customers. While individuals are of course different, people do have some similarities in terms of their habits, lifestyles, preferences, where they are located, or in the case of b2b, what type of business they are in, etc. An understanding of these similarities can be used to divide a total market into subgroups (segments) each of which will consist of customers and consumers (buyers and users) who share similar characteristics and are different from people in the other subgroups. This process is called market segmentation.

There are many ways to segment markets and this chapter has briefly described the use of geographic, demographic, geo-demographic, psychographic and behavioural segmentation in the case of consumer markets and macro- and micro-segmentation approaches in the case of b2b markets. It is up to marketers to decide which of the segments are attractive enough to target. This is the process of targeting or target marketing.

A number of different targeting strategies have been described: undifferentiated (mass) marketing, differentiated marketing, concentrated marketing, niche marketing and customised marketing. A useful way to think of these is as a continuum from undifferentiated, where there is no targeting and the product is considered suitable for all (e.g. copper), to totally customised, in which the product is provided on an individual basis (e.g. a handmade wedding dress).

Once they have identified one or more potential target markets, marketers need to research customer/consumer perceptions of their own and competing brands so that they can develop better suited products and determine the best mix of marketing activities for that market segment (or segments). This is called positioning. Positioning is about understanding customer and consumer perceptions of the brands on offer. These are then plotted on a perceptual (brand) map. An in-depth understanding of the brands competing in the target market(s) is essential in determining the best positioning strategy.

Positioning is not a one-off activity. It may become necessary to reposition the brand later in order to minimise competition. Marketers should carry out regular checks on their brands' actual and perceived positions and those of key competitors.

The chapter ends by bringing all these concepts together into the complete segmentation-to-positioning five-stage process, which starts by identifying the total potential market, goes on to the identification of market segments, the selection of target market(s) and the identification of the positions of competing brands within the target market(s), and finishes by establishing one's own position within the target market(s).

CHALLENGES REVIEWED

Now that you have finished reading the chapter, look back at the challenges you were set at the beginning. Do you have a clearer idea of what's involved?

HINTS

- Segmentation and targeting strategies.
- Differentiated or undifferentiated?
- Perceptual mapping.
- Segmentation bases.

READING AROUND

JOURNAL ARTICLES

Walker Reczek, R., Summers, C. and Smith, R. (2016) 'Targeted ads don't just make you more likely to buy – they can change how you think about yourself', *Harvard Business Review*, 4 April. Available at: https://hbr.org/2016/04/targeted-ads-dont-just-make-you-more-likely-to-buy-they-can-change-how-you-think-about-yourself (accessed 12/04/16).

MAGAZINE ARTICLES AND BEST PRACTICE GUIDES

Davidson, N. (2012) 'Ecover's makeover', *Admap*, December. London: WARC.

Franklin, E.T. (2012) 'Consumer segmentation: subculture targeting', *Admap*, June. London: WARC.

Puddick, M. (2012) 'WARC best practice guide: how to write brand positioning statements'. Available at: www.warc.com/ (accessed 14/04/13).

BOOKS AND BOOK CHAPTERS

Brown, E. (2012) 'Networks', in *Working the Crowd: Social Media Marketing for Business* (2nd edn). Swindon: BCS – The Chartered Institute for IT, pp. 49–59.

Hallighan, B. and Shah, D. (2009) *Inbound Marketing Get Found Using Google, Social Media and Blogs (New Rules Social Media Series)*. London: John Wiley and Sons.

ONLINE RESOURCES

www.youtube.com/watch?v=eNVde5HPhYo – This promotional video was released to build anticipation for the launch of the Fiat 500L compact car aimed at new mothers. 'The Motherhood' is a sharp-witted rap about the trials and tribulations of becoming a mum. Read more at: www.campaignlive.co.uk/article/1190261/mums-rap-attitude-keeps-real

WEBSITES

www.artscouncil.org.uk/what-we-do/research-and-data/arts-audiences/arts-based-segmentation-research/ – the UK Arts Council explains how segmentation works in the arts – with a quiz.

www.caci.co.uk – for information on Acorn.

www.experian.co.uk – for information on Mosaic.

www.sportengland.org/about-us/ – Sport England segments sports players (and non-players).

www.strategicbusinessinsights.com/vals – for information on VALS psychometric segmentation.

TEST YOURSELF

1   What are the three main assessment criteria for market attractiveness? (See p. 134)

2   What is target marketing? (See p. 134)

3   Explain what a market segment is. Why do marketers segment their markets? (See p. 135)

4   What are the main criteria for assessing the usefulness of a market segment? (See pp. 137–138)

5   What are the main bases that can be used for segmenting consumer markets? (See pp. 139–147)

6   What is social grading and how is it measured? Is it the same as social class? (See pp. 143–144)

7   What are the main bases that can be used for segmenting business markets? (See pp. 148–150)

8   What is positioning? (See pp. 156–157)

9   What is the difference between mass marketing and niche marketing? (See pp. 153–154)

10   Under what conditions is mass marketing an appropriate marketing strategy? (See p. 155)

11   What is the five-stage process from market segmentation to positioning? (See pp. 162–163)

REVISION TOOLS

Want to test yourself even more? Review what you have learnt by visiting
https://study.sagepub.com/masterson4e

- Practise for exams with **multiple choice questions**
- Revise key terms with **interactive flashcards**

MINI CASE STUDY: WHO'S LISTENING?

Read the questions, then the case material, and then answer the questions.

QUESTIONS

1   Using the list of consumer segmentation bases given earlier in this chapter, segment the market for broadcast radio. Remember to explain your segmentation choices.

2   Suggest at least two other bases, not specifically mentioned in the chapter, that might be helpful in segmenting this market. Remember that segments should consist of *people* not products. Justify your choices.

3   Look at the descriptions of BBC Radio stations below. Describe their primary target audiences. Drawing on the information in the case and your own experience, can you identify other market segments, outside of that primary audience, who might listen to that station?

4   Look at the list of BBC radio stations given below. Which radio stations do you think the Smith family would listen to and why?

The Smith family live in a comfortable, if a little worn, semi-detached house in a pleasant, leafy London suburb. Mrs Vicky Smith is a music teacher and a skilled pianist. Mr George Smith is a lorry driver and away from home at least two nights a week. They have three children all of whom love music – but of different types. Megan is 17 and loves to dance. Ben is 14 and football mad although he also likes hip hop and rock music – the heavier the better. Ellie is 12 and also sports mad, especially football and tennis. She loves pop music, keeps track of what's in the charts and listens to lots of new releases – especially from girl bands. The family also have a dog who likes all ball games and seems to like music too – though it's possible any noise would do. They leave the radio on for her when they go out.

There's a retro-styled digital radio in the kitchen and Vicky keeps the radio on while she prepares meals and does housework. So does George though they disagree on which station to listen to. She likes jazz for housework and comedy shows or current affairs for cooking. Vicky prefers the radio to the television as she can keep looking at what she's doing rather than have to look at a screen. George likes 'anything with a beat' – especially the hits of the 1990s. Sometimes he dances which drives the kids mad. They retreat to their bedrooms where they can listen to their own music through their phones or iPods or Internet radio. Ben likes to try and drown out his father's oldies by playing rock music really loud or sometimes hip hop if he's feeling particularly competitive. His parents hate hip hop but Megan sometimes joins him – especially if she can persuade her brother to dance. Ellie plugs her earphones in and loses herself in a world of pop. Usually she listens to her favourite bands' albums but she also makes endless playlists, spending hours adjusting them and swapping them with friends – though she rarely plays friends' lists preferring to stick to her own.

When Vicky is lesson planning or marking, she likes to listen to classical music, ideally without advert breaks.

When he's working, out on the road, George's guilty pleasure (which he doesn't admit to) is Radio 2; he enjoys the presenters' banter, relies on the traffic news to avoid delays and often calls in his own updates under the pseudonym 'Big G'. Of course if there's a match on he'll listen to sports radio for the live commentary. He also likes to think of Ben and Ellie watching the match on television at home. Long distance driving can be a lonely business and the radio really helps.

Megan has a Saturday job in a local cafe. They play Radio 2 there as well – she's learnt to block it out. Ben listens to it sometimes too when they have some old rockers from the 1960s or 1970s on – Megan despairs.

BBC RADIO STATIONS

BBC Radio 1

Broadcasts a popular combination of music and entertainment aimed at 15-29 year olds. Also features digestible news, documentaries and advice for young adults.

BBC Radio 1 Xtra

1Xtra is a digital station known for the best black music and a strong focus on new music and live gigs. Also features entertainment, documentaries and news aimed at younger audiences.

BBC Radio 2

Attracts in the region of 13 million listeners with a mix of music and speech based content including documentaries, comedy, live concerts and religious programming. Well known special campaigns include support for BBC Children in Need and the 500 Words short story competition for children.

BBC Radio 3

With a focus on arts and cultural broadcasting, BBC Radio 3 is best known for classical music but also hosts programmes dedicated to jazz and world music alongside a range of quality documentaries and drama.

(Continued)

(Continued)

BBC Radio 4

BBC Radio 4 is a speech based station offering in-depth news and current affairs. In addition, the station broadcasts a wide range of factual and entertainment programmes, plays, readings, comedy shows and the popular serial drama, *The Archers*.

BBC Radio 4 Extra

This digital-only network is fuelled by the BBCs extensive archive of speech based entertainment content including award-winning comedy and drama.

BBC Radio Five Live

Radio 5 Live provides round the clock coverage of news and sporting events together with supporting analysis and discussion, interviews and phone-ins.

BBC Radio Five Live Sports Extra

5 Live Sports Extra provides extended live coverage of selected sporting events.

BBC 6 Music

BBC Radio 6 Music offers an eclectic mix of music based entertainment content that celebrates alternative pop music and culture from the 60s onwards

BBC Asian Network

BBC Asian Network provides a wide range of speech and music content for British Asian communities.

BBC Nations and Local Radio

The BBCs regional radio services for England and the Channel Islands, Scotland, Wales, and Northern Ireland include more than 40 stations.

REFERENCES

BBC (n.d.) 'Inside the BBC: What we do: Radio'. Available at: www.bbc.co.uk/aboutthebbc/insidethebbc/whatwedo/radio (accessed 06/03/17).

Bruning, E.R., Hu, M.Y. and Hao, W. (2009) 'Cross-national segmentation: an application to the NAFTA airline passenger market', *European Journal of Marketing*, 43 (11/12): 1498–522.

Clark, S. (2004) 'Advertising in schools', *The Times Education Supplement*, 25 June. Available at: www.tes.co.uk/article.aspx?storycode=396901 (accessed 08/04/13).

Davidson, N. (2012) 'Ecover's makeover', *Admap*, December, London: WARC.

Dibb, S. and Simkin, L. (1996) *The Market Segmentation Workbook: Target Marketing for Managers*. London: Routledge.

Dibb, S. and Wensley, R. (2002) 'Segmentation analysis for industrial markets: problems of integrating customer requirements into operations strategy', *European Journal of Marketing*, 36 (1/2): 231–51.

Du, R.Y. and Kamakura, W.A. (2006) 'Household life cycles and lifestyles in the United States', *Journal of Marketing Research*, 43 (1): 121–32.

Haley, R.I. (1968) 'Benefit segmentation: a decision-oriented research tool', *Journal of Marketing*, 32 (Jul): 30–5.

Kern (2013) 'The gnome experiment'. Available at: **www.gnomeexperiment.com** (accessed 08/05/13).

Lindgren Jr, J.H. and Shimp, T.A. (1996) *Marketing: An Interactive Learning System*. Fort Worth, TX: The Dryden Press.

Louden, D.L. and Della Bitta, A.J. (1993) *Consumer Behavior* (4th edn). New York: McGraw-Hill.

Monbiot, G. (2013) 'Hey advertisers, leave our defenceless kids alone', *Guardian*, 15 April. Available at: **www.guardian.co.uk/commentisfree/2013/apr/15/advertisers-leave-defenceless-children-alone** (accessed 08/02/17).

NRS (National Readership Survey) (2015) 'Social grade'. Available at: **www.nrs.co.uk/nrs-print/lifestyle-and-classification-data/social-grade/** (accessed 20/02/16).

Office for National Statistics (2015) 'Statistical bulletin: families and households 2015', 5 November. Available at: **www.ons.gov.uk/peoplepopulationandcommunity/births deathsandmarriages/families/bulletins/familiesandhouseholds/2015-11-05#living-alone** (accessed 17/04/16).

Ogilvy Public Relations (2013) 'Case study: Kern the gnome experiment'. Available at: **www. ogilvyprlondon.com** (accessed 08/05/13).

Rogers, E.M. (2003) *Diffusion of Innovations* (5th edn). New York: The Free Press.

Romaniuk, J. (2012) 'Five steps to smarter targeting', *Journal of Advertising Research*, 52 (3): 288–90.

Rothschild, M.L. (1987) *Marketing Communications*. New York: DC Heath.

Shapiro, B.P. and Bonoma, T.V. (1984) 'How to segment industrial markets', *Harvard Business Review*, May–June: 104–10.

Quinn, L., Dibb, S., Simkin, L., Canhoto, A. and Analogbei, M. (2016) 'Troubled waters: the transformation of marketing in a digital world', *European Journal of Marketing*, 50 (12): 2103–33.

Wells, W. and Gubar, G. (1966) 'Life cycle concept in marketing research', *Journal of Marketing Research*, 3 (4): 355–63.

PART ONE   THIS IS MARKETING

PART TWO   MAKING SENSE OF MARKETS

PART THREE   THE MARKETING MIX

PART FOUR   MANAGING MARKETING

MARKETING RESEARCH

5

MARKETING RESEARCH CHALLENGES

The following are illustrations of the types of decision that marketers have to take or issues they face. *You aren't expected to know how to deal with the challenges now*; just bear them in mind as you read the chapter and see what you can find that helps.

Degree to job: Virgin

- You run a travel agency. You have found a fabulous hotel in the Swiss Alps that you have never used before. However, the hotel wants to know how many rooms to reserve for you for next season. What information do you need to work this out, and how will you collect it?

- Your company's skateboard sales have been falling steadily over the last two years. How would you make a case to a sceptical managing director that the expense of research into the causes of the fall would be worthwhile?

- The editor of a lad's mag, a monthly magazine read by men and women (e.g. the men's wives and girlfriends), has invited you to research the attitudes of readers to its contents. How would you do this?

- Your company is hoping to launch a new beer and wants to find out what would be popular across Europe. This is difficult because different European countries traditionally drink different types of beer. However, recently you have seen an Italian drinking British beer, a British man drinking French beer and a Swede drinking German beer. You need to get views from a huge number of beer drinkers to be sure you get the complete picture. It is not practical to interview every beer drinker in Europe. What could you do?

INTRODUCTION

Successful plans must be based on good intelligence. Before changing something, it is important to fully understand exactly what it is, and how it works, currently. To understand a marketing situation, and its future possibilities, you must have good information about it, i.e. you have to conduct marketing research.

The environmental analysis discussed in Chapter 2 (the marketing environment) is only possible if there is sufficient data available. The segmentation processes described in Chapter 4 are totally dependent upon sound market intelligence. How can a company design products, develop advertising campaigns, set prices, choose outlets, encourage customer loyalty or build

ACTIVITY

Reflecting on previous chapters, write a list of all the things you might need to research in the following situations:

- starting up a small, top-quality ice cream business and hoping to sell to local businesses (shops, restaurants, etc.)
- a top brand of perfume is losing market share
- a firm of accountants is considering setting up a new office in a different town.

If you can, compare lists with someone else. Why do you want to know these things?

its brands without information about its customers, its competitors and the worlds they inhabit?

This chapter will outline the research process, list typical areas for marketing research and examine the techniques used by researchers to gather data. Much of this data is personal, some of it is sensitive and so market researchers have to be careful of their research subjects' wishes, rights and potential reactions. Market researchers should be honest, open and, above all, ethical in their dealings with research subjects.

Finally, the chapter briefly considers one of the main purposes of all this research and analysis: forecasting marketing trends.

DEFINITIONS

Marketing research covers the investigation of a broad range of activities (see below). The terms 'marketing research' and 'market research' are today used interchangeably – although some might argue that market research is narrower in scope, focusing on customers and consumers, whereas marketing research covers the whole of the marketing process.

The Market Research Society (MRS) definition embraces all types of data gathering and investigations for market and social research:

> Research is the collection and analysis of data from a sample of individuals or organisations relating to their characteristics, behaviour, attitudes, opinions or possessions such as consumer and industrial surveys, psychological investigations, observational and panel studies. (Market Research Society, n.d.)

This definition uses various research techniques as illustration. These will be explained below. It also refers to a sample. Sampling is an important concept in marketing research. It is rarely possible to investigate everyone in the world, or even everyone in your target market, so researchers assess a subset, or sample, of the people (or products, or whatever the thing to be researched is) instead. It is important to ensure that this sample is big enough and broad enough to be fully representative of the whole – otherwise the resulting research will be flawed. Sampling methods are explained in more detail below.

10 step guide to sampling

Philip Kotler offers a much shorter definition. Marketing research is: 'the systematic design, collection, analysis and reporting of data and findings relevant to a specific marketing situation facing the company' (Kotler et al., 2012).

sample

a smaller number of people, or cases, drawn from a population that should be representative of it in every significant characteristic

Note the phrase 'specific marketing situation' here. Marketing research is not a general activity, it is targeted, it has specific objectives. There is a good reason why it is being done.

THE USE AND VALUE OF MARKETING RESEARCH

Marketing research is a planned activity. It is carried out methodically so that the results are supported by evidence that can be checked by others. Marketing research provides vital information for key marketing decisions, e.g. which products should be developed, how they should be packaged, what price should be charged, how they should be distributed, who they should be aimed at, what benefits and features customers would want and how the products should be promoted. In order to make these decisions, marketing managers need to know (among other things): what competitors currently offer, what their reactions might be to these new products, what would make customers buy these products in preference to those of their competitors and how retailers will respond (e.g. will they be prepared to stock the new products?) Without marketing research it would be very difficult to make such decisions. Marketing research is so important to good marketing that organisations spend billions on it each year.

---

research focus

Muntinga, D.G., Moorman, M. and Smit, E.G. (2011) 'Introducing COBRAs: exploring motivations for brand-related social media use', *International Journal of Advertising,* **30 (1): 13–46.**

These researchers used an instant messaging service (IM) to conduct online interviews in order to explore a range of different motivations for engaging in online brand-related activity.

THE MARKETING RESEARCH PROCESS

Marketing research is a continuous process of information gathering and analysis into which ad hoc marketing research activities may also be fitted as and when management problems arise. Exhibit 5.1 shows the stages involved in the marketing research process.

1   Recognise the marketing management problem.

The starting point for the research process is the recognition of a marketing problem. Perhaps there has been a loss of sales or market share? It could be that there are problems with distribution or that customers are choosing to shop elsewhere.

2   Define the research problem.

Once the marketing management problem has been recognised and understood, it needs to be restated as a research problem. This may require some background information. For example, a local authority may be concerned that few people shop locally, preferring large, out-of-town superstores and malls. Neighbourhoods are becoming run-down as shops close. The research problem, at its broadest, is to find out why customers shop outside their local community. More specifically, the research will investigate:

who tends to shop outside, what local shopping is available, customer attitudes to the local facilities, what might make people change their shopping habits, and what are the costs and benefits involved from the points of view of the shoppers, the local shop owners, the supermarket owners and developers, etc. These are research questions to be answered.

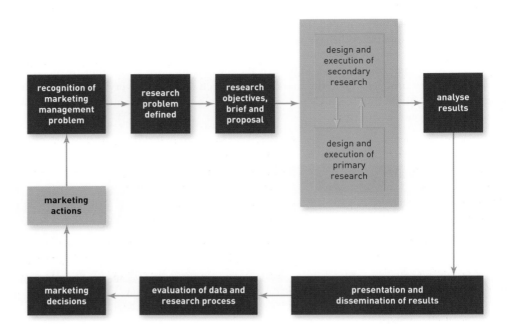

EXHIBIT 5.1 The marketing research process

3　Set research objectives, write research brief.

The next step is to set research objectives. These provide a clearly defined direction for the research activity. From the objectives, basic decisions can be made as to the form the research will take, including the use of both secondary and primary research (see below). Management will need to think through the resources required and set a suitable budget. There is a trade-off to be made here between cost and certainty. The more information managers have, the better the decisions they can make, but costs rise as the research goes on and on, and so a reasonable budget must be set.

Organisations do not always undertake their own research. Frequently, they employ research agencies to carry out some or all of the research tasks. These agencies will need to be thoroughly briefed on what is required. The agency then expands the brief into a complete research proposal, i.e. a document that details exactly what they propose to do. An agreed proposal makes it much less likely that misunderstandings will arise in the future and also encourages the agency to take more responsibility for the research.

4   Carry out research (design and execution).

Secondary research (also known as desk research) should always be considered *before* primary research (also known as field research) is undertaken. If the right information already exists, then it may be possible to answer a number of the research questions and address the research problem through secondary research alone. This would make primary research unnecessary, saving time and money.

There are many sources of secondary information and the Internet has made them easier to find and to use. There are also many primary research methods, the most commonly used being surveys (see below for primary and secondary research).

5   Analyse results.

As the data from the research is gathered, it is collated and analysed. The type of analysis will depend on the nature of the data and the information and answers required. Analysis, especially qualitative analysis, can be very subjective. However, it is important for analysts to be as objective as possible. Quantitative analysis claims greater objectivity thanks to the mathematical techniques it employs, but even this is dependent upon the skills of, and the decisions made by, researchers and analysts.

One way of looking at analysis is to think of it as a sense-making process. Analysis is the means by which raw data (e.g. the number of people who shop out of town on a Tuesday) is converted into valuable information (e.g. which are the most popular shopping days and why) that can be used for marketing decisions.

6   Present and disseminate results.

There is little value in researchers keeping their findings to themselves. After the sense-making process of analysis, the results need to be shared and made available to all staff who could benefit. Some of the results may be considered confidential and so restricted access is needed. However, the more usual problem is to ensure findings are distributed widely, are well understood and acted upon. Researchers are expected to comment on the quality of the findings (in terms of confirming their accuracy, validity and reliability, see p. 000) and make appropriate recommendations related to the findings to management.

7   Evaluate data and research process.

Evaluation should not be limited to the results themselves but should extend to the whole research process. Has the research brief been fulfilled? Has this been done within budget? On time? Have the results shed light on the management problem? Could it have been done better?

8   Make marketing decisions and carry them out.

The purpose of research is to make well-informed decisions and to improve marketing actions, e.g. raise prices or develop a new product. These changes will elicit a response from the market which may then form the basis of a new marketing research cycle.

secondary research
(desk research)

the search for good-quality data that has been validated and is now published for use by others

primary research
(field research)

carried out specifically for the research task in question

176

ETHICS IN MARKETING RESEARCH

Good marketing research always takes account of the ethics of the situation. Over recent years, professional body (e.g. the Market Research Society) codes of conduct have been strengthened by changes in laws and regulations covering data protection and freedom of information. Codes of behaviour for researchers are about honesty, openness and respect for respondents' privacy, and are mostly common sense. There have been some unscrupulous marketing research practitioners in the past and the activity continues to carry the stigma created by unethical salespeople claiming to be carrying out research as a selling tactic. When approaching potential respondents, a researcher should clearly identify who they are, that they are carrying out research, and the broad purpose for which the research is being conducted. Confidentiality should be assured or, if it is not, the respondent's permission must be acquired. Similar ethical considerations should be borne in mind when recording, analysing and reporting research findings. The storage of data will be affected by legal controls such as those covered by the UK Data Protection Act 1998.

---

research focus: classic concept

Brien, R.H. and Stafford, J.E. (1968) 'Marketing information systems: a new dimension for marketing research', *Journal of Marketing*, **32 (Jul): 19–23.**
An article that emphasises the need to view marketing research as an integrated system rather than ad hoc research projects.

A full version of the Market Research Society Code of Conduct can be found on their website (www.mrs.org.uk). Other professional bodies related to marketing research in other countries will also have their own versions of the codes.

AREAS OF MARKETING RESEARCH

Marketing research is used to investigate a number of different marketing areas including:

- the marketing environment
- competitors
- consumer behaviour
- business buying behaviour
- sales
- distribution
- products and brands
- pricing
- advertising and promotions
- media habits.

MARKETING ENVIRONMENT RESEARCH

Organisations need to understand the wider environment in which they are operating. For example, an analysis of social trends may reveal opportunities for new products while an in-depth understanding of government's attitude to businesses may enable a company to foresee a business threat such as tighter (or looser) new regulations. Research in this area can be quite general and is most likely to be secondary. (See Chapter 2 for more on the marketing environment and PRESTCOM analysis.)

COMPETITOR RESEARCH

It is clearly important for an organisation to know as much as it reasonably can about who its competitors are and what they are doing. This includes not only their past and current activities, but also indications of their future plans.

CONSUMER BEHAVIOUR RESEARCH

Customer and consumer research is largely concerned with their decision-making processes, attitudes, preferences, repurchasing patterns and with how consumers use products. Why do some people buy and others don't? Why do some shop around and others remain loyal to one supplier? What role do brands play in consumers' lives? Analysing consumer behaviour has led to a large and valuable body of knowledge that draws heavily on other disciplines such as psychology and sociology (see Chapter 3).

digital focus: mind over matter

The popular fizzy drinks Pepsi® and Coca-Cola® (Coke®) are practically identical in terms of chemical composition. The chances are you know which you prefer ... but could you tell them apart in a blind taste test? In the 1970s and into the early 1980s, PepsiCo ran a classic series of advertisements based around a taste test challenge. PepsiCo had always felt they had the better product as tasters routinely preferred Pepsi to competitor brands. In the ads, Coke fans were shown testing two un-labelled drinks only to be shocked when the sample they claimed tasted best (and identified as Coke) was revealed as Pepsi. Today Coke is still the global market leader. Perhaps consumers failed to be convinced by the ads, or perhaps there is something so powerful about the way we *think* about our preferred brand that it changes the way we respond to its taste? If only we could look inside consumers' heads.

The latest developments in neuromarketing research may offer just such an opportunity. The goal of neuromarketing is to study how the brain is physiologically affected by advertising and marketing strategies. Sophisticated neuroimaging techniques such as functional magnetic resonance imaging (fMRI) and electroencephalography (EEG) are used to monitor changes in activity in different areas of the brain as subjects are exposed to various stimuli.

Neuromarketing research agency Visionone

More than 30 years after PepsiCo unveiled the Pepsi challenge ads, Samuel McClure and a team of researchers from Texas re-ran the classic taste test experiment using fMRI to explore brain activity during exposure to anonymous and labelled samples of both Pepsi and Coke. When consumers weren't aware which brands they were testing, patterns of brain activity suggested both products tasted equally good. However, when consumers knew which brand they were drinking, Coke appeared to stimulate more activity in the areas of the brain thought to be involved in complex judgements and decisions. Taken together these results are a significant step towards proving the power of branding.

Source: McClure et al. (2004)

ACTIVITY

The cola blind taste test is perhaps one of the most famous pieces of commercial research ever, although it was used mainly as advertising for Pepsi. Pepsi claimed that in blind taste tests the majority of people preferred the taste of Pepsi. Yet they still buy more Coca-Cola. Why do you think that is?

Try this at home. Can you tell the difference? Are you surprised by which tastes best?

© Dave Pickton

Over recent years, there has been an explosion of customer data collection activities fuelled through the growth and availability of more advanced technologies. Modern computing power, in terms of storage and processing of data, has meant that companies can easily capture data on all customer transactions: what is bought, by whom, how frequently, by what means and where. Tesco, for example, makes good use of customer transaction data to segment their customer base and provide highly targeted offers based on buying and usage behaviour. Social media listening helps firms identify and track important conversations taking place online. For example, alerting sales teams if a prospect mentions the company name or identifying key influencers who have shared or amplified the impact of content produced by the firm.

Toys R Us uses social data

amplification
sharing via social media networks that enhances the reach of digital content

research focus

Schweidel, D.A. and Moe, W.W. (2014) 'Listening in on social media: a joint model of sentiment and venue format choice', *Journal of Marketing Research,* **51 (4): 387–402**
    The authors demonstrate that the inferences marketing researchers obtain from monitoring social media are dependent on *where* they 'listen' and that common approaches that either focus on a single social media venue or ignore differences across venues in aggregated data can lead to misleading brand sentiment metrics.

multinationals

corporations with subsidiary companies in other countries which have significant power although they answer to the parent company

public sector

government-owned organisations

BUSINESS BUYER BEHAVIOUR RESEARCH

In business markets, goods and services are bought either for use and consumption within the customer organisation or for resale. This is a vast area of research because it involves all organisations that buy and sell from each other, from one-person companies to huge multinationals and government corporations. Business-to-business (b2b) research includes research into government and public sector organisations and their buying behaviour as well as into commercial companies. Institutions such as local authorities and hospitals are large buyers and users of goods and services and may have complex buying procedures and decision-making criteria.

digital focus: social media listening

Argos is the UK's leading multi-channel retailer, offering more than 33,000 products through its website and mobile channels alongside its established network of high street stores and traditional telephone order service. In 2013 Argos rolled out the first of its new digital store formats replacing catalogues with touch screen tablets and introducing a raft of fresh new design features including a seamless online payment system and a pioneering FastTrack same-day home delivery service.

With more than 40 years' experience as a UK high street fixture Argos knew its customers had certain expectations of their in-store experience. Whether they embraced the changes or hated them, Argos anticipated they'd have plenty to say about it on social media. The store wanted to be able to track, analyse and respond to this valuable feedback quickly and efficiently.

A comprehensive social media listening and analysis service provided by Brandwatch provided the solution, offering both an overall view of the general **sentiment** towards the changes but also filtering and segmenting data by store location and uncovering insights into key demographic variables. For example, analysis of social comment from men revealed more interest in the hi-tech features of the new stores, whereas women spoke more positively about the new approach to customer service. While Londoners embraced the changes overall, they were also the most likely to complain about queues.

'Listening': Social media research

Argos can now very quickly identify which store is performing best, and praise for staff in a particular store can be fed back directly to the store manager. This approach also identifies issues that can be actioned almost instantly, plus it reveals the varying tastes and preferences of customers around the country, so that Argos can deliver a locally tailored experience for its consumers.

(With thanks to Brandwatch and Argos)

SALES RESEARCH AND FORECASTING

One of a marketing manager's most important and most complex tasks is sales forecasting. Developing a new product, entering a new market or making changes to any of the elements of the marketing mix is risky. Organisations need to predict how customers will react and also what competitors' retaliatory strategies might be. A costly failure can be disastrous for an organisation. Equally, standing still with no change brings its own risks. Marketing management is about basing decisions for change on sound information obtained through professional marketing research.

It is hard to predict sales precisely but the better the information the forecast is based on, the better the chance that it will be accurate. Most sales forecasts are based on previous sales figures so that is the first piece of information required. Managers will want to know about the total market sales (i.e. the sales of competitive products as well as their own) so they can work out an overall market growth rate and their own market share. They will also need to factor in such things as changes in the marketing environment (see Chapter 2) and new product launches (their own and competitors').

Of course, the past is not always an accurate guide to the future and forecasts of future sales are a vital part of business planning. There are a number of ways businesses can try to see ahead. A customer survey of purchase intentions is an excellent way although it is more practical for b2b than for consumer goods. The salesforce are also a good source of information, although they tend to underestimate in order to get a lower sales target (and possibly to earn more commission by over-achieving it).

sentiment analysis
aims to identify the feelings (i.e. attitudes, emotions and opinions) underlying user-generated content

market growth rate
the percentage increase in total sales within a category or market

survey
direct questioning of market research subjects

consumer goods
goods that are bought/used by individuals rather than by companies

Methods of estimating future sales vary according to how frequently a product is likely to be purchased and should incorporate first time, replacement and repeat sales (Kotler et al., 2012). For example, washing machines and cars are infrequent purchases whereas coffee is a frequent purchase. Taking washing machines as an example, people setting up their first home may be buying for the first time. Later on, they may need to replace that machine. Knowing the likely life of the machine will help the company to estimate when that will happen. For FMCG (fast-moving consumer goods) such as shampoo, repeat sales may be the most important element of the forecast.

Forecasting can be defined as the estimation of the future value of a variable (most commonly sales). A key assumption is that a relationship does exist between the variable being forecast (the dependent variable) and the other one or more variables that are being measured against, i.e. the independent variable(s). For example, it is assumed that growth in sales is in some way related to advertising. Spreadsheets may be used to plot trends and compounded growth rates.

Marketing activities are designed ultimately to deliver sales and so sales forecasting is a key input to marketing planning.

DISTRIBUTION RESEARCH

distribution

the processes involved in moving goods from the supplier to the customer or user

Distribution research is carried out by manufacturing companies and producers into their use of intermediaries (warehouse operators, wholesalers, insurance and financial brokers and agencies, retail store outlets) to find out how to get the best service for customers. There may be many intermediaries in a supply chain (e.g. in the food chain, from farm to fork). Distribution research can discover where companies could improve their selling functions or increase the selling effectiveness of their distribution outlets, perhaps by helping distributors with promotions or providing training in the use of products.

Manufacturing firms require information to assist them with decisions such as: the kinds of outlets to sell through; which territories to sell in and what field supervision and training are required. For retailers, research is crucial to help with management decisions about siting new stores, in-store layouts, car parking, stock quantities, deliveries, etc.

As with all these categories of research, it is common for companies to appoint research agencies to investigate their selling activities and the effectiveness of sales outlets and distribution networks. Some research companies undertake research like this under their own initiative and sell their findings to interested companies, e.g. AC Nielsen's retail audits.

PRODUCT AND BRAND RESEARCH

unique selling proposition (USP)

a clear point of differentiation for a product/service

Much of product research is about testing the design concept, performance, ease of use, reliability, special features, appearance and packaging of products. Researchers also ask customers and consumers about brand superiority, in terms of qualities, higher prices and appeal. This helps to create distinctive brands and unique selling propositions (USPs). Many of the products we use daily have been tested with customers by marketing researchers before their release onto the market. New product development is an important part of marketing and marketing research has a key role to play in each of the stages of development (see Chapter 6), whether this be research into new technologies, competitor products, screening, concept testing, market potential analysis, market segments, consumer preferences, etc. Marketing research has been fundamental to the expansion of many industries, including computer gaming, digital television and mobile phones; however, FMCG industries such as food and drink consistently top the list as the most researched categories.

Research is not confined to physical, manufactured goods but also extends into the service industries (see Chapter 7). These industries (e.g. financial services, travel, tourism and leisure, media, public services and utilities) have generated considerable work for marketing researchers. Marketing research has helped insurance companies and banks such as Aviva, Virgin Money and HSBC to provide new services and products both online and offline. In the travel sector, low-cost airlines such as Norwegian Air, easyJet and Ryanair were developed in response to well-researched customer needs. Customers are regularly asked for their opinions on a range of services from beauty care and therapy to second-hand book sales.

Larger companies usually have their own market researchers who regularly and systematically check the performance of the company's own products. Market analysts use audit data (see 'Secondary research' on p. 182), sales data and other secondary sources in this to monitor markets, looking for customer and usage trends, and sometimes spotting gaps in the market that may be profitable opportunities for the company.

PRICING RESEARCH

Product sales are often highly sensitive to price movements and so pricing research is important to many firms. Research tests customers' reactions to price changes, competitors' price changes, price promotions, seasonal prices, and differences in expected price bands for different sizes, packaging and quantities. Even prestige, branded products, such as Gucci and Calvin Klein, are susceptible to price competition when there are reasonably priced quality substitutes available. Demand can be price elastic when there is choice, as there is with many household cleaning products (see Chapter 10 for an explanation of elasticity). The manipulation of prices is risky because of the competitive forces in play, so pricing research is done to establish just how much customers would be prepared to pay.

ADVERTISING AND PROMOTIONS RESEARCH

Advertising and promoting big brands such as Nike and Reebok is very expensive and so companies use marketing research to help ensure they meet their objectives and reduce the risks. Marketing research not only uncovers customers' desires and needs, it also provides data such as customers' personal details, which companies can use to target their mail-order offerings. Customer data feeds into crucial marketing decisions such as which market segments (see Chapter 4) to target and how best to appeal to them. Research in this area includes pre- and post-testing of communications, tracking studies, media planning research, readership/viewership/listenership surveys, exhibition and sponsorship evaluation, and direct marketing communications research, including the use of e-communications and the design of customer offers.

MEDIA HABITS

Not only do marketers need to know who their customers might be, they also need to know how best to communicate with them. This is where an understanding of their media

Discovering customer needs through research

substitutes
other products that might be bought as alternatives; they satisfy the same or similar needs

price elastic
when the demand for a good changes significantly after a price change, e.g. price goes up by 10%, demand falls by 20%

elasticity
a significant response to changes in a marketing variable, most commonly price; if the demand for a product is price elastic, sales volumes will change by a greater percentage than the percentage change in price, e.g. if the price goes up by 5%, sales fall by 7%; therefore if the price rises the sales revenue actually falls

pre-testing
evaluating the effectiveness of an aspect of a marketing campaign with its target audience before release

post-testing
evaluating the effectiveness of an aspect of a marketing campaign with its target audience after release

tracking
marketing effects are monitored over time

habits comes in; what, where, when and how much they read, watch and listen to. Media habits are in many ways an integral part of our behaviour, we consume media constantly and there is a huge amount of data collected almost continuously (on the Internet this is done automatically). All the main media have audited data covering their use. In the UK, the Broadcasters' Audience Research Board (BARB) provides information on television viewing habits, the National Readership Survey (NRS) covers major newspapers and magazines, the Radio Joint Audience Research (RAJAR) provides information for radio and there are similar audience measurement organisations for cinema and video, and out of home (OOH) media. The UK Online Measurement Company (UKOM) provides measurement and analysis of online audiences across multiple devices and platforms. Online audience measurement can be particularly challenging as typically website impression data (as measured by server and cookie counts) exaggerates the number of *people* who may have actually been exposed to online content; material may not have been loaded by a browser or a viewer may not have scrolled down far enough to see it. A combination of machine measurement techniques and survey data is needed in order to provide a comprehensive view of who visits what, what else they visit and what devices they use. All the main media – from the local press to national TV, from poster sites to websites – have detailed profiles of their own audiences (which they use to encourage advertisers). But not only is media habit information vital in itself – it is also collated with other research data to create much richer insights into customer behaviour. For example, 'Touchpoints' is a consumer-centric, multimedia database which provides details of consumers and their media behaviour, giving a unique view of people's daily lives and their media usage. The TGI covers 18 broad product/service areas of 4,000 brands in over 500 product fields involving over 720,000 interviews annually in over 60 countries. Information is collected on respondents' demographics (e.g. age, sex, income, education, etc.), their attitudes, beliefs, values and opinions, and on their consumption of press, satellite, cable and digital TV, radio, cinema, OOH and the Internet.

impressions
the number of times ad content is displayed

SECONDARY (DESK) RESEARCH

The terms 'desk research' and 'secondary research' have become interchangeable so, for the purposes of this chapter, the term 'secondary research' will be used to embrace 'desk research' as well. Secondary research is the search for good-quality secondary data that has been validated and already published in some form. Secondary data sources may be internal (i.e. the organisation's own records) or external. Companies, government institutions and international bodies such as the Organisation for Economic Cooperation and Development (OECD) and the World Trade Organisation (WTO) maintain databases of current information useful for trade. Firms like Mintel, Keynote and the British Market Research Bureau collect data on markets, products and customers which they sell on to other interested organisations. Exhibit 5.2 shows internal and external sources of secondary and primary data.

Whenever data from another source is used, researchers have to be careful to acknowledge that source, and to get permission from publishers or data owners.

Secondary research is important in establishing what is already known so that researchers can build on that information rather than just rediscover it. Information about past events, and the dates they occurred, can be helpful in establishing the background of significant

	Internal sources	External sources
Secondary data collection	Customer records Sales reports Retail outlet/dealer's feedback Financial figures about customers, suppliers and dealers Research and development studies Production and technical records Management reviews Marketing intelligence assessments	Trade and consumer press Websites and social media sites Commercial and industrial reports Government publications Trade association reports Other companies' reports Search engines and directories Market reports Retail audits
Primary data collection	Current customer feedback Current customer complaints Sales interviews and daily feedback Current delivery situation Current state of stock turnover Current feedback from marketing, discounts and promotional activity State of current production levels to keep pace with dealer and customer demand Current research and development activity to give competitive edge	Observing behaviour: • watching customers and situations • surveillance by electronic means Questioning respondents: • asking questions in personal interviews • asking questions by telephone • using mailed questionnaires • using web-assisted interviewing • using video links to ask questions Carrying out experiments: • carrying out product trials in a laboratory setting • carrying out consumer tests, e.g. eye tracking • carrying out trials in the field, e.g. a sample of respondents trying a product at home or in a public place within a specified period

EXHIBIT 5.2 Examples of secondary and primary data sources

product and market developments. This information can also be used to help forecast future patterns or trends (assuming past and current assumptions hold). The volume of secondary data available increases year on year and modern technology, e.g. databases and the Internet, makes it widely available and easier to access.

The starting point for secondary research is usually the organisation's own records. If there is insufficient relevant information available internally, then researchers will look for alternative, external data sources.

The advantages of secondary data collection include:

- it is non-reactive – i.e. it can be carried out without alerting any other organisation or business

- it is unobtrusive because it only seeks out what is already available

- the issue of confidentiality in the use of materials is not usually a problem (so long as copyright permission has been obtained)

ethical focus: whose data is it anyway?

It seems that almost everything we do online, whether it's buying groceries, booking a ticket, registering a warranty or taking out a new phone contract, involves handing over some of our personal information. It can be frustrating and time consuming to fill in yet another online form, but have you ever stopped to consider what information about you is being captured by companies and agencies even *without* your knowledge?

Developments in information technology make it easier than ever for organisations to collect and analyse information about our behaviour. Firms argue they use insights from data analysis to develop products that better meet our needs, or to provide the right offer, to the right customer at the right time. But does that always mean better value for consumers? Have you noticed how the best offers are often reserved for new customers, so that regular switching is often required to ensure the best deal?

More than 100 countries and territories around the world have now adopted comprehensive data protection or privacy laws to protect personal data held by both governments and private companies. By law UK organisations must be up-front about how data is to be used, take appropriate steps to protect personal data, and there should not be any secret purposes for data being collected. But how many of us take the time to read all the small print, for example when we download and install a new app? Little surprise then that 85% of people remain concerned about how their personal information is passed or sold to other organisations, and 77% worry about the security of their personal details, according to a recent survey carried out by the UK Information Commissioners Office.

Midata is a UK government project involving businesses and consumer groups that aims to give consumers better access to and control of their own personal data. So far midata is helping consumers obtain key information – for example utility and phone bills – in a digital format that makes it easier to compare services and find the best deal. In 2013, the midata innovation lab was set up to allow businesses and expert organisations to work together to develop experimental apps based on data voluntarily donated by a panel of consumers. One prototype app, named 'relative calm' enables relatives and carers to access a dashboard of data to see if an elderly or vulnerable person is getting out of bed each morning, keeping their home at a safe temperature and not taking out unusual amounts of money from their bank.

'In the digital age the information that we generate as we go about daily life is a source of huge potential value', said Professor Sir Nigel Shadbolt, the chair of the midata programme.

Do you think greater control and access to your own personal data could help make you more comfortable sharing it?

Sources: Department for Business, Innovation and Skills (2013); Banisar (2014); ICO (n.d.)

- accountability is rarely a problem because such published data has been vetted by previous research and reviewers, so the data collected can be used to back up one's own opinions and statements about what is known about the research problem at hand

- it is an economical method whose costs (e.g. database access or the price of a market research report) are usually known very quickly

- it is a speedy research method as the data has already been collected.

In any research project, secondary data should be collected first, i.e. before any primary research is undertaken. Secondary research is usually much cheaper and if the data you want already exists, why collect it again? Researchers use primary research methods to fill in gaps; to find out things that secondary research could not tell them.

However, there are limitations to secondary data. The data have been compiled for the original publisher's own purposes. So the data collected are relevant to that organisation and might not be applicable to studies currently being conducted by others. Data might be biased or have left out things that were not relevant to the original research project. The secondary data might also be out of date, depending on how many years ago it was collected. It may just be wrong: sloppily collected or collated. Always check data against multiple sources.

COMMERCIALLY AVAILABLE RESEARCH

There are a number of commercial organisations (such as Mintel, Nielsen, TNS and Keynote) which conduct research and publish substantial reports which other researchers and client companies can then purchase.

Nielsen, for example, provides data about the total sales of retailers' and manufacturers' brands in many product categories. A product's barcode contains information such as contents, manufacturer, price and country of origin. Each product is scanned at the store's checkout and this information can then be used by marketing research agencies to compile retail audits.

Kantar Media's TGI is derived from a questionnaire of over 45 pages, sent out to representative consumers (consumer panels). The selected consumers, usually in their own homes, answer questions or perform small tasks and return their responses to the research agency. In this way information is obtained about respondents' general purchasing habits, lifestyles and needs. The surveys cover a comprehensive range of topics, such as brands consumed, levels of income and expenditure. Information collected in this way can be sold to businesses that are interested in any of these consumer topics. More information on TGI can be found on Kantar Media's website (**http://kantarmedia-tgigb.com**). Governments are also a good source of secondary data, for example YouGovProfiles is a segmentation and media planning tool for brand owners and agencies (**www.yougov/ findsolutions/profiles**).

PRIMARY RESEARCH

When relevant secondary data is not available, information has to be gathered directly from individuals and the market. This is known as primary research. Researchers always begin with secondary research as this is cheaper and usually quicker. Primary research is then used to fill in the gaps or examine findings in greater detail.

External primary research may involve dealers, suppliers, customers, consumers, trade associations, industry groups and government institutions. This primary data is useful in building up pictures of levels of satisfaction with the products and services and of general attitudes towards an organisation and its activities.

retail audit
a research implement that provides information on retail product sales, e.g. value, volume, market/ brand share

Kantar Ctar consumer research

consumer panels
a primary research technique that seeks the views, attitudes, behaviour or buying habits of a group of consumers

primary data
first-hand data gathered to solve a particular problem or to exploit a current opportunity

ACTIVITY

Go to the library, or search online, for examples of recent market research reports and company directories. Look for company directories such as Kompas and Dunn and Bradstreet, and market research reports such as Mintel and Keynote. If you are searching online, you will probably need to do so through a library's service, e.g. a university library, as the market research reports are often subscription-only although government reports (including EU) may be freely accessible.

What information do they provide? What other examples containing useful marketing information can you find and what do they cover?

Advances in computing have made gathering, recording and analysing information much easier and quicker. Researchers can involve substantially greater numbers of respondents, or respondents who might be difficult to reach by other means. Computer-based research can also have the advantage of providing a record of what was said. There are a number of websites, e.g. SurveyMonkey and SmartSurvey, which automate questionnaire production and distribute questionnaires online. Although the basic service may be free, they charge for the more sophisticated features that are usually required by professional or academic researchers (including students).

b2b focus: a primary research illustration

Simply Software is considering selling hardware maintenance services. Initially, they send an email to their entire salesforce asking how many customers have enquired about such services. Next they ask the sales team to sound out their customers at their next visit. Additionally, they could write to members of organisations such as the Computer Users' Association. While waiting for responses, they check their own records of customer usage and complaints and assess competitive offerings via a web search.

If there is sufficient interest in the new service, the company will need to design it to fit with customer needs. To find out what would appeal to customers, it could invite groups to come in and talk about their current hardware service arrangements: what's good and what's not; what extra services they would like; and what they would be prepared to pay. Again they could consult the salesforce and other key employee groups. They could send a questionnaire to current customers.

This scenario makes use of a variety of research techniques and approaches: internal data analysis, web searching, salesforce information, trade association information, focus groups, face-to-face interviews and a survey. This use of multiple methods is sometimes called 'triangulation': gathering the information that the company needs from a variety of sources and perspectives to ensure that it is as full, and as accurate, as possible.

There are two broad approaches to primary research: quantitative and qualitative, which should be seen as mutually supportive. Each has its advantages and both can be of benefit to markets in terms of problem-solving and decision-making. Quantitative research is numerical, *measures* market phenomena and usually involves statistical analysis. By contrast, qualitative research deals in words and does not attempt to count things; instead it provides an understanding of how and why things are as they are.

quantitative research

seeks numerical answers, e.g. how many people have similar characteristics and views

qualitative research

investigates people's feelings, opinions and attitudes, often using unstructured, in-depth methods

CONTRASTING QUANTITATIVE AND QUALITATIVE RESEARCH

Quantitative research has the reliability of numbers and statistically proven large-scale results while qualitative studies help to understand respondents' attitudes, motivations and behaviour. For example, quantitative research might be used to find out how much of a product is bought, when it is bought and where. This information shows marketing managers how and what customers have purchased, from which they can deduce what customers are likely to consume in the near future. However, should the marketing team want to know *why* people buy what they do, numbers alone will not suffice. A qualitative approach is better at discovering such customers' purchase intentions. The customers would need to be interviewed and probed for in-depth answers.

Qualitative and quantitative research should be seen as mutually supportive. For instance, as quantitative surveys taking in large numbers of people are expensive to conduct, a smaller-scale exploratory qualitative study is often conducted first to see whether a quantitative survey might be worthwhile and to assist with the design of that survey. For example, if the exploratory study unearths only very limited demand for a new product, then the need for an expensive quantitative survey is questionable.

QUALITATIVE RESEARCH

Qualitative research helps researchers to find new or different ways of looking at problems. Unlike quantitative research, qualitative research techniques 'do not attempt to make measurements, [but] seek insights through a less structured, more flexible approach' (Birn et al., 1990). It is used to 'increase understanding, expand knowledge, clarify the real issues, identify distinct behavioural groups' (Gordon and Langmaid, 1988). Qualitative research is about finding out what people think and feel and it is often used as a means of developing the design of a quantitative research programme, e.g. by helping to design the questions for a survey. It can be exploratory, i.e. a small-scale attempt to find out the particular circumstances of a market and its customers. It can be relatively unstructured, e.g. an interview where the interviewees are encouraged to discuss answers freely and so unearth a greater wealth of information for the researchers. It can be descriptive, as in the narratives offered in biographical or phenomenological research. It can be explanatory in nature, trying to discover why people do particular things, unearthing their attitudes and motivations. It may cover a broad range of companies or consumer types or it may look at one or two particular instances in depth.

The most common qualitative research methods are in-depth interviews and focus groups both of which are covered in more detail later in this chapter.

QUANTITATIVE RESEARCH

Quantitative research requires much larger numbers of respondents than qualitative research. Its aim is to find out how many people have similar or specific characteristics and views. If there are large numbers of respondents, a quantitative survey is used to collect the data. It would be too time-consuming and costly to cover a large number of respondents with a qualitative approach. Use of questionnaires is a popular technique adopted, and these can be cost-effective in reaching many people when posted, faxed, emailed or completed online. The answers are then subjected to analyses using statistical computing software (e.g. SPSS or Microsoft Excel).

The largest type of quantitative study, and the most complete way of collecting data, is to conduct a full-scale census of the entire population within a country. Full-scale census surveys are used by governments all over the world as aids to planning and forecasting. Each census provides a large amount of information that gives reliable statistical data about population characteristics. The heads of households, or chief income earners, in

exploratory (research)
initial research to see whether a more comprehensive study is needed

biographical research
an individual's story or experiences told to a researcher or found in other materials

phenomenological research
describes the experiences of individuals concerning some specific phenomena or occurrence

in-depth interviews
one-to-one research interviews; commonly used in qualitative research

focus groups
a qualitative research technique using a group discussion overseen by a moderator, used to explore views, attitudes and behaviour with regard to a marketing issue; common in advertising research

SPSS (Statistical Package for the Social Sciences)
a software program for statistical analysis

census
a survey that includes all members of a population

10 steps to questionnaire
design

each household have to fill in the census questionnaire. The process is expensive and time-consuming so population censuses are only conducted every 10 years in the UK.

It is impossible for market research organisations to draw data from every member of the country's population in the way a census does. Respondents do not have to cooperate and, anyway, the costs involved would be huge. Therefore, they question a sample of the population. Each member of that sample group may represent hundreds, or even thousands, of people. It is therefore vital to choose your sample carefully to ensure you have the same balance of characteristics (sex, age, background, etc.) that are representative of the statistical population that is being studied. Sampling is considered later in this chapter as it is such an important part of the survey process. However, before leaving the issue of the use of census data, it is worth noting here that researchers use the term population in a particular way and this does not necessarily mean the whole population of a country. Marketing researchers are concerned with the research population. If the research only needs to be focused on a particular group of people, such as attendees at a specific concert, then this would be the relevant research population. While it may still be inappropriate to survey all of them for cost and time reasons, a census would be a survey of all of these people, not of everybody in the population at large. From a research perspective, the important consideration is the definition of the research population which might be used for a census or from which a sample can be drawn.

customer profile

a description of the firm's customer base, used to target customers more accurately

The strength of quantitative research lies in the way statistical analysis is used to explain marketing phenomena. Marketers can base their decisions on statistically proven facts with known margins of error. The development of computer-aided simulations and database applications has greatly enhanced the ability of marketing researchers to build customer characteristics from geo-demographic data (see Chapter 4 for more information on market segmentation and geo-demographics) and purchasing records to build up more accurate customer profiles.

research focus

Stewart, D.W. and Hess, M. (2011) 'How relevancy, use, and impact can inform decision making: the uses of quantitative research', *Journal of Advertising Research*, 51 (1): 195–206.
   This paper reviews the current state of use (and value) of quantitative research in advertising. It concludes that the value of quantitative research is well established but its use is less than might be expected. The authors discuss the reasons for this.

PRIMARY RESEARCH METHODS AND TECHNIQUES

Primary research is original research, i.e. it is not reliant on previously published information. There are two major forms of primary research:

- asking questions (surveys and interviews)
- watching how people behave (observation).

	Advantages	Disadvantages
Email survey (quantitative)	Cheaper than offline methods Good for international surveys Versatile and very quick Can link to website	Poor email lists can make it hard to reach a representative sample Brevity of responses May be seen as spam
Website surveys and studies (quantitative or qualitative)	**Intranet** sites are low cost and easily accessible *within* an organisation **Internet sites** have similar advantages to email surveys Easily accessed Social networking groups contain lots of information and can facilitate extensive discussion	Respondents select themselves Little control over sample Reliance on people to find the website Vested interests may distort the findings
Postal survey (quantitative)	Self-administered so lower cost A large number can be surveyed Possibility of enclosures	Limited to short questionnaire (otherwise people will not fill it in) Hard to ask follow-up questions or probe deeper Low response rates
Telephone survey (quantitative or qualitative)	Allows follow-up questions Avoids cost of travel Can choose time to call Computer-assisted telephone interviewing (CATI) for automated data collection	Intrusive Hang-ups Time-consuming CATI is more expensive to set up than using phone
Face-to-face interviews (quantitative or qualitative)	Flexibility: questions can be flexed Visual materials and other aids can be used Allows follow-up questions and probing: greater depth Personal relationship: builds trust Computer-assisted personal interviewing (CAPI) is faster and more accurate	May be expensive (e.g. travel, time) Time-consuming Interviewees may cancel appointments at short notice CAPI is more expensive to set up and more staff training is required
Focus groups (qualitative)	Flexibility: 'moderator' can encourage conversational directions Visual materials and other aids can be used Allows follow-up questions and probing: greater depth Discussion encourages more ideas	Needs good control by the 'moderator' otherwise group dynamics can cause a loss of direction Can be problematic to get a truly representative sample of individuals Time-consuming to set up
Consumer panels (usually quantitative – but may be qualitative)	Consumer can do product testing or give responses from home Regular panels: good response rates Automate response through Internet links	Expensive and time-consuming to set up Can be problematic in getting a truly representative sample of individuals

(Continued)

EXHIBIT 5.3 (Continued)

	Advantages	Disadvantages
Use of observational equipment and recorders (e.g. cameras/CCTV) (quantitative)	Can be always-on Captures actual behaviour Useful in everyday and test situations Less intrusive than human observer	Much information is irrelevant Time-consuming to review Requires monitoring of respondents in test situations (more researcher time)
Autonomic response measurement (e.g. eye tracking, galvanic response, pupilometer, tachistoscope, neuro-measurement – see p. 195) (qualitative)	Measures natural, unconscious responses Can be used before market release Alternative materials and treatments can be tested	Laboratory situations Needs specialised equipment Limits number of respondents

EXHIBIT 5.3 Comparison of common primary research methods

QUANTITATIVE SURVEYS

Quantitative surveys are what most people think of when they think of market research. Surveys involve asking respondents questions and recording their responses. There are a number of different ways to administer a survey and a range of techniques available to the researcher. Respondents may complete the survey forms themselves (e.g. if it is sent by post or emailed or is online) or they may be asked questions by a researcher (e.g. on the phone or face to face), who then completes the questionnaire on their behalf. The following are some of the more popular methods:

- email surveys
- postal surveys
- telephone surveys
- face-to-face surveys
- web surveys
- omnibus surveys
- panels
- syndicated surveys.

Most surveys employ some form of questionnaire answered individually or, less commonly, in pairs (duos) or small groups. The last three on the list above have some special characteristics which are explained below.

OMNIBUS SURVEYS

omnibus survey

a large questionnaire that provides data for multiple clients

In an omnibus survey research agencies collect information on behalf of a number of their business clients at the same time and on a regular basis. A new sample of respondents is recruited each time (one of the key differences between this and a 'panel' – see below). Typically, clients pay to have one or a series of questions put into a larger questionnaire.

Such a questionnaire might contain different sections relating to lifestyles, consumption habits, financial circumstances, ownership of motor vehicles, etc. In the motor car and financial services industries, where manufacturers and institutions are very protective of their corporate reputations, omnibus surveys are useful in helping to hide from the respondents the purposes for which the answers to the questionnaire are required. When reporting the findings, the research agency will just report back the responses to the specific questions asked by the client and not the full questionnaire results.

PANELS

Panels are most often thought of as consumer panels but can equally be industrial or b2b. Groups of people are recruited to respond to a specific survey over a period of time, and some are set up permanently by research agencies who only have to recruit new members if existing ones drop out or if they choose to increase the size of the panel. They can be expensive to set up but relatively cheap to run and maintain. A big advantage is that once recruited, high response rates can be assured and the same group of people are available throughout the research process. Consumer panels are frequently used for surveying buying habits and usage behaviour of grocery goods and for researching media habits such as watching TV, listening to the radio and reading the press.

SYNDICATED SURVEYS

Syndicated surveys are similar to omnibus studies in that they are undertaken on behalf of a range of clients who pay into the syndicate. The difference here, however, is that where omnibus research involves a questionnaire composed of questions from different clients and each client only sees the responses to its question(s), syndicated research is designed by the research agency as a complete piece of research which is sold to each of the clients with full results from the research made available at a cost. For example, an organisation with a small research budget may buy into a syndicated advertising tracking study along with other organisations as a cost-effective way of finding out how its own and others' advertising is being received by the target market.

syndicated research
data consolidated information from various studies

QUESTIONNAIRE DESIGN

Questionnaires are possibly the most common research tool and are especially used in quantitative surveys. The questionnaire is a flexible tool for the market researcher who can use it to obtain important information about consumer behaviour, attitudes to products, shopping habits, media habits and many other marketing-related issues. Quantitative researchers often use standardised questionnaires with samples of several hundreds or even thousands of respondents. Such questionnaires consist of highly structured questions for ease of coding and statistical analysis. Designing questionnaires looks easy but designing good questionnaires is a highly skilled task. Questionnaires should always be pilot tested with typical respondents for whom the questionnaire was constructed. Such testing invariably shows ways to make the questionnaire more effective.

questionnaire
a set of questions for use during a survey

Researchers often use email, or links to websites, to administer their questionnaires. This means that information can be collected much faster and that physical distance is no obstacle. Through email and the web it is no more expensive to contact people on the other side of the world than it is to talk to people in the next office.

Computerised questionnaires have other significant advantages over their old-fashioned paper counterparts. The computer does away with that tedious (and confusing) business of 'if you ticked yes, now go to question 44b, otherwise go to question 16'. Each answer can determine what the next question will be.

The information collected from all the respondents is then downloaded, collated, statistically analysed, cross-related and systematically grouped into the types of categories that will allow researchers to make meaningful statements to their clients about the findings.

A questionnaire should be easily understood by the people who have to answer the questions, otherwise they are likely to give incorrect or misleading answers. It is therefore usually better to use everyday language and simple wording.

Guidelines for the wording of questionnaires (based on Fink, 1995):

- use complete sentences
- avoid abbreviations and acronyms
- avoid slang and colloquialisms
- take care with jargon and technical expressions (will the respondent understand?)
- ask an expert researcher to review the questionnaire
- test the questionnaire on a typical respondent
- avoid two-edged questions, e.g. 'do you buy milk and eggs?' – these may be hard to answer accurately
- avoid introducing bias or strongly emotive language, e.g. 'do you think that the way supermarkets encourage food waste is criminal?'
- avoid negative phrasing as these questions are harder to answer and may be misinterpreted, e.g. 'did you enjoy the film?', not 'did you not enjoy the film?'

Keeping language simple and making the questionnaire easy to complete is especially important for self-administered questionnaires (i.e. questionnaires that will be completed without a researcher present to provide guidance). Generally speaking, the less trouble a questionnaire is to fill in, the higher the response rate is likely to be.

OPEN OR CLOSED?

closed questions
questions that expect a one-word (usually yes or no) answer

open-ended questions
questions that invite the respondent to comment rather than just give a one-word answer

categorical data
also known as 'nominal' data, data that has no numerical value and so cannot be statistically analysed although each category may be counted, e.g. gender, star sign, hair colour

Closed questions can be answered in a single word (often yes or no). They are useful for getting a definitive answer or pinning things down and are easier to code and analyse than open-ended questions. An open-ended question gives the respondent more freedom to answer the question in their own way. Open-ended questions are useful for opening up a subject and discovering more about it. They are much used in qualitative research.

Although they are easier to analyse, closed questions can seem more difficult to write because the researcher has to know the possible answers in advance: not such a problem for 'yes' or 'no' questions, or for categorical data such as which gender a person is or where they live, but trickier if a scale of answers is required, for example, the question 'How often have you visited this place?' requires the researcher to have a good idea of what might be the maximum number of visits. If the questionnaire allows for possible answers of '1–2; 3–4; 5–6; 7–8; more than 8', and in fact lots of people have visited 20 or more times, the resulting data will be of poor quality.

Closed questions:

'What is your age?'	16-25	26-35
'Do you have a bank account?'	Yes	No
'Do you own a car?'	Own	Don't own

Scale questions:

Likert scale

Superdry is a fashionable brand

1	2	3	4	5
Strongly agree	Slightly agree	Neither agree nor disagree	Slightly disagree	Strongly disagree

Comments:_____
_____
_____

Osgood's semantic differential scale

Was Rosannica Restaurant's service:

Reliable   _ _ _ _ _ _ _ _ _   Unreliable
Friendly   _ _ _ _ _ _ _ _ _   Unfriendly
Expensive   _ _ _ _ _ _ _ _ _   Inexpensive

Comments:_____
_____
_____

Rank order scale

Please rank in order of preference each of the following university facilities:

Sports facilities   ☐
Medical centre facilities   ☐
Library facilities   ☐
Parking facilities   ☐
Restaurant facilities   ☐

Comments:_____
_____
_____

Open-ended questions:

'What did you enjoy about the play last night?'
_____
_____

'Describe your feelings concerning the news about brand X'
_____
_____

'What do you think the level of competition will be like in the next five years?'
_____
_____

EXHIBIT 5.4 Examples of ways of asking questions

OBSERVATION TECHNIQUES

observation

a primary research technique that involves watching how subjects behave in their normal environment

participant observation

a primary research technique in which the observer becomes involved with their subjects rather than remaining apart

Observation, as the name suggests, is about watching how people behave rather than asking them questions about their behaviour. Simple observation involves watching and recording people and their activities: perhaps using products or doing their shopping. A 'pantry audit' is an example of simple observation. Researchers list all the products or brands that are kept in someone's home. A useful observation for a toy manufacturer is watching children play with their toys to see exactly how they behave and enjoy themselves. For a restaurant owner, watching people use their services can be highly insightful. Participant observation, which is a variant, requires the researcher to become involved in the activity or task being observed, e.g. the researcher might accompany the respondent on a shopping trip.

An advantage of using observation as the research approach is that there should be no researcher or response bias in the observation process, although the recording of the observed behaviour may cause problems. Technology helps to overcome this problem. Those being observed can be filmed or sound-recorded unobtrusively (though this should always be done with their permission, of course). For example, television viewing habits can be monitored electronically as the television is turned on and channels changed.

Other measurement techniques include:

- eye movement camera – used for such things as assessing advertisement designs by electronically tracking exactly what the eye is looking at (see Exhibit 5.5)

- tachistoscope – used to show images very quickly which can be used, for example, to measure brand image awareness

- pupilometer – used to measure pupil dilation (the size of the pupil in the eye); the larger the pupil, the more it indicates how much the image being viewed is liked

- facial scanning technology – used to copy test adverts over the Internet

- psycho-galvanometer – used to measure changes on the surface of the skin when the respondent is viewing images or answering questions or performing a task

- neuro-monitoring – there is a growing area of research which involves the measurement of brainwave patterns as respondents are presented with different messages or images and using different media.

The immense advantage all these techniques share is that they measure unconscious responses. These are biological changes that are automatic and well documented for their reliability.

WEB ANALYTICS

marketing metrics

'measurements that help with the quantification of marketing performance, such as market share, advertising spend, and response rates elicited by advertising and direct marketing' (Chartered Institute of Marketing)

Thanks to the web, it is easier now than ever before to collect up-to-date, detailed, data on customer behaviour. Organisations have access to masses of data; sometimes more than they know how to deal with.

In order to make the most of this wonderful potential information, it is important to plan the data collection carefully. Key questions to be answered when planning include:

- what marketing metrics are needed?
- how might the necessary data be collected?
- which of those methods will be most effective in terms of cost, accuracy and time?
- who will be responsible for the data collection (e.g. in-house or agency)?

- how will the data be stored?
- how will it be analysed (data mining)?
- what reports should be produced to assist managers in their decision-making?

data mining

using specialist software to analyse large amounts of data (held in a database) to identify patterns or relationships in that data

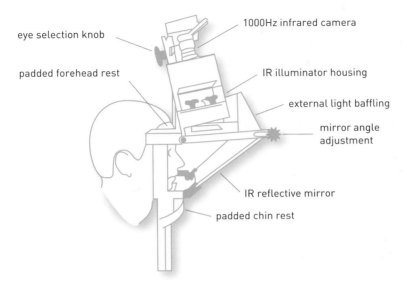

EXHIBIT 5.5 Example of a stationary eye-tracking system; alternative systems are smaller and can be more conveniently head mounted. The latest systems use small cameras placed unobtrusively (and unobserved) in front of viewers

Ryan and Jones (2012) suggest seven key performance indicators (KPIs) for websites:

1   conversion rate; the number of visitors who make a purchase, or book an appointment, etc.
2   page views
3   absolute unique visitors
4   new vs. returning visitors
5   bounce rate: the number of visitors who leave the site immediately, having only looked at the first page (the 'landing page')
6   abandonment rate: the number of visitors who do not complete an action, typically leaving without checking-out the items in their basket
7   cost per conversion, including advertising.

Website visitors and email recipients leave a digital trace that can be tracked and analysed, making online marketing communications much easier to measure than offline (Charlesworth, 2009) although it is still hard to tie online promotional activity directly to offline sales (see Chapter 8). The two most common ways to collect information about website visitors are through web access logs, which are created and held by the organisation's own web server, and page tags (embedded code) which send data to the organisation's analytics service provider. There are a number of commercial organisations which provide analysis services, e.g. Google (**www.google.com/analytics**) and Yahoo (**http://help. yahoo.com/l/us/yahoo/ywa/**). The information may be supplemented through 'cookies'

Web analytics tagging & tracking

(see digital focus box below). By these means, organisations can find out: where in the world the person browsing is located, how they came to the site (e.g. directly or through an advert or via a search engine – in which case they can also see the search terms entered) and their journey through the site (Ryan and Jones, 2012).

digital focus: do you like cookies?

World Wide Web

the graphical user interface
to the Internet

The main point of the **World Wide Web** is that it's user friendly. We surf at will, tracking down interesting clips and articles, looking for information on our favourite things (shows, people, brands, etc.), playing good games, finding the best product deals. Cookies help this to happen.

Cookies are small files which are stored on your hard drive and are available to the browser (e.g. Internet Explorer or Firefox). They are used to tailor your experience of the Internet and help make it more personal. It's how sites are able to greet you by name and show you what's new since your last visit. This sounds good, so why are they controversial and why has the EU passed a law restricting their use?

Most cookies are harmless and enhance your online experience. The problem cookies are called 'persistent third party cookies'. They come from a different site: one that you may not even know about. They can be used by advertisers and trackers to record your browsing habits, following you wherever you go, even when you've moved off the site where you encountered the cookie. They arrive in various forms, e.g. through adverts, widgets or embedded content (often videos).

The EU Directive on Privacy and Electronic Communications came into force in May 2012 and it requires users' explicit consent before data can be stored on their computers. That's what's behind all those pop-ups telling you that a site uses cookies. Do you click and read the details of *how* they are used?

This information is, of course, very helpful for improving the website design, making it stickier (so people stay longer), placing links appropriately to help them to the right pages and identifying any page that commonly causes them to leave the site, but it can be used more strategically to improve overall business performance. According to a recent IBM Executive Report, an effective customer analytics strategy can help drive top-line growth, avoid unnecessary costs and increase customer satisfaction (Teerlink and Haydock, 2011). The Internet can provide masses of information on customers but, too often, the insights gleaned from web analytics stay in the IT department instead of being used more widely to help grow the business.

SOCIAL MEDIA DATA ANALYTICS

Social networks like Twitter, Facebook, Linked-in and Instagram create a huge volume of largely unstructured data from the flow of comments and information passed between participants. Social network data analytics aim to identify patterns and extract meaning from this data that can be used to help firms understand and profile their audiences more effectively. Special software can be used to analyse text and the sentiment or feelings users express when they communicate in social networks. New data visualisation techniques can be used to assess the strength of connections between members (or nodes) in social networks and to provide valuable insights into how influence occurs. These emerging technologies are being incorporated into a number of practical social media management tools, for example, L'Oréal uses Traackr, an online influencer relationship management software platform, to identify the best connected beauty vloggers and bloggers.

QUALITATIVE STUDIES

Qualitative techniques include:

- interviews
- focus groups
- projective techniques
- ethnography.

research focus

Levy, S.J. (2012) 'Marketing management and marketing research', *Journal of Marketing Management,* **28 (1–2): 8–13.**
As a practitioner and an advocate of the use of qualitative methods of research, the author notes specific instances of their applications and sums up the awareness he has gained about marketing management and the use of marketing research.

IN-DEPTH INTERVIEWS

Interviews (in-depth interviews) are ideal for gaining detailed information on a topic from a limited number of people. The decision about who to interview clearly depends on the objectives and nature of the study. Sometimes it is appropriate to interview loyal customers or fans and sometimes the researcher may want to talk to people who never buy the brand. Expert interviews can be very useful in getting in-depth information and an industry view. For example, students often want to interview marketing managers or advertising agencies for their projects. Denscombe (2000) suggests two questions to be answered before choosing interviews as a research technique:

1   Does the research really require the kind of *detailed information* that interviews supply?

2   Is it reasonable to rely on information gathered from a small number of informants?

Interviews provide depth of information, but not usually breadth.

Interviewers usually start by asking a few general questions or putting up a problem situation or case scenario for the interviewee to respond to. Although interviewers vary in approach and style, they should always create a situation where the respondent feels at ease and can talk freely about the subject, thereby generating more information and insights for the interviewer. The aim is to encourage the respondent to freely express her or his opinions, attitudes, experiences, interpretations and motivations. Interviews are time-consuming and can take from one to several hours. A voice or video recorder can be helpful if its use is agreed with the respondent. Analytical software such as NVivo can be useful when analysing interview transcripts.

Face-to-face interviewing.

Source: iStock.com/wdstock

global focus: elusive data

Marketing research in less developed countries (LDCs) can present particular problems. Often, there is very little secondary data available, and what there is may be out of date or unreliable. Population censuses are expensive and so poorer countries are unlikely to do these often, if at all. Few houses, especially in rural areas, may have phones and so the telephone directory will be a slim volume. (In many LDCs, people in remote areas are more likely to have mobile phones than landline telephones.)

This lack of secondary data also affects primary research as it is hard to obtain an accurate sampling frame. As a consequence, convenience samples are often used.

The actual collection of primary data can also be difficult in itself. In some countries, women still play a subservient role to their men and would not be permitted to talk to a man – certainly not alone. So who do you send to do the interview? The obvious answer would be a woman. But how will you find a trained female market researcher in a country where women do not work outside the family? In such countries, people can also be reluctant to talk to strangers at all, especially about personal matters.

On the other hand, countries that have not always enjoyed the privilege of free speech may prove a researcher's dream. Response rates to surveys can be very high – though whether this is because people are accustomed to cooperating with official enquiries, or just because they find being asked their opinion on consumer products a novelty, is as yet unclear.

Focus group
smartphone testing

FOCUS GROUPS

A focus group comprises a number of respondents (usually 6–12 people) led by a professional researcher who is called the facilitator or moderator. The researcher starts by asking questions or prompting the group members to respond to the words, sights, sounds and touch of visual images, or the actual products themselves in order to get the group discussion flowing freely about the subjects or objects. By observing the interactions and recording the discussions, the researcher can gain useful insights about the groups' intentions and feelings towards the subjects or objects.

PROJECTIVE TECHNIQUES

Projective techniques use indirect questions to understand respondents' perspectives better. Examples of projective techniques include:

- word associations – one word is said and the respondent supplies her/his own immediate associated word in response

- picture associations – respondents are shown a range of pictures and asked to choose those that best represent the item being researched, e.g. the pictures that best represent a particular brand

- sentence completion – respondents are asked to complete incomplete sentences, e.g. Brand X soap is the most …

- cartoon test or thought bubbles – a cartoon or picture is shown and the respondent has to fill in the captions or thought bubbles

- third-person techniques – the respondent is asked what they imagine a specified other person, e.g. a friendly Martian, might say about something

- personalisation of objects – e.g. respondents are asked to imagine if the brand was a celebrity who it would be

- collages – respondents are asked to create a collage representing the research item from a pile of pictures.

ETHNOGRAPHY

Ethnography is a research approach in which time is spent with consumers in their own environment, e.g. at home with a family to understand mealtimes. It can sometimes be more effective than focus groups because it shows how consumers do things in a natural setting rather than talking about what they do in the artificial context of an interview room or laboratory.

Ethnographic research relies on techniques such as observation, video diaries, photographs, interviews in normal surroundings, and analysis of objects or materials that someone uses as part of their job or when taking part in activities such as preparing a packed lunch.

Ethnography is particularly useful for exploring consumers' unmet needs and can help marketers identify new product opportunities. Ethnographic research can be time consuming. Although it need not involve full immersion in a subject's life, researchers do need to establish trust with research subjects so that they behave as they would do under normal circumstances. Typically a great deal of data is collected and that can make analysis complex and potentially expensive.

> **ethnography**
>
> the description, or interpretation, of the patterns of behaviour in a social group or setting; the researcher will immerse himself or herself in a variety of ways into the culture of the group to be studied

Focus groups can give useful insights into people's views and feelings.

Source: ESB Professional/Shutterstock.com

NETNOGRAPHY

As the term suggests, netnography is an adaptation of traditional ethnographic research techniques to the study of online behaviour. The term was coined by Robert Kozinets who has also refined and developed a specific approach and recommendations on how to locate online communities and topics, filter and analyse data, and navigate ethical grey areas, for example how to obtain subjects' voluntary consent to be observed and techniques for protecting participants' anonymity (Kozinets, 2002, 2015). Netnography is similar to ethnography in that it is typically naturalistic, immersive and descriptive and involves a variety of methods. However, it is usually much faster and simpler – and therefore more cost-effective – to carry out research in online contexts. Distance is no barrier to participating in an online community and a wealth of freely expressed consumer opinions and behaviours, for example in discussion threads on public chat forums or consumer review sites, are easily accessible, searchable and downloadable.

Stacy Graiko:
ethnographic research

PRE-TESTING, TRACKING AND POST-TESTING

Marketing communications, especially advertising campaigns, can be expensive to implement. While a planned programme of pre-testing, tracking and post-testing can also be expensive, it is usually a lot less costly than a failed campaign.

Pre-testing is a way of assessing the likely effectiveness of marketing communications campaigns before the firm commits to the expense of running them. People are asked for their responses to different advertisements – most usually in a focus group convened by the agency. Alternatively, they may be asked about brand names or promotional offers. Direct marketers pre-test a number of different offers and creative treatments to assess which ones different types of people are most likely to respond to positively. Post-testing (i.e. afterwards) can provide further observations about the marketing communications effects.

Tracking is simply the testing process that measures what is going on over a period of time. Such testing is commonplace in the marketing communications industry where pre-testing may be used to evaluate and select advertising concepts, tracking is used to measure changes in recognition and recall of the advertising, branding and attitudes, and post-testing is used to assess the overall effect of a campaign.

recognition

being aware of something, e.g. a product or an advert, when shown

recall

remembering things (e.g. products, brands, adverts); may be prompted (i.e. aided by stimulus material such as part of an advert) or unprompted (i.e. unaided)

population

a complete group of people, cases or objects which share similarities that can be studied in a survey

SAMPLING

A sample is a smaller group of research subjects used to represent the whole of the research population to be studied. Qualitative research samples are small and are used to explore subjects or consider them in depth rather than to draw general conclusions about the research population as a whole, whereas quantitative research samples should be large enough, and representative enough, to allow researchers to draw general conclusions about the population being studied.

The sampling process consists of four steps:

1   Define the research population.
2   Determine the appropriate sample size.
3   Choose a sampling method.
4   Select the sample.

The first step in sampling is to define the research population from which the sample will be drawn. The second step is to determine the appropriate sample size. How many people need to be surveyed? Then the researcher must choose a sampling method and finally select the actual research subjects (people, products, companies, etc.) to be approached.

It is important that the characteristics of the sample should be as close to those of the population as possible, as the sample is meant to be representative of the population from which it is drawn.

There are several sampling methods available to researchers (see below). Random sampling (or probability sampling) approaches are well suited to statistical analysis. Non-random (or non-probability) methods can deliver quantified results but care has to be taken in making presumptions about how representative they are of the wider population. Subjects chosen through a probability sample should have a quantifiable chance of being selected. This is not true of a non-probability sample where the researcher may not know the probability of any one subject being selected – and some may have no chance at all. It is a subjective approach.

For example, imagine that a firm wants to find out how children spend their money. Clearly, they cannot question all the children in the country, so they will try to find a representative sample, or subset. Then they can ask this smaller group of children questions and scale-up to get a close approximation of the picture across the whole country. First, they establish (perhaps through a smaller qualitative study) that the key factors that influence what children buy are:

- their gender (boy or girl)
- their age.

The country's child population breaks down as follows:

52% are girls

20% are 0–3 years

20% are 4–6 years

30% are 7–12 years

30% are 13–15 years.

The names they select for the survey (perhaps 1,000 names from the total million or so) should also be: 52% girls, 20% 0–3, etc. This will then be a suitably representative sample of the whole.

RANDOM (PROBABILITY) SAMPLING METHODS

Just as the name suggests, the people or things selected for a random sample all have an equal chance of being chosen. Just like the numbers on a roulette wheel, each is equally likely to come up. Before they can be selected, however, the researcher must have a complete list of the entire research population (a sampling frame). If someone is missing, then clearly they cannot be chosen and the sample will not be entirely random.

random sample
a probability sample

sampling frame
a list of the actual members of a population from which a sample is then chosen

SAMPLING FRAME

The sampling frame might be a telephone directory, an electoral register, a list of members of a club, or any other list that represents the research population as a whole. The list should contain accurate records of the entire research population and it needs to include contact details. It is usually very difficult to obtain a complete and accurate sampling frame but, without it, probability sampling is not possible. Consequently, most researchers find they have to use a non-probability sampling method such as purposive sampling (see below).

purposive sampling
a non-probability sampling method, which means that every member of the research population does *not* have an equal chance of being picked; the researcher uses their judgement to choose the units to be studied

There are a number of different types of random sampling including:

- simple random sampling
- stratified random sampling
- systematic random sampling
- area or cluster sampling.

Simple random sampling

simple random sample

the Rolls-Royce of sampling
methods, every member of
the population has an equal
chance of being selected;
this can be expensive and
often difficult

For simple random sampling, every member of the population should have an equal chance of being selected. This complete randomness can be quite difficult to achieve in larger populations and so there is a useful variant on this pure simple random sampling: systematic random sampling.

Systematic random sampling

systematic random
sampling

uses the whole population as
a sampling frame but draws
subjects from it at regular
intervals, e.g. every
10th name on the list

For systematic random sampling, each individual in the sampling frame is identified by means of a number and then regularly spaced numbers are chosen until the sample has been filled. The first name should always be drawn by simple random sampling (see above) and after that, names are chosen at regular intervals, e.g. every seventh name on the list, to make up the desired sample size.

Stratified random sampling

stratified random
sampling

the research population
is divided into mutually
exclusive groups and
random samples are drawn
from each group

A sample of individuals is selected by dividing the population into mutually exclusive groups and then random samples are drawn *from every group*. For example, the population could be sorted according to social grades (A, B, C1, C2, etc.) or income levels, respondents are then drawn randomly from each group. (Be aware, though, that classifying people according to their social grade has always been one of the most dubious areas of market research investigation, even though it is still one of the most widely used classification systems.)

Area or cluster sampling

area or cluster sampling

the research population
is divided into mutually
exclusive groups (e.g.
geographical region:
perhaps by postcode) so
that a random sample of the
groups can be selected

A sample of clusters is selected by dividing the population into mutually exclusive groups (e.g. geographical region: perhaps by postcode) so that a random sample of the groups can be selected – the sample is of groups not of individuals. For example, England could be divided into counties and then a sample of those counties chosen at random (e.g. Cornwall, Lancashire and Kent), hence only people from those counties (and not other counties) are interviewed. This process can have several stages, selecting further subsets of the groups.

NON-PROBABILITY SAMPLING METHODS

Random samples are expensive, time-consuming and risky. An inaccurate sampling frame or too many non-responses can invalidate the research. Consequently most researchers use non-probability sampling methods. Commonly used methods include:

- purposive sampling
- convenience sampling
- quota sampling.

Purposive (judgemental) sampling

This is a non-probability sampling method, which means that every member of the research population does not have an equal chance of being picked. For example, if the experts within a particular industry are well-known, the researcher can simply choose from these people to represent the expertise of the industry. Knowledge gleaned from these experts would be more useful than knowledge from a larger sample of people who are less expert in the particular field. In another example, we know that there are a vast number of retail outlets selling food in Britain, but there are only a few national supermarket chains (e.g. Tesco, Wal-Mart/ASDA, Sainsbury's, Morrison's and Waitrose). So a purposive sample of large retail firms would include these stores.

Convenience sampling

A convenience sample is picked on the basis of convenience to the researcher. Organisations sometimes use their own employees to evaluate new products or prototypes that their research and development departments have come up with. Universities and colleges carry out market research surveys based on convenience samples of students and visitors to their campuses.

convenience sample
a sample picked on the basis of convenience to the researcher, e.g. work colleagues

Convenience sampling lends itself to qualitative research, where consumer information can be obtained fairly quickly, inexpensively and effectively from convenient respondents who are close to hand. The rationale is to select the most accessible members of the population from which to conveniently draw the sample. Unless the members of the population are reasonably uniform (e.g. in expectations, socio-demographic make-up, etc.), there can be problems as the sample may not be representative of the population. In such a case a quota sample (see below) would be a better method.

Quota sampling

In marketing research it is common practice to use quota samples. The population is divided into relevant categories, e.g. train travellers, car drivers, bus passengers, etc. Researchers then question a set number of people from each category. That number should be set to reflect the proportions of the total research population. This sampling method is often used in street surveys where each researcher will be given a quota of respondents, e.g. asked to find 30 train travellers, 15 male and 15 female, to take part and, of these, 10 should be from each of three income brackets.

quota sample
picks respondents in proportion to the population's profile, e.g. if 25% of the population are under 25 and female, then researchers set a quota of 25% females under 25 for the sample

As another example, a survey of the manufacturers of paints should include a selected number or quota of the large companies, such as Dulux. In consumer studies, quotas can be set based upon socio-economic and demographic characteristics such as age, race, gender and education attained.

ethical focus: reaching out

Recruiting the right people to interview is a crucial, but can be a difficult, part of the research process, especially if the people you need to interview are hard to find or unlikely to want to talk to you. This is often the case with vulnerable people like the homeless or mentally ill.

One answer to this is a technique known as 'snowballing'. It lets the participants recruit each other.

(Continued)

(Continued)

Ipsos MORI's Participation Unit explored various approaches as part of a methodological trial assessing the impact of different interviewee recruitment methods on a particularly hard-to-reach group: occasional drug users. Thanks to the snowballing technique, peer interviewers were able to interview a wide spectrum and diversity of drug users in locations most researchers could not usually reach. In contrast, interviewees recruited by professional market research agency staff were all participants in rehabilitation programmes. Of course, there are drawbacks to using peer interviewers and appropriate training has to be provided to ensure that there is no bias in the way the interviews are conducted.

It does seem that snowballing can get answers from places that more traditional approaches would never reach.

TEST MARKETING

test market

a subset of a market in which a product offering can be sold for a short period of time in order to predict demand and to try out and refine the marketing mix

A test market is a mini-market – a smaller version of the whole market, in which changes to any or all elements of the marketing mix can be tried out, e.g. new products, promotions, distribution, retail display, pricing, etc. If the marketing mix is successful in the test market, then it can be rolled out to the real market with more confidence. In the UK, television advertising campaigns are sometimes tested in one of the television regions before going national. However, not all countries have regionalised television (e.g. Germany, for instance, does not), so TV adverts are more difficult to test.

The use of test marketing is a recognition of the difficulties of researching matters, as a scientist might, by controlling conditions in order to test one particular variable (e.g. the price, or the communications medium). In the world of marketing and social research, variables cannot be controlled in the field. The test market therefore needs to be as close as is reasonable (or variations accounted for) to the whole of the market. While the variables cannot be controlled, they are at least presumed to have approximately the same effect in the test market as they would in the full market. Test marketing may be particularly useful when launching a new product or significantly changing or experimenting with changes to the marketing mix.

QUALITY OF MARKETING INFORMATION

Wrong information or missing information is no use at all. Sound marketing decisions can only be made on the basis of good quality information. The data must be:

* timely
* accurate
* reliable
* valid.

TIMELINESS

It is important that research is finished on time. If it is late, then it may be too late to be of any use. For example, the management problem may have become acute or the marketing environment may have changed. Out-of-date data is worthless.

ACCURACY

Accuracy is about correctness or precision. Clearly it is desirable to have absolutely accurate data. However, this is not always possible (complete accuracy is rare) and comes at a high cost. Frequently, researchers have to make estimates and it is important that they make it clear when this is the case. Relying on inaccurate data can lead to poor decisions, but if we know how inaccurate a figure may be, then we can make allowances. For example, if a thermometer consistently shows boiling water to be 91°C, instead of 100°C, then we know it is inaccurate and by how much.

RELIABILITY

Reliability refers to the consistency of results. If a piece of research is repeated with an identically composed sample, would it produce the same results? In the example above, does the thermometer read 91°C each time? Even though the measurement is inaccurate, if it returns the same result, it is reliable.

VALIDITY

Validity is a key concept in assessing the quality of research. Research should deliver evidence that can be used to answer the research problem. 'Internal validity' is an indicator of whether the research measures what it claims to measure. It is no use using a barometer (which measures pressure) if you want to measure temperature. That requires a thermometer. If research has 'external validity' it means that generalisations can be made from the research carried out on a sample to the wider population from which the sample is drawn.

Researchers have ways to deal with issues of validity which are beyond the scope of this book. Just remember the importance of taking care over the research design to ensure the research outcomes are valid.

---

research focus

LaPointe, P. (2012) 'The dog ate my analysis: the hitchhiker's guide to marketing analytics', *Journal of Advertising Research*, 52 (4): 395–6.

While the age of big data allows for more in-depth insight into consumer behaviour and enables more sophisticated targeting, it is also important to be aware that this is just a small portion of consumers' shopping and buying behaviour. Using marketing analytics as a predictive tool is complex and over-analysis can lead to skewed results. When applying marketing analytics it is vital to be mindful of scale, relevance, validity and reliability and to not forget that gut instinct still goes a long way.

SUMMARY

Marketing research is a crucial aspect of marketing. It provides the basis for all marketing decisions.

Good marketing research is essential to the objectives and successes of both profit and not-for-profit organisations. The procedures used are well-established forms of collecting, analysing and conveying information about people and markets. Markets can be described and analysed in detail so that opportunities can be taken, the performances of organisations assessed and competitors' activities tracked. Marketing research is, therefore, indispensable for the marketing intelligence purposes of organisations and in helping them to develop their marketing strategies.

Marketing research starts with secondary data which should be collected before any primary research is undertaken. The broad categories of qualitative and quantitative research have been described along with the many and varied primary research methods that fit into these categories. The decision of which method or methods to use is a direct function of the information needed which, in turn, is a function of the marketing management problem the researcher is trying to solve.

CHALLENGES REVIEWED

Now that you have finished reading the chapter, look back at the challenges you were set at the beginning. Do you have a clearer idea of what's involved?

HINTS

- Sources of secondary information, internal records, primary research approaches.
- Objectives of research.
- Appropriate qualitative research methods.
- Sampling.

READING AROUND

JOURNAL ARTICLES

Barker, M. (2003) 'Assessing the "quality" in qualitative research: the case of text-audience relations', *European Journal of Communication*, 18 (3): 315–35.

Earls, M. (2003) 'Advertising to the herd', *International Journal of Market Research*, 45 (3): 311–36.

Tarran, B. (2003) 'The birth of an idea', *Research* (the magazine of the Market Research Society), August: 22–4.

MAGAZINE ARTICLES

Noble, T. (2013) 'Neuroscience in practice', *Admap*, March. London: WARC.

BOOKS AND BOOK CHAPTERS

Belk, R., Fischer, E. and Kozinets, R.V. (2013) *Qualitative Consumer and Marketing Research*. London: Sage.

Burcher, N. (2012) 'Listening', in *Paid Owned Earned: Maximizing Marketing Returns in a Socially Connected World*. London: Kogan Page, Chapter 2, pp. 33–54.

Clow, K.E. and James, K.E. (2013) *Essentials of Marketing Research*. London: Sage.

Parsons, E. (2009) 'New technologies of marketing research', in E. Parsons and P. Maclaran, *Contemporary Issues in Marketing and Consumer Behaviour*. Oxford: Butterworth Heinemann, Chapter 11, pp. 117–96.

WEBSITES

www.barb.co.uk – Broadcasters Audience Research Board, e.g. market research applications.

www.cia.gov/library/publications/the-world-factbook – the CIA's world factbook, for country information.

www.mrs.org.uk – home of the Market Research Society.

www.surveymonkey.com – online survey tool.

Market research reports – *Mintel*, *Keynote* and *Euromonitor* are commonly found in university libraries or can be accessed online by subscription.

TEST YOURSELF

1   Why is marketing research sometimes referred to as market research? (See p. 172)

2   If marketing managers know about their customers from past purchases, why do they need to conduct marketing research? (See p. 173)

3   What are retail audits and consumer panels? (See pp. 180 and 185)

4   What is meant by defining a research problem? (See p. 173)

5   Define random sampling. (See p. 201)

6   What are the advantages of secondary data over primary data? (See pp. 183–184)

7   What is qualitative research? (See p. 186)

8   What is the difference between simple random sampling and stratified random sampling? (See p. 202)

9   List three qualitative research techniques. (See p. 197)

10   Name three commercial market research organisations. (See p. 185)

REVISION TOOLS

Want to test yourself even more? Review what you have learnt by visiting
https://study.sagepub.com/masterson4e

- Practise for exams with **multiple choice questions**
- Revise key terms with **interactive flashcards**

MINI CASE STUDY: MAKING MONEY

Read the questions, then the case material, and then answer the questions.

QUESTIONS

The company have asked you, as a marketing researcher, to help them identify profitable and long-lasting new business areas. You need to think through this research project.

(Continued)

(Continued)

1   In no more than two sentences, explain the purpose of your research project.

2   a)   List 10 pieces of information that you will need in order to complete the project.

    b)   Why would they be helpful?

You don't need to actually find the information at this stage, just work out what you need to know, e.g. what industries do De La Rue operate in? Sometimes it helps to use questions to describe what you're looking for.

3   Which of those 10 pieces of information (or data) are quantitative and which are qualitative?

4   a)   Identify which things can be found out using secondary research.

    b)   Where might you find them?

For the remaining items on your list, the ones that are going to need primary research, suggest a primary research method(s) to uncover the required information. *If the answers to all your questions are available from secondary sources, think of two more pieces of information that are not already published.*

5   Justify your choices.

Have you ever heard of De La Rue International? Do you have any of their products? Actually, you almost certainly do. De La Rue prints more banknotes than any other company in the world.

    That might sound like a dying business. After all, cash is being replaced by cards, contactless payments, Internet transactions, but even people with a wallet full of cards and a smartphone crammed with apps still need cash and it is still the preferred method of payment in many countries. Demand for banknotes may be falling, but De La Rue's printing presses are still kept busy: if you stacked the banknotes they produce every week, the pile would reach the top of Everest – twice.

    'Even though we're using credit and debit cards more than ever, people still have cash in their wallet', says chief executive Martin Sutherland. 'It's convenient, it's free at point of use, classless – not everyone has a bank account – and most of all, it's reliable. Cash is the payment mechanism of last resort, it will still work when there's a power cut or the card reader won't scan'.

    About 85% of De La Rue's business is with foreign markets. The company designs, produces or issues banknotes for about 140 countries and frequently wins awards for its innovative and hard to counterfeit designs. They won 'banknote of the year' three years running for their colourful Kazakh notes. Note designs are regularly updated and sometimes countries commission notes to mark special occasions as Guyana did with a new $50 note to help celebrate their fifty years of independence. 'Producing banknotes is a genuinely artisan process', Sutherland says, adding that De La Rue's designers will visit and photograph countries as well as meet local people to better understand the essence of those areas.

    They have a long-term contract with the Bank of England which is important not just for the revenue it ensures, but also because the prestige of this client reassures others and helps them to win new business. One of their more recent innovations is called 'active'; a visual affect where depending on how you view a note, it looks a different colour.

    These frequent updates are necessary because the longer a design is in circulation, the more time the forgers have to work out how to reproduce it. Some of the security measures De La Rue builds in to its products are confidential but the more obvious ones include a strip of silver foil running through notes, holograms and ultraviolet inks. Banknotes also use engraved images because they are harder to reproduce; 'You don't want something that can be done on a laser printer', says Sutherland. It takes a huge amount of skill to produce a banknote

    New technology is important in banknote printing if banks are to keep ahead of the counterfeiters. One of the latest innovations is the introduction of polymer banknotes, like the latest British five pound note (printed by De La Rue of course). These polymer notes, which have already been adopted in a number of other countries, are stronger, longer lasting and more difficult to forge.

Note printing

Source: David Levenson/Corbis Documentary Getty Images

De La Rue are a long-established printing business. The founder, Thomas De La Rue, is generally recognised as the inventor of the modern English playing card having patented a better way of printing them. They are a world leader in high security printing and payment systems technology: 70% of De La Rue's £472 million annual revenues comes from banknotes, making them the biggest commercial banknote printer in the world, but this is not the only part of everyday life the company touches. They design and produce passports, security and tax stamps on products such as alcohol and tobacco, postage stamps, cheques, vouchers and they also manufacture currency counting machinery and money dispensers.

With an eye to the future, De La Rue is looking for other, related products to make and sell and also for new markets – though the specialised nature of their business means that they will always be a b2b company as their products are not suitable (or even legal) to sell to consumers. While most of their customers (and certainly the biggest ones) are governments or government departments, they do have some corporate clients who buy promotional vouchers and other printed items that require the kind of security and anti-counterfeiting systems that De La Rue can provide.

Sources: Parsons (2014); Tovey (2015); De La Rue (2016); Wintle (n.d.)

REFERENCES

Banisar, D. (2016) *National Comprehensive Data Protection/Privacy Laws and Bills 2016* (28 November 2016). Available at: http://ssrn.com/abstract=1951416 **or** http://dx.doi.org/10.2139/ssrn.1951416 (accessed 04/05/16).

Birn, R., Hayne, P. and Vangelder, P. (1990) *A Handbook of Market Research Techniques*. London: Kogan Page.

Brien, R.H. and Stafford, J.E. (1968) 'Marketing information systems: a new dimension for marketing research', *Journal of Marketing*, 32 (Jul): 19–23.

Charlesworth, A. (2009) *Internet Marketing: A Practical Approach*. Oxford: Butterworth Heinemann.

De La Rue (2016) 'Bank of Guyana celebrates 50 years of Guyana's independence with a new $50 banknote', 12 May. Available at: www.delarue.com/media-centre/latest-news/2016/2016-05-12 (accessed 08/02/17).

Denscombe, M. (2000) *The Good Research Guide*. Buckingham: Open University Press.

Department for Business, Innovation and Skills (2013) 'Businesses get creative with consumer data at the "midata" Innovation Lab launch', press release, 10 July. Available at: www.gov.uk/government/news/businesses-get-creative-with-consumer-data-at-the-midata-innovation-lab-launch (accessed 04/05/16).

Fink, A. (1995) *How to Ask Survey Questions*. London: Sage.

Gordon, W. and Langmaid, R. (1988) *Qualitative Research: A Practitioner's and Buyer's Guide*. Aldershot: Gower.

ICO (Information Commissioner's Office) (n.d.) *Guide to Data Protection*. Available at: https://ico.org.uk/for-organisations/guide-to-data-protection/data-protection-principles/ (accessed 04/05/16).

Kotler, P., Keller, K., Brady, M., Goodman, M. and Hansen, T. (2012) *Marketing Management* (2nd edn). Harlow: Pearson.

Kozinets, R.V. (2002) 'The field behind the screen: using netnography for marketing research in online communities', *Journal of Marketing Research*, 39 (1): 61–72.

Kozinets, R.V. (2015) *Netnography: Redefined* (2nd edn). Abingdon: John Wiley & Sons, Inc.

LaPointe, P. (2012) 'The dog ate my analysis: the hitchhiker's guide to marketing analytics', *Journal of Advertising Research*, 52 (4): 395–6.

Levy, S.J. (2012) 'Marketing management and marketing research', *Journal of Marketing Management*, 28 (1–2): 8–13.

Market Research Society (n.d.) 'Standards and guidelines'. Available at: www.mrs.org.uk/standards/revised_code_definitions.htm (accessed 06/03/10).

McClure, S.M., Li, J., Tomlin, D., Cypert, K.S., Montague, L.M. and Montague, P.R. (2004) 'Neural correlates of behavioural preference for culturally familiar drinks', *Neuron*, 44 (2): 379–87.

Muntinga, D.G., Moorman, M. and Smit, E.G. (2011) 'Introducing COBRAs: exploring motivations for brand-related social media use', *International Journal of Advertising*, 30 (1): 13–46.

Parsons, A. (2014) 'De La Rue: licensed to print money', *BBC News Business*. Available at: www.bbc.co.uk/news/business-27888665 (accessed 04/06/16).

Ryan, D. and Jones, C. (2012) *Understanding Digital Marketing* (2nd edn). London: Kogan Page.

Schweidel, D.A. and Moe, W.W. (2014) 'Listening in on social media: a joint model of sentiment and venue format choice', *Journal of Marketing Research*, 51 (4): 387–402.

Stewart, D.W. and Hess, M. (2011) 'How relevancy, use, and impact can inform decision making: the uses of quantitative research', *Journal of Advertising Research*, 51 (1): 195–206.

Teerlink, M. and Haydock, M. (2011) *Customer Analytics Pay Off*. IBM Institute for Business Value. Available at: ftp://ftp.software.ibm.com/software/au/201301/Transform_6Customer_analytics_pay_off_Executive_Report.pdf (accessed 01/03/17).

Tovey, A. (2015) 'Cash is king for the future, says UK banknote printer De La Rue' *The Telegraph*, Finance, 30 December. Available at: www.telegraph.co.uk/finance/newsbysector/industry/12061880/Cash-is-king-for-the-future-says-UK-banknote-printer-De-La-Rue.html (accessed 04/06/16).

Wintle, A. (n.d.) *World of Playing Cards*, 'Thomas De La Rue: a brief history of De La Rue's playing cards'. Available at: www.wopc.co.uk/delarue/index (accessed 04/06/16).

WHAT THIS PART IS ABOUT

When they have completed their research and analysis, and understand their marketing environment and their customers, marketers make plans to satisfy those customers' needs. At the heart of these plans is a set of tools known as the marketing mix. The marketing mix is traditionally referred to as the 4Ps: product, promotion, place and price. The 4Ps are not enough for today's more complex product offerings though, so three more have been added to take account of the nature of services (see Chapter 7). The 7Ps add physical evidence, people and process to the original four. All the marketing mix elements must be blended together to produce an integrated plan of action to build brands and deliver long-term profits.

The marketing mix sounds deceptively simple, but a product is so much more than the item you buy. The product that is offered to customers includes its packaging, its brand and its supporting services and the decision to buy it may have more to do with those things than with the make-up of the item itself. Promotion is so much more than just advertising and is much more subtle than simply saying 'buy this'. Place is about getting the right products to the right people at the right time and about making it as easy as possible for customers to buy our products. Without a price, a product is a gift. Set the wrong price (either too high or too low) and products may not sell at all. The success of a service product may be largely reliant on the people that provide that service or the process that delivers it. Some services, e.g. restaurants, are heavily reliant on other products (peripheral products) such as the food served or on the décor of the restaurant. Both of these would be considered physical evidence.

Decisions about the marketing mix elements should not be made in isolation. The Ps need to fit with each other. An exclusive product, such as a designer suit or a Bang & Olufsen music system, commands a high price, is sold in upmarket shops, or delivered to your door in a smart van, and should be high quality. An everyday product, such as shampoo or cat litter, should do its job reliably, be inexpensive and be widely available. If just one of the Ps is out of sync, then the whole of the product offering will be devalued.

PART THREE

THE MARKETING MIX

PRODUCT

PRODUCT CHALLENGES

The following are illustrations of the types of decision that marketers have to take or issues they face. *You aren't expected to know how to deal with the challenges now*; just bear them in mind as you read the chapter and see what you can find that helps.

Degree to job: innovation director

- You are a manager in a large confectionery company which has just taken over another company. You now have too many chocolate products which are proving to be complex to manage. You have been asked to recommend which should be kept and which dropped. How will you decide?

- You are the marketing director of a large car company. The finance director wants to cut the product development budget. She cannot see why you need to keep launching new models so often. Can you convince her that this is necessary?

- You are given the task of managing a well-known and long-established brand of jeans. The brand is showing its age and sales are slowly falling year on year. What might you do to halt the decline and revitalise the brand?

- You are a salesperson at an electronics retailer. You stock the same PCs as everyone else and cannot change the basic products themselves. How can you make it more attractive for customers to come to your store rather than go to your rivals?

- You have recently been appointed marketing manager for a manufacturer of kitchen appliances (fridges, microwaves, dishwashers, etc.) and have just discovered that your products have built-in obsolescence, i.e. they are made to last five years only and then they have to be replaced. It would be easy to make them so that they lasted longer, but then you would not make the replacement sales. What is your position on this?

INTRODUCTION

Product is one of the 4Ps of the marketing mix: the central elements of a marketing plan. The other 3Ps are promotion, place and price, and these 4Ps together are the basic tools marketers use. (Services marketers extend these 4Ps to 7Ps – see Chapter 7.) They must be carefully planned out so that they all work together in order to meet companies' targets for sales and profit.

Defining the marketing mix

- Product
- Promotion
- Place
- Price.

Products are developed to meet customer needs and so those needs must first be researched and understood. The product can then be targeted at a specific market segment and a marketing mix developed to support its desired positioning (see Chapter 4). Product managers, or brand managers, use the marketing mix to design marketing programmes for their products and develop good customer relationships to ensure their brands' ongoing success.

product manager

the person responsible for the marketing of a specific product or product line

Some products are tangible (i.e. they have physical substance, they can be touched), e.g. shoes, golf balls, books, and some are intangible (without physical substance, they cannot be touched), e.g. insurance or a dental check-up. The tangible products are often referred to as goods, while the intangible products are referred to as services. However, no product is completely physical; all have service elements to them, e.g. after-sales service, warranties, guarantees, installation assistance. Equally, very few services are pure service; most have a physical element to them. When you have your car cleaned, the cleaner uses detergent, wax, etc. When you eat in a restaurant, you are served food. Goods providers often use the service aspects of their products to differentiate them from the competition, whereas service providers may try to use the products associated with their services to do this.

goods

tangible products, i.e. those with physical substance

This chapter will concentrate on tangible products, i.e. goods (the ones you can actually touch), leaving services to be dealt with in more depth in the next chapter. It will consider what makes a new product a success in the marketplace and why so many fail. Most companies sell more than one product and the entire range must be managed so that individual products contribute to the success of the brand. Product managers use a number of analysis tools and these will be considered here, along with the strategies they feed into.

Branding is one of marketing's most popular tools and much has been written about the power of the brand. Branding was perhaps the primary competitive weapon of the 1990s, and in the twenty-first century it has become almost ubiquitous – everyone wants a brand. This chapter will consider branding as an integral part of the product offering. Chapter 11 will revisit branding and its place in the whole of the marketing mix and in marketing strategy.

WHAT IS A PRODUCT?

A product can be described as a bundle of attributes or characteristics. A loaf of bread may be large, sliced and wholemeal, or it may be small, white and unsliced. These are its physical attributes and they provide benefits to the person who buys and/or eats the loaf. For example, the loaf may be good value for money, good for your health or convenient for sandwich making. Products exist to satisfy people's needs. The primary purpose of bread is to satisfy hunger; a watch satisfies our need to know the time; a car satisfies the need to travel from one place to another and washing powder cleans clothes. The product's attributes (or characteristics) must satisfy the customer's needs.

Customers judge the value of a product by weighing up all its aspects – the total product offering. The total product may have to satisfy a range of needs, e.g. Diet Pepsi has to quench thirst, taste good, be low calorie, be convenient to drink and convey a suitable image. Needs range from the simple (e.g. quench thirst) to the elaborate (e.g. convey suitable image). Some of these needs are fulfilled by basic product characteristics, e.g. the water in Diet Pepsi satisfies thirst, but some needs require more than just product ingredients. For instance, Pepsi's image is largely created by its advertising and its convenience is down to the size and design of the can or bottle. Whether or not an exchange (see Chapter 1) will take place, i.e. a sale be made, depends upon the customer's judgement of the total product's value. The customer's perception of a product's value may differ greatly from the company's perception and is dependent upon all the elements of the marketing mix, i.e. the 4Ps (product, promotion, place and price). Customers have expectations of products that go beyond product performance. They may expect helpful product support, clear instructions and a fair price. They may also want their purchases to be ethically sound: non-exploitative, safe to use and environmentally friendly. The marketing mix must therefore be well planned and integrated to create a total product offering that matches, or exceeds, the customer's expectations and needs.

There are a number of ways in which products may fail to match consumer expectations, for example: the product may not meet the basic need for which it is being bought (i.e. it may not work well enough), it may not suit the customer (too tight, too bright perhaps), the customer's friends and family may not like the product, the customer may have expected better quality, the product may take up too much time, either to buy, to install or to learn how to use it, or even the product may never arrive or may arrive too late – this is a common fear of Internet shoppers. Products that disappoint are unlikely to be bought again or recommended to others.

total product offering
the total package that makes up, and surrounds, the product, including all supporting features such as branding, packaging, servicing and warranties

research focus

Lukas, B.A., Whitwell, G.J. and Heide, J.B. (2013) 'Why do customers get more than they need? How organizational culture shapes product capability decisions', *Journal of Marketing*, **77 (1): 1–12.**

It is a fundamental marketing principle that products should be designed to match customers' needs, yet many products are over-designed, i.e. they *more* than meet those needs. This paper examines why.

THE TOTAL PRODUCT OFFERING

Thanks to modern manufacturing techniques, most products can be copied by competitors with relative ease – and often made more cheaply than the originals. Firms rarely compete on the basis of their products' physical features alone; they offer their customers much more than that. One product may offer better value than others, or better after-sales service, or come in a handier packet, or it may enhance the customer's image (perhaps because it is a more desirable brand). Mass-produced products are usually differentiated from each other by their additional characteristics rather than by their fundamentals.

CORE BENEFITS (OR THE CORE PRODUCT)

A product's main reason for existence is called its core benefit. This is the simplest possible answer to an expressed need: no frills, no branding or packaging, no warranties or service promises, just the most basic reason why that product would be needed. The core benefit of a food product is to provide nutrition or satisfy hunger. A coat is needed to keep a person warm. Medicine is meant to cure or relieve an illness.

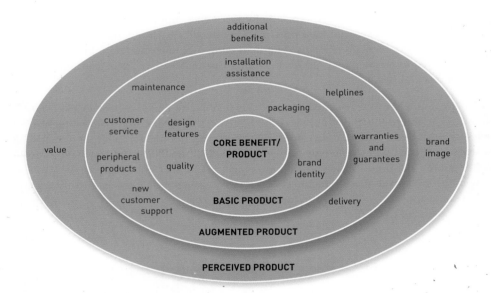

EXHIBIT 6.1 The total product offering

Many people claim that there is no such thing as a new need; just new or different ways of solving an old problem, i.e. satisfying that need. For example, riding horses was an improvement over walking from one place to another, trains replaced the horses, then came cars, then aeroplanes. The transport problem is being solved in new and different ways. Electric light replaced gas for lighting, which in turn had replaced paraffin and candles, which in turn had replaced tallow wicks. The core benefit of all these things is to light the dark.

Marketers must be sure that their products satisfy a need in its most basic sense. Products that do not offer a sound core benefit will usually fail. No matter how precious the metals they are made of, or how many jewels are used to decorate them, watches must keep good time. No matter how cheap it is, a washing powder that does not get clothes clean has little chance of success; it does not deliver the core benefit it was bought for.

A product's primary task is to fulfil its basic function; to satisfy that core need. The next stage is to consider how to enhance its appeal to customers. This requires a thorough understanding of what customers want from this type of product, as well as awareness of what is already being offered by the competition.

In a monopoly situation, where there is only one provider, that company can get away with offering just the bare minimum. If there is no choice, customers have to put up with whatever is available, however poor the product. When there are multiple suppliers, they have to compete with each other for customers. There will therefore be a variety of products available, all designed to meet the same basic needs. Customers have choices as to what to eat or wear, which hamburger or trainers to buy. With choice comes the opportunity for customers to express their individuality in the way they make this choice. They will choose the products and services that have the most value to them. An understanding of how customers see value gives the organisation a chance to make a product offer that matches consumer preferences better than the competition's products do.

Most products on sale offer the same core benefit, and so the choice is often made on the basis of what else the products offer; on their points of difference. It may be the flavour of the burger, the type of bun it comes in, the restaurant where it is served, the extras, the way it is packaged. These things all form part of the total product and are illustrated in Exhibit 6.1 above.

BASIC PRODUCT

The basic product is the product stripped down to its essentials: its features (for shower gel this might be scent, ingredients, etc.), quality level, visual identity (e.g. brand name and logo) and packaging (is the shower gel in a bottle or a squeezy tube that hangs?). These things are the means by which the core benefit (e.g. cleansing) is delivered and, to the consumer's thinking, they add up to the product itself. These product attributes may be used to judge the product against competitors' offerings and assess how well it meets the customer's needs.

monopoly

a market in which there is only one supplier

basic product

a bundle of essential characteristics; a product described in terms of the features that deliver its core benefit (e.g. the ingredients of a soft drink – fizzy orange) without reference to service or other more sophisticated elements

visual identity

all the outward trappings of the brand, e.g. logo, name, colours and packaging

These products all share the same core benefit, though they differ in other ways.

© Dave Pickton

global focus: I'll have the usual please

Unfortunately, you may not be able to get your usual product abroad. There is an ever-increasing number of global brands available but, although they may look the same as the ones at home, there are sometimes subtle differences.

Take Coca-Cola, for example. The US drink is not quite the same as the one you can buy in parts of Asia, where it has more sugar added. McDonald's? Well, you can hardly sell hamburgers in India where the cow is sacred, so those burgers are made of lamb instead. Then there's the strange story of the Mars bar. Mars was founded in the USA – and Britain. The first company was the US one, and it was so successful that its founder could see no reason to change. However, as is the way of the world, his son wanted to make improvements. Frustrated by his father's blocking his ambitions, the son emigrated to England where he set up his own company.

Mr Mars Senior's bestselling line in the USA was Milky Way. The new British company started with the same product but called it the Mars bar instead. Eventually father and son, and the two companies, were reunited. However, the Mars bar and Milky Way are still confused – if you know someone who is going to the USA, ask them to bring you a Mars bar and see what you get.

AUGMENTED PRODUCT

The next level of the total product model contains supporting features. Among these are guarantees, service network, delivery, after-sales service and credit facilities. These can be an important source of differentiation from the competition. They enhance the product offering and can be used to counter objections or resolve doubts in a customer's mind. For example, a guarantee reassures a customer who is worried about quality and a credit agreement helps convince a customer who is concerned about the price.

As such extras are not physically part of the product, they can usually be changed without modifying the basic product itself. Fiat offered a 12-year anti-perforation warranty on the bodywork of its cars. The cars were the same as in previous years, so the basic product was the same, there was no change in production, only the augmented product changed – and could easily be changed again. Despite there being no change in the way the cars were produced, Fiat will have incurred some costs in this alteration to the augmented product, especially if there were claims made under the warranty. A balance always needs to be struck between increased cost and increased perceived value.

PERCEIVED PRODUCT

The outer ring of the total product model (see Exhibit 6.1) is the perceived product. Customers' perceptions of a product vary, e.g. different customers have different views on what a product is worth or how fashionable it is. Perception involves the way in which we interpret our world and is built from our life experiences and our personalities. We have different likes and dislikes, different tastes – that is largely why suppliers offer us a choice of products.

One of the big challenges of marketing is to ensure that customers perceive a product in the way that is intended. If there is a mismatch of customer perception and supplier intention, then there is a problem. For example, when Sunny Delight was launched, it was positioned as a healthy drink for children – as one that children would like the taste of and parents would feel was doing them good. Children did like the taste but parents did not share Procter and Gamble's view of the product's healthy qualities. There was a rethink, a redesign and a relaunch.

Products provide more benefits than just the core ones. A car's core benefit may be flexible travel – there is no need to go to specific departure or arrival points, such as bus stations or airports, at specific times, and they also carry one or several people, with luggage if required. All cars provide this benefit and so a customer's choice of car will depend upon the other rings in the total product model (see Exhibit 6.1) and upon individual preference. Some people want fast cars, some want safe cars, some want cars that keep them cool, some want enough room for the whole family and others want cars that are easy to park. In a competitive market, the customer's perception of the total product (is it fast, safe, roomy, etc.?) is the main determinant of their choice.

A NOTE ON BRANDS

The American Marketing Association defines a brand as the 'name, term, design, symbol, or any other feature that identifies one seller's good or service as distinct from those of other sellers'. Branding spans two levels in the total product model. A brand's visual identity is part of the basic product: the brand name, and its distinctive appearance helps customers to recognise and differentiate the product and signal its level of quality. Brand image is also an important part of the customer's perception of the product and so fits into the model's outer ring. Branding is covered in more detail in Chapter 11 and the role of promotion to communicate a brand's distinctive characteristics and associations is explained in Chapter 8.

PRODUCT TYPES

There are millions of different types of product available so product managers find it helpful to group similar products together so they can more easily compare and contrast competing products (Exhibit 6.2).

CONSUMER PRODUCTS

The following are some common product categories. There is overlap and some products may fit more than one category. For example, shampoo is both a non-durable good and a convenience good – and it is usually categorised as FMCG.

Durable goods

These products are expected to last a considerable length of time. They are not used up all at once but can be used repeatedly, for example a washing machine is expected to wash many loads of clothes; a car should be able to make a large number of journeys.

Non-durable goods

These products are used up in the process of consumption. They do not last. Fruit is eaten. Soap dissolves.

Service products

Services cannot be stored at all. Normally they are used there and then. You watch a film and are left with only a memory (and possibly a ticket stub). You get off the bus and have no further claim on it. Services present marketers with particular challenges and will be discussed in more depth in the next chapter.

impulse goods

spur-of-the-moment purchases, i.e. not pre-planned, e.g. flowers bought at the station on the way home

emergency goods

goods infrequently purchased but needed at short notice, e.g. rain capes, sun hats, plasters

shopping goods

carry a relatively high risk, perhaps because they are a high price or it may be that the cost of product failure is high

Convenience goods

These are products that customers buy frequently and think little about. They are relatively cheap and have many close substitutes so they need strong branding and/or eye-catching colours and designs to make them stand out from the crowd. There are a number of sub-categories of convenience good:

- Impulse goods are spur-of-the-moment purchases, i.e. not pre-planned, e.g. an ice cream bought while in a queue or flowers bought at the station on the way home.

- Staple goods (or essential goods) are purchased regularly, perhaps always kept in the cupboard or fridge (e.g. coffee, milk, shampoo).

- Emergency goods are infrequently purchased but needed at short notice (e.g. rain capes, sun hats, plasters). Such products may be location-specific (rain capes sell well at Disney World and Wimbledon) and have a high value to customers at that time, so their prices can be higher than other convenience goods.

ACTIVITY

© Dave Pickton

Classify the products in the photo. Are they:

- impulse goods?
- staples?
- emergency purchases?

FMCG are a form of convenience good, but in this case looked at from the retailer's point of view. They are the products that move off the shelves quickly and so need frequent restocking, e.g. toothpaste, washing-up liquid, instant coffee.

Shopping goods

Shopping goods carry a higher associated risk for a customer than convenience products do. They may be more expensive or it may be that the costs (either monetary or in terms of inconvenience or loss of self-esteem) associated with product failure are high. Customers usually shop around to find the right car, stereo, furniture, necklace or lawn mower (hence the name shopping goods). For many, shopping for such things is an enjoyable leisure activity in its own right. Customers are likely to spend some time over the decision-making process, assessing the options, seeking information and opinions, trying things out. These products are therefore sometimes referred to as high-involvement purchases, i.e. the customer gets very involved in the decision-making. For more on decision-making processes, see Chapter 3.

Speciality goods

Speciality goods are unusual, and often quite expensive, products which appeal to a relatively limited customer set. They are commonly sold in niche markets, for example: model aeroplanes, high spec computers, wedding clothes, horses and classic cars. Speciality goods may be high-risk and so customers may need extensive emotional support and encouragement from the supplier before they buy. This often means that they are sold through limited outlets (see exclusive distribution in Chapter 9) by highly trained staff.

high-involvement purchases

purchases that customers expend time and effort on, usually high cost or high risk, e.g. cars, holidays, wedding dresses

speciality goods

unusual, probably quite pricey, products

Consumer products	Examples
Durable goods	Fridges, bicycles
Non-durable goods	Fresh food, toiletries
Services	Theatre seats, haircuts

Convenience goods:
   Impulse buys
   Staples
   Emergency
	Snacks, flowers
	Bread, washing-up liquid
	Headache pills, tissues

Shopping goods	Mobile phones, cars
Speciality goods	Antiques, sports cars
b2b/industrial products	**Examples**
Capital goods	Fork-lift trucks, computers
Accessories	Screwdrivers, hard hats
Raw materials	Flour, steel
Sub-assemblies/components	Engines, wheels
Supplies	Stationery, paper cups
Services	Cleaning, accountancy

EXHIBIT 6.2 Product types

b2b AND INDUSTRIAL PRODUCTS

Businesses and other organisations buy enormous amounts of products. While a consumer is likely to buy one car at a time, a business might buy a whole fleet. Some products are sold to both consumer and business markets (though the selling process will be different), e.g. stationery items, others are designed specifically to meet the needs of organisational customers, e.g. hand dryers.

Capital goods

capital goods
(fixed assets)

substantial purchases that
are not used up in one go
but are expected to be used
multiple times

Capital goods are durable products (i.e. they are designed to last for a number of years), such as machinery and buildings. They are usually high cost, bought infrequently and carry high potential risk. Consequently, great care is normally taken over these purchases.

Accessories

These are smaller capital items, e.g. chairs, shelving, hand tools such as screwdrivers. They support the production process. As they are lower cost, they represent a lower financial risk to a company. However, some accessories are essential and their failure may have far-reaching consequences so not all are low risk. For example, a hand tool that breaks may cause serious injury. The total product still plays a part in the differentiation of such products.

Raw materials

generic products

goods that have no
discernible difference from
each other; often used to
mean unbranded goods

Raw materials are goods that will be processed, and added to, by the manufacturing process. Together they become the finished article. For example, cotton is knitted into socks; crude oil is refined and becomes petrol (and a number of other products); water, hops and yeast are brewed into beer. At this level it may be difficult to distinguish one supplier's products from another since, by their nature, raw materials may be similar – though some may be higher quality than others. They are often generic products; however, service, delivery terms, technical assistance, financial arrangements and many other aspects can be exploited to make the organisation different and thus the preferred supplier (see Exhibit 6.1).

Sub-assemblies, components and parts

These products have already been through a manufacturing process but are not finished goods. They are bought by businesses to incorporate into their own products. For example, Levi's buys denim fabric to make into jeans, Nokia buys microchips for its mobile phones and Siemens buys condensers to put into its fridges.

Supplies

Numerous minor items are used in the production process, and they are important in the smooth running of the whole process. Companies depend on such things as soap, stationery, pens, copier paper and cleaning materials. These are not capital goods as they are non-durable (i.e. they are used up relatively quickly rather than being reused over and over).

Services

Manufacturing businesses rely on efficient machinery so maintenance and repair services are important to them. All workplaces need regular cleaning. Buildings must be painted and repaired. In addition, there are a large number of business services, such as consultancy, accountancy, legal advice and IT support. The special nature of services is discussed in Chapter 7.

There are many different ways to categorise products and different markets have their own preferred descriptors. The product types presented above refer to basic products. However, most products are not generic products – they are branded.

BRANDING

'A brand is an idea or an image of a product or a service provided by the organisation. Branding is the marketing of this idea or image so that more and more people recognise it and become aware of the brand' (CIM, n.d.). This section will discuss branding as part of the total product offering. The strategic nature of branding, and how strong brands are built, will be considered in Chapter 11.

The function of a brand

WHAT IS A BRAND?

Brands are differentiated by their unique names, logos and packaging and other meaningful associations held in customers' minds that make up the brand image (see Chapter 11). The term 'branding' seems to originate with American ranchers, who branded their cattle to assert their ownership. Each branding iron was unique and made an indelible, identifying mark. That mark was an assurance that the animal in question was from that particular ranch and came to be used as a guide to the quality of the beef. Business branding originates with skilled workers who made especially good tools or leather, and later with manufacturers who could provide consistent quality. They realised that their superior goods were worth more than their rivals' so they labelled their products to make them easily recognisable. Through the latter part of the twentieth century, branding developed alongside marketing as a managerial process, although some of today's well-known brand names existed as company names long before they became part of a branding strategy, e.g. Bank of Scotland, Swan Vesta matches, Daimler motor cars, His Master's Voice records (HMV), De Kuyper. A strong brand brings with it a wealth of quality, value and high performance cues and some even become intrinsic parts of consumer lifestyles.

The growth of branding as a strategy has caused a change in emphasis within organisations. Companies used to be centred on the production of goods or services. The emphasis was very much on quality and efficiency (see Chapter 1 for production and product orientation); now the value of brands is understood and they are protected and nurtured.

THE ADVANTAGES OF BRANDING PRODUCTS

Companies invest millions in the development and protection of their brands. A strong brand is seen as key to commercial success, providing the following advantages (and more):

- high brand equity
- increased product awareness levels
- the ability to charge a premium price

brand equity
the monetary value of a brand

- reduced susceptibility to price wars
- competitive edge
- a sound basis for building strong customer relationships
- higher likelihood of repeat purchases
- retail leverage
- the fact that new products have a better chance of success thanks to the brand name.

Brands must be built in order to become strong and benefit from the advantages listed above. It is not enough just to attach a name and a logo to a product. Nor do brands automatically maintain their strength. They must be nurtured and carefully managed (see Chapters 8 and 11 for more on building brands).

HIGH BRAND EQUITY

A well-known brand adds value to a product both from the customer perspective and from the company's. Brands may be the most valuable assets that a company has. For more on brand equity, see Chapter 11.

INCREASED PRODUCT AWARENESS

Clearly, it is crucial that potential customers should be aware of a product. It is the first stage on their journey to buying it (see sequential models in Chapter 8). One of the key roles of advertising is to build that awareness and an easily recognised brand makes that task much easier. Product and packaging design play key roles here as well, by making the product more visible and reinforcing the brand's values.

PREMIUM PRICING AND REDUCED SUSCEPTIBILITY TO PRICE WARS

premium price
a relatively high price

A good brand name helps a firm achieve a premium price for its products. Think of the differences in the prices of trainers. The well-known brands, e.g. Nike and Reebok, can charge much more for their products than lesser-known brands. It is not just a question of having a well-known name. The strength of the brand depends upon the values associated with it in that particular market. Marks & Spencer is a well-known brand but they cannot get away with charging Nike prices for their trainers, even if the quality is comparable.

Without a brand, a firm will have to settle for a commodity position in the market where low prices alone drive sales. Some firms actively choose this position, e.g. the makers of generic pharmaceuticals, but it does not sit well with the concept of marketing as a series of complex management tasks leading to greater success for the organisation. In very price-conscious markets, e.g. children's shoes and clothing, or in economic downturns, marketers can come under great pressure to compete on price but this might devalue their brand (assuming it already has a reputation). Aaker (2002) argues that pressure to compete on prices can even undermine attempts to build up a brand as one of the main impetuses for branding, i.e. the differentiation from the competition that allows a firm to charge premium prices is removed.

COMPETITIVE EDGE

A branded product simplifies shopping by assisting with a customer's product adoption process (see Chapter 3). If the marketing communications have worked well, then the potential customer will already have built up a set of associations with the brand, short-circuiting a lot of the information searching that they might otherwise have to do. This is good for customers as they save time and effort (this assumes that their image of the brand is correct) and is certainly an advantage to the branded product as it is likely to be preferred to other unknown or less well thought of products.

BUILDING CUSTOMER RELATIONSHIPS

The strength of the customer's relationship with a brand is central to that brand's growth. The relationship is normally between the customer and the brand itself rather than between the customer and the brand's owner, which may even be a company that the customer has never heard of. There are many big companies which own many brands that do not bear their owner's name. For example, Diageo is the owner of a large number of drinks brands (Smirnoff, Baileys, Guinness, Johnny Walker, Captain Morgan) and yet 'I'll have a Diageo please' is never heard in bars (see 'Brand types' in Chapter 11).

The importance of this brand relationship has prompted companies to develop various relationship-building activities which establish a two-way flow of communication with their customers and encourage them to integrate brands into their lives. Examples of these activities include club memberships, Facebook pages, Twitter accounts, fan pages and other website activities, loyalty schemes and reward cards, branded events (e.g. the V Festival), registration of warranties, and promotional products such as T-shirts and bags with the brand name and logo on.

product adoption process
the stages a buyer goes through before purchasing a product

ACTIVITY

What do these car marques say to you? What ideas or images form in your mind in connection with each of the brands?

How does Porsche's logo compare to that of Mercedes or Mini? What do the differences say about each brand's personality?

Source: David MG/Shutterstock.com

Source: Charnstir/Shutterstock.com

Source: 360b/Shutterstock.com

The Porsche, Mini Cooper and Mercedes logos are the registered trademarks of each respective corporation. Use of the logos here does not imply endorsement of the organisations.

reward cards
similar in appearance to credit cards, used to register points given away with purchases (e.g. Nectar card, Tesco Clubcard)

Brand communities

The number and strength of brand communities is increasing rapidly, thanks to the Internet in general and social media in particular. Membership of a brand community is a significant part of a growing number of people's social lives. Muniz and O'Guinn (2001: 412) first coined the term 'brand community' and they defined it as 'a specialised, non-geographically bound community, based on a structured set of social relations among admirers of a brand'. Brand communities are characterised by a set of shared attitudes towards, and beliefs about, the brand (shared consciousness), rituals and traditions connected with the brand and a sense of moral guardianship for the brand. A brand that is liked well enough to inspire a community to grow around it clearly has a number of loyal consumers and therefore this is generally held to be a positive thing for the brand – though members of brand communities can be the brand's greatest critics as well as its greatest fans. Brand communities can be very possessive towards brands and the importance of understanding their views is illustrated by the reaction of loyal customers to the introduction of a new recipe for Coca-Cola. They boycotted the product and sales slumped so badly that the original recipe had to be reinstated. New Coke lasted about three months.

Experiential marketing

One way in which marketing programmes aim to strengthen customer–brand relationships is by creating immersive experiences that bring products and brands to life, for example in stores, at events or online through the use of interactive branded websites, games and apps. Experiential marketing programmes aim to connect with customers on both a rational and emotional level, ensuring the product or service is always remembered. For example, Nike is a pioneer in the use of movement tracking technology through the use of multi-sports tracking sensors embedded in watches and wristbands. The company has even developed Nike Fuel, its own universal measurement of movement. Through the Nike+ community customers can set goals, track their progress and connect and compete with other runners online and at larger scale events and experiences such as the worldwide Nike Women Victory Tour.

REPEAT PURCHASES

Most human beings instinctively avoid unnecessary risk. Buying things represents at least a financial risk in that money may be wasted if the product is not fit for purpose. There are other possible risks too. For example, there is ego risk if the product is unflattering (e.g. clothes) or ridiculed by others (e.g. an unpopular scent), or physical risk if the product turns out to be unsafe (e.g. faulty machinery). A brand that has been bought before and found to be satisfactory reduces these risks and so people are more likely to buy that trusted brand again.

A good experience of a brand results in a happy customer who continues to purchase. Conversely, a bad experience can lead to an unhappy customer who may very well reject future offerings bearing this brand, no matter how attractive the offering appears to be. Worse still, they may tell their friends, family and acquaintances of their bad experience, influencing them against the brand. Attraction and retention are key words when thinking about the development of a brand.

RETAIL LEVERAGE

In many countries, large retailers have enormous power when it comes to setting prices and dictating terms of purchase and sale. Tesco, for example, is one of the largest companies in the world, much larger than many of the manufacturers who supply it. Tesco therefore has a great deal of buying power (see Chapter 9). However, there are some branded products that are so popular that even a retailer as powerful as Tesco is unlikely

experiential marketing

provides customers with in-depth, personally relevant experiences with products to create a lasting impression either online, in the physical world or both

Nike+ Run Club app

to leave them off its shelves, e.g. Heinz Tomato Ketchup, Heinz Baked Beans, Kellogg's cereals, Coca-Cola, Kleenex tissues.

NEW PRODUCT SUCCESS

Even the most innovative and high-quality new products struggle to make headway in today's markets. Many entrepreneurs have launched seemingly superb products only to watch them fail. A strong brand gives that vulnerable new product a much better chance of success. The customers can call on their experience of previous products of the same brand, and transfer those brand values to the new product.

brand values
how a brand is perceived by the market

This reduces the risk associated with trying something new and so the new product is more likely to make it into their evoked set of products, and therefore they are more likely to try it. Take the BBC iPlayer, for example. It was launched into a market that was struggling to gain consumer acceptance. ITV and Channel 4's catch-up TV services were not attracting sufficient viewers but the BBC's new product changed the market profile completely by reassuring reluctant viewers and encouraging them to try the catch-up service. Now all three services are doing well and others, e.g. Sky, have joined them. The market has continued to grow further with new products for recording and catch-up viewing on numerous devices from set-top boxes, smartphones and games machines such as the Nintendo Wii.

For more on branding, including brand components, types of brand, branding strategies and brand equity, see Chapter 11.

---

research focus

Belén del Rio, A., Vazquez, R. and Iglesia, V. (2001) 'The effects of brand associations on consumer response', *Journal of Consumer Marketing*, **18 (5): 410–25.**

This paper studies the dimensions of brand image by focusing on the value of the brand as perceived by consumers. Four categories of functions are identified: guarantee, personal identification, social identification and status. These functions are shown to have a positive influence on the consumer's willingness to recommend the brand, pay a **price premium** and accept **brand extensions**.

PRODUCT DEVELOPMENT

New products are the lifeblood of a company. Competitors improve their product offerings all the time and customers usually prefer to buy the latest thing. They want this year's fashions, the technology with the latest features, the most convenient household products, the healthier version or the greener version or just the more economical one. This philosophy of constant innovation, especially in consumer goods markets, has been adhered to by leading companies for many years. However, it is important to plan and to manage the process carefully. Too much innovation too quickly can be disruptive and make product lines too complicated to manage effectively. As the complexity of the management task increases, so the organisation's costs rise and its profit margins shrink. To maximise its profit potential, the company needs to be sure that any additional products add more value than the costs they create.

Developing consumer goods

ethical focus: built to last?

It's always frustrating when a product breaks or stops working, but have you ever stopped to wonder if failure might be all part of the plan? The idea of built-in obsolescence isn't new. All kinds of products from light bulbs and washing machines to PCs, printer ink cartridges, video games and even motor cars *could* be designed to last as long as possible, but in practice they are built to last just long enough. This is a marketing idea, not a technological limitation. Some of the earliest lightbulbs ever produced are still burning brightly more than 100 years after they were created having burned for more than a million continuous hours. Modern LED or energy saving bulbs are sold at a premium on the basis that they outlast traditional filament bulbs, yet few promise anywhere near that length of service.

As prices of domestic appliances continue to fall, it is often cheaper in the short term to buy a new product than get an old one fixed. But what is the real cost of such a throwaway mentality? The new appliance is using valuable resources in its manufacture, while the old one may be adding to a landfill site somewhere. In the very long term, it could cost us the ability to make such things at all.

In the gadget industry, critics suggest we are close to crisis point. The majority of contemporary smartphone devices cannot even be opened to replace a battery. Apple has introduced proprietary screws to prevent devices from being serviced by independent repair shops. Add in software upgrades that aren't compatible with existing hardware and the time it takes for a brand new gadget to become outdated or just plain dysfunctional is surprisingly short.

Consumers aren't the only losers here, the environment is too. Due to a lack of clear economic incentives and methods, globally only a fraction of smartphones are sold or traded for a new one. These unwanted ecologically damaging devices languish in drawers for a while before ending up in landfills.

Sources: Spinks (2015); centennialbulb.org (n.d.)

Innovation is expensive and depends upon the support of top management and an organisational culture that encourages new ideas. The new product development process can take a number of forms. It may be an informal exercise in encouraging ideas, or a formal, structured approach with its own staff and facilities dedicated to the research of changing customer needs and the development of new ways to fulfil them.

New products do not have to be totally new inventions. In fact, truly new products are very rare. Even those that seem to be so innovative, e.g. tablets, iPhones, music downloads, are really just improvements on previous music (gramophones, CD players, tape machines) or communications products (landlines, fax machines, telegrams). Most new products are modifications of previous offerings rather than new-to-the-world products. So the PC manufacturers make their laptops lighter and with better screens, mobile phones have more features, skirt lengths go up (or down), processed food has less fat or less sugar or more vitamins, etc.

THE IMPORTANCE OF INNOVATION

Some industries compete largely on the strength of their new ideas (e.g. computer games, mobile phones, convenience foods), and for firms in these industries it is particularly important to invest in research and development. They need original, well-researched product ideas in order to stay competitive. Just how innovative an organisation and its products are depends on a number of things, including:

- how old the product, or the technology the product is based on, is – the older the technology, the more likely it is to be replaced; newer technologies may be able to be refined

- the size of the organisation – small firms are often more inventive, it is easier for new ideas to get heard; unfortunately, they often lack the resources to develop an idea fully and so may lose out to a larger firm

- how competitive the market is – having lots of competitors may drive a firm to innovate; however, monopolies are more likely to have the money, if they see the need

- how quickly consumer tastes change – anything that could be considered a fashion item will change frequently; anything that customers will tire of (films?) will be replaced regularly.

New products can be used to:

- increase or defend market share by offering more choice within the range or by updating older products (e.g. Ford has developed people-carrier versions of most of its models; mobile phone makers frequently release new models)

- appeal to a different market segment (e.g. Guinness bitter, Häagen-Dazs frozen yoghurt)

- maintain a reputation as a leading-edge company (e.g. Apple iPhones and watches)

- diversify into new markets and thereby spread risk (e.g. Dyson hairdryers)

- improve relationships within distribution channels (e.g. Allied Domecq offering its Baskin-Robbins franchisees further franchise opportunities in Dunkin' Donuts and Togo's)

- make better use of resources such as production capacity (e.g. some chocolate bars can be made on the same production machinery as others)

- even out peaks and troughs in demand (e.g. ice cream parlours selling baked potatoes; Father's Day was invented by greetings card companies).

TYPES OF NEW PRODUCT

Most new products' newness stems from innovation in the basic, augmented or perceived product rather than from true innovation in the product's core (see total product offering). Very few are designed for an entirely new purpose, i.e. to meet a new need or one that was not met by any product before.

New products can be classified as follows:

- *Innovative product*: likely to be a technological or medical breakthrough, e.g. Biodiesel (a vegetable oil-based fuel), satnav, laser eye surgery, e-books. There are relatively few of these types of new-to-the-market products and services. Innovative new products may be protected by a patent, requiring imitators to obtain a licence to produce their version or risk being sued.

- *Replacement product*: more common than innovative ones. The customer need has been satisfied by a previous product but the replacement product does it better (or at least differently), e.g. multimedia devices are replacing CD players just as they (more or less) replaced record players and tape decks; the latest iPhone model supersedes the one before.

- *Variant product*: many companies frequently introduce new, related products to their ranges. These may be temporary or more permanent additions, e.g. Kit Kat Chunky (long term), Ford Fiesta Zetec Red and Black (special editions).

- *Me-too product*: these are imitations of products already on the market, e.g. the many tablets and other multimedia devices that followed the iPad and Kindle on to the market. It makes sense to let others do the costly market research and development first – to let them take the risks.

- *Relaunched product*: this is not really a new product at all. Rather, the physical characteristics of the basic product may not be altered (or only slightly) but the total product offering has changed. There will be a different marketing strategy, perhaps changing the emphasis on product benefits, e.g. Airtime, the group video chatting service originally launched in 2011, was relaunched as a free iOS and Android app in 2016.

digital focus: clockwork power

As the pace of technological change gathers speed, there are, apparently, fewer and fewer areas where customers might be surprised by new-to-the-world ideas. New and wonderful electronic gizmos, both for entertainment and for more serious applications, are everywhere and have become the norm. Yet it is still possible to be surprised. Take, for example, the Bayliss wind-up radio, which exploited old clockwork technology, applied modern techniques and produced a fully portable power source that is now being exploited elsewhere – e.g. in powering laptop computers, satellite navigation systems and even for recharging mobile phones by use of a device included in a pair of hiking boots (every step generates power for the user's phone).

Initially, Trevor Bayliss found it next to impossible to find a manufacturer prepared to back him. They were unable to see the potential of his radical, old idea.

THE PRODUCT DEVELOPMENT PROCESS

Proposed new products are evaluated at each stage in their development process. If an idea is not going to make it to launch, then it is better to eliminate it as early as possible. The product's development costs mount up as it moves further through the development process and as these costs increase, failure results in greater financial (and possibly reputational) loss.

It can be dangerous to rely on customers to judge a new-to-the-world product idea. Sometimes new products fulfil a need that it had not occurred to customers *could* be met, and so it is not really possible to assess customer reaction accurately before they see the finished item. People were perfectly happy with landlines before mobile phones were introduced and it took a little while for them to realise how important it was to be permanently in touch. Portable music was unheard of before Sony brought out the Walkman – now no train journey is complete without earbuds and a personal playlist.

The model in Exhibit 6.3 shows the stages of the product development process. Product development should not be seen as a one-off or ad hoc activity but as a continuous process.

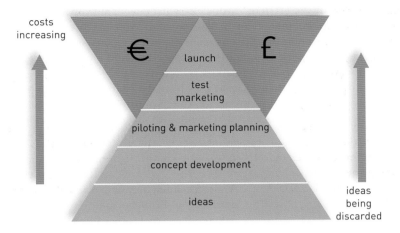

EXHIBIT 6.3 New product development process

That way, there will be a consistent stream of new product ideas available to be taken to the next stage and ready to replace older products when their time comes.

Constant monitoring and evaluation are essential in this product development process. The aim is that only the right products should progress while those with little chance of commercial success are deleted as early as possible. The number of products in development reduces at each stage as some are rejected. However, the costs associated with the development of each product mount as it goes through the stages. So the costs associated with the product development process escalate, and the number of viable product ideas reduce, as time passes.

IDEA STAGE (GENERATION AND INITIAL SCREENING OF IDEAS)

Ideas for new products may be generated internally or externally. Some companies are technology led, e.g. Dyson and Apple, and get the inspiration for most of their new products from their own product research. They have substantial research and development departments whose job it is to design technologically advanced products. Other companies, particularly the more market-orientated ones, take their lead from their customers and look to develop products that match explicitly stated customer needs. Others may employ a marketing agency which specialises in new product ideas.

Market research seems a sound way to find ideas for new products and it will certainly help establish customers' views on the firm's existing product offering and, by establishing what is wrong with it, suggest new ideas. It is better at uncovering customer needs than at finding specific product solutions, as customers are rarely able to imagine the design of a product that does not exist.

The rise of the Internet and social media in particular has of course made it easier than ever to enlist the help of others in the idea generation process. Crowdsourcing is a term used to describe the practice of seeking input from a large number of people, typically via the Internet. Starbucks Coffee Company has pioneered the practice of crowdsourcing since the launch of its successful platform, MyStarbucksIdea.com, in 2008. The site's introduction

Ted Talks:
designing for humanity

crowdsourcing
where companies or individuals engage a large number of people (a crowd) to contribute to a specific project or cause often related to efficiency, innovation or problem-solving

states simply, 'You know better than anyone else what you want from Starbucks. So tell us'. In its first year of operation more than 70,000 consumers did just that: submitting ideas for better products, ways to improve the customer experience, and providing valuable feedback on products and experiences. Starbucks saves time and money on market research and avoids costly mistakes by implementing hundreds of user generated ideas each year. Customers are keen to share their ideas as they have the chance to create a better product for themselves and to feel part of an active and supportive community of like-minded people. Customers can get annoyed when companies make changes without asking their opinion. By *engaging* instead of simply *serving* the crowd, Starbucks has created a win-win situation for the company and its customers (Gurley, 2014).

There are many techniques to generate new product ideas: from brainstorming (a lively group session where ideas spark other ideas and all are captured, none discounted or disparaged), to analysing customer complaints and competitive products, to establishing original research facilities. 3M (the makers of Scotch Tape and Post-it Notes) deliberately encourages a culture of creativity and allows its employees to spend some of their time on personal projects that may, or may not, produce ideas the company can use.

At the start of the development process, the focus is on generating as many ideas as possible. The impractical ones are then quickly discarded while the possibles will progress to the next stage.

ACTIVITY

Be a market researcher briefly.

1   Ask some of your friends, family or classmates what new communications products they would like. *Do not lead or prompt them.*

2   Then try asking them what is wrong with the products they already own (computers, mobile phones, telephones, etc.) and if they can think of any improvements to them.

How many new product possibilities have you discovered? Which technique generated more?

digital focus: Google's global student app challenge

When it comes to solving a problem, it's generally held that two heads are better than one, but why stop there? In 2014 Google launched its Admob Student App Challenge – a crowdsourcing contest for great app ideas. There are regional and global prizes available to entrants who pour their imagination and creativity into building an app (either Android or iOS) using the Admob platform, which also allows the apps to earn money. Students must also submit a business plan.

The first challenge took place in 2014 and received hundreds of entries from 90 countries. By the time shortlisted apps were announced to the world they had already been downloaded more than 300,000 times. The first global winner was Johns Hopkins University student Phani Gaddipati who devised an electronic flashcards app to help with revision. Similar in style to the old-fashioned paper flashcards, users can create their own cards and organise them into stacks to test recall and record and monitor performance. While prizewinners including Phani enjoyed a trip to San Francisco and the chance to host their apps on Google Play, the real winner was Google itself. What better way to demonstrate the potential of its Admob platform to ambitious developers worldwide?

Sources: AdMob by Google (n.d.); ideaCONNECTION (n.d.).

CONCEPT STAGE (DEVELOPMENT AND TESTING OF THE PRODUCT CONCEPT)

A product concept is much more than just an idea. The product has to be thought through from both technical and consumer, or end-user, points of view. This may involve the production of drawings, detailed descriptions and theoretical models – all of them trying to assess whether the idea will work. As well as testing the product design and consumer reactions, the concept should be examined to see whether or not it fits in with the organisation's marketing strategy. Is it a product that will add to and complement the company's existing range of products?

In the motor industry many ideas are floated but get rejected quickly. Those that have potential are passed to the design studio where the proposed car is mocked up, perhaps even as a full-size model that can be seen in three dimensions. Individuals, both inside and outside the organisation, are then shown the model and asked for their opinions.

The product concept is tested both for its viability as a product and as a business proposition. Business analysis involves reviewing costs and sales projections in order to arrive at a profit forecast and to assess the likelihood of this product meeting the company's objectives for it. Products that meet the company's criteria move on to the next stage: product development.

Essentials of product design

research focus

Jindal, R.P., Sarangee, K.R., Echambadi, R. and Lee, S. (2016) 'Designed to succeed: dimensions of product design and their impact on market share', *Journal of Marketing*, 80 (4): 72–89.

This research examines the relationship between product design and market share. Drawing from diverse disciplines such as marketing, industrial design and engineering, the authors conceptualise design as being composed of three distinct product-level dimensions: function, form and ergonomics. Empirical results from several different sources in the US light vehicle industry reveal an important strategic trade-off concerning design capabilities. Firms can either 'design for satisfaction', by investing in both function and ergonomics, or 'design for delight', by investing in form design capabilities so as to reap market share rewards.

PROTOTYPING AND PILOT PRODUCTION

A prototype is a test product. Prototyping and/or pilot production of a product is very costly and so only products with good potential are allowed to get this far. Such products have passed concept tests and are now ready for production, but first the company may make a prototype (or prototypes) in order to conduct further tests. These tests check the safety of the product, its durability, usability, etc. Car manufacturers such as Volvo use crash test dummies to see what happens when the car crashes at various speeds. Toy manufacturers call children in to play with the new toy to see how well it stands up to their misuse. Computer games companies employ people to play and test their prototypes to ensure good gameplay and eliminate bugs and crashes. Many organisations use computer simulations for this stage, especially if the prototype would be expensive to make and/or would require an actual production facility. The results from these tests are used to refine the design before production starts.

Uber driverless cars

Crash Test Dummy

Source: iStock.com/uatp2

Full-scale production is very expensive and so most companies start by making one, or a small number, of the products so that they can test their production plans and make any necessary changes before committing to large-scale manufacture. These initial pilot runs may involve making the product entirely by hand, as setting up a working production line is expensive and time-consuming and may be a waste if the product does not make it to the next stage of the development process. Critical evaluation now takes place, assessing the product in its approximate final form.

MARKETING PLANNING

The marketing planning process may have already begun – sometimes product development stages overlap at least a little. The marketing department have to work out what price to charge, how much advertising and other communication will be required and where and how the product will be sold. They will develop a formal product marketing plan that sets out the product's proposed positioning, their sales targets and other formal marketing objectives. See Chapter 12 for more on the drawing up of marketing plans.

TEST MARKETING STAGE

Concepts will only progress this far if the company believes that those products will sell. They may now be made in small quantities and sold to a small, selected market, usually a geographic region, in order to obtain information about customer reactions. A test market is the market in miniature. The area chosen should represent the whole market as closely as possible in all its key characteristics, e.g. demographics, lifestyles, media, outlets, competition. Not only the product itself, but also all the related marketing mix activities are tested. If the mix works well, then the product may be launched immediately afterwards. Alternatively, the test marketing exercise may suggest modifications to the mix, or that the product should not be launched at all.

Test marketing is expensive and time-consuming and also has the disadvantage of allowing the competition to assess the new product. Competitors may even attempt to spoil a test market, perhaps by deliberately lowering the price of their own products in that area, or launching their own, local promotional campaign. Some have even been known to launch special, limited edition versions of their own products in order to spoil the sales and market research data from the test market.

Test marketing is not essential, only desirable, and the drawbacks may outweigh the benefits. If the new product is a simple modification of an existing one, and the market is already well known and understood, then the product may be launched without exposure to a test market.

LAUNCH (COMMERCIALISATION)

This is the final stage in the product development process. The company is now committed to full-scale manufacture and distribution, and has many decisions to make before the product is ready to be shipped out. All marketing mix elements must be finalised: prices set, promotion booked, packaging arranged, the distribution chain set up and all the operational issues involved in supplying the product to the market resolved. The company's personnel will need to be trained on the new product and enthused about it. Timing is crucial to a successful product launch and therefore there must be a detailed project plan. Companies trading internationally will have to decide which countries to launch in first. Very few will roll out a new product in all their markets at the same time as that would place too great a burden on even a multinational's resources.

The launch of a new-to-the-world product (or even a major innovation on an old one) is a time for the company to celebrate. They might host an event for customers, staff and journalists with the intention of gaining publicity for the new product. The launch of a new consumer product needs to be well publicised as its initial reception and the speed with which early sales build up are often crucial to its long-term success.

New products are launched regularly. The continued existence of many large high-tech corporations relies upon the successful launch of their next product. The producers of computer games frequently battle to be the first to launch the latest technology. Sega used to be a major player in this market, producing its own consoles and equipment, but now they have to be content to produce software for other manufacturers' platforms. Fall behind on the technology and billions of pounds' worth of sales can slip into the hands of competitors. So much depends on the effectiveness with which target markets have been researched, and consumer expectations matched.

New products are launched to replace old ones that no longer have significant markets. Most new products will, unfortunately, fail despite companies' best efforts in their development. There are many reasons for these new product failures including:

- failure to meet consumer expectations of the product (new software often suffers from this)
- consumers' resistance to change: this is simply a preference for the product already used to meet the need – if it still works, why change it?
- insufficient investment in its launch: new products usually need substantial marketing communications budgets to support them and, if they are truly innovative, consumers may need to be educated in their use
- inadequate market research: resulting in a product that does not actually meet an unfulfilled need
- production difficulties: leading to inadequate supply or poor product quality
- distribution issues: for example failing to persuade sufficient retailers to stock the product
- bad timing: a product that takes a long time to develop may be launched into a market that has already moved on, or in which a competitive product is already well established. For example, Google Lively launched in 2008 some five years after its rival Second Life; the timing was doubly bad as 2008 saw the beginning of an economic recession, the product was withdrawn in January 2009. Alternatively, the product may just be ahead of its time – as it could be argued Sinclair's electric car was in the 1980s or the original e-books that failed to catch on in the 1990s.

The time in between a product's launch and its deletion can be viewed as the life of that product and one of the tools available to aid managers with their product planning is the product life cycle.

b2b focus: getting the drinks in

Consumers of premium spirit brands, such as Bacardi light rum and Gordon's gin, can be fierce champions of their favourite brand, claiming it has superior taste and that they can always pick it out. Such spirits are rarely drunk neat though – they are mixed with something else and that something else is usually a larger measure than the alcohol. Take gin and tonic or rum and coke, for example – in both cases there is more mixer than spirit in the drink. How can the superiority of the chosen spirit be best preserved? The answer clearly lies in a premium quality mixer. Mixers are complementary products. They are most commonly bought to go with another product, gin or rum for example.

The Fever-Tree range of mixer drinks was developed to fill this perceived gap in the market. There was a clear need for the product: consumers wanted more natural drinks and most existing mixers were highly artificial and stuffed with additives. Fever-Tree used only the best, exotic natural ingredients, even producing the world's first naturally low-calorie tonic water (no artificial sweeteners; just a blend of fruit sugars, citrus, aromatic botanicals, natural quinine and spring water).

However, it is one thing to come up with a great idea, but quite another to make it into a success. The challenge was to get it to the consumers. To do that, Fever-Tree needed to convince retailers to stock it. They began with sales calls to upmarket hotels and restaurants, including The Ritz and Claridges, but they needed a supermarket stockist if they were to make significant inroads into this market. Positive media coverage in papers such as the *Sunday Times* helped convince Waitrose to stock Fever-Tree and the brand's market share soon increased by a percentage point (a significant amount in a market as large as this one).

Fever-Tree is now available from Tesco, Sainsbury's, Harrods, Fortnum and Mason and many smaller retailers, cafes and bars. It is served in six out of the top 10 restaurants in the world (as voted for by *Restaurant* magazine in 2008). World-renowned chef Ferran Adria turned Fever-Tree Premium Indian Tonic Water into a course in itself: 'Sopa de Fever-Tree tonica'. In the USA, the world's largest mixers market, Fever-Tree was awarded 'Best New Product' at the 2008 Tales of the Cocktail awards. Fever-Tree also won the new brand (SME) award at the Marketing Society's Golden Jubilee Awards 2009.

THE PRODUCT LIFE CYCLE

product life cycle

a product analysis tool based on the idea that a product has life stages: introduction, growth, maturity, decline, deletion

The product life cycle concept is one that has many opponents and many supporters. On the one hand, it has limited usefulness as a management tool since it provides no absolute answers, on the other hand, it does help analyse the market for a product and so can be a helpful decision-making aid. Criticisms of the product life cycle model are discussed below. The position of a product in its life cycle can indicate whether there are likely to be further significant increases in sales or not – and provide pointers on what to do in order to maximise those sales.

The model in Exhibit 6.4 illustrates how products move through a series of stages from introduction to a market to their final replacement with another product. The product's progress is mapped out in a similar way to a human being's progress through life: birth, growing up, reaching maturity, declining into old age and ultimately death – or, in the product's case, deletion. The length of each of the stages varies considerably from product to product; some take a long time to be accepted and so the first, introduction stage may be extensive; some will have long, slow growth, others very rapid and short-lived growth, etc. High fashion products may display a life cycle with very rapid progress through introduction, growth and maturity and equally rapid, if not more rapid, decline and deletion. The difficulty in predicting how long a product will spend in each stage is one of the arguments against the product life cycle model.

THE STAGES OF THE PRODUCT LIFE CYCLE

Introduction

At the introduction stage, sales are low (initially zero) and the product is usually making a loss. The challenge is to get people to try the product. The people most likely to try it are the innovators (see the section on the diffusion of innovations (production adoption) model in Chapter 3) and so marketing efforts are usually directed at them.

innovators
people who are most receptive to new ideas and are first to try out new products

Growth

Sales increase during the growth stage, as does customer understanding and appreciation of the product. This stage is critical to the product's long-term survival as it is now that customers decide whether to make the product one of their regular purchases (in the case of FMCG) or not. Shopping goods such as televisions, are clearly not regular, repeat purchases but consumers may decide to buy a second or third one – or may need a replacement product. Aggressive pricing and intensive promotional campaigns are often used during this stage as competitors fight to capture, and retain, customers.

The product's design is likely to be set during the growth stage. Faults should have been fixed and necessary design improvements made. This is the time to introduce new members of the product range, add features and maybe lower prices. A product with more features may attract more customers. The early majority (see Chapter 3) should be buying the product by now.

early majority
a substantial group of customers who follow early adopters in buying a new product or service

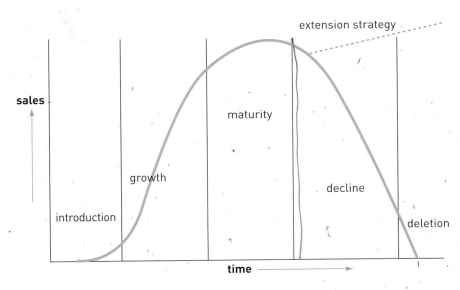

EXHIBIT 6.4 Product life cycle

Maturity

Sales peak during the maturity stage of the life cycle although their growth rate slows as this is now a relatively stable market. Development and launch costs should have been covered so this is the stage at which the greatest profit may be made. Competition hots up in the maturity stage. The market is likely to have been split into numerous segments, for example when chocolate was first introduced to Europe, it was just sold as cocoa to be made into drinks. In today's mature confectionery market, just think how many different types of product, aimed at different types of people, are chocolate-based.

Mature products are likely to be more standardised and also more sophisticated than the original basic ones. This standardisation, along with the increase in volume, makes manufacturing easier and cheaper. However, there may still be a number of product variations. For example, kitchen furniture may have a standard, modular design but come in a choice of colours, finishes, handles, etc. There may also be special editions available for limited time periods.

This is also the time to look for an extension strategy in order to delay decline.

Extension strategies

It may be possible to extend the profitable life of a product which is starting to decline. The product might do better in another market, e.g. in another country or aimed at a different age group. Guinness is a classic example of how successful re-targeting can extend the life of a product. Many years ago, Guinness was regarded as an old person's drink, with its slogan 'Guinness is good for you'. There was a distinct problem: its market was dying – literally. Award-winning advertising helped to make the drink trendy and more appealing to a younger market segment, and so it lives on today.

The product may need to be repositioned in order to bring in new customers. This may be a physical repositioning (e.g. changing the product ingredients, perhaps by reducing the amount of sugar in a soft drink) or a perceptual repositioning (usually with the aid of a marketing communications campaign). Lucozade, for example, was known for many years as a drink for invalids to 'aid recovery'. The product's owners then repositioned the drink as an energy boost for sports people and it assumed a much more youthful, isotonic personality. The brand personality has been changed yet again to become a mixture of a health drink and an energy drink. Each change has been to target different market segments.

Product sales may be increased by persuading existing customers to use more of it, e.g. by finding new uses for it, perhaps in different combinations with other products, or by using the product in a different way (e.g. 100 uses for WD40, or Rice Crispies made into a dessert for children's parties).

There are numerous strategies to try but they need to be planned and implemented before the product goes too far into decline. Despite marketing departments' best efforts, sadly most products do eventually decline and die.

Decline

The decline stage, which companies try to delay for as long as possible, is characterised by falling sales. This may not be as catastrophic as it at first appears, as there are numerous

---

extension strategy

means of prolonging the product life cycle

brand personality

a set of human character traits associated with a brand, e.g. bubbly, elegant or friendly

examples of products being well managed in their decline and producing very satisfactory profits for some years. This time can also be used to prepare the market for the successful introduction of the old product's replacement.

In the decline stage, everything starts to wind down. Product ranges and features are cut to a minimum, with unprofitable products and less popular features being phased out and so the customer has a lot less choice. Unless an extension strategy can be found quickly, or the product gains cult or classic status (as some music or fashion products might), it will eventually die.

Deletion

The final stage in a product's life cycle is its end – the deletion stage, when the decision is taken to withdraw the product from sale. The product may be costing more to maintain and support than it brings in. The market is shrinking, as sales are falling, profits are declining and new, alternative ways of satisfying customer needs and wants are available.

Pony traps, hula-hoops (the plastic toys, not the snack), cassette players and typewriters are all products that were introduced, grew, matured and declined, and no longer have any significant commercial value (apart from occasional reappearances as novelty items). They were all replaced by other products that better satisfied customers' needs.

Deleting a product is a big decision and there a number of things to consider before it is reached:

- Is the company prepared to risk losing other business because of this? Some customers may be so upset to lose one of their favourites that they shop elsewhere.

- What effect will the deletion have on the rest of the product range? Would it leave a gap that would drive customers to competitors? For example, if a restaurant stopped offering a salad bar, customers might go elsewhere for the sake of the one salad eater in their group.

- Will the product's disappearance upset loyal customers?

- What residual problems may the company be left with? For example, previously sold products may still have warranties and will require support.

Take, for example, an airline that has decided to delete a service. Frequent users of this service may have accumulated a substantial number of Air Miles, which they are now no longer able to use. These will continue to show as a debt on the airline's books until the customers use them and yet these customers can no longer use them as there are no flights. There is a serious customer relations issue here. Since the Air Miles have no expiry date, this debt can apparently exist forever. The airline can solve the problem by converting the value of the Air Miles into shopping vouchers, which the customers can spend at home. Microsoft and most other software companies give notice before discontinuing support for their obsolete products. Many users do not upgrade to the latest versions of the software and they must be supported for a reasonable time. Eventually products enter the 'limited support phase' and the company makes renewed attempts to get them to upgrade to the newer products.

research focus: classic concepts

Levitt, T. (1965) 'Exploit the product life cycle', *Harvard Business Review,* **43 (Nov–Dec): 81–94.**
   Levitt reviews the product life cycle and suggests ways of turning it into an effective instrument of competitive power.

Enis, B.M., LaGarce, R. and Prell, A.E. (1977) 'Extending the product life cycle', *Business Horizons,* **20 (Jun): 46–56.**
   The paper questions the concept of the product life cycle, particularly in accepting inevitable decline, and proposes that the product life cycle can be extended further. It proposes strategies for each stage of the life cycle and for its extension.

USING THE PRODUCT LIFE CYCLE AS AN INPUT TO PLANNING

It is difficult to determine exactly where a product is in its life cycle. The product life cycle model is just one of many inputs into the decision-making process and managers have to rely on their judgement and experience.

The product's life stage can be helpful when making marketing plans. Should new features or even new models be introduced? Should the price be changed? Is it time to step up promotional activity? Should promotions be persuasive rather than informative? Should the product be offered more widely or perhaps distribution should be cut down?

A product's life is governed by market forces and managerial decisions. Its life can be terminated or extended. Aspects of the product can be changed to help it adjust to changing market conditions, e.g. new competition, changing customer tastes or reduced incomes. The product life cycle model is an aid to understanding products and their markets, and a useful tool for helping to manage product portfolios. A company with too many products in the decline stage would need to think of ways to extend some of those products' lives rapidly or to hurry the introduction of some new ones. If they had paid more attention to the mapping of their products' life cycles earlier, then they might have avoided the problem by ensuring that new products were in the pipeline ready to replace these older ones. Equally, a company with most of its products in the growth stage would be in a high-risk category because of the high expenditure needed to support them in what is likely to be a competitive marketplace.

The product life cycle model was originally devised for generic products, i.e. the product type, not the individual branded item (shoes, not Clarks shoes). It is often, however, applied to product classes or specific brands. The idea behind the product life cycle is that products have an inbuilt life that can be mapped and so its application to one specific branded product (e.g. Samsung Galaxy phones, but not iPhones or other competitors) can be difficult. It is possible that one brand is out of step with its competitors, i.e. it is following a differently timed life cycle. The reason for that is likely to lie with its marketing mix, i.e. it is likely to be an internal cause rather than an external one which would affect other similar products as well – perhaps a poor marketing campaign has destroyed the product's image or a health scare has affected this one product but not others. For this reason, as well as to ensure that you are comparing like with like, it is always important to be clear what you are analysing. Is it hatchbacks, cars or Volkswagens?

The product life cycle model can also be related (though not precisely) to the stages of market diffusion (see Chapter 3). In the early stages of a product's life, its buyers will largely be innovators, i.e. the risk takers who are happy to try a new product and who like to own the latest thing. In the growth stages of the product life cycle, customers may be early adopters or the early majority. These people may have a special interest in, or knowledge of, such products and are quite adventurous in their product choices. The majority of customers will buy the product during its maturity phase – this is when sales peak. In the early stages of decline, most customers will be from the late majority and the laggards categories. These are people who prefer to wait until a product is tried and tested (by other people) before they buy it and may even wait until it is a product that other people will be surprised that they do not have.

It is often claimed that product life cycles are getting shorter. Certainly, high technology products, such as computers, have noticeably short lives as newer, improved models seem to come out almost immediately after purchase. Some products have always had short lives, such as fashion items, but others seem to live on forever. There is no sign of a significant decline in the demand for bread, for example, and that has been around for thousands of years. The belief in shorter product life cycles can become a self-fulfilling prophecy if decisions on product development and management are based on it. This might lead companies to withdraw or sell off products before their time. Equally, this perception that products have shorter lives can encourage companies to step up research and development and so decrease the time between innovations, and to introduce more and more new products as quickly as possible (Rifkin, 1994), which, given the expense of development and the frequency with which new products fail, may be a costly exercise.

CRITIQUE

The product life cycle model has many critics. Its simplicity leads many to say it cannot possibly represent accurately the situation in a complex and dynamic marketplace; it is certainly true that not all products follow this exact pattern. Some just never seem to die, for example, gin, cutlery and bread have been with us for centuries. They have been adapted, e.g. the gin may be purer, the cutlery may now be dishwasher-proof and the bread now has E numbers, but those products live on. Others, of course, never actually grow to maturity. It is estimated that at least 50% of new products fail within a year of their launch: they die before they have lived. So the product life cycle is a model of a *successful* product, not a failure.

Product life cycles vary in the time they take to run their course. The lives of some highly successful products are so short that they cannot be mapped before they are over. High fashion products fall into this category.

Dhalla and Yuspeh (1976) claimed that the product life cycle was dangerously misleading and often caused companies to delete products that could have been profitable for many more years with the right adjustments to their marketing mix. Lambkin and Day (1989) argued that the traditional product life cycle framework is an oversimplification. It is not only changes in consumer demand but also the firms' competitive situation and supply side changes that must be taken into account, to fully understand and predict how a market situation is likely to evolve over time.

A product can defy the rules of the product life cycle through clever repositioning, perhaps even taking up a position outside its current category, as the Fox network did in the USA when it aired a cartoon aimed at adults in a prime time television slot normally reserved for family sitcoms. When a breakaway position such as this works, the product redefines its competition. *The Simpsons* cartoon is the longest-running sitcom ever in the USA (Moon, 2005).

PRODUCT PORTFOLIO MANAGEMENT

Few companies sell just one product; some sell thousands. Their products are collectively referred to as their product portfolio, and this needs careful management.

The number of product lines a company sells is referred to as product breadth. Within each line, there will be several products (product depth). For example, the Ford Fiesta is one product line, while the Ford Focus is another. The Fiesta line has a number of models (Studio, Style, Zetec, Titanium, etc.), which may have different engines and other features. That is its depth. The product manager lays down guidelines for the consistency required within each line, both in terms of product features and in terms of marketing activities. Products may be introduced, dropped, modified or replaced. Sufficient resources must be allocated (e.g. budgets for advertising, research, customer support). The manager must also agree what contribution to profits the product ought to make and this will become a target or sales objective. The company must have enough cash-generating products to support the cash eaters.

A number of management tools have been developed to help managers to judge the performance of individual products and brands, or ranges of products and brands, or strategic business units (SBUs). Then decisions can be taken on the various products' futures.

Although these product portfolio analysis tools may appear simple, they require considerable research, calculation and analysis. The Boston Consulting Group matrix (BCG matrix) considers the growth of the market and the size of the product's share of that market relative to the market leader's share (see Exhibit 6.5). The GE-McKinsey matrix uses market attractiveness and competitive position (see Exhibit 6.6).

BOSTON CONSULTING GROUP (BCG) PORTFOLIO MATRIX

The Boston Consulting Group (BCG) portfolio matrix shows the relationship between cash-generating products and cash-eaters. This model plots products, or SBUs, in a matrix formed by two axes: market growth rate and relative market share. It is important to note that this is the growth rate of the *whole* market; it takes into account all sales within that category, including competitors' sales. So, for example, if the matrix was being drawn up for Nestlé's chocolate products, then the market would be chocolate generally and Cadbury's, Mars and many other brands would be added in when working out its size and growth rate. The market needs to be carefully defined and this may not be easy. For example, are Green and Black's chocolate bars part of the chocolate bar (countline) market, or a general chocolate market, or confectionery, or snacks, or organic foods?

Once the market has been defined, the market growth rate is calculated by working out the percentage increase (or decrease) in sales from the previous year.

---

product line

a product and all its variants (models, colours, styles, sizes, etc.)

product breadth

the number of product lines a company supports

product depth

the number of items within a product line

strategic business unit (SBU)

a distinct part of an organisation that has an external market for its products

product portfolio analysis

the process of comparing products/services to see which are deserving of further investment and which should be discontinued

Boston Consulting Group (BCG) portfolio matrix

a product portfolio analysis tool involving classifying products, or SBUs, according to their relative market share and market growth rate, as stars, cash cows, problem children or dogs

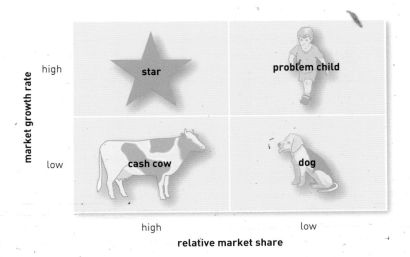

EXHIBIT 6.5 Boston Consulting Group portfolio matrix

Source: The BCG Portfolio Matrix from the Product Portfolio Matrix © 1970, The Boston Consulting Group, printed with permission.

For example:

current market sales	£2,200,000
minus last year's sales	− £2,000,000
equals sales increase	= £200,000
as a percentage of last year's sales	$\underline{£200,000 \times 100}$
	£ 2,000,000

market growth rate = 10%

High growth markets are attractive to companies as they offer a better chance to increase sales; the company's sales just have to move with the market's and they will go up. Exactly what constitutes high growth for a market, and what is low, is uncertain. Traditionally, the mid-point is often taken as 10% and so it can be construed that anything over that may be high and anything below it may be low (Doyle, 2002). However, different markets are likely to vary considerably and so a judgement must be made.

The other axis is labelled 'relative market share' and measures the product's success (in terms of sales) against the market leader in its field. The dividing line between high and low is where the product has an equal share with the market leader. To the left of the line (high), the product is the leader in the market. The further left it is, the greater its relative share and so its leadership. To the right of the line represents a relative market share lower than the market leader. The further it is to the right, the smaller its relative share and the weaker its relative position. The company's product(s) are placed in one of the four boxes of the model and thereby categorised as stars, problem children (sometimes referred to as question marks or wild cats), cash cows or dogs. The boxes are not absolutes. The products do not always have to be in the middle of a box. For example, a product in the medium growth market may be categorised as a dog but placed towards the top of the box, or as a problem child but near the bottom of the box.

It may be more profitable to have a small share of a large market than it is to have a large share of a small market (so a problem child in a large market can be more valuable than a star in a smaller one), and so the BCG portfolio matrix should also be refined by careful definition of the appropriate market and to reflect market size.

STAR

stars

a category within the Boston Consulting Group portfolio matrix; products or SBUs (strategic business units) with high market share in a high-growth market

Products in rapidly growing markets in which the company has a high relative market share are called stars (e.g. Apple's iPhone, Amazon's Kindle). They generate a large amount of cash but are also expensive to support. They are good investments as they have high earning potential both at the present time and in the future. That investment is likely to be needed if the company wants to retain its market position, as competitors such as Samsung Galaxy or Kobo Aura will be trying to emulate stars.

Stars therefore often require high promotional expenditure and perhaps additional product development in order to keep their competitive edge. If this is managed successfully, then when the market's growth rate slows down (as markets inevitably do), these stars will become cash cows.

CASH COW

cash cows

a category within the Boston Consulting Group portfolio matrix, products or SBUs (strategic business units) with relatively high market share in low-growth markets

Products in slow growth, or even static, markets in which they have relatively high market share are called cash cows. They need little promotion although under-investment can turn them into dogs (see below) so they should not be taken for granted. The company's objective is likely to be to hold this position in order to obtain maximum return on investment (ROI). The profits from cash cows can be used to invest in stars, which are high maintenance, or problem children (who need help).

PROBLEM CHILD

problem children

a category within the Boston Consulting Group portfolio matrix; products or SBUs (strategic business units) with relatively low market share in high-growth markets

Products in this quadrant are in a rapidly growing market but hold a relatively low market share. They are also called question marks or wild cats. The market looks attractive (as long as it keeps growing) and just maintaining current market share will increase sales as the company would then have the same percentage of a bigger market. However, the company may be unsure how the market will develop or whether it can acquire enough customers to make further investment here worthwhile. Small companies often suffer by having too many problem children in their portfolios.

Problem children will require heavy investment in a successful marketing mix if they are to develop into stars. Left alone, they will almost certainly become dogs as the market growth rate declines. If they prove to be too much of a drain on resources, they may be sold or deleted from the portfolio

DOG

dogs

a category within the Boston Consulting Group portfolio matrix, products or SBUs (strategic business units) with relatively low market share in low-growth markets

Dogs are in stagnant or slow-growing markets and have relatively low market share. When a dog gets old it may be kindest to put it to sleep but, from a company's perspective, there may be sound reasons to keep it alive. It might be an effective loss leader or barrier to market entry by competitors or it might still be generating profits. It can be quite difficult to judge just when a product has reached the end of its useful life and, ideally, rather than just phase it out, it is often worth trying to sell it on to another company. One company's dog can become another's cash cow or even a star if they are operating in different markets or market segments.

Attempts are sometimes made to relate the BCG portfolio matrix to the product life cycle. Problem children may be in the introduction phase, stars are in the growth stage, cash cows are generally mature products and dogs are in old age (decline). However, this is not necessarily the case and to characterise a problem child as being in the introductory phase may be unhelpful if the product has in fact been around for some time. Additionally, the match is of limited help in analysing the product portfolio.

Here is a saying that may help you to remember the BCG matrix: *milk the cow to feed the problem child, in the hope that it will grow up to be a star. And shoot the old dog.* (Although you may, of course, find reasons not to do that last bit!)

GE-MCKINSEY MATRIX

This is another classic portfolio analysis tool which is also known as the market attractiveness, market strength matrix. This nine-box matrix is a systematic approach to determining which products or SBUs are the best ones for investment. Rather than rely on managers' forecasts, the company judges how well a product may do in the future on the basis of two, currently known factors: the attractiveness of the industry or market it is in and its competitive strength within that industry or market.

GE-McKinsey matrix
a portfolio analysis tool developed by McKinsey & Co and GE involving classifying product lines or SBUs (strategic business units) according to their competitive position and market attractiveness

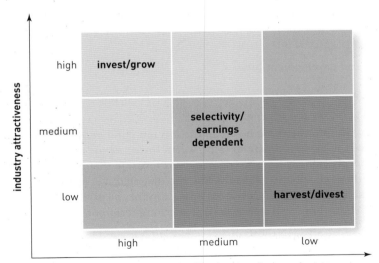

EXHIBIT 6.6 GE-McKinsey nine-box matrix

Attractiveness can be defined in a number of ways depending on the particular circumstances of the company, for example:

- market size
- market growth rate
- ease of market entry
- competition
- profitability
- social and environmental impact
- technological requirements
- legal implications
- energy and other resource requirements.

The business's competitive position may be calculated by assessing its:

- market share
- market share growth rate
- management team's skills and competences
- product quality
- brand strength
- distribution channels
- promotional effectiveness
- production capacity
- production efficiency
- unit costs
- research and development success.

These criteria are then weighted according to their relative importance to the company and the market.

Products that fall into the three boxes in the top left-hand corner of Exhibit 6.6 would appear to have the growth potential to be worth investing in. Those in the three boxes on the diagonal are borderline. The company may invest in them if it has sufficient funds, or it may let them go (divest). Those below the diagonal, i.e. in the bottom right-hand corner, are likely to be sold off (divested) or kept in the portfolio only if they can generate sufficient short-term cash (harvested). Their long-term potential is poor.

Placing products or SBUs in these three categories is a good starting point for strategic analysis, but sound managerial judgement is still needed to ensure the right decisions are made. For example, a strong brand that dominates an unattractive market, perhaps a slow-growing one, may still be a far better prospect than a weak brand in a highly attractive market and yet they both fall into the selective investment section of the matrix (Coyne, 2008).

There are many different portfolio analysis tools and organisations will have their favourites – even their own variants. The BCG portfolio matrix (see above) and the GE-McKinsey matrix are, however, the basis for many of these more modern techniques.

research focus

Gluck, F.W., Kaufman, S.P., Walleck, A.S., McLeod, K. and Stuckey, J. (2000) 'Thinking strategically', *McKinsey Quarterly*, June. Available at: www.mckinsey.com/insights/strategy/thinking_strategically (accessed 14/05/13). The Boston Consulting Group portfolio and the GE-McKinsey matrices were radical innovations of their time. They are included here as they formed the basis for many other portfolio analysis tools, e.g. MACS (Market Activated Corporate Strategy) and the Portfolio of Initiatives.

CRITIQUE

It has been argued that portfolio analysis tools over-simplify what are actually complex situations. Ironically, some of these tools have now grown so complex that they cannot meaningfully be applied in real life. Some of the criticisms are briefly outlined below.

First, they merely provide a snapshot of the company's portfolio at a single point in time. The next day, things may have changed. Also, they ignore products in development that have yet to be launched into the market.

Second, consider how market share is calculated. At best, it is a guesstimate, often based on knowledge of one's own business and estimates of competitors' sales, sometimes informed by industry analysts (usually only when the stock market has a keen interest). How, then, is it possible to calculate market share accurately or to compare the relative growth of one market to another in order to map the company's portfolio? Furthermore, is market growth the best criterion for analysis? Perhaps profitability is more important?

Third, these tools fail to recognise any interdependencies between elements of the company's product portfolio. For example, a dog may be essential to the sales of a cash cow if they are complementary products such as an inkjet printer and print cartridges.

This is not to say these tools are not useful as a systematic approach to portfolio analysis. They are a sound base for further exploration of issues and subsequent management decisions. Also, these product portfolio tools can be useful when allocating resources, but it is important to recognise their general limitations and not follow them blindly.

SUMMARY

There are many different types of product and each has particular characteristics that influence its marketing, but all must deliver a core benefit. Competitive advantage often comes through differentiating aspects of the total product, rather than just the basic product, and the service elements of a product can be a key selling point (as can the product elements of a service – see Chapter 7). Branding is today a key differentiator and this is often at the heart of the customer's choice of product and may even inspire loyalty to a particular product.

Management of a product portfolio is a huge marketing challenge. Products are launched, build sales and eventually die. There are a number of portfolio analysis tools which can help managers to judge a product's contribution to the company and to decide what course of action to take next. In this chapter we have briefly considered two of them: the Boston Consulting Group portfolio matrix and the GE-McKinsey matrix. There are criticisms to be made of these tools, as there are of the product life cycle concept, but they all provide useful insights to help manage the product offering.

complementary product
one that is required by another product, e.g. a printer needs paper, a DVD player needs DVDs

portfolio analysis
the process of comparing SBUs (strategic business units) or products/services to see which are deserving of further investment and which should be discontinued

CHALLENGES REVIEWED

Now that you have finished reading the chapter, look back at the challenges you were set at the beginning. Do you have a clearer idea of what's involved?

HINTS

- Product portfolio management.
- Importance of innovation.
- Product life cycle – extension strategies.
- Total product offering – augmented and perceived product, particularly service aspects.
- Is this right? Can preserving our environment be compatible with making products? Would customers pay more perhaps for products that lasted longer? Would they choose your company over others if it had a more responsible attitude? Bear in mind that there are likely to be laws about manufacturers' responsibilities for disposal of old products soon.

READING AROUND
JOURNAL ARTICLES

Gottfredson, M. and Aspinall, K. (2005) 'Innovation vs. complexity', *Harvard Business Review*, 83 (12): 62–71.

Hewer, P. and Hamilton, K. (2012) 'Exhibitions and the role of fashion in the sustenance of the Kylie Brand mythology: unpacking the spatial logic of celebrity culture', *Marketing Theory*, 12 (4): 411–25.

Ramanujam, M. and Tacke, G. (2016) 'In product development, let your customers define perfection', *Harvard Business Review*, 9 May. Available at: https://hbr.org/2016/05/in-product-development-let-your-customers-define-perfection (accessed 18/08/16).

Rubinstein, H. (1996) '"Brand first" management', *Journal of Marketing Management*, 12 (4): 269–80.

BOOKS AND BOOK CHAPTERS

Haig, M. (2011) *Brand Failures: The Truth About the 100 Biggest Branding Mistakes of All Time* (2nd edn). London: Kogan Page.

Haig, M. (2011) *Brand Success: How the World's Top 100 Brands Thrive and Survive* (2nd edn). London: Kogan Page.

Hart, S. (2008) 'New product development', in M.J. Baker and S. Hart (eds), *The Marketing Book* (6th edn). Oxford: Butterworth Heinemann, Chapter 13, pp. 260–80.

Hartley, R.F. (1995) 'A giant fails to cope', in R.F. Hartley, *Marketing Mistakes* (6th edn). New York: John Wiley, pp. 57–73.

ONLINE RESOURCES

Ledbetter, Charles (2005) 'The era of open innovation', a TED talk. Available at: www.ted.com/talks/charles_leadbeater_on_innovation (accessed 12/02/17).

WEBSITES

www.cim.co.uk – the Chartered Institute of Marketing.

www.designcouncil.org.uk – the Design Council, includes articles on product design.

TEST YOURSELF

1 Define a product. (See p. 216)

2 What is meant by the term core product? (See p. 218)

3 How can products be differentiated? (See p. 225)

4 Which usually attracts higher customer involvement – convenience goods or shopping goods, and why? (See p. 222)

5 What does FMCG mean? (See p. 221)

6 Why are strong brands so important to companies? (See pp. 225–226)

7 Draw the product life cycle diagram. (See p. 238)

8 What is an extension strategy? Give two examples. (See p. 240)

9 Is the product life cycle universally applicable? If not, why not? (See p. 243)

10 Draw the BCG matrix. (See p. 244)

11 What should you do with a dog? (See p. 246)

12 Why is innovation important? (See p. 230)

REVISION TOOLS

Want to test yourself even more? Review what you have learnt by visiting
https://study.sagepub.com/masterson4e

- Practise for exams with **multiple choice questions**
- Revise key terms with **interactive flashcards**

MINI CASE STUDY: EVERYONE HAS TO GROW UP SOMETIME, EVEN THE LYNX LAD

Read the questions, then the case material, and then answer the questions.

QUESTIONS

1 Identify the Unilever product lines mentioned in this case study. List the products mentioned within each line.

2 Draw and label a total product offering diagram for Axe/Lynx. Make sure it is specific to the brand – no general terms.

(Continued)

(Continued)

3   How have Unilever involved consumers in this brand? What marketing theories/concepts underpin this consumer involvement?

4   How might the product life style model be helpful to companies selling men's grooming products? Make sure you apply the theory specifically to men's grooming.

Lynx

Source: Christopher Elwell/ Shutterstock.com

There was a time when teenage boys wouldn't think of using even the most manly of deodorants and as for hair products, well they were clearly for girls. Now boys want to smell good, look good and have their skin feel good. This attitude change is largely due to some clever marketing and some of the cleverest of that marketing came from a very closely targeted Unilever brand.

One of the first body sprays for young men, Axe was first launched in France in 1983. Axe came in three fragrances: Amber, Musk and Spice. Two years later, it hit the shelves in the UK as Lynx (there was already a brand called Axe in the UK). Since then, the Lynx/ Axe Institute of Attractiveness has created dozens of fragrances supported by iconic advertising. It was all about making average young men appealing to stunning women.

It's been over thirty years since then and things have changed. Young men still want to impress women, of course they do, but they are no longer concerned that using grooming products will diminish their manly appeal or earn them mockery from their mates. In fact, it seems the ladies like it. However, the Axe/Lynx generation have grown up and grown out of the brand and Unilever can see a more lucrative potential market in slightly older men: men with more money to spend and perhaps a nostalgic fondness for the Africa or Apollo fragrances of their youth.

Rik Strubel, global vice president of the Lynx and Axe brands, called the 2016 relaunch the biggest repositioning of the brand in the last twenty years; 'We have been catering to teenage guys and we are now talking to his older brother, who is in university'.

The brand had conducted a survey of 3,500 men in 10 markets. It found that young men's confidence was low. Only 5% of men in the UK described themselves as attractive (this was one of the lowest country scores, US men were three times more likely to think they were attractive).

The new Lynx/Axe products were innovative. Rather than choose one scent, they encouraged men to buy several. The idea behind these daily fragrances was that men would use a different body spray according to their mood or what they were doing. There would be a different scent for work or for going out; Signature for the evening perhaps and Adrenaline for weekends (rather like women use perfume). This new premium range was developed with the help of Anne Gottlieb (the nose behind fragrances at Marc Jacobs, Calvin Klein, and Tom Ford) and presented in more stylish packaging.

Each body spray had matching shower gels and deodorants. There were also new hair products for different looks, for example Natural Look Flexible Hold Cream 'for the casual (un)done look' and Urban Messy Look Matt Gel. These hair products were supported by styling advice on the website.

Unilever's survey had found that men still feel an overwhelming pressure to conform to old masculine stereotypes despite the contemporary emphasis on individuality and social acceptance. According to Strubel, Axe/Lynx's marketing activity was aimed at empowering men, enabling them to be themselves. The message behind the new campaign was that this was now a brand for all (confident) men, regardless of colour, sexual orientation, (dis)ability or appearance. Nic Owen, managing director of ad agency 72andSunny Amsterdam, added that the brand's positioning was about 'inspiring and supporting' men, helping them to be the most attractive version of themselves. The previous magic-sex-potion positioning gave way to a wider definition of attractiveness. It was no longer just about sexual attraction but about being a better, more confident person who was successful in life – not just as a babe magnet. As Owen said, 'It's [about] making young men more attractive human beings, rather than the "spray and get laid" area'.

In 2015, Unilever were a global market leader in men's grooming with $4.5 billion of sales. However, they had made no inroads into the shaving market. In 2016 that changed when the giant multinational bought a small Californian company called Dollar Shave Club. The company had only been going for about four years, had projected revenues of just $200 million and was only just in profit.

Analysts had expected Unilever to buy a much larger, better established company but Paul Polman, Chief Executive of Unilever, explained that they wanted the more innovative and disruptive brand. 'We will be disrupters ourselves'. Dollar Shave sold razors through online subscriptions and had a projected sales increase of 32% that year.

'This is much more than just a razor company', Polman said. 'Male grooming is a $40bn market that is growing faster than personal care, so we see this as a huge opportunity'.

Unilever hoped that the small company's e-commerce expertise, and existing subscribers, would help it to gain market share for all its grooming products, especially in China where online sales were increasing rapidly.

Large consumer goods companies such as Unilever are finding it harder and harder to increase sales. They have extremely large and varied portfolios already and are constrained by the economic slowdown in emerging markets and weak demand in Europe and North America. Repositioning Lynx/Axe is one response to this, acquiring new businesses is another. In both cases, Unilever are signalling their confidence that men's grooming is a market that still has potential.

Sources: Carvell (2016); Daneshkhu (2016); Oakes (2016); Lynx (n.d.); Unilever (n.d.)

REFERENCES

Aaker, D.A. (2002) *Building Strong Brands*. Sydney: Simon & Schuster.

Admob by Google (n.d.) '2016 AdMob student app challenge'. Available at: www.google.co.uk/admob/challenge.html (accessed 25/05/16).

American Marketing Association (n.d.) 'Dictionary'. Available at: www.ama.org/resources/Pages/Dictionary.aspx?dLetter=B (accessed 28/04/16).

Belén del Rio, A., Vazquez, R. and Iglesia, V. (2001) 'The effects of brand associations on consumer response', *Journal of Consumer Marketing*, 18 (5): 410–25.

Carvell, N. (2016) 'Lynx is back to dominate your grown-up grooming regime', *GQ*, 25 July. Available at: www.gq-magazine.co.uk/article/lynx-daily-fragrances-review (accessed 14/08/16).

Centennialbulb.org (n.d.) 'Home of the world's longest burning lightbulb'. Available at: www.centennialbulb.org/ (accessed 25/05/16).

CIM (Chartered Institute of Marketing) (n.d.). 'What is marketing?'. Available at: www.cim.co.uk/more/getin2marketing/what-is-marketing/ (accessed 28/04/16).

Coyne, K. (2008) 'Enduring ideas: the GE–McKinsey nine-box matrix', *McKinsey Quarterly Strategic Thinking*, September. Available at: www.mckinsey.com/insights/strategy/enduring_ideas_the_ge_and_mckinsey_nine-box_matrix (accessed 20/02/14).

Daneshkhu, S. (2016) 'Unilever sharpens focus with push into personal care' *Financial Times*, 21 July. Available at: www.ft.com/content/f2ace74a-4f3d-11e6-88c5-db83e98a590a (accessed 14/08/16).

Dennis (2010) 'Life's bloopers: foreign brand names', *True North Strong and Free*, Canada. Available at: http://tnsf.ca/bloopers/index.php?Page=FB (accessed 03/08/13).

Dhalla, N.K. and Yuspeh, S. (1976) 'Forget the product life cycle concept!', *Harvard Business Review*, 54 (1): 102–12.

Doyle, P. (2002) *Marketing Management and Strategy*. Harlow: FT/Prentice Hall.

Enis, B.M., LaGarce, R. and Prell, A.E. (1977) 'Extending the product life cycle', *Business Horizons*, 20 (Jun): 46–56.

Gluck, F.W., Kaufman, S.P., Walleck, A.S., McLeod, K. and Stuckey, J. (2000) 'Thinking strategically', *McKinsey Quarterly*, June. Available at: www.mckinsey.com/insights/strategy/thinking_strategically (accessed 14/05/13).

Gurley, G. (2014) 'Starbucks crowdsourcing success'. Available at: https://blog.betterific.com/2014/03/25/starbucks-crowdsourcing-success/ (accessed 25/05/16).

ideaCONNECTION (n.d.) 'Crowdsourcing brilliant student app ideas'. Available at: www.ideaconnection.com/open-innovation-success/Crowdsourcing-Brilliant-Student-App-Ideas-00577.html (accessed 25/05/16).

Jindal, R.P., Sarangee, K.R., Echambadi, R. and Lee, S. (2016) 'Designed to succeed: dimensions of product design and their impact on market share', *Journal of Marketing*, 80 (4): 72–89.

Lambkin, M. and Day G.S. (1989) 'Evolutionary processes in competitive markets: beyond the product life cycle', *Journal of Marketing*, 53 (3): 4–20.

Levitt, T. (1965) 'Exploit the product life cycle', *Harvard Business Review*, 43 (Nov/Dec): 81–94.

Lukas, B.A., Whitwell, G.J. and Heide, J.B. (2013) 'Why do customers get more than they need? How organizational culture shapes product capability decisions', *Journal of Marketing*, 77 (1): 1–12.

Lynx (n.d.) 'Lynx find your magic'. Available at: www.lynxmalegrooming.co.uk/ (accessed 14/08/16).

Moon, Y. (2005) 'Break free from the product life cycle', *Harvard Business Review*, 83 (5): 86–94.

Muniz Jr, A.M. and O'Guinn, T.C. (2001) 'Brand community', *Journal of Consumer Research*, 27 (4): 412–32.

MyStarbucksIdea (n.d.) 'Learn more'. Available at: www.starbucks.com/coffeehouse/learn-more/my-starbucks-idea (accessed 25/05/16).

Oakes, O. (2016) 'Lynx launches major rebrand aimed at slightly older, more sensitive men', *Campaign*, 13 January. Available at: www.campaignlive.co.uk/article/lynx-launches-major-rebrand-aimed-slightly-older-sensitive-men/1379139#9o4X2yYq2UxxuRKk.99 (accessed 12/08/16).

Rifkin, G. (1994) 'The myth of short life cycles', *Harvard Business Review*, 72 (11): 11.

Spinks, R. (2015) 'We're all losers to a gadget industry built on planned obsolescence', *The Guardian*, 23 March. Available at: www.theguardian.com/sustainable-business/2015/mar/23/were-are-all-losers-to-gadget-industry-built-on-planned-obsolescence (accessed 24/05/16).

Unilever (n.d.) 'Lynx'. Available at: www.unilever.co.uk/brands/our-brands/lynx.html (accessed 14/08/16).

PART ONE   THIS IS MARKETING

PART TWO   MAKING SENSE OF MARKETS

PART THREE   THE MARKETING MIX

PART FOUR   MANAGING MARKETING

SERVICE PRODUCTS

7

SERVICE PRODUCTS CHALLENGES

The following are illustrations of the types of decision that marketers have to take or issues they face. *You aren't expected to know how to deal with the challenges now*; just bear them in mind as you read the chapter and see what you can find that helps.

- You are at the bank asking for a loan to help your chauffeuring service through a slump. If you are refused the loan, then you will have to sell off some of your limousines at a fraction of their value to you. It is unlikely that you will ever be able to afford to buy such cars again. The bank manager is not impressed with your business. He says it can never be a source of real wealth as it does not make anything. What could you say to convince him that the business is worthwhile?

- You manage the check-in operation for a major airline. You are visiting your staff at Gatwick airport when 10 of your planes have to be withdrawn from service for safety checks. The queues of angry passengers are building up and you can see staff at a competitor's check-in looking smug and preparing to lure some of your customers away. What are you going to do? How can you come out of this with an even better reputation for great service?

- You are the marketing manager for a company that makes office furniture. Despite being one of the best recognised brands in your home business-to-business market, you have recently lost a couple of big orders to a foreign rival whose prices are much lower. To make matters worse, their furniture is just as well designed and as good quality as yours. Their brand name is as well recognised too. The production manager has shown that there is no way your company can match their low prices. You need a way to make customers value your products more highly. What are the possibilities?

- You used to sell cars but now you are a travel agent and you have two, difficult, potential customers in front of you: a bride and groom who want to fly an entire wedding party to a Caribbean island and put them up in a smart hotel. This would be a major sale but they are nervous about signing the agreements and want to be reassured that everything will be just perfect. When you were a car salesperson, you would have shown them the car and taken them for a test drive in it, but your budget does not stretch to flying the couple to the Caribbean – and anyway it is currently the monsoon season. How will you reassure them and make the sale?

slump

when an economy experiences a severe fall-off in sales, usually accompanied by unemployment, lower prices and low levels of investment, sometimes called a depression

INTRODUCTION

Products come in many forms, from ice creams to consultancy, from photocopiers to physiotherapy. Many products have no substantial physical form: we cannot pick them up, put them away in a cupboard, sell them on to someone else. Hairdressing, cleaning, insurance, maintenance, teaching – these are all service products and they are just as real, and potentially just as profitable, as the products that you can touch.

The study of services marketing encroaches into other disciplines rather more than most marketing topics do, incorporating aspects of design, human resource management and operations. Europeans sometimes use the term 'service management' instead as a more accurate, and less restricting, description (Grove et al., 2003). There is no clear defining line between the sale of a service, its production and its use. These aspects of a service product are often inseparable.

Take hand car washing as an example. A motorist pulls into a petrol station, or parks in a car park, and is approached by a young man who asks if she would like her car washed. She says 'yes' and the same young man produces bucket and sponge and gets to work. That young man has sold the service and delivered the service and his customer has used the service all within a very short space of time. In fact the provision of the service (the young man wielding bucket and sponge), and the use of the service (the car becoming clean) happen simultaneously. It is possible to build in a delay between sale and consumption, if, for example, there had been a queue for car washes, but often the whole process happens all together.

So service products are indeed rather different from the goods we studied in the last chapter, although they still have to be priced, delivered and promoted. This chapter will explore those differences, the challenges they present and the recognised ways of overcoming them. It will also show why service products are so important to all businesses today – to goods manufacturers as well as to service companies.

DEFINITIONS

Services
marketing defined

A defining feature of service products is that they are intangible (they cannot be touched) as opposed to goods, or physical products, that are tangible. Unfortunately life, and business, is rarely that straightforward. Few products are exclusively tangible or intangible. A car is a solid object but it comes with a warranty which is not. The car needs insurance and will need servicing in the future. It may be wise to have a roadside recovery package such as that offered by the AA in the UK or ANWB in the Netherlands. The availability, price and quality of these additional services are often important factors in a customer's decision to buy a car and are all part of the total product offering.

services
intangible products

Similarly, many things that are classed as services have substantial physical products at their heart.

Take the restaurant business, for example. A key determinant of the diner's satisfaction will be the food itself. The surroundings and the service are important, but if the food is no good then the restaurant is no good either. So although marketers, and governments and other interested parties, like to distinguish between goods and services, there are significant overlaps between the two.

There are a number of definitions of services, most of them having at their heart this idea of intangibility. According to Palmer (2005: 2–3), services are:

> The production of an essentially intangible benefit, either in its own right or as a significant element of a tangible product, which through some form of exchange, satisfies an identified need.

Another defining feature of a service is that the customer does not actually own anything as a direct result of receiving the service:

> Any activity or benefit that one party can offer to another which is essentially intangible and does not result in the ownership of anything. Its production may or may not be tied to a physical product. (Kotler et al., 2001: 535)

Here is an alternative definition:

> A service is an activity which benefits recipients even though they own nothing of significance extra as a result.

This simple definition encapsulates the key ideas of conferring a product benefit, no rights of ownership and of services being processes, or activities, rather than material things.

THE IMPORTANCE OF SERVICES

Services are becoming more and more important to both businesses and consumers. The majority of business start-ups are service businesses, although admittedly many of them are very small.

Service businesses are sometimes criticised on the grounds that, unlike manufacturing businesses, they do not produce any increase in wealth. Restaurant or hotel customers spend their money and are poorer – they have nothing of ongoing value in exchange. Food has been eaten, sleep has been had, but customers own nothing new that they can sell on. This idea dates back to Adam Smith, an eighteenth-century economist who argued that intangible products did not create anything of real value unlike the products of manufacturing or agriculture (Palmer, 2005). However, service customers contribute significantly to the income of a country. Some countries are even said to have service economies, i.e. they rely on service businesses for the bulk of their wealth. For example, approximately 80% of UK, Dutch and French gross domestic product (GDP) is generated by services. In Germany, the figure is approximately 70% (CIA, n.d.). One of Britain's main foreign currency earners is the City of London, where banks, insurance companies and other financial institutions carry out their business. However, hotels and restaurants also bring huge amounts of money into most European capitals, largely thanks to visiting tourists. The more traditional services still have their part to play – even highly paid city bankers have to eat.

With rapid developments in digital technology, some products that used to be packaged goods are now sold on a subscription basis, as services. This is particularly true in media industries where, for example, streaming media and download services are replacing

gross domestic product (GDP)
a way of measuring an economy; the total value of all goods and service purchased in a country

subscription
regular purchase payment, usually as part of an ongoing contract to buy something, e.g. a monthly magazine

traditional physical products like, books, CDs, DVDs or printed newspapers. In the digital economy many goods are entirely weightless and others are shrinking every year as new advances enable miniaturisation. The microchip inside a novelty greetings card probably contains more computing power than the entire planet did in 1945 (Coyle, 1999) and yet good service is still worth its weight in gold.

KNOWLEDGE-BASED ECONOMIES

The trend towards service industries is at its most advanced in the MDCs (most developed countries), such as the UK, Germany, France and the USA, but it is notable worldwide. The MDCs could be said now to have moved beyond service economies and into a new era of knowledge-based activities where expertise is prized above all else. These are nations of consultants, financiers and lawyers, who outsource more basic services such as call centres and computer programming to other countries which possess skilled workforces (particularly in IT).

So Europe has become a continent of knowledge-based workers who are paid for their expertise while other countries, with cheaper labour costs, do the manufacturing. Current thinking is that it is a company's intellectual capital that is its most valuable asset, rather than the more tangible things it owns. This, as Handy (2002) points out, can cause a problem because companies do not actually own their employees. They are not slaves. They are free to leave and take their expertise with them. Handy quotes a story about the world-renowned advertising agency Saatchi & Saatchi. The board fired Maurice Saatchi, one of the agency's founders, who duly left, taking major clients and some of the agency's best staff with him. These things did not belong to the company or its shareholders.

REASONS FOR THE GROWTH IN THE SERVICES SECTOR

There are a number of reasons behind this rise in the popularity of service businesses, including:

Growth of the service sector

- more employment in knowledge-based industries such as consultancy and IT

- increased consumer leisure time and consequent demand for leisure services

- the popularity of outsourcing services as a cost-cutting and efficiency measure

- displaced workers setting up their own small businesses, notably consultancy, training and coaching

- complex modern products requiring support services

- the fact that the service element is now often the key (if not only) way to differentiate a goods item (physical product).

First, the knowledge workers and other highly skilled service staff, who are the backbones of advanced economies, have to keep their knowledge and skills up to date. ('Knowledge worker' is a term first used by Peter Drucker to describe people who work with information rather than in more traditional industries. Knowledge workers may be thought of as the ultimate service industry employees.) Such personnel need ready access to detailed information banks as they are insatiable users of information services and they also need training, even coaching and mentoring. Corporate coaching is a service that has taken off in the last few years. Experienced business people, with specific coaching training, help hard-pressed executives to make the most of their talents and their time.

Second, people in the more developed nations have larger incomes and a lot more free time to spend it in. This means that the demand for leisure activities, largely services, has gone up. Hotels, restaurants, cafés, bars and health clubs have been the main beneficiaries of this new-found wealth, closely followed by retailing. So many people love to shop! This increase in disposable income also means that many people can afford to pay others to do things that most of their grandparents would have done themselves: mending pipes, fixing windows, cleaning, gardening, laying patios, decorating, etc. However, many services are considered luxuries, e.g. restaurants and travel, and these suffer badly during hard times such as recession.

The increased popularity of outsourcing has also encouraged new service businesses to start up. Company profits are under closer scrutiny as more businesses are publicly quoted or are registered as limited liability companies – meaning they have shareholders who demand higher profits. Consequently, today's businesses are always looking for ways to cut costs and one of the recommended routes to lower cost operations is to focus on the core business and outsource as much of the rest as possible. Many businesses employ other companies to perform key tasks such as delivery, installation, maintenance, call centres, even new product development, as well as more peripheral, but nonetheless important, activities such as cleaning, vehicle fleet management and staff training. All the above-mentioned examples are services and this outsourcing has created a lot of new businesses whose core business is to provide these services.

outsourcing
the subcontracting of a business process, e.g. delivery or maintenance, to another organisation

Outsourcing is not without its drawbacks, however. Although costs may be saved up front, there may be further expense incurred if the outsourcing goes wrong. Firms who outsource customer contact activities, such as call centres or Internet order taking, are handing over a significant part of their customer relationship to another company. They are trusting the outsource partner to care for their company's image and reputation, and not to set up a rival business and poach their customers.

The outsourcing of work to other countries where land and labour costs are cheaper boosts those countries' economies and helps to turn them into viable markets for the home country's products. However, outsourcing to other countries can sometimes create a level of dissatisfaction in the home country. In the UK, for example, some banks and insurance companies are endeavouring to create competitive advantage by making a virtue of returning all of their call centres to the UK.

This trend towards setting up operations in lower-cost countries has meant that the displaced workers of Western Europe, North America, Japan and other post-industrial nations have had to seek alternative employment. Many have turned to self-employment, either in a new industry or as consultants or trainers to their old one. Service businesses are often relatively cheap to set up as many require little in the way of heavy machinery, land or premises. A cleaning service needs mops, buckets, brushes, polish, etc., and maybe a small van to travel from place to place, but little else. A consultant may only need an office, a car and communications equipment. Many service businesses are small and so the investment needed to start one up is also small. It is actually an advantage to be small in some types of service, particularly where personal service is prized (e.g. decorators). Recent years have seen a huge increase in the number of self-employed workers and small business owners, many of whom are offering services.

Another reason for the increase in service products can be found in the world of physical products. Modern technology has created ever more complex products, such as laptops, MP3 players, hard disk recorders, intelligent cars and all the technical paraphernalia (routers, Bluetooth devices, scanners, etc.) that surround computers. Such complex products can be prone to breakdowns and so they need maintenance and repair services. Some, such as heavy industrial plant or highly technical products, need training courses for users before they can even be started up.

As advanced production techniques have made products more standardised, it is often the service aspects (the support: helpdesks, training, service engineers, etc.) that are the means of differentiating one product from another. Customers frequently choose a more expensive supplier on the grounds that they believe the installation or the ongoing service will be better. They are wise enough to recognise that the cost of their new central heating boiler, car or PC does not end at the point-of-purchase. They take account of the ongoing service costs and the hassle factor when deciding what to buy and from whom (see Chapter 3 for more on how customers make purchase decisions).

POP (point-of-purchase) see point-of-sale (POS)

Training and support is another major growth area. Services are people-intensive and rely on the skills of those who provide them. All these lawyers, accountants, nurses, IT technicians, plumbers, consultants and trainers need to be trained and supported themselves and so we have a self-perpetuating cycle of service (see Exhibit 7.1).

EXHIBIT 7.1 Circle of service creation

Most of today's products have a strong service element, which may be the source of their competitive advantage. Equally, many services have a physical product element and this may be the source of theirs, although skills are a more common determinant of the quality of a service. Service products can use physical elements within the offering, and physical products can use service elements, to add to the satisfaction provided by the product.

THE NATURE OF SERVICES

A cut and blow dry needs shampoo. A car service needs filters. A consultancy project produces a report. A night's sleep in a hotel room means there must be a bed. There are very few pure services (i.e. with no physical element at all) in existence, just as there are increasingly few pure goods (i.e. with no service element). Whether a product is primarily a good or a service makes a great deal of difference to the way in which it will be marketed.

Exhibit 7.2 presents a continuum upon which example products are placed according to their degree of physicality.

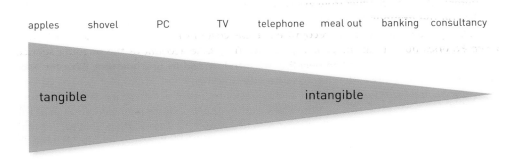

EXHIBIT 7.2 A product continuum, tangible to intangible

Apples bought in a shop have the benefit of all the retail and distribution services that got them there. However, apples picked on a pick-your-own farm or from your own garden have no service element. A shovel will probably be bought from a shop but requires no maintenance or other services, unlike a PC where the warranty and back-up service may be important. Televisions may well be chosen for their features: Android, curved screen, ultra HD, etc., but they are no use without a signal from a broadcaster. Restaurants are selected for their standards of service and their ambience as much as for their food. Banking uses few tangible features: cash, cards, the bank building itself. Online banking is even less tangible. The ultimate intangible product is perhaps consultancy. Although consultants usually provide a written report at the end of their work, it is not the writing down that clients are really paying for but the ideas contained within the report – the consultant's expertise.

The overlap between goods and services is so large and yet so difficult to pinpoint that some marketers have expressed doubts as to whether services marketing is a distinct marketing area at all (see the section on service logic at the end of this chapter).

CHARACTERISTICS OF SERVICES

Throughout much of this book, goods and services are treated similarly. A service is a product and it needs pricing and promoting just as any product does. As Theodore Levitt said, 'There are no such things as service industries. There are only industries whose service components are greater or less than those of other industries. Everybody is in service' (cited in Kotler, 2003: 167). However, the provision and marketing of services present some additional challenges. Many of these arise from the nature of services – the way they differ from goods.

Services have a number of defining characteristics which set them apart from goods. The following are typical service characteristics and will be discussed in the section that follows:

- services confer benefits
- services are intangible – they have no (or little) physical form and so cannot be touched
- services are time and place dependent – they cannot be stored or moved
- the service provider is part of the service
- the consumer is part of the service
- services are inconsistent
- services cannot be owned.

Some academics believe that the distinctions between goods and services have become so blurred that even these key characteristics are unreliable and should be revised (Grove et al., 2003). It is certainly true that technology has made a difference. Some Internet services can, in a way, be stored. Purchases can be left in a shopping basket and paid for later, downloads can be bought and then watched later. The Internet has also meant that the service provider and customer do not always have to be together. Think of Internet banking, for example. So it may be best to consider these as typical characteristics of traditional services, some of which can be mediated by technology.

SERVICES CONFER BENEFITS

Just like goods, services are designed to meet customer needs and so services also have core benefits. The core benefit from having your car serviced is the prevention of a breakdown. The core benefit from a haircut is to look better. The core benefit from most medical services is to feel better. There may be additional benefits, e.g. the car being worth more, but marketers must ensure that the service provides the core benefit well. Once you have had a bad haircut, you do not usually go back to that hairdresser no matter how good the coffee was – unless the service recovery was really good, of course. (Service recovery will be examined later in the chapter.)

This does not mean, however, that service products can be analysed in exactly the same way as physical products. Chapter 6 presented a total product offering model, with outer rings comprising largely service elements or other intangibles. While the idea of a core benefit from services is useful, much of the rest of the total product offering model needs modification when applied to services.

The concept of the total service product offering is illustrated in Exhibit 7.3 using the example of a concert.

Music fans go to concerts in the hope of being entertained, having fun, socialising and maybe leaving the venue feeling exhilarated or even inspired. Those are the benefits that they are looking to the concert to provide. The second ring of the model shows the things

Characteristics
of services

service recovery

trying to retrieve a situation
caused by a bad product or
poor service encounter

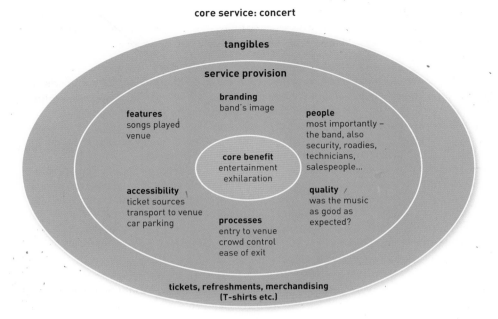

core service: concert

tangibles

service provision

branding
band's image

features
songs played
venue

people
most importantly –
the band, also
security, roadies,
technicians,
salespeople...

core benefit
entertainment
exhilaration

accessibility
ticket sources
transport to venue
car parking

quality
was the music
as good as
expected?

processes
entry to venue
crowd control
ease of exit

**tickets, refreshments, merchandising
(T-shirts etc.)**

EXHIBIT 7.3 Total service offering for a concert

that may contribute to that core benefit. Clearly, the band itself is a major factor, along with what they play (features) and how well they play it (quality). The sound system will also contribute to the quality of the event and technicians (people) will be important to ensure that sound and lighting work properly. The thrill of the concert may be spoilt if the audience has to queue for hours to get out of car parks or on to buses at the end (accessibility) or if crowd control is too aggressive (processes). The idea of branding a band is not novel. Bands can effectively be considered as brands – many have logos and merchandising (branded goods such as T-shirts and posters) is typically a key part of concert activity. The experience will be enhanced if good refreshments are available (tangibles). These tangibles are represented in the third ring of the model.

SERVICES ARE INTANGIBLE

Services are, at their core, intangible. You cannot smell them, touch them or throw them at anyone. However, some services are more intangible than others (see Exhibit 7.2). For example, a dental check-up is almost completely intangible. The only products involved could be the dentist's instruments. The dentist's skill is the most important element and that has to be taken on trust. On the other hand, a meal in a restaurant has a lot of tangible things associated with it, especially the food. This intangibility makes services harder to market than goods. Potential customers feel more confident buying something that they can see and feel – and take back if necessary. So one of the key challenges for marketers is to reduce the perceived risk involved in buying a service by making it appear more tangible, often by emphasising the peripheral products used in carrying out the service. Restaurants usually try to convince potential diners that the food is really good. Beauticians stress the benefits of the products they use.

peripheral products
a secondary product often provided as part of a service, e.g. the complementary mints at the end of a meal, shampoo at the hairdressers

ethical focus: free-downloading

If you cannot see it, touch it or smell it, can you steal it? Police in West London arrested a man for stealing a wireless broadband connection. He was sitting on a garden wall outside a house (not his own), using his laptop and the house owner's broadband. Many people would claim that this was a victimless crime. The broadband subscriber did not have to pay more because extra use was made of his connection, and his service was not affected in any way. It is not difficult to password-protect a connection and so, if people want to prevent others from using their broadband, then perhaps they should secure the connection?

In a further blow to attempts to police these connections, Internet Service Providers are encouraging their users to make the connections available to others and so build up national wireless access. They advertise 'hot spots' where any of their broadband customers can access the Internet by **piggybacking** on someone else's connection.

At the Emmys in 2015, host Andy Samberg gave out a valid username and password for subscription TV service *HBO Now*, encouraging the audience to use it. About half of all Netflix users don't actually have a Netflix account of their own – they share someone else's. The CEO of HBO (Home Box Office) said publicly that HBO weren't bothered by people sharing log in details despite their online services gaining the bulk of their revenue from subscriptions rather than advertising – though that might change if too many people did it. HBO's stated business plan for its *HBO Now* service is to build addicts; people who can't live without their favourite TV shows.

The police, and consumer groups, maintain that it is unacceptable to use services without the subscriber's permission. They argue that the freeloaders, by getting services without paying, increase the costs for those who do pay – and someone has to pay or there will be no service provided.

Is it acceptable to use someone else's broadband service or not? Do you share an account for Netflix or any other subscription service? Who pays?

Sources: Topping (2007); Lynley (2014); Gammell (2015); Tuttle (2015)

piggybacking

when one company uses the distribution channels already established by another company, usually, but not always, in an overseas market

Promotional merchandise is one of the tangibles at a rock concert.

Source: iStock.com/Green Pimp

Making use of online reviews posted by previous customers is one way to reduce the risk associated with the purchase of intangible service products. Tripadvisor has become particularly influential in the travel and hospitality sector, with 83% of travellers using reviews to pick the right hotel (Tripadvisor, 2017). Most people read between 6 and 12 reviews prior to booking while over 50% claim they won't commit to booking until they have read online reviews (Tripadvisor, 2017).

Even a small improvement in a firm's ratings can make a big difference to its profits. Research by Cornell University's Centre for Hospitality showed that when a hotel's reputation increases even one point on a five point scale, it is able to raise prices by as much as 11% without losing bookings (Anderson, 2012). It is particularly important for new businesses, and firms new to using online reviews, to deliver excellent customer service. Early reviews can be disappointing, especially if a glossy brochure or PR buzz around a launch has set customer expectations too high. Over time customer comments tend to become more positive as previous reviews help to set customer expectations. Eventually reviews settle down to a more accurate average (Melián-González et al., 2013).

Intangibility also presents marketers with a serious competitive issue. It makes it more difficult to protect a service from imitation. The inventors of physical products can apply for patents to safeguard their product in the early years while they recoup their development investments. Patent laws, and the rigour with which they are enforced, vary from country to country but few countries' laws, if any, include service products. Other intellectual property laws, such as copyright and trade mark registration, offer some protection but are even harder to enforce.

patent
a legal protection for inventions that prohibits unauthorised copying

SERVICES ARE TIME AND PLACE DEPENDENT (THEY CANNOT BE STORED OR MOVED)

Services are transient. They happen at a particular time and cannot be stored for later sale or use. You cannot buy a service to keep in the cupboard and use at your convenience like you might a tin of soup or a bottle of shampoo. Planes and trains leave at specific times and customers have to be on board if they want to travel. The train or plane operator has to sell seat tickets before departure. If seats remain unsold, they have lost potential income. This perishability of services, as some writers refer to it, greatly complicates the planning of service operations.

The management of peaks and troughs of demand is more difficult for service providers. Whereas a retailer or a manufacturer has a stock room in which to keep surplus products until demand picks up again, service providers just lose business if they do not have enough products. The retailer or manufacturer can stockpile in anticipation of a future peak in demand, fans for the summer perhaps, and so keep their workforce employed, but a hairdresser cannot get ahead by doing extra haircuts and keeping them for later. Service providers may need to employ seasonal staff and lay them off again when demand is low – a reason why so many students find jobs in the holiday industry. Another way that service providers can manage these peaks and troughs is through changing the price (see price discrimination in Chapter 10) to attract extra customers when business is slack or to increase profits in times of high demand.

Additionally, for most services, the number of customers that can be served at any one time is limited and so services often involve appointments, e.g. for the dentist, or queuing and service customers are more often turned away than are customers for goods. There are a limited number of tickets for a concert. There are a limited number of seats on the plane.

Service products cannot be moved like physical products which can be bought in one place and then transported to another location. Few services can be delivered long distance (though modern electronic technologies do facilitate this for some services). A hotel room cannot be moved; you must sleep in the hotel. A play is not performed whenever and wherever you want; it must be at the theatre and at a scheduled performance time.

The time dependency of many services makes accurate demand forecasting essential. Without it there will be unsold seats or dentists with nothing to do. Late customers cause significant problems. If a customer misses an appointment or is late for it, then this can cause serious scheduling problems. The person who was to perform the service (the hair-dresser, the lawyer, the bank manager) will be left with extra time that they could have used more profitably while any revised scheduling may impact on the quality of service for subsequent customers.

digital focus: internet banking

Modern technologies have overcome some of the difficulties normally found in the marketing of services. In particular, technology has helped address the issues of inconsistency and inseparability (the service provider having to be there to deliver the service).

In the virtual world, consumption can take place without both provider and customer being in the same place at the same time. Automation also improves service consistency, although the differences in consumers and their skills may make them experience the service differently. This has a major advantage in terms of opening hours. Internet banking, for example, is available 24/7 without staff having to be there.

First Direct, now a division of HSBC, was a pioneer of telephone banking and was also among the first to move into Internet banking. Customers can manage most aspects of their accounts online: view balances and statements, transfer money, pay bills and set up direct debits. First Direct has no branches, which means it makes considerable cost savings.

The website helps First Direct in other ways too: the technology provides a more consistent service delivery than a person would; imagery and branding are more tightly controlled; and a record of transactions is created automatically. On the other hand, customers are at the mercy of the unpredictability of the Internet service itself and this may affect their perception of the service. Also, an Internet service is quite easy to copy, making it harder for brands to differentiate themselves from the competition.

Do you bank online? What other online services do you use and how does each distinguish itself?

THE SERVICE PROVIDER IS PART OF THE SERVICE

A service provider is an intrinsic part of the service. It is rarely possible to disassociate the person or organisation that performs the service from the service itself. This is often referred to as the inseparability of services and it is a key difference between services and physical products. Customers frequently buy products with no knowledge at all about how and where they were produced and by whom. Do you know which company made the bread for your sandwich? Have you visited their factory? Do you know the name of the baker?

In the case of personal services, such as dentistry, the service provider must actually be physically present at the point that the service is consumed, e.g. the tooth is filled. This is not true for all services. The less personal the service, the more likely it is that it can be performed remotely. For example, an Internet user may shop in the middle of the night, while all the online retailer's staff are asleep. Technology is often the facilitator of remote services. The first telephone users had to ask an operator to connect the call. Early databases needed technicians to search them.

Technology allows service providers to cut costs. Traditionally, services have been very staff intensive, much more so than manufacturing, and this is expensive, especially in the more developed nations where wages are high. Thanks to advanced telecommunications, organisations can move their customer service operations to other countries where staff costs are lower and often employment law is less stringent. A number of British companies have call centres in India, for example.

Thanks to the Internet, organisations can get their customers to do some of the work for themselves, e.g. placing orders online or filing tax returns electronically. This offloading of work on to the customer is not a particularly new idea and it is not solely due to technological advance. Self-service in supermarkets and cafés has the same cost-cutting motivation.

THE CONSUMER IS PART OF THE SERVICE

The consumer of the service is part of the experience whether or not they perform a part of the service themselves, e.g. by serving themselves in a petrol station. Because the production

Most personal services, such as beauty treatments, require both people to be present.

Source: iStock.com/andresr

Some services have been delegated to customers so that the service provider does not need to be present.

Non-personal services are less likely to require the presence of both people, e.g. windows are often cleaned in the householder's absence.

Source: iStock.com/Andrew_Howe

and consumption of services cannot be separated, the consumer has to be considered as an element of the production process and their actions, reactions or inaction need to be taken into account in the service offering's design. This brings into sharp focus the emphasis that is now placed on customer relationship management (CRM). Not only has the importance of customer loyalty been recognised in successful marketing, but also the way in which building relationships is a fundamental part of the service offering. Early work in recognising the shift of marketing emphasis from goods to services and the roles of relationship marketing can be found in the publications of such authors as Grönroos and Gummesson in the late 1970s and 1980s.

For most service customers, ease of use of a service will be important. They do not want to be overly involved in the service delivery. If an investment service is too complicated or there are too many forms to fill in, then the potential customer may be put off. Most people shop at the supermarket that is the closest to them or has the best parking. Consumers value service convenience, which they measure in terms of the time and effort they have to expend on the service. Berry et al. (2002) proposed five categories of service convenience:

service convenience
a measure of how much time and effort consumers need to expend to use the service offered

- decision convenience
- access convenience
- transaction convenience
- benefit convenience
- post-benefit convenience.

First, there is the question of the ease of decision-making. People are more likely to consider performing a service themselves (e.g. DIY) than they are to consider making a physical product. Service providers must ensure that there is enough information available, and in the right form, to inform this decision as well as the choice of supplier.

Second, the customer may consider how easy it will be to ask for the service, e.g. do they have to go to the restaurant or can they order by phone and have their food delivered? Is the website easy to navigate or is it disjointed and slow?

The third category is transaction convenience: how long will it take to pay and how secure is the payment? Often you have to pay for services before you actually receive them, e.g. you have to buy a ticket for a play. If it takes too long to pay (perhaps there is a queue) people may give up. E-tailers suffer particularly from this as many shoppers abandon their baskets before the check-out.

e-tailers
online retailers

Next is benefit convenience: the time and effort that the consumer has to expend in order to actually receive the core benefit of the service while the service is happening, i.e. during the service encounter. For example, the benefit of a taxi ride would be considerably reduced if the customer had to walk the last mile of their journey. If the food takes too long to come, customers may walk out of a restaurant. This is the one point of the service process where customers do not always mind spending extra time. If the service is a hedonistic one, e.g. a holiday, then customers may well be happy to prolong the experience.

service encounter
the time during which a customer is the recipient of a service, e.g. the duration of a meal in a restaurant

Finally, there is post-benefit convenience. Customers want hassle-free ongoing benefits from the service provided and not to have to return to complain or to have the fillings replaced in their teeth too quickly (see service recovery later in this chapter).

OTHER PEOPLE MAY ALSO BE PART OF THE SERVICE

Consumers' enjoyment of a service is also affected by other people, particularly other consumers, and especially if the service is one that is offered to a group rather than just to individuals. For example, a play can be spoilt by someone else's mobile phone.

A train journey can be turned into a distressing rather than relaxing experience by the bad behaviour of fellow passengers. Equally, a holiday may be so much more fun thanks to good company. It can be hard for service providers to control the behaviour of their customers and sometimes their very attempts at control cause a problem for others, e.g. the puzzled old ladies who are no longer allowed to take their nail scissors onto aeroplanes because of increased security measures.

ACTIVITY

Imagine you are a holiday rep at a Mediterranean beach resort. You are based in a large hotel that is popular with both young people, who want to go out clubbing, stay out late and then stay in bed until the afternoon, and with families. What problems might you anticipate and what can you do to resolve them?

Local people have complained about the behaviour of both groups of customers. Is that your concern? What can you do about it?

SERVICES ARE INCONSISTENT

Physical products aim for consistency in quality, packaging and features and many can rely on advanced manufacturing techniques to help them deliver it. Even physical products are not infallibly the same though as there may be flaws in ingredients or components. Nature is not always as bothered about consistency as some fussy humans are either – fruit and vegetables come in various shapes and sizes, and often with blemishes despite farmers' best efforts. Sometimes inconsistencies are viewed positively, as in home-baked goods, where the slightly irregular shapes are proof that they are genuinely hand prepared, but usually consumers prefer standard products.

Services are difficult to standardise. Their intangibility means that consumers cannot know how good they are until the service has been delivered. A customer can try on clothes before they buy, but if they employ a plumber to mend a leak, they will not know whether it was worth it until the plumber has finished the job. One of the ways that customers reduce the risk of non-performance (e.g. the pipe still leaks) is by relying on *past* performance as a guide to the future (something that financial services adverts point out that you should not do). If the plumber did a good job last time, then probably this job will also be good. If expectations are not met, if the standard of work is inconsistent, then the customer will be unhappy with it, and possibly bitter arguments and negotiations will ensue. It is not as easy as just putting the trousers back on the rail and trying another pair, the quality of the work is often a matter of judgement.

Service products are dependent upon humans, and humans are not always consistent. It is rare that two haircuts are exactly the same. In a restaurant, you might order the same food as before but it is unlikely that it will be prepared and served by the same staff – and, even if it is, it could still be a little different.

Consistency is something that many services strive for, but few deliver. It is more important for some services, e.g. financial ones, than it is for others. Lawyers and accountants rely upon documentation to try to provide consistent services. Automation has made a huge difference here. For example, services provided online are more likely to be the same than offline ones; however, this consistency comes at the price of an inflexibility that does not always provide the service that customers actually want as anyone that has tried to fill in an online form that does not ask the right questions will know.

Another way to provide more consistent service is by following strict procedures. Service owners devise a plan for their employees to follow so that each service encounter will be as similar to the previous one as possible. Fast-food chains have tight controls over what their staff do. Kitchen staff walk along set paths from fryer to sink to serving hatch. Bells ring when it is time to turn the burger or take the chips out of the fat. Nothing is left to chance. This heavily proscribed way of working has the added advantage that trained chefs are not required. The work, however, is repetitive and can soon become boring. Staff turnover is often high in such restaurants.

Simple flow charts or more detailed customer journey maps are often used to work out how best to provide a consistent, quality service (see Exhibit 7.5 below) or there may be a service blueprint. These tried-and-tested procedures are part of what a franchisee is paying for when they buy their business idea from the franchiser.

blueprint

an original, or master, plan for how to make or do something

franchisee

a person or company who has bought a franchise

franchiser

owner of a business idea or product who grants a licence to someone else to market or operate it

The best service providers go to great lengths to ensure that they provide a high-quality service, one that customers can rely on – and still they will receive some complaints. Customers are no more consistent than staff. Some like their burgers overcooked, others do not. One customer will love their haircut, but it will not suit her friend. There are diners who like loud music in restaurants and there are those who complain that they cannot hear their companions talk – and those may actually be the same people but at different times, or with different companions. Services are often inconsistent in their reception as well as in their delivery and so all service businesses must be adept at handling complaints if they are to be successful (see service recovery later in this chapter).

SERVICES CANNOT BE OWNED

This lack of ownership is largely a function of the intangibility of the service. There is nothing to actually own. A client pays for the beautician's skill (and the creams etc.) but at the end of the treatment has nothing more than a good feeling (and better skin) to take home. Service clients are paying for expertise, experience, advice, skills, knowledge and the benefits these bring. The benefits may last, but the service itself is of limited duration. Of course, it is possible to augment the service offering with additional items (peripheral products), some of which may be physical goods. For example, in the case of hairdressing or beauty treatments, the client may be able to purchase hair care and beauty goods for use at home.

DIFFERENT TYPES OF SERVICE

The services sector is a very large one and so it is easier to study if it is broken down into smaller groupings or subcategories. Traditionally, similar activities have been grouped together, e.g. the UK government uses the following categories:

- retail, hire and repair
- media and creative services
- health and social care services
- personal services
- IT and telecommunications services.

While this is easy to do, it is a business-based categorisation rather than a customer-based one and therefore not market-orientated. A marketer would prefer to see the groupings based on customer needs and the way the services are used rather than the type of skills and resources needed to provide them. However, classifying activities in this way can lead to some very broad categories which are not particularly useful for marketing. Palmer (2005: 52) suggests that it would be better to group them along the lines of 'processes by which customers make decisions, methods of pricing and promotional strategies'.

Additionally, there are problems when classifying some large and diverse organisations. For example, Tesco would be classed as a retailer even though it also offers IT and banking services. That category of retail is so broad anyway, incorporating organisations as diverse as Galeries Lafayette, Lidl, Holland & Barrett (a health food chain) and individually owned corner shops – all, incidentally, food retailers but with very little in common in terms of their business operations.

retail
selling goods to customers for their own use, i.e. not for resale

Academics tend to place services on a continuum according to their nature – most commonly their degree of intangibility (see Exhibit 7.2). Dibb et al. (2006) propose a different five-category classification scheme:

1 Type of market.
2 Degree of labour intensiveness.
3 Degree of customer contact.
4 Skill of the service provider.
5 Goal of the service provider.

In this schema, type of market would typically be 'consumer' or 'business' and a description of the core activity, e.g. consumer legal advice. The degree of labour intensiveness would be classed as either high or low depending on how automated it was. The degree of customer contact would also be classed as high or low, with healthcare being an example of a service with a high degree of customer contact and the postal service being an example of a low level of customer contact. Dibb et al. (2006) consider the skill of the service provider in terms of professional or non-professional. Accountancy is a professional skill whereas dry cleaning is not. The rationale behind this is that professional services are more complex and their practitioners have to be sure to comply with more regulations than non-professionals do. Clearly, there is a cross-over area here as it is not only the traditional professions, such as lawyers, doctors, accountants, who are highly regulated as anyone who works with children in the UK will

ACTIVITY

The following services vary in terms of how reliant they are on goods. Try placing them on a scale from pure service to high use of (peripheral) products. Then categorise them using any of the systems mentioned above:

- banks
- insurance companies
- hotels
- casinos
- restaurants
- travel agencies
- airlines
- colleges
- crèches
- debt collectors
- doctors' surgeries
- plumbers
- management consultancies
- cleaners
- stockbrokers
- garages
- personal trainers.

vouch. The final classification category, the goal of the service provider, refers to whether they are a profit or non-profit organisation (e.g. charities, the National Health Service).

There is no general agreement on a classification system for services and it may well be that service products are so diverse that any system will be flawed. It is important to remember that these categorisations are meant to assist the study and marketing of services and, if they do not do so, then there is little point to them. Choose a category or system that fits the service you are considering, and do not be afraid to choose a different one in a different situation.

Another consideration in categorising services as an aid to marketing them well is to think about the degree of involvement of both the service provider and the consumers. In considering the nature of services in the section above, it was identified that both the service provider and the consumer are integral parts of service provision but the extent of their involvement in the process will vary: some services require high levels of direct involvement by the provider (e.g. dentistry) and some low levels (e.g. online ordering). Similarly, this is the case with the level of involvement by the consumer. It is possible to consider the marketing implications of each in defining the service provision.

RETAILING AND E-TAILING

In many of the more developed countries, shopping is a major pastime. This is a relatively new phenomenon. Shopping used to be considered a chore rather than a leisure activity. This change in shopping's status has significant implications for retailers and for retailing's place in marketing. Is it a service or is it a form of personal selling or is it the final stage in the distribution channel? (See Chapter 9.) So which P of the marketing mix should we put it in: product, promotion or place? The answer is, of course, that there are aspects of retailing which fit into all of these categories although this chapter is mainly concerned with retail as a service to the consumer: a provider of goods and services and a leisure activity.

As the main source of goods, retailing has a special place in the services spectrum. Its *raison d'être* is to provide other products and it is difficult to separate it out from those products. So there are two issues of inseparability here: the service provider (in this case the retailer) is an integral part of the service and so are the goods they sell. Retailers will be judged on the quality of both.

Whereas traditional retailers are tied to a particular place, a high street or out-of-town shopping centre perhaps, there are other retailers who are not. Mail order (or catalogue)

personal selling

communication between a salesperson and one or more prospective purchasers

companies have sold their goods and services through the post for many years. Their business is based upon the convenience of bringing the shop to the shopper's own home. A modern variant of home shopping is provided by the Internet. The number of purchases made over the Internet is growing steadily but still the vast majority are made offline. According to the Office for National Statistics (2016), online sales account for less than 14% of all retail sales in the UK. The majority of Internet sales are made by pure play retailers, i.e. Internet only businesses, but household goods retailers and department stores are showing the fastest growth rates.

pure play

an organisation that only sells online, e.g. Amazon, eBay

A C T I V I T Y

Refer back to Exhibit 7.3 of the total service offering. Re-draw the diagram for a retailer of your choice.

digital focus: going shopping

Why don't Primark sell online? They did briefly trade online in the summer of 2013, by which time most of their competitors were well established on the Internet, but it was only a trial and hasn't been continued.

There are massive advantages to selling online: reaching new markets, saving money on expensive high street properties, employing fewer staff, centralising warehousing and improving stock control. A website is so much cheaper and easier to manage than a chain of shops. Many of Primark's high street rivals have both: they are **bricks and clicks** operations, not pure plays, and the growth is mainly in online sales.

In Primark's stores, clothes fly off the shelves – and perhaps that success is part of the problem. Primark's business model is based on cheap, disposable high fashion. Customers go back again and again because they want the latest thing – not things that will last. The store changes its ranges many times in a season. You get the look, wear it until you are tired of it, then go back to the store and get something else. **Stock turnover** is high – and that can be a nightmare for an online retailer.

One of the common complaints made about websites is that they often display items that are out of stock or, even worse, they send substitute products that customers just don't want. How could Primark keep a website up to date while continuing to constantly offer new clothes? They would have to change item listings hourly – and still they would be running the risk of upsetting their loyal customers. Perhaps it is better to have those customers come to the shop and browse. Let them see how cheap and lovely the clothes are – and buy multiple items because they can't decide which one they like best.

Primark is owned by Associated British Foods and their Chief Executive said: 'as you can imagine, the margins are so small that it can be difficult to sell a £3 t-shirt when you're spending the same amount just to ship it. The shipping costs for an online business are the key reason why online-only retailers can't compete with us'.

Many consumers believe online shopping is cheaper; many businesses are online because costs are lower – but these things may not always be true.

Source: Neville (2013)

bricks and clicks

an organisation, usually retail, that operates both online and offline, e.g. John Lewis, Tesco

stock turnover

a measure of the frequency with which items for sale need to be replenished

As the Internet becomes a mass marketplace, ease of use becomes more and more important: high quality and service convenience are demanded by e-shoppers too. The early Internet shoppers were computer-skilled bargain hunters, but this is no longer true. Today's online shoppers are motivated by the convenience of shopping from home at any time of the day or night, and having products delivered to their door. Ease of use is paramount and numerous customers give up and abandon their shopping baskets before they make it all the way through to the check-out pages (Jayawardhena et al., 2003). If the process takes too long, it may not only negate the service convenience advantage, but also anger the customer to the point that they never return.

THE SERVICES MARKETING MIX
THE OTHER 3PS

The traditional marketing mix of 4Ps (product, promotion, place and price) needs some expanding in order to cope with the distinctive qualities of services. In 1981, Bernard Booms and Mary Jo Bitner proposed the addition of a further 3Ps: physical evidence, participants (people) and process (cited in Bitner, 1990).

Service companies have an even greater need to build customers' trust in the products they offer than goods providers do. They need to reassure customers that the service will be a quality experience, especially as most of the time the service is bought untried. One often used strategy to overcome fears associated with the service product's intangibility is to turn it into something more tangible. The surroundings in which a service is delivered are a key part of customer satisfaction. The ambience of the restaurant, the plates, the music, the state of the toilets – all these things contribute as much to a meal out as the quality of the food. These more tangible aspects of services are called physical evidence and they are important contributors to customer satisfaction. These things are largely within the control of the staff who get blamed when things go wrong. However, if the service environment is good, and seems well organised, customers are less likely to blame the staff for service failures, even when it is really their fault (Bitner, 1990).

The second P of this extended marketing mix is more commonly referred to as 'people' rather than as 'participants' (the original term). Delivery of a service is usually reliant on staff and so they are important, but the customers and consumers also affect delivery of a service and so they are included in the mix too.

Then there is the question of the actual provision of the service: the process. When a customer buys a product, such as a DVD, it is put in a bag, taken home and watched whenever the new owner feels like watching it. They do not actually see the product being made, they just buy the end result. However, a service only exists while it is being delivered. When a customer goes to the cinema, the only thing that gets taken home is memory. If it was a bad film, there is not much they can do about it. The actual process of watching the film is the chargeable thing. Exhibit 7.4 illustrates the 7Ps of the services marketing mix.

The first 4Ps of the marketing mix were introduced in Chapter 6 and have their own individual chapters in this book. The extra 3Ps of services marketing are discussed individually below.

P	Description	Examples
Product	The core service offering	Haircut
Promotion	Advertising and other tools	Student discount, press advertisement, business cards
Place	Where the service is delivered Intermediaries involved in service delivery	The salon franchises (e.g. Toni and Guy)
Price	The money part of the exchange	May be scaled according to stylist's experience
People	Who deliver the service and who receive it	Hair stylist, junior, receptionist, service consumer
Process	How the service is delivered	From booking the appointment to leaving the salon – and beyond
Physical evidence	The tangible aspects of the service	Shampoo

EXHIBIT 7.4 The 7Ps of services marketing

PEOPLE

It is the organisation's people who deliver the service, and their attitudes, skills and efficiency often determine how satisfied customers are. It is therefore important that customer-facing staff should be well trained, appropriately turned out and courteous. It is often people that build relationships rather than companies. (In some industries, employees have to sign a contract preventing them from working in the same area for a specified time period after they leave in an attempt to prevent them from taking customers with them.)

If the service personnel are on the end of a telephone line, then it is a good telephone manner that is essential. If they are communicating by email, it is their written communication and efficiency that are important.

Technology does not replace people completely in the delivery of most services, it just makes them more remote (and may mean the company needs fewer of them). The loss of the personal touch means that it can be harder to build customer relationships. The Internet has the potential to remove all human interaction from transactions, reducing them to mere routines (Pincott and Branthwaite, 2000). Amazon and other online retailers work hard to build relationships with their customers. They personalise web pages, greet their returning visitors by name and track them through the site so that they can make pertinent recommendations. However, there is growing evidence that too much personalisation is unpopular with some customers, who find it intrusive and who do not want so close a relationship with their bookseller (O'Connor and Galvin, 2001).

The quality of a service is largely dependent upon the skills of the people who provide it, and so the quality of the people who provide a service is even more important than the quality and skills of those who make products. Good, up-to-date training is important. Faulty products may be caught by quality control before they leave the factory, but there are no second chances with services. It is not possible to rewind and start again.

research focus

Echeverri, P., Salomonson, N. and Åberg, A. (2012) 'Dealing with customer misbehaviour: employees' tactics, practical judgement and implicit knowledge', *Marketing Theory*, 12 (4): 427–49.
The 'people' element of the marketing mix refers to both customers and service providers. This paper looks at the range of ways in which frontline staff deal with difficult customers.

PROCESS

Process is the way in which the service is provided. Burger King is self-service whereas Pizza Express offers waiter service. The processes involved are different, although each scenario is capable of providing competitive advantage.

How bookings are made and how customer enquiries are handled is part of the service process. This is an aspect of service management that is becoming increasingly out-sourced and automated through ticket agents, and Internet and telephone sales. This outsourcing is potentially damaging for the customer relationship as customers may actually build relationships with the firm's subcontractor rather than the firm itself. This makes the customers harder to retain in the future. Even worse, it has been known for companies that started as subcontractors to expand and take on the whole business themselves (e.g. plumbers contracted to a home services company could decide to take on the customers themselves).

The service encounter, which determines the perceived quality of the service, should be carefully thought through. Customer journey mapping is a technique used extensively in services design. The aim is to create a visual representation of how customers interact with an organisation. The service provider tries to step in to the customer's shoes to document each key point of interaction, known as a touchpoint, from the user's perspective. Research is carried out to examine customer actions, needs, expectations and perceptions at each stage of the journey to help the firm understand how its processes impact the customer experience. Customer journey mapping can identify problem areas or 'pain points' in the customer journey and pinpoint 'moments of truth' – where there is the opportunity to make or break the relationship. This is particularly important when firms make use of multiple channels (website, catalogues, retail store and mobile app) and as a result customers can weave many different winding paths from awareness to purchase and beyond.

Joining a gym, for example (see Exhibit 7.5), begins with a phone call to explore membership options and book an appointment to view the facilities. What impression is created by the person who answers the phone? Their courtesy and helpfulness, and perhaps how quickly a tour can be arranged will be the first point at which the experience could go wrong.

Customer process	Phone up for prices	Visit gym	Application	Induction
	'How long do I have to sign up for?' 'Can I pay per visit?'	'Will I fit in?' 'Are they all super fit?'	'How long is this going to take?'	'What shall I wear?' 'I hope they don't weigh me!'
Company process	• Reception takes call • Takes customer contact details for sales team call back	• Guided tour (sales team)	• Complete application form • Personal profile and goals sheet	• Safety briefing (instructor) • Personal programme
Aim	Tour booking	Completed application	Signed contract Set up payment	Health & Safety Upsell personal training
Experience	I had to explain twice and dislike the hard sell	Friendly guide and met a nice lady Lots of people like me here	Took ages – I didn't know what to write and no staff to help	Worried about being watched I wasn't the only one with no idea what to do!
Improvements	• Dedicated sales line New training (listen to customer needs) • A make or break touchpoint	• Set up buddy system for new customers • Select guides with great people skills	• Reduce form length – basics only Complete personal profile after induction	• Set expectations beforehand (new confirmation letter/email) • Book inductions in quiet periods where possible

EXHIBIT 7.5 Simplified customer journey map for joining a gym

When the customer arrives at the gym, the welcome they receive is important. This is the start of the service encounter, a positive tour experience is likely to play a big part in a prospective member's decision to join. Each stage in the process must be carefully managed so as to meet customer expectations.

research focus

Minkiewicz, J., Bridson, K. and Evans, J. (2016) 'Co-production of service experiences: insights from the cultural sector', *Journal of Services Marketing*, 30 (7): 749–61.
This paper explores the way organisations collaborate with customers to facilitate consumption of cultural experiences through the lens of co-production. It finds that cultural organisations are co-producing service experiences with their customers, as revealed through a number of key processes: inviting customers to actively participate in the experience, engaging customers and supporting customers in the co-production of the experience.

ACTIVITY

PHYSICAL EVIDENCE

Although fundamentally intangible, most services do have a tangible element (just as goods, i.e. physical products, frequently have intangible service elements). Even dentists give you appointment cards and occasionally free toothpaste, and they certainly have instruments and a chair, and reception and waiting areas designed to look pleasant and comfortable.

These tangible aspects are known as physical evidence and are key in shaping the customers' perception of the quality of the service. Physical evidence takes many forms. It may be a peripheral product, e.g. the oil used in a car service or the soap provided in a hotel. It may be the surroundings in which the service is delivered – the ambience. This comprises décor, music, colour scheme, etc., which is particularly important in places of entertainment such as bars and restaurants (see servicescapes below for more on the environment in which a service is delivered). It may be a ticket or a contract, the physical proof that you have paid for the service. Tickets may sound trivial but they play a vital role in reassuring customers that their flight, theatre seat or concert is booked. There is no real need for an airline to issue a ticket as they have the passengers' details on their computer system, but the ticket (even an e-ticket) tells the customer where to go to catch the plane and is a chance to check that the flight is correctly booked. For the same reason, airlines usually send a confirming email as do online retailers who want to reassure customers that their order has been received and will be dispatched.

servicescape

the total environment in which a service is experienced

SERVICESCAPES

The environment in which the service is provided and experienced plays a significant part in the overall effect and assessment of the service. Consumers do not typically go to too much trouble in analysing individual components (unless prompted to do so), but instead experience a totality. Booms and Bitner (1981) proposed the concept of the servicescape to describe the total (and frequently complex) environment in which the service encounter takes place. They defined servicescape as:

> The environment in which the service is assembled and in which the seller and customer interact, combined with tangible commodities that facilitate performance or communication of the service. (Booms and Bitner, 1981: 56)

Upmarket servicescape: a luxury service such as a trip on the Orient Express demands luxury surroundings.

© Dave Pickton

The ambiance, décor, staffing, layout, accessories, and so on contribute to the total experience of the service encounter of a theatre or bar or other service offering. The environment is one that helps to define the service, distinguish it from competitor offerings and ultimately generate customer satisfaction or dissatisfaction. Take Abercrombie and Fitch, for example. This is not just any shop. Customers go there for the experience as much as for the clothes. The ultra-trendy décor is inspired. Lighting is dim (apart from strategically placed spots so that shoppers can see the clothes on offer), music is loud (check their website for playlists), the assistants are all young and good-looking (they are cast rather than hired), and bare-chested male models often adorn the entrance. There are queues both outside the shop and inside for the tills where people queue for up to an hour just to pay.

global focus: dream flight

People are fond of saying that 'you get what you pay for' and it does seem to be true of air travel. International airlines compete fiercely for passengers and, while budget operations like Ryanair cut all the costs they can to offer the lowest headline price, at the premium end of the market Emirates, British Airways and Cathay Pacific look for ways to make the journey more luxurious. They want passengers to actually look forward to the flight rather than just seeing it as a way to get somewhere.

Flying can be stressful so airlines look for ways to reduce that stress and make the flight more enjoyable. Air France, British Airways and Virgin Atlantic all offer spa treatments in their airport lounges giving passengers the chance to chill before they board their flight. Many up-market airlines put premium cosmetics products such as Clarins and Elemis in their complimentary inflight amenity bags. Emirates goes a step further by offering first class passengers a spa shower on its A380 aircraft as well as facials and massages in its Dubai lounge. All this is a wonderful for first and business class passengers, but what about economy?

Emirates' latest innovation is aimed at the cheaper seats. The airline has launched an interactive amenity kit for economy class passengers which they hope will provide a more comfortable travel experience than that of their rivals. These kits use augmented reality (AR) technology to provide immersive content on mobile devices.

The kit bags come in six designs inspired by the six regions in Emirates' global network – Australasia, Latin America, Middle East, Africa, Europe and the Far East. The designs incorporate the colours and patterns of each of these regions. Their contents include: eye mask, earplugs, toothbrush and toothpaste, and socks – each tailored to the design on the bag. The bags themselves are made of Neoprene material (a strong, water resistant fabric) so they have a number of follow on uses for travellers.

However, the really innovative part of the kit is its AR app. Blippar has created exclusive content for Emirates including activities and health tips for a more comfortable and relaxing travel experience. The app works with Emirates' inflight entertainment system so that passengers across *all travel classes* can enjoy over 2,500 channels of entertainment and free Wi-Fi on their mobile devices. They just download the app and scan their kit bag. The content will be refreshed every six months so frequent flyers shouldn't get bored.

Some reality has also been augmented in airport servicescapes. San Jose Airport teamed up with Google to test their Tango technology. Tango enables mobile devices to establish their position relative to the world around them without GPS or other external signals. This paves the way for location-based AR mobile applications that know exactly where a user is.

The San Jose app helped users to find their way around the terminal and displayed augmented reality billboards with destination information outside each departure gate. App users could also see various 3D images floating around the retail area; a 3D shark swimming outside of the Sharks Cage restaurant and pints of beer floating outside the pub. Perhaps the cleverest use of the augmented reality was to search for a shop or restaurant based on its proximity to your current location and the time of your flight. The app used photographic quality images of the airport to show the way to the selected shop or restaurant making sure there was plenty of time to eat or shop and still make the flight.

Do you think augmented reality adds value to a service? Or is it just a gimmick?

Sources: Emirates Media Centre (2016); Future Travel Experience (2016); Garcia (2016)

ACTIVITY

Compare and contrast the online servicescapes of two competing Internet retailers – perhaps one you know well and one that is new. How do you decide if the retailer is trustworthy? How does visual design, content and imagery affect your interest and enjoyment (especially if you've never shopped with them before)? What features make the site easier or harder to navigate? What aspects do you think could be improved?

In a virtual or online situation, the environment becomes the website and the situation surrounding the electronic device. Servicescapes thus become composites of what the service provider offers and what the consumer brings to the service encounter. Again, this emphasises the potential for inconsistency in the service offering as different customers interact in different ways and at different times with the service being offered.

Characteristics of the e-servicescape, like the layout of the site and the images used, can help to build consumers' feelings of trust in an online retailer, just like the experience of walking into a long-established and reputable store. Harris and Goode (2010) identified three key dimensions of the e-servicescape: 1) aesthetic appeal 2) layout and functionality and 3) financial security, which contribute to consumers' confidence in and intention to purchase from the site.

SERVICE QUALITY

Service companies need to build the customer's trust in the services they offer. They need to reassure the customer that the service will be a quality experience. Given that services are intangible and inconsistent (see the 'Characteristics of services' section above), it is all the more important to pay particular attention to the quality of service offered. Many papers and articles have been written on customer expectations and perceptions of service quality. Perhaps the most famous model used to measure service quality is SERVQUAL (Parasuraman et al., 1988), which employs five dimensions that contribute to service quality:

1   Tangibles (see physical evidence above)

2   Reliability (how dependable is the service, can its performance be relied upon?)

3   Responsiveness (speed of response and helpfulness of staff)

4   Assurance (confidence in the service offering, credibility and consistency)

5   Empathy (good customer understanding).

Customers are asked to complete a questionnaire that uses a series of questions related to the five dimensions listed above. Importantly, SERVQUAL has two parts: the first asks about the service in general and the second part asks the same questions about the specific service received. For example, if the service was a restaurant, Part A would be about restaurants of a similar type more generally and Part B would ask about the specific restaurant whose service quality was being measured. The reason why this is significant is that Part A gives an indication, a benchmark, against which the service being evaluated can be assessed. Gaps between expectations in general and the perception of the service offered in particular can be highlighted and improvements made where relevant.

It is important to assess service quality against the right benchmarks. There would be little point in trying to assess the service quality of a small, local restaurant against what may be expected of a particularly high-class, expensive restaurant of the type run by celebrity chefs.

Customers and consumers do not expect perfection. Typically, they have a tolerance range and are willing to accept anything that falls within it. Things can and do go wrong. What is usually important is what the service provider is able to do about it and this is where service recovery comes in (see below).

research focus: classic concepts

Parasuraman, A., Zeithaml, V.A. and Berry, L.B. (1988) 'SERVQUAL: a multiple-item scale for measuring consumer perceptions of service quality', *Journal of Retailing*, 64 (1): 12–40.

In the first article, the authors, experts and key researchers in the field of service quality, develop a scale for measuring service quality.

Parasuraman, A., Zeithaml, V.A. and Malhotra, A. (2005) 'E-S-QUAL: a multiple-item scale for assessing electronic service quality', *Journal of Service Research*, 7 (3): 213–33.

In this second article, the authors modify the scale to assess service quality on the web, which they use to measure service quality delivered on e-tailing sites.

BRANDING SERVICES

Branding started in the world of the physical product, at a time when manufacturing processes had advanced to the stage at which consistency and quality could pretty much be assured. Services tend to be inconsistent, which makes them harder to brand. However, there are lots of famous service brands today: British Airways, Avis rent-a-car, HSBC, Hilton Hotels, McDonald's, J. Walter Thomson, Wetherspoons, etc. Brands are seen as a badge of quality. Consumers have been educated by the physical products companies to understand this and so, in our age of the brand, service companies are able to switch things around and create brands that confer quality – rather than products of quality that therefore deserve brands.

A good brand not only reduces the customer's perceived risk, it actually enables a company to charge a higher price for its services.

ACTIVITY

Identify 10 major service brands. It may help if you look at adverts in the press (or try a web search) to jog your memory. Try to identify examples from a range of different sectors, such as travel/tourism, financial services, high street and online retailing, telephony and communications, etc. Consider the ways in which the companies have created and promoted their brands and what you think those brands represent. What message do they convey to customers?

ethical focus: McLibel

McDonald's is one of the largest and best-known brands in the world. The company's revenues exceed those of a number of smaller, less well-off countries. There are over 25,000 McDonald's restaurants in the world and about 40 million people eat there every day. But not everyone loves McDonald's. Towards the end of the twentieth century, protests against their products, and the means of producing them, were growing steadily. Still, McDonald's fans outweighed the critics massively and so the company seemed secure.

Then, one day in a flat in North London, a postman and a gardener wrote a little pamphlet lambasting McDonald's for its unethical products, employment practices and means of production. They handed it out to passers-by on the local streets and got vegetarian restaurants to display it. The pamphlet was fairly innocuous, a little out of date and, according to Naomi Klein, clearly the product of a 'meat is murder' vegetarian attitude. It was therefore unlikely to worry the core McDonald's customer. McDonald's really should have let it go, but they didn't, they sued.

The two activists, Helen Steel and Dave Morris, had little money and were denied legal aid. In court, these two quite ordinary-looking people had to face a battery of top lawyers on the other side. The trial was the longest in the history of English law – and the newspapers gleefully reported on it every day. Helen and Dave's views, previously only communicated to the few Londoners who had bothered to read the pamphlet, were now written up with commentary by leading journalists and posted on the web for the world to see and blog about. As for the original pamphlet, that had become a collector's item. More recently, in 2005, a documentary film was made about the McLibel two. Who won and who lost the case is largely irrelevant. This was one of the biggest corporate PR disasters of all time and its effects are still being felt – and seen – in McDonald's current marketing strategies.

For the full story of the McLibel trial, visit www.mcspotlight.org/case.
Sources: BBC News (1999); Haig (2003)

SERVICE LOGIC IN CONTEMPORARY MARKETING

Ever since service marketing research became established in the 1970s, the service context has been recognised as an opportunity to approach customers in fundamentally different ways (Grönroos and Gummerus, 2014). Established goods-focused marketing thinking emphasises the importance of building value into the product (see Chapter 6 for more on total product offering) and communicating that value to consumers. That value is exchanged for money at the point-of-purchase (if the price is right). By contrast, in a service context, even though a great deal of effort goes in to the design of a service product, its *value* can only be determined *by the customer* as they use the service for themselves – this is known as 'value-in-use' (Vargo and Lusch, 2004). Importantly, because service providers are able to interact with customers, they have the opportunity to directly influence customers' experiences and the value they derive from each encounter.

value proposition

a promise of value to be delivered by an innovation or feature designed to make a company or product attractive to customers

customer engagement

a customer's connection to a brand – this may have cognitive (thinking), affective (feeling) and/or behavioural (doing) aspects

As a result service marketing is often more concerned with the process of actively keeping the promise made to consumers than with making that promise, or value proposition, compelling in the first place. Service marketing emphasises the things firms do *with* customers not *for* or *to* them. This key idea of co-creating value with customers, which emerged from service marketing research, has far wider implications for marketing more generally, especially as digital and social media technologies enhance opportunities for all firms to interact with customers (see Chapter 8 for more on customer engagement.)

As contemporary marketing emphasises the importance of building relationships with customers, service thinking has become even more prominent. The term service-dominant logic (S-D logic) made famous by Vargo and Lusch (2008), refers to a more radical claim that *all business is* underpinned by a service orientation, defined as the application of knowledge and skills to benefit someone else. From this perspective, there is no distinction between goods and service. Instead all marketing is service, and goods (tangible products) are just one way of distributing that service to customers. For example, an iPhone is one way in which Apple shares its expertise with customers alongside an extensive range of online applications and services, a support team to call on when things go wrong and sophisticated logistics that ensure phones and accessories arrive with the customer on time and in one piece. To successfully adopt an S-D logic therefore a firm needs to focus not only on customers' desires (in order to offer a compelling value proposition) but also on customers' practices – what they do and what support they need to get genuine value-in-use.

service-dominant logic (S-D logic)

the idea that all organisations are primarily concerned with the exchange of services rather than physical products

Microsoft: value co-creation workshop

research focus

Luca, N.R., Hibbert, S. and McDonald, R. (2016) 'Towards a service-dominant approach to social marketing', *Marketing Theory,* **16 (Jun): 194–218.**

Recently, social marketing has moved away from traditional marketing management approaches towards service-orientated theory, integrating concepts from other disciplines, to account for the distinctive nature of social change and develop an ecological perspective. This article considers the applicability of service-dominant logic to social marketing, with a particular emphasis on how a systems perspective can offer new ways to address challenges of social change.

SERVICE RECOVERY

Nobody can guarantee that all service encounters will run smoothly or as intended. Things go wrong. Trains, boats and planes run late and are delayed. A financial transaction may contain errors. The food may not taste as it should in a restaurant. The plumber may not fix a leak or an electrician may charge more than expected. These things may occur despite the best efforts of the service provider and may be simple but unfortunate mistakes.

Service recovery

One bad service encounter is a serious thing that may lead to a significant loss of custom, not only from the person directly affected but also from others if that person tells family and friends of the bad experience or shares their frustration on Twitter. Bad news travels fast, especially via social media! A poorly handled customer complaint can have a significant negative impact on a firm's reputation. Consequently, service recovery is very important. If the service does go wrong, then the customer's concerns must be handled with great care. Good customer relationships are even more important to service businesses.

A complaint should be looked at as an opportunity to provide great service. It is often possible to turn the situation around and impress the customer after all. Bars and clubs may apologise profusely and take things off the bill or offer free drinks. Airlines may upgrade seats to first class or offer free tickets for another flight. The result can be a more satisfied customer than the one who received good service in the first place. Firms' need to monitor social media channels closely so that they are ready to act quickly to prevent a potential

Virgin Trains Twitter
service recovery

public relations crisis. Virgin Trains grabbed the headlines for all the *right* reasons when train staff were able to respond within minutes to a teenager's distress Tweet sent from a toilet cubicle that had run out of paper. By intervening quickly and going the extra mile to meet one customer's needs, Virgin gained a great deal of very positive free media exposure for its business.

While poor service encounters need to be avoided, service recovery provides opportunities for greater customer satisfaction if dealt with well. Encouraging customers to state their complaints may seem counter-productive but analysis of complaints can be an important research activity that can avoid customer disappointment at the time of the service delivery and can be built into overall improvement plans to avoid future complaints by other customers.

research focus

Hocutt, M.A., Bowers, M.R. and Donavan, D.T. (2006) 'The art of service recovery: fact or fiction', *Journal of Services Marketing*, 20 (3): 199–207.
   As it is impossible to ensure all customer experiences are positive, it becomes all the more relevant to understand the importance of what companies do about poor customer experiences. Bad experiences may be spread to others through word of mouth, creating even lower levels of customer satisfaction and loyalty. Service recovery is, therefore, a critical concept. If handled well, service recovery can lead to greater levels of customer satisfaction.

SUMMARY

Services are aspects of the total product offering. While it is convenient to think of physical products and service products as different, in reality they are part of the same product continuum (Exhibit 7.2), in which services have greater intangibility than physical goods. From a marketing perspective, it is always wise to consider what services may be added to enhance physical products and what physical products can be used to enhance the service offering.

In MDCs there has been a significant economic shift from manufacturing output to service provision. For this reason, the economies of MDCs place great reliance on services and on those companies that provide them. In marketing, therefore, it is important to recognise the distinctiveness, and key characteristics, of services. This chapter has highlighted the nature of services and identified seven particular characteristics: the customer gains some benefit from them; they are mostly intangible; they are time and place dependent (they cannot be stored); the service provider is an intrinsic part of the service itself; the consumer is also an intrinsic part of the service itself; services are inconsistent; and there is no resulting ownership of anything significant.

The interest in services marketing has led to an expansion of the traditional marketing mix from 4Ps to 7Ps by the inclusion of physical evidence, people and process. While the 7Ps clearly relate to services, many physical products also contain elements of services and therefore the 7Ps can be used for all types of products.

This chapter also highlighted a number of other key concepts, such as service convenience, service encounter, service quality, servicescape and service recovery as important considerations when marketing services. Branding is a strategy that evolved in the world of physical goods, but it has more recently been successfully applied to services. Branding is covered in greater depth in Chapters 6 and 11.

CHALLENGES REVIEWED

Now that you have finished reading the chapter, look back at the challenges you were set at the beginning. Do you have a clearer idea of what's involved?

HINTS

- The UK and most other MDCs are service economies so talk about how much income service businesses generate, the jobs they create and how they facilitate other businesses.

- Service recovery – remember that people often think more highly of a company that treats them really well after a mistake has been made than they do of companies who have never made mistakes.

- There are a number of answers to this problem – an obvious one relies on offering a better service; think about peripheral products, processes and how to exploit the skills of your people (who have the advantage of being more local).

- This is about the intangibility of services and how that makes them high-risk purchases. You need to reduce the perceived risk somehow, e.g. by emphasising the tangible aspects of the service being offered (such as the hotel's facilities) and the brand values of the airline, and/or by reference to previous satisfied customers. Do not forget about what guarantees and assurances you can offer.

READING AROUND

JOURNAL ARTICLES

Berry, L. (1980) 'Services marketing is different', *Business*, 30 (3): 52–6.

Grönroos, C. (1997) 'From marketing mix to relationship marketing: towards a paradigm shift in marketing', *Management Decision*, 35 (4): 322–39.

Grove, S.J., Fisk, R.P. and Joby, J. (2003) 'The future of services marketing: forecasts from ten services experts', *Journal of Services Marketing*, 17 (2): 107–21. (A journal article that gave insights into the future of services marketing that you can read and compare with your knowledge of what has actually happened.)

BOOKS AND BOOK CHAPTERS

Chaffey, D. and Smith, P. (2012) 'Remix', in *Emarketing Excellence: Planning and Optimising Your Digital Marketing* (Emarketing Essentials) (4th edn). Oxford: Routledge, Chapter 2, pp. 49–100.

Gummesson, E. (2008a) 'Exit services marketing – enter service marketing', in M.J. Baker and S. Hart (eds), *The Marketing Book* (6th edn). Oxford: Butterworth Heinemann, Chapter 23, pp. 451–71.

Gummesson, E. (2008b) *Total Relationship Marketing* (3rd edn). Oxford: Butterworth Heinemann.

ONLINE RESOURCES

Emmy host giving HBO Now password away: www.youtube.com/watch?v=rvJlVk-Jvzw

WEBSITES

www.hospitalityassured.com – a website for an organisation (Hospitality Assured) dedicated to raising standards in the hospitality industry. Check out *The Standard* with its 10 key steps to achieving service and business excellence.

TEST YOURSELF

1   Define services. (See p. 258)

2   Why should marketers be more concerned in today's economies with the marketing of services? (See p. 259)

3   What does the product continuum describe? (See p. 263)

4   Identify the seven characteristics that describe the nature of services. (See pp. 263–264)

5   What is meant when we say that services are inconsistent? (See p. 271)

6   Dibb et al. propose a way of classifying services based on five criteria. What are they? (See p. 273)

7   What is meant by the consumer being part of the service? (See p. 269)

8   What is 'service convenience'? (See p. 270)

9   What are the 7Ps? (See pp. 276–277)

10   Why is physical evidence important to the marketing of services? (See p. 280)

11   Why is it important to assess service quality and what is SERVQUAL? (See p. 282)

12   Why is service recovery an important concept? (See p. 285)

REVISION TOOLS

Want to test yourself even more? Review what you have learnt by visiting
https://study.sagepub.com/masterson4e

- Practise for exams with **multiple choice questions**
- Revise key terms with **interactive flashcards**

MINI CASE STUDY: ROCK PLANET

Read the questions, then the case material, and then answer the questions.

QUESTIONS

1   Identify and explain examples of the 7Ps at work in the case study.

2   What is Rock Planet doing well? Where does it fall down?

3   Using the 7Ps to guide you, recommend three improvements the restaurant can make. You should explain and justify your ideas.

The Rock Planet restaurant opened with a burst of publicity and a celebrity launch party just over a year ago. For the first few months it was the place to eat, although even then there were mutterings about slow service and rude waiters. Now it's a familiar London landmark, particularly popular with tourists who like the inexpensive set lunch menu. Its reasonable prices and rock star connections also attract the young for celebrations such as birthdays and leaving parties. The bouncers look formidable, but they've never been known to refuse anyone entrance unreasonably.

The restaurant is usually full, so diners wait in the bar, which is loud and crowded. A 1960s-style jukebox adds to the din. Customers get a Rock Planet buzzer, one of five designs (each a model of an artist), which lights up and sings when their table is ready. Flamboyant waiters shake cocktails in dramatic style against a backdrop of rock memorabilia. Electric guitars adorn the walls alongside pictures of their famous former owners. One of Jimi Hendrix's guitars has pride of place above the bar. To its right, under thick glass, is a scrap of paper on which John Lennon jotted some of the words to 'She Loves You'. On the left is one of Will-i-am's hats.

The rock décor is carried through to the restaurant, as is the music. All the waiters are young and dressed up. There are the teddy boy suits and the flared skirts and short socks of the 1950s, glam rock, grunge and some of the latest club styles. The restaurant serves fast food American style: hamburgers (and a veggie burger), fries, salads, chicken and ribs. It also does take-aways and delivers within a five-mile radius.

The biggest complaint is that food doesn't come to the table fast enough – something that is rubbed in by the lights that flash on a neon map of the USA to tell the waiters when an order is ready for collection. However, many diners find the friendly service makes up for their building hunger. And they tend to order more drinks. Home-delivery customers have to order at least two hours before they want the food.

Rock Planet is a place where people like to celebrate their birthdays and so the staff have a birthday routine. They dance through the restaurant carrying sparklers and then, when they reach the birthday table, they sing 'Happy Birthday' and encourage the rest of the diners to join in. The birthday boy or girl is presented with a cupcake with an everlasting candle on it and a small bag of inexpensive Rock Planet merchandise.

Further entertainment comes from the Rock Planet Moments. Each day, the manager chooses three dishes to be the special recommendations of the day. When the 20th order for that dish is delivered to a table, there is a fanfare and lights flash. The lucky diner gets the featured dish on the house and a complementary cocktail (alcoholic or non-alcoholic) of their choice. For the 50th order, the diner gets their whole meal free.

Very lucky diners may get to sit at a table next to the stars. The restaurant is owned by a group of well-known musicians who make a point of eating there as often as possible. Sometimes, you might even get 'Happy Birthday' sung by a megastar.

One of the biggest challenges for the management is keeping the place clean. It's a large, busy restaurant and lots of children eat there. Inevitably this means that there are spills and it can be hard to get them cleaned up while people are eating. The toilets are checked every hour but they still sometimes run out of towels or soap. The floor seems always in need of a clean. The problem in the bar is even worse. Staff have trouble fighting their way to tables to collect glasses and wipe down tabletops. A dropped tray of glasses means dangerous glass on the floor, so staff are reluctant to collect too many at once. Frequently the bar staff run out of clean glasses altogether.

Rock Planet has had some bad reviews recently. Critics say the food is unimaginative and of low quality, the restaurant too loud and too dirty, the service too slow and the waiters often get the orders, or the bill, wrong. But apparently the diners disagree – it's still packed out every night.

Note: Rock Planet and this case study are entirely fictional.

REFERENCES

Anderson, C. (2012) 'The impact of social media on lodging performance', *Cornell Hospitality Report*, 12 (15): 6–11. Available at: http://scholarship.sha.cornell.edu/chrpubs/5/ (accessed 14/10/16).

BBC News (1999) *McLibel Duo Gain Part Victory*. Available at: news.bbc.co.uk/1/hi/uk/308453.stm (accessed 20/05/13).

Berry, L.L., Seiders, K. and Grewal, D. (2002) 'Understanding service convenience', *Journal of Marketing*, 66 (3): 1–17.

Bitner, M.J. (1990) 'Evaluating service encounters: the effects of physical surroundings and employee responses', *Journal of Marketing*, 54 (2): 69–82.

Booms, B.H. and Bitner, M.J. (1981) 'Marketing strategies and organization structures for service firms', in J.H. Donnelly and W.R. George (eds), *Marketing of Services*. Chicago: American Marketing Association, pp. 51–67.

CIA (Central Intelligence Agency) (n.d.) *The World Factbook*. Available at: www.cia.gov/library/publications/the-world-factbook/fields/2012.html (accessed 11/05/16).

Coyle, D. (1999) *The Weightless World: Strategies for Managing the Digital Economy*. Cambridge, MA: MIT Press.

Dibb, S., Simkin, L., Pride, W.M. and Ferrell, O.C. (2006) *Marketing Concepts and Strategies* (5th edn). Boston: Houghton Mifflin.

Echeverri, P., Salomonson, N. and Åberg, A. (2012) 'Dealing with customer misbehaviour: employees' tactics, practical judgement and implicit knowledge', *Marketing Theory*, 12 (4): 427–49.

Emirates Media Centre (2016) 'Emirates introduces the world's first interactive amenity kit in Economy Class', 17 July. Available at: www.emirates.com/media-centre/emirates-introduces-the-worlds-first-interactive-amenity-kit-in-economy-class# (accessed 15/08/16).

Future Travel Experience (2016) 'San Jose Airport and Google team up to explore potential of augmented reality technology', August. Available at: www.futuretravelexperience.com/2016/08/san-jose-airport-and-google-team-up-to-trial-augmented-reality-technology/ (accessed 15/08/16).

Gammell, K. (2015) 'How streaming TV has become a Free for almost everyone', *The Guardian*, Money, 18 July. Available at: www.theguardian.com/money/2015/jul/18/streaming-tv-sharing-subscriptions-stealing (accessed 22/05/16).

Garcia, M. (2016) 'Flying fabulously: airlines indulge pax vanity with luxury products', APEX, 8 August. Available at: http://apex.aero/2016/08/08/flying-fabulously-airlines-indulge-pax-vanity-luxury-products (accessed 15/08/16).

Grönroos, C. (1984) 'A service quality model and its marketing implications', *European Journal of Marketing*, 18 (4): 36–44.

Grönroos, C. and Gummerus, J. (2014) 'The service revolution and its marketing implications: service logic vs service-dominant logic', *Managing Service Quality*, 24 (3): 206–29.

Grove, S.J., Fisk, R.P. and Joby, J. (2003) 'The future of services marketing: forecasts from ten services experts', *Journal of Services Marketing*, 17 (2): 107–21.

Haig, M. (2003) *Brand Failures: The Truth about the 100 Biggest Branding Mistakes of All Time*. London: Kogan Page.

Handy, C. (2002) *The Elephant and the Flea*. London: Arrow.

Harris, L.C. and Goode, M.M. (2010) 'Online servicescapes, trust, and purchase intentions', *Journal of Services Marketing*, 24 (3): 230–43.

Hocutt, M.A., Bowers, M.R. and Donavan, D.T. (2006) 'The art of service recovery: fact or fiction', *Journal of Services Marketing*, 20 (3): 199–207.

Jayawardhena, C., Wright, L.T. and Masterson, R. (2003) 'An investigation of online consumer purchasing', *Qualitative Market Research: An International Journal*, 6 (1): 58–65.

Kotler, P. (2003) *Marketing Insights from A to Z: 80 Concepts Every Manager Needs to Know*. New York: John Wiley & Sons.

Kotler, P., Armstrong, G., Saunders, J. and Wong, V. (2001) *Principles of Marketing* (European edn). Harlow: Pearson Education.

Luca, N.R., Hibbert, S. and McDonald, R. (2016). 'Towards a service-dominant approach to social marketing', *Marketing Theory*, 16 (Jun): 194–218.

Lynley, M. (2014) 'HBO's CEO doesn't care that you are sharing your HBO password', *Buzzfeed*. Available at: www.buzzfeed.com/mattlynley/hbos-ceo-doesnt-care-that-you-are-sharing-your-hbo-password?utm_term=.peogQXG5k#.khw0J7M4O (accessed 22/05/16).

Melián-González, S., Bulchand-Gidumal, J. and González López-Valcárcel, B. (2013) 'Online customer reviews of hotels: as participation increases, better evaluation is obtained', *Cornell Hospitality Quarterly*, 54 (3): 274–83.

Minkiewicz, J., Bridson, K. and Evans, J. (2016) 'Co-production of service experiences: insights from the cultural sector', *Journal of Services Marketing*, 30 (7): 749–61.

Neville, S. (2013) 'Primark unlikely to continue with Asos online collaboration', *The Independent*, 6 November. Available at: www.independent.co.uk/news/business/news/primark-unlikely-to-continue-with-asos-online-collaboration-8923652.html (accessed 23/05/16).

O'Connor, J. and Galvin, E. (2001) *Marketing in the Digital Age*. Harlow: FT/Prentice Hall.

Office for National Statistics (ONS) (2016) 'Statistical bulletin: retail sales in Great Britain: Apr 2016'. Available at: www.ons.gov.uk/businessindustryandtrade/retailindustry/bulletins/retailsales/apr2016#internet-sales-in-detail (accessed 26/05/16).

Palmer, A. (2005) *Principles of Services Marketing* (4th edn). Maidenhead: McGraw Hill.

Parasuraman, A., Zeithaml, V.A. and Berry, L.B. (1988) 'SERVQUAL: a multiple-item scale for measuring consumer perceptions of service quality', *Journal of Retailing*, 64 (1): 12–40.

Parasuraman, A., Zeithaml, V.A. and Malhotra, A. (2005) 'E-S-QUAL: a multiple-item scale for assessing electronic service quality', *Journal of Service Research*, 7 (3): 213–33.

Pincott, G. and Branthwaite, A. (2000) 'Nothing new under the sun?', *International Journal of Market Research*, 42 (2): 137–55.

Topping, A. (2007) 'Man using laptop on garden wall charged with wireless theft', *The Guardian*, 23 August, p. 3.

Tripadvisor (2017) 'How reviews help your business', 20 March. Available at: www.tripadvisor.co.uk/TripAdvisorInsights/n2150/how-reviews-help-your-business (accessed 08/03/17).

Tuttle, B. (2015) 'The real rules for sharing passwords at HBO Now, Netflix, Amazon Prime, and Hulu', *Time: Money*. Available at: http://time.com/money/4043147/hbo-netflix-amazon-prime-share-account-password/ (accessed 26/05/16).

Vargo, S.L. and Lusch, R.F. (2004) 'Evolving to a new dominant logic for marketing', *Journal of Marketing*, 68 (1): 1–17.

Vargo, S.L. and Lusch, R.F. (2008) 'Service-dominant logic: continuing the evolution', *Journal of the Academy of Marketing Science*, 36 (1): 1–10.

PROMOTION (MARKETING COMMUNICATIONS)

8

PROMOTION CHALLENGES

The following are illustrations of the types of decision that marketers have to take or issues they face. *You aren't expected to know how to deal with the challenges now*; just bear them in mind as you read the chapter and see what you can find that helps.

Degree to job:
Groundwork Charity

- You are a marketing manager responsible for a new range of chilled fruit drinks. What budget would be appropriate for the launch?

- You run a small, specialist soft drinks firm. Your marketing budget is a tiny fraction of that of your major competitor and you certainly cannot afford television advertising. How will you get your brand noticed by potential customers?

- Disaster! You are the public relations manager for a major airline. The check-in staff and baggage handlers have gone on strike leaving thousands of passengers stranded at an international airport. They are angry and frustrated. What will you do now? What will you do later when the crisis has passed?

- You are an advertising account manager and one of your clients is a multinational snack food manufacturer whose account is worth £30 million per year to your agency. In the past, most of that money has been spent on advertising during children's television programmes but recently there has been a consumer backlash against adverts, and junk foods, which target young children. You need to advise your client on their future marketing communications strategy.

INTRODUCTION

Promotion is one of the 4Ps of the marketing mix and an essential part of the total product offering. No matter how good your product is, if people do not know it is good, then they will not buy it. Equally, no matter how good your promotion is, if your product is poor, then people will not *continue* to buy it. Some form of promotion, or marketing communication, is necessary to make customers aware of the existence of the product, help create its brand identity, and persuade them to try it and even to incorporate it into their lives.

To be effective, promotional activity must be based on a sound understanding of how and why products are bought, consumed or used and of current market trends. Clearly, this involves in-depth research as well as an understanding of the principles of buyer behaviour (see Chapters 5 and 3 respectively). Marketers segment their potential audiences (using the techniques discussed in Chapter 4) in order to select the best group(s) at which to aim their communications.

DEFINITIONS

In marketing, 'promotion' refers to communication designed to persuade others to accept ideas or concepts; to consider the benefits of products or to motivate people to take action. It rarely results in an immediate sale. Promotion's role is to move people closer to a purchase decision.

This chapter will examine the reasons why it is necessary for organisations to communicate, who they communicate with, how they can get their message across and how they can get consumers engaged and involved with their brands. It will also consider the regulatory environment within which marketers operate (with particular reference to UK regulatory bodies). The chapter concludes with a brief section on setting marketing budgets.

THE PROMOTION MIX

There are many promotional tools or activities and the traditional way of categorising all of them is as the promotion mix, which (traditionally and at its most basic level) comprises:

promotion mix
traditionally, advertising, PR, sales promotion and personal selling

- advertising
- public relations (PR)
- sales promotions
- personal selling.

Just as there are 4Ps in the marketing mix, product, promotion, place and price, there are also four main elements to the promotion mix (although unfortunately they do not all start with the letter P).

Although advertising is sometimes used as an alternative term for promotion or marketing communications, in its stricter sense the term describes any *paid* form of *non-personal* presentation of ideas, goods and services by an *identified* advertiser. Most advertising consists of paid-for promotional messages carried by the mass media (TV, radio, press, cinema, posters and websites); however, search and social media platforms such as Google and Facebook offer greater potential for targeting and now represent a significant share of UK advertising spending (Spanier, 2016). Public relations (PR) uses different activities designed to promote goodwill and enhance and protect reputations and brand image. These activities may include providing news and feature stories for the media, running events, sponsorship, or building relationships with influential individuals and groups. PR may use the same media (e.g. television, radio, the Internet) as advertising but in a very different way. While advertisers buy space or airtime and control (within the regulations) what goes into it, PROs (Public Relations Officers) have to persuade journalists to include stories about their brands and cannot control what those journalists say. Media coverage resulting from PR activity is therefore earned (rather than paid for); company/brand-related stories, activities or events have to be newsworthy.

mass media
communications channels that reach a large, relatively undifferentiated audience, e.g. posters, the Internet, press; plural of mass medium

Sales promotions are short-term special offers and other added-value activities intended to induce buyers to buy, or try, a product. Such offers include two for the price of one, money-off coupons and instant wins. Many brands make use of their own packaging or websites and social media channels to promote such offers. The promotional channels that a company owns or controls directly are known as owned media.

Personal selling, as the name suggests, is the most personal of the promotional tools. It involves persuading customers of the benefits of products and services, usually on a one-to-one basis. Such personal communication is costly – imagine sending a salesperson out to sell single bottles of shampoo to individuals. Consequently, it is an approach favoured in business-to-business (b2b) sales where the order quantities are higher. Similarly, it would be a waste of television advertising if it was used to sell ball bearings as the vast majority of those who saw the ad would not be interested, so it would be more efficient to send sales representatives to the few companies that might want to buy them.

Different techniques are needed in different markets, in different situations and to achieve different ends. More information about the use of paid, owned and earned media channels can be found in the section on marketing communications media.

MARKETING COMMUNICATIONS OR PROMOTION?

The terms 'marketing communications' and 'promotion' mean the same thing. Promotion is the older name and fits within the mnemonic the 4Ps. In this chapter (as in life), the two terms will be used interchangeably.

Each tool in the promotion mix has certain strengths that will be outlined below. Some organisations – e.g. Nike, Cadbury and Volkswagen – emphasise advertising and public relations efforts in their promotion mixes. Others, especially those engaged in b2b marketing, choose personal selling as a significant promotion mix ingredient. Smith & Nephew, Johnson & Johnson and 3M sell healthcare products to hospitals and all tend to favour personal selling in these situations. This is, in part, because of the more complex nature of the decision-making (see Chapter 3) and the need to identify and nurture different stakeholders.

MANAGING PROMOTION

A key part of a marketing communications manager's job is to plan and coordinate the promotion mix elements:

- setting objectives for what the elements are intended to accomplish
- setting budgets that are sufficient to support the objectives
- designing campaigns that will achieve those objectives
- checking the results of the campaign regularly to ensure that it is on track to achieve the marketing communications objectives (evaluation and control).

CAMPAIGNS

A campaign is a series of coordinated marketing activities designed to achieve specific objectives, e.g. to reposition a product or to educate people about its correct use or to raise a brand's awareness levels. Each of these objectives needs a different set of promotional activities. Educating people about products' use is quite different from raising brand awareness: different messages call for different techniques. Managers must decide what emphasis to put on interpersonal versus mass communication, whether to select a push strategy or a pull strategy (see below), which media channels to use and how much importance to place on each of the different promotion mix elements.

As well as being internally coordinated, all of a company's campaigns should fit with each other. Managers need to be able to think in a joined-up way. It is counter-productive to have one campaign's message or 'feel' contradicting another's. Consequently, the design of campaigns starts higher up. It begins with the development of overall marketing communications objectives and a promotional strategy.

push strategy
a promotional strategy aimed at distribution channels

pull strategy
a promotional strategy aimed at end customers or consumers

[handwritten margin notes: Brand awareness / positive brand attitude / stimulate purchase / build loyalty / build trust / Inform / persuade]

MARKETING COMMUNICATIONS OBJECTIVES

An objective is something that an organisation wants to achieve: a target to aim for. Well-chosen marketing communications techniques are capable of achieving many positive things for a company, but clearly it makes sense to think through exactly what the organisation wants to achieve before designing, and then spending money on, a campaign. The objectives of a Ryvita campaign were to 'reposition crispbread from diet to delicious healthy food while normalising the product and the user' (White, 2013). Objectives may also express what the intended audience should *think, feel* and/or *do* differently as a result of the campaign. For example, Heinz's Classic Soup campaign won a silver award in the Design Business Association's (DBA) 2009 Design Effectiveness Awards. The campaign's objectives were to:

  reinvigorate the brand (*the overarching aim*)

  'remind consumers that Heinz provides good, nourishing food made with wholesome ingredients' (*think*)

  'make the range feel relevant to a contemporary audience and get consumers to "fall in love" with Heinz again' (*feel*)

  get people to eat more soup (*do*). (DBA, 2009)

Without clear-cut objectives it is impossible to know whether a campaign was a success or not. It really is not enough to produce an attractive campaign that people like, or even one that wins awards. Companies expect their advertising to help their business. They expect it to achieve something worthwhile.

THE IMPORTANCE OF TARGETED OBJECTIVES

A strategy is the means by which a firm tries to achieve its objectives. Objectives are fundamental in providing strategic direction for an organisation and can only do this if they are clearly stated, compatible with each other, known, understood and followed (Pickton and Broderick, 2004). A marketing manager must set the promotion objectives before deciding on the best promotion mix.

In order to set realistic objectives, the firm needs a clear statement of its target market. However, a promotional campaign may not be aimed at the entire market; it may even be aimed at people who are not part of the market at all. Promotional campaigns reach out to target audiences.

target audience
the people, or organisations, that are selected to receive communications

TARGET AUDIENCE OR TARGET MARKET?

Target markets are customers (i.e. the people who buy goods and services). The term is also used to refer to consumers or users (who may or may not have bought the product themselves). However, in marketing communications, everyone involved in the purchase decision, however indirectly, needs to be understood and addressed. The people that organisations want to talk to are target audiences and may include potential agents, distributors, retailers, opinion leaders and formers, journalists, employees, the government, present and potential shareholders – anybody who is important to the organisation. So the term 'audience' is broad and may, or may not, include the market.

For example, Domino Pizza's target market is broad and encompasses families, singles and students, but the target audience for a very successful campaign was:

> customers of competitor stores (specifically Pizza Hut)
>
> lapsed or occasional pizza eaters who have (through experience) low expectations of home delivered pizza. (Makin, 2002)

The target audience is often more specific and narrower than the target market and closely targeted communications tend to be more effective:

- products are sold to target *markets*
- marketing communications are addressed to target *audiences*.

A good deal of marketing has international dimensions. Although not all organisations are global, many audiences are and major brands try to maintain consistency in their worldwide positioning. How disappointing to visit a foreign country and find that your favourite designer is considered downmarket, or that your beer is thought to be poor quality. Marketers have to take into account a varied international audience when designing their marketing communications strategies.

PROMOTIONAL STRATEGY

There is no one clear definition of the term 'strategy'. Over the years strategy has acquired a number of meanings, and academics and practitioners are not in total agreement. Engel et al. (1994) used the term 'promotional strategy' to refer to a controlled, integrated programme of communication methods designed to present an organisation and its products or services to prospective customers, to communicate need-satisfying attributes, to facilitate sales, and thus to contribute to long-term profit performance. Pickton and Broderick (2004) emphasised the need to consider a range of target audiences when determining strategy and not just to focus on customers.

PUSH AND PULL STRATEGIES

One way of understanding the different promotional emphases of various organisations is to think of them as push or pull. Who are the target audiences? If the campaign is directed towards consumers or end-users, then it is hoped that by demanding the product, they will pull it through the supply chain. If, on the other hand, the campaign is directed at intermediaries, e.g. retailers, then its purpose is to persuade them to push the products.

Targeted promotion

In some companies, marketing efforts and tactics are aimed primarily at the trade, such as wholesalers, distributors and retailers. In this case, advertising and sales promotion, selling effort, as well as pricing strategies, are aimed at generating trade interest and demand for the company's products. This promotional focus is designed to push a product into, and through, the distribution channel. Push strategies are common in the industrial sector and also in the field of medicine. Medical sales representatives from companies such as Astra-Zenica promote (push) products very strongly to general practitioners and support this push with promotional material from the marketing department. This promotional material may include brochures and branded merchandise. Next time you visit your doctor, observe the different promotional materials in the surgery, such as posters, Post-its, pens and mouse mats.

Conversely, a pull strategy focuses a company's marketing efforts on the final customer or consumer. The objective of this strategy is to generate sufficient consumer interest and demand for the company's products to be pulled through the distribution channels. The goal is to generate demand at the retail level in the belief that such demand will encourage retailers and wholesalers to stock the product.

Although we see push and pull as distinctive strategies, it is usually not a case of deciding between one or the other, but more of determining where the balance should be. An effective marketing communications strategy often uses a combination of push and pull.

The strategy is implemented through the marketing communications mix, which is considered in more detail later.

push
common usage descriptor for part of a push strategy

pull
common usage descriptor for part of a pull strategy

THE MARKETING COMMUNICATIONS PROCESS

An understanding of the communications theory that underpins the marketing communications process is helpful in ensuring that messages arrive safely. Schramm (1955) was among the first to model the communications process and the model presented in Exhibit 8.1 is based on his initial, simple model.

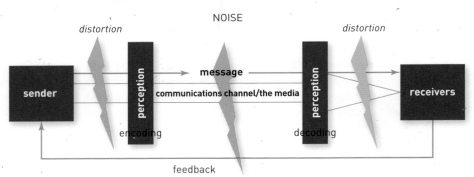

EXHIBIT 8.1 Simple communications model – after Schramm (1955)

There are two principal participants (or sets of participants) in the communications process:

1   The sender is the originator or source of the message. This is the company which is doing the advertising, such as BT or Coca-Cola. Although in practice, agents or consultants may actually do a lot of the work on behalf of the sender.

2   Receivers are the people to whom the message is sent, the target audience(s).

Advertising will be used for the purposes of this explanation; however, the model is applicable to all forms of marketing communications. The advertiser wishes to communicate with a chosen target audience. The message is the actual information and impressions it wishes to send. This message is coded into an advert by the agency's creative team (they make the ad). It can then be sent. The 'media/channels' are the means used to carry the message, e.g. in the case of advertising this may be by television, radio, cinema, etc.

The challenge of marketing communications is to ensure that this process communicates the right message, in the right way, to the right people, in the right place, at the right time. Communication only actually takes place when the receiver understands the message and, ideally, acts upon it. This may not be a physical action – it may be a change of attitude (a frequent objective of advertising) – but something happens to the receiver as a result of receiving the message – even if it is only an increase in knowledge.

Senders are not usually telepathic. They cannot transmit pure thought so they have to put the message across through a commonly understood code, such as words, pictures, symbols and/or actions. Senders *encode* messages, using their skills and resources (e.g. film studios or printers). Encoding is the first step in the communications process. Ideally, the sender's intended message is transmitted, although in reality this does not always occur. Have you ever tried, unsuccessfully, to express an idea? You know what you intended to say, but the words that came out of your mouth failed to reflect your thoughts or worse, your idea was misunderstood? Media advertising is an expensive business. An advert that does not come across well to its target audience is a major waste of time and money. That is why agencies, and their clients, put so much into getting them right.

Messages that are encoded badly get distorted and are not received correctly: distortion is a coding problem, a lack of skill, or care, either on the part of the sender (who encodes) or the receiver (who decodes).

The message may get distorted at either end of the channel. For example, the press release may be badly written, the prize for the sales promotion poorly selected, the salesperson might be disagreeable that day or the problem may lie with the poor language skills of the receiver or their lack of attention. In marketing communications, it is up to the sender to try to ensure that the way the message is coded is suitable for the intended target audience.

Distortion is not the only barrier to communication. There are a number of other things that may get in the message's way: poor television reception, graffiti on a poster, a computer going down, crackle on a telephone line, the receiver having a headache – this is all noise.

There is no excuse for poor coding by professional communicators such as advertising agencies. However, decoding happens at the other end of the channel and the receivers' decoding skills are less certain. Whether or not the message is correctly received depends upon the receivers' interpretation of the message transmitted. The sender hopes that the message received is identical to the one transmitted, but this is not always the case.

creative team
an art director and a copywriter; they work together to create ads

distortion
a barrier to communication; poor coding skills, e.g. a badly devised ad or a badly worded sales promotion, that prevent the message from being received correctly

barrier to communication
anything that gets in the way of a message and prevents it from being received correctly

noise
a barrier to communication, usually from an external source, e.g. technological breakdown

Levels of coding skill and external noise are easier to deal with than the distortion that comes from perceptual problems. Perception is how we see the world. Our perception is built up over the years through all of our experiences. Without it, we would be unable to interpret the world around us. Think of a newborn baby. It knows nothing and may well misinterpret its world. How puzzling those new shiny toys must be – especially the ones that make its mother shout when it reaches for them. There is no understanding, no ability to interpret external stimuli, without learning and experience. As no two people's lives are exactly the same, their perceptions will not be the same either and this can cause communication problems. The person whose experience includes severe seasickness may view a boat sailing out to sea with dread, while others might see that as an invitation to relaxation or adventure. Images used in advertisements must be selected with care.

Individual perceptions are influenced by selective attention and selective distortion (see Chapter 3).

After the decoding process, the receiver responds to the message. The receiver may show interest in the message and may accept everything that is communicated without question. However, the receiver may also react unfavourably to the communication or may totally ignore it. From the marketer's perspective, the message will not be effective unless it elicits the desired response. This may be covert (unseen), such as a favourable attitude change towards a product or increased awareness or knowledge of a product. Sometimes the response is overt, such as redeeming a coupon, or returning a form to order a product or to receive more information. The sender needs to know that the message has been understood: feedback is the response from a receiver back to the sender.

feedback
a part of the two-way communications process whereby the receiver sends a message back to the original sender

Feedback can sometimes, especially with advertising, be hard to pick up. The change in the receiver may be slight, e.g. an increased awareness of the shampoo on offer. The original Schramm model portrayed one-way communications; there was no feedback. This is no longer accepted as correct. Effective marketing communication is two-way. It should be a dialogue, not a monologue.

This two-way communication may be asymmetric (uneven) or symmetric (even) regarding the balance of power between sender and receiver. In two-way asymmetric communication, there is communication from a sender to a receiver with little or delayed feedback, producing a non-direct dialogue, such as in most mass media advertising. In two-way symmetric communication, there is a direct dialogue between the sender and the audience who play equal parts in the communication. Two-way symmetric communication leading to mutual goodwill and understanding between an organisation and its publics has been the goal of PR since Grunig and Hunt first proposed their highly influential four models of public relations in 1984 (see research focus box below). Traditionally, personal selling activities have this major benefit. A face-to-face communications scenario involves both verbal and non-verbal feedback to people. This allows effective salespeople to continuously adapt and improve their pitch. Today, new technologies are creating opportunities for better interactivity and near immediate response across a wide range of communications media. Interactive digital television, QR codes, social media hashtags and mobile apps are just a few examples. While this enhanced interactivity may improve understanding, it is still questionable just how equal and balanced any form of persuasive communication, even PR, can really be. Will one party always have more control than the other?

research focus: classic concept

Grunig, J. and Hunt, T. (1984) *Managing Public Relations*. **London: Thomson Learning.**
Still considered by many PR people to be the foundation for PR theory, this book sets out four models of PR:

1   press agency/publicity (one-way communications)
2   public information (one-way communications)
3   two-way asymmetric communications
4   two-way symmetric communications.

ENGAGEMENT

Increasingly, brand owners recognise the importance of consumer participation in brand-building. Tuten and Solomon (2015) suggest that participation might be considered the fifth 'P' of modern marketing. From this point of view, communicating a promotional message to a target audience effectively is just the start of a process of consumer or customer engagement.

The term engagement has become something of a twenty-first-century marketing buzzword but it is not always used consistently, especially among marketing practitioners. A Facebook 'like' may simply be a way of getting a special offer, whereas someone participating in a forum is likely to be far more invested in the company. Clearly there are significant differences in the degree of consumer involvement (see Chapter 3) and the extent to which a customer may feel connected or committed to the brand in question.

It's also important to think about different aspects of engagement: cognitive (thinking), emotional (feeling) and behavioural (doing). For example, 'liking' a Facebook page to get a free pizza voucher is primarily behavioural engagement although it may also stimulate thinking about the great value on offer from your favourite chain. It may or may not lead to a deeper emotional connection whereas involvement in an online brand community often leads to the development of deeper passion for a favoured brand.

Sashi (2012) developed a model of engagement as a cycle which emphasises the value of social media at each stage in the process.

- *Connection* is essential, if you cannot connect or communicate with customers then genuine engagement is not possible. Connections are made between customers seeking-out sellers (including visiting a website) or sellers reaching out to customers (e.g. through promotional activity).
- *Interaction* can happen on or off line, in a store or on the web. For example, GoPro's online community lets consumers give feedback on product performance and share videos with other users.
- *Satisfaction*: the customer will only continue to interact if they are satisfied.
- *Retention*: a dissatisfied customer is unlikely to return. Someone who is consistently satisfied or is delighted by a single experience is far more likely to be retained.

- *Commitment*: consumers become committed to a brand either because it's too costly to switch or because they have developed an emotional attachment. For example, the Nationwide Building Society may offer better rates to keep long-term customers. On the other hand, many Apple fans are too emotionally attached to ever switch.

- *Advocacy*: according to Sashi, consumers are only likely to champion a brand when emotional bonds have been formed.

- *Engagement* includes consumers in the process of creating value. According to Sashi both delight and commitment are required for genuine engagement.

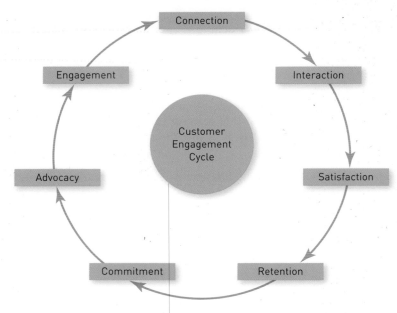

EXHIBIT 8.2 A model of engagement (Sashi, 2012)

Source: Republished with permission of Emerald Group Publishing ltd., from Management Decision, Sashi, C.M, 50 (2), 2012; permission conveyed through Copyright Clearance Center, Inc.

Working towards consumer engagement can therefore deliver a number of benefits to a business (Brodie, 2011, 2013) including greater commitment, trust, emotional involvement and identification with the brand – ultimately enhancing brand loyalty.

Lego creative consumer engagement

INFLUENCING CUSTOMERS

Influencing and encouraging buyers to accept or adopt goods, services and ideas are among the key objectives of marketing communications. Some argue that the ultimate effectiveness of promotion is determined by its impact upon product adoption among new buyers or increases in the frequency of current buyers' purchases. However, a single promotional activity rarely causes an individual to buy a previously unfamiliar product and so, to have realistic expectations about what promotion can do, product adoption should be viewed as a multi-stage process rather than a one stop quick fix.

In Chapter 3, the six stages of the consumer buying process were identified as:

1   need or problem recognition
2   information search
3   evaluation of alternatives
4   purchase decision
5   purchase
6   post-purchase evaluation.

Throughout this process the consumer deliberately, or unconsciously, adopts various attitudes, or has various mind-states, in relation to the product/service offer. The nature and objectives of marketing communications need to alter to take account of these in order to encourage the correct purchase, or re-purchase, decision.

Several models, known as hierarchy of effects models, have been developed to illustrate the activities required to take a consumer from the state of unawareness about the product to one of willingness to purchase the product or service.

AIDA is a simple model commonly used by marketing professionals. According to this model, potential buyers go through a psychological or behavioural process before purchasing a product. AIDA is an acronym for:

Attention

Interest

Desire

Action

It incorporates various psychological processes. Attention (or awareness) is a cognitive process; it relates to how and what we think and believe. Interest and desire are affective processes; they relate to our emotions, how we feel about something. Finally, action takes the form of manifest behaviour (i.e. actually doing something) – we buy the product or tell others about it.

AIDA AND SETTING PROMOTION OBJECTIVES

Although a simple model, AIDA can be helpful when setting promotion objectives and is a good way to demonstrate how these sequential models work.

Attention

In the initial stage, say for a new product, the promotion objective is to get the product seen and, ideally, talked about by the target audience. For example, an effective advertisement must grab attention from the very first viewing or hearing. If the target audience's attention has not been caught, then whatever follows will be of little use.

hierarchy of effects models

describe the stages individuals go through when making a purchase or consumption decision

AIDA

a sequential model showing the steps that marketing communications should lead potential buyers through: attention, interest, desire, action

Interest

After the audience's attention has been gained, their interest in the product must be aroused. This may be achieved by creating an understanding of the benefits of the product in relation to the personal need(s) of customers, and focusing the message on how the product or service being advertised actually meets these needs. Much modern advertising tries hard to be entertaining and to generate interest in the product behind the advert in that way. The main objective of the interest stage is to motivate individuals to want information about the product: its features, uses, advantages, disadvantages, price and location, etc.

Desire

At this stage, a company tries to appeal to the target audience's wish to fulfil some need. While it is usually best to aim advertisements (or other promotional material) at moving the audience from one stage to the next, interest in, and desire for, the product can often be established simultaneously.

Action

As the name suggests, the action stage aims to get individuals to do something such as purchase the product or service. This is often helped by making it easier for the potential customer to take action. This can be done by giving a phone number, an Internet address or closing with a note saying that credit cards are accepted. Personal selling and sales promotion are particularly effective at closing sales, the latter by offering an additional incentive to buy, e.g. money off or a free gift with purchase.

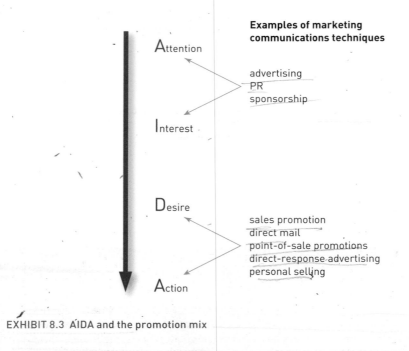

EXHIBIT 8.3 AIDA and the promotion mix

AIDA AND THE PROMOTION MIX

Think about the sequential nature of AIDA. It comprises a number of stages that follow on, one from the other. However, it is not always necessary for organisations to start promotional campaigns at the top of the hierarchy, at the attention or awareness stage. The product may have been around for a while and everyone has already heard of it.

The choice of promotion mix will depend on where in the response hierarchy the organisation wishes to direct its promotional effort. For example, if the firm's primary objective is to catch the audience's attention, then advertising is often the most effective promotional tool. Advertising can also be very effective at creating and holding interest, and at reinforcing positive aspects of the product to develop post-purchase satisfaction. PR is also extensively used to raise interest levels in a product. Personal selling tends to be effective at creating desire and motivating purchase. Sales promotion is good at closing the sale, for example by making a time-limited offer: 'half price this week only'.

Hierarchical models such as AIDA describe the step-by-step process through which individuals move when exposed to marketing communications; these encompass the cognitive (thinking), affective (feeling) and conative (doing) steps.

Russell Colley (1961) developed a hierarchy of effects model known as DAGMAR (Define Advertising Goals for Measured Advertising Results). In this he stressed the importance of setting objectives against each element within the hierarchy (or at least those that were relevant to the promotional campaign being devised). Although his focus was on advertising objectives, his ideas are equally appropriate across all marketing communication tools (see Exhibit 8.4).

DAGMAR

an acronym for Defining Advertising Goals for Measured Advertising Results; a hierarchy of effects model describing the stages individuals go through when making a purchase, or consumption, decision

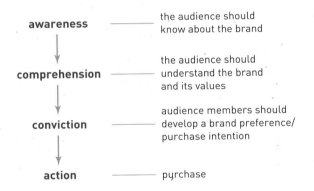

EXHIBIT 8.4 DAGMAR: a hierarchical model

research focus: classic concept

Colley, R. (1961) *Defining Advertising Goals for Measured Advertising Results*. **New York: Association of National Advertisers.**

Colley introduced DAGMAR to the world in this article. He argued that advertising outcomes can be improved by first recognising that a hierarchical process of communications is involved, then setting appropriate advertising goals related to this process. (Others have criticised Colley's specific hierarchy and even whether any specific hierarchy exists that covers all eventualities.)

Coca-cola & Snapchat
Christmas cards

paid media

channels of communication in
which advertisers buy space,
e.g. television, magazines,
social media sites

owned media

channels of communication
which belong to or are
controlled by the client
company, e.g. an in-house
newsletter, company website
or brand Facebook page

earned media

channels of communication
outside marketers' direct
control that are used to talk
about or report on brands,
issues, organisations;
traditionally PR media,
e.g. newspaper columns/
editorials (not advert
space), an individual's
blogs, individual social
media pages

viral marketing

an electronic form of
word-of-mouth marketing
that spreads rapidly (like a
virus) within the population

MARKETING COMMUNICATIONS MEDIA

Over the last few decades, massive technological change has altered our media habits dramatically. Where once mass media had the potential to reach large swathes of the population in one go, audiences are now fragmented, split between hundreds of TV channels, radio stations and magazines. The Internet challenges traditional notions of publisher and reader now that individuals can blog, post on social media sites and send instant messages.

There are a number of ways of classifying modern media but perhaps one of the most useful, and marketing-orientated, is POEM: **P**aid, **O**wned or **E**arned **M**edia.

The term paid media refers to channels for which the brand has to pay a fee to the media owner, e.g. TV or press. This includes traditional mass media advertising where there is a charge for ad space and some hybrid marketing communications techniques ('hybrid' here refers to a blend of advertising and PR) such as sponsorship. The sponsor pays a fee for the privilege of being associated with the thing being sponsored (the sponsorship 'vehicle') such as a sports team or an event. (For more on sponsorship, see below.)

The main advantages of paid media lie in their access to a large audience, their broad creative scope and their relatively good control over how and when the brand is presented to their target audience. They are often used at the outset of a campaign to drive awareness and encourage the discovery of owned media channels (see below). The main disadvantage is that these paid media have become increasingly cluttered with brands and messages, making it hard to stand out from the crowd and be heard above all the noise.

Owned media are owned and/or controlled by the brand owners themselves, e.g. corporate websites, blogs, newsletters and brochures as well as office or retail premises. Clearly brand owners have almost absolute control over how the brand appears and what is said about it in these media, but they may not gain the attention that paid media can, especially among new audiences. Owned media channels typically represent a key opportunity for brands to engage with existing customers and consumers. Many branded websites are designed to provide immersive experiences and compelling content that may also stimulate social media sharing (see earned media below) that in turn increases the reach of brand messages. Earned media are when other individuals become the channel for communicating brand messages. The content of earned media is outside of the control of the brand owner, the authors may be customers, consumers or critics, e.g. professional journalists or bloggers (public relations coverage is the original earned media). Brands have always tried to get customers to recommend their products to friends and to talk about them enthusiastically. More recently, they have aimed for greater brand engagement by trying to ensure consumers see brands as intrinsic parts of their lives or essential to their lifestyle. Word of mouth (WOM) and viral marketing have been valuable techniques for a long time but the popularity of social media has opened up new opportunities for brands to reach farther, faster. WOM and viral brand exposure have to be earned, they do not happen automatically. (See below for word of mouth and viral marketing examples.)

The main disadvantage of earned media lies in the brand's lack of control over what is said about it. This has been a major worry for many brand owners who fear that the brand's image will be hijacked by bloggers and social media networkers who may poke fun at it or show it in a bad light. In practice, this rarely happens. Most of the tribute adverts on sites like YouTube really are tributes and even when people do poke fun at an ad, or lambast it, as they did with Brad Pitt's ad for Chanel No. 5, the resultant publicity may not be harmful. In fact, individuals' willingness to comment on and share brand-related content may be an important way to express personal identity in digital environments. Schau and Gilly (2003) argue that 'we are what we post', noting that individuals choose carefully which brands they wish to be digitally associated with through social media. Brands have been quick to exploit these new consumer behaviours. For example, BMW, as part of a sponsorship programme of leading European ski resorts,

recently installed motion tracking video cameras to record skiers tackling a tricky slalom course and offered free use of automatic cameras at picturesque viewpoints. Images and video could be later downloaded and shared (along with subtle BW branding) and skiers could take part in a virtual competition race to win a BMW four-wheel drive vehicle. Skiers personal data collected from digital ski-lift passes was also used to produce a record of each day's activity including altitudes, descents and total distance covered. By tapping into consumers' inherent competitive instincts and desire to capture and share their experiences through social media, BMW was able to dramatically extend the reach and impact of its sponsorship with minimal paid media investment.

Media planners aim to blend paid, owned and earned media to broaden a campaign's reach, create a buzz and deepen audience engagement. A good example is the Compare the Meerkat series of ads (for www.comparethemarket.com) starring Aleksandr Orlov, a Russian meerkat, and his family and friends. The campaign started life in paid media as a TV advert but thanks to a compelling companion website and carefully coordinated promotional and social media activity its characters have taken on a life of their own. Even Sergie, head of IT and often the butt of Alexandr's jokes, has his own Twitter feed with over 15,000 followers, and the official You Tube channel has more than 24,000 subscribers; this is owned media. In 2010 Alexandr's catchphrase 'simples' was added to the *Collins English Dictionary* and his autobiography generated more pre-orders than the former UK Prime Minister Tony Blair's memoirs. More recently the character's razor-sharp wit has been showcased in TV interviews on ITV's *This Morning* and *Good Morning Britain* shows where Alexandr got the better of Piers Morgan. These events along with the countless social media shares and mentions surrounding them are classed as earned media.

An important point to understand about this classification of paid, owned and earned media is that the classification is dependent upon how the medium is used rather than the medium itself. A TV advert is using paid media, a TV interview on a chat show is using earned media, and if the company has its own TV channel, that is owned media. An advert placed on someone else's website or on a search engine such as Google is using paid media; a brand communication on the brand's own website or social media page is using owned media; while a mention in someone else's blog or an online review, or a sharing on social media, e.g. a re-tweet, is classified as earned media.

reach
the number (or percentage) of the target audience exposed to an advert or other promotion during a campaign; also referred to as coverage or penetration

Owned media opportunities

MEDIA CLASSES

A media class is a type of media, e.g. television or press. Media classes can be broken down into different media vehicles, e.g. specific programmes or titles. Exhibit 8.5 lists examples of the media currently available – although new ones appear all the time. Of the traditional advertising mass media, press takes in the most money despite being a less expensive medium than TV – there is just so much more of it. The picture is constantly changing, though. New digital TV channels keep appearing. These are cheaper vehicles than terrestrial television and can be targeted more closely as many channels are very specialist and so appeal to clearly defined audiences, e.g. a home improvement channel is clearly a good place to advertise DIY equipment.

TV	Posters	Underground stations
Newspapers	Magazines	Video games
Cinema	Buses	Trains
Video	Taxis	Telephones
CD/DVD	Search engines	Mobile phones
Radio	Websites	Cars/vans/lorries
Email	Directories	DOOH screens (Digital Out Of Home)
Shop fronts	Escalator steps	Beer mats
Pavements	Post-it notes	Promotional gifts
Sides of buildings	Packaging	Clothing, e.g. T-shirts
Skywriting	Blimps	Road signs
Tickets	Notice boards	Blogs and wikis
Outdoor screens	Windows	Bar optics
Social networking sites	Rubbish bins	Bus shelters
Laser projection	Students' heads (transfers or shaved into hair)	Anything else that could carry a promotional or persuasive message

EXHIBIT 8.5 Examples of promotional media

ACTIVITY

Take a walk around your local high street or shopping centre. Note down the different types of ambient media you find.

The Internet, along with other digital technologies such as iTV (interactive television) and mobile phones, may still be referred to as new media – although digital and mobile are becoming more accepted terms as the newness wears off. The technology behind digital media has a number of advantages:

- interactivity
- faster response times

- more direct communications
- greater possibilities for interaction between audience members and user- generated content
- the ability to put the message across in a more sophisticated way.

The term ambient media was originally applied to unusual outdoor media. It is becoming more widely used now to describe any outdoor media, although some ambient media may actually be indoors. Used in this broader way, the original, and still the biggest, ambient media are poster sites. Advertising is getting everywhere and the discovery of new media possibilities is a great source of differentiation and a way to cut through the noise created by communications overload. More unusual ambient media include cars, laser light shows, people, tickets, stairs, postcards, balloons and skywriting.

WORD OF MOUTH AND VIRAL MARKETING

One of the most powerful ways to transmit a message is through word of mouth/viral marketing. When friends and relatives talk positively about a product or service, it sounds so much more convincing than when the words come from an actor on television who has been paid. Some adverts are deliberately designed to stimulate word of mouth, to get people talking, tweeting, blogging and posting on social media sites.

T-Mobile has been particularly good at this in recent years. It started with a flashmob on Liverpool Street station and progressed to Josh's band, a look-a-like Royal wedding viral video and beyond. These brand experiences are designed to showcase brand values and build consumer relationships with the brand; however, their ability to stimulate word of mouth or to go viral broadens their reach and makes them so very much more effective as marketing tools.

Electronic media, such as email, SMS and social media, lend themselves well to word-of-mouth advertising as they make it easy to pass a message on. Advertisers look for ways to engage their audience and encourage them to pass the message on. They hope to create a buzz. This encouragement may involve some financial reward (e.g. by offering customers money-off vouchers for passing messages on to their friends), or may just be based on entertainment value (known as organic WOM).

THE MARKETING COMMUNICATIONS MIX

Marketers have a large number of promotional tools which they can use to achieve their communications objectives. Historically these tools, or techniques, have been organised into four broad categories: advertising, public relations, sales promotion and personal selling. This is known as the promotion mix (or marketing communications mix). However, increasingly, other categories are being added that either do not fit neatly into these four or that some people feel deserve their own category heading. Examples include direct marketing, sponsorship, experiential marketing and packaging. The number of promotional activities available to marketers is growing all the time.

These promotional tools involve either direct (i.e. personal) communication, usually on a face-to-face basis or on the telephone (and, perhaps, through video-conferencing and email),

---

new media
makes use of modern technologies, e.g. the Internet, iTV, mobile phones, CD/DVD

ambient media
unusual out-of-home (OOH) media, e.g. lasers, tickets, promotional clothing, tattoos, pavements

ACTIVITY

Check YouTube for tribute adverts and other user-generated advertising content. Try Cadbury's, BMW, Mini, Sony and McDonald's as starting points and then see what's new.

direct marketing
'all activities that make it possible to offer goods or services or to transmit other messages to a segment of the population by post, telephone, email or other direct means' (Chartered Institute of Marketing)

sponsorship
giving financial aid, or other resources, to an individual, organisation or event in return for a positive association with them, e.g. the Coca-Cola Cup

ACTIVITY

Collect or identify as many examples of promotional material from one organisation as you can. How do they differ? Why do you think they differ? Who are the audiences?

or indirect (i.e. non-personal) communication via a medium such as television, magazines or radio, or through packaging, leaflets, etc. It is the responsibility of the marketer to determine which approach is best for each situation.

Whichever element, or elements, of the promotion mix organisations choose, the purpose is to communicate a message to an appropriate target audience in order to elicit a favourable response, such as purchasing a product or changing an attitude. The term 'integrated marketing communication' is used to emphasise that all elements of the promotion mix should be coordinated and systematically planned to complement each other.

The separate elements of the promotion mix will now be discussed in more depth under each of the four basic headings that were introduced at the start of this chapter, namely:

integrated marketing communications

the process of ensuring that all elements of the promotion mix are complementary in order to avoid mixed messages and strengthen the brand

- advertising
- public relations (PR)
- sales promotions
- personal selling.

b2b focus: our treat

Although much of marketing and marketing communications theory focuses on consumer goods, particularly fast-moving consumer goods (FMCG), a significant amount of marketing communications is conducted between businesses. Interestingly, the big FMCG manufacturers' primary contact is with trade, not end customers. Managing trade contacts (e.g. wholesalers and retailers) is quite different from dealing with end customers and consumers. For example, whereas a consumer might want one bottle of wine, a retailer may want many cases of different types. Such major sales warrant a different approach. The supplier may send a sales representative to call personally or use techniques such as telesales, direct mail (post, fax or email) or trade exhibitions, either to make sales or to set up appointments for the rep to call.

telesales

making sales calls by telephone

Relationships are even more important in b2b and some companies go to great lengths to foster them, often at great expense. Major sporting and cultural events offer corporate hospitality packages to help companies entertain their guests: Pimms and strawberries in a private marquee along with centre court tickets at Wimbledon; trackside seats at F1 events along with the opportunity to meet the drivers; a trip to the Olympics, World Cup Final, the opera or the Chelsea Flower Show (all liberally hosted by your account representative of course). Some companies go further and arrange their own bespoke events. Themed parties can take guests anywhere from Hogwarts to the Wild West

Consumer marketers like to say 'the customer is king', but business customers are even more likely to be treated royally.

ADVERTISING

Advertising is a broad term for any *paid* form (i.e. paid for by the advertiser) of *non-personal* presentation of ideas, goods and services by an *identified* advertiser. Communication by advertising is transmitted to a target audience through various forms of media, which include television, radio, cinema, press, posters and the Internet. Other marketing communication tools also use these media (notably PR) and so it becomes even more important to coordinate promotional activities through integrated marketing communications planning.

The major benefit of mass media advertising (e.g. television) is its ability to communicate to a large number of people all at once, e.g. all the existing and potential consumers for McDonald's fast food.

Mass media advertising can be eye-catching but its effectiveness is hard to measure.

Source: Pop Paul-Catalin/Shutterstock.com

Traditional mass media advertising is indirect and non-personal (i.e. not individually addressed). It allows marketers to send a uniform message with great frequency. However, it does have several disadvantages. Even though, for example, the cost per person reached by the advertising may be relatively low, the total financial outlay can be extremely high – especially for commercials shown during popular television programmes such as *Coronation Street* or the *X Factor*. These high costs can limit, and sometimes prohibit, the use of this type of advertising in an organisation's promotion mix. It should be remembered that not all companies have huge marketing communications budgets like Nike or Coca-Cola (and that even these aim for effectiveness and efficiency in using their companies' budgets). However, television advertising is now within the reach of those with a smaller budget thanks to the many digital channels available. Costs can also be kept down by focusing on specific regions.

frequency
the number of times that an average member of the target audience is exposed to an advert during a campaign

Additionally, the non-personal nature of the advert makes it harder to measure, or even receive, a response from the audience, making this effectively a one-way means of communication. Technology is helping to overcome this limitation. Interactive television, mobile and Internet advertising all make two-way communication so much easier.

HOW DOES ADVERTISING WORK?

Over the years, researchers have designed a number of models to investigate how advertising and other marketing communication tools work. Two of the more popular ones, AIDA and DAGMAR, are outlined above. The truth is that we still do not know exactly how advertising works – but we do know that good advertising can have positive effects on customers and on sales. Many of these explanatory models are sequential, showing the customer moving through stages, beginning by becoming aware of a product and ending with a sale or some form of post-purchase re-evaluation. Such models are essentially about persuasion, about moving people on to the next stage. Although these sequential models have been much criticised in recent years, they are still helpful to marketing communicators seeking to understand their customers and to help them to make the right decisions.

research focus: classic concept

Jones, J.P. (1990) 'Advertising: strong or weak force? Two views oceans apart', *International Journal of Advertising*, **9 (3): 233–46.**
This article reviews the conventional view of advertising – the strong theory – which is all but universally believed in the USA and which sees advertising as a dynamic force operating as an engine for brand innovation and other types of change in the marketplace. Andrew Ehrenberg's theory sees advertising as a weak force. This paper argues that a good deal of confusion has been caused by an uncritical belief that the strong theory operates in all circumstances. As a result, advertising has been associated too much with over-promise and under-delivery.

ADVERTISING OBJECTIVES

Marketers use advertising in a number of ways. Most consumer advertising is product (or brand) advertising; however, there are other forms, for example corporate, that communicate the values and ideas of organisations.

Advertising is rarely the best tool for closing a deal, so advertising objectives tend to relate to the early stages of sequential models like AIDA. Advertising can create awareness of a brand, ensure improved knowledge of that brand and its attributes, create a more favourable image, stimulate positive attitudes and achieve many other things, but product advertising's underlying objective is usually sales and its ultimate function is to sustain a brand and make it profitable.

The problem with trying to measure advertising's effectiveness on sales alone is that it is hard to prove that the advert really did cause the increase in sales. Of course, there is a lot of anecdotal evidence to suggest that advertising has a positive effect on sales. Sales do tend to rise during an advertising campaign – and then to fall off soon after. However, that is not conclusive proof. There could be any number of other reasons why the sales rose, e.g. a competitor was short of stock, there was a price reduction at major retailers, a journalist wrote a good review. Conversely, it might be unfair to judge the advertising as bad just because sales do not rise. It may not be the advertising's fault. Many companies today advertise just to keep up. It is not so much a question of trying to increase sales, but of protecting their market share. If they stop advertising, they hand an advantage to the competition.

THE ESSENTIALS OF ADVERTISING

A way of simplifying our study of advertising (and of marketing communications as a whole) is to consider its four essential elements (media, message, creative execution, audience), as identified in Exhibit 8.7, and discussed in turn in the section that follows.

audience profile

a detailed description of audience characteristics used by marketing communicators to tailor their promotional efforts

Audience

Get the right message to the right audience and you have a good ad. It sounds simple, but unfortunately it is not. Advertising agencies put a lot of time and effort into understanding audiences and into developing audience profiles. If you want to communicate effectively with someone, it helps to know them well.

Objective	Situation/use
Awareness or attention	Usually of a new product
Recognition (or prompted recall)	A form of awareness – particularly important for a new product, where the purchase decision is made at the point of purchase, e.g. anything sold in a supermarket
Recall	Another form of awareness – the ability to remember the product rather than just to recognise it; useful where decisions are made in advance of purchase, e.g. seeing a film at the cinema
Reminder	For established products that may be being overlooked
Repositioning	Altering the way the brand is viewed by the target audience, e.g. Baileys is an anytime drink, not just an after-dinner liqueur
Differentiation	Making the brand stand out from the competition
Information	Telling the audience something about the brand, e.g. that it has new features
Build brand image	Associating desired qualities with the brand, e.g. that it is innovative or youthful
Image change	A form of repositioning, altering the market's perception of the brand, e.g. Old Spice is for young, sexy men
Education	Telling the audience what the product is for or how to use it – especially new products
Stimulate word of mouth – or create a buzz	Getting people talking about the brand
Go viral	Enticing people to pass the ad on, or to comment on it, electronically, e.g. re-tweet or share on Facebook
Information gathering	For example, direct-response advertising gives audience information back to the advertiser
Attitude change	Changing a negative to a positive, e.g. 'Volvos are not for me' to 'That's a cool car'
Attitude reinforcement	Encouraging positive attitudes, e.g. 'I like brand X'
Correction of a misconception	Giving the audience a new angle, e.g. 'I can't afford a new car' to 'That's cheaper than I thought'
Trial stimulation	If a person never tries your product, then they can never become a regular purchaser
Sales	Purchase of the new product

EXHIBIT 8.6 Typical categories of advertising objectives

Remember that a target audience is not the same as a target market. The audience for an advert is the people at whom the message of the ad is aimed. They may be part, or all, of the target market, or they may not. Sometimes adverts are deliberately aimed at influencers rather than actual purchasers, e.g. many toy ads are (rather controversially) aimed at toy consumers (children) rather than customers (parents). In the past, anti-smoking campaigners have also aimed at children, urging them to nag their parents into giving up. Trade audiences are often wider. Take, for example, an advert in a trade magazine for cars. It could be aimed at the fleet manager (who manages the company's car fleet), professional buyers (who negotiate terms of purchase), the company owner or the finance director (who may make the ultimate decision), the people who have cars (who may push for new ones) or the PR department (which guards the company's image) – in fact at any member of the decision-making unit (see Chapter 3).

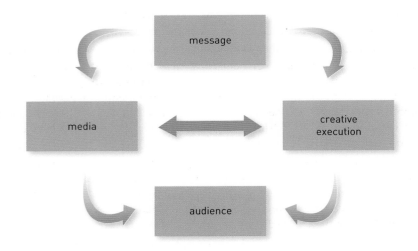

EXHIBIT 8.7 Advertising essentials

Message

advertising proposition

what the overall advert should say to the target audience, the impression that should be left in their minds (this is not the slogan; the whole of the advert should communicate the proposition)

Once the advertisers have established exactly who it is they want to talk to, they can develop the correct message to achieve their advertising objectives. They develop an advertising proposition: what the advertising should say and the impression it should create, but not necessarily phrased in the way that the ad will say it. For example, the message that this is a fun beer that enhances sociability while also providing refreshment might result in the slogan 'refreshes the parts other beers cannot reach'. The slogan is the clever, catchy form of words that goes into the actual ad. It is part of the creative work and is written by a copywriter (copy just means text, i.e. the words in an ad).

copywriter

someone who writes the words for promotional materials, e.g. adverts

copy

text

Creative execution

The advert's message is not normally put across through words alone, there are visual elements to most advertising that assist its transmission: a picture, a scene, colours, designs. There may also be music, other sound effects, acting – all of these form part of the creative execution. This is the heart of the advert. Advertisers appeal to our emotions (e.g. through humour or sex) and/or to our rational side (e.g. through value for money or product features), in order to interest us in their products.

creative execution

the way an advert is designed in order to put the message across

There are a number of common execution approaches including those below. Look out for these and others as you see and listen to advertisements. Think of them as movie genres, as types of advertising – adverts may well combine aspects of a number of these executions and some, e.g. music, are not standalone. They are presented here as advertising executions, but some are also useful to other marketing communication tools, such as PR, to get messages across.

- *Slice of life*: a real, everyday situation shows the product in normal use, e.g. a little boy plays his separated parents off against each other and persuades them both to take him to McDonald's.

- *Animation and CGI*: cartoon characters can liven up a dull product, deal with an embarrassing subject, e.g. cartoon bears and toilet rolls, meerkats and insurance.

- *Endorsement*: uses supposed experts, or past users, to verify the merits of the product, e.g. 'my washing has never been so white'. Testimonials are commonly used in Internet advertising. There is more space to print endorsing statements, making them more credible. Testimonials are reassuring in a medium where lack of trust is a problem. References in blogs are even more reassuring as they have the impartiality of word-of-mouth advertising, which is perhaps why less scrupulous advertisers sometimes write these themselves.

- *Celebrity*: attracts attention, gives the product credibility. Sometimes celebrities are endorsing the product, e.g. Cheryl Cole and Susan Sarandon have proved 'worth it' for L'Oréal, but sometimes their involvement in the ad is more peripheral, e.g. Jenson Button, Rory McIlroy and Jessica Ennis were seen in adverts for Santander, but are we meant to believe they actually bank there? David Beckham promotes H&M but does he really shop there?

- *News style*: common in press adverts, makes the advert look more like part of the publication.

- *Fantasy*: catches the imagination, particularly useful when the product cannot be shown in use, e.g. Smirnoff vodka ads. Advanced CGI has made many fantasy executions even more fantastical, e.g. a Coca-Cola advert had someone disappear into a vending machine and emerge in a completely different world.

- *Spoof or parody*: catches attention through humour, e.g. Specsavers parodied the Lynx ads; the original Gary Lineker Walker's crisps ads played on his good guy reputation.

- *Demonstration*: shows how the product works, e.g. how Flash can clean a floor so quickly. These can be more imaginative than a straight demonstration and may be combined with a fantastical element, e.g. in a Mini convertible ad, a man was surrounded by threatening hoodies every time he tried to close the roof, but they disappeared when he desisted. Eventually we got the message: 'leave it open'.

- *Comedy*: engages the audience – so long as they get the joke. Humour can be very effective and entertaining but it must be used carefully to ensure it does not offend. Also, jokes are not as funny the second, third, fourth time around so these ads may have limited lives. There are numerous examples. Try Volkswagen's Darth Vader ad with its follow-up 'The Dog Strikes Back', or any of the Lynx ads.

Humour and culture in international business

- *Audience participation*: advertising is no longer content with actors on a screen; some adverts invite the actual participation of target audiences or are mini films of events. T-Mobile staged a flashmob at Liverpool Street station but the main point was that it would be filmed, not only by their agency for use as an advert, but also by commuters (on their phones) for sharing. Coca-Cola's Coke Chase advert invites the audience to decide who wins the race. This kind of active audience engagement reinforces messages and creates a buzz.

- *Music*: often a key part of the creative execution, it creates mood, attracts attention, reinforces a message, inspires word of mouth and makes the ad more memorable. Music is not a stand-alone execution, of course – it is most commonly in the background – but it can be a major element as in the Cadbury's gorilla ad (Phil Collins, 'In the Air Tonight'), John Lewis's 2011 'never knowingly undersold' ad (Paloma Faith, 'Never Tear Us Apart'), or Xbox 360's ad (Lily Allen, 'The Fear') which made more of the music by featuring Lily Allen singing along with hundreds of Xboxers (so there was a celebrity element too).

Advertising media

The final essential of advertising is the media: the carriers of the message. Without media, no one will ever hear or see the ad. The right choice of media is essential to the effectiveness of a campaign. It has to be appropriate to the target audience and to the message.

media vehicle

the TV programme, newspaper, magazine, poster site, film, etc. in which adverts appear

media class or media category

type of media, e.g. television, press, posters, cinema

There is little point in advertising in *Cosmopolitan* if you are trying to reach elderly men (though there may be some point if you are trying to reach younger men as, apparently, a large number of them read it; they do not buy it, they just read their girlfriends' copies). It is important to establish the readership/viewership profile of media vehicles and match this to your audience profile. Newspapers, TV channels, etc., provide guides to assist with this and to help sell their advertising space.

The choice of media also affects how the message comes across. If your message is a complex, informative one, perhaps explaining the technical advantages of a new computer system, then a 30-second TV ad just will not do. You need the space and copy possibilities of the press. However, if you want your new jeans to catch the eye of the younger generation, then the creative scope offered by a cinema ad may be the best thing (and then you can cut it down to show on TV as well).

Posters can have great impact.

© Dave Pickton

Advertisers must choose a media class (the inter-media decision, e.g. television or Internet or press) and then a media vehicle (the intra-media decision, i.e. the actual TV programmes or websites or magazine titles). This decision is based on the creative scope a medium offers and its audience profile. For example, a TV advert aired during *Big Brother* would allow the advertisers to use colour, sound and movement (actors, props and/or animation) to create an impact on a young audience. An ad or a page on Instagram could use interactivity to engage a sociable, IT-literate audience.

research focus: classic concept

Rust, R.T. and Oliver, R.W. (1994) 'The death of advertising', *Journal of Advertising*, **23 (4): 71.**
'Advertising is on its deathbed and it will not survive long, having contracted a fatal case of new technology'.
A prophecy from 1994 that mass media advertising will be superseded by interactive media.

PUBLIC RELATIONS (PR)

Traditionally, PR was perceived to be a corporate function. Today, there are a number of types of PR, and marketing communications has embraced and adapted the various elements of the discipline. Creating and maintaining goodwill and a good reputation are just as relevant to product brands as they are to corporations as a whole.

Raising the visibility of organisations and encouraging interest in them are important functions of marketing communications. In recent times, public relations has assumed a greater significance at both the corporate level and within the promotion mix.

WHAT IS PUBLIC RELATIONS?

According to the Chartered Institute of Public Relations (2013):

> Public relations is the planned and sustained effort to establish and maintain goodwill and mutual understanding between an organisation and its publics.

Reflecting on this definition, the words *planned*, *sustained effort* and *mutual understanding* need emphasising. Good public relations involves conducting planned programmes with clear objectives, so that results can be assessed and understood. Good public relations involves sustained activity over time. The objectives of creating and maintaining goodwill are not achieved by short-term activities alone. Finally, good public relations requires mutual understanding between the organisation and its various publics. In public relations, the organisation receives as well as transmits information, listens as well as speaks (Jefkins, 1989).

THE SCOPE OF PUBLIC RELATIONS

Public relations can raise awareness, inform, interest, excite, educate, generate understanding, build trust, encourage loyalty and even help generate sales (Pickton and Broderick, 2004). PR can raise visibility and also help develop corporate and product credibility in ways that other promotional tools cannot. It can also be used to enhance the effectiveness of advertising.

Any solid management planning relies on research and analysis, and PR is no exception. The planning and management of PR is a systematic process of identifying PR tasks, setting objectives, defining PR publics, integrating PR within the promotion or marketing communications mix, scheduling, managing the implementation of PR techniques and assessing their effectiveness.

inter-media decision
the choice of media class

intra-media decision
the choice of media vehicle

publics
PR term for target audiences, the groups of people with whom the organisation communicates

PR TECHNIQUES
Media relations/publicity

Publicity can stimulate demand for goods or services by generating news about them in the mass media. This is done by means of news releases, press conferences and events or publicity stunts (e.g. the Red Bull Stratos project, in which Felix Baumgartner jumped to Earth from a helium balloon in the stratosphere).

Good media relations encourage media coverage and favourable, positive publicity. Equally valuably, they also discourage negative coverage. This is an important function of professional public relations specialists and involves developing strong personal relationships with editors and journalists. Media releases contain information about the organisation and its products or brands in the hope of obtaining positive editorial coverage and are sent to journalists who may, or may not, use all (or more usually part) of the content. Publicity may use the same mass media as advertising. However, unlike advertising, the media costs are not paid for directly by the company, nor does publicity identify itself as coming directly from the company; it can therefore have greater impact as it has the appearance of coming from an impartial source.

Publicity can be an impressive and effective promotional tool. However, as it involves a third party, such as a newspaper reporter or editor, who has the power to determine the nature of the message, a firm has little control over its timing and content. An extreme example of this is the publicity – good, bad or indifferent – a company's products get in *Which?* consumer magazine. *Which?* regularly evaluates products and publishes the results of the tests. Companies have no control over the tests or the resultant publicity. Visit www.which.co.uk for examples.

ACTIVITY

Press releases are often written in the same format as articles suitable for publication. Time-strapped editors sometimes print them with little or no amendment. Browse through a newspaper or magazine and try to find stories that may have been placed by a commercial company (the weekend glossies or special interest magazines are often the best source). What's the objective behind the story?

Publications and brand journalism

content marketing
the creation and distribution of entertaining, helpful or informative material (usually online or mobile) in order to attract and engage a clearly defined audience

The PR department or agency is often responsible for this increasingly important task, although advertising agencies and, increasingly content marketing specialists also offer the service. Organisations produce a variety of publications, e.g. employee newsletters, financial reports, consumer magazines, brochures and media packs as well as a great deal of digital content. The dramatic rise in popularity of social media has resulted in many organisations struggling to keep pace with the demand for 'brand journalism' – in fact many journalists have found second careers publishing on behalf of brands. Publishing quality content is not only an important way of communicating with key stakeholders, it can also make a big impact.

Video content marketing

Websites and social media sites

When customers want to find information about a product, they are very likely to Google it. Websites are important sources of information. Brand owners provide information, entertainment and incentives through their own websites and through social media sites. These sites may be managed by an in-house team or by an agency, which may be a PR, advertising or specialist digital firm. Constant monitoring and updating is vital if digital content is to remain accurate and prove valuable to potential customers. The majority of social media content is user-generated so systematic social media listening (see Chapter 5) is becoming an increasingly important activity for many firms. Typically firms make use of web-based software to track conversations and trending topics and to flag up any potential problem situations where prompt intervention may help limit the damage to a firm's reputation.

digital focus: all the best jobs in the world!

Governments the world over are always under pressure to cut costs and deliver good value for taxpayers' reluctantly handed over money. They rarely have the budget for flashy advertising campaigns or star endorsers but a standard government information website has limited effect. Clearly PR is needed – but that may have a high price tag too, especially if your audience is global.

In 2009, the Queensland Tourist Board came up with a great idea for maximum impact with minimum funding. They harnessed the power of social media to create a campaign that captured the world's imagination – and all for the price of a website and some classified ads.

Their objective was to create international awareness of the islands of the Great Barrier Reef. Their idea was a competition with a very special prize: the best job in the world. The job was caretaker of beautiful Hamilton island. Duties were to feed fish, collect mail, clean the pool – and write a weekly blog.

They placed job ads in the classified sections of newspapers around the world and created a website where applicants were asked to post 60 second job application videos. The winner of a popular vote was guaranteed a place on the shortlist along with the tourist board's top picks and all were flown to Australia for the interview. Islandreefjob.com received 4 million hits per hour on its first day and had more hits than Google in the UK (where the eventual winner came from).

TV news programmes around the world picked up on this picturesque good news story. Videos of the Great Barrier Reef and its islands were broadcast at prime time (at no further cost to Queensland) in the USA, Canada, Europe, Japan – just about all the countries targeted by the Tourist Board as likely sources of visitors.

Success breeds imitation. In 2013, the Australian Tourist Board resurrected the idea but this time there were six jobs across Australia and an explanatory video starring the winner of the original competition. The jobs included Chief Funster for New South Wales, Wildlife Caretaker in South Australia and Western Australia's Tastemaster (they make a lot of wine in WA). More than 330,000 people from 196 countries expressed interest in the six dream jobs and more than 40,000 video entries were uploaded.

The idea caught on outside Australia too. Belvedere vodka asked for 1 minute video applications for a global brand ambassador to travel the world teaching bartenders to mix innovative cocktails. Two lucky Canadians got paid to hike, paddle and ride horses coast to coast using outdoor supplier Woods gear while blogging along the way. Facebook users chose the Irish winner of the Budweiser Dream Job competition. He received €40,000, plus a €5,000 equipment bursary as well as mentoring sessions with experts in his chosen field (film-making). In the UK, the National Trust used similar techniques to find a farm manager and conservationist for recently acquired land on Great Orme in North Wales. The prize was a £1 million farm for £1 per year in rent plus a lot of hard work.

Can you out-imagine the Australians? What would you do to get the world buzzing and blogging about a tourist destination?

Sources: BBC News (2016); Tourism Australia (n.d.)

Corporate communications

Aspects of corporate communications that fall into the category of PR include corporate identity programmes, corporate image management, corporate advertising, some internal communications and some communications with other publics or stakeholder groups.

Public affairs and community relations

This involves contact with the government and government agencies, special interest and professional groups, as well as the local community, with a view to building and maintaining local, national and international relations.

Lobbying

An approach associated with public affairs and media relations. It aims to build and maintain positive relations with, for example, group leaders, legislators and officials, through negotiation and persuasion.

Sponsorship

Sponsorship is a business relationship in which one organisation provides funds or other resources/services to another organisation (or an individual) and gains commercial advantage through being linked to them. It may be on a relatively small scale directed at a local activity, or involve millions of pounds. Typical sponsorship vehicles include sports (events, teams and individuals), television programmes and the arts.

Product placement

This is another promotional tool that is growing in importance. How many times have you downloaded a film or watched a recorded TV programme and zapped through the adverts to the start of the film itself? The marketing communications industry is aware that adverts, whether on television or in other media, can irritate some of the audience. This, as well as clutter in the marketplace, was the impetus behind product placement. Today, a wide variety of brands is placed within television programmes and films, either appearing naturally as part of the background, props or set or more closely integrated into the script or storyline itself. There are considerable commercial benefits to be obtained when brands are seen being used (and thus, by implication, endorsed) by actors and celebrities, although the audience is not always fully aware that this is effectively advertising. The communications process can be quite subtle. More recently, media coverage of major releases including the James Bond franchise has been critical, for example when 007 swapped his signature vodka martini (shaken) for a swig of Heineken beer in *Skyfall* thanks to a deal reportedly worth $45 million (Barber, 2015).

Sponsorship

Source: iStock.com/Tasfoto NL

research focus

Dens, N., De Pelsmacker, P., Wouters, M. and Purnawirawan, N. (2012) 'Do you like what you recognize? The effects of brand placement prominence and movie plot connection on brand attitude as mediated by recognition', *Journal of Advertising*, 31 (3): 35–53.
   This paper examines the relative effectiveness of different forms of brand placement in movies.

Branded content

A natural progression from media sponsorship and product placement, branded content is more common in the USA than in Europe, where it has been slow to take off. It is still in the early enough stages of development to have a number of different names. In the USA, it is more likely to be called branded entertainment and it is also sometimes called 'advertiser-funded programming'. Branded content is a logical progression from sponsorship. Instead of selecting a suitable event to sponsor, the advertiser creates one. For example, Heinz, having discovered that their products were most often consumed by families eating together, created a family cooking television programme. Betway, sponsors of West Ham football club, created a six-part series which took fans behind the scenes at the club.

branded entertainment
leisure activities, most commonly television or radio programmes, paid for by an advertiser in order to draw attention to its products

Events management

This is the staging of events such as conferences or festivals. They may be one-offs or something that occurs regularly. If a new product is to be launched, there may be internal announcement meetings. External events may be staged to attract, hopefully, favourable publicity and extensive media coverage.

Some events are designed around the brand with the objective of showcasing the brand's values and involving the audience with the brand more deeply. One of the earliest examples of this is the V Festival. This music festival goes beyond sponsorship, it was designed specifically for Virgin and has run every August since 1996.

ACTIVITY

Visit an exhibition. Observe and evaluate all the activities that are going on. Consider the organisation of the exhibition as a whole – the number of stands, layout, visitor attendance, exhibitor attendance, promotional/informational materials, atmosphere and all the supporting services.

- Evaluate the whole event from a visitor's perspective.
- Evaluate the event from an exhibitor's perspective.
- What recommendations would you make for future exhibitions?

Crisis management

Dealing with unforeseen events is an important facet of PR and is often referred to as damage limitation. It may involve product recall. Volkswagen and Renault both had to recall thousands of cars after the emissions scandal of 2015; Mars had to recall products in 55 countries after plastic was found in a Snickers bar. Some companies have had to deal with major ecological disasters. BP's reputation (and profits) suffered badly as a result of the Deepwater Horizon oil spills in the Gulf of Mexico. The crisis can be caused by management or celebrity endorser indiscretion as when Gerald Ratner rubbished his company's jewellery products. Gillette, Gatorade, GM Motors, Accenture, and AT&T aborted campaigns and terminated their contracts with Tiger Woods after his squeaky clean image was tarnished by the revelation of an extra marital affair.

digital focus: Starbucks takes its eyes off the wall

Great PR is all in the timing but even with the best laid plans, you need to be ready to respond in the moment if things don't quite turn out as expected. A promotional event might be easily overshadowed by a breaking news story or, as in the case of Starbucks, a well-meaning stunt might be hijacked by angry protestors – resulting in the brand hitting the headlines for all the wrong reasons.

When Starbucks decided to invest in a huge digital display screen next to one of its pop-up cafés in front of the Natural History Museum in London, it hoped for a wall full of feel-good festive greetings as customers tweeted to #spreadthecheer. When something went wrong with moderation, the screen started pulling in live content automatically, before comments had been checked.

Starbucks had already received bad publicity after being drawn into a row over corporate taxation. With resent-ment growing among UK consumers, the wall quickly became a target for angry tweets, some with offensive language: 'Hey #Starbucks PAY YOUR ————— TAX'. Another wrote, 'If firms like Starbucks paid proper taxes, museums wouldn't have to prostitute themselves to advertisers'.

Blaming a 'temporary malfunction with the content filtering system', Starbucks was quick to apologise and managed to retain its Natural History Museum sponsorship. Lesson learned, there is a time and a place for campaigns centred on user-created content ... and it is not in the middle of a national media scandal!

Sources: *The Telegraph* (2012); Tojagic (2012)

SALES PROMOTION

Organisations spend more of their marketing budgets on sales promotion than they do on advertising. Clearly, then, this is a very important promotional weapon, so what exactly is it? The Institute of Promotional Marketing (IPM), the professional body that represents all the major sales promotion practitioners in the UK, gives this definition of promotional marketing (sales promotion):

> Promotional Marketing is any marketing initiative, creating a call to action that has a direct and positive impact on the behaviour of a targeted audience by offering a demonstrable, though not necessarily tangible, benefit. (IPM, n.d.)

Sales promotion adds value to an exchange. It works by making a product into a better deal. It offers something extra for free or money off or the chance to win something else and most people, it seems, like to think that they have got something for nothing. It could perhaps be free conditioner with your shampoo, or money off a badly wanted computer game or an instant-win competition. Sales promotions are intended to induce buyers to purchase, or try, a product, or to improve the effectiveness of marketing channel members (e.g. retailers or wholesalers).

research focus

Cleeren, K., van Heerde, H.J. and Dekimpe, M.G. (2013) 'Rising from the ashes: how brands and categories can overcome product-harm crises', *Journal of Marketing,* 77 (2): 58–77.

This is an examination of how different marketing actions mitigated the negative effects of having to recall an entire line of faulty products.

Carrillat, F.A., d'Astous, A. and Lazure, J. (2013) 'For better, for worse? What to do when celebrity endorsements go bad', *Journal of Advertising Research,* 53 (1): 15–30.

This experimental study examined what is the optimal decision for a company whose brand is endorsed by a celebrity immersed in a scandal.

Advantages of sales promotion as a marketing communications technique include:

- It has been shown to work. Sales promotion campaigns usually produce notable increases in sales, or trial of a product.

- This effectiveness can be measured, and therefore proved, quite easily. A sales promotion's impact on sales is more directly attributable to the promotion (rather than other activities) because it is a short-term offer and because there is usually some easy means to collect data, e.g. counting money-off coupons handed in, or counting competition entries.

- It can be closely targeted. Thanks to computer databases, a special offer can be directed at specific groups of people within particular market segments, e.g. online retailers might send out incentives to people who have registered but never bought.

- It is manageable within a smaller budget. By managing the length of time the promotion is available, and the number of winning entries or coupons or free products available, sales promotion can maximise the effectiveness of a limited budget. This is a very important aspect of sales promotion, although it must be managed carefully or the costs can get out of hand.

- It has an almost immediate effect. The fortunes of brands and companies are increasingly volatile. Sales promotions can be devised, implemented and take effect far more quickly than other forms of promotion.

- It creates interest. Sales promotion brings in an element of novelty and excitement, which customers enjoy and to which, more importantly, they respond.

SALES PROMOTION OBJECTIVES

Sales promotion is usually used to achieve short-term objectives such as to:

- introduce a new product
- encourage greater usage
- combat or offset competitors' marketing efforts
- stimulate a product trial.

It should be fully integrated with other promotional tools to form a cohesive plan that supports the organisation's long-term objectives. Many sales promotions are seen as down-market and therefore unsuited to campaigns that are promoting an upmarket image. Also, some types of promotion would be too expensive to fund if extended to high-priced goods, and so BOGOF promotions, for example, tend to be found on low-priced products such as toiletries, food and drinks. Sales promotion is at its most effective in the latter stages of the buying process. Promotions are good at prompting action.

There are three categories of sales promotion: consumer, trade and salesforce.

CONSUMER PROMOTIONS

Trial is regarded as the most important action objective for almost every brand. In FMCG, getting a customer to buy for the first time is harder than getting repeat purchases. Customers making high-involvement purchases may also want to try them out, e.g. test driving a car. Sales promotions are a good way to stimulate trial, to add value and to reassure.

Consumer promotions are generally one of three types: save, win or free. For example:

* samples – standard or trial-size giveaways
* coupons, e.g. 25p off your next purchase
* premiums – an extra, free item, e.g. BOGOF
* special offers, e.g. half price this week
* bonus packs – extra quantity or larger product, e.g. 25% bigger bar
* multipacks – cheaper than buying separately
* competitions, e.g. answer the following questions …
* prize draws, e.g. check the number by ringing/writing in
* instant wins, e.g. Kit Kat's 'Win a Million' promotion
* points to collect, e.g. Avios or Nectar points
* tie-ins – giving a different product away, e.g. McDonald's Happy Meal gifts
* cause-related promotions – the seller gives a donation to a worthy cause for every product sold, e.g. Pizza Express donates to the Venice in Peril Fund every time one of its Veneziana pizzas is sold
* self-liquidating special offers, e.g. a cereal company offering a set of breakfast bowls in return for £10 and four tokens.

Consumer sales promotion programmes may be paid for by the retailer but are commonly financed by the manufacturer. They are often supported by advertising, point-of-sale (POS) promotions (also known as point-of-purchase (POP)) and merchandising activities within retail outlets.

TRADE PROMOTIONS

Consumer goods suppliers spend a great deal on trade promotions to distributors, including retailers, as part of their push strategy.

self-liquidating special offer

a sales promotion that pays for itself (usually because the company making the offer has bought the promotional items in vast quantities and so obtained a substantial discount)

point-of-sale (POS) promotion

the general term for any type of promotion found where the sale takes place; most usually associated with retail outlets

merchandising

selection and display of products within a retail environment

Supermarkets use a lot of sales promotions.

© Dave Pickton

Promotions by manufacturers to their distributors, generally called trade promotions, are often some form of price promotion because the main factor motivating distributors is their reseller profit margin.

Price promotion is often used to stimulate trial, i.e. persuading the distributor to stock a product for the first time. There are three main types of trade trial promotion:

1   *New line fees* (slotting allowances): these are cash payments or a proportion of the shipment (consignment of goods) donated free, which amounts to a price inducement, in return for stocking a new product or offering a new service for a specified period of time.

2   *Price-offs*: these are straight reductions in the selling price to the distributor and are sometimes called off-invoice promotions.

3   *Returns*: the manufacturer agrees to buy back unsold quantities of the product. Distributing on consignment is an extreme form of this. The distributor pays nothing to the manufacturer until the product is sold (also known as sale or return).

trade trial promotions
sales promotions aimed at members of the supply chain, e.g. a prize for selling 100 cases of wine

Price promotions are also important in encouraging repeat purchase by distributors. There are four types:

1   *Price-offs*: as described above, but on the understanding that part of the discount will be passed to the end customer or consumer, or that the distributor will provide extra display, advertising or both.

2   *Joint promotions*: these are agreements by which the manufacturer and distributor both contribute funds towards promotional expenditure. The proportion of contribution may vary.

3   *Sales contests*: competitions in which retailers or other trade partners can win attractive prizes.

4   *Sales education*: this is applicable mainly to industrial products and services, or to the more technical types of consumer durable. Manufacturers train the retailer's or wholesaler's staff and all parties benefit from the increased sales.

SALESFORCE PROMOTIONS

Manufacturers have a salesforce to motivate. Salesforce promotions include monetary rewards, such as bonuses, and non-monetary rewards, such as prizes, training programmes, motivational meetings and selling aids.

WHAT CAN GO WRONG?

Sales promotions must be very carefully planned. There is a code of practice to abide by, and laws on gambling and competitions to be obeyed. For example, if someone has to pay to enter, then that is gambling and, in the UK, a licence is required to run gambling games. Hence that

Promotional display
Source: ROBYN BECK/AFP/Getty Images

familiar phrase, 'no purchase necessary'. There is a thriving sales promotion industry in the UK and, as the details of promotions can get quite complex, it is usually advisable to enlist expert help for anything but the simplest of offers. Some of the scenarios that might arise are outlined below.

- Over-redemption:

    o bad promotion design, e.g. the classic case of the Hoover flights promotion. Hoover offered a free flight to New York with every vacuum cleaner purchase. Unfortunately, the vacuum cleaner was cheaper than the flight and people flocked to electrical appliance stores instead of to travel agents. That promotion is reported to have cost £48 million.

    o error in administration, e.g. Pepsi's Philippine subsidiary promised one million pesos (about £25,000) for bottle caps bearing the winning number 349. When PepsiCo had paid out £8 million, it realised something was amiss – there were far too many winners. The withdrawal of the offer provoked riots.

- Misredemption: one of the advantages of sales promotion is the accuracy of its targeting. You can send a coupon to precisely the person you want to redeem it, but can you prevent it from being passed on to someone else?

- Malredemption: the likely number of winners for any promotion is carefully worked out and budgets are set. Lottery syndicates are encouraged but, if a promotion requires the collecting of a set of something, beware: joint efforts (and swaps arranged through newspaper columns or on the Internet) could blow the budget.

- Faulty pack design: some sales promotions require a special pack design to disguise which one is the winning pack. This packaging must be designed with great care. If someone swallows a prize notification ticket when upending a packet of crisps into their mouth (as has happened), then trouble will ensue.

- Pilfering: if the pack design is not good enough to disguise a winner, the chances are it will never make it out of the shop. Bored sales assistants enjoy trying to spot a winning pack.

- Lost in the post: many samples fail to reach the right target. They may arrive but be picked up by another member of the household. There have been complaints that some of the promotional items that land on doormats are dangerous to young children who may think that they are toys or sweets, when they are not.

Sales promotions need careful, worst-case scenario planning – and professional indemnity insurance.

PERSONAL SELLING

There is talk of outlawing door-to-door selling in the UK. This will be good news for many people, who feel threatened and coerced by such salespeople, and bad news for the unprofessional sales organisations whose behaviour has prompted the ban. Putting to one side the ethical problems associated with extreme forms of personal selling, it has a major role to play in the promotion mix of many companies. Personal selling is an oral presentation, in a conversation with one or more prospective purchasers, for the purpose of making sales.

Personal selling involves informing customers of the benefits of products, and persuading them to buy through personal communication in a potential exchange situation. It includes such things as a salesperson explaining a product's features, a technician demonstrating a new MRI scanner to relevant hospital personnel, and even the person at the supermarket who gives you a free sample of a new luxury ice-cream while telling you something about it.

Personal selling differs from other forms of communication in that messages flow from a sender to a receiver directly (often face to face). This direct and interpersonal communication lets the sender receive and evaluate feedback from the receiver immediately. This communications process, known as dyadic communication (between two people or groups), allows the message to be tailored more specifically to the needs of the sender and receiver than do many of the other media.

dyadic communication
a dialogue between two people or two groups

Reaching a limited number of people through personal selling efforts costs, proportionately, a considerable amount more than it does through advertising. However, in many situations it is thought to be worth it because of the immediate feedback and its greater persuasive impact on customers.

global focus: doing business abroad

Company representatives and salespeople have to learn the business conventions of other countries in order to do business there. Failure to do so can leave an impatient North American hanging around for hours in a South American office wondering what has happened to the meeting or a disappointed European waiting for a contract that they believe has been promised by a Japanese firm but which never materialises.

Many Latin Americans have a different attitude to time than do their North American counterparts. In the USA, meetings should start on time. Further south, they can see no point in starting before everyone is ready. The Japanese dislike saying an outright no, as it seems rude, and are also concerned not to lose face by admitting that they do not have the authority to say yes. Either or both of these situations can leave a European with the false impression that they have made a sale.

In many countries business is a much more personal interaction than it is in the West. Arabs prefer to do business with people they know. The Japanese too spend time getting to know people and building trust before they commit to any business dealings. Much time may be spent on the golf course before business is even mentioned.

Conducting business in some countries is particularly awkward for women. There are many countries, notably Arab and African ones, where women are still not accepted as equals in the workplace. On a positive note here, Western women tend to be treated as representatives of their companies first, their countries second – and their sex third. So they do get on rather better than local women do and it is by no means impossible for women to strike deals in such countries. Some Western companies refuse to bow to local custom and send their female employees as trailblazers.

SALESPEOPLE

To develop a salesforce, a marketing manager needs to decide what kind of salesperson will sell the firm's products most effectively. Various authors classify sales roles in different ways. Some classify sales jobs into two broad categories: service selling, which concentrates on getting sales from the existing customer base, and developmental selling, which aims to convert prospects into customers. Others refer to three basic roles: order taking, order supporting and order getting. From reading the above, you will understand that there are many sales roles and, in reality, these roles may not be discrete. Salespeople now have to perform many tasks and activities daily (not just selling), which involve numerous skills, such as:

- buyer/seller team coordinator
- customer service provider
- buyer behaviour expert
- information gatherer
- market analyst and planner
- sales forecaster
- market cost analyst.

research focus

Storbacka, K., Ryals, L., Davies, I.A. and Nenonen, S. (2009) 'The changing role of sales: viewing sales as a strategic, cross-functional process', *The European Journal of Marketing*, **43 (7–8): 890–906.**
 The role of sales within the promotion mix is constantly changing. This study revealed that the twenty-first-century sales function is changing in three interrelated aspects: from a function to a process; from an isolated activity to an integrated one; and from operational to strategic.

STAGES OF SELLING

A number of sequential steps go into making a sale. These are illustrated in Exhibit 8.8.

prospecting
looking for prospective customers

cold call
when a salesperson calls on a prospect without an appointment

Prospecting is about finding potential customers. Exhibitions are good sources of prospects, as are direct-response promotions. Websites are often used to identify people who are interested in a brand or product category. It is important that a salesperson should prepare before approaching a prospect. They need to know what kind of person they are dealing with, why they might want the product and what their likely hot buttons are. The next step is to get the appointment. This may be arranged in advance (e.g. over the phone) or the salesperson may cold call. The next step is a big one. Although, in Exhibit 8.8, it is labelled 'making the pitch', there is more to it than that. First, the salesperson should find out what the customer wants, then he or she can draw attention to the most appropriate products and their benefits. The best salespeople are good listeners. It is unlikely that the product will fit the customer's needs perfectly – there will be some objections raised (e.g. it is too expensive, it is the wrong colour, it is too heavy or too light). The salesperson must address these concerns honestly, and perhaps convince the customer that the things the product lacks are unimportant. Now comes the close. This is the part that many salespeople find the hardest: they just have to ask for the order. Finally, there is the follow-up: making sure the product is delivered, that it works properly and, of course, checking if the customer needs anything else. This could be the start of a long and profitable relationship.

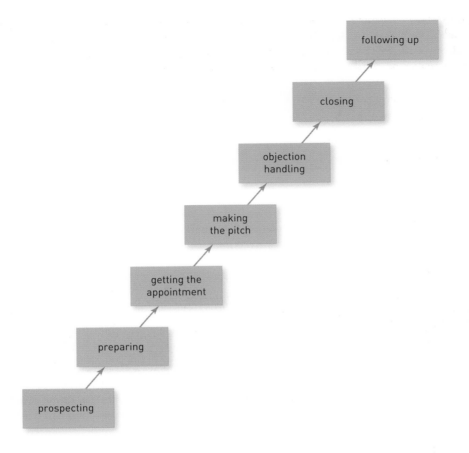

EXHIBIT 8.8 Personal selling

Not all steps are used in all sales situations. The retail sales assistant, for example, will be in a very different situation from a key accounts salesperson who works for a manufacturer of heavy industrial equipment.

ethical focus: closing techniques

Salespeople employ a number of closing techniques to persuade customers to place orders. Some are more effective than others and some are less ethical than others. Good salespeople are honest and straightforward. If customers like and trust them, they are far more likely to buy from them.

Some examples of closing techniques are:

- the straight close, e.g. 'So would you like one?' followed by silence
- the deadline close, e.g. 'There is only the one left in stock and I don't know when we'll be able to get more'

(Continued)

(Continued)

- the assumptive close, e.g. 'So I'll get it delivered next week then'
- the alternative close, e.g. 'Would you like the blue or the green?'
- the no problem close, e.g. 'Order it now and you can cancel it later if you change your mind'
- the sympathy close, e.g. 'I just need one more order to make my sales quota this month'.

sales quota
target number (or value) of sales set for a salesperson

Look out for these next time you're out shopping. You may even be able to add to the list.

DIRECT MARKETING COMMUNICATION

It is not always easy to fit all the elements of the marketing communications mix into four broad categories. Where to put direct marketing (or more accurately in the context of promotion, direct marketing communication) is one such problem, as it can make use of advertising as well as sales promotions and personal selling.

Most promotional tools are aimed at mass audiences but there are weaknesses with the mass approach and so many companies have adopted a more direct approach to their markets. They are motivated not just by cost advantages but also by opportunities to improve quality and service provision.

direct marketing communication
promotional material designed to prompt a direct response from the recipient to the sender

Direct marketing communication establishes personal contact with prospects and customers to encourage a direct response. Early direct marketing communication focused on providing a telephone number or a response card in advertisements (i.e. direct-response advertising). Today, direct mail, telemarketing, door-to-door, email and interactive website forms are among the main direct-response media used.

direct mail
promotional material delivered by post

Direct marketing has outgrown its early roots and has become a sophisticated marketing tool used for building relationships with customers. Direct-response advertising is now only a part of the huge direct marketing industry. The Institute of Direct and Digital Marketing's (IDM) definition emphasises the importance of building customer relationships and the value of customer data: 'planned recording, analysis and tracking of individual customers' responses and transactions for the purpose of developing and prolonging mutually profitable customer relationships' (IDM, 2010). The primary objectives of direct marketing are to build and sustain a mutually rewarding relationship with individual customers, to reduce media cost and to improve the effectiveness of marketing communications and the measurement of results.

direct-response advertising
'advertising, or selling, through any medium inviting the consumer to respond to the advertiser' (IDM Direct Marketing Guide)

Undoubtedly, direct marketing has grown and developed because of rapid advances in computing and communications technology, transportation and changing market conditions. Technology has facilitated the collection, storage, analysis and retrieval of customer data.

A database is effectively an electronic filing system with extensive cross-referencing and processing capabilities. This data is used to identify prospects for a company's products. These prospects are then targeted for marketing and sales activities, usually by being placed on specific lists. Take the example of a department store. It may have lists for men, women, parents, customers of specific cosmetics companies, people who buy designer clothes, people who have its store card, people who do not have its store card, people who have responded to a particular campaign or offer, people who purchased electrical goods such as televisions or household appliances. This information is gathered from purchases made in store, data provided by customers when they fill in forms (such as applications for store cards, credit agreements, competition entries) and bought in from other sources (there are companies that specialise in buying in data and selling it on).

The targeted customers may be sent mailings, telephoned, emailed or just added to a list to receive regular newsletters, updates, etc.

Databases have been used for years to analyse customer buying patterns, refine communications campaigns and identify prospects for other products and services. The technology has, of course, become more sophisticated and powerful, and so have the uses to which it can be put. Today, many companies have data warehouses and use data mining software to sift through the enormous amounts of data stored in them and make the connections between the data. For example, a company can match up customer profiles in different parts of the country with past sales at specific times of year and use this link to identify new ranges that might sell well. There is almost no limit to the connections data mining might make – as long as the data exists in the database, of course.

These sophisticated computer systems are at the heart of customer relationship management (CRM). Organisations have more information on customers than they ever had before, as well as the technology and techniques to use it to understand and serve their customers better and ensure the experience is consistent across multiple channels. There really is very little excuse for poor customer service today and yet it does still exist in some places. Have you ever received a standard response to a query that really just did not answer it? It can be a mistake for an organisation to become over-reliant on automation.

data warehouse
a large database holding copies of customer and environmental data taken from the organisation's other systems and designed specifically to make it easier to raise queries and produce reports

FACTORS AFFECTING MEDIA CHOICE IN DIRECT MARKETING COMMUNICATIONS

No one medium always achieves the highest response at the lowest cost, and it is generally true that those media that elicit a higher response also tend to be the most expensive. For example, telephone responses are potentially the highest of any media, but the costs are also the highest.

To assess the media for a direct marketing campaign, the framework AIMRITE can be used as a decision-making aid (Pickton and Broderick, 2004).

- *Audience*: does the media reach the desired target audience?
- *Impact*: does the media have sufficient impact to ensure the message has a chance of getting through the clutter?

ACTIVITY

Obtain a direct-response press or magazine advertisement or a piece of direct mail. Critically appraise the media choice made, using the AIMRITE framework (although you are not likely to be able to assess the end result).

- *Message*: does it help ensure the message is clearly communicated?
- *Response*: does it make responding easy?
- *Internal management*: does it enhance the efficient management of the campaign?
- *The end result*: what are the costs and projected likely revenues? Taking the above into account, and looking at the average response rates for the chosen media, how likely are you to hit target for the campaign?

SEARCH MARKETING

Most online experiences begin with a search engine, so any business that wants to drive traffic to its website will want to be as close to the top of the list of search results. Search marketing incorporates aspects of both advertising and PR as well as some specific techniques and technologies so it doesn't fit neatly into the four marketing communications mix categories. To make sense of search marketing it helps to think about two kinds of search results returned in response to a user's query.

organic search results

the natural consequence of a search engine applying its algorithm to find the most relevant answers to a user's query; they do not include advertisements

search algorithm

the often complex sets of rules that a search engine applies in order to filter and prioritise web pages

search engine optimisation

a range of techniques employed to improve visibility of websites as high as possible in the list of search results

The first category of results, known as organic search results, is prioritised according to a complex set of rules, known as search algorithms. The exact rules applied to filter results are, of course, a closely guarded secret, but broadly speaking, the relevance and quality of content contained on the site are considered along with the authority of the source. Search engine optimisation involves researching the keywords and search terms potential customers might use, providing good quality, relevant content and ensuring the site is seen as authoritative, for example through links to other popular, high quality online sources.

The second category is paid search results; effectively advertisements that have been served-up along with the organic search results. It isn't always easy for users to distinguish paid search results from organic results. Google currently displays paid results at both the top and the bottom of the first screen in exactly the same colour and format as organic results with just a small 'ad' symbol to distinguish them. Google adwords is by far the leading platform for paid search worldwide. Google selects which ads to display based on a match between keywords included in the query and those selected by the advertiser. In theory, this is a win-win situation as the user only receives ads that are relevant to their needs right now, whereas the advertiser is able to reach audiences who have actually declared an interest in the products they sell. The advertiser only has to pay when a user clicks on the ad – a system known as pay-per-click. Successful paid search campaigns also involve careful keyword research. Popular adwords such as 'Holiday' or 'Spain' are typically more costly than less common terms. It pays to identify more specific search terms like 'Andalusian self-catering holiday' that are more likely to deliver better quality leads.

MARKETING COMMUNICATIONS REGULATIONS

Throughout Europe and elsewhere, marketing communications are subject to constraints and regulations. Some controls are set by law and others are self-imposed voluntarily by the marketing communications industry itself. The balance of legal and self-regulations varies from country to country. Collectively, the UK regulations seek to uphold four guiding principles. Promotions should be:

- legal
- decent
- honest
- truthful.

These principles are used to produce a series of codes of practice covering different media and types of promotion. These codes can be seen on the Advertising Standards Authority (ASA) website at www.asa.org.uk.

Despite attempts to ensure that these principles are maintained, there are examples of some dubious practices. Regulatory bodies police the industry and, where necessary, require that promotions are withdrawn if they contravene the principles above. Legal action can be taken in extreme cases.

ethical focus: breaking the code

It's in the nature of human beings to push boundaries to see how far they'll stretch, and advertisers are no different. In the UK, the ASA and OFCOM are there to maintain standards.

The UK's most complained about ad to date is a KFC Zinger Crunch ad showing workers at an emergency helpline talking with their mouths full of chicken. The main cause for complaint was their appalling table manners and the example they set to children. There were 1,679 complaints but the ASA decided it was up to parents to teach their children manners, not advertisers: complaint not upheld.

A Carphone Warehouse ad attracted complaints from 145 people including some of its competitors. Ads in a range of media, including TV, press and on a CD, promoted a new TalkTalk telephone package with 'free broadband forever'. The complaint was that it was misleading to suggest that the broadband was free when it involved an 18-month contractual commitment to the calls package, a connection charge of £29.99, ongoing costs of £9.99 per month plus line rental (£20.99 in total) and a disconnection fee of £70. The complaints were upheld.

The most complained about advert of 2015 was for Money Supermarket and featured a man in denim shorts and high heels prancing down a street. Many viewers found this distasteful and overly sexual. The complaint was not upheld. In fact, of the 10 most complained about ads of 2015, only the tenth one was banned. That was an ad for XLS Medical, a slimming aid, which featured two women exchanging text messages before heading off on holiday. After seeing a photo of her friend who had lost weight, the other woman was unhappy about not being able to fit into her holiday wardrobe. The ASA upheld the complaints because the ad 'presented an irresponsible approach to body image and confidence'.

464 people complained about PayPal's Christmas ad in which two children were worried that their parents hadn't been shopping for Christmas presents. Complaints expressed concern that the ad revealed the truth about Father Christmas. The ASA did not uphold the complaints; however, PayPal did change the scheduling of its commercial.

John Lewis upset some animal lovers with a hugely popular Christmas advert which showed a little boy pinning a Christmas stocking to his dog's kennel on a windy, snowy day. Many thought this endorsed leaving animals out in the cold and was unacceptable but the ASA did not uphold the complaints.

To find out more about the advertising codes, and for examples of complaints, visit www.asa.org.uk.

In general, it is up to the media owners (TV, radio, cinema, newspaper and magazine owners, etc.) to decide whether or not an item is likely to contravene the codes of practice, and to refuse to run the promotion where this may happen. In the case of TV and radio, any advertising should be pre-vetted – that is, checked before transmission, but in the case of most other promotions, such pre-vetting is impossible because of the volume of advertisements involved and so checks are made after the promotions have been circulated. Members of the public are encouraged to make complaints, which are subsequently investigated. In the case of the UK, a great deal of voluntary self-regulation is relied on to enhance the legal controls. The Advertising Standards Authority is responsible for regulating advertising, sales promotions and direct marketing (including the Internet). There are also numerous other professional bodies representing the different elements of marketing communications, which also have their own codes of professional practice. Most other countries have similar arrangements although the extent, and nature, of the control exerted vary significantly.

SETTING THE MARKETING COMMUNICATIONS BUDGET

Marketing communications should be seen as an investment. It can, however, be quite expensive and so attention should be paid to getting the budget right. Setting the promotional budget is not an exact science. Various techniques are used by organisations, the five most popular ones being:

- arbitrary method
- affordable method
- competitive parity method
- objective and task method
- percentage of sales method.

Budgeting methods between organisations vary in popularity. While the percentage of sales method is reputed to be a favoured approach in larger organisations, small businesses are more likely to use arbitrary or affordable approaches.

ARBITRARY METHOD

Rather than a method, this is an approach to arriving at a budget figure. It is more a judgement that seems right at the time. It is unlikely to be based on any significant criteria and is more likely to be based on a gut feeling or intuition. It is an educated guess – but, remember, it may have been made by a very experienced marketing director.

AFFORDABLE METHOD

In essence, this means that the company will spend on promotion what it thinks is reasonable and can afford. Organisations using this approach, like the arbitrary approach, are more likely to reflect a view that marketing communications are an expense rather than an investment.

The affordable method causes problems with long-range planning. The company cannot guess the funds that will be available in the future to spend on promotion. Also, in times of recession or hardship, very little will be spent on promotion, and yet this is most likely to be the time when extra spending would be of benefit.

COMPETITIVE PARITY METHOD

A budget is set that matches, exceeds or is in proportion to competitors' budgets. Care has to be taken in applying this method. For example, not all companies have the same objectives. Some may want to become the market leader (market share objective), while others may wish to become more profitable (profitability objective). A company's nearest competitor may be much bigger or much smaller than it is. Simply matching expenditure in this situation would not be sensible. Setting the budget as an appropriate proportion would be a better approach.

OBJECTIVE AND TASK METHOD

The objective and task method determines a budget based on what the various communications activities need to achieve. In essence, objectives are set and then the marketing communications tasks to achieve the objectives are decided upon. By calculating the costs of those tasks, a budget is set.

Although this method may appear to be the best, it is a method that is rarely applied in its entirety. Difficulties in implementing this approach include:

- the company may not be able to afford the budget arrived at
- it is time-consuming (and therefore expensive to prepare)
- the task may not actually achieve the objective anyway, e.g. the planned PR campaign may not raise the company's credibility as intended.

PERCENTAGE OF SALES METHOD

The percentage of sales method is probably the most popular method. It is the classical approach partly because it is easy to calculate. It links marketing communications expenditure directly to levels of sales by allocating a fixed percentage of turnover to marketing communications.

turnover
the monetary value of sales; also called revenue or sales revenue

However, there are difficulties. What percentage should be used and how should the turnover be determined? The percentage may be based on previous practice, on competitor allocations or on industry averages. Turnover could be based on historic sales, last year's sales or sales averaged over a number of years. It could be based on current sales levels, or it could be based on forecast sales (which may, of course, be wrong).

Perhaps unsurprisingly, in practice, most organisations use a combination of all these approaches to set their budgets.

SUMMARY

This chapter has introduced some basic concepts and models that support marketing communications decisions. The key model to understand is the communications process, since marketing communications, or promotion, is a communication process. This involves an understanding of the sender, the message, the media and the receivers.

Organisations can use a variety of promotional tools to communicate with potential customers, whether consumer or organisational. The major promotional tools are advertising, PR, sales promotion and personal selling. To these can be added direct marketing and sponsorship, together with many other activities such as packaging and events. Collectively, these are known as the promotion or marketing communications mix.

The organisation can use its promotion mix to develop both push and pull strategies. With a push strategy, the organisation directs its promotional efforts at marketing channel members. These then push the product forwards to the final buyer. With a pull strategy, the organisation directs its promotional efforts at the final buyer to develop a strong demand for the product that is used to pull a product through the marketing channel. Most organisations use a combination of push and pull.

The purpose of all marketing communications is to create a response from potential buyers. One response model, also known as a hierarchy of effects model, is AIDA (Awareness, Interest, Desire and Action). Each promotional tool has different degrees of effectiveness in eliciting these different responses.

One approach does not fit all. There is no single optimal promotion mix and no one accepted scientific approach to determining the promotion mix. Many factors need to be considered, such as: the objectives of the marketing plan; the size and characteristics of the target market/audience and their buying decision process; the type of products being promoted; the objectives of the promotional efforts; and competitors' promotional efforts.

CHALLENGES REVIEWED

Now that you have finished reading the chapter, look back at the challenges you were set at the beginning. Do you have a clearer idea of what's involved?

HINTS

- See 'setting the marketing communications budget'.
- Think beyond mass media advertising to other promotional tools and more targeted media.
- Time for crisis management – see 'publicity' and 'media relations'.
- Think about repositioning and take great care not to be misleading in your approach – check the advertising code carefully.

READING AROUND

JOURNAL ARTICLES

Bergkvist, L. and Zhou, K.Q. (2016). 'Celebrity endorsements: a literature review and research agenda', *International Journal of Advertising*, 35 (4): 642–63.

Fulgoni, G.M. (2016) 'In the digital world, not everything that can be measured matters: how to distinguish "valuable" from "nice to know"', *Journal of Advertising Research*, 56 (1): 9–13.

Garretson Folse, J.A., Netemeyer, R.G. and Burton, S. (2012) 'Spokescharacters: how the personality traits of sincerity, excitement, and competence help to build equity', *Journal of Advertising*, 31 (1): 17–32.

Gupta, S. (2015) 'In mobile advertising, timing is everything', *Harvard Business Review*, November. Available at: https://hbr.org/2015/11/in-mobile-advertising-timing-is-everything (accessed 20/08/16).

Van Kuilenburg, P., De Jong, M. and Van Rompay, T. (2011) '"That was funny, but what was the brand again?" Humorous television commercials and brand linkage', *International Journal of Advertising*, 30 (5): 795–814.

Wiid, R., Grant, P.S., Mills, A.J. and Pitt, L.F. (2016) 'No joke: understanding public sentiment toward selling and salespeople through cartoon analysis', *Marketing Theory*, 16 (Jun): 171–93.

MAGAZINE ARTICLES

Carter, S. (2013) 'A creative legend's lesson to planners', *Admap*, February. London: WARC.

Cooper, A. (2013) 'Keep sponsorship local', *Admap*, March. London: WARC.

Freeman, W. (2014) 'Six of the best product placements in video games', 13 July. Available at: www.theguardian.com/technology/2014/jul/03/six-of-the-best-product-placement-video-games (accessed 02/09/16).

BOOKS AND BOOK CHAPTERS

Abilasha, M. (1999) 'Celebrities in advertising', in J.P. Jones (ed.), *The Advertising Business*. London: Sage, Chapter 17, pp. 193–208.

Burcher, N. (2012) *Paid Owned Earned: Maximizing Marketing Returns in a Socially Connected World*. London: Kogan Page.

Hackley, C. (2010) *Advertising and Promotion* (2nd edn). London: Sage.

Levinson, J.C., Meyerson, M. and Scarborough, M.E. (2008) *Guerrilla Marketing on the Internet: The Definitive Guide from the Father of Guerrilla Marketing*. Irvine, CA: Entrepreneur Press.

JOURNALS

International Journal of Advertising

Journal of Marketing Communications

MAGAZINES

Admap

Campaign

Marketing Week

PR Week

VIDEOS

AMC TV, *Madmen* – TV series, available on DVD.

BBC4 (2008) *Hard Sell programmes 1–6* – Phil Jupitus narrates a series exploring 50 years of British TV advertising.

WEBSITES

www.asa.org.uk – the website for the Advertising Standards Authority; check out the complaints and adjudications.

www.brandrepublic.com – access to news stories and feature articles.

www.creativeclub.co.uk – (subscription-only); excellent source for current advertising.

www.theidm.com – the Institute of Direct and Digital Marketing; go to the knowledge centre and browse.

www.warc.com – (subscription-only) the World Advertising Research Centre: journals, case studies, papers on best practice and much more.

TEST YOURSELF

1   List and explain the key elements in the communications process model. (See pp. 298)

2   Identify sources of noise in the communications process. (See pp. 299)

3   What are the main elements, or tools, of the promotion mix? (See pp. 294)

4   What are the advantages and disadvantages of mass communication and interpersonal communication? (See pp. 306)

5   Define push and pull strategies. (See pp. 297)

6   What are the problems with using 'increase sales' as a promotion objective? (See pp. 312)

7   How is advertising controlled or regulated in the UK? (See pp. 332)

8   What is the AIDA model and how can it be used to set promotion objectives? (See pp. 303)

9   Explain how personal selling is a two-way communications process. (See pp. 300)

10   Explain and give examples of the major types of consumer sales promotion. (See pp. 322)

11   What is direct-response advertising? (See pp. 330)

12   Discuss the strengths and limitations of each budgeting method. (See pp. 334)

REVISION TOOLS

Want to test yourself even more? Review what you have learnt by visiting
https://study.sagepub.com/masterson4e

- Practise for exams with **multiple choice questions**
- Revise key terms with **interactive flashcards**

MINI CASE STUDY: A FLY-AWAY SUCCESS STORY – RED BULL GIVES YOU WINGS

Read the questions, then the case material, and then answer the questions.

QUESTIONS

1   Analyse Red Bull's marketing communications strategy in terms of: objectives, target audience and brand positioning.

2   Red Bull make excellent use of paid, owned and earned media. Identify examples of each and discuss how they support each other to maximise audience reach.

3   How well integrated are Red Bull's marketing communications activities? What pulls them together?

How do you become a market leader? One way is to create a whole new category and then launch your brand into it with a bang. That's what Red Bull did back in 1987 and they are still leading the energy drinks market that they created. In 2012 they sold 5.2 billion cans.

Strong brands like Red Bull don't happen by accident. The company has invested a lot into its marketing: a lot of thought and effort, although not really such a lot of money. Compared to companies like Coca-Cola and Pepsi, their marketing budget is tiny, yet a can of Red Bull can cost over twice as much as a can of cola.

It all started in the 1980s when Austrian entrepreneur Dietrich Mateschitz visited Thailand and was impressed and energised by a local drink. He adapted the ingredients to better suit Western tastes and launched it in 1987 as Red Bull, Europe's first energy drink. The first press ad claimed that it was so awesome polka dots would fly off your tie.

1988 saw Red Bull's first sponsorship deal: the Red Bull Dolomitenmann: 'one of the toughest extreme sport relays on the planet', a marathon event combining mountain running, paragliding, kayaking and mountain biking. More extreme sport sponsorships followed – snowboarding, mountain biking and cliff diving – but this wasn't enough for Red Bull. The brand wanted to be even more involved in the exciting lifestyle represented by these high-risk challenges, and so they began creating their own events. They became an integral part of the action rather than just standing on the sidelines.

Red Bull run a number of different contests and events such as a soapbox race and the Red Bull Flugtag. Flugtags challenge contestants to build flight machines which are then launched (or crashed) off a 30-foot plat-form into water. The flight record for one of these amateur machines is 207 feet, their crashes are spectacular and prizes are awarded not just for length of flight but also for imaginative design and humour. Flugtags have been held all round the world and attract huge crowds at the actual event – though the bulk of the audience watch online via Facebook or YouTube. Two years on, that record-breaking flight in Minneapolis had over half a million views on YouTube.

Red Bull
Flugtag

In 2012, Red Bull launched a man into space – and then threw him out. Felix Baumgartner set the world record for skydiving when he fell approximately 39 kilometres, reaching an estimated speed of 1357.64 km/h (843.6 mph), or Mach 1.25. He was the first person to break the sound barrier without being inside any form of vehicle. The event was watched live around the world – and then watched again and again on YouTube. The space dive made sense both for daredevil Felix and for Red Bull. It was a logical progression from what they had done before. Over the years, Red Bull's association with daring stunts and extreme sports has successfully created an independent, edgy image that has served it well. More recently, the brand has added creativity to its image with its involvement in contemporary culture through events such as Word Clash street poems and Art of Can which invited would-be artists to create sculptures using Red Bull cans – inspired recycling! (www.redbull.com/en/stories/1331580470607/red-bull-art-of-can-inspired-recycling).

Through these events Red Bull carries on an intense conversation with its youthful and independent-minded target audience. The brand is part of their lives, providing entertainment, excitement, challenge. The buzz around Red Bull is regularly stoked by another high-risk brand experience but it is the audience and their engagement that has really built that brand strength.

Red Bull has extended its do-it-yourself approach to events into media. Now they have an online TV channel (www.redbull.tv/Redbulltv) where you can watch sports and entertainment programmes and listen to music. It's all free – but it's also all heavily branded. The Red Bull Media House provides web clips, documentaries and photos for other publishers. The official Red Bull website looks more like a sports site with tabs for mot-orsports, biking snowboarding and surfing. It also has games and music. The emphasis is clearly on what Red Bull does as a brand, not on the product itself. This is lifestyle branding at its best.

Red Bull's promotional activities are so well integrated that they seem like one long, continuous campaign. While their focus is on events and branded content, they do also make use of paid media. The famous tag line, 'Red Bull gives you wings', is frequently seen on television, in the press and on other web pages. They use the

(Continued)

(Continued)

different promotional tools for different purposes. The adverts create awareness and build brand image through their humour and consistency. Sponsorship of sports like Formula 1 builds credibility by association and the Red Bull branded events and online content, e.g. the Red Bull Air Race and Last Man Standing 48-hour Motocross, differentiate the product and engage the audience.

Red Bull promises to deliver energy. It will wake you up, enhance your performance. The universal appeal of this brand promise helps the brand to cross international boundaries. The drink may have started in Austria, inspired by a Thai tonic, but now it is boosting energy levels all over the world.

brand promise

the way the brand sets out to fulfil a customer need, e.g. Pepsi might promise to be thirst quenching

REFERENCES

Barber, N. (2015) 'Does Bond's product placement go too far?', BBC News, 1 October. Available at: www.bbc.co.uk/culture/story/20151001-does-bonds-product-placement-go-too-far (accessed 01/03/17).

BBC News (2016) 'The stunning £1m farm you can rent for £1 a year', BBC News, 18 May. Available at: www.bbc.co.uk/news/uk-36324031 (accessed 8/9/16).

Brodie, R.J., Hollebeek, L.D., Jurić, B. and Ilić, A. (2011) 'Customer engagement: conceptual domain, fundamental propositions, and implications for research', *Journal of Service Research*, 14 (3): 252–71.

Brodie, R.J., Ilic, A., Juric, B. and Hollebeek, L. (2013) 'Consumer engagement in a virtual brand community: an exploratory analysis', *Journal of Business Research*, 66 (1): 105–14.

Carrillat, F.A., d'Astous, A. and Lazure, J. (2013) 'For better, for worse? What to do when celebrity endorsements go bad', *Journal of Advertising Research*, 53 (1): 15–30.

Chartered Institute of Public Relations (2013) 'What is PR?'. Available at: www.cipr.co.uk/content/careers-cpd/careers-pr/what-pr (accessed 14/02/17).

Cleeren, K., van Heerde, H.J. and Dekimpe, M.G. (2013) 'Rising from the ashes: how brands and categories can overcome product-harm crises', *Journal of Marketing,* 77 (2): 58–77.

Colley, R. (1961) *Defining Advertising Goals for Measured Advertising Results.* New York: Association of National Advertisers.

DBA (2009) *Heinz Classic Soups,* Design Business Association Effectiveness Awards 2009. Available at: www.warc.com (accessed 13/12/09).

Dens, N., De Pelsmacker, P., Wouters, M. and Purnawirawan, N. (2012) 'Do you like what you recognize? The effects of brand placement prominence and movie plot connection on brand attitude as mediated by recognition', *Journal of Advertising*, 31 (3): 35–53.

Engel, J.F., Warshaw, M.R. and Kinnear, T.C. (1994) *Promotional Strategy* (8th edn). New York: Irwin.

Grunig, J. and Hunt, T. (1984) *Managing Public Relations.* London: Thomson Learning.

IDM (2010) Institute of Direct Marketing website. Available at: www.theidm.com/resources/jargon-ouster (accessed 15/05/10).

IPM (n.d.) 'Definitions'. Available at: www.theipm.org.uk/insights/definitions-faq.aspx (accessed 01/03/17).

Jefkins, F. (1989) *Public Relations Techniques*. London: Heinemann.

Jones, J.P. (1990) 'Advertising: strong or weak force? Two views oceans apart', *International Journal of Advertising*, 9 (3): 233–46.

Makin, C. (2002) *Domino's Pizza: Building a High Street Brand Through a Change in Media Strategy*, IPA Effectiveness Awards, Best Interactive. Available at: www.warc.com (accessed 01/09/03).

Pickton, D.W. and Broderick, A. (2004) *Integrated Marketing Communications* (2nd edn). Harlow: FT/Prentice Hall.

Rust, R.T. and Oliver R.W. (1994) 'The death of advertising', *Journal of Advertising*, 23 (4): 71.

Sashi, C.M. (2012) 'Customer engagement, buyer–seller relationships, and social media', *Management Decision*, 50 (2): 253–72.

Schau, H.J. and Gilly, M.C. (2003) 'We are what we post? Self-presentation in personal web space', *Journal of Consumer Research*, 30 (3): 385–404.

Schramm, W. (1955) 'How communication works', in W. Schramm (ed.), *The Process and Effects of Mass Communications*. Champaign, IL: University of Illinois Press, pp. 3–26.

Spanier, G. (2016) 'Facebook ad sales to overtake Channel 4 and Sky in the UK', *Campaign*, 12 May. Available at: www.campaignlive.co.uk/article/facebook-ad-sales-overtake-channel-4-sky-uk/1394548 (accessed 02/09/16).

Storbacka, K., Ryals, L., Davies, I.A. and Nenonen, S. (2009) 'The changing role of sales: viewing sales as a strategic, cross-functional process', *European Journal of Marketing*, 43 (7–8): 890–906.

The Telegraph (2012) 'Starbucks Twitter campaign hijacked by tax protests', Technology, 17 December. Available at: www.telegraph.co.uk/technology/twitter/9750215/Starbucks-Twitter-campaign-hijacked-by-tax-protests.html (accessed 28/09/16).

Tojagic, S. (2012). 'Starbucks Twitter campaign goes horribly wrong', *Branding Magazine*, 19 December. Available at: www.brandingmagazine.com/2012/12/19/starbucks-spread-the-cheer-twitter-campaign/ (accessed 28/09/16).

Tourism Australia (n.d.) 'Best jobs in the world'. Available at: www.tourism.australia.com/campaigns/global-youth-project.aspx (accessed 08/09/16).

Tuten, T.L. and Solomon M.R. (2015) *Social Media Marketing* (2nd edn). London: Sage.

White, T. (2013) 'Ryvita crisp bread: ladies that crunch', IPA Effectiveness Awards 2012. Available at: www.warc.com/Content/ContentViewer.aspx?MasterContentRef=03ed9049-99e0-420e-a5f1-24dd648b8d0c&q=ryvita+ladies+that+crunch&CID=A97315&PUB=IPA (accessed 02/09/16).

PART ONE   THIS IS MARKETING

PART TWO   MAKING SENSE OF MARKETS

PART THREE   THE MARKETING MIX

PART FOUR   MANAGING MARKETING

PLACE

PLACE CHALLENGES

The following are illustrations of the types of decision that marketers have to take or issues they face. *You aren't expected to know how to deal with the challenges now*; just bear them in mind as you read the chapter and see what you can find that helps.

- Imagine that you work for Reebok. Your objectives are to increase the number of sales made in your home market and to maintain the relative exclusivity of the brand. How can you use the stores to achieve your objectives?

- A journalist you know is writing a story about the increase in direct marketing and has come to you, as a marketing consultant, for some advice. You have told her that getting the right product to the customer on time is critically important. In reply, she has asked you to explain why, if it is so important, all manufacturers do not take responsibility for every aspect of deliveries themselves.

- You are the Export Manager for a French wine company. You know that Australian and American wine producers are seen as more technologically advanced and better value. How can you compete?

- Your small furniture company is located in a small industrial estate in Cornwall. You know that your products have great potential if only consumers could see them. Unfortunately the major retailers tell you that you cannot make enough furniture to be worth their while working with you. How can you develop to get around this?

- You are the headteacher of a large secondary school which is always in need of cash. A snack food manufacturer wants to install vending machines in the school to sell crisps, chocolate and biscuits. They will stock and maintain the machines and give the school 15% of the takings. What do you need to consider before accepting or rejecting the deal?

INTRODUCTION

Where did you buy your last T-shirt? Do you know where it was made and how it got from there to you? Billions are spent on products every year but few people look beyond the places where they buy things. They do not think about the plantation that their bananas came from or the factory in which their television was made. For a marketer, place includes *all* the activities and all the organisations involved in getting goods from their point of origin to their point-of-sale.

Place is one of the elements of the marketing mix and is really more accurately referred to as distribution, but then the marketing mix would not be the 4Ps; it would be 3Ps and a D which would be far less memorable.

Many of the activities involved in managing product distribution are crucial to effective targeting and positioning (see Chapter 4). For example, placement in an upmarket store sends an upmarket message that helps build a brand image in customers' minds. The timely arrival of goods is seen as good customer service. Contrarily, late arrival of goods, or the arrival of the wrong goods, or of goods in poor condition can undermine all the good work of the product managers and marketing communications managers and cause customers to reject a brand completely. There is a significant management challenge here: a challenge requiring the management of both time and space.

This chapter looks at some key elements of the exchange relationship (see Exhibit 9.1), in particular how this idea of place brings together sellers and buyers, products and the needs they are designed to fulfil. It will discuss the importance of time, space, information, bargaining power and what sellers have to do to match buyers' expectations. By the end of the chapter, you will begin to realise just how much work has been done to put those trainers in your local sports shop or to make your next dream holiday a reality.

THE IMPORTANCE OF DISTRIBUTION

marketing opportunity

a chance to reach a particular group of customers with a product offer

All businesses depend on marketing opportunities to meet potential customers' needs. Opportunities, whether taken or missed, are what shape the future of the enterprise.

Changes that affect the way products are distributed frequently bring new marketing opportunities, e.g. to reach new customers or to launch new products. These may be technological changes. For example, widespread use of the Internet has changed the way in which many products are delivered to customers. Online newspapers have largely replaced print and offer the advantages of continuously updated and instantly accessible news and information. Music can be downloaded or streamed instead of bought on CD. Opportunities may arise from changes in the competitive environment, such as a company withdrawing from a market and so freeing up its channels of distribution. Changes in the political and regulatory environments can affect how and when companies get products to customers, e.g. the relaxation of Sunday trading laws or the granting of new licences. All of these things provide marketing opportunities.

b2b focus: an opportunity to become one of the most successful companies in the world

Most of today's laptops and PCs are based on the architecture which was originally developed for the IBM PC launched in 1981 (the only sizeable alternative architecture is Apple), but IBM was not the first to make a personal computer.

Towards the end of the 1970s, IBM, which was the market leader for large business computers, realised that it had to get into the growing market for small home and personal computers quickly or it would miss out on a huge opportunity. That meant, unusually for IBM, contracting out some of the development. IBM was one of the largest companies in the world and many companies did not want to get involved in a project where the power was so one-sided. However, IBM's decision to work with others presented major, and unusual, marketing opportunities for smaller firms who were prepared to develop components and software for the new PC.

This proved a golden opportunity for two little known companies: Intel and Microsoft. Microsoft produced the original PC Disk Operating System. (DOS has, of course, long since been replaced by Windows). Microsoft was handed a new product development contract but the real value lay in the chance to have a Microsoft operating system sold with every IBM PC globally. So this was really a distribution (or place) opportunity.

IBM sold its PC business to Lenovo who went on to become a market leader. Lenovo is just one of a large number of companies (e.g. Dell, Toshiba, Acer, Fujitsu, Siemens, Hewlett Packard) who make computers which depend on Microsoft Windows – and Microsoft is now one of the largest, and most profitable, companies in the world.

Sources: Bellis (2007); IBM (n.d.)

In a competitive environment, the customer can shop around so companies want to be their first not second choice. The tension between consumer needs and business capabilities creates a constant dynamic for change. One of the key roles for marketing management is the creation of attractive opportunities for exchange and that means monitoring the changes carefully and getting the place right.

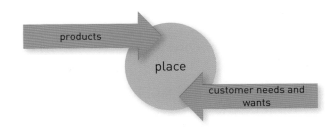

EXHIBIT 9.1 The exchange relationship system

CHANNEL MEMBERS

A supply chain is a network of businesses and organisations through which goods pass to get to their final destination (see Exhibit 9.2). In most developed markets, these networks will be extensive and have many participant businesses. A global business, such as Ford or Renault, has a supply chain that runs through a number of countries. Each of the businesses within that chain is likely to have further international suppliers so that the whole network spans the world. So, Ford buys raw materials and parts from a number of other businesses and sends cars on to a number of resellers.

Marketing communications inside the marketing channel are important as a way of: motivating intermediaries, managing intermediaries dealing with conflicts, building trust between channel members.

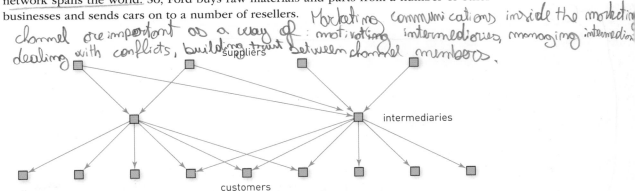

EXHIBIT 9.2 Example of a supply chain: suppliers, intermediaries, customers

Channel decision and other decision in the marketing mix e.g. pricing, promotion (handwritten)

As companies have got larger, and marketing has become global, so warehouses and distribution networks have grown. It may appear to be cheaper (thanks to economies of scale) to put one huge warehouse in the Netherlands and use it to send goods all over Europe, but this will use more petrol (a scarce resource) and cause more pollution. Bigger is not always better.

A distribution channel (sometimes called a marketing channel) is a product's route through the supply chain. The distribution channel is a specific product's path through the supply chain. Its shape is determined by the product's manufacturer in order to meet their marketing objectives. For example, Rolex watches target quite a small customer group (the relatively affluent), offer high-quality service and want to project a quality image. Consequently, Rolex generally uses upmarket retail partners with comparatively few stores. This is called selective distribution (see 'Designing the supply chain' below).

channel members
the businesses that make up a distribution channel; intermediaries

To summarise, a supply chain includes all of the channel members while a specific distribution channel is limited to just one group of channel members chosen to deliver a particular product to a particular market.

BUYERS: CONSUMERS, BUSINESSES AND OTHER ORGANISATIONS

This group is at the end of a supply chain. Its members do not sell the product on but buy it to be used by themselves or their organisations. (For more on customer types see Chapters 1 and 3.)

SELLERS: MANUFACTURERS, RETAILERS, WHOLESALERS, RESELLERS

Manufacturers and producers are the major group of sellers and many of the largest manufacturers have global product recognition. For example, Hewlett Packard is one of the world's leading computer printer manufacturers. Its products are sold to customers in different markets through a global network of outlets, some of which are retailers selling to end-user customers, and some of which are resellers selling the products on. Coca-Cola is known globally as a producer of soft drinks, although in many countries the drinks are produced by another company under licence rather than by Coca-Cola itself.

resellers
a business that buys products in order to sell them on to another business further down the marketing channel

Products are transformed as they move through the supply chain, i.e. each company in the chain uses its expertise and resources to change them in some way before passing them on. For example, German manufacturer FAG buys steel and transforms it into ball

intermediaries
businesses that form part of the distribution channel, passing goods on towards the end customer

bearings, which it then sells to motor manufacturers across the world. Those manufacturers sell their motors to quarry plant manufacturers, who make equipment to extract material from the earth. At each stage, value is added to the bought-in product, i.e. it is transformed into something that can be sold at a higher price (e.g. steel into ball bearings – or fresh peas into frozen ones). The length of a product's supply chain is determined by the complexity of the final product and its user's needs.

Magna Park in Leicestershire is Europe's largest distribution park.

© Dave Pickton

Intermediaries within the part of the supply chain that makes up the distribution channel (or marketing channel) also add value to the product. They deal in finished products, in bars of soap and televisions rather than ingredients or sub-assemblies such as vegetable fat and electrical components. Distribution channel members may, for example, re-package goods, take them to more convenient places for sale or offer extra services such as delivery, installation or advice on the product's use.

The seller that most consumers buy from is the retailer. The retailer is usually the last member of the supply chain before the end customer. Retailers may operate from shops, catalogues, phones, direct-response adverts in the press or on television, or websites (or increasingly through a combination of these outlets). Retailers use their market knowledge to select products that their customers will want to buy. When they do this well, business is good; if they do it badly, the business will do badly too.

research focus

Teller, C. and Dennis, C. (2012) 'The effect of ambient scent on consumers' perception, emotions and behaviour: a critical review', *Journal of Marketing Management*, 28 (1–2): 14–36.
  Based on a critical literature review and a field experiment in a regional shopping mall, the researchers investigate the effectiveness of ambient scent. Interestingly, the researchers cast doubt on previous studies and the impact scent has on shoppers in a shopping centre environment.

Retail organisations come in all sizes. The biggest retailers, such as Wal-Mart and IKEA, are global household names and can offer consumers products from around the world. The smallest are corner shops or businesses run from home.

Retailers buy goods in and sell them on, transforming them and adding value to them (partly through providing a more convenient way to buy them) in the process. This transformation turns the buying business into a selling business. An illustration of this is Tesco's transformation of Heinz beans. Tesco buy millions of cans of beans which arrive at its distribution depots packed in cartons and on pallets. These pallet loads are opened so that individual cans can be stacked on the supermarket's shelves. Tesco sell the individual cans of beans to the final customer. In an IKEA store it may be the customer who has to take the product from the stack of products in the warehouse, which directly passes the cost of the work to the customer.

Wholesalers are one step further away from the final customer than retailers are. They usually buy products to sell on to other members of the supply chain and they support smaller retailers by holding stock in a more convenient location, thus reducing the delivery time from the manufacturers. Most retail wholesalers (e.g. cash and carries) also transform the products by breaking down the quantities supplied by the manufacturer. In this respect they are quite similar to the retailer. Wholesalers are invaluable to small FMCG retailers, such as corner shops, who otherwise would need large stockrooms and would have large amounts of cash tied up in stock.

Wholesalers are currently in decline and the main reason for this is the growth of large retail businesses, such as the big supermarkets and high street multiples, which generate significant economies of scale by buying in bulk direct from the manufacturers. This makes it more difficult for the wholesaler to sell their products at prices that earn sufficient profit.

In business-to-business (b2b) markets, many different businesses carry out the breakdown of bulk function. They are called resellers.

breaking down

in distribution, unpacking goods (or putting them into smaller boxes) for easier handling

cash and carry

a wholesaler whose main customers are small retailers who visit the premises, pay for their goods and carry them away; cash and carries do not deliver

high street multiples

chains of shops, such as WH Smith and Boots

Type of retailer	Description	Examples
Market traders	Stall in open or covered market, low rent, few facilities, may move location regularly, specialist or variety; markets are traditional across the world but have fallen out of favour in the UK; some have been repositioned upmarket and there is also an upsurge in farmers' markets	Leicester market (traditional), Borough market (more upmarket), Columbia Road market (flowers and plants)
Independents	The majority of shops are independent but, in the UK and many other industrialised nations, they account for only a small proportion of sales; they have fewer resources and usually less expertise than the large high street multiples	One-off newsagents, restaurants, hairdressers
Multiples and chains	Have a standardised image; they may specialise in a specific range of goods (e.g. women's fashion) or may stock a wider range or be service providers	Topshop, Marks & Spencer, Toni and Guy, Starbucks, Slug and Lettuce, Shell
Supermarkets, superstores and hypermarkets	Usually multiples, common in food but also found in specialist categories such as golf or hardware; hypermarkets are usually out of town	Tesco, Aldi, PC World
Convenience stores	Smaller than supermarkets and with more limited stock but easier for shoppers to pop in to; local shops and garage forecourt shops	Spar, Londis, Tesco Metro, BP Connect
Department stores	A collection of shops or departments under one roof; the store is centrally owned although parts may be rented out	House of Fraser, Debenhams, El Corte Inglés, Printemps, Vendex
Discount stores	Traditionally large, warehouse-like shops with cheap prices; their cost savings come from: lower rents (they are often out of town), minimum service levels, rudimentary display and bulk purchase; increasingly moving online for further cost savings and wider reach	Lidl, Mountain Warehouse
Warehouse clubs	Large stores offering wholesale prices to members only; members may be individual and/or trade; a cross between a cash and carry and a discount store (see above)	Costco, Sam's Club (USA)
Voluntary chains	A network of individually owned shops which club together to benefit from economies of scale and to gain marketing advantages	Mace, Spar
Franchises	A type of multiple, the outlets are individually owned but licensed by a larger company to sell their products	Body Shop, Domino's Pizza, Merry Maids (cleaning service)
Factory outlets	May be large and out of town (and grouped into a factory outlet or shopping village) or smaller and more central; originally sold seconds but are now also used to get rid of excess stock; paradise for bargain hunters	Bicester Outlet Village, Cheshire Oaks, The Galleria Outlet Centre
E-tailers	Primarily sell online; many offline retailers also sell online (bricks and clicks), few are pure Internet businesses (pure plays)	Amazon, Ocado

EXHIBIT 9.3 Types of retailer

FACILITATORS: AGENTS AND LOGISTICS SERVICES

This group of businesses smooths the flow of products through the supply chain. Members of this group usually have specific expertise in a market, or other specialist resources.

Agents are businesses that represent other businesses in a particular market. Smaller businesses often use locally based agents as a means of entering new or distant markets because the agent has knowledge of the market and access to local facilities. The agent can thus reduce the costs and risks associated with entering the new market. These businesses do not usually actually purchase products so they cannot be classed as resellers. They take orders and are paid a commission.

The housing market provides a good example of how agents work. In this market, the buyers and sellers tend to be individuals or families with just one house to sell. The estate agency does not take ownership of the house at any point; it brings buyers and sellers together by communicating the property's details to potential buyers and showing them around the house. The agency then charges the seller a commission for any subsequent sale of the property.

The final category of participants is that of the businesses that transport and store products for the various members of the supply chain. They are known as logistics services, and include warehouses, distribution depots and transport services.

logistics
the flow of goods and services through the supply chain

The simplest way to deliver something is by mail or courier. Small transport companies can deliver bigger items. If large quantities of products need be moved around, then the logistics business will also need to be a big company. These businesses have specialist facilities and knowledge. Some, e.g. UPS, have grown to a global scale and can take products to market anywhere in the world. The vast majority of logistics businesses, however, are much smaller.

Companies who use specialist logistics companies do so primarily to reduce costs. By concentrating on just this one specialist function, logistics businesses benefit from economies of scale (e.g. they can use larger lorries and so make fewer trips) and so are able to deliver goods more cheaply than most manufacturers can. They also transport a large enough volume of products frequently enough to make it worthwhile investing in specialist storage and transport. For example, XPO Logistics refrigerated trucks and cold-storage depots protect perishable goods in transit across the world.

There are drawbacks to contracting out deliveries. For a mail-order company, the only face-to-face contact with the customer may come at the point of delivery and then that is not with one of its own employees. The customer service provided by the logistics company is therefore a major determinant of customer satisfaction, but it is not in the seller's control. Apart from the impact this has on customer relationships, there are a number of marketing opportunities lost here, for example, the lorries and packaging may not bear the seller's name. To get around this, many major retailers who contract out their distribution insist that the transportation company paints its vehicles in the retailer's corporate colours. Those Marks & Spencer lorries you see on the motorway actually belong to Norbert Dentressangle and are driven by that company's staff.

Eddie Stobart is a well-known logistics contractor.

© Dave Pickton

ethical focus: peril on land and sea

Billions of dollars' worth of goods are stolen each year while being transported. They end up on the black market, transferring revenue from legitimate businesses to criminal and even terrorist activities and reducing countries' tax revenues. Cigarettes and alcohol are common targets as they are valuable and easy to sell. Pharmaceuticals are frequently stolen and end up on the streets instead of in the hospitals which is costly and dangerous for businesses, health authorities and for the public.

While there are significant thefts from warehouses, most distribution-related crime involves thefts from lorries or other means of transport. Europol (the EU's law enforcement agency) has identified six different types of cargo crime:

- hijacking – both lorry and load are stolen, the driver is often threatened
- lorry theft – stealing an unattended vehicle
- load theft – stealing the load while a vehicle is parked
- deception/diversion – tricking the company into delivering to the wrong address
- bogus transport companies – a company wins a contract to deliver and then disappears with the goods
- warehouse crime – theft from storage facilities.

The precautions that distributors have to take to avoid losing cargo cost money and create hassle. Road haulage companies may have to re-route lorries away from high risk areas, limit stops, monitor trucks through GPS tracking and call the driver if there is an unscheduled stop, fit strong locks and seals, use branded lorries (easier to trace than plain ones), vet staff carefully and pay for expensive insurance.

While lorries are more common targets, piracy is more likely to make the headlines. In recent years, parts of the world have become dangerous for shipping. West and East Africa, parts of South East Asia, the Far East and some of the areas around India and Bangladesh are particularly piracy prone. Somalian waters are patrolled by warships from a number of Western navies, for example a combined EU force (named Atalanta) has been operating there since 2008. This is of course extremely expensive for the governments involved showing how seriously they take the issue of piracy.

Somalian pirate attacks have declined – but piracy has increased on the West Coast of Africa, particularly around Nigeria, out of reach of the military patrols. The pirates, who are well armed and frequently violent, have attacked vessels up to 120 miles offshore. They are well organised and often well informed. One band of Nigerian pirates managed to board a chemical tanker, sail it to another location and offload part of its chemical cargo into a waiting tanker.

The annual cost of piracy has been estimated at between $12 billion and $18 billion – and someone (someone else) has to pay for that.

Sources: Manners-Bell (2014); International Chamber of Commerce Commercial Crime Services (2016); EUNavfor Somalia (n.d.)

THE RIGHT SPACE AND TIME

Customers choose where and when to buy something. For example, if they want a sandwich, they go to a sandwich shop – probably at lunchtime. If they want shoes, they go to a shoe shop at a convenient time. The sandwich shop and the shoe shop are fixed, geographic spaces – geography is the simplest idea of place. Whether the specific sandwiches and shoes are available may depend on the season (e.g. fewer sandals around in the winter).

It also depends on the opening times of the shops and whether the customer has time to get there. So another fixed point, a point in time, can be added to the concept of place.

In our increasingly technology-driven world, these concepts of space and time have become more flexible. Thanks to the Internet, customers can shop at any time of day or night. They can stay at home and have everything delivered to them – although not always immediately.

ACTIVITY

Think about something important that you bought recently. How did you choose the place that you bought it from? Did you just go somewhere you'd been before, or did something else affect your choice?

Place, or distribution, is often summed up as *getting the right product to the right place at the right time*. No matter how good the product, if it is not available when and where the customer wants it, then there will be no sale. So if the shop is closed, or too far away, or if the salesperson calls at a bad time, or the website cannot deliver fast enough, customers are likely to make their purchases elsewhere. The time and place of the sale are important parts of the product offer.

RIGHT SPACE

There is an old saying, which has been attributed to a number of famous retailers, that there are three secrets to business success: 'location, location, location'. So how do businesses, not just shops but all the other members of the supply chain too, choose their locations?

According to McGoldrick (2003), the most important consideration is the firm's target market. Who are they, where are they, and where do they want to buy things? Other considerations include the competition and costs.

There are several questions businesses need to ask when choosing the right location for retail premises:

- Are there enough of the right type of customers there?
- Where do they go now? What would make them switch?
- Is it easy to get to? Is there good public transport? Car parking?
- Will staff be able to travel there at a price they can afford (this can be a problem with some of the more exclusive areas and also out of town locations)?
- What are the costs involved?
- How many competitive outlets are there? Is there enough business to support a newcomer?
- Are there complementary businesses nearby? For example, customers of a real meat butcher may be good prospects for an organic vegetable shop or a good bakery.
- Is there a suitable building available in the right timescale?
- Do you need planning permission? Is it likely to be granted? If the premises were used for another purpose before, then you are likely to need permission for 'change of use'.
- Has there been a similar business in the area? How did it do? Many people take over a failing business, e.g. a restaurant, and then fail too. It is important to analyse why the previous business failed *before* starting up.

ACTIVITY

Find a map of your local area. Where would you want to open the following types of retail outlet:

- an upmarket restaurant
- a bar
- a clothing store
- a DIY store
- a sweet shop?

What problems might you face, i.e. what are the constraints?

- What legal restrictions are there? For example, it may be a conservation area making it difficult to alter premises, or it may be residential only, or certain types of business may be prohibited, e.g. bars.

- For chains, what impact will the new outlet have on existing ones? Is it too close? Will it take away trade?

- What does the location say about your business? Does it project the right image?

Sometimes it's the location that makes the marketing opportunity: a high street with no food store, a vacant shop near a school, a residential area with no bars or restaurants, an out-of-town site large enough to take a superstore with parking. These are places where there is little or no competition and where the retailer could reasonably expect to make good profits.

If a clothing retailer wants to attract the rich and fashionable, then its stores will need to be in exclusive locations, such as Bond Street in London or the Quadrilatero della Moda in Milan. The image of an area and its surroundings (e.g. residential or business) is a good indicator of the type of customer likely to be found there.

If, however, the retailer depends on high sales volumes, then they will need to be somewhere busy, like London's Oxford Circus or a popular shopping mall. Here they are also more likely to get passing trade (i.e. people who are just passing on their way somewhere else but who might pop in).

Of course, retail premises in prime locations are expensive, the preserve of flagship stores of well-known brands. These premises often play an important role in communicating an upscale brand image or creating immersive brand experiences. For example, Nike's UK flagship store Niketown in London's Oxford Street is the only place in the country where the brand's entire range is displayed. As the name suggests, the shop is laid out like a town, with separate buildings, one dedicated to each sport, surrounding a central square where inspirational sporting images are projected onto a giant 360-degree screen. The store also hosts special events, its own running club and personal appearances from star athletes. It has become a tourist destination in its own right and a site of pilgrimage for dedicated brand fans and sneakerheads.

The use of temporary, pop-up stores is an increasingly popular strategy for brands keen to engage with customers in a particular location, at a particular point in time, without the costs associated with permanent premises. Pop-up stores come in different forms; a mini store within a store, a traditional bricks and mortar building or a stand-alone kiosk at a music festival, for example. Even the humble food van is making a comeback. Gourmet wood-fired pizza vans and prosecco bars are another form of pop-up premises with the added benefit of being infinitely mobile. The launch of a pop-up store is often a public relations opportunity in its own right, supported by stunts or other special events designed to build anticipation and the sense of an opportunity that's not to be missed. Recently the US brand, Fruit of the Loom, known for its sensibly priced, packaged underwear sold in

Event experiences and engagement

supermarkets like Wal-Mart, decided to prank its customers with a fake high-end lingerie store, exotically named 'Frùt'. Customers lured in by all the trappings of a luxury retail environment could touch and feel the products and see them displayed in stylish surroundings. They were more than happy to pay twice as much – until they got to the till and the real brand behind the store was revealed. In the UK, frozen food brand Birds Eye's pop-up restaurants in London, Manchester and Leeds caused a stir on social media by offering guests the opportunity to 'pay-by-picture' by posting images of their meals on Instagram using the tag #BirdsEyeInspirations.

A busy location with lots of passing trade is a popular place for many retailers of low-value goods – they need a high volume of sales in order to make profits. There is usually a newsagent and a café near a railway station. People want things to read and eat on train journeys. When they miss their train (or it is delayed), then they want a drink and a snack to while away the time. In the early days, McDonald's used to snap up sites near highway intersections – often in the middle of nowhere. It had realised that the bulk of its customers came by car, usually on their way somewhere else, and could be tempted to take a break by the sight of those famous golden arches. Other fast-food retailers would sometimes set up shop anywhere McDonald's did – just because McDonald's was so good at picking locations.

Clusters of similar businesses are quite common. Some areas become known for certain types of shop. For example, London's Tottenham Court Road is full of PC dealers, the Lanes in Brighton is known for antiques, Hatton Garden is the place for jewellery. Clearly, these retailers are not trying to avoid the competition, rather they seem to revel in it. So why do they do it? Again, it is about volume of customers. If an area is known for a product type (e.g. PCs), then customers will flock there and not bother to go anywhere else. They know that they will have a wide choice in that one place.

Any retail business has to decide whether its strategy will be to take its stores to the customers or to try to attract customers to its stores. Desirable as it may be to set up shop in a busy area with lots of the right type of customer, it is not always possible to find suitable premises there and so it may be necessary to attract customers away from their usual haunts. This was the idea behind the first of the out-of-town superstores. There were no sites big enough to house the vast stores that the retailers had in mind in the town centres, and so they went out of town – making sure there were good roads and ample parking, of course.

Intermediaries further up the supply chain (e.g. wholesalers, agents, distributors) may deliver goods to their customers and that makes a big difference to how they choose their location. In fact they may choose to be nearer their suppliers. It is unlikely that they will be reliant on passing trade and so they can afford to be in a more out of the way place. Good transport links are important, as is cost-effectiveness of course.

One of the advantages of the Internet is that it enables businesses to be closer to the customers – right in their homes. It is important not to forget that any goods ordered will need to be delivered, though, so the location of warehouses still needs to be thought through carefully.

RIGHT TIME

To deliver what customers want when they want it requires flexibility in the supply chain and that usually means higher operating costs. Think about how food is sold. A large supermarket stocks over 20,000 different products. Millions are spent weekly on food and drink. The only thing that stops some shops being permanently open is government legislation. Laws vary across Europe, for example some countries restrict trading hours on Sundays, while many governments leave this decision to local authorities. The Internet overcomes these restrictions on shopping of course, although even the largest supermarkets do not deliver 24/7. These long opening hours create the impression that people can buy anything they want at any time. Stores have to live up to this expectation by trying to ensure that their whole range is always in stock. Stock costs money to buy and to store so accountants always try to minimise stock levels and the working capital that is tied up in that stock. Overstocks (stock that is not sold) are expensive as they have to be sold off cheaply or binned. This is especially a problem with perishable goods such as food. There is therefore a tricky balancing act with stock: stores need enough to meet demand without running out, but not so much that there is a lot of waste. Stock, or inventory, management is a very difficult process.

Making sure that goods are always available requires good logistics planning. This is a complex process with lots of scope for mistakes which may lead to stock-outs or overstocks. An empty space on a shelf means lost sales – missed opportunities for both retailer and manufacturer. If customer demand was constant, then logistics would be much easier, but unfortunately demand fluctuates with people's changing tastes, the weather, changes in competitive offerings, items on the news, new campaigns – the list is endless. Imagine buying food for a small seaside café early in a Scottish summer. How would you know how much ice cream to get in? How much soup and other warming dishes? Will the demand be for iced lattés or for hot chocolate? Alternatively, take pity on department store buyers at Christmas. If they buy too many Christmas goods, they are left with stock nobody wants in January. If they buy too few, they have missed valuable sales and gained frustrated customers.

Fernie and Sparks (2004) identified five key aspects of logistics management:

1   suitable storage facilities for stock

2   keeping the right amount of stock – not too much or too little

3   good communications throughout the distribution channel so that suppliers can respond quickly to requests for products

4   transport that is capable of carrying the required quantities of products safely to their destinations

5   packaging that will protect the product in transit and storage while being easily handled – so boxes should not be too big or heavy, or too small as small packages take longer to pack.

Some products need specialist storage facilities, e.g. refrigeration or a dust-free atmosphere. All need to be located conveniently, to be secure and to be accessible for onward transportation. Retailers used to keep their stock on the premises so that they could refill shelves quickly, but only the smallest do this today. Retail space is expensive and so is better used for displaying goods rather than storing them. Large retailers have their own distribution centres situated close to clusters of stores so that they can restock easily. Some manage these themselves, e.g. Amazon, but others contract out to logistics specialists such as DHL.

Keeping the right amount of stock requires good sales forecasting. Most retailers and wholesalers use computerised stock control programs fed with data from electronic point-of-sale systems (EPOS). Bar-coded products are scanned at checkouts, or by hand-held scanners

---

working capital

net current assets, i.e. available cash and anything that can raise cash in the short term (e.g. stock)

stock-out

when a supplier runs out of a particular product

distribution centres

large warehouses that repackage goods into smaller units and ship them to trade customers; they may be exclusive to one large retailer

EPOS (electronic point-of-sale)

a computerised system that collects sales data at a retail checkout

in warehouses, and stock figures are adjusted automatically. This information can then be communicated, either by the Internet or the company's own system (Intranet), to other members of the supply chain. Replacement stock may be ordered with no further human intervention at all.

Transporting goods may sound straightforward but it is not. Some town centre shops are difficult to access and deliveries may only be permitted at certain times (usually out of

hours) so as to prevent traffic hold-ups. There are restrictions on lorry size and how long drivers can drive for. The thoughtless driving of lorries with the company's logo emblazoned on the side is a PR problem. There are environmental considerations: trains and boats are considered less polluting than road or air, but boats are slow and so are unsuitable for the shipment of perishable goods from a distance. In many countries, there is a growing consumer preference for local products. Not only are they perceived as fresher, but also their purchase is seen as supporting the local economy and as less polluting because they have travelled a shorter distance.

Source: Peter Macdiarmid/Getty Images News/Getty Images

Packaging has a number of functions within the supply chain. It may have a promotional role (see Chapter 11) and even be an intrinsic part of the product, e.g. an individual ice cream tub, a toothpaste tube or a bottle for shower gel. Its logistics role is protecting the goods during transit, storage and handling, and making them easier to handle, stack and secure.

DIFFERING VIEWS OF PLACE
THE CONSUMERS' VIEW

Generally speaking, shoppers do not think very much about place or the management of the supply chain. Shoppers just want goods and services to be easily available. Shoppers' perceptions are thus largely focused on the last link in the supply chain, usually the retailer (Piercy, 2002). People rarely think about where clothes come from or what had to happen to make it possible for them to buy them where they did. The most important goal of distribution is to ensure that the right goods are available when and where the customer wants them.

There are times when shoppers will be very interested in the source of goods, usually on health or ethical grounds. Shoppers who want organic food want reassurance from the retailer that the original source is reliable and truly organic. The UK supermarket Waitrose grows its own produce on a 4,000 acre country estate thus ensuring the traceability of many of the products it sells. Others are now following suit.

Many shoppers are increasingly concerned about ethical issues. For example, many shoppers in developed countries do not approve of the use of child labour. Sellers can respond by collectively organising to reassure shoppers that their products are ethically produced. The Rugmark label is an example of one such scheme. Retailers subscribe to a neutral third-party organisation that checks the product's source to ensure that it does not use child labour. Only products that meet the specification can bear the label.

Clearly, the design, and ongoing management, of the distribution channel are extremely important. The specific design will vary from product to product and will be discussed later in this chapter. Consumers need more than just quality goods and services; they also need a reassuring purchase experience so that they feel they can trust their suppliers and are comfortable with their purchases.

Organisations buy more things than consumers do and, just like consumers, they want to know where their goods and services come from and to buy them from suppliers they can trust.

ethical focus: FAIRTRADE

The FAIRTRADE Foundation, which awards the FAIRTRADE Mark, is made up of different organisations, such as Oxfam, the World Development Movement and Christian Aid. The FAIRTRADE Foundation is a member of the standard-setting umbrella organisation FAIRTRADE Labelling Organization International (FLO). The FAIRTRADE Mark shows consumers that the farmers and workers who produced the products received a fair and stable price. They also have safe working conditions, stronger rights and treat their environment with care.

FAIRTRADE products include cocoa, coffee, tea, sugar, bananas, orange juice, honey and cotton. Any end product that is awarded the FAIRTRADE Mark must meet strict conditions of production and the Foundation has independent assessors to check that these conditions are being met.

Through such third-party schemes, the concerns of the consumers are passed up through the supply chain to the original source of the products. The customer can be satisfied that the farmers and workers who grew the products are getting a better deal. In this way, the FAIRTRADE Mark meets consumers' need to avoid exploiting poorer workers in the developing world.

FairTrade Ugandan coffee

THE ORGANISATION'S VIEW

Does a business see the supply chain in the same way as the shopper? It depends on the business, what it is buying (or selling) and what it intends to do with that purchase. A small cafe needs paper serviettes which will have to be bought in. These are low-value items with limited impact upon the business. This is a tactical, not a strategic, decision. It is likely that the café owner will simply add serviettes to their shopping list for the next visit to the cash and carry (a form of wholesaler). In this respect, the business is acting like a typical consumer and will be just as frustrated if the serviettes are not in stock.

On the other hand, a multinational buying electrical components to build into its products is likely to see the supply chain in a very different way from an individual shopper. The components will affect the quality of the finished products and the buyer will have to answer to others for their purchase decision and so will seek a different level of reassurance about the goods and the buying situation – quite likely in writing. They will also be treated differently. Organisational buyers rarely go to the shops. Instead, salespeople visit them at the buyer's convenience and the purchases are delivered.

Organisations have a view both up and down the supply chain. They may be at its end for some purchases, in its middle (as intermediaries) for others, and, if they are manufacturers, at the start of it for some. At times they are buyers, at others they are sellers.

As buyers, organisations want the best suppliers for each item that they buy. Larger organisations usually have formal systems to assess potential, and existing, suppliers – especially those who will supply critical components. For example, vendor rating involves evaluating sellers' performances against a set of predetermined measures. These measures may include reviews of the product range (both the current offerings and potential new ones), product quality, production capability and capacity, pricing and delivery. In this way the company tries to make its supply chain as effective and efficient as possible (Lysons and Gillingham, 2003).

vendor rating

a vetting process to help buyers identify where there may be potential benefits or difficulties associated with a particular supplier

The supply chain can make or break a business and so its design is a strategic decision which requires the best information available. When things go wrong in the supply chain, all the companies involved in the production and delivery of the goods suffer. Sometimes the damage can be permanent. The BSE (mad cow disease) crisis in the early 1990s is still affecting sales of British beef across the world. It is therefore considered good practice to view other channel members as partners rather than mere suppliers or customers.

THE PARTNERSHIP VIEW

It has become normal practice for businesses to organise partnerships both upwards and downwards in the supply chain. This is most evident in retail. In larger stores, tills are linked to a head office computer which checks stock quantities against predetermined levels and produces an order that is transmitted automatically to the supplier's computer. The supplier then takes responsibility for delivering the order to the store. There is a considerable degree of trust built into such relationships. The retailer benefits from reduced stock risks while the supplier sells more goods on a regular basis and so both benefit.

A seller that always delivers quality goods on time, with no subsequent problems, at a price that is acceptable to the market, develops a reputation as a good company. This can help it to develop its business beyond its existing set of customers or to strengthen its defences against possible newcomers to the market. Good suppliers help make the buyer's business better too. Additionally, large businesses may support suppliers in the development of new products or in helping to establish new ways of trading.

PLACE MANAGEMENT

In its simplest form, place management is only concerned with the moment at which an exchange of value happens. In reality, although the moment may be simple, there is usually some preparation needed to make the exchange possible. Take for example the sale of a bar of chocolate at a kiosk. If the owner of the kiosk had not previously been out and bought it (usually from a wholesaler), then there could be no sale. This also holds true for the wholesaler, who would have had to purchase the bars from the manufacturer. This simple example shows how the supply chain extends away from the final exchange in a series of prior exchanges. If this chain is broken at any stage, then the final exchange is at risk. Ensuring that the chain is in place and delivering the expectations of all businesses involved is an important part of the management function.

In a small business, the buying and selling tasks are likely to be only part of a manager's job. In a larger organisation, these functions are likely to be carried out by specialists in dedicated departments. The sales team or sales department has a crucial role in the firm's relationship with customers and potential customers. Having taken the orders and made the delivery promises, it is also usual for sales departments to organise the physical delivery of the product to the customer. The buying department, or merchandising department, has specialist personnel who buy particular types of product, e.g. homewares, children's fashion, men's grooming products.

Finding, and keeping, the right place for the final exchange usually requires the development of successful long-term business partnerships within the distribution channel. Only rarely will it benefit a business to change sellers regularly. There is usually much more to be gained from working together over a long period.

THE SUPPLY CHAIN AS A NETWORK OF PARTNERS

Substantial networks, both horizontal and vertical, may have to be developed in pursuit of the best place design (Michel et al., 2003). Consider the linkages necessary for a pick-your-own (PYO) fruit farm to reach its market. Initially it might seem that there could not be a simpler form of exchange. After all, customers just take the food from the ground and pay for it. However, if we look backwards up the supply chain, there are a considerable number of other participants in the process. For a crop such as strawberries, most PYO farms will buy in the plants from a dedicated nursery that has grown the plants from seed. The growth of the plants can be further encouraged by the use of fertilisers bought from agricultural merchants. Next the potential customer has to be told about the opportunity to pick fruit, and so another relationship is needed to develop the promotional aspects of the business. This may be with a local printer or the local newspaper. The place where the exchange happens affects all other aspects of marketing function.

DESIGNING THE SUPPLY CHAIN

The design of the supply chain is a strategic management function. Its consequences are long-term and far-reaching. A well-designed supply chain can reduce costs by minimising overlaps between channel members and cutting out redundant parts of the network. It can also increase companies' responsiveness to market conditions, enabling them to restock or deliver more quickly.

No one channel member can control the entire supply chain. Until relatively recently, marketers focused exclusively on the chain downwards (towards the final customer) from them, i.e. their distribution channel. However, all the sellers in the supply chain have an impact upon each other and so the network does need to be considered as a whole – despite its sometimes awesome complexity. 'Chain' is perhaps a misnomer as it suggests linearity, a set of links with a beginning and an end. A supply chain is really more of a network (see Exhibit 9.2). There are many different branches and routes through. Each of the network's members has something to offer and something to gain. In addition, the businesses in a network all have customers to whom they address their efforts and for whom they design a product offering. These customers may become sellers in their turn. The supply chain is built upon a succession of negotiated agreements between buyers and sellers.

There are three key words in supply chain design: effectiveness, economy and efficiency. These three words shape the objectives for the operation of any supply chain. If the goods are not in the right place at the right time, then the exchange is not likely to take place and the supply chain is not effective. If there are too many costs being added to the basic product by the various players, then the final product will be too expensive and not economical and the customer may choose to buy from another source. Lack of efficiency at any stage will add to these costs and thus put the whole exchange process at risk. It takes a coordinated effort from all channel members to create an effective, economical and efficient supply chain.

digital focus: showrooming

Times are hard for high street stores. As if it wasn't bad enough trying to sell to price-conscious, recession-hit consumers, they also have to deal with new competitors and new ways to shop.

'The staff at Jessop's would like to thank you for shopping with Amazon', read a sign in the window of a newly closed Jessop's store. The specialist camera retailer had gone into liquidation and clearly blamed the online competition. They weren't the only multiple to blame technological advancement for their demise. DVD rental firm Blockbuster found it couldn't compete with video on-demand services and HMV lost out to downloaded music. Their shops were often full so how could this happen? Well, there may have been people in the shops, but they weren't all customers; many were just showroomers.

A showroomer is someone who goes into a shop to browse and try out the merchandise, then checks for the prices online and buys it cheaper from somewhere else, usually an online retailer. Sometimes, they even make the purchase on their mobile while still in the store. Research by design agency Foolproof found that 24% of people showroomed while Christmas shopping and 40% of them took their business elsewhere. Online retailers can afford to charge less for the same products because they don't have to pay those expensive high street rents nor the staff salaries.

Mobile assised shoppers

So how can high street shops fight back? Some have tried charging a browsing fee but even genuine shoppers are understandably reluctant to pay. Others, e.g. specialist sports stores, make sure they offer valuable expertise and excellent service. You have to have a really thick skin to walk out of a shop to find a cheaper price if an assistant has measured your feet, watched you run to assess your gait, asked you about your exercise programme, advised you on it and then recommended the perfect running shoes for you. Though probably some die-hard showroomers still will.

There is an interesting twist to this tale. Online retailers and the physical stores have a symbiotic relationship. The online stores sell more if shoppers have been able to see, feel and try out the goods. Amazon recognise this and opened their first high street bookstore in Seattle in 2015: a pure play moving into bricks and clicks. Watch this space.

Source: Campbell (2013)

The choice of supply chain members depends on the product, the market and the tasks to be undertaken. If there are many stages in the process of manufacturing a product, the supply chain is likely to have many members. It does not stop there. Many other companies may become involved before the final customer takes delivery of their product.

Take aeroplane manufacture as an example. There can be hundreds of companies involved in the production of these large and complex products which the manufacturer, e.g. Airbus, sells to airlines or governments. To make the planes into passenger carriers, these organisational customers need other products, e.g. catering, cleaning, refuelling, airport, services, films. The providers of all these purchases form part of the airline's supply chain. To further complicate the issue, companies may need to find different partners, and design different channels, in different countries as distribution infrastructures are not the same the world over.

Some products need special handling. Take ice cream, for example. Just as consumers need freezers to store the product, so does every business involved in moving the product from the manufacturer to the

ACTIVITY

You are planning a twenty-first birthday party for 400 guests. Identify the different businesses that you will need to work with to make the event a success. How will you choose each of the businesses?

retailer. There has to be a transport system capable of moving the product in its frozen condition. Not every transport business has such resources and this limits the potential number of partners. The same idea applies to other types of product. For example, specialist companies transport industrial gasses in specially designed bulk tankers. The specific needs of the supply chain can thus create niche marketing opportunities.

MASS MARKETING OR SELECTIVE MARKETING?

Managers must take account of the nature of the market when designing a distribution channel. The wider the range of potential customers, the wider the supply chain.

exclusive distribution

the distribution channel has only one or two specially selected outlets within a specified area

Exclusive, luxury goods, such as designer clothing, would normally have the most restricted distribution channels, i.e. exclusive distribution. In extreme cases, the designers may only support one or two outlets for their products, often those directly owned by the designer. This allows them to keep very close control over their distribution.

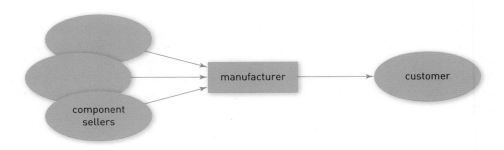

EXHIBIT 9.4 Exclusive distribution

intensive distribution

products are available at numerous outlets

selective distribution

the distribution channel is restricted to a few outlets

Where there are many different types of customer, perhaps in different locations, then the pattern of connections becomes more complicated. Such situations call for intensive distribution, in which numerous outlets are used. In between these two extremes, there are products that are available in a number of places, but not all. This is termed selective distribution.

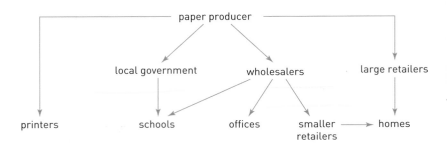

EXHIBIT 9.5 Multichannel distribution

Note: Each member of the supply network will have numerous contacts with other businesses.

A company like Nike could not have become as large as it has by using selective or exclusive channels – it had to be intensive. Nike operates its own stores and has a large number of major retail partners, both specialist sportswear outlets (such as Sports Direct) and clothing stores. The range offered in the general clothing stores is limited so as not to challenge the specialist sports sector. This use of different types of channel to reach the same potential target group is also known as multichannel distribution (see Exhibit 9.5).

multichannel distribution the use of different types of channel to reach the same target market

research focus

Kabadayi, S., Eyuboglu, N. and Thomas, G.P. (2007) 'The performance implications of designing multiple channels to fit with strategy and environment,' *Journal of Marketing*, **71 (4): 195–211.**

This paper investigates whether multiple channel systems make their greatest contributions to firm performance when their structures are properly aligned with their firms' business-level strategies and with environmental conditions.

SHORT, SIMPLE CHAINS OR LONG, COMPLICATED CHAINS?

Exclusive, selective and intensive distribution are to do with the breadth of the distribution channel, i.e. how many members it has at each level in the channel. When designing a channel, it is also important to think carefully about its depth, i.e. how many levels (or intermediaries) there will be between the producer and the final customer (see Exhibit 9.6).

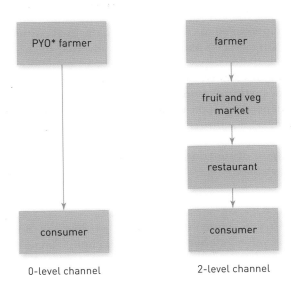

EXHIBIT 9.6 Distribution channels: simple

The simplest distribution channel is the one that connects the producer directly to the consumer. Contrast this with the multiple channels design between a paper manufacturer and its customers in Exhibit 9.7.

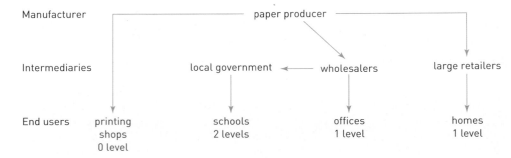

Manufacturer	paper producer			
Intermediaries		local government ← wholesalers		large retailers
End users	printing shops 0 level	schools 2 levels	offices 1 level	homes 1 level

EXHIBIT 9.7 Distribution channels: multiple

Note: To achieve the broadest market coverage some suppliers use many intermediaries while smaller, or more specialist, suppliers will use only some of the intermediaries available. Each member of the supply network will have numerous contacts with other businesses.

direct sales

when a manufacturer deals directly with customers rather than through intermediaries in the supply chain

A zero-level supply chain, straight from farmer to customer.

© Dave Pickton

The shortest channel has no intermediaries at all. The producer sells direct to the end customer. This is called a 0-level channel or direct selling (direct sales). If there is one intermediary between the producer and the end customer, we call that a 1-level channel, while two intermediaries make a 2-level channel, etc. The longer the channel, the less control the producer has over how its products are presented to consumers (or to the final customer organisations in the case of b2b markets). Many producers advertise to consumers even though they do not deal directly with them. This is part of building a brand name and, as well as impressing consumers, this makes their goods more attractive to intermediaries who are more likely to stock them. A company such as Heinz is entirely dependent upon retailers to make sales to consumers. It redresses the power imbalance through marketing communications campaigns designed to persuade end customers to ask for its products when they go to the shop. Even the largest of supermarkets would not want to be without Heinz baked beans and ketchup.

disintermediation

reducing the number of intermediaries in a supply chain with the aim of increasing control and lowering costs

reintermediation

when a firm seeks to gain competitive advantage by reintroducing or adding a supply chain intermediary

DISINTERMEDIATION

Sometimes suppliers try to shorten their supply chains by expanding up or down the chain. They may buy other intermediaries, for example a supermarket might buy a farm, or they might just cut out a level in the chain by dealing directly, for example by selling online through their own website rather than through a shop. Disintermediation reduces the number of intermediaries between producer and end-user, often in a bid to increase control and/or profits. Re-intermediation is when a firm seeks to gain competitive advantage by reintroducing or adding an intermediary. For example, independent fashion boutiques working through an ASOS marketplace pay a commission on every sale in return for access to the ASOS global online audience and extensive online promotional support.

global focus: cheap sources of supply

Everybody likes a bargain and retailers try really hard to deliver good ones. The combination of customers wanting cheap prices and retailers wanting to beat their competitors' prices puts severe pressure on manufacturers to keep costs down. Gone are the days when Marks & Spencer proudly proclaimed that it used only British suppliers. M&S, like almost every other chain store, looks abroad for lower cost items.

So why are those imported skirts and T-shirts so cheap? How can that be when the transportation costs must be so much higher? Partly it's due to differences in currency values and living standards, but often the main differences are that labour is cheaper and there are fewer, costly regulations to be complied with. A garment factory in Bangladesh that made clothes for European high street brands, including Primark, Benetton, Bonmarche and Matalan, collapsed killing at least 80 people and injuring up to 800 more. This prompted calls for these multimillion pound Western businesses to take more responsibility for the way their clothes were produced.

It isn't just clothing manufacturers that can be criticised for cutting costs to the point where supply chain members cut corners. In 2013, Britons were shocked to find that much of the beef they had bought in supermarkets was in fact horse – something not commonly eaten in Britain. To the media's apparent surprise, the British public's main issue with this was that they had been mis-sold rather than that they had inadvertently eaten an animal usually considered a pet rather than a source of food. The supermarkets' defence was that their supply chains were so long and complicated, and crossed so many borders, that they hadn't known where this meat originated, relying on the next business up the chain to do the checking.

How much responsibility do you think retailers should take for what goes on further up the supply chain? How much responsibility should we as consumers take? Should we think rather harder about why those clothes (or those ready meals) are so cheap and perhaps just refuse to buy them?

Horsemeat scandal

OVERSEAS OPERATIONS AND MARKET ENTRY OPTIONS

Most marketing textbooks include a substantial section on market entry options, but it is important to remember that marketing efforts do not finish once a market has been successfully entered. Very few organisations enter international markets with a short-term involvement in mind. Breaking into a new market is a complicated and costly business and most who take on the challenge will be hoping that they are setting up a long-term, profitable part of their business.

The first choice facing any seller who wishes to trade internationally is whether to:

- make the products at home and export them, or
- make the products abroad.

Many firms start by exporting. This is an easier route, with lower financial risks. Manufacturers can continue to use their existing facilities (perhaps expanded) and suppliers, just as they have always done for their domestic markets. They find an agent or distributor with knowledge of the target market and use them to sell, arrange delivery of, and service products overseas. This is known as indirect export. Larger, or more experienced, firms may handle the export themselves (direct export), sending personnel overseas as required. As business builds and becomes more profitable, and as the firm's knowledge of the market

ACTIVITY

Visit the Heinz website at www.heinz.com. What is its business purpose? How does it try to achieve this?

domestic market

a company's home market, i.e. markets in the same country as the company itself

indirect export

using a third party (e.g. an export management company), based in the firm's home country, to sell products abroad

direct export

when a company makes products in its home country for sale abroad and then manages the overseas sales and marketing of them itself

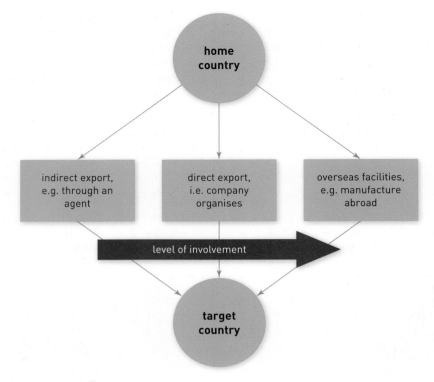

EXHIBIT 9.8 Market entry and operational options

grows, it may set up facilities overseas – perhaps a sales or servicing office, an assembly plant, even a fully-fledged factory.

How to enter an overseas market becomes a more complex choice for service marketers who, because of the nature of services (which are intangible and cannot be stored – see

Indirect export	Direct export
The least effort for the exporter, as long as the trading partner performs well	Requires more effort, finance and resources from exporter, e.g. logistics management
Lowest risk option	Higher risk than indirect export as more investment is required, but still low risk compared to setting up more substantial overseas operations
Usually the easiest exit strategy (can cancel agreements, depending upon terms of contracts, and withdraw from market)	Ease of market exit depends on the degree of involvement, i.e. how much the firm has invested in the operation
Little or no customer contact	Owns the customer relationship, but has to manage customer-facing staff from a distance
Gains no market experience and is reliant upon agents to feedback data	Builds up market experience within the exporting organisation

EXHIBIT 9.9 Comparison of direct and indirect export

Chapter 7), can rarely make the product at home and export it. Electronic services, such as banking and credit card transactions, can indeed be hosted in one country while sold and used elsewhere, but services which require the personal touch, e.g. medical care or maintenance, generally cannot. So the choices for service marketers depend upon the nature of the service. Most service companies will have to set up operations overseas if they wish to sell their product there (see 'Services' below).

In global markets expansion is often crucial to long-term business success. A larger organisation can reduce its overall costs thanks to economies of scale. These cost reductions can then be used to increase the business's competitiveness (usually by lowering prices, although there are other ways, e.g. increasing advertising) and/or its profit margins. The world's biggest retailer, Wal-Mart, has cost reduction as a key objective and although it has not always been successful in its overseas developments, it is globally feared by all of its competitors.

To become a global business a company needs to consider carefully the extension of its supply chain and the development of the new distribution channels needed. In order to grow, it will need suitable partners to help provide the benefits that new customers seek.

global focus: delivery terms

Different countries have different trading practices. In some it may be customary for the buyer to arrange delivery of the goods, while in others it is the seller who does this. In some countries it is common practice to pay for the goods up front, whereas in others this might be considered sharp practice. It is therefore hardly surprising that this is an area where misunderstandings frequently arise.

To minimise such misunderstandings, in 1936 the International Chamber of Commerce devised a set of rules for the interpretation of international terms and conditions. These became known as **incoterms** (international commercial terms) and although they have been revised many times since, incoterms are still helping to simplify international trade today. They set out how activities, costs and risks are to be split between the buyer and seller and range from everything being the responsibility of the buyer to the other extreme, where everything is the responsibility of the seller.

The chosen incoterm appears as a three-letter code in the contract followed by the relevant place, e.g. EXW London ('ex works') means that the buyer is collecting the goods from the seller's premises in London and is responsible for transportation costs, taxes and duties from that point onwards. In contrast, DDP Paris ('delivered duty paid') makes the seller responsible for costs and delivery to the buyer at their address in Paris.

The latest revision was in 2010 and so the set of rules now in force are known as Incoterms 2010. There are 11 terms grouped into two categories based on the method of transport. Seven of the terms apply to all forms of transport and the remaining four terms apply only to sales that only involve transportation over water.

For a more detailed explanation of what they mean, see **www.bdpinternational.com/wp/wp-content/uploads/Incoterms-2010-EU.pdf**

Sources: UK Government (2012)

incoterms
a set of rules governing the delivery terms for international sales

SOURCES OF POWER AND CONFLICT IN THE SUPPLY CHAIN

The different routes through the supply chain to the final customer are known as distribution channels. Each business involved is known as a channel member. Any supply chain is dependent for its success on the individual contributions of its members, which are selected for their resources and skills. Each member has some power in the particular distribution channel of which it is a part (see Exhibit 9.10). Businesses with greater power have significant advantages. An extreme example is provided by Marks & Spencer. By 1996 Marks & Spencer had grown to be the world's fifth largest retailer and was making profits of £1 billion (€1.4 billion) per year. Under the chairmanship of Sir Richard Greenbury, the company was proud to announce that the vast majority of its products came from British sources. Unfortunately, the company's financial performance stalled and then collapsed. As profits slumped, Sir Richard was replaced and the management of Marks & Spencer's operations was severely overhauled. One result of these changes was a new approach to buying products. The old 'Buy British' strategy went and, as a result, several of Marks & Spencer's old suppliers collapsed. In this channel, Marks & Spencer was the dominant player and even had the power to close down other members' businesses. This example illustrates the importance of the relationships between channel members. In most cases businesses recognise that being too dependent on another business is potentially dangerous (in fact, Marks & Spencer did, at one time, have a policy of never allowing a supplier to become dependent upon its orders so as to avoid this situation). Most businesses aim to have a variety of different customers, which spreads the risks and reduces the chance of collapse if one partner fails.

referent power
influence over others gained through superior knowledge or expertise

In the example above, Marks & Spencer had power because of its size and consequent financial strength. Most businesses do not have sufficient resources to control the whole supply chain. There are, however, other sources of power that channel members can use to gain advantage in their relationships. The main source of power, outside that of financial influence, is knowledge or expertise. This is known as referent power.

EXHIBIT 9.10 Factors influencing the relationship between buyers and sellers

Businesses that are expanding into new areas look for partners that have knowledge of that particular market. This knowledge will help reduce mistakes and build relationships that may lead to further profitable developments. Customers expect shop assistants in specialist stores to be well informed. This is the basis of specialist retailing across the globe: from fashion shops where the merchandisers are expected to be aware of trends and details, to delicatessens where staff should know a Serrano from a Parma.

legitimate power
influence over others conferred by law or regulations

A third source of power in the supply chain comes from specific regulations or laws that are used to regulate markets. This is also known as legitimate power. This form of power can be used to increase control over the other channel members. This is definitely the case when one partner owns a patent on the required item. This type of power is commonly found in pharmaceutical markets where drug companies can legally protect their investment in new products for a number of years.

Branding is another way of gaining legal support for products as the law can be used to protect a brand from imitators. There have been cases of retailers allegedly copying a manufacturer's branded product and selling it as if it were the retailer's own product. ASDA was found guilty of this when it copied the McVitie's Penguin biscuit bar. The court took the view that such activities were intended to mislead the customer as to the origin of the product, and were therefore unacceptable. This case illustrates the problems that can arise between channel members when one challenges the power of another's brand. (For more on branding, see Chapters 6 and 11.)

digital focus: is Taylor Swift ever, ever getting back together with Spotify?

Many of Taylor Swift's most famous hits are inspired by break-ups. Unfortunately, her split from Spotify has been far from harmonious. Ms Swift's relationship with Spotify has been fraught since she pulled her entire catalogue in 2014 in protest against the all-you-can-stream music service she claims devalues music. Swift wrote at the time, 'Music is art, and art is important and rare. Important, rare things are valuable. Valuable things should be paid for'.

Taylor Swift
Source: JStone/Shutterstock.com

Spotify claims it pays around 70% of its revenues to record labels although artists themselves can expect to receive a much smaller slice of the pie. Many established stars have backed Swift, voicing concerns for the future of music if new artists, struggling to get a break in the business, are unable to make meaningful revenue from streams while they build up enough of a following to generate income from live shows. Several big-name artists like Gwen Stefani, Beyonce, Coldplay and Drake have experimented with delaying the release of their albums onto the streaming service, effectively creating a stream-free window in the immediate post-launch period in a bid to stimulate sales.

It was nine months before Adele's hugely successful album *25* was released on any music streaming platform. In that time it had sold more than 18 million copies globally. While there is little doubt Adele has a rare talent, the success of *25*, coupled with a dramatic rise in the popularity of traditional vinyl (sales hit a 28-year high last year), are perhaps signs that the tide is turning against disposable downloads. Are music lovers opting once again to buy and own their favourite music ... at least that should be music to Taylor Swift's ears?

Taylor Swift vs Spotify

Sources: Engle (2014); Luckerson (2016); McIntyre (2016); Morris (2016)

A well-designed supply chain should limit the potential for conflict between the channel members. Any conflict reduces effectiveness in the supply chain and may ultimately lead to channels being closed off. Failure to resolve conflict between members, or ending up in law courts, is a failure in the management of the buyer–seller relationship.

MARKETING FUNCTIONS IN THE SUPPLY CHAIN

As a product passes along the supply chain, its costs rise, partly because the activities carried out at each stage (e.g. transport, storage, re-packaging) have to be paid for, but also because each intermediary needs to make a profit. This is why the shorter the channel, generally speaking, the lower the final price. At each point in the chain, both parties to an exchange want good value and so customers must value the product at a greater price than the seller paid for it and so be prepared to pay more for it (see Chapters 1 and 10 for exchanges and customer value). The members of the supply chain make their contributions to the eventual product experience in a number of ways.

STOCK HOLDING

just-in-time (JIT)

a lean manufacturing and stocking approach where little or no stock is held

For a retailer, having stock available is critical to success because usually no stock means no sales. Stock that does not sell is a waste of the retailer's money, so every effort is made to minimise this. This often means putting pressure on sellers to hold stocks away from the retailer's stores but ready to be called in at short notice if required. This just-in-time (JIT) or quick response (QR) approach reduces the retailer's waste but increases the seller's financial risk if the products do not sell.

digital focus: drone delivery service

When global Internet retailer Amazon first announced plans for its Prime Air drone delivery service, many dismissed it as a Black Friday PR stunt. Amazon claims the 'future service' will deliver packages up to five pounds in 30 minutes or less using unmanned aerial vehicles or drones. Smart 'sense and avoid' technology will enable multiple drones to be safely flown out of a pilot's line of sight for distances of up to 10 miles.

If this sounds like a scene in *Back to the Future*, be assured that Amazon CEO, Jeff Bezos, is taking the future of distribution very seriously indeed. Prime Air has attracted a team of leading engineers and pilots, including a former NASA astronaut, and hundreds of millions of dollars are thought to have been invested.

Drones have already proven effective means of transporting small packages. In July 2015 an Australian manufactured drone (called Flirtey) delivered medical supplies to a rural health clinic in Virginia, USA. The demonstration run was sanctioned by the US Federal Aviation Authority in partnership with NASA. More recently Amazon has announced plans to begin testing delivery drones in the UK with the full support of the UK government and Civil Aviation Authority. While the US authorities had been unwilling to relax laws restricting drone flights to a pilot's line of sight, the UK authorities have been more encouraging, entering into a partnership with Amazon to permit more ambitious testing. An Amazon spokesperson emphasised the importance of safety: 'We're not going to launch until we can demonstrate safety, and that's what this programme is going to do'.

It seems almost inconceivable that in the early years of Internet commerce, it was normal to wait weeks for the delivery of online purchases. Amazon's free five-day delivery service was a game changer then, just as its drones may be tomorrow: 90% of Amazon parcels weigh under 2.5kg making them perfect for drone delivery. This isn't just another bold Amazon statement but potentially a chance to retain crucial competitive advantage in an industry that is relentlessly driving down delivery times and transforming consumer expectations of service quality.

So long as it rings the right doorbell.

Sources: Gibbs (2015); Tovey (2016); Woolf and Gibbs (2016)

Drone Delivery Service
Source: Mopic/Shutterstock.com

Amazon drone delivery

TRANSPORTATION

Clearly, there must be the means to get the product to the customer. Consumers often visit stores themselves and so they take care of the transport of their purchases themselves.

Businesses are likely to require delivery. Transportation is often contracted out to logistics services who are outside the buyer–seller relationship (see 'Channel members' above) or companies may use couriers, or even the post office. Online bookseller Amazon may now have its own warehouse (it did not originally, but relied on others to fulfil orders), but they outsource their deliveries.

For some products the task of transportation is complicated by the nature of the product itself (e.g. moving natural gas from the North Sea to homes). The transportation system for this example includes production platforms, pumping stations and thousands of miles of pipeline. Without that specialist transportation system this market could not exist.

INFORMATION GATHERING

This is a function that is undertaken by all participants. Information gathering does not necessarily require a formal market research project as all businesses obtain information on the markets that they serve as the result of their day-to-day operations. Many small businesses fail to recognise the value of this by-product of their work and therefore lose out on numerous marketing opportunities. Successful businesses, however, will analyse the information to shape the ways in which they approach their customers, both current and potential. More sophisticated analysis can be a source of further competitive advantage. For example, some large supermarkets feed meteorological forecasts into special software to anticipate future demand for key products (coleslaw or charcoal in hot weather) and then work with suppliers to make sure stores have enough of those items on the shelves.

In some cases, the information is shared with other members of the supply chain. This sharing activity helps to improve the efficiency and effectiveness of the chain as a whole, and is evidence of healthy relationships between the participants.

COMMUNICATING

This function helps to develop efficiency in the supply chain. If information can be shared quickly, then the costs of operation can be reduced. Most major retail businesses use EPOS systems to capture information from their stores. Such systems use the barcodes on products to identify the items and quantities that have been sold. This data is then sent to a head office computer that adds up all of the individual stores' information. If more stock is needed, the central computer can place an order with the seller's computer using an EDI (electronic data interchange) system. Replacement products can thus be ordered without any human effort. These systems can work 24 hours a day, seven days a week, and are a major force in the globalisation of retailing.

globalisation
the process of growing to a worldwide scale; it often involves the standardisation of offerings and cultural convergence

Some firms are harnessing the power of social media to improve communications throughout the supply chain, for example by posting updates about weather conditions that could impede delivery or wholesalers sharing automated inventory updates with resellers. Social media can also encourage greater collaboration among supply chain partners, for example by supporting transparent group discussions and sharing data and knowledge to improve supply chain efficiency and forge stronger supply chain relationships.

Constantly swapping business partners is inefficient. It leads to additional costs in selecting and evaluating prospective candidates. The development of long-term relationships helps to create trust and facilitates the exchange of information between the partners. In the longer term, this reduces the costs in the supply chain and brings financial benefits to all members.

PROMOTING

All buyers and sellers in the supply chain will promote their goods and services to each other. The final consumer does not see the majority of such promotional efforts, but they are vital to the development of the various relationships in the supply chain.

Promotional activities can be very sophisticated and behind the scenes, such as a manufacturer giving the retailer a retrospective discount dependent on the volume of product sold in a particular period of time. Alternatively, the effort can be blatant, such as Debenhams' Blue Cross Sale advertisements that announce 20% discounts on specific days (often on Tuesdays to boost sales in the quieter part of the week). Some retailers combine the two forms, such as KwikSave's '£1 off Beefeater Gin' promotion. In this case, the product is a brand of Allied Domecq, a wine and spirit distribution company. This company sees it as in its own interests to support the retailer in promoting its product in preference to those of its competitors.

The possible objectives and the various methods for these promotional activities are discussed more fully in Chapter 8.

DIGITAL CHANNELS

Supply chains become ever more complex, ever harder to manage. New members join, although sometimes they are uninvited. Others leave. The concept of place is a dynamic one and it is one of management's major challenges to keep up with it.

For the marketer, new technology allows new services to be created and these will need to be distributed to customers. These new opportunities also bring potential dangers. In a digital world, it is very difficult to control the distribution of a digital product. Many people think nothing of listening to pirated recordings. Services such as Napster grew from individuals illegally copying CD-based music and making it available through the Internet. With physical products a counterfeiter has to create a manufacturing facility, and that takes resources. With digital products the copying and distribution can be done at the press of a button. In the future, marketers will have to pay more attention to protecting the distribution of their digital products if they are to secure the maximum return on their investments.

ELECTRONIC DISTRIBUTION

One of the biggest changes the Internet has brought to our lives is through electronic distribution: all kinds of Internet downloads including mobile apps, e-books, or software updates and even cloud-based services and online gaming are examples of weightless products that are digitally distributed. The possibilities are growing daily. The Internet offers 24/7 access to services delivered directly to the receiver's PC. This level of convenience is something that store-based retailers cannot match and gives e-tailers (using e-distribution) a distinct market advantage.

research focus

Xing, Y., Grant, D.B., McKinnon, A.C. and Fernie, J. (2011) 'The interface between retailers and logistics service providers in the online market', *European Journal of Marketing*, 45 (3): 334–57.

The growth in online shopping has presented challenges for physical distribution service quality provided by retailers and logistics service providers. Through interviews with retailers, logistics service providers and experts, this paper examines issues regarding electronic physical distribution service quality.

BUSINESS-TO-BUSINESS (B2B)

Over the last decade, the revolution in communications technology has affected almost all businesses. As defined in this chapter, the concept of place has two major components: time and space. The Internet has affected both of these.

In the b2b sector, some small businesses still use paper-based ordering systems. Salespeople may collect orders personally and forward them to a central sales office. However, smartphones and other handheld electronic devices are rapidly replacing the old systems. The Internet creates opportunities for customers to send in their orders without visits from salespeople who can then concentrate on relationship building. Online customers can choose the time when the ordering will take place and can be shown a much wider variety of products than any sales representative is able to carry.

It is this capacity for carrying information, and for transmitting it so speedily, that makes the Internet so effective as a channel for communication. Buyers can surf the net looking for potential suppliers from anywhere in the world. Similarly, suppliers can also use the Internet to find potential customers. Some facilitating businesses exist simply as portals, allowing sellers to post their products on the host site (for a fee, of course). This saves the buyers search time and the sellers gain access to a worldwide marketplace.

portal
a website that acts as a gateway to a number of other sites

BUSINESS TO CUSTOMER (B2C)

Many retailers who never before used direct marketing techniques, such as catalogues or telesales, are now online – albeit reluctantly in some cases. In the UK, it is now almost unheard of for any major retailer not to have a web presence (there are a few chains holding out, e.g. Fenwicks, Primark).

Initially, customers were reluctant to shop online as they did not trust the technology. They were worried about credit card fraud, whether the goods would ever turn up, whether they would be in good condition, what they could do if they wanted to return something. Advances in security, the experience of others, and the appearance of known and trusted companies and brands online have reassured them, and convenience has won shoppers over. Far from being the bargain hunters that the early e-shoppers were, today's time-starved consumers are prepared to pay extra for their groceries, in the form of delivery charges, so that they can shop from home (Huang and Oppewal, 2006). Offline sales are still greater but online sales are growing rapidly. According to the European Commission (2015), the value of retail e-commerce in the EU grew by 13.4% in 2014 to a total of €370 billion. The share of e-commerce in the total retail sector is significantly lower in Europe than in the USA: in 2014, electronic sales accounted for 7.2% in the EU compared to 11.6% in the USA. Most consumers still buy from retailers located in their own countries – even though the Internet has opened up the world to them. Only 15% of consumers purchased online from another EU country, while nearly three times as many (44%) bought something online locally.

The willingness of consumers to shop online has had a knock-on effect in b2b markets. Previously, it was necessary to have shops, often large ones and often chains of them, if you wanted to sell to consumers. Now products can be sold from a website without the need for such expensive investment. This has changed the competitive nature of many markets (e.g. booksellers). It is easier for new competitors to enter markets and it is easier for producers to sell direct. Internet retailers are judged by the impression their website makes. It is much cheaper to build an impressive website than an impressive shop, and so smaller companies can compete much more easily with larger ones.

There are snags, of course. Manufacturers have little or no experience of dealing with consumers. They still need to break down bulk as consumers will not want to buy a case of mayonnaise, just a jar. Then there is delivery. This is where many of the direct sellers fall down and where they lose the trust of their customers. In the early days, Internet-ordered goods were frequently late, wrong, damaged or 'no-shows'. It is still vital to get the right goods to the right customer at the right time – and that is not such an easy task.

CUSTOMER TO CUSTOMER (C2C)

One of the most radical changes that the Internet has made to supply chains is the introduction of another channel member – the consumers themselves. Some consumers have always passed on goods in a small way, usually second-hand goods, maybe some unwanted gifts (or more dubiously acquired items), but this activity was so small-scale that it barely registered in the commercial world. The web has provided the means for individuals to access thousands, even millions, of other individuals and so has opened the way for a host of small-scale exchanges and facilitated the birth of numerous businesses.

Some businesses tap into this potential by offering services for individual sellers. For example, Amazon marketplace is a forum where individuals can offer books and other items for sale, either through a listing or by auction, but without the risks inherent in running an Internet business as Amazon manage the site and collect the payments for them (for a commission of course). Another global example is eBay, which claimed to have 162 million buyers and 900 million listings in 2016 (eBay, n.d.). Their phenomenal reach is often cited as the reason for the collapse of a number of small antiques and collectibles shops.

SUMMARY

Effective place management is vitally important to the marketing function. The elements of space and time are combined to create opportunities in which buyers and sellers can come together. A clear understanding of the buyer's needs, not just from the product but also from the exchange itself, helps the seller to shape an offer that maximises the chances of an exchange.

Most exchanges will use existing supply chain networks. These are formed from different types of business that are connected by their own exchange relationships. These networks have many forms, from the simple (farmer direct to consumer) to the complex (Boeing building a new aeroplane). As the networks become more sophisticated, so there is more likelihood that the members will begin to operate as business partners. These partnerships may be for a particular project or on a long-term basis.

Each business in the supply chain has its own skills and capabilities. These are a source of business power in its relationship with the other members of the network. In most cases there is little open conflict, but there is usually some tension because of the opposing profit objectives.

In the twenty-first century, business exchange relationships are increasingly global. Changes in communications and physical distribution have made this growth possible. As the geographical distances between buyers and sellers have increased, the management of the physical movement of goods has become progressively more important and more complex. In recent times there have been massive technological changes, and these changes in communication and transportation technologies have had a massive impact on our ideas

c2c (consumer to consumer)

business dealings between consumers, e.g. on eBay

physical distribution

the process of moving goods and services between businesses and consumers

of place. As technology continues its rapid development, marketers will need to be open to change if they are to maintain their business's effectiveness.

Successful management of place also requires an understanding of its role in the marketing function. Place offers opportunities for information gathering, for testing new products, for trying out promotional techniques and for getting feedback on pricing strategies.

A manager's ability to create, sustain and develop relationships is a fundamental skill in generating business success. To manage place well requires that you manage relationships well. These relationships will be both internal (with other departments that affect the flow of products through the business) and external (with customers and suppliers) (Gadde and Håkansson, 2001).

Getting all the activities that come under the heading 'Place' right will set the scene for a successful exchange. For that to happen, marketers must ensure that the right goods get to the right customer in the right time and space.

CHALLENGES REVIEWED

Now that you have finished reading the chapter, look back at the challenges you were set at the beginning. Do you have a clearer idea of what's involved?

HINTS

- Breadth of distribution coverage and merchandising support – see also 'Marketing functions in the supply chain'.
- Marketing functions in the supply chain.
- How do the members of the supply chain add value? (Also branding.)
- The importance of building relationships through the supply chain.
- Junk food and child obesity problems – what responsibilities do schools have to the children in their care?

READING AROUND

JOURNAL ARTICLES

Pearson, M.M. (1981) 'Ten distribution myths', *Business Horizons*, 24 (3): 17–23.

Teller, C. and Dennis, C. (2012) 'The effect of ambient scent on consumers' perception, emotions and behaviour: a critical review', *Journal of Marketing Management*, 28 (1–2): 14–36.

Vukadin, A., Lemoine, J.-F., and Badot, O. (2016) 'Opportunities and risks of combining shopping experience and artistic elements in the same store: a contribution to the magical functions of the point of sale', *Journal of Marketing Management*, 32 (9–10), Academy of Marketing Conference 2016: The Magic of Marketing.

BOOKS

Harvard Business School (2011) *Harvard Business School on Managing Supply Chains*. Boston: HBR Press.

MAGAZINES

Retail Week, UK

ONLINE RESOURCES

BBC, *Mary Queen of Shops* – retailing insights. Available at: www.bbc.co.uk/programmes/b007mwv9/clips.

Ted Talks, Mick Mountz (2011) 'What happens inside those massive warehouses?' Available at: www.ted.com/talks/mick_mountz_the_hidden_world_of_box_packing.

Ted Talks, Rose George (2013) 'Inside the secret shipping industry'. Available at: www.ted.com/talks/rose_george_inside_the_secret_shipping_industry.

WEBSITES

www.bdpinternational.com/wp/wp-content/uploads/Incoterms-2010-EU.pdf – this site provides a useful simple summary of incoterms with explanatory diagrams highlighting buyers and sellers' risks and costs.

www.dhl.co.uk/en/logistics – see the range of services offered by one of the world's largest logistics companies.

www.ethicaltrade.org/ – Ethical Trading Initiative – respect for workers worldwide.

TEST YOURSELF

1   What is a supply chain and what is its purpose? (See p. 345)

2   How can a manufacturing business be both a buyer and a seller? (See p. 346)

3   What is the main function of an agent? (See p. 349)

4   Why do major supermarkets, such as Tesco and Sainsbury's, have Internet stores when they have invested so much in physical supermarkets? (See pp. 350–354)

5   How can a firm use the concept of place to help it position its business against those of its competitors? (See p. 351)

6   Heinz engages in direct marketing communications to the final consumers of its products. Why it is unlikely to engage in direct delivery of its products to those customers? (See pp. 345–348)

7   Why would businesses want to create long-term relationships with their suppliers? (See p. 357)

8   Why is it important that the supply chain should be responsive to customers' needs? (See p. 355)

9   What is meant by the term 'disintermediation'? (See p. 362)

10 Why is product expertise important to businesses? (See p. 359)

11 What is the difference between direct export and indirect export? (See p. 363)

12 Why does the physical nature of the product sometimes affect the choice of supply chain participants? (See pp. 359–362)

REVISION TOOLS

Want to test yourself even more? Review what you have learnt by visiting
https://study.sagepub.com/masterson4e

- Practise for exams with **multiple choice questions**
- Revise key terms with **interactive flashcards**

MINI CASE STUDY: HONEST, TASTY AND REAL – DORSET CEREALS

Read the questions, then the case material, and then answer the questions.

QUESTIONS

1   How would you categorise Dorset Cereals' distribution strategy before and after the re-positioning exercise? Why?

2   Discuss the advantages and drawbacks of a brand like Dorset Cereals being stocked by large supermarkets such as Tesco and Sainsbury's.

3   Revisit the section headed 'Marketing functions in the supply chain' above. How can Dorset Cereals and its retail partners manage these marketing activities to the best, mutual advantage? What would you expect them to do?

Muesli has gone through a rejuvenation of late and Dorset Cereals is largely responsible. Back in the early 2000s, muesli was worthy but rather dull. Everyone knew it was good for them but not everyone wanted to eat it. Supermarkets stocked the big brand names, such as Alpen, and their own-label products. Health food stores stocked the real deal but it was often compared to sawdust or cat litter.

Dorset Cereals had been around since 1985 and was sold in most of the specialist health food shops such as Holland and Barrett. However, their sales figures were flat even though healthy cereals were the only category in the cereal market showing a healthy growth. The breakfast cereal market generally was saturated. Cereals had been so well marketed that it was hard to find new customers or ways to grow the business. Also, it was dominated by large multinationals like Kellogg's and Nestlé who filled whatever space remained on supermarket shelves once their own-label products had been displayed.

According to Mintel (2008), grocery multiples like the well-known supermarkets account for 94% of all breakfast cereal sales. There are a number of niche players who sell through health food shops or even, like Mymuesli, online, but if they wanted to make any serious inroads into the market at all, Dorset Cereals needed to be on the supermarket shelves. To achieve that they needed a radical brand makeover.

They researched the market and interrogated their own brand, establishing its values clearly. They realised that the supermarket's shelves were already full of cereals that claimed to have natural qualities and healthy ingredients but none of them claimed to taste good! Dorset Cereals repositioned itself as 'honest, tasty and real'. This new positioning was encapsulated in a radical new brand identity. A simple, eye-catching leaf icon adorned the improved packaging. The leaf symbolised the natural ingredients of the muesli and was easily recognisable even when re-coloured for different recipes, or turned into a cellophane window on the pack through which the product could be seen. It soon came to represent Dorset Cereals in the minds of both consumers and trade.

Previously, the muesli had been packaged in basic plastic bags that:

- faded into the background on shelves and so were rarely noticed
- would not stay upright on display stands and so looked a mess in store and irritated shopkeepers
- failed to protect the product well enough in transit causing wastage
- regularly spilt cereal across kitchen tables to the intense annoyance of consumers.

The new packs were bigger and made from recyclable card. They stood out, stood up and kept the cereal in good condition while being transported, stored and displayed in store. They also featured the kind of quirky copy that makes a good breakfast-time read.

(Continued)

(Continued)

© Ros Masterson

Armed with this new look, the company approached the major supermarket chains, some of whom (notably Waitrose) took the brand on trial. With its more appealing brand identity, it flew off the shelves and further orders were placed. Soon it stopped being the preserve of upmarket stores like Waitrose, and became a staple on the shelves of Tesco, Sainsbury's, Morrison's and the rest. At the same time, the Dorset Cereals sales team persuaded a number of high-end, independent retailers to stock the brand and so they kept up the muesli's luxury image. In a later development, the company launched individual portion catering packs for hotels and restaurants and so broke into yet another new market thanks to imaginative packaging.

As a result of the improved distribution, Dorset Cereals' market share more than doubled, outstripping competitors' mueslis and even growing the breakfast cereal category overall.

By making their cereal look more exciting, Dorset Cereals had got people more excited about breakfast.

Sources: Mintel (2008); WARC (2007)

REFERENCES

Bellis, M. (2007) *The Unusual History of MS DOS the Microsoft Operating System*, about.com, part of the New York Times Company. Available at: inventors.about.com/library/weekly/aa033099.htm (accessed 18/04/07).

Campbell, A. (2013) 'The peril of showrooming', *BBC News Magazine*, 21 April. Available at: www.bbc.co.uk/news/magazine (accessed 08/05/13).

eBay (n.d.) 'eBay by the numbers', *About eBay, Company Fast Facts*. Available at: www.ebay-mediacentre.co.uk/global-facts (accessed 06/09/16).

Engle, P. (2014). 'Taylor swift explains why she left Spotify'. *Business Insider UK* 13 November. Available at: http://uk.businessinsider.com/taylor-swift-explains-why-she-left-spotify-2014-11?r=US&IR=T (accessed 28/09/16).

EUNavfor (n.d.) Available at: http://eunavfor.eu/ (accessed 04/10/16).

European Commission (2015) 'Digital contracts for Europe: unleashing the potential of e-commerce', *Communication from the Commission to the European Parliament, the Council and the European Economic and Social Committee*, 9 December. Available at: http://ec.europa.eu/justice/contract/files/communication.pdf (accessed 06/09/16).

Fernie, J. and Sparks, L. (2004) 'Retail logistics: changes and challenges', in J. Fernie and L. Sparks (eds), *Logistics and Retail Management: Insights into Current Practice and Trends from Leading Experts* (2nd edn). London: Kogan Page, pp. 1–25.

Gadde, L.E. and Håkansson, H. (2001) *Supply Network Strategies*. London: Wiley.

Gibbs, S. (2015) 'First successful drone delivery made in US', *The Guardian* (online) 20 July. Available at: www.theguardian.com/technology/2015/jul/20/first-successful-drone-delivery-us (accessed 19/09/16).

Huang, Y. and Oppewal, H. (2006) 'Why consumers hesitate to shop online: an experimental choice analysis of grocery shopping and the role of delivery fees', *International Journal of Retail and Distribution Management*, 34 (4/5): 334–53.

IBM (n.d.) *IBM Archives 1981*. Available at: www-03.ibm.com/ibm/history/history/year_1981.html (accessed 18/04/07).

International Chamber of Commerce Crime Services (2016) 'IMB Piracy Reporting Centre'. Available at: https://icc-ccs.org/piracy-reporting-centre (accessed 4/10/16).

Kabadayi, S., Eyuboglu, N. and Thomas, G.P. (2007) 'The performance implications of designing multiple channels to fit with strategy and environment,' *Journal of Marketing*, 71 (4): 195–211.

Luckerson, V.L. (2016) '11 wildly popular albums you can't get on Spotify', *Time*, 29 March. Available at: www.time.com http://time.com/4274430/spotify-albums/ (accessed 28/09/16).

Lysons, K. and Gillingham, M. (2003) *Purchasing and Supply Chain Management*. Harlow: FT/Prentice Hall.

Manners-Bell, J. (2014) *Supply Chain Risk*. London: Kogan Page.

McGoldrick, P. (2003) *Retail Marketing*. Maidenhead: McGraw-Hill.

McIntyre, H. (2016) 'Six months old today, Adele's "25" is showing few signs of slowing down', *Forbes*, 20 May. Available at: www.forbes.com/sites/hughmcintyre/2016/05/20/six-months-old-today-adeles-25-is-showing-few-signs-of-seriously-slowing-down/#ef965f44b771 (accessed 18/09/16).

Michel, D., Naudé, P., Salle, R. and Valla, J.P. (2003) *Business-to-Business Marketing*. Basingstoke: Palgrave Macmillan.

Mintel (2008) *UK Breakfast Cereals Market Report*. London: Mintel.

Morris, C. (2016) 'Vinyl record sales are at a 28-year high'. *Fortune*, 16 April. Available at: www.fortune.com http://fortune.com/2016/04/16/vinyl-sales-record-store-day/ (accessed 28/09/16).

Piercy, N. (2002) *Market-led Strategic Change*. Oxford: Butterworth Heinemann.

Teller, C. and Dennis, C. (2012) 'The effect of ambient scent on consumers' perception, emotions and behaviour: a critical review', *Journal of Marketing Management*, 28 (1–2): 14–36.

Tovey, A. (2016) 'Can Amazon's drones deliver the Back to the Future world?', *The Telegraph*, 31 July. Available at: www.telegraph.co.uk/business/2016/07/31/can-amazons-drones-deliver-the-back-to-the-future-world/ (accessed 19/09/16).

UK Government (2012) 'Guide: Incoterms'. Available at: www.gov.uk/incoterms-international-commercial-terms/what-the-terms-mean (accessed 05/04/13).

WARC (2007) 'Design Effectiveness Awards', Design Business Association. Available at: www.warc.com/ArticleCenter/Default.asp?CType=A&AID=HomeEC90615&Tab=A (accessed 30/12/09).

Woolf, N. and Gibbs, S. (2016) 'Amazon to test drone delivery in partnership with UK government', *The Guardian*, 26 July. Available at: www.theguardian.com/technology/2016/jul/25/amazon-to-test-drone-delivery-uk-government (accessed 19/09/16).

Xing, Y., Grant, D.B., McKinnon, A.C. and Fernie, J. (2011) 'The interface between retailers and logistics service providers in the online market', *European Journal of Marketing*, 45 (3): 334–57.

10

PRICE

PRICE CHALLENGES

The following are illustrations of the types of decision that marketers have to take or issues they face. *You aren't expected to know how to deal with the challenges now*; just bear them in mind as you read the chapter and see what you can find that helps.

- You run a medium-sized business, a second-hand car dealership. A competitor, the showroom on the other side of town, reduces its prices. Should you do the same? What will happen if you don't and if you do?

- You have decided that it is a good time for your business to grow. The business is fashion design and is just getting known. You need to make more money to fund that growth: to make sample garments for the shows and to give away to celebrities. Could changing prices help at all? Should you put them down, or up?

- You have developed a new product. It is brand new, a technological breakthrough: an instant transportation system. It will make most other forms of transport redundant. How do you know how much to charge for it?

- You work for a large chain of furniture stores. Business is slack and competition for the few customers buying furniture is fierce. Your boss suggests offering credit deals to low-income households who would find it hard to borrow money from a bank as they are too great a risk. What are the potential drawbacks to this idea?

- Yours is a multinational company with branches in most countries. Incomes and currencies vary. How can you set prices for your televisions that will maximise profits in the richer countries without losing business in the poorer markets?

INTRODUCTION

Price is often a seriously undervalued part of the marketing mix. On the one hand, this is a great shame as many companies miss out on the competitive edge that the creative use of pricing brings. On the other hand, it is a good thing for the marketers who do appreciate the finer points of pricing. Pricing can be a devastating competitive weapon.

While some notable retailers, such as Lidl, Asda and Tesco, clearly continuously research prices, very few companies base their pricing decisions on serious pricing research or revise their prices often enough, most thinking that it is good enough to set them once a year, along with the budgets (Cox, 2001). Other common mistakes include not taking into account the rest of the marketing mix and focusing too much on costs.

Price is the odd one out in the 4Ps of the marketing mix. The other three elements can be perceived as costs but the price of the goods and services a firm sells is a direct determinant of its profit – and most businesses' primary aim is to make high profits. Pricing strategy, therefore, is a key part of a firm's overall marketing strategy and one that has a direct effect on the bottom line.

As an alternative to, or in combination with, other marketing mix elements, a company can use pricing to improve the customer's perception of the product's value. Lowering the price is not the only way to do this; in fact, it might be counter-productive, making the product seem cheap. This is where creativity and judgement come in. This chapter will attempt to show how that works.

Through most of this chapter, price will be used in the simpler sense of the money charged for a product (unless otherwise stated). However, there is more to price than the price tag. The price to the customer is everything they have to give up to obtain the product. This includes time, effort and alternative purchases. The chapter will begin by considering the implications of the price of a product and how it affects a business. It will move on to look at the different influences on price setting and how prices can be used to help achieve marketing objectives. Pricing strategies and tactics for both new and existing products will be covered alongside some of the additional complexities of pricing in multiple countries. Prices are not fixed once and for evermore, so it is important to understand the implications of changing prices. The chapter then makes a brief excursion into economics for price elasticity of demand – an important concept for marketers as it helps them to forecast sales at different price levels. It finishes by considering the impact of the Internet on pricing.

WHY IT IS SO IMPORTANT TO GET THE PRICE RIGHT

profit

the difference between what something costs to make and the price for which it is sold

The price of the goods and services a firm sells is a major determinant of its profit – and most businesses' primary aim is to make high profits. Pricing strategy, therefore, is a key part of a firm's overall marketing strategy. Even not-for-profit organisations usually need at least to cover their costs if they want to continue their existence. In hard times, companies may be focused on survival rather than on profits, but then too, they need to pay careful attention to their pricing strategies. As the one part of the marketing mix that delivers money to the firm, rather than takes it out, price is always important.

costs

what an organisation pays for the goods and services it receives; see also direct costs, indirect costs, variable costs and fixed costs

The prices an organisation charges have a direct bearing on key corporate and marketing objectives, as described below.

WHAT IS PROFIT?

objective

a goal or target

Profit is what's left over when all the bills have been paid.

sales revenue − costs = profit

sales revenue (turnover)

the income a firm receives from the sale of goods and services

So to make the most profit, you need to get in as much money as possible (revenue):

sales revenue = sales volume × selling price

… and pay out as little as possible (costs).

Here's an example of how to work out profit:

> Kidzone clothing sells 100 T-shirts at £5.00 each. Each T-shirt costs £1.00 to make, distribute and sell.

Sales revenue from the T-shirts is:

> 100 (volume) × £5 (price) = £500

Total cost is:

> (volume) × £1 (cost) = £100

The company's profit is:

> £500 (sales revenue) − £100 (total cost) = £400

PROFIT AND REVENUE

It is easy enough to sell a lot of something – just sell it really cheaply. Firms that use this technique will lose out on profit, of course. So why not set the price really high? Now the firm will not sell anything at all. This much is obvious, but what is not so easy is finding the spot in the middle: the highest price at which the most people will buy. This is the price that will earn the most profit.

Generally speaking, marketing focuses on maximising sales revenue, rather than on keeping costs down. However, if the costs are too high for the price, no amount of clever marketing can make up for it.

sales revenue
the income a firm receives from the sale of goods and services

Finance people have been known to dismiss marketing as an unnecessary cost. The marketers' response is that marketing expenditure is an investment in the firm's future. It is true, however, that pricing is the only part of the marketing mix that does not involve financial outlay.

IMAGE

'Pile it high, sell it cheap' is a motto that has been attributed to various supermarkets. Is this a strategy designed to promote an upmarket or downmarket image? The strategy of reducing price, and so selling large volumes, appears a downmarket ploy. Price affects image.

SURVIVAL

A sure way to go out of business is to set prices lower than costs. Firms may get away with this in the short term (see 'Contribution pricing' and 'Loss leaders' later in this chapter), but keeping prices too low for too long is a recipe for disaster.

Pile it high, sell it cheap.

© iStockphoto.com/Juanmonino

b2b focus: selling Irish cheese to the French

© Jlwarehouse/Shutterstock.com

The Little Milk Company is a cooperative of ten, family run organic dairy farms in Munster and Leinster, Ireland. Individually, the farms were small and easily pushed on price by milk retailers. Collectively they form a sizeable organisation producing 3 million litres of milk per annum – and they have considerably more bargaining power.

Most milk is sold through the large supermarket chains who use their market power to keep prices low. Farmers have complained for years that the prices are so low that their dairy herds are unsustainable. According to the Royal Association of Dairy Farmers, every week three to four farmers give up dairy farming saying that they can no longer make milk production work financially. In 2015, a group of farmers organised protests outside the worst offending supermarkets; inside they staged a 'trolley-dash', emptying the shelves of milk which they then donated to charity.

The problem is that the farms are so small in comparison to the supermarkets. That's why joining forces makes such good sense. As well as negotiating as a group, The Little Milk Company found a great way to add value to their product: they transformed their organic milk into award-winning cheeses. Their organic Irish brie, cheddar and wedding cake cheeses are now in demand not just across Ireland but in other parts of Europe too – including that renowned home of fine cheeses: France.

Pat and Angela Mulrooney, founder members of The Little Milk Company, have been organic dairy farmers for many years. They decided that the best way to protect their business was to process the milk into other products: 'as a primary producer you become a **price taker** especially with a commodity product like milk, we wanted to become **price makers** so we decided to do something about it'.

Initially a purchasing group, they found the transition into a co-operative relatively straight forward. Their marketing strategy aims to get closer to consumers, shortening the supply chain and giving them more control over their products, and especially over their prices.

Sources: Butler and Brignall (2015); Irish Organic Farmers & Growers Association (n.d.); The Little Milk Company (n.d.)

price makers
another term for price leaders

price takers
another name for price followers

MARKET SHARE

If a company wants to increase sales, this is likely to mean taking customers away from a competitor (unless the overall market is growing in which case all companies may be able to grow). Any increase in one firm's market share means a decrease in another's. One of the most common ways to do this is by undercutting competitors' prices (see 'Market penetration' and 'Predatory pricing' below).

PRICING VIEWPOINTS
WHAT IS A PRICE?

A basic definition of price is:

> The money charged for a product or service.

That does sound obvious and there is more to it than that. Think about what you *really* pay for a product, say a laptop. There is the price of the computer itself, but then there are other things too: peripherals, software, maybe service agreements. The customer and the salesperson may see the price differently. The customer may have gone into the store to buy a laptop and have a price in mind for that. The salesperson may see the laptop as the starting point of a deal that will include numerous extras, and over a much longer period. They will try and sell extended warranties and service agreements as well as additional software and a higher specification computer.

A more comprehensive definition of price is:

> Everything that a customer has to give up in order to acquire a product or service.

This second definition takes account of the added costs associated with the purchase. For example, buying a new pair of shoes takes time: going to the shop, trying them on, maybe taking them back. It costs additional money for transport, maybe for lunch too. Then there may be accessories to buy, such as cleaner, protector, a handbag. It takes effort. It involves giving up alternatives that the money could have bought (opportunity cost). It takes an investment of brain power and judgement to ensure you get the right pair. There is also the actual money paid for the shoes.

To illustrate the complexities of pricing decisions, Lancaster et al. (2007) consider three differing perspectives on pricing: the economist's, the accountant's and the marketer's. There is also the customer's view, of course.

opportunity cost

alternatives that could have been had/done instead, e.g. the opportunity cost of a lunchtime sandwich may be a pre-packed salad, and an evening at the cinema costs a night's study

THE ECONOMIST'S VIEW OF PRICING

In a free market, a product's price would be set by the forces of demand and supply (see Chapter 1). The idea is that the price goes up, and down, until it settles at the point where buyers are prepared to buy just exactly the same amount as sellers are prepared to sell (see Exhibit 10.1).

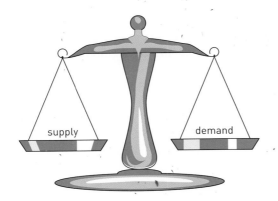

EXHIBIT 10.1 Price in the balance

If there are more buyers than products, the price goes up until enough buyers fall out of the market and demand equals supply again. If there are more products than customers, the price falls until more customers are attracted into the market.

Take the example of a fruit and vegetable stall in a market towards the end of the day. The trader shouts out his or her prices, gradually reducing them until he or she attracts customers. At an auction, the potential buyers bid against each other, pushing the price up: the more buyers there are, the higher the price goes. If there is only one potential buyer, then the price stays low.

However, that is not the way business is done in shopping malls. The economist's view is more theoretical than the real world. In practice, shops and suppliers cannot change prices so dynamically; their prices are largely fixed in advance. The concept of supply and demand remains useful, though. Clearly, the higher the price of a product, the fewer people will be prepared to buy it, and so if a firm wants to clear out old stock, then it will usually reduce the price. The consequent increase in sales is evidence of the law of supply and demand.

Drawbacks in the economist's view of pricing include the following:

- It assumes that the firm's main objective is to maximise short-term profit. This is not always true, as they may want to break into a new market, or they may be a not-for-profit organisation, or in an industry where excess profits are unacceptable (e.g. electricity supply). There are many reasons why a firm may choose to make less profit than it could.

- It assumes all companies have perfect information concerning competitor prices.

- Price is not the only thing that influences demand, and it is complicated to work out a demand function using all of the possible variables, e.g. marketing communications, competitors' prices. Therefore, demand forecasts are never 100% accurate.

THE ACCOUNTANT'S VIEW OF PRICING

Accountants want to make sure that the price of a product or service covers all its costs, so that a profit can be shown (see 'Cost-based pricing' below). Drawbacks in the accountant's view of pricing include:

- It can be hard to work out all the costs involved.

- Focusing solely on the firm's own costs means ignoring the market and the power of the rest of the marketing mix. People may be prepared to pay more, especially if the brand is strong, or there has been a good advertising campaign, or a firm has shops in better locations, or all the competitive products are twice that price. This could be a missed opportunity for profit.

THE CUSTOMER'S VIEW OF PRICING

Price–quality relationship

Customers usually want the best quality at the lowest price. For a customer, the price has to represent good value:

perceived value = perceived benefits – price

Drawbacks in the customer's view of pricing include:

- Quality costs money – there has to be a trade-off between the two; the highest-quality products cannot be sold at the lowest prices.

- People's perception of the value of a product differs – e.g. some people will pay a lot more for branded goods such as Nike, while others will not.

THE MARKETER'S VIEW OF PRICING

Marketers see pricing as an opportunity to gain competitive advantage. It is vital to take account of what the market can bear: how much people are prepared to pay, and how much competitors are charging. Drawbacks in the marketer's view of pricing include:

- Marketers may want to set a price that does not actually cover the costs of making a product. Clearly, this can only be sustained in the short term or the firm will make a loss (see 'Loss leaders' and 'Contribution pricing' later in this chapter).

research focus

Bertini, M. and Gourville, J. (2012) 'Pricing to create shared value', *Harvard Business Review*, **90 (6): 96–104.**

In this article, the authors highlight that most companies 'use pricing to extract what they can from every transaction' and provide examples to illustrate their point. They consider this antagonistic, destructive and dated approach in an environment where today's consumers are not passive price-takers and will abandon companies who take advantage. They contend that 'value neither originates with nor belongs solely to the firm. Without a willing customer, there is no value. Therefore, value must be shared by a firm and its customers'.

PRICING IN THE MIX

Clearly, it is important to have a good product, but a product without a price is a gift. So, there must be a price. The key question is how much and the answer must take account of the rest of the mix. The price sends a message, just as the promotion, distribution channels, product and its packaging do. People do not expect Harrods to be cheap, but what about Aldi? Which is likely to sell the highest quality goods? The price sends a message about quality. Customers associate a high price, sometimes mistakenly, with high quality.

While a high price can attract wealthier consumers who value quality, those sales may come at too high a cost to the company. When Sainsbury's relaunched its premium range of Taste the Difference products, it made good use of its association with celebrity chef Jamie Oliver to emphasise the high quality ingredients and sophisticated flavours that made the products worth paying extra for. Ultimately the advertisements were a little too successful. Research revealed cost-conscious consumers were being put off in the belief their shopping would be too expensive at Sainsbury's. Jamie Oliver was soon back on TV screens promoting affordable family meals 'for a fiver' backed-up with recipe cards and itemised shopping lists available in store.

ACTIVITY

Visit a high-end department store, such as John Lewis or Galeries Lafayette. Go into the electricals department and find examples of expensive, and cheaper, products in the same category (e.g. coffee machines, blenders, digital video cameras, headphones and hi-fi systems). What are the differences in terms of packaging, materials used, presentation? Could you tell which was cheaper before you looked at the price tag?

Now go to a larger electrical superstore, like Currys, or have a look online at www.amazon.co.uk or www.ao.com. Can you find the same brands? If you can't find them, find the most similar thing you can and compare that with your impression of the more expensive department store brands.

Sainsbury's Brand Match

Certain styles of promotion are associated with cheaper or more expensive products. When prices are rock bottom, the advertisers often shout – literally or through their choice of bold colours. There is more sales promotion (money-off coupons, two for the price of one, etc.) at the lower end of the market. Top fashion brands tend to advertise in glossy high-fashion magazines such as *Vogue* (if they advertise at all – public relations is more their forte).

research focus

Dinsmore, J.B., Dugan, R.G. and Wright, S.A. (2016). 'Monetary vs. nonmonetary prices: differences in product evaluations due to pricing strategies within mobile applications', *Journal of Strategic Marketing*, 24 (3–4): 227–40.
In two studies, the authors found that consumers perceive apps with monetary prices as being less novel than apps featuring a non-monetary price (banner advertisements). These inferences regarding product novelty affect customer purchase intent.

PRICING OBJECTIVES

Pricing objectives can be grouped under two main headings:

- financial return, e.g. maximising revenue, recovering an investment made (usually in developing the product)
- market-orientated, e.g. positioning, maintaining brand image, building market share, enticing customers to the store, rewarding customers for loyalty.

The financial objectives are largely inward-looking, while the market-orientated ones look to the external environment. Some of these objectives are really short term, e.g. 'enticing the customer into the store', and some should normally be long term, e.g. 'maximising revenue'. There may also be an ethical element to the setting of prices, e.g. governments may make services affordable to target social groups, such as the low paid, even pricing on a sliding scale to encourage those on low incomes to take advantage of services such as school dinners or education. Some companies also deliberately keep prices low for specific groups, e.g. IKEA's flatpack houses were only made available to people with combined incomes of under £35,000.

There are numerous pricing techniques that are used to meet these objectives.

PRICING TECHNIQUES
STRATEGIES, TACTICS AND METHODS

Textbooks and commentators cannot seem to agree on which of the various ways of setting prices are strategies, tactics or methods. Some have apparently given up on categorisation altogether.

PWC: customer value based pricing strategies

Pricing strategy

In this book, a pricing *strategy* is defined as being medium to long term and having a significant impact on the company's overall marketing strategy, or even corporate strategy. A pricing *tactic* is defined as a short-term action, or one with limited impact beyond the product being priced. Pricing *methods* are mechanical ways to set prices. They are a good starting point, or a good way to check that the price arrived at is sane, but, marketers would argue, not a way to set prices in isolation. It is also important to check out the ways price can be used to greater effect via a specific strategy or tactic. Some pricing techniques, e.g. market skimming (see later in this chapter), could be used as strategies (longer term) or tactics (shorter term).

PRICING METHODS

There are three key elements to price setting: competitors' prices, customers' perceptions of the product's value and costs.

A business's costs must be covered, but too great an emphasis on costs in a pricing strategy leads to missed opportunities. It is vital to take account of what is going on in the market. What are competitors charging? How much do customers want to pay? Exhibit 10.2 shows the key influencers on the pricing decisions.

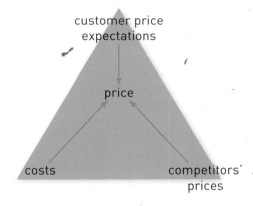

EXHIBIT 10.2 Price setting

For a car manufacturer, there would be substantial costs in buying the materials required to make the cars. In the long run, these must be covered by the pricing of the car or the company will be out of business. Costs of supplies are an important consideration. The company buys in engine parts, sheets of metal, mirrors, etc., and then adds value to them by turning them into a functional car. They have to pay wages, rents and other bills in order to do this. So additional cost is incurred here. But then there is the question of value. Is the car only worth the sum of its parts? Of course not, otherwise why bother to put it together at all? It is worth more as a car than as a pile of materials and sub-assemblies, but how much more?

Competitors and customers have a key role to play in determining how much value has been added by turning the parts into a car. Is it a better or worse car than the competition's? How much are customers prepared to give up for it?

Most methods of pricing can be classified as either:

- market-based pricing (taking account of competitors and/or customers), or
- cost-based pricing.

MARKET-BASED PRICING

There are a large number of different market-based pricing methods, including:

- customer value pricing
- psychological price barriers
- auctions
- going-rate pricing
- tenders
- cartels.

Customer value pricing

customer value pricing

pricing a product or service according to the value placed on it by the customer

A product is only worth what someone will pay for it. The price is the company's estimate of the product's value. The customer may place a different value on the product. The trick is to make these two concepts of value balance, so that the firm is paid a fair price and the customer gets a good deal. This is a difficult balancing act. The seller will have invested a great deal of time, money, effort and creativity into its offerings. They have great value. The customer has many choices as to what to buy, and will consider their relative values. The seller can increase the value of its offering in a number of ways, e.g. through added features, better quality, a superior brand image, better service, home delivery. Increases in value are usually created through the other elements of the marketing mix – one of the reasons why it is so important to coordinate all marketing mix elements.

In customer value pricing, the price is based on what customers value a product at, i.e. what it is worth to them, rather than on what it cost the firm to make. If the balance between value and price is right, then customers will see that the price they are being asked to pay is justified even if that price is higher than the competition's.

ACTIVITY

How much are you prepared to pay for:

- lunch
- a jacket
- a pair of shoes
- a concert ticket?

Work out your own psychological price barriers. Then, the next time you buy such things, see how well the products available match up to your budget.
    You are likely to find a range of prices, e.g. lunch can cost anything from a sandwich at less than £2 to a fancy restaurant meal at £50 plus. Where do you fit in this range and what affects the price barriers you have identified? (See also 'Product line pricing' later in this chapter.)

Psychological price barriers

psychological price barrier

the top price a customer is prepared to pay

psychological pricing

the idea that prices ending in certain numbers (usually 9s) appear to be considerably cheaper than slightly higher ones, e.g. £9.99 seems more than 1p less than £10.00

Many people have a budget in mind before they go out to buy something. They may exceed the budget by a little, but there will be a price beyond which they will not go. That is their psychological price barrier. Some marketers set prices by conducting research to establish just where that barrier is. Then they set prices just below it.

Psychological pricing is a related concept (see 'Pricing tactics' below).

Auctions

Auctions used to be the preserve of art galleries and antique dealers, but the advent of the Internet has changed all that. Now auctions are a way to get products cheaper – online.

Bandyopadhyay et al. (2001) attribute the success of auctions on the Internet to simplicity, real-time price negotiation and the large number of participants. There are a number of variants on the traditional auction, in which buyers keep bidding until only one is left in, e.g. some goods are sold by 'reverse auction'. At a reverse auction, suppliers make the bids, undercutting each other, and the customer takes the final offer and so gets the best price. (For a full explanation of Internet auctions, see www.ebay.co.uk.)

Going-rate pricing

Competitors' prices have to be taken into account when setting prices. Charge twice as much as the competition and the firm will make no sales; charge half as much and it is missing an opportunity for profit (as well as possibly sending the wrong message about quality).

Some established firms are considered to be price leaders or price makers: they set the prices that the others, the price followers or price takers, follow. Price leaders are often the largest competitors in the market but sometimes a smaller company is recognised as having particular expertise, and even larger firms will follow its lead. This happens quite often in the financial services industry.

Going-rate pricing is one of the most common ways of choosing a price. It is especially favoured by new entrants to a market who need to make sure that they set their prices at a realistic level in comparison to those of the competition, and who have no track record to guide them.

Advantages of going-rate pricing are that it:

- avoids price wars (see below)
- makes use of the expertise of more established firms.

Disadvantages are that it:

- assumes that competitors got their sums right and set the best price – they may not have
- firms have different cost bases; it is quite possible that Coca-Cola can charge 23p (€0.32) per can and still make a profit whereas it may cost a new competitor 25p (€0.35) just to make the drink and can it.

Tenders

There are numerous types of tender, but the basic premise of all of them is that a number of firms bid for a contract. The contract is usually awarded to the lowest bidder although this is not always the case – non-price criteria may be taken into account. This type of pricing is common in government, particularly for public works contracts such as road or bridge building, where the tender system is seen as being open and above reproach.

Tenders may be by sealed bid (when a firm does not know what the others are bidding) or open.

Cartels

A cartel is a group of companies that get together and fix prices between them. Cartels are most common in oligopolistic markets where they justify their joint price setting by saying that it avoids price wars. When companies get together and choose a mutually acceptable price, it tends to be higher than it would have been had they had to compete with one another. So it is cosy and safe for business, but not always good news for consumers.

---

price leaders
set prices for a market; other firms follow their lead

price followers
firms that set their prices in accordance with others in the market, notably a price leader

price war
two or more firms keep undercutting each other in an attempt to build market share until one or the other backs off or goes out of business

tender (tendering)
where firms bid for a contract and, usually, the lowest priced bid wins

cartel
a group of companies that get together and fix prices between them

oligopoly
a situation where the market is dominated by a small number of very large companies

Probably the most famous cartel is OPEC (the Organisation of the Petroleum Exporting Countries). In the 1970s and 1980s, OPEC set the prices for the world's crude oil. Now there are other countries involved, but the 14 OPEC members (Algeria, Angola, Ecuador, Gabon, Indonesia, Iran, Iraq, Kuwait, Libya, Nigeria, Qatar, Saudi Arabia, United Arab Emirates, Venezuela) still 'ensure the stabilization of oil markets in order to secure an efficient, economic and regular supply of petroleum to consumers, a steady income to producers and a fair return on capital for those investing in the petroleum industry' (OPEC, n.d.).

Cartels are considered an anti-competitive practice and are illegal in the EU; however, that did not stop five truck producers colluding to fix prices and coordinate the introduction of new emissions technologies for 14 years. In 2016, they were fined €2.93 billion, sending a clear message that such practices would not be tolerated (European Commission, 2016).

research focus

Jobber, D. and Shipley, D. (2012) 'Marketing-orientated pricing: understanding and applying factors that discriminate between successful high and low price strategies', *European Journal of Marketing*, 46 (11/12): 1647–70.
The paper aims to test seven marketing-orientated factors that have the potential to discriminate between the setting of successful high and low prices. The study supports a marketing-orientated theory of price determination based on market, customer and competitor factors.

COST-BASED PRICING

Many marketers warn against placing too great an emphasis on costs when setting prices. However, they are important. If a firm does not cover its costs, then, sooner or later, it will go out of business. The downside of focusing on covering costs is that the firm may miss out on profit, but determining the cost of a product may not be straightforward. There are different types of cost as shown below.

Types of costs

total costs

all product costs, i.e. direct + indirect, or fixed + variable

direct costs

costs that are clearly due to the making of a particular product, e.g. cocoa and sugar are direct costs of chocolate bars

indirect costs

costs that cannot be attributed to a particular product as they are not directly associated with its production or sale, e.g. the running costs of the chief executive's car

- total costs – the sum of all costs
- direct costs – costs that are clearly due to the making of a particular product, e.g. cocoa and sugar are direct costs of Cadbury's Dairy Milk
- indirect costs – costs that cannot be attributed to one particular product as they are not directly associated with any one product's production or sale, e.g. the running costs of the chief executive's car
- variable costs – costs that go up as production increases, e.g. electricity bills
- fixed costs – costs that do not vary with production, e.g. insurance premiums.

Costs are either fixed or variable *and* either direct or indirect. Examples include:

- electricity is usually a variable, indirect cost – it costs more as production increases, but it is hard to work out just how much electricity went into the making of a particular product
- raw materials are variable, direct costs – you need more flour to make more cakes, and you still know just how much flour it takes to make a cake

- rent is usually a fixed, indirect cost – it does not vary month on month, and contributes to a number of different products

- highly specialised machinery may be a fixed, direct cost – the nozzle that pipes the perfect star on top of the coffee creams in the chocolate factory, perhaps.

Cost plus pricing

Cost and price are different. Costs are monies that a firm has to pay to its suppliers. Prices are what they charge customers for the products/services they sell. The 50p a customer pays for a chocolate bar is a cost to him or her, but a price to the shop that sells it. Clearly, prices should be higher than costs – at least most of the time.

There are a number of pricing methods that take the costs of making the goods, or of delivering the service, and then add on an amount to arrive at a price. It is therefore now necessary to take a slight detour into accounting, to see briefly how cost plus pricing is used in making decisions.

Cost plus pricing methods include:

- mark-up pricing
- full-cost pricing
- contribution pricing.

Mark-up pricing

This pricing method is common in retail as it is a relatively straightforward way for a shop to set prices: calculate the direct cost of the product, then add on an amount to cover indirect costs and provide a profit. For example, a boutique buys in dresses for £50 each. The £50 is the direct cost, but there are other costs involved in running the shop (heating, lighting, rent, wages, etc.). To price the dresses, it uses a simple formula, perhaps adding on 300% of the direct cost. This should mean that each dress sold covers *all* costs, and makes a profit.

direct cost	£ 50.00
mark-up	£150.00
selling price	£200.00

Advantages of mark-up pricing are that:

- it is a relatively simple way for retailers (and some other businesses) to set their prices
- unlike full-cost pricing (see below), mark-up takes account of demand. Retailers do not apply the same mark-up to all products – they are usually adept at varying prices to take account of the popularity of products.

mark-up pricing
the price is set by adding a percentage (a mark-up) to the direct cost

Disadvantages are that:

- the mark-up may not be high enough to cover all the indirect costs, especially if some products remain unsold
- a retailer knows the (direct) cost of products but it is not always so simple; direct cost per unit varies depending upon the level produced, e.g. there may be a discount available for buying a larger quantity, so costs come down (economies of scale).

So we need to know the demand for the product before we can set the price, and demand is largely determined by price. What output level shall we pick to get our cost base? It is a vicious circle (see Exhibit 10.3).

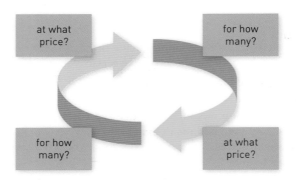

EXHIBIT 10.3 The vicious circle of price setting

Full-cost pricing

This is also known as absorption costing.

Full-cost pricing is as it sounds: work out the total unit cost (i.e. the *total* cost per product) of making the product, then add a further amount, and that's the price. For example, the local pizzeria adds up the costs of all the ingredients on its four seasons pizza, adds in an amount for wages and the running costs of the restaurant, then adds 100% for profit.

per pizza	direct costs	= £0.75
	indirect costs	= £1.25
	total cost	= £2.00
	+100%	= £4.00, so that's the price

Advantages of full-cost pricing are:

* all production costs are covered by the price
* cost increases get passed on to the customer in the form of a price increase, so profit margins (in percentage terms) remain the same
* it may be the only way to price a job for which the amount of work cannot be predicted, i.e. the price is set retroactively, when all the costs are known, e.g. for a research and development project.

Disadvantages are as follows:

* direct costs, such as ingredients, are easy enough to allocate to a product (a baker knows how much flour was used in each loaf), but if a salesperson sells a range of products, of differing values, how much of his or her salary, company car costs, etc. should be added to the cost of each item? And just imagine how complicated that would

be to work out for each of a thousand products sold by a hundred salespeople, all on different salaries. Then there's the other staff, buildings costs, etc. This allocation of indirect costs to a product is often quite arbitrary – what percentage of the chief executive's car costs should be allocated to each Dream bar?

- it ignores the market forces of demand and supply (although changing the profit margin can help to account for this) and the price sensitivity of customers – they may be prepared to pay more, or they may not be prepared to pay that price at all, in which case a way would have to be found to reduce the costs

- if a firm gets more efficient (i.e. fixed costs per unit go down – perhaps because you have installed more modern equipment), then their price goes down too, but if the product was selling well at a higher price, why lower it? In practice, a firm might not lower prices in this circumstance, but that would mean that it was no longer naively adhering to the firm's cost plus pricing policy and had allowed some market awareness to creep into its price setting by adjusting its profit margins.

Contribution pricing

Mark-up pricing uses direct costs as a basis on which to set the price. Full-cost pricing uses the total cost as a basis. Contribution pricing is based on variable costs.

It is being included here with the other cost-based pricing methods, but this one is rather different. Really, within the classifications given earlier in the chapter, contribution pricing is usually used as a pricing tactic. It is something that can only be used in the short term – usually just for one order. Try to use it all the time, on all products, and the company will rack up the losses and go under. However, it is also a way to price loss leaders (see below).

The idea behind contribution pricing is that, as long as the product is sold for more than its variable cost, it is making a contribution towards the fixed costs and profits.

Contribution pricing is often used for one-off orders. For example, the Alpha Company's monthly fixed costs (FC) are £3,000 and variable costs (VC) are £3 per product. It regularly sells 2,000 alarm clocks each month.

So:

fixed cost per product, i.e. average fixed cost (AFC) = the fixed costs divided by the sales volume, i.e.

$$= \frac{£3000}{2000} = £1.50$$

total cost per unit $= \text{AFC} + \text{VC}$

$$= £1.50 + £3.00 = £4.50$$

ACTIVITY

Using the full-cost pricing method, work out the price for a box of chocolates when:

fixed costs (rent, etc.)	= £40,000 per month
variable costs (ingredients, etc.)	= £1 per box
sales volume	= 100,000 per month

The accounts department has set 25% as the profit margin.

(The answer is at the end of the chapter.)

---

total costs

all product costs, i.e. direct + indirect, or fixed + variable

contribution pricing

pricing method based on variable costs

variable costs

costs that go up as production increases and down when it decreases, e.g. electricity bills

loss leader

a product that is sold at a loss, usually to tempt shoppers to make other purchases

contribution

the amount of money remaining from the sale, when the variable costs have been paid

fixed costs

costs that do not vary with production levels, e.g. insurance premiums

A new customer, Beta Holdings Ltd, wants to buy 500 clocks, but is only prepared to pay £4.00 per clock. This will not cover the total cost of making the clock, but it will cover the variable costs – anything over £3.00 makes a contribution. Should Alpha accept the order? It depends on:

- whether the fixed costs are actually already covered by other orders

- whether they have enough capacity to make the new order

- how much goodwill the acceptance of this order will generate – will Beta Holdings turn into a regular customer, maybe at a better price?

- how much bad feeling may be created if other, regular, customers find out and feel over-charged.

This is similar to the technique that economists call marginal cost pricing. Marginal cost is the cost of making *additional* units. So, in the example above, Alpha would work out what additional cost was involved in making the extra 500 clocks – it would need components, would use more electricity, and perhaps would have to pay some overtime. Often, these additional costs will be the same as the variable costs of the order.

However, it is possible that Alpha would have to buy more machinery and, in that case, the additional cost (marginal cost) would be more than just the variable cost as additional fixed costs would be incurred too.

Advantages of contribution pricing are that:

- in a highly competitive business, a company may have the opportunity to achieve significant extra business by putting in a low bid

- it may mean keeping workers on when otherwise they would have been laid off, causing hardship for them and their families

- it keeps workers' skills honed – if they spend time idle, or doing other work, they are likely to get out of practice and will not be so efficient in the future

- if you let workers go, your competitors may snap up the best of them

- idle machinery sometimes seizes up and may require more maintenance in the future

- idle machinery is a wasted investment and still costs money in service agreements, etc.

A related concept is that of loss leaders (see below).

TARGET PROFIT PRICING

It would be useful for the firm to know how much, i.e. what sales volume, it has to sell in order to cover its costs. Then it can see if it is likely that the product will sell that many, and so if it is worthwhile. Clearly, price is one of the main determinants of how many products people will buy. The law of supply and demand (as well as common sense) tells us that higher prices result in lower sales, and vice versa.

The firm can work out the required sales volume, *at a given price*, that will cover costs. This is called the breakeven point.

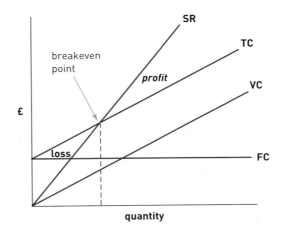

Key
SR = sales revenue
TC = total cost
VC = variable cost
FC = fixed cost

EXHIBIT 10.4 Breakeven

Breakeven analysis

Breakeven analysis can be done graphically (see Exhibit 10.4) or as a calculation.

A breakeven chart is a clear, visual way of analysing a firm's profit at various levels of output, and a set price. By drawing a new chart, managers can see the impact of a change in price on the firm's profits, breakeven point and margin of safety. If costs change, a new chart will also show the impact of that. Increases in costs will push the breakeven point higher; increases in price will result in a lower breakeven point.

At any given price, the firm will break even at the point where total cost (TC) = total sales revenue (SR). Further graphs can be drawn to work out the breakeven points at different prices.

If it sells a larger quantity than the breakeven point, it makes a profit. If sales fall below breakeven, it makes a loss.

If you would like to try drawing a breakeven chart, have a go at the additional activity at the end of this chapter (Appendix: Additional cost-based pricing activity).

Margin of safety

If a firm sells more than is required to break even, then that extra quantity is referred to as its 'margin of safety'. In Exhibit 10.5, a firm sells 100,000 products, but breaks even when it sells 75,000. The margin of safety is 25,000. The significance of this is that the firm knows how many sales it can afford to lose before it hits crisis point.

Setting a target profit

When firms use target profit pricing, they want to set a price that will result in a defined overall profit. This method of price setting is popular with the privatised utilities, which have a duty to provide fair prices and not to make excess profits. On a normal breakeven chart, firms set a target profit by finding the point at which the difference between sales revenue and total cost equals the target profit. Then they simply draw a line down to the quantity axis and read off the sales volume required to achieve that target profit (see Exhibit 10.6).

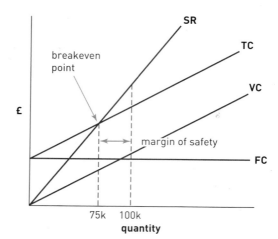

Key

SR = sales revenue
TC = total cost
VC = variable cost
FC = fixed cost

EXHIBIT 10.5 Margin of safety

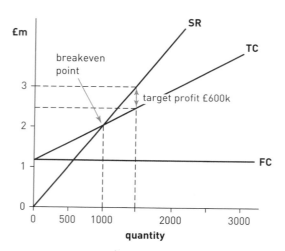

EXHIBIT 10.6 Roadrunner Co. target profit chart

Target profit pricing can also be calculated. The formula for this is:

$$\frac{\text{fixed cost} + \text{profit target}}{\text{contribution per item}}$$

= required level of output

For example, the Roadrunner Co. wants to make £600,000 profit on its bicycles. Fixed costs total £1.2 million, while variable costs are £800 per bike. The bike is priced at £2000.

| contribution | = selling price – variable cost |
| | = £2000 – £800 = £1200 |

$$\frac{1,200,000 + £600,000}{£1200} = 1500 \text{ bicycles}$$

So it knows that if it sells 1500 bicycles at a price of £2000 each, then it will make £600,000 profit (see Exhibit 10.7). Alternatively, it could read this figure off a breakeven chart by finding the point at which the SR and the TC lines are £600,000 apart.

Remember that a breakeven chart works for one price only – you need to draw a new chart to try out the profit target at a new price.

Drawbacks to breakeven analysis include:

- it assumes that all the products made will be sold
- it is a static model – if costs change, then a new chart has to be drawn
- as with all analysis tools, its effectiveness depends upon the quality of the figures it uses: rubbish in = rubbish out
- it is actually more complicated than the example in Exhibit 10.6 shows because fixed costs are not always linear. They can increase (e.g. when the capacity of a machine is reached and a new one has to be bought) (see Exhibit 10.7).

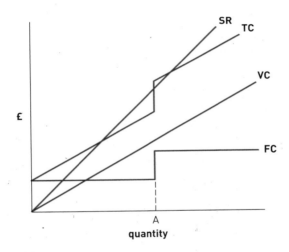

EXHIBIT 10.7 Stepped breakeven chart

PRICING STRATEGIES
NEW PRODUCT PRICING STRATEGIES

The price is one of the most difficult things to get right for a new product. Many products fail because they are either too expensive, and therefore do not sell, or too cheap and so the company is unable to meet its costs. Small businesses often charge too little for their products and it is one of the reasons that so many of them fail. It is much harder to explain a price increase to customers than it is to explain a decrease. It is often difficult to raise a price once a product has been launched on to the market as customers by then have a view of the right price and are reluctant to pay more. This is why so many new products declare that they have an introductory price. This leads customers to expect a price rise in the near future.

The two major new pricing strategies are:

1   market penetration
2   market skimming.

Market penetration

When a company first enters a market, it needs to build market share. A low price should tempt people to try the new product. If they like it, they will buy it again. So a product trial may lead to product adoption. The main objective of a penetration pricing strategy is to establish the product in the market: to build a customer base.

Advantages of market penetration pricing are that:

* it encourages people to try a product
* it encourages retailers to build up stocks – then they will not have room for competitors' products.

Disadvantages are that:

* it may provoke retaliation from existing companies
* it is not suitable for products with a short product life cycle as there may not be enough time to recover from the initial, low revenue.

The big disadvantage to the consumer is, of course, that the price does not stay low forever. New credit cards offer low, or no, interest. Then, when they are established, the 'introductory offer' disappears and they hope that their cardholders will not bother to change cards again. Many of the broadband service companies (such as BT and TalkTalk) and TV subscription companies (such as Virgin Media and Sky) also offer introductory prices for the first few months with a price increase specified thereafter.

Market skimming

This is really the opposite of penetration pricing. Firms following a skimming strategy set their prices higher than they need to, in order to maximise profits. The key to the success of a market skimming strategy is that there should be no significant competition – otherwise people will just buy the cheaper alternative. The company may be launching an entirely new product or entering a new market.

This strategy works well where:

* there is insufficient market capacity and competitors cannot make more of the product
* there are no competitors (either because they do not exist at all or, perhaps, they have no distribution in that particular geographic area)
* demand for the goods in question is relatively price inelastic
* a high price is seen as an indicator of high quality.

Advantages of market skimming are:

- early cash recovery – this is particularly important if this is a new product and the firm has made a significant investment in its development; it needs to get its money back before other firms copy the invention and the market becomes more crowded. This is something that pharmaceutical companies are particularly keen to take advantage of before their patent protection runs out.

Disadvantages are that:

- there is a high danger of encouraging other firms to enter the market – they see high profits being made and they want to make them too
- depending upon the type of product and the market in question, there may be an ethical issue over charging high prices, e.g. for prescription drugs, or in less-developed countries.

GENERAL PRICING STRATEGIES

General pricing strategies are:

- prestige pricing
- pre-emptive pricing
- product line pricing
- price discrimination.

Prestige pricing

Prestige pricing sets a high price for a product. Unlike price skimming, this is an ongoing strategy – the product stays expensive throughout its life. The high price is designed to associate an image of quality and high status with the product. This high price is itself an important motivator for consumers. Customers with higher incomes are less price sensitive and more interested in buying high-quality, prestigious products that enhance their image. Promotional strategies revolve around these aspects of the product, helping to justify the high price in the customer's mind. Typical prestige brands include Chanel, IBM, Bang & Olufsen, Cartier and BMW.

Pre-emptive pricing

A company following a pre-emptive pricing strategy sets low prices to deter new entrants to the market. This is especially suitable in markets where there are few other barriers to entry, e.g. the company does not hold a patent and/or entry costs are low. (For more on barriers to entry, see Chapter 12.)

Pre-emptive pricing should not be confused with predatory pricing (see 'Pricing tactics' below). Pre-emptive pricing is a perfectly legitimate strategy, whereas predatory pricing, which sets prices below costs in order to drive another firm out of business, is illegal in many countries including Britain.

prestige pricing
pricing a product high in order to enhance its status

pre-emptive pricing
setting prices relatively low in order to deter others from entering a market

predatory pricing
also known as **destroyer pricing** or extinction pricing, it is when a dominant company sells products at a loss with the intention of driving a rival firm out of the market

Rolls-Royce: a prestige product sold at a prestige price and here being used to provide a special service.

© Dave Pickton

The calculation and allocation of costs to particular products are not always straightforward and a company accused of predatory pricing may have a defence against such accusations. The use of loss leader pricing (again, see 'Pricing tactics') also complicates the issue.

Product line pricing

Many companies develop product lines, rather than just single products, and these lines may be named and branded distinctly. A company's product range may contain a number of product lines, e.g. Ford produces the Ka, Fiesta, Focus, Fusion, Mondeo, Galaxy, Maverick ... and all of these lines have a number of models with different engine sizes, different finishes and different features.

The product manager has to set price steps within the product lines. How much more will a customer pay for a Focus with a 1.6-litre engine rather than a 1.4? How much extra should be charged for a Zetec? There will be some overlap between the top of one line and the bottom of the next one up, but how much can they overlap without the top of the line losing business?

Some sellers use well-established price points for the products in their line: so a restaurant's main courses may be premier price (for a particularly special dish, such as lobster), top price (for more expensive ingredients such as entrecote steak), mid-price (for most dishes) and low price (perhaps for vegetarian options).

Price discrimination

Price discrimination can be dangerous, but can also be very profitable. It relies heavily upon market segmentation (see Chapter 4). Price discriminators charge different prices *for the same products* to different market segments. The most common segments used are time, geography and age. Some examples are outlined below.

- Time-based discrimination:
    - many train services are more expensive if you want to travel before 9.30 am
    - British Airways' return economy air fare from London to Sydney is over a thousand pounds more over Christmas, than it is in October (BA, n.d.)
    - many entertainment venues give a discount if you book in advance.

- Geographic discrimination (though exchange rates need to be taken into account when comparing prices in different countries):
    - CDs are cheaper in the USA than they are in many European countries
    - cars are often cheaper in mainland Europe than they are in Britain and cheaper in the north of Britain than in the south
    - Some less developed nations are allowed to buy drugs for a fraction of their normal price.

- Age discrimination:
    - children travel on public transport at reduced prices
    - OAPs get discounts on cinema and theatre tickets
    - if you are 27 or under, you can get a one-month Inter-rail ticket, valid for trains in 30 European countries, for about two-thirds of the price that over-27s pay (InterRail, n.d.).

The key to successful price discrimination is that customers should not be able to move between segments. It is surprising how many teenagers will happily take a couple of years off their age in order to get a cheaper bus fare. If people can move themselves into a cheaper segment, they will.

Dynamic pricing is a form of price discrimination that makes use of sophisticated data analysis to adjust the price of online goods and services offered to individual customers on a minute by minute basis, sometimes within the same browsing session. All kinds of data can be used to personalise an offer:

- Cookies that store information about browsing history and previous purchases can identify return customers and encourage them to buy again by offering a better deal. Alternatively new customers could be lured in with lower prices on the first few purchases.

- Search terms and patterns may indicate a customer's readiness to buy. For example an initial search for 'wireless headphones' indicates someone in the early stages of the decision-making process. Evidence of hopping back and forth between competitor sites or a search for 'best price Bose Soundsport' suggests a credit card is poised for purchase. Customers who check flight prices frequently may see the price go up. This might suggest tickets are selling out but more likely, the firm is taking the opportunity to charge a higher price to a determined customer.

- Postcode information can be used to identify customers living in affluent areas who can afford to pay more.

- Location information can also be used to adjust prices where there is strong local competition.

dynamic pricing makes use of customer profile and web browsing data to adjust online prices on a user per user basis

Online pricing strategies

Easyjet's dynamic pricing

research focus

Shapiro, S.L, Drayer, J. and Dwyer, B. (2016) 'Examining consumer perceptions of demand-based ticket pricing in sport', *Sport Marketing Quarterly*, **25 (1): 34–46.**

Dynamic ticket pricing (DTP), a new revenue management (RM) strategy in sport, has grown in popularity. This study examined consumer perceptions of demand-based pricing over time, to assess the influence of attitudes on perceived value and purchase intentions. Results indicated that time, team performance expectations, fairness perceptions, seat location and ticket market influenced perceived value of the ticket.

In the European Union, borders are easy to cross, and there is no duty on goods brought in for personal use. Europeans frequently visit neighbouring countries to get a better deal – on a car, on alcohol and cigarettes, on Christmas presents. It gets harder to maintain different prices in different countries when people are able to travel freely.

The Internet has been a major blow to the price discriminators. Now, consumers can surf the web looking for bargains. They can check out prices all over the world and either buy online or use their superior pricing knowledge to drive down high street prices.

INTERNATIONAL PRICING

All the pricing methods, tactics and strategies covered in this chapter are valid in international marketing too, but here they are overlaid with all the difficulties of competing in a foreign environment. Goods and services sold in another country normally have to be priced in that country's currency. However, in business-to-business (b2b) deals, there may be arguments for pricing a contract in either the buyer's or the seller's currency – or even in a third-party currency such as the US dollar. Rates of exchange fluctuate and so it can be difficult for a company to maintain consistency in its pricing across countries: €120 may equate to £80 one day and £75 the next. Clearly, if the price has been set at the level that represents a fair exchange, then such fluctuations are not desirable.

PARALLEL IMPORTING (THE GREY MARKET)

parallel importing
when someone outside of the official supply chain sells goods that were bought abroad (usually more cheaply)

grey importing
when someone outside the official supply chain buys goods (usually very cheaply) in another country for sale in their home country

Adapting prices to suit local income levels may sound like good business practice but it does have a downside. If a product is cheaper in one country than in others, then there is a danger that people will buy it in the cheaper country and then export it themselves to the more expensive one. Companies sometimes find themselves competing against their own products. In order to prevent this, either the product must be varied or the price must be pitched at a level that makes parallel importing (also called grey importing) unattractive. Different prices can still be charged so long as the difference is small enough that the additional cost of exporting means that it is not worthwhile. Many companies go to the courts to try and stop parallel importers but this is often unsuccessful and always time-consuming and expensive. It is better to avoid the problem entirely through judicious use of the marketing mix.

Sometimes companies set different prices in different countries deliberately in order to maximise profits (see 'Price discrimination' above) and sometimes prices differ as a result of exchange rate changes or the actions of third parties, such as retailers. Varying prices across the world, and particularly across regions, such as the EU, can cause significant problems for a company. For example, they may have a negative effect on the product's image or they may provide the opportunity for parallel importing, i.e. when trade customers buy in a cheaper country and then import the goods themselves, thus undercutting the manufacturer and undermining their positioning strategies.

global focus: cheap imports

Where do they come from, those piles of branded goods in the local market? How can Superdrug afford to sell perfume so cheaply? How does Hong Kong based www.strawberry.net ship premium beauty products hundreds of thousands of miles to customers in Europe and still undercut local retailers? Sometimes the goods are legitimate supplies – perhaps excess stock or the end of lines that the manufacturers are selling off. Sometimes their route to market is murkier – grey in fact. Grey importing is when someone outside the official supply chain buys goods, often in another country, for sale back home. Some of these products come from less-developed countries where prices have to be lower (otherwise people could not afford to buy them). This price discrimination tempts buyers from the more expensive markets who know they can then substantially undercut the manufacturer's recommended price and still make a profit.

There are further complexities to setting prices in foreign currencies:

- it may be harder to get reliable market information as the company is less familiar with this foreign market or because the information does not exist in the form that the company is used to (many third-world countries do not collect the market data that more developed countries do)

- prices in different currencies, and in multiple markets, require a lot of management time to monitor and to compare to competitive prices
- pricing laws vary from country to country (e.g. many Muslim countries do not allow credit, some governments will not allow foreign companies to undercut local ones).

PRICING TACTICS

Shorter-term, limited impact or special situation pricing options include:

- predatory pricing
- psychological pricing
- loss leaders
- promotional pricing and discounts.

PREDATORY PRICING (DESTROYER PRICING, EXTINCTION PRICING)

This pricing tactic is considered an anti-competitive practice in a number of countries, including the UK, the USA and the EU, so it is against the law; however, it is notoriously hard to prove).

> Predatory pricing occurs when a dominant undertaking incurs losses with the intention of removing a rival and/or deterring other potential competitors. (Office of Fair Trading, 2002)

Google has been the subject of a number of lawsuits over the free supply of Android and its search engine. The larger firm can carry this because it benefits from economies of scale. There have been some notorious and controversial examples of predatory pricing in the airline business and also in publishing but they are hard to prove and prosecutions are rarely successful.

digital focus: Microsoft vs. Netscape

A long time ago, when Microsoft was still a relatively small company, it started giving away Internet Explorer. In fact, it was argued that in some cases Microsoft effectively paid people to use Internet Explorer in preference to their existing browser, by giving them free software and marketing assistance. The strategy was crucial to the company's success in taking the market leadership away from arch-rival Netscape, which was, up until then, the most popular web browser. 'Even though Netscape constantly revised its pricing structure, it was impossible to stay competitive with "better than free"', testified Netscape CEO James L. Barksdale in the Justice Department's anti-trust suit against Microsoft.

Sources: France and Hamm (1998)

PSYCHOLOGICAL PRICING

A surprisingly large number of products are priced at X pounds and 99 pence or X euros and 99 cents: £4.99 and £9.99 are particularly popular prices. The idea, of course, is to fool the customer into thinking that the item is cheaper than it really is: £1000 sounds so much more than £999 – or so the theory goes.

This links to psychological price barriers (see above). If a customer's top price for a bunch of supermarket flowers is £3.00, then it makes sense to price some at £2.99. The customer feels he or she got a good deal and the supermarket has only lost out on a penny.

LOSS LEADERS

This tactic is often employed by retailers as a means of getting customers into a shop. Getting customers into the shop is a major retail objective as, once inside, they are more susceptible to the in-store promotional displays and impulse buys. A loss leader is a product, prominently displayed and advertised, that is priced well below its normal price, even below its cost to the seller. It is a lure.

Advantages are that:

- the lower price provides a competitive advantage
- this can build the brand if people associate the company with value for money
- there may be opportunities to sell complementary products, upgrades or follow-on goods/services, e.g. a maintenance agreement
- it stimulates word-of-mouth promotion.

How can businesses afford to do this? Well, as with contribution pricing this is not a tactic that can be employed for everything. Profits from the other items on sale have to cover the losses of the loss leader. Some retailers even put their other prices up in order to compensate, so watch out.

PROMOTIONAL PRICING AND DISCOUNTS

Seasonal sales and special offers are types of sales promotion.

© Dave Pickton

Short-term special offers are really sales promotions rather than price reductions, so see Chapter 8, which covers marketing communications, for discussion of those. Discounts are often part of the pricing policy, especially if offered as a matter of course, for a reason. For example, many firms give a discount for bulk purchase.

A number of supermarkets give a fixed percentage reduction to customers who buy six bottles of wine or offer six bottles for the price of five. Clearly, this is to encourage people to buy more, and, if they do buy more, then the supermarkets can afford to charge a little less and still make a good profit.

Many restaurants have a table d'hôte menu: two, three or even four courses for a fixed price. The restaurant can afford to offer diners a good deal because this helps with its ordering and planning. If it knows that a lot of people will order the same dish, then there is less waste, and so less cost.

ethical focus: not so happy hour

'The binge drinking girl who suffered liver failure at just 14' (*Daily Mail*)

'Italian children's binge drinking blamed on Britain' (*Daily Telegraph*)

It's not something the UK really wants to be known for, but some British youngsters are notorious for their binge drinking. Doctors worry that youthful drinkers are heading for long-term health problems. Local communities and police see them as troublemakers or potential victims of unscrupulous attackers. Pubs and clubs see a lucrative business opportunity. So what can, or should, be done?

A number of government-funded promotional campaigns have tried to reach youngsters with messages about health risks, about personal danger when drink makes them vulnerable, and even about making them see how ridiculous drunks look. One ad showed a night out in reverse. A young woman with messed up hair and smudged make-up, wearing ripped clothes covered in drink and vomit stains, staggers out of her front door on broken heels. A young man pours curry down his chest, rips his clothes and beats himself up. The strap line reads: 'You wouldn't start a night like this so why end it that way?'

Taxes on alcohol are high, making prices higher. This is partly to make it less affordable and partly because the taxes on alcohol sales raise valuable revenue for the government. If people drank less, the Treasury would actually suffer. Even so, there is talk of raising prices further to discourage excess drinking.

There are rules governing the sale of alcohol. In the UK you have to have a licence to sell it. Only over-18s can buy it. It can only be drunk in designated places such as bars and restaurants. Some councils have now banned drinking in the street, for example. In Sweden, the rules are even stricter.

The UK has regulations governing alcohol advertising, e.g. advertising cannot suggest that having a drink makes you more attractive or more capable. It must not target young people and so all the actors or models must look over 25. The ads mustn't plug into youth culture – as some alcopops advertising used to do. In France, mass media alcohol advertising is banned altogether.

Drinks manufacturers have pledged to encourage more moderate drinking. Some cans and bottles carry advice to 'enjoy this drink sensibly'. Diageo, who makes brands such as Guinness and Smirnoff, has run sensible drinking campaigns (though with a rather smaller budget than their brand advertising campaigns). At the same time, pubs are running sales promotions designed to get young people to drink more: happy hours where drinks are half price, buy one get one free promotions, reduced prices, loyalty cards – you can probably think of others.

The government has tried several times to introduce stricter rules on alcohol sales promotions but most are resisted by the powerful drinks lobby. One such initiative involved setting a minimum price per unit of alcohol but, although a minimum pricing law was passed by the Scottish Parliament, they struggled to introduce it in the face of strong objections from the Scottish Whisky Association among others. Legislation was rejected for the rest of the UK.'

So what is the answer? Who is responsible? Should we rely on the drinks trade to police itself and on young people to take care of themselves? Should these promotions be banned? Should alcohol advertising be banned? Should the sale of alcohol be further restricted?

Would higher prices make young people drink less?

CHANGING THE PRICE

For many businesses, changing prices is expensive and time-consuming, so it is not something they want to do frequently. They have to rework the figures, recalculate VAT, redraw breakeven charts and work out new profit forecasts. Mail-order companies have to reprint their catalogues (the larger, glossier ones can cost as much as £5 or more each).

Restaurants have to reprint their menus. Shops have to change price labels and tills have to be reprogrammed.

So, given the trouble and expense involved, why would a firm change its prices? There are a number of possible, pressing reasons:

- a substantial change in business costs, perhaps because raw materials have become cheaper or new production techniques have become more efficient (a lower price can be charged), or materials or wages have become more expensive (an increase in prices is needed to compensate)

- an imbalance between supply and demand, i.e. customers want to buy more than the company has to sell; if there's a shortage, then prices may rise – possible causes include production hold-ups, such as strikes, shortages in materials, machine breakdowns, and the product suddenly becoming fashionable (the latest craze)

- an imbalance between supply and demand, i.e. customers do *not* want to buy as much as the company has to sell; if there's a surplus, then prices may fall – possible causes include a bumper harvest, a better product hitting the market, a health or safety scare (e.g. news stories about red meat being bad for you caused a massive drop in the sales of beef, pork and lamb)

- a change in competitors' marketing, e.g. a price decrease, a major advertising campaign, new stores opening up

- a changed economic situation, e.g. inflation

- new laws, new taxes or other government pressure, e.g. government-appointed regulators review the prices charged by privatised utilities (BT, water companies, gas and electricity providers)

- as a result of a change in the firm's marketing strategy, e.g. as part of a repositioning exercise

- an opportunity to make more sales revenue.

See 'Effect of elasticity on pricing decisions' below for how price can be manipulated to make more sales revenue: sometimes by raising prices and sometimes by lowering them.

PRICE WARS

A price war is a destructive spiral of reducing prices. It starts with one seller trying to undercut competitors by reducing prices. Others follow suit, meaning that the first firm has to reduce prices again in order to maintain its competitive advantage. So it goes on, sometimes until the weaker competitors (those with fewer financial resources) go out of business (see Exhibit 10.8).

In the short term, a price war is popular with consumers, but it is bad for business and, in the longer term, it is bad for consumers too.

Price cut! Blackberry

Businesses lose profits – they are cutting prices and, because others are matching their price cuts, they are not gaining market share. So they are just selling the same amount but at a reduced price. Eventually, either firms will go out of business, thus reducing consumer choice, or the firms involved will call a truce. Then they may have to put prices back even higher to recoup the profits they lost during the price war.

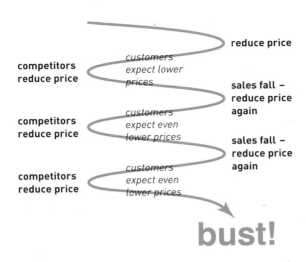

EXHIBIT 10.8 Price wars

digital focus: price matching, price beating

Listen to the TV ads, check out what's happening at the checkout. Shop in major supermarkets, online or in-store, and you will see how improved pricing research, technology and developments in EPOS (electronic point-of-sale) are affecting the price you pay at the till. Asda maintains that baskets of goods bought there are consistently cheaper than its rivals. Waitrose sends out money-off your total shop vouchers that vary according to how much you usually spend. They are finely judged to tempt you back more regularly to spend a little more. This claim is based on continuous independent market research. Sainsbury's tries to tempt you back to shop with them next time by printing out a whole variety of money-off coupons at the same time as your receipt; offers personalised to you based on your shopping habits and how much you have spent.

By contrast, Aldi embarked on a TV campaign in which they directly compared their own brands to **brand leaders** on a range of products. Rather than claiming they can offer the same brand at a lower price, they are saying, why buy the leading brand when the Aldi versions are as good if not better and will cost you less?

Such price comparisons, of course, are not confined to the high street and shopping centres. E-tailers can show price comparisons and offer deals even more easily. Shopping search engines and price comparison sites such as Kelkoo, Megashopbot, comparethemarket.com, moneysupermarket.com and pricerunner.com can search out the best prices for your chosen product. Go on to the Amazon website and a comprehensive listing of prices from different suppliers available through Amazon will be listed for you to choose between. Looking for a bargain? Try out the 'coupon' sites such as Groupon or Vouchercloud and Dealcloud.

brand leader

the brand with the highest sales within its particular market

Price comparison websites

PRICE ELASTICITY OF DEMAND

Price elasticity of demand is a measure of price sensitivity, i.e. it measures how many more, or fewer, products are sold when the price changes (see Exhibit 10.9).

Price elasticity

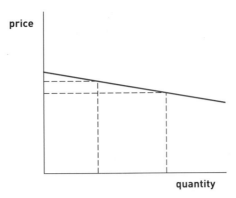

EXHIBIT 10.9 Price elasticity of demand

**price elasticity
of demand**

a measure of the degree to
which demand for a good
changes when its price is
changed

price inelastic

the percentage change
in demand is less than
the percentage change in
price, e.g. price goes up
by 10%, but the demand is
unaffected or is effected to a
lesser extent

We know from basic demand theory (and from common sense) that if the price of a product goes up, then fewer people will want to buy it, and vice versa. If a product's demand is very sensitive to a change in price, i.e. when the price goes up just a little, then far fewer products are sold and it is said to be price elastic. If the product's sales do not vary by much when the price changes, then its demand is said to be price inelastic (see Exhibit 10.10).

The steep curve is a price inelastic demand curve for a product such as cigarettes. As they are addictive, few people give up, even after a significant price increase.

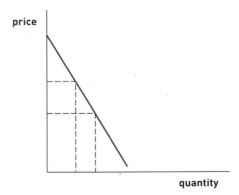

EXHIBIT 10.10 Price inelasticity of demand

CALCULATING ELASTICITY

In order to calculate elasticity, the price *change* and the quantity *change* first need to be expressed as *percentages* of the *original price and quantity*:

$$\text{Price elasticity} = \frac{\% \text{ change in quantity demanded}}{\% \text{ change in price}}$$

The bigger the answer, the greater the elasticity. For example, Le Café is considering increasing the price of its café latte. It wants to know whether this price increase will achieve the aim of increasing revenue. This depends on how many customers stop buying the lattes because they are too expensive. Last time it increased the price, it went from £1.50 to £1.65, and Le Café sold 480 cups a week instead of 600. Price elasticity can help.

Step 1: work out price change

£1.65 – £1.50

= 15p

Step 2: to express the price change as a percentage, divide the change in price by the original price then multiply by 100

15p/150p × 100

= 10%

Step 3: work out quantity change

480 – 600

= –120 (i.e. 120 fewer lattes sold)

Step 4: to express the quantity drop as a percentage, divide the change in quantity by the original quantity then multiply by 100

–120/600 × 100

= –20% (don't worry about the minus – it will be explained later)

Step 5: now substitute the figures into the elasticity equation

$$\frac{\% \text{ change in quantity demanded}}{\% \text{ change in price}}$$

–20/10

= –2

If the answer is a number bigger than 1 (ignore the minus sign for the moment), the product's demand is elastic. The product is significantly sensitive to price changes and raising the price will lead to a large fall in sales. This is the case with the café lattes.

So, if you are the marketing manager of Le Café, you need to be wary of increasing the price. A better way to increase revenue would be to *decrease* the price, then a lot more people will buy the product, and the increase in the volume of lattes sold will outweigh the price decrease per latte.

If the answer is below 1, then the product in question has an inelastic demand curve. Raising the price will not put many people off and revenue should increase.

The minus sign just means that when price rises, demand falls, i.e. they have a negative relationship. If demand rose with price (as in the case of some antiques, works of art, shares), then there would be no minus sign.

EFFECT OF ELASTICITY ON PRICING DECISIONS

Although few marketing managers work out the exact elasticity of their products' demand curves, elasticity is a concept that everyone involved in setting prices needs to be aware of. It is a vital consideration when changing prices as it determines whether lowering, or raising, prices is most likely to result in a revenue increase.

If a product has a price *inelastic* demand, then putting prices up will result in increased total sales revenue. Very few customers will stop buying the product, and their loss will be amply covered by the higher price that remaining customers pay.

If a product has a price *elastic* demand, then to increase revenue, the price should be lowered. Many more people will buy the product. So many that they will compensate for the lower price. Of course, competitor activities need to be taken into account as well.

Most essential goods (bread, petrol, power, etc.) are not particularly price sensitive (inelastic). Whereas inessentials (cream cakes, bubble bath, meals in restaurants, etc.) are usually more sensitive to price changes (elastic).

This can be seen from the demand curves in Exhibits 10.9 and 10.10. The shallow curve is for a product with a price elastic demand, i.e. it is very sensitive to a change in price. A small price change results in a large change in the quantity of the product demanded.

FACTORS AFFECTING THE PRICE ELASTICITY OF DEMAND

- *Necessity or luxury?* To an economist, a luxury is anything inessential: chocolate, bubble bath, ready-made meals, DVDs, etc. Really luxurious products, such as diamonds, sports cars, top designer clothes, etc., are termed prestige goods. Generally, necessities and prestige goods have inelastic demand, while luxuries have elastic demand.

- *Close substitutes*: if there are many alternative products available, then the demand will tend to be elastic. A substitute is something that a customer could buy instead, e.g. there are lots of different makes of ballpoint pen or pencils.

- *Habit forming?* If it is, then the demand will tend to be inelastic, e.g. cigarettes.

- *Time period*: many products are more responsive to changes in price (i.e. more elastic) in the long term. It takes a while for people to find an alternative, although they eventually will. Also, higher prices will encourage new competitors into the market, and so more choice will be available.

- *Frequency of purchase*: the more often customers buy the product, the more impact a price increase has on their budget, and therefore the more price elastic the demand is, e.g. a student may have a favourite brand of beer, but if the price goes up, he or she may have to switch to a cheaper one.

- *Customer loyalty*: if a brand is well established, then it may have loyal customers who are reluctant to change. The demand will be inelastic.

- *Price level*: elasticity varies along the demand curve. When something is already very cheap (e.g. matches), making it cheaper may have little effect. Similarly, if something is too expensive for most people (e.g. a Rolls-Royce), making it even more expensive may have little effect on demand. So very expensive goods may have price inelastic demand above a certain level, but elastic below a certain level. Imagine £20 off trips to Australia – it is not enough to make a difference, but £200 off might. Necessities are

prestige goods
high-status goods, e.g. Rolls-Royce, Rolex

usually price inelastic at lower price levels, but may become elastic at higher levels as more alternative products become economically viable, e.g. cakes instead of bread, or would people take a bus to work if it cost the same as a taxi?

- *Stage of the product life cycle*: a new product may have price inelastic demand on introduction (little competition), be more price elastic during the growth phase, less elastic during maturity (assuming brand loyalty has been built up) and have a high level of price elasticity in its decline.

It is important for a company to know how demand for its product will react to a change in circumstances. This chapter has only considered elasticity in terms of price, but the concept can be applied to all marketing variables.

OTHER ELASTICITIES OF DEMAND

There are numerous different kinds of elasticity that can be calculated: advertising elasticity of demand measures how responsive sales are to a change in the advertising budget; income elasticity measures the response to a change in people's earnings. Of particular significance is cross-elasticity of demand. This measures the change in one company's sales in response to the change in price of a competitive product. For example, Coca-Cola would expect to sell more if Pepsi raised its price. Calculating the cross-elasticity would help Coca-Cola to know how many more cans to produce.

---

research focus

Bezawada, R. and Pauwels, K. (2012) 'What is special about marketing organic products? How organic assortment, price, and promotions drive retailer performance', *Journal of Marketing*, **77 (1): 31–51.**
This paper investigates the demand elasticities of marketing mix elements in the sale of organic foods.

PRICING ON THE INTERNET

What makes pricing on the Internet different is the availability of information and the degree to which customers can participate in price setting – or even turn into sellers themselves. eBay has been a phenomenal success, attracting many more customers than offline auctions do and even becoming a way of life for some devotees (and destroying the businesses of some others, e.g. sellers of collectibles). The Internet empowers bargain hunters who can more easily search out the best offers available (Wright and Jayawardhena, 2001) and at the same time provides a more convenient shopping experience for the time-starved.

There are a number of factors that combine to make Internet prices lower than their offline equivalents:

- *price transparency*: the availability of digital shopping agents (see below) and cost comparison websites makes it easier for customers to seek out the best deals

- *informed consumers*: consumers with easier access to information make more considered purchasing decisions, especially in fast-moving sectors such as technology, driving down prices for goods approaching the end of the product life cycle

shopping agents
programs which search the Internet and then display a table of comparative prices for a specified item

- *international competition is increasing*: it is no longer cost-prohibitive to ship goods internationally although some consumers underestimate the costs of import tax and customs charges for higher value items (and some just ignore them); there is also the cost of returning any faulty or unwanted goods

- *reverse auctions*: sellers bid for the buyer's business which encourages suppliers to undercut each other

digital start-up

a newly opened online business

- *new business models*: digital start-ups often use low prices to gain a customer base. Many new online businesses are funded by venture capitalists, prepared to take a longer-term view of their investment. The company can charge less and sustain a loss for some time. Other online service providers, like Spotify, use a 'freemium' model, offering a basic version for free and charging a premium for more advanced features.

- *lower costs*: cutting out intermediaries (e.g. retailers) or getting customers to do some of the administration (e.g. filling in order forms or printing tickets at home) effectively cuts out costs

- *high price elasticity* (i.e. price sensitivity, see above for a more detailed explanation): online markets appear to be more price sensitive than their offline equivalents

- *frequent price changes*: e-tailers can respond more quickly and easily to changes in competitive prices or in other market conditions. Firms can also make individual personalised offers on a user-by-user basis (see dynamic pricing above).

efficient market

a market in which prices adjust quickly, and frequently, in response to new information (in economic theory)

In the early days of the Internet, economists gleefully anticipated the realisation of something that had, until then, been only a theory: an efficient market. In an efficient market, buyers have ready access to pricing information for all their choices of products to buy. The Internet provides this thanks to the ease of searching numerous possible suppliers, its interactivity (which enables real-time auctions), the ease with which prices can be changed and the availability of shopping agents. Shopping agents are software programs which search the Internet and then display a table of comparative prices for a specified item, e.g. Google Shopping. Interestingly, despite the opportunities to shop around, not all Internet shoppers choose the lowest possible price due to factors such as brand familiarity, trust and perceived service levels.

There has been much debate as to whether the Internet is really a different marketplace or just a different marketing channel. Does it reach a new set of customers or just reach the same ones in a different way? Whether it is a new market or not, most of the old rules still apply to it – and that includes the pricing strategies, tactics and methods discussed elsewhere in this chapter. Sometimes, however, it does provide a new way to implement the old ideas. Take price discrimination, for example. Companies need to exercise care here, though, as consumers are likely to perceive the charging of different prices on this basis as unfair and therefore to trust the suppliers less in the future (Grewal et al., 2004). The music industry has come in for a lot of criticism because of its pricing policies, both online and offline. For example, Apple iTunes customers used to be charged differently for downloads according to the country revealed

ACTIVITY

Search the web. What's the best price you can find for the latest Samsung Smartphone model?

by their email address – a practice which resulted in an EU investigation of the record companies responsible for the differing charges. Apple were forced to change their EU pricing strategy; however, four years later, Apple was one of several technology companies called in front of the Australian government to explain why their prices were so high.

SUMMARY

Pricing is a much neglected marketing tool. Too many firms take a mechanical approach to the setting of prices, often purely on the basis of costs. Far too few organisations review their prices regularly enough and so they miss marketing opportunities.

Pricing is a competitive weapon that should be deployed alongside the rest of the marketing mix. A product's price sends a message – of quality, of desirability, of status, of a good buy. It has to vary according to place of purchase – wholesale, retail, Internet. It is a key part of the brand.

Common pricing objectives include maximising revenue, maintaining brand image, building market share, recovering an investment made (usually in developing the product), enticing customers to the store, and rewarding customers for loyalty.

Pricing methods are largely either cost-based or market-based. Too great an emphasis on cost can lead to missed profit. Market-based methods take account of what the market can bear, but the price must always be high enough to cover costs in the long run.

Pricing strategies and tactics overlap. There are specific strategies for new product pricing. Firms following a market penetration strategy set their prices low. A market skimming strategy employs high prices. General pricing strategies include: prestige pricing, where a high price is set to confer status; pre-emptive pricing, where a lower price is set to discourage competition; product line pricing, where related products are sold at a variety of prices; and price discrimination, which charges different prices for the same product to different market segments.

market penetration strategy
encouraging existing customers to buy more of a product in order to increase sales of existing products in existing markets (part of Ansoff's growth matrix)

Pricing tactics include psychological pricing, which sets a price that sounds cheaper (e.g. £999) and loss leaders, which are products sold very cheaply but made up for by the profits of others.

Elasticity is a key concept when changing prices. Products with price inelastic demand will earn more revenue if the price is increased. Prices for products with price elastic demand should be lowered if the firm wants to increase its sales revenue.

CHALLENGES REVIEWED

Now that you have finished reading the chapter, look back at the challenges you were set at the beginning. Do you have a clearer idea of what's involved?

HINTS

- Profit margins and price wars.
- Price elasticity of demand and the impact of price on image.
- New product pricing strategies – skimming.
- Think about why the banks will not make the loans – can these people afford to pay them back? What will happen if they cannot make the payments?
- Remember parallel importing. The product may need simplifying in order to reduce costs.

READING AROUND

ARTICLES

Dean, J. (1976) 'Pricing policies for new products', *Harvard Business Review*, 1 November. Part of the HBR Classic concepts series.

Khomani, N. (2015) 'The top tricks supermarkets use to confuse customers', *The Guardian*, Consumer Affairs, 16 July. Available at: www.theguardian.com/money/2015/jul/16/the-top-tricks-supermarkets-use-to-confuse-consumers (accessed 30/09/16).

Kumar, N. (2006) 'Strategies to fight low cost rivals', *Harvard Business Review*, 84 (12): 104–12.

Porter, M.E. and Kramer, M.R. (2011) 'Creating shared value', *Harvard Business Review*, 89 (1/2): 62–77.

WEBSITES

There are numerous websites that you can go to for price comparisons to find cheaper prices. For example:

www.comparethemarket.com

www.kelkoo.co.uk

TEST YOURSELF

1 How does price affect a product's brand image? (See p. 385)

2 How do the forces of supply and demand affect prices? (See p. 383)

3 Complete this formula: perceived value = perceived benefits … (See p. 384)

4 List three possible objectives of a pricing strategy. (See p. 386)

5 List the three key influencers on pricing decisions. (See p. 387)

6 What is a psychological price barrier? (See p. 388)

7 Whose prices are taken into account in 'going-rate pricing'? (See p. 389)

8 Which type of cost is mark-up pricing based on? (See p. 391)

9 If a new customer wanted to place a large order but would only accept a low price, what would you take into account when deciding whether or not to take the order? (See p. 394)

10 What are the drawbacks to breakeven analysis? (See p. 397)

11 Briefly describe two major new product pricing strategies. (See p. 398)

12 Explain price elasticity of demand. (See p. 407)

REVISION TOOLS

Want to test yourself even more? Review what you have learnt by visiting
https://study.sagepub.com/masterson4e

- Practise for exams with **multiple choice questions**
- Revise key terms with **interactive flashcards**

MINI CASE STUDY: 'TAXI!' OR IS IT 'RIDE-SHARE!'

Read the questions, then the case material, and then answer the questions.

QUESTIONS

1   Are taxi fares set using cost based or market pricing methods or both? *Explain* your answer and *illustrate* it with examples from the case study.

2   What is the theory behind 'surge pricing'? How does it work in practice and what are the arguments for and against it?

3   Is Uber following a penetration pricing strategy or could their pricing be said to be predatory? What other pricing strategies and tactics are employed in the taxi industry? Assess their effectiveness in London and/ or in your hometown.

Source: Kaspars Grinvalds/Shutterstock.com

One of London's most iconic sights is the ubiquitous Black Cab – but for how much longer? London's Black Cab fleet is facing threats from competition old and new.

Black Cab drivers have always had to lure passengers away from the much cheaper buses, tubes and over-ground trains. The arrival of 'Boris Bikes' (liveried cycles that can be hired from one docking station and returned to another), didn't worry them. Public transport was slower, less convenient and not 24 hour, the bikes required fitness and the courage to brave London's traffic. They had fought the mini cab battles years before and won. Mini cabs were just ordinary (often scruffy) cars with ordinary drivers. They had to be booked in advance, not hailed on the street, and the drivers didn't have the much lauded 'knowledge' that Black Cab drivers did.

Now some tube trains and buses run all night. Central London congestion charges have made it easier to get around by bike. New train lines have improved services across the city. And Uber has arrived.

Originally Uber offered chauffeur-driven prestige cars but they soon changed the business model and started to compete directly with taxis. Uber's online platform is an example of disruptive technology. It connects people needing lifts with the nearest available cars available for private hire. Uber drivers could charge less for the same journey, were more convenient and the app that allows you track your driver on a map was a novelty that smartphone-addicted Londoners just loved. A 20-minute, two-mile trip in a Black Cab costs about £14. In an Uber it's more like £8. Black Cabs usually charge according to how long the journey takes – something that it is often hard to estimate given London's heavy traffic. With Uber, riders know in advance what the fare will be.

In the thirty years to 2015, during which time London's economy doubled in size and its population increased by almost 2 million people, the number of Black Cabs rose from 19,000 to 22,500. In the seven years between 2009 and 2015, the number of Uber drivers rose from none to over 25,000. Yet Uber claimed that it wasn't adding to big cities' pollution problems by increasing car use, quite the reverse in fact. Many people used Uber at the start of train or bus journeys to get to and from stations.

The Uber business model relies on a massive increase in both drivers and riders, the result of which is more work (and more money) for the drivers at a cheaper price for the passengers. This works by cutting the amount of time that the drivers are idle while waiting for a fare. In three years, Uber drivers in New York saw their idle time on the platform almost halve: from 36 minutes per hour, to just 20 minutes.

Uber's aim is to have its ride-sharing cars constantly on the move in a 'perpetual journey'. To that end, UberPool knits together riders' journeys so they can share cars. Strangers share cars making it a sort of public transport/ taxi hybrid. It is even cheaper than the original Uber service. Uber claims that UberPool will significantly reduce

(Continued)

(Continued)

private car ownership. A recent Uber study in Paris concluded that taking UberPool for a year would be cheaper than owning a car. Cities could change beyond all measure if millions of parking spaces are no longer required.

Despite this, Uber has powerful critics. London's mayor, Sadiq Khan, wanted new regulations, such as a written English test for licensed taxi drivers, that he said would level the playing field for ride-sharing platform Uber and the iconic Black Cab. Why? Well the Black Cab drivers accused Uber of taking short cuts with safety and exploiting drivers in order to undercut their prices – and they were losing business of course. Many believed that Uber was determined to drive them out of business altogether by making it impossible for the Black Cab drivers with their higher overheads and regulated prices to make a decent living. They may have a point, Uber executives refer to Black Cabs as 'heritage' and in February 2016, Black Cab drivers were invited to join the Uber platform free for the first year.

London's Black Cab drivers are renowned for a number of things. On the plus side, their knowledge of London streets and back streets and how to avoid traffic jams is encyclopaedic; their cabs have to be well maintained and their conversational skills are legendary. On the down side, they are said to sometimes refuse to take fares, 'I'm not going south of the river this time of night mate', overcharge and their conversational skills are legendary (they tend to have strong opinions so that one can go either way – if you want a demonstration of this, ask a Black Cab driver about Uber). Most Londoners love the Black Cabs while also moaning about how hard it is to get one and how expensive they are, so a cheaper alternative, with benefits, was bound to be tempting.

It's not just London cab drivers who are up in arms about Uber, New York's cabbies also lost out when Uber arrived but later fought back with upgraded technology in the cabs and a snazzy app they hoped would out-uber Uber.

Uber started in California and has spread across the world causing controversy wherever it goes. In Nairobi it engaged in a price war with a local ride-sharing firm Little Cab. In August 2016 it suspended services in Abu Dhabi after several drivers were arrested on vague charges. After two years of trading, the company gave up in China and sold to rival firm Didi Chuxing. Uber admitted that it had been losing more than $1 billion a year in China, spending huge sums to subsidise discounted fares.

One of the more controversial things about Uber is its surge pricing: if demand for taxis is high, the price goes up. Other taxis also charge more at different times. For example, London's Black Cabs charge more after 22.00, at weekends and public holidays and even more at Christmas. Longer journeys have a higher rate per minute as do journeys to or from Heathrow airport. There is a charge for booking by phone or online. Mini cabs may charge more for a long journey to somewhere that they are unlikely to get a return fare. You will probably pay more for a luxury car or a car that seats more people.

Uber would argue that surge pricing is just market forces at work and that the higher price persuades some passengers to wait for a cheaper time or use an alternative means of transport, leaving the available cars for those who can afford the price and thus evening out demand. Disgruntled passengers may call it 'price gouging' – exploiting the market. But then they can always get a Black Cab – can't they?

Sources: Bull (2015); Mohammed (2015); BBC (2016); Hawkins (2016); Knight (2016); Sullivan (2016); Wesangula (2016)

REFERENCES

BA (n.d.) *Buy Travel*, British Airways. Available at: www.britishairways.com/travel/fx/public/en_gb (accessed 18/09/16).

Bandyopadhyay, S., Lin, G.B. and Zhong, Y. (2001) 'Under the gavel', *Marketing Management*, 10 (4): 24–8.

BBC (2016) 'Uber sells Chinese business to Didi Chuxing', *Business*, 1 August. Available at: www.bbc.co.uk/news/36938812 (accessed 29/09/16).

Bertini, M. and Gourville, J. (2012), 'Pricing to create shared value', *Harvard Business Review*, 90 (6): 96–104.

Bezawada, R. and Pauwels, K. (2012) 'What is special about marketing organic products? How organic assortment, price, and promotions drive retailer performance', *Journal of Marketing*, 77 (1): 31–51.

Bull, J. (2015) 'Fare trade: breaking down London's taxi debate', *London Connections*. Available at: www.londonreconnections.com/2015/fare-trade-breaking-down-londons-taxi-debate/ (accessed 29/09/16).

Butler, S. and Brignall, M. (2015) 'Dairy farmers call for supermarket boycott as milk price falls', *The Guardian*, Business, 6 August. Available at: www.theguardian.com/business/2015/aug/06/dairy-farmers-call-for-supermarkets-boycott-as-milk-price-falls (accessed 04/10/16).

Cox, J. (2001) 'Pricing practices that endanger profits', *Marketing Management*, 10 (3): 42–6.

Dinsmore, J.B., Dugan, R.G. and Wright, S.A. (2016) 'Monetary vs. nonmonetary prices: differences in product evaluations due to pricing strategies within mobile applications', *Journal of Strategic Marketing*, 24 (3–4): 227–40.

European Commission (2016) 'Antitrust: Commission fines truck producers €2.93 billion for participating in a cartel', press release, 19 July. Available at: http://europa.eu/rapid/press-release_IP-16-2582_en.htm (accessed 18/09/16).

France, M. and Hamm, S. (1998) 'Does predatory pricing make Microsoft a predator?', *Business Week*, 23 November. Available at: www.businessweek.com (accessed 03/04/13).

Grewal, D., Hardesty, D.M. and Gopalkrishnan, R.I. (2004) 'The effects of buyer identification and purchase timing on consumers' perceptions of trust, price fairness, and repurchase intentions', *Journal of Interactive Marketing*, 18 (4): 87–101.

Hawkins, A. (2016) 'Yellow taxis have a new weapon in their war against Uber: gadgets', *The Verge*, 26 September. Available at: www.theverge.com/2016/9/26/13035642/nyc-taxi-cab-android-touchscreen-tablet-verifone (accessed 29/09/16).

InterRail (n.d.) Untitled. Available at: www.interrail.eu/interrail-passes/pass-benefits/interrail-youth-discounts (accessed 03/03/17).

Irish Organic Farmers & Growers Association (n.d.). 'The Little Milk Company – organic dairy farmers are doing it for themselves!'. Available at: iofga.org/wp-content/uploads/The-Little-Milk-Company.docx (accessed 04/10/16).

Jobber, D. and Shipley, D. (2012) 'Marketing-orientated pricing: understanding and applying factors that discriminate between successful high and low price strategies', *European Journal of Marketing*, 46 (11/12): 1647–70.

Knight, S. (2016) 'How Uber conquered London', *The Guardian, The Long Read*. 27 April. Available at: www.theguardian.com/technology/2016/apr/27/how-uber-conquered-london (accessed 29/09/16).

Lancaster, G., Withey, F. and Ashford, R. (2007) *Marketing Fundamentals*. CIM Workbook. Oxford: Butterworth-Heinemann.

The Little Milk Company (n.d.) [online] Available at: www.thelittlemilkcompany.ie/ (accessed 04/10/16).

Mohammed, R. (2015) 'The taxi industry can innovate, too', *Harvard Business Review*, February 13. Available at: https://hbr.org/2015/02/the-taxi-industry-can-innovate-too (accessed 02/03/17).

Office of Fair Trading (2002) 'OFT fines Scottish newspaper publisher for predatory pricing'. Available at: www.oft.gov.uk/news-and-updates/press/2002/pn_58-02#.UfzqZ5LVCSo (accessed 03/08/13).

OPEC (n.d.) 'Mission statement', Organisation of the Petroleum Exporting Countries. Available at: www.opec.org (accessed 18/09/16).

Shapiro, S.L., Drayer, J. and Dwyer, B. (2016) 'Examining consumer perceptions of demand-based ticket pricing in sport'. *Sport Marketing Quarterly*, 25 (1): 34–46.

Sullivan, J. (2016) 'Uber suspends services in Abu Dhabi', *BBC Business*, 29 August. Available at: www.bbc.co.uk/news/business-37211268 (accessed 29/09/16).

Wesangula, D. (2016) 'Uber and Little Cab's battle to control the streets of Nairobi', *The Guardian*, Sustainable Business, 16 September. Available at: www.theguardian.com/sustainable-business/2016/sep/16/uber-little-cabs-kenya-nairobi-battle-taxi (accessed 29/09/16).

Wright, L. and Jayawardhena, C. (2001) 'Netting the consumer: the e-direct marketing imperative', *Proceedings of the Marketing Science Conference*. Cardiff: University of Cardiff.

APPENDIX: ADDITIONAL COST-BASED PRICING ACTIVITY

ACTIVITY: DRAWING A BREAKEVEN CHART

You will need proper graph paper, a ruler, pencil, rubber and calculator for this.

The Roadrunner Co. produces racing bicycles:

fixed costs (FC) add up to £1.2 million

variable costs (VC) are £800 per bike

the bike sells for £2000

1   The first challenge is to decide on the scale for the graph. In real life, you would know current output levels and could use those as a guide. Otherwise, it is really trial and error. Draw the (vertical) *y* axis along the short side of your paper. For our Roadrunner example, let's label the *y* axis £m, and take it up to £4m, and the (horizontal) *x* axis (quantity of bicycles) to 3500.

2   Now, plot the fixed costs. This is the easy one – fixed costs do not change so we draw a straight, horizontal line across from the *y* axis at £1.2 million. Label this line 'FC'.

3   Next, draw the variable costs line. VC are £800 per bike, so pick a number (any number between 1 and 3500) and work out the VC at that level of output.

For example, 500 × £800 = £400,000.

Now make a small mark at the point where 500 on the *x* axis meets £400,000 on the *y* axis. Repeat for another random point, say 2000:

2000 × £800 = £1,600,000.

Next, taking 0 (bottom left corner of the graph) as your starting point, just join the dots to make a variable cost line (it should be a straight, diagonal line; if it is not, then check the two calculations). Label this line 'VC'.

Why use 0 as a starting point? It is because if you don't make any products, then there will be no variable costs – they are ingredients and raw materials, remember.

4   The next line to draw is the total cost (TC) line and there's a cheat's way to do this.

Take a ruler and lay it along the VC line, then carefully move it up, keeping the angle the same, until it crosses the y axis at the start of the FC line. Then draw a straight diagonal line, starting at the y axis. This line should be parallel to the VC line. Label this line 'TC'.

Why does the total cost line start at the FC line? Because total cost = fixed cost + variable cost, so it can never be *less* than fixed cost.

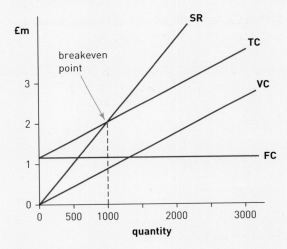

EXHIBIT 10.11 Roadrunner Co. breakeven chart

5   The sales revenue (SR) line is drawn in a similar way to the VC line. Pick two numbers (any two numbers within the scale of the graph). Work out the revenue at those sales volumes (quantity × price), then, using 0 as a starting point, plot a straight diagonal line that joins all three points. Label this line 'SR'.

6   Now you're ready to read off the breakeven point. X marks the spot, i.e. it is where the sales revenue and total cost lines cross. Draw a line down to the quantity axis – the answer should be 1000.

Of course, if the company wants to know what happens if the price is increased to £2100, it will have to draw a new line for sales revenue.

As an alternative to the graphical method, the firm might calculate breakeven points using this formula:

Fixed costs

Contribution *per item*

Let's revisit the Roadrunner Co. figures:

fixed costs are £1.2 million

variable costs are £800 per bike

price is £2000

contribution = selling price – variable cost

$\dfrac{1,200,000}{1200}$ = £2000 – £800 = £1200

= 1000

So, it needs to sell 1000 bicycles at £2000 in order to cover all its costs, i.e. to break even.

ACTIVITY: ANSWER TO FULL-COST PRICING ACTIVITY (SEE P. 393)

total cost = fixed costs + variable costs

fixed cost per unit (box) $= \dfrac{£40,000}{100,000} = 40\text{p}$

total cost per unit (box) = 40p + £1 = £1.40

price, i.e. total cost + 25%

= £1.40 + (£1.40 × 25%)

= £1.75

WHAT THIS PART IS ABOUT

The final section of this book draws together all the previous areas and shows what marketers actually do with the resources at their disposal. Branding is a major weapon in a marketer's armoury and so Chapter 11 looks back at previous chapters on the marketing mix and shows how the marketing mix elements combine to build brands. Chapter 12 explains the marketing planning process and how it is used to manage marketing activities and to achieve marketing goals.

Modern organisations are highly reliant upon marketing and successful marketing is dependent upon the skills of marketers. There is a wide range of different roles within marketing: research and analysis, logistics planning and management, account handling, brand management, new product development, price setting – it would take too much space to list them all here. However, we do want you to share our enthusiasm for marketing and to find your ideal marketing role. So we have put an extra, bonus, section on this book's companion website that explains what marketers do in more detail and how your career might develop.

Go to https://study.sagepub.com/masterson4e

We wish you good luck in your future marketing career!

PART FOUR

MANAGING MARKETING

PART ONE   THIS IS MARKETING

PART TWO   MAKING SENSE OF MARKETS

PART THREE   THE MARKETING MIX

PART FOUR   MANAGING MARKETING

BUILDING BRANDS: USING THE MARKETING MIX

BRAND-BUILDING CHALLENGES

The following are illustrations of the types of decision that marketers have to take or issues they face. *You aren't expected to know how to deal with the challenges now*; just bear them in mind as you read the chapter and see what you can find that helps.

Degree to job: Volkswagen

- Aphrodite is a small, well-known confectionery brand that wants to change its image to that of a supplier of high-quality, special-occasion sweets. The marketing director has asked you to review current marketing activities to ensure that they support this new market position. What do you need to check?

- You are the marketing manager for a well-known designer fashion brand. A chain store has approached your company with a view to placing a large order. The finance manager is delighted and is prepared to discount the price. However, the managing director has some concerns. Do you think this order should be accepted? Do you want to impose any special terms and conditions?

- A friend owns two coffee bars, one in Leicester and one in Edinburgh. She now works in Edinburgh as that coffee bar is new and has no manager yet. Since she left, takings at the Leicester restaurant have dropped right down and she doesn't know why. She has asked you to help her find the problem. Do you know what to do?

- You are the brand manager for a range of jams that are one of the oldest brands in the world. The range has distinctive and well-recognised packaging. However, the packaging is not recyclable and you are under pressure to change it. You are worried about losing your brand's competitive advantage. What do you need to consider? What can you do?

INTRODUCTION

The marketing mix is at the core of any marketing plan. The most commonly used schematic for the marketing mix is the 4Ps which has the advantage of being both widely recognised and easy to remember.

The marketing mix is a set of tools and should be treated as such. No one element can stand alone; they must all support each other. If they conflict, target markets will be confused, objectives will not be met and the brand's image will be diluted. Marketing managers blend their marketing mixes to make an integrated plan that will achieve their marketing objectives.

This chapter focuses on brands and how they are built and nurtured with the marketing mix. The mix is summarised, demonstrating how the techniques fit together and showing how they can be integrated to build brands. The idea of branding as an integral part of a modern product was introduced in Chapter 6. In this chapter, it is examined as a strategy that employs all elements of the marketing mix.

Brand overview

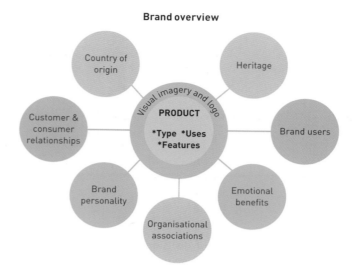

EXHIBIT 11.1 Brand overview

Adapted from Aaker, D.A. (2012) Building Strong Brands. London: Simon and Schuster.

ethical focus: Pret a Manger

While branding is most often discussed in connection with promotional activities, building a strong brand requires much more than a clever campaign – a strong brand must 'walk the walk' as well as 'talk the talk'. The UK's Pret a Manger chain of gourmet sandwich shops is a good example of an organisation that has built a successful brand by ensuring each element of the marketing mix aligns with what matters most to its customers. Pret does not invest as heavily in advertising as many of its competitors (take Subway, for example) and yet its logo is instantly recognisable and its distinctive attributes well understood. This success is due in no small part to the compelling story Pret has to tell about its business and the vision and values that underpin it.

The chain was inspired by the Parisian *traiteurs* that sell gourmet ready to eat food at affordable prices to people too busy to cook for themselves. The store's design was based on the upmarket steel-and-chrome of the sandwich bars typical of New York in the 1980s. The concept must have seemed the epitome of sophistication in comparison with the dingy cafes and sandwich bars typical of Britain's high street at the time. The first Pret store was unveiled in the upmarket London suburb of Hampstead in 1984, and since the very beginning Pret has distinguished its offer through a commitment to quality, freshly prepared food, carefully sourced ingredients and the swift and efficient service demanded by its time-pressed urban clientele. Pret builds kitchens in or very near to every store and famously donates any unsold food to the homeless at the end of each day. Through its foundation trust the firm supports charities that work to 'break the cycle of homelessness' and provides apprenticeships to help vulnerable people get back into employment.

Pret's clear brand vision guides every strategic decision the firm makes; from the location of their stores in busy metropolitan neighbourhoods, to investing in state of the art contactless and mobile payment technology (Pret customers are busy people who embrace the latest gadgets), to ensuring there are always enough team members in shops to prevent queues. Pret's distinctive approach often earns the brand exposure in newspapers and social media as it creates news opportunities and cultivates a sense of community and connection with customers who identify with the brand and its values as well as appreciating the taste of its products and the quality of service they've come to expect.

Using design to tell brand stories

BRANDING

Brands are important assets for many companies, and building and maintaining their strength is a key marketing task that involves all of the marketing mix. A brand is more than a design or a concept. It is a combination of attributes which together promise customers the solution to their problems, the answer to their needs, a means to express themselves – or even to create a better world. Brands are a major component of both the value consumers perceive in products and the value they gain from their consumption, possession or use. Branding has seemed to be the saviour of mass-produced products which often have little or no other means of differentiation. The credit for the success of many modern products has been attributed to their branding, but the brand can also cause a product to fail (Haig, 2003). If a brand's image deteriorates, then its sales may suffer as Levi's, Burberry and Doc Martens have all found – though clearly it is possible, with clever brand management, to recover.

research focus

Cleeren, K., van Heerde, H.J. and Dekimpe, M.G. (2013) 'Rising from the ashes: how brands and categories can overcome product-harm crises', *Journal of Marketing*, 77 (2): 58–77.

Product-harm crises can cause major revenue and market-share losses, lead to costly product recalls, and destroy carefully nurtured brand equity. The authors analyse 60 fast-moving consumer goods (FMCG) crises that occurred in the United Kingdom and the Netherlands to assess the effects of post-crisis advertising and price adjustments on the change in consumers' brand share and category purchases, the extent of negative publicity surrounding the event and whether the affected brand had to publicly acknowledge blame. The authors provide context-specific managerial recommendations on how to overcome a product-harm crisis.

BRAND MANAGEMENT: CONCEPTS AND TERMINOLOGY

Branding has given rise to a host of concepts and terms that are often used slightly differently by different people. There are many different ways to look at a brand and many books and papers dedicated to the subject. The following section will consider:

- brand image
- brand identity
- visual identity
- brand personality
- brand associations
- brand authenticity.

This is by no means an exhaustive list of branding terms (see the glossary and reading around for a more complete investigation of current terminology). These have been chosen to give a broad view of how to build and manage a brand along with insight into current brand management thinking.

Strategic brand management

BRAND IMAGE

The target market's perception of the brand is called the brand image and it is this that really matters. This is what people really think of the brand and, in an ideal world, it would match the image the brand team wanted people to have. A brand's power stems from the collective nature of consumer and customer perceptions. One person's perception cannot create a powerful brand; it takes numerous people accepting the brand truth and reinforcing it in their everyday lives (Holt, 2004). Whether or not the image held in people's minds matches that which the firm intended will depend upon how well the brand team have constructed the brand identity, and the extent to which that identity is successfully expressed in each element of the marketing mix. The brand image is also subject to outside influences. Brands exist independent of their owners who cannot control everything that is said about them or how they are used. A person forms a brand image on the basis of all their experience with the brand – not just the official brand communications.

brand identity

the distinguishing characteristics and ideas the company wants its customers to associate with the brand

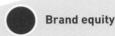
Brand equity
The financial value of a brand

Brand image
The way the market actually perceives a brand

Brand identity
How the brand owner wants a brand perceived; embodies brand attributes, associations and visual identity

EXHIBIT 11.2 Brand image

BRAND IDENTITY

Brand identity can be defined as the distinguishing characteristics and ideas the company wants its customers to associate with the brand, i.e. it is aspirational, though customers may or may not actually form that desired image. The brand identity is constructed by the company, or 'brand owner'. Product attributes, e.g. the quality of the item and its features, contribute to a brand's identity but there is much more to a brand than just a product. The parent or corporate brand may be a key component of a product's brand identity, e.g. Apple, and all that it represents, is a strong part of the iPhone's identity. The brand may have a constructed personality (see below). Brand meanings is

corporate brand

a company brand name

Apple: our signature

ethical focus: sweet and innocent

The Innocent brand is one of the big success stories of the 2000s. It has grown from a virtually unknown fruit drink found in just a few stores to a must-have for every food shop and sandwich store of note. The makers of Innocent smoothies take great care to ensure that the product is as high quality as it can be – pure fruit, no additives and no concentrates – but that is only part of their appeal.

Innocent: success story

Strong ethical values are central to the distinctive brand identity that has played such a key role in building the Innocent brand. The distinctive, apparently hand-sketched, fruits or shapes with halos logos have a childlike quality and are reassuringly simple looking. The brand embodies a light-hearted, effervescent and fun personality perhaps mirroring the youthfulness of the brand's founders, three Cambridge University graduates who established the business while still in their early twenties. The fun personality is also expressed in the brands' advertising, the tone of voice used in social media communications and most strongly through the packaging, which also showcases the brand's ethical stance. Take the time to read an Innocent pack and you will not only find out exactly what's in your drink, but also what isn't, for example:

© Innocent. Picture courtesy of Innocent

1   No concentrates

2   No stabilisers

3   No flavourings

4   No GM stuff

5   No preservatives

6   No added sugar

7   No E numbers

8   No funny business

You may also find such things as a picture of a fireman's hat (drawn by Kat, aged 26$^1/_2$) alongside a little story about energy entitled *smoky bacon*.

A brand identity such as Innocent's demands that the firm behave in an environmentally friendly way. The individual-size smoothie bottles are made of 50% recycled plastic and the brand's ethical credentials are further strengthened by sourcing bananas from plantations certified by the Rainforest Alliance and donating 10% of its profits to charities.

One important bit of information that you won't find prominently displayed on Innocent smoothies packaging is that the brand is owned by Coca-Cola, one of the largest and most powerful corporations in the world. The brand's founders claim they haven't sold out and that Innocent's mission to 'taste good and do good' can be realised more efficiently with the financial backing of Coca-Cola (though they act now in a non-executive advisory role). Can Innocent remain true to its core brand values and retain its innocence or has the brand sold its soul?

a catch-all term for the many other elements that comprise a brand's identity. Symbols can be powerful tools in brand development. Logos are fiercely protected by their brands' owners. Other symbols, such as the meerkats for Compare the Market.com and McDonald's Golden Arches, are instantly recognisable. Brands can also be symbolic of more abstract ideas, e.g. Ben and Jerry's has a hippy feel. Brands may be metaphors for other concepts, e.g. Harley Davidson can represent freedom. All these things, and more, are embodied in the brand identity. The brand identity is constructed by the company, or 'brand owner' and is based on four main constructs; brand as person, brand as product, organisational associations and other brand meanings (see Exhibit 11.3).

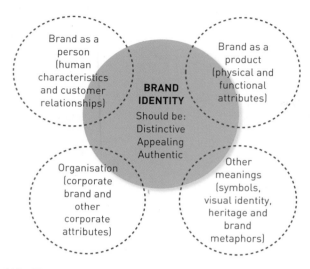

EXHIBIT 11.3 Brand identity

Adapted from Aaker, D.A. (2012) Building Strong Brands. London: Simon and Schuster.

VISUAL IDENTITY

The most obvious attribute of a brand is its visual identity. The name, logo, packaging and physical appearance of branded products clearly distinguish them from non-branded alternatives. A brand's visual identity may also provide cues to other important associations (see below) the brand owner hopes to create. For example, Pepsi is blue because it is different from Coke and also refreshing and modern. Hovis packaging has an old-fashioned look because it is a traditional brand. Unleaded petrol comes out of a green-handled pump because it is more environmentally friendly.

Mars has a strong visual identity.

Source: iStock.com/darios44

BRAND NAMES

There are historical reasons behind most corporate brand names. Companies often start out with the owner's name (e.g. Mars, Cadbury, Sainsbury, Guinness, Ford, Mercedes, Marks & Spencer, Dior). This remains the corporate brand name as it is well known and people make associations with it. In the 1990s, however, there was a management craze for renaming organisations, i.e. changing their brand names. There were a number of reasons behind this, including:

- a more attractive name that either described the organisation better or enhanced the brand identity
- a name that was more acceptable (or just easier to pronounce) in international markets (e.g. Jif household cleaner became Cif)
- distancing the organisation from its past (e.g. Andersen Consulting became Accenture after a scandal).

Not all of these re-namings were successful. Take Consignia, for example. This was the new name chosen, after extensive consultation and market research, for the Royal Mail service. There were good reasons for wanting to change the name. The business had changed and was no longer merely a mail service. They operated call centres, courier services and logistics services and so the name no longer described the business that well. It was limiting their ability to add new services. Also, the organisation wanted to grow its business in overseas markets, beyond the rule of Queen Elizabeth II, where there might even be other 'Royals' and 'Royal Mails' to cause confusion. Finally, it wanted to revamp its image and be seen as a modern business rather than one stuck in the nineteenth century. Consignia was chosen because it does not actually mean anything in any language, but it sounds attractive and relevant.

It was a disaster. The organisation and its branding consultants severely underestimated the British public's attachment to the old name, and the media's will to sink the new one. Within about three years, the old name was back.

People do not like change. They get used to a brand and its look, and can react surprisingly strongly to management improvements. Such updates therefore need to be handled very carefully.

BRAND ASSOCIATIONS

There is much more to most brands than meets the eye. While a branded product may *look* much the same to everyone, individuals are likely to *think* and *feel* and *behave* very differently towards it. People form a range of different functional and emotional associations with brands in their minds. Brand associations may relate to physical or functional properties of a product based on experience, e.g. very shiny hair after using that brand of conditioner. Others are formed by what is known about or learned from the organisation that makes a product or even how or where a product is produced. Other associations may be formed based on what other people who use the brand are like or perhaps the values that an individual perceives the brand to embody or represent. Individuals also experience and remember feelings associated with brands and can identify very personally with some brands. The particular mental representations formed by individuals are, of course, beyond the direct control of a brand owner. Nevertheless by developing and expressing a distinctive, appealing and authentic brand identity, that encompasses positive and desirable brand associations, there is a greater chance of a positive brand image being formed.

BRAND PERSONALITY

A brand can be described in a similar way to a person. Brands may be young (e.g. FCUK), mature (e.g. Epicure), rebellious (e.g. Virgin), understated (e.g. Liberty), classy (e.g. Aston Martin), forceful (e.g. Nike), caring (e.g. Body Shop) – any personality descriptor that can be applied to a person can be (and probably has been) applied to a brand. Not all brands are endowed with human characteristics, but many of the most successful are. These human

ACTIVITY

characteristics are sometimes referred to as the brand personality. Marketers develop their brands' personalities as part of their brand identity, which may be articulated in a brand personality statement, e.g. 'This is a chocolate bar that bites back. It's edgy and assertive while being absolutely dependable – a bar you want on your side'. This is not meant as a slogan for an advertising campaign, although it might help inspire one. This is the way the brand team brings its product to life, it helps to predict how the brand will behave and how customers might relate to it.

Some brands can be described as 'anthropomorphic', i.e. their human characteristics are so strong that they can seem like actual people – and behave accordingly. Brand owners reinforce these human characteristics to deepen consumers' brand relationships. Social media are a valuable tool here. Brands have their own pages and profiles; they tweet thoughts for the day and jokes. They want to be liked; they want to be your friend.

BRAND AUTHENTICITY

The world has become a more cynical place. Consumers just don't trust brands, especially big brands, the way they used to. It's not just the major scandals such as VW's emissions tests cheating or BP's major oil spill, it's also the everyday shattering of illusions with revelations about pink sludge in hamburgers, or child labour in trainer factories or just the sheer weight of E numbers and sugar involved in some foods. All these things bring consumers up short and make them reconsider their loyalties. Consumers want to believe. No wonder brands feel the need to prove their credentials. They have to demonstrate that they live up to expected standards, behave consistently in the context of their brand values and are true to their heritage.

Brands are the heroes of their own stories. Stories that are started by the brand owners but continued by consumers, distributors and the media. Social media play an important part in building this brand narrative as consumers contribute their own stories and brand experiences to the sum of knowledge about the brand.

> Brand narrative is the ongoing connecting dialogue between company and customer. It is where marketing communications has moved to: away from pure brand image advertising to experiential branding. (Dahlen et al., 2010)

Consumers will not want to be part of the story, or propagate it, unless the brand is authentic, i.e. it is communicating and behaving in a way that is consistent with the identity and values it represents (see ethical focus: sweet and innocent).

global focus: tell me a true story

Brands were originally just owners' marks, then they became badges of product quality, then they moved on to be a means of differentiation from the competition. More recently they have incorporated certain emotional and social values, e.g. Nike's 'Just do it', L'Oréal's 'Because you're worth it', Ford's 'Go further'. Now all the cool brands want to be 'authentic'. Brand authenticity is described by Interbrand as 'an internal truth and capability', a 'defined heritage' and a 'well-grounded value set' (*The Economist*, 2015). That is why so many brands are keen to tell you their story.

Most companies started with a product set and then built a brand around it. They now find themselves re-examining their history and trying to build a story that demonstrates the brand's credentials – or is it the credentials they wish the brand had?

An increasing number of websites and adverts play upon the brand's history, dusting off old photos of founders (e.g. Jack Daniels) and early products (e.g. VW Beetle) to prove that they have always been there for us. Their heritage and country of origin often play a large part in this story. Story-telling comes more easily to some brands than to others of course, but imagine you had the good fortune to own a brand that revolves around stories and whose own story is known worldwide, is strong and consistent – instant authenticity – which may be why a survey by PR firm Chen and Wolfe found Disney to be the most authentic brand in the world.

Source: iStock.com/CTRPhotos

The Disney studios themselves have quite a story behind them of course, going all the way back to Mickey Mouse, but all their products have their own great stories. They are much loved films after all!. So instead of weaving a story around a brand in order to sell more products, Disney launch products straight from a story. Imagine a doll company coming up with the idea of an ice princess doll (leaving aside the fact that they would probably feel the need for a range, perhaps including a sun princess and a snow queen), then devising a campaign that encouraged young girls to interact with the doll, maybe even giving her a storyline: a family, a home, a prince. What a lot of work and it might not catch on. How much better to take inspiration from a highly successful film, say *Frozen*, and launch your princess into a world that already loves her and knows her story.

Now you've got the world talking.

Sources: Burns (2015); *The Economist* (2015); Czarnecki (2016)

BRAND EQUITY

A good brand image has a value. Branded goods usually carry higher prices than unbranded ones. Compare the prices of lesser-known brands of sportswear with those of Nike and Adidas. This value is known as brand equity and it is a difficult thing to calculate even though it is often one of the company's most valuable assets.

High brand equity is clearly a desirable thing and the brand's marketing mix should be designed with this in mind. For example, frequent price promotions, such as discounts or sales, indicate low brand equity and will do nothing to build it up, whereas brands that have a high price, high distribution intensity, pleasant shopping environment and large advertising budget are likely also to enjoy significant brand equity (Yoo et al., 2000).

One way to value brands is to examine takeover bids. Companies usually have to pay more than the value of a firm's physical assets in order to buy it. They pay for goodwill (ongoing business prospects) and they pay for brands. In 1988, Nestlé paid £2.5 billion ($3.6 billion) for Rowntree's, which was much more than the company was apparently worth (Smith, 2006), in a deal that gave it rights to one of the biggest-selling chocolate snacks of all time: KitKat. Unfortunately, this technique does not help put a value on the balance sheet of a company that is not subject to a takeover bid.

global focus: the world's top brands

According to *Forbes*, a leading business magazine, the world's most valuable brands (measured in billions of US dollars) in 2016 were:

1	Apple $154.1b		6	Toyota $42.1b
2	Google $82.5b		7	IBM 41.4b
3	Microsoft $75.2		8	Disney $39.5b
4	Coca-Cola $58.5		9	McDonald's $39.1b
5	Facebook $52.6b		10	GE $ $36.7b

IT and electronics companies continued to dominate the listings. Nine of the top 10 brands are from the USA, only Japanese Toyota spoiling their perfect 10. Samsung (South Korea) came in 11th place and BMW (Germany) was 14th.
Source: *Forbes* (2016)

price premium

a high price charged to give the impression of superior quality

An alternative way to value a brand is to ascertain how much extra customers are prepared to pay for the branded good rather than an unbranded one. So, how much more would you pay for a KitKat than for an unheard-of chocolate wafer biscuit? That price premium can then be multiplied by the number of bars sold (say in a year) to arrive at the brand equity. Neither these, nor the many other valuation methods tried, are entirely satisfactory. However, it is generally agreed that strong brands do have value – we are just not sure how much.

research focus

Hennig-Thurau, T., Houston, M. and Heitjans, T. (2009) 'Conceptualizing and measuring the monetary value of brand extensions: the case of motion pictures', *Journal of Marketing*, **73 (6): 167–83.**
Valuing brands is complicated; valuing brand extension potential is even more so but Hennig-Thurau et al. have developed a means to measure the monetary value of brand extension rights in the context of motion pictures (i.e. movie sequel rights) and to calculate the effect of variations of key product attributes, such as the continued participation of stars, on this value.

BRAND TYPES

There are a number of different types of brand in the marketplace today (see Exhibit 11.4) each of which has advantages and disadvantages. Most of Cadbury's products have an individual brand name as well as the corporate name. Cadbury's name is the badge of quality, while the individual name is an identifier for a particular recipe of confectionery. A purely descriptive name for Cadbury's Flake would be too long and would not differentiate the product from those of the competition. Heinz, however, traditionally sticks to straightforward descriptions of its products alongside its corporate brand name, e.g. Heinz baked beans, Heinz tomato ketchup. The company relies on its own name to help establish the desired brand image. Even Heinz, who traditionally used their corporate brand name only, have now caught the brand name fever though, by introducing, or acquiring, some range brands (e.g. Weight Watchers and Linda McCartney).

Own-label brands are a big success story. Once the poor relation of branding, seen as inferior to manufacturer brands, they now take up the bulk of supermarket shoppers' trolleys. They are popular with retailers (and some wholesalers) because they enable them to earn better profits. These products are not manufactured by the retailers, just badged by them. The advantage to the manufacturer is that it can use up spare capacity this way. However, these brands can be the cause of friction in the supply chain if the manufacturer believes that the own-label product is too similar to its own (see ethical focus: the lookalikes).

Generic products are less common in FMCG than they used to be. Nowadays, they are more likely to be pharmaceuticals and they can be controversial. Many life-saving drugs, e.g. for cancer or for AIDS, are very expensive and well beyond the reach of third-world countries. Some companies, notably in India, ignore patents and make copies of these drugs and sell them for a fraction of the normal price. Is this a crime or a public service?

own-label

products that bear a retailer's brand name, e.g. Tesco; sometimes called 'private brands'

patent

a legal protection for inventions that prohibits unauthorised copying

Corporate umbrella brands	The products use the corporate name	e.g. Heinz, Next
Range brands	Groups of related products share a brand name	e.g. Taste the Difference (Sainsbury's), Lean Cuisine (Nestlé)
Individual brands	Each product has its own brand name	e.g. Twix (Mars), Bold (Procter & Gamble)
Own-label (private) brands	Products bear the retailer's (or wholesaler's) name	e.g. Tesco, Marks & Spencer
Generic (unbranded) products	A product descriptor with no brand or owners' name	e.g. Ibuprofen

EXHIBIT 11.4 Brand types

BRAND ARCHITECTURES

The types of brands a company uses, and the way they relate to each other and to the corporate brand, are often referred to as their brand architecture. There are a number of brand architectures in use today but the best known are the branded house and the house of brands (Abraham and Taylor, 2011). According to the World Advertising Research Centre's best practice briefing (WARC, 2012), a house of brands comprises a set of stand-alone brands, e.g. Mars owns Dolmio, Pedigree Petfoods and Uncle Ben's. This architecture helps firms to position different products clearly and to maximise their impact in their target markets. It is also useful for a diverse portfolio where the company needs to distance some brands from each other. For example, customers may not be happy to buy the same brand of chocolate and dog food. A branded house (which is sometimes known as monolithic) uses a single master brand to span a set of products, known as sub-brands. This master brand reassures potential purchasers while the sub-brand serves as a descriptor, e.g. Virgin (master brand): Virgin Trains, Virgin Atlantic, Virgin Mobile, Virgin Media, Virgin Money (sub-brands).

BRAND STRATEGIES

The choice of brand type can almost be said to be a strategy in itself. It certainly has far-reaching consequences for the company's marketing. However, there are some specific strategies that relate to branding.

brand architecture

the structure of an organisation's **brand portfolio** which shows how their brands relate to one another; it typically includes master and sub-brands

branded house

a form of brand architecture which uses a single master brand to span a set of products, known as sub-brands

house of brands

a form of brand architecture which comprises a set of stand-alone brands with their own names and identities, although there may be a reference to the owning brand

Branding strategies are used 'to differentiate products and companies, and to build economic value for both the consumer and the brand owner' (Pickton and Broderick, 2004: 242). The following are some of the more commonly used strategies.

- Co-branding is when two companies' brand names appear together, as on PCs when the brand name of the chip manufacturer appears alongside the PC maker (e.g. 'Intel inside'). Either or both brands should benefit from this as the good reputation of one rubs off on the other.

- Multi-branding is a strategy employed by companies that have multiple products within the same category. This gives the customer the illusion of choice. They can switch brand but still be buying from the same supplier. For example, Procter & Gamble has many different brands of washing powder: Ace, Dreft, Bold (Bolt), Ariel, Dash, Fairy, Daz, Bonus, Vizir and Tide. These are not all available in all countries, and each lays claim to slightly different properties, but they all clean clothes.

The above are ongoing strategies. However, one of the great advantages of a strong brand is that it can be used to launch new products with a far greater chance of success. According to Kotler (2003), there are three ways to introduce more products under the auspices of an existing brand:

1 *line extension*: introducing product variants under the same brand name, e.g. a new flavour or colour

2 *brand extension*: using the brand name on products in a new category but within the same, broadly defined market, e.g. a biscuit company starting to produce cakes

3 *brand stretching*: using the name on products in a different market, e.g. a cigarette company making clothes.

For example, when Robinsons launched a new summer fruits drink flavour, that was a line extension. When Mars started making ice cream bars, that was a brand extension. The king of brand stretching is Richard Branson of Virgin, taking a brand name originally chosen for the music industry and launching it into airlines, drinks, trains, radio, cosmetics, mobile phones, etc. – that is really stretching a brand!

These new product strategies carry different levels of risk. The lowest risk would appear to be the line extension. It can be anticipated that existing, loyal customers will try a new variant of a product they already buy. However, all that is happening here is that they are substituting the new version for the old. There is no overall increase in sales. Line extension does have a role to play, though. It is essential to many brands that new versions be introduced or the line will become boring. Chocolate manufacturers launch new bars. Perfumiers introduce new scents or packaging. Drinks companies try out new flavours. New versions of products replace those that have reached the end of their lives and no longer sell well. A good brand manager anticipates that decline, and has the new variant ready in advance of it (refer to the section on the product life cycle in Chapter 6 and above).

Brand extension carries a higher risk of failure. People loved Mars ice cream. It was such a success that other chocolate manufacturers followed suit. So would you buy any kind of food from Mars? How about frozen ready meals? Baked beans? Breakfast cereal?

digital focus: making Angry Birds fly further

Rovio was founded in Finland in 2003 and had just two employees. Now the company employs more than 500 staff and has offices in China, the USA and Sweden. How did that happen? Rovio is the company that made those birds angry – and let them fly!

Angry Birds is one of the most successful paid-for apps ever. It is available on numerous platforms and in numerous versions; from Brazilian birds to Star Wars. According to Michele Tobin, the company's vice president, brand ad partnerships and advertising in the Americas, its success was based on 'a lot of science, a lot of trial and error and a little bit of magic'.

The existence of over 260 million Angry Birds players across the globe suggests that there may be substantial opportunities for Rovio to expand into other sectors. The company is pursuing brand stretches into theme parks and films. It already sells books and consumer products such as clothing, toys and accessories and has an online store as well as a bricks and mortar store in Helsinki.

Rovio has an impressive animation studio where it produces a weekly cartoon series called Angry Birds Toons. The cartoon is available on a range of media: there is a dedicated channel on Rovio's website, a new button within its games and smart TV apps for appliances made by firms like Samsung and Roku. MTV, the Cartoon Network and Comcast Xfinity on demand have also signed up to broadcast the series, which will be aired in nations from Brazil and India to Germany and the USA.

Each new Rovio game now contains customised, integrated adverts. They favour brands that add value to the games, for example by offering rewards or additional content: 'For us, it is all about how to deliver a better experience that will benefit both the advertiser and our fan base', said Tobin. 'Because we're a multi-faceted media company, we can do some pretty interesting things not only in the game, but outside the game'.

One example of this was an initiative undertaken with McDonald's in China. In a twist on the premise of Angry Birds, the idea was that pigs had stolen food from McDonald's. Television adverts told this story, and giant, empty burger boxes and packs of French fries began to appear in Beijing and Shanghai. The fast-food chain's famous golden arches were turned into slingshots, and limited-edition merchandise was available in branches. This multimedia campaign also used geo-location technology on smartphones to tell fans who were near a McDonald's store that they would receive special in-game rewards and content if they just went inside.

The Rovio company was built on just one game, one idea, but Angry Birds has been an amazing success and prompted huge brand love. One good brand can launch many popular products.

Source: Whiteside (2013)

Unilever successfully extended its Lynx brand. The original Lynx was just a deodorant, but now a wide range of grooming products are available under that brand name. Sometimes a brand carries with it associations that would be unhelpful to the new product. Companies may then actively try to disassociate the two. So Levi's did not call its cotton trouser 'Levi's' but Dockers instead. Sometimes, a company opts for a new range brand name, perhaps coupled with the corporate brand (e.g. Tesco Finest).

The riskiest of these three strategies is brand stretching. Often, the stretched brand breaks. Xerox computers were never as popular as the company's copiers and printers. *Cosmopolitan*'s move into the health food sector (with a range of low-fat dairy products) did not work, nor did its Cosmo Spirit Cafés (Anon, 2003). The strategy does work for some, however, even without a new range brand name. Yamaha successfully added musical instruments, home audio/video equipment, computer peripherals and sports equipment to its motorcycle range. Many retailers have successfully moved into financial services, offering credit cards, loans and insurance. Usually they do not run these services themselves, of course, but license others to do so, lending their name to the enterprise.

research focus

Caldieraro, F., Kao, L.-J. and Cunha, M. (2015) 'Harmful upward line extensions: can the launch of premium products result in competitive disadvantages?', *Journal of Marketing,* **79 (6): 50–70.**
Companies often extend product lines upwards (i.e. by adding premium products) in response to competitive threats and with the goal of increasing demand. In this research, the authors make the case that upward line extensions aimed at matching a competing product may lead consumers to reassess their perceptions about the brand and the attributes of products. Ultimately, this can result in a loss of demand, market share and profit for the extending firm.

GLOBAL BRANDING

Although it is rare to find globally standardised products, there are a number of global brands. A global brand may not have (in fact, almost certainly will not have) a completely standardised marketing mix, but it will have the same brand personality the world over and that personality will be expressed through a visual identity that is standard in its essential design, even though there may be some variance in packaging, languages used, etc.

No logo & corporate brands

Take McDonald's, for example. The golden arches are a well-recognised symbol throughout the world. Ronald McDonald has clowned his way through restaurant openings from New York to Shanghai. The writing beneath the arches may be in another language, or even another alphabet, but the brand identity is nonetheless the same. The products are not exactly the same though, and nor is the marketing mix. In India, Hindus do not eat beef products and so the burgers have to be made of something else, originally mutton but now the Maharaja burgers are chicken. Veggie burgers are also available in India, where the staff who make them wear a different uniform and prepare them separately from the meat (this is an example of a different process). The veggie burgers are also sold in other countries where there is a significant demand for vegetarian foods (e.g. some European countries), but are not generally available in the USA. In predominantly Muslim countries, the burgers are called beefburgers rather than hamburgers because Muslims do not eat pig products and the word 'ham' is therefore off-putting (even though there is no ham in the burger – the name comes from Hamburg where the recipe originated). In Australia, you can get a McOz: a quarter pounder with beetroot, tomato, lettuce and onions.

McDonald's, Beijing.

© Dave Pickton

Prices vary according to local costs, ingredients and income levels. Promotions have to be in the right language and suited to local audiences. In some countries, McDonald's own their own restaurants; elsewhere they are franchised. Some outlets, e.g. in Japan, sell ranges of branded toys and other products; others do not. Yet McDonald's is held, quite rightly, to be the epitome of a global brand. Its image is consistent, as is its positioning.

research focus: classic concepts

Levitt, T. (1983) 'The globalisation of markets', *Harvard Business Review*, **61 (May–Jun): 92–102.**

Ohmae, K. (1989) 'Managing in a borderless world', *Harvard Business Review*, **67 (May–Jun): 152–61.**
These classic papers address the challenges of marketing worldwide in interlinked economies. The papers have at their hearts the inescapable view that marketing should no longer be thought of at a local level alone and suggest how to handle marketing across borders.

BRAND LOYALTY

A company's loyal customers consistently choose that brand over any other. This brand loyalty has to be earned by the company and can be destroyed much more quickly and easily than it can be established. Loyalty is important because loyal customers make the best brand ambassadors, spreading positive word of mouth and so encouraging others to buy the product, and because repeat purchases mean a steadier, more reliable volume of sales for the company in question. Quality is crucial, both in the product itself, and in any supporting service. Poor service will lead to disappointment in the purchase and a reluctance, if not a downright refusal, of a company's loyal customers to consistently choose that brand over any other.

brand loyalty
the attachment that a customer or consumer feels to a favourite product

A customer who repeatedly purchases the same brand may, or may not, be loyal to it. True loyalty comes from an ongoing relationship, not from convenience. So a customer who shops in their local supermarket every week may do so out of convenience rather than loyalty. It may sound like this does not matter, as the sales are made anyway, but what happens when another store opens nearby? Does that supposedly loyal customer stay with the shop they have always used or do they switch? Also, where do they shop when they are away from home? Truly loyal customers will stick with their store and that makes them valuable.

Brand loyalty is based on an emotional bond between the customer and the brand. It can be very personal and powerful, and is usually formed on the basis of past experience, past brand encounters. When Coca-Cola launched New Coke in the USA in the 1980s, the reaction from customers was phenomenal. The product had been extensively blind taste-tested in the marketplace and had been almost universally described as having a superior taste to original Coke. However, when the new version replaced the old, public reaction was violent. Street protests took place to demand that the old recipe be reinstated. Customers were so emotionally involved with the brand, it meant so much to them, that the change was felt as a personal blow. They felt betrayed and so their loyalty was tested to the limit. Wisely, just 79 days after the launch, Coca-Cola changed back – and apologised.

It is far more expensive to win a new customer than to keep an existing one and so it is cost-effective (as well as nice) to build these emotional linkages, and hence brand loyalty. Wise companies calculate the customer lifetime values (the net present value of all their purchases of the brand, past and future), rather than just looking at short-term sales. This approach is not without its drawbacks, however. The very act of calculation tends to reduce exchanges to transactions rather than relationships (Peelen, 2005), and without a good relationship with customers it is unlikely that the company will retain customers for a lifetime anyway.

Brands as lovemarks

ACTIVITY

Pick a favourite product – one that you are loyal to (a chocolate bar, drink, restaurant, brand of sports equipment, TV programme). Make a list of what might cause you to buy, watch or consume something else instead.

A strong brand is a good starting point for building brand loyalty, but the loyalty does not happen automatically. Loyalty comes out of a good, mutually beneficial relationship and its foundation is trust. This trust must go both ways. Clearly, customers must trust the brand. They must feel comfortable with it, secure that products will do what they are supposed to, that the quality will be maintained, that their brand experience will be the same as it was the last time they made a purchase, and the time before, and the time before that. Equally, the company must display some trust in its customers. A company that treats customers as if they are trying to con it will never build a relationship with those customers, will never gain their loyalty. This demonstration of trust can be an explicit part of the offer, or it may be demonstrated on an individual basis as part of the brand's customer service. For example, Virgin Wines will leave a delivery of 12 bottles of wine on a customer's doorstep if they are out when the delivery driver calls. If the wine is stolen, they replace it with no questions asked. Similarly, they encourage their customers to try wines by offering to refund any bottles that the customer does not like. Clearly, it would be easy to take advantage of this but, as the company has been making those offers for a large number of years now, it would seem that Virgin customers are generally honest and so the company's trust is not misplaced.

Customer satisfaction is a key contributor to loyalty, but not all satisfied customers will be loyal. For example, you may have really enjoyed the last holiday you took – the flight, hotel, resort and value were all great – but you will probably want to go somewhere else next time. Satisfied customers will have a positive attitude towards the company and will probably intend to buy from it again. This, however, may not be enough to clinch the actual sale. A positive attitude is only a predisposition to behaviour; other things often get in the way and cause a person to do something else. They may even go out with the intention of buying one thing but come home with another. (For more on attitudes and their relationship to behaviour, see Chapter 3.)

Customers remain loyal because they value what they get from a firm (Reichfeld, 1994). This value mainly comes from product quality, functionality and style, service and support. These things are not all within the control of the marketing department, so if a company wants to build loyalty, it needs all departments to work together to achieve this. There needs to be an integration of customer-related activities across the whole organisation. This is easier for companies with a customer focus (see Chapter 1).

research focus

Matzler, K., Pichler, E., Füller, J. and Mooradian, T.A. (2011) 'Personality, person–brand fit, and brand community: an investigation of individuals, brands, and brand communities', *Journal of Marketing Management*, 27 (9–10): 874–90.
This paper, based on research with car enthusiasts attending a 'brandfest', investigates the links between personality traits, product attachment, brand trust and loyalty, and the desire to be part of a brand community.

The meeting of customer needs is at the heart of good marketing. Marketers have to get inside their customers' heads and see the offering through their eyes. If the offering is noticeably better than that of the competition, then competitive advantage will be created. For example, it may be better quality, or cheaper, have a better image or be more readily available. The marketing mix will be more effective if it is well integrated, i.e. each element fits with the others so that there are no contradictory signals (see 'Mixing it' below). Resources are always a constraint on marketing activities. There is no point in designing a mix that the company does not have the resources (finance, expertise, time or a suitable infrastructure) to implement.

THE MARKETING MIX: A REPRISE
FIRST THERE WERE 4PS: THE TRADITIONAL MARKETING MIX

Each of the 4Ps is covered in more depth in its own chapter (Chapters 6–10). This chapter focuses on integrating the elements of the marketing mix to build brands and also introduces some of the additional complexities associated with international marketing. Exhibit 11.5 summarises the 4Ps and shows how they can fit together.

Product	Price	Place	Promotion
Features (characteristics, attributes)	Price range	Intermediaries (retailers, wholesalers, etc.)	Advertising
Range	Discounts	Coverage	Personal selling
Support services	Allowances	Order processing	Public relations
Brand	Negotiation policy	Stock control	Sales promotion
Design	Credit policy	Delivery	Direct marketing
Packaging	Price changes	Transport	Sponsorship

EXHIBIT 11.5 The 4Ps: key variables

PRODUCT

It may seem obvious just what a product is (a pen, a car, a ring, a bar of chocolate, etc.), but there is rather more to it than that.

Products of the same type, e.g. cars, and even produced by the same manufacturer, e.g. Ford, are differentiated by features, quality, size, speed, shape and colour. They have different features (engine size, braking system, colour, interior trim, etc.) and come in different sizes for different drivers (small car, small family car, family car, executive, limousine, van, minibus, people carrier, etc.). All these things are characteristics (or attributes) of a particular car and so a product could be said to be a bundle of characteristics. It is the quality of these features, coupled with the workmanship that goes into the product, that determines its quality. Quality is something that most customers look for in a product, even though they cannot always afford to buy the best. This is an example of how the marketing mix integrates. The best components, such as those that go into a Rolls-Royce (e.g. walnut veneer dashboards), cost more than others (e.g. plastic dashboards). This means that a higher price will have to be set for the products that have the higher quality components. Some customers will be willing and able to pay that price (so long as the quality really is better), some will not. Those who do buy a Rolls-Royce will be buying not just a car but an exclusive image as well. They will therefore expect impeccable service, both before and after the sale.

Most consumer products are adapted in some way to suit the needs of different countries although there is some convergence of global tastes and preferences, largely due to improved communications and the efforts of multinational and global companies. This allows manufacturers to standardise products in certain categories. For example, Gillette's Mach 3 was developed as a world product. It is a standard shaving system designed to meet the needs of men who want a quicker, closer shave – whatever their nationality.

There are some products that look the same and are assumed to be the same, but even Coca-Cola is not the same in all countries, e.g. it has more sugar in India than it does in Europe. There are many more standardised products in b2b and industrial markets. Raw ingredients such as vegetables, commodities such as salt, metals, minerals and gemstones are all more likely to be standard, as are many office and computer supplies.

Companies provide a range of products, of differing quality, with different features, different images and different levels of support, to match the prices that different customers are prepared to pay for that product type.

A product is a bundle of characteristics but, of course, that is not what customers really want to buy. What the customer really wants is the *benefit* that the product brings. People do not just buy cars, they buy means of transport or status symbols. They do not really buy rings because they want small bands of metal, they want tokens of affection, gifts, decorated fingers, symbols of their engagement. Marketers must concentrate on the benefits their products bring to their purchasers – the product features and quality are really just the means by which those benefits are delivered.

Products have a number of levels, which together make up the total product offering. Customers may decide between two products on the basis of any of the attributes listed in Exhibit 11.5, e.g. customer support, but they will not buy a product that does not deliver the core benefit required. A pen must write, chocolate must taste good, a car must go.

The basic product is the product itself and includes features, components and quality level. Remember that this may be a physical product or a service product. Service products also have features, components, quality levels, etc. Take a dry cleaning service, for example. It may be local (a feature), include ironing (a component), be standard or gold service (quality), and be given back to the customer in a plastic bag or a strong clothes carrier (packaging). The perceived product is the product as the customer actually sees it, which may not be in quite the way the supplier intended. For example, a restaurant may wish to be thought of as upmarket, but its target market may just think it is over-priced. The augmented product is the surrounding support for the product, including all support services, delivery and installation.

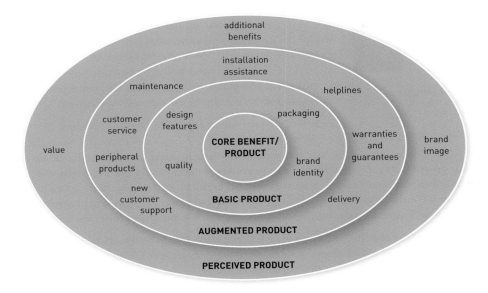

EXHIBIT 11.6 The total product offering

Take a shirt as an example. Its core benefits are that it covers nakedness and provides some warmth. As a basic product, the shirt is blue, fashionably styled, available in most sizes and made of 100% cotton of the highest quality. The supplier offers a no-quibble, money-back guarantee if the shirt fails to live up to expectations. This augments (adds to) the product. If the shirt in question also happens to be made by Armani, how does that affect the perception of it?

Previously, firms tried to differentiate themselves from their competition through tangible product advantages: their products might be better quality, come in more colours, have additional features, etc. Competitive strategies centred upon developing a product that was demonstrably superior to competitors' products and then updating it regularly in order to maintain that superior position. However, as markets have become more competitive, tangible product differences are harder to maintain and so the augmented product has become the main source of competitive edge for many companies – providing their unique selling propositions (USPs).

unique selling proposition (USP)
a clear point of differentiation for a product/service

The term USP originally stood for 'unique selling point' and was first used by Rosser Reeves, whose idea was that advertising worked best when it made one clear point. Unfortunately, the phrase was picked up and reinterpreted as meaning that a product must have a unique feature, something that it is increasingly hard to maintain (Pickton and Broderick, 2004). The word 'point' caused confusion and consequently 'unique selling proposition' is the

Famous faces can help make brands famous too.

© spatuletail/Shutterstock.com

definition now generally preferred. The USPs of today are most likely to be derived from additional services or from branding. (For more on services, see Chapter 7.)

The brand is part of the augmented product and is one of the best ways to differentiate a product from its competition. Towards the end of the twentieth century, branding came to be seen as the main contributor to a company's competitive edge. The emphasis was on brand value. Leading brands battled for the loyalty of consumers: few more fiercely than the big sportswear companies, Nike, Reebok and Adidas, who spent millions on promoting their brands. They competed as fiercely to sponsor the best, or in some cases the most photogenic, sports stars as those athletes competed themselves.

Some highly successful organisations are just brands – they don't actually make anything and may franchise the selling operation too. For example, Virgin has lent its name to a number of products (vodka, cola, cosmetics) that it has very little to do with. At the beginning of the twenty-first century, the brand's power began to look less sure. Customers want more value than a brand alone can give. Strong brands have become part of their consumers' lives, moving from being a part of the consumers' identity and a way to declare certain values to the world, to a defining personal characteristic.

Products may be at different stages in their product life cycles in different countries, although these differences are reducing as the forces of globalisation gather force. Exporting has long been seen as a means of extending a product's life cycle but, with the convergence of life cycles internationally, the general shortening of product lives and the trend for global brands to launch new products simultaneously in multiple countries, this is becoming less common.

PROMOTION (MARKETING COMMUNICATIONS)

Consumers have a wide choice of products on which to spend their money. Sellers try to influence that choice through the use of promotion. This is the part of the marketing mix that is primarily concerned with communication, which is why it is now more commonly known as marketing communications. Marketing communications is thought to be a better term as it is a more accurate description and because there was always the possibility of confusion between promotion and sales promotion. Marketing communications and promotion are interchangeable terms and this book uses both.

The promotion mix traditionally comprises:

- advertising
- public relations (PR)
- sales promotion
- personal selling.

Direct marketing communication and sponsorship can be added to these.

Advertising uses paid media (advertisers buy space or air time in which to show their adverts), e.g. television, radio, cinema, Internet, leaflets. Media relations is a large part of public relations (PR) and this uses earned media, mainly through media releases, the placing or seeding of stories, press conferences or briefings, and publicity stunts. Although PR does not use paid-for space or air time, it would be a mistake to describe PR as free. PR agencies do not work for free and there are printing and other costs to account for as well.

Media vary in their availability and quality. Some countries have no national press, some have no local press. In remote parts, television reception may be poor. The Internet is still banned in parts of the world (although this is hard to enforce in practice). In recent years, many companies have made their first foray abroad via the Internet which is an excellent direct sales medium provided that the product in question does not require too much personal support.

Walls ice cream displays from around the world.

© Dave Pickton

Organisations use a range of PR activities, including exhibitions, hospitality, sponsorship and product placement. All of these are designed to build relationships with audiences and promote understanding of the organisation and its activities. Trade fairs and exhibitions are often important to firms who are trying to get established in an overseas market. These provide the perfect place to demonstrate products, meet potential buyers and agents, and check out the competition.

Short-term special offers (money-off coupons, multibuys, competitions, free trials, etc.) are called sales promotions and are a popular choice, especially among FMCG retailers. Personal selling ranges from sales assistants in shops, through door-to-door salespeople and telesales, to the high-level account managers who sell large capital items (such as bridges and mainframe computers) to governments and the boards of multinational clients.

All these activities must be integrated so that they support, rather than contradict, each other. The same message and tone should come through from each activity. This is an important part of building brand image. As well as being integrated with each other, marketing communications activities must also fit with the rest of the marketing mix as the message comes through from all of the mix, not just from explicit communications. Harrods sells quality products at premium prices, and its communications must be similarly upmarket. A gaudy advert in a downmarket magazine offering a BOGOF would detract from its carefully cultivated image. (For more on marketing communications, see Chapter 8.)

While promotional strategies may be global, differences of language and environment mean that they can rarely be absolutely standard in their detail. Adverts, packaging and promotions will all have to be translated. Different images, and actors, may need to be used if locals are to relate to them. Some countries insist on local actors appearing in all adverts and there are numerous other regulations that affect what promoters can and cannot do, country by country. There are a number of ways around these problems. Television and cinema adverts may be dubbed (although this does not help overcome the foreign looks of the actors). Some companies develop pattern adverts. These have a consistent look and tone, although some images and the slogan may be written for a specific audience.

hospitality

hosting clients (e.g. providing refreshments in a private room) at events

BOGOF

buy one get one free

pattern adverts

partial standardisation of advertising, useful in international marketing; the adverts have the same look and feel although some images and the slogan may be written for a particular place or purpose

b2b focus: marketing communications

The biggest promotional tool in b2b is personal selling. Firms who operate in b2b markets, rather than consumer markets, usually have fewer customers who buy more. This makes the expense of salespeople worthwhile. Salespeople can explain complex products and build relationships with their customers. They are an important source of competitive edge and repeat business.

Trade shows and exhibitions are important in business markets. Most industries have these (e.g. Internet World, the Motor Show, the Boat Show). They are good for networking, product demonstrations, identifying prospects, building contact databases, entertaining customers and checking out the competition.

Businesses do use advertising to market to other businesses, but they use different media. Television would be overkill. Most adverts appear in the specialist trade press, such as *The Grocer, Computing, Accountancy Age, Environmental Engineering* and *The Hat* magazine or on the Internet. Sometimes businesses will do some consumer marketing to help their trade customers sell products on. So diamond miners might promote jewellery to increase the derived demand for diamonds.

PLACE (DISTRIBUTION AND LOGISTICS)

Place is perhaps the least descriptive of the marketing mix titles and therefore the most likely to cause confusion. Place refers to the whole distribution process – from customer enquiry to after-sales service. In consumer marketing, the place where the actual sale happens is part of that, but it is not the whole story. In b2b, the sale often takes place on the customer's premises, where a salesperson has called.

marketing channel

another term for distribution channel

The marketing channel, or distribution channel, illustrated in Exhibit 11.7, is a three-level channel (i.e. there are three links in the chain between the manufacturer of the product and the eventual customer).

EXHIBIT 11.7 Example marketing channel for clothing

Designing the most effective and efficient marketing channels is an important part of marketing management. The longer the channel, the more removed the producer of the product is from its customers and the more opportunity there is for things to go wrong. Most manufacturers have little or no customer contact; it is the retailer who builds a relationship with the customer. This lack of contact makes it harder for manufacturers to get to know what their customers think of the products, what they would like to see changed, what new products they might like. It also means they have to work harder to build brand loyalty.

The shortest channel is a zero-level (0-level) channel. This means direct sales – there are no intermediaries. The product's producers deal with the customer themselves.

Marketing managers have to work out not only the length of a channel, but also its breadth. How many retailers, distributors, etc. will handle the product? The answer will partly depend on whether this is an exclusive or a mass-market product. Is it cheap or expensive? Again, the mix intermingles. The nature of the product helps to determine the nature of the channel.

Channel design is only the beginning. The supply chain for a product may be complex, spanning several countries, and will require careful ongoing management. Good relationships throughout the chain are essential for long-term success. Distributors need support and encouragement if they are to choose to push the right product forward.

Indirect exporters leave the job of getting goods to customers to someone else, but companies with a more direct involvement have to organise distribution themselves. This can be a difficult task as distribution channels, and the nature of the intermediaries available, can vary enormously. The Japanese distribution infrastructure used to be so fiendishly complicated that some would-be exporters claimed it was an unofficial barrier to trade. (For more on place, see Chapter 9.)

Place is about getting the right product to the right customer at the right time. A lot goes on behind the scenes to ensure that this happens.

ACTIVITY

Given the availability of the Internet, its relatively low cost and the fact that most households now have access to it, why don't all manufacturers sell directly to customers? Why do they let their products be sold through traditional marketing channels at all? What is it that they may not be able to do, or not do as well as wholesalers and/or retailers?

Think this problem through from the point of view of:

- a PC manufacturer such as Hewlett Packard
- an FMCG manufacturer such as Kellogg's
- a car manufacturer such as Renault
- a shoe manufacturer such as Havaianas.

mass market
a homogeneous market, i.e. there is no distinction between segments

digital focus: channel conflict

The Internet has opened up new markets for all members of the supply chain, from raw materials suppliers through to retailers. This freer market access brings new competition with it, both from companies at the same level in the supply chain and from those at different levels who were not previously seen as competitors at all. Organisations can reach previously inaccessible markets, e.g. overseas markets, and at the same time the distinction between levels is blurring as wholesalers and manufacturers sell directly to consumers.

For example, a number of sportswear retailers have set up Internet sites to offer their customers an alternative way to buy sporting goods. In the world of e-commerce, these retailers may have to deal with competition from retailers in other countries (although in practice, many retailers cannot cope with supplying overseas orders and so only deliver to specific locations). Most of these retailers get their stocks from wholesalers, who can also now sell sports goods directly to consumers as can the sportswear manufacturers.

Wholesalers and manufacturers do not operate from smart high street stores and so, in the past, were not equipped to deal with end customers. Now they can. With an Internet site, they can cut out the retailers and sell direct.

This merging of customer bases is a cause of channel conflict. Supply chain members are able to compete with other members higher up, or lower down, the chain. Some manufacturers choose not to compete. They may offer products direct to customers but make sure that the deal is not as good as can be obtained at online retail sites. There is sound reasoning behind this strategy, and it is often to do with order administration and the problems of dealing with thousands of customers when you are only used to dealing with tens of customers.

PRICE

Price is the one element of the marketing mix that does not need a budget. The other three Ps all cost significant amounts. Price brings the money in.

At one level, the price is what a business charges its customer for the goods and services it provides. However, the product that the customer is buying may actually cost more than the price suggests. This may be because of hidden costs, such as a computer upgrade required before the software will run, or it may be more subtle, like the time it will take the customer to install the new software (time is money), or the loss of the benefits they would have got if they had bought a different package. So the organisation needs to bear these other things in mind when setting the actual price.

The price of a product is usually the most significant part of the value that a customer hands over in exchange for a product. Therefore, the perceived value of the product must be at least equal to the price. Other elements of the mix can be used to increase the perceived value and therefore allow the charging of a higher price, e.g. attractive or useful packaging, a free gift or an additional feature such as the bonus disks that come with some DVDs.

Organisations with trading partners or customers overseas, have to choose a currency in which to price contracts for sale. Given that marketing is about meeting customer needs, it would seem to be good marketing practice to price in the customer's currency. However, this has some disadvantages for the seller in terms of costs and practicalities of converting the customer's currency into their own. In practice, many contracts are priced in a well-accepted, stable, easily convertible currency, such as the US dollar – whether or not one of the parties is American.

Goods and services that are sold directly to end-users or consumers, rather than through marketing channels, will normally have to be priced in the local currency.

The price of a product sends a message to potential customers: high quality, cheap and cheerful, bargain, or somewhere in between. It is important that this message accords with the actual product. If Rolls-Royce halved its prices, people would be likely to think that the quality had dropped significantly. If Toshiba drops the price of its computers because a new model will be out soon, people may see this as a bargain and snap them up. The price and the product must match up if marketing is to work successfully.

Prices must also be in accord with place. If a restaurant wants to charge high prices, it usually needs not just good food, but also to be in a prime location. Perhaps then the restaurant critics will give it good write-ups (which is good PR). (For more on price, see Chapter 10.)

PACKAGING: THE FIFTH P?

Whether or not we grant packaging the status of a fifth P, it is certainly a very important part of the product offering. Packaging transcends the traditional 4Ps, playing a part in each and every one.

It is part of the product. Many products have to be packed or they cannot be sold. For example, the product may be liquid (e.g. cough syrup), dangerous (e.g. acid), potentially damaging (e.g. hair dye), delicate (e.g. contact lenses) or perishable (e.g. foodstuffs). As well as protecting the product, the packaging may be there to protect consumers. Childproof tops protect the young from accidental ingestion of harmful medicines. Tamper-proof packs prevent the malicious from poisoning, or otherwise spoiling, products.

Sometimes the packaging is more than a means to contain the product; it is an integral part. Products such as toothpaste turn packaging into a feature: pump or tube? Food can be packaged in different ways and this turns it into different products. For example, peas may be sold in tins, jars, packets, vacuum packs or their original pods. Individual drinks cartons have straws attached to make them easier to drink on the go.

Some packs are deliberately made attractive so that people will use them rather than put the product into something else (e.g. some of Marks & Spencer's desserts come in glass bowls). This can be good promotion too if the pack has the product's name on it. How many people, even in cafés, bother to decant ketchup out of the bottle rather than have it sitting on the table advertising Heinz?

Packaging can be a key consumer decision criterion, especially for commodity products. Take milk as an example. Milk can be packaged in a number of ways: glass bottle, plastic bottle, paper carton, tin or packet (for dried milk). Some customers may choose the milk with the carton that is easiest to open, or the one that pours best, or keeps the milk freshest longest, or survives freezing.

Innovative packaging can confer competitive advantage. A supplier who invents a new and better way of packaging has an advantage over its competitors – at least until they catch up. Imagine having been the first to put fruit juice into a small carton with a straw, milk in an easy-pour carton, shampoo in a sachet or tissues in a pocket-sized pack.

The packaging is a key part of the brand's visual identity and so is jealously guarded by brand owners. Coca-Cola watches competitors carefully and is quick to object if any rival product looks too similar to its own (e.g. the first can design for Sainsbury's Cola bore too close a resemblance). Distinctive packaging becomes associated with the product and is the means by which the product is recognised: Jif's lemon juice is packed in a yellow plastic lemon. Perrier has a distinctive green bottle.

Internationally consistent packaging has the advantage of being recognisable to travellers and so is especially important for products that might be bought by visitors to a country: camera film, headache pills, toiletries, suntan lotion, etc. They may not speak the language well enough to ask and so the sight of a familiar package will reassure them and give that product a competitive edge over others.

Packaging is sometimes referred to as the silent salesperson because of its marketing communications role. Packaging sends a message about the product inside. This may be explicit (i.e. it may be a slogan or on-pack promotion) or it may be implied through the packaging's style. Advertisements often contain a pack shot, usually at the end of the ad. It is hoped that this image of the pack will stay with the consumer and then, when they see it in the shop, they will remember the message of the advert. This is particularly useful for products that rely on recognition, i.e. when customers may browse shelves looking for a suitable product to buy (this applies to most FMCG).

Packaging is also informative. It states country of origin, lists ingredients, gives instructions for use and carries warnings (e.g. not suitable for children under three).

The packaging can also be used to persuade people to use more of the product. Allegedly, Domestos increased its sales substantially by changing the instruction 'use sparingly' to 'use

on-pack promotion
a promotional offer printed on the product's packaging

pack shot
a picture of the product, in its packaging, used in an advert to aid recognition

liberally'. Foodstuffs regularly carry recipes designed to encourage cooks to see how else the product can be used. Imaginative packaging can help to sell the firm's other products, e.g. by including other products in the recipes, attaching a trial-size packet of biscuits to the coffee (or vice versa). There are many possibilities.

Packaging can be varied to give a company more pricing options. Refill packs are cheaper than original products. Larger sizes are often better value.

Good packaging is essential to protect products during distribution. Secondary packaging (large cartons and palettes) may be needed here to make sure goods are easy to handle, can be stacked safely, and arrive at their destination in good condition. Sometimes this secondary packaging can be turned to good promotional advantage. Packets of crisps, which are notoriously hard to keep on the shelves (they sell fast and so run out, and they also slip about), are normally supplied to retailers in large brown boxes. One innovative crisp company decided to use these boxes to give their crisps an edge. They perforated a hole in one side of the box so that, when the hole was punched in, customers could reach into the box and pull out the crisps. The boxes had become display stands (all bearing the crisp manufacturer's name and logo, of course). Shops no longer had to unpack the crisps and restock the shelves. When a box was empty they just brought in the next box.

ethical focus: the lookalikes

A number of manufacturers have taken retailers to court over own-label brands that just look too much like the real thing. The complaint may be about the make-up of the product itself or it may be about the packaging – an infringement of the brand is potentially even more damaging than a rip-off of the product itself.

Tesco, Marmite and Asda's own brand yeast spread – packaged inspiration.

© Dave Pickton

• United Biscuits, makers of the much-loved Penguin, sued ASDA over its Puffin bars.

• Coca-Cola's objection to Sainsbury's Classic Cola can resulted in a redesign.

• Kellogg's has complained about the package design of Tesco's breakfast cereals.

• ASDA was in trouble over the appearance of its own-label versions of popular spirits such as Archers and Malibu.

Lookalikes

The original manufacturers have put millions into brand development and don't see why these retailers should cash in. It is difficult to decide where to draw the line – when is it a product inspired by the original and when is it a cheap imitation?

Packaging must be especially carefully designed for overseas markets. The following should be taken into account:

• any laws and regulations governing its composition, recycling, the languages used.

• cultural issues that may affect the size of the packet, the colours used – and the languages used.

- education and literacy levels in the country – how should the instructions be written? Perhaps they should be diagrammatic? Dangerous products (e.g. pharmaceuticals) must be especially carefully explained.

- transport – one of packaging's main functions is to protect the goods during transit. How rough is the handling likely to be?

THE EXTENDED MARKETING MIX: 7PS

The 4Ps do not provide enough scope for the support of modern products, many of which have a strong service element. The 7Ps were developed as a marketing mix for services, but 7Ps are really more appropriate than 4Ps for all but the simplest products today. Exhibit 11.8 shows examples of the use of the additional 3Ps.

Example products	Examples of physical evidence: the tangible aspects of the service	Examples of people: who deliver the service	Examples of process: how the service is delivered
Car cleaning	Car shampoo, sponges	The cleaners	While you shop
Restaurant meal	Food, tables, cutlery	Cooks, toilet cleaners	Self-service
Car hire	The car, maps	Receptionist, mechanics	Car delivered to home address
Personal computer	Retail environment	Shop assistants, helpline operators	Assistants' approach to customers in store, call-queuing systems

EXHIBIT 11.8 Examples of use of the additional 3Ps

The first three products in Exhibit 11.8 are services, while the last one is a physical product, a PC, but it still has a number of service elements that are important to the customer. Retailing is itself a service and so the shopper is a service user. With a product like a PC, there may be more service elements involved: helplines, installation assistance, maintenance, etc. Contrast this with an FMCG purchase, such as soap powder. There is no installation help or maintenance required for this product, but there is still a retail service to be provided. Also, check the side of the box. Many FMCG products do offer advice lines or similar services – all are designed to try to establish a relationship with the customer and offer a better service.

These additional 3Ps must also be integrated into marketing plans. They too should support the rest of the mix, not clash with it.

PHYSICAL EVIDENCE

Physical evidence includes peripheral products, such as free peanuts on a bar, products that are part of the service, such as ice in a drink, the décor of the place where the service is provided – and anything else that is tangible, but not the actual physical product itself.

The physical evidence may be the key thing in setting customer expectations. A smart, trendy bar with genuine art on the walls, expensive-looking furniture and waiters in tuxedos sets the expectation of superior service, a good wine list, high prices and a classy clientele. Contrast that with a typical local pub or bar, with posters and a wide-screen TV on the walls, a footrest around the base of the bar, hard-back chairs, a jukebox and the bar staff in T-shirts. Quite a different customer expectation is set. Customer expectations are extremely important in marketing, and particularly in services marketing. A customer who has been let down, i.e. has received a service that does not meet their expectations, is an unhappy customer. They are liable to complain and to say unflattering things about the product to their friends. Often, if they had received the same service but had known what to expect beforehand and chosen it anyway, then they will be quite content with that situation.

So physical evidence is an important aspect of customer service and must match the rest of the mix if expectations are to be met.

PEOPLE

Most services require people to deliver them and to receive them. Although there are an increasing number of services delivered electronically, e.g. Internet messaging, where people's involvement is limited to the original set-up and maintenance of the service and dealing with queries and complaints, people remain an important asset for most service providers. The quality of the service is liable to be largely dependent upon the quality of the people involved in its delivery and so, once again, the people must match the rest of the mix. A high-class restaurant needs silver service waiters; a burger joint does not.

The people who deliver the service are an integral part of its marketing mix, as are the people who receive that service. Customers are part of the interaction and influence the way a service operates. For example, it is quite possible for two people to eat the same meal in the same restaurant and experience the same service but one will love it and one hate it. This is equally true of concerts, haircuts and service from shop assistants.

PROCESS

Process starts long before a service is actually experienced. It starts with the prospect's very first contact with the service-providing organisation. This may be reading a brochure, visiting a website, making a phone call or calling into an office or shop. The process of service delivery is key to customer satisfaction and therefore to the stimulation of positive word of mouth and repeat business. The restaurant can be the smartest in the world, the staff the best trained and friendliest, but if customers find their booking has been lost, or if the food takes hours to arrive, they will not be happy. In a pizza restaurant, however, there may be no advance bookings and customers may be expected to queue. Customers may be happy to do this, especially if they are able to sit in the bar and have a drink, listen to music, read the menu. That is all part of the process.

Once again, the process has to be right, and fit with the rest of the marketing mix, if the product is to be a success. (For more on the 7Ps, see Chapter 7.)

MIXING IT (INTEGRATING THE MARKETING MIX)

Each element of the marketing mix should support the others. They should build to a consistent whole that accords with the organisation's brand values and so builds the brand's image. For example, an upmarket, exclusive fashion brand would:

- require high-quality products, made with top-class fabrics, that are well styled and well made, perhaps finished by hand (product)
- command premium prices (price)
- be sold in more exclusive, fabulously done-up stores (place, physical evidence)
- be sold by smart, fashionably dressed staff (people)
- provide an alteration service to achieve a perfect fit (process)
- be promoted in a tasteful, creative way, perhaps with adverts placed in fashion and life-style magazines, and with suitably upmarket celebrities wearing the clothes (promotion).

However, a mass-market clothing brand might:

- use cheaper fabrics and mass-production techniques while keeping fancy trims to a minimum
- undercut competitors' prices
- be sold everywhere
- be carried home in cheap carrier bags
- be promoted extensively, in newspapers and magazines that the customers read, on billboards, even on flyers.

flyer
a short brochure

These mixes send clear, but very different, messages about the company's offering. If the messages are contradictory, then customers will become confused. You cannot charge a high price but use cheap materials (at least not for long). If your products are on sale every-where, they lose their exclusive image (this is why Levi's was so keen to stop Tesco selling its jeans, and why perfumers such as Calvin Klein do not want their products sold in high street stores such as Superdrug).

The marketing mix is used to implement marketing strategies and plans. It is the mar-keter's toolkit, and deciding how to use each tool is a key part of the marketer's job. Those decisions are made in the light of the organisation's objectives and its overall strategy to meet those objectives. Look back at the above example: if a brand wants to maintain its upmarket position, then clearly it must be in the best shops and be made of high-quality materials. The desired market position informs the choice of how to use marketing tools. With the marketing purpose firmly in mind, marketing managers are able to design effective marketing programmes, which must be based on a well-coordinated marketing mix.

VARYING THE MIX THROUGH A PRODUCT'S LIFE

Marketers do not decide on the best marketing mix for a new product and leave it at that forever. The mix has to be varied over time in response to, or in anticipation of, the chang-ing marketing environment (see Chapter 2) and the brand's circumstances. The product life cycle (which was introduced in Chapter 6) provides an illustration of how the optimal marketing mix may change over time (see Exhibit 11.9).

The product life cycle model was originally devised for generic products, i.e. the product type not the individual branded item (e.g. shoes, not Clark's shoes). It can, however, be applied to individual, branded products as well.

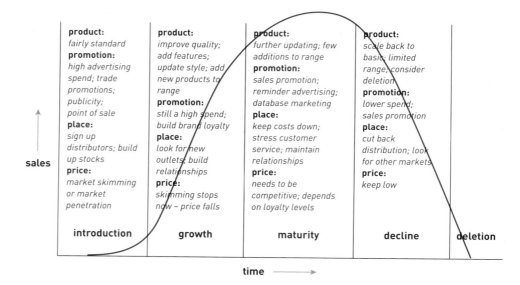

EXHIBIT 11.9 Mixing it through the product life cycle

INTRODUCTION

Products are often very expensive to launch. The research and development that goes into a new product can cost hundreds of thousands or even millions, and will have to be recouped in the early life of the product. Initially, the promotion budget will be at its highest. People do not know about this new product and so they must be told. There may be no distribution channels and so those need to be built up. If the product is a new invention (e.g. 3D films, space flights or domestic robots), then the company may be able to use a price-skimming strategy to help recover some of its costs more quickly (see Chapter 10). However, the prospect of large profits will encourage competitors into the market (unless the new product is protected by patents – though often even these are not enough).

GROWTH

During the product's growth stage, organisations should be focusing on building brand loyalty and encouraging repeat purchases. They might introduce new products or lines and add more advanced features to existing products. A lower price may attract new customers or encourage existing ones to buy more. However, if the initial strategy was penetration pricing, perhaps for a me-too product, then prices may now be put up. Distribution coverage is vital to build up sales. A good push strategy (i.e. promoting the product to members of the distribution channel) may encourage retailers and other intermediaries to stock the product.

me-too product

a new product that is an imitation of an existing, competitive one

MATURITY

By this stage there are likely to be a larger number of competitors in the market and so competition for customers is fierce. Promotion strategies will be geared towards maintaining market share and extending this profitable maturity stage for as long as possible.

Good customer service and the rewarding of loyal customers will help to retain them. Generally, the price of a mature product needs to be competitive, but if the firm has done a good job of building brand loyalty, then demand may now be more price inelastic. If its customers are truly loyal, truly committed to the brand, then the firm may actually be able to charge a slightly higher price than its competitors.

DECLINE

When a product is in decline, ranges and features are cut to a minimum. Unprofitable products, and less popular features, are phased out. Expensive promotion is unlikely to be worthwhile and so the marketing communications budget is cut. If there is no immediate replacement on the way, then some distributors may be dropped. Demand for the product is likely to be very price elastic and so prices need to stay low in order to make sales. The exception to this is when a product has built a highly loyal following (perhaps it has gained the status of a cult product), where a few people may be prepared to pay high prices to obtain their beloved product before it disappears forever.

research focus: classic concept

Levitt, T. (1965) 'Exploit the product life cycle', *Harvard Business Review*, **43 (Nov/Dec): 81–94.**
    The product life cycle is a well-accepted concept in marketing although it needs to be applied wisely. In this article, the author demonstrates the significance of product life cycle to marketing planning in each of the stages of the cycle.

CRITICISMS OF THE MARKETING MIX

The mix has been at the heart of marketing since the 1960s, but it is not universally acclaimed. There are those who find the 4Ps too limiting and so add further elements to the list. Some authors feel the fifth P should be packaging, others that it should be people. The element of people is formally included in the 7Ps of services marketing but packaging still moves around.

Jones and Vignali (1994) added an S, for service. It is today recognised that all products have a service element and that this is key to their acceptance and success. Customer service must be at the heart of a market-orientated organisation and the responsibility of everyone in the company, not just the marketing team. Grönroos (1997) considered that to view service as a separate element of the marketing mix would be disastrous for an organisation as it would isolate customer service as a distinct function apart from the rest of the organisation rather than being fully integrated at its core. This would downgrade its importance.

Modern marketing stresses the importance of building good relationships with customers and intermediaries, and so one problem with the marketing mix is that it emphasises techniques rather than customers and their needs. We could see relationship building as part of promotion, but this brings a danger of inducing customer cynicism. Card-based loyalty schemes are viewed by many as mere sales promotion – and customers are likely to have cards, and collect points, from all competitors.

The marketing mix has occasionally evolved into other letters. For example, Lauterborn (1990) proposed the 4Cs:

- customer needs and wants
- cost to the customer
- convenience
- communication.

The 4Cs have the advantage of being more customer focused. However, the 4Ps are indelibly lodged in the minds of several generations of marketers and are likely to be the preferred model for some time to come.

The development of faster and better methods of manufacture has led to the vastly increased level of choice being offered to the customer. This change from a supply-dominated market-place to one where customers demand certain things, and are prepared to look for what they want, comes from the certain knowledge that those things will be available from one of the many possible sources now competing for their business. Increased distribution of goods and services nationally, internationally and globally, presents vast choice to customers. The challenge in such a world is to find customers in the first place, and to hang on to them in the future. This is one of the objectives of branding.

Brand strength is important and so maintaining and building this strength is an essential part of managing a brand. Strong brands sell more easily, both initially and to loyal customers, and are therefore valuable organisational assets.

SUMMARY

Branding is one of the most important marketing strategies to emerge in the late 20th century and is still key to the success of many companies, especially consumer goods companies, today. A strong brand is a valuable asset, leading to higher sales, greater profit and often more loyal customers. However it takes a lot of work to build a brand, and even more to keep it strong.

This chapter has looked at the components of a brand, each of which must be protected and nurtured if brand equity is to be built and maintained. It has considered different types of brand and of brand architectures. It has introduced the concept of brand personality and the more recent idea of brand authenticity.

There are numerous branding strategies which can be key to an organisation's competitive position. These are implemented through a brand plan as part of the overall marketing plan (see Chapter 12).

Most marketing plans rely heavily on the marketing mix for their implementation. The 4Ps has been the most commonly used framework for many years but this is always extended to 7Ps when considering services marketing. As so many products now have service elements to them (warranties, guarantees, after-sales service, retailing, etc.), the 7Ps framework has become generally preferred for all products – tangible and intangible ones. Packaging is another important marketing tool and is often proposed as the fifth P.

Although they remain the most popular frameworks, the 4Ps and 7Ps models are not without their critics, mainly on the grounds that they are insufficiently customer-focused.

A brand's marketing mix should be integrated, each element working with the others to present a united front and support the organisation's marketing objectives. An uncoordinated mix sends conflicting messages to target customers and is much less effective in terms of building brand values and achieving marketing goals.

CHALLENGES REVIEWED

Now that you have finished reading the chapter, look back at the challenges you were set at the beginning. Do you have a clearer idea of what's involved?

HINTS

- The marketing mix must be integrated so all elements should support the organisation's desired position in its market.
- See 'Contribution pricing' in Chapter 10 but also remember that price is seen as a determinant of quality.
- The 7Ps of services marketing are key determinants of the attractiveness of services to customers.
- This is an ethical question – how important is the environment to your firm? Are there ways to maintain the brand identity even when changing packaging (Nestlé managed it with KitKat, for example)?

READING AROUND

JOURNAL ARTICLES

Napoli, J., Dickinson-Delaporte, S. and Beverland, M.B. (2016) 'The brand authenticity continuum: strategic approaches for building value', *Journal of Marketing Management*, 32 (13–14): 1201–29.

Patterson, A., Khogeer, Y. and Hodgson, J. (2013) 'How to create an influential anthropomorphic mascot: literary musings on marketing, make-believe, and meerkats', *Journal of Marketing Management*, 29 (1–2): 69–85.

BOOKS AND BOOK CHAPTERS

Aaker, D.A. (2012) *Building Strong Brands*. London: Simon and Schuster.

Baker, M. (2008) 'The marketing mix', in M.J. Baker and S.J. Hart (eds), *The Marketing Book*. Oxford: Butterworth Heinemann, Chapter 12, pp. 147–59.

de Chernatony, L. (2010) *From Brand Vision to Brand Evaluation* (3rd edn). Oxford: Butterworth Heinemann.

Haig, M. (2006) *Brand Royalty: How the World's Top 100 Brands Thrive and Survive*. London: Kogan Page.

Holt, D. (2004) *How Brands Become Icons: The Principles of Cultural Branding*. Boston: Harvard Business Review Press.

Klein, N. (2000) *No Logo*. London: Flamingo.

WEBSITES

www.cim.co.uk – the Chartered Institute of Marketing.

www.interbrand.com – Interbrand.

TEST YOURSELF

1 What do the terms 'brand image' and 'brand identity' mean? (See pp. 428)

2 How can you assess brand equity? (See pp. 433)

3 Explain the difference between a 'branded house' and a 'house of brands'. (See pp. 435)

4   Define and give examples of: corporate brands, range brands and individual brands. (See pp. 435)

5   What is the difference between a line extension, a brand extension and a brand stretch? (See pp. 436)

6   What are the main arguments for local adaptation of global brands? And for standardisation? (See pp. 486)

7   What are the 7Ps? (See pp. 451)

8   What are the characteristics of a well-designed marketing mix? (See pp. 488)

9   Give examples of marketing tactics appropriate for a product in its growth phase in the product life cycle model. (See pp. 453)

10 How can packaging give a product a competitive advantage? (See pp. 448)

11 Why is it important that all elements of the marketing mix match and support each other? (See pp. 452)

12 What faults can you find with the marketing mix as a framework for marketing activity? (See pp. 455)

REVISION TOOLS

Want to test yourself even more? Review what you have learnt by visiting
https://study.sagepub.com/masterson4e

- Practise for exams with **multiple choice questions**
- Revise key terms with **interactive flashcards**

MINI CASE STUDY: SMALL OBJECTS OF DESIRE

Read the questions, then the case material, and then answer the questions.

QUESTIONS

1   Identify the elements of Apple's brand identity.

2   Was the launch of the iPhone a line extension, a brand extension or a brand stretch? Explain your answer and then discuss the advantages of this strategy.

3   What evidence is there that Apple enjoys a high level of brand loyalty? What advantages does this bring the company?

4   What meanings do you associate with the Apple brand? What has Apple done to help create these connections? What other experiences have influenced your image of the brand?

5   Should electronics manufacturers take responsibility for the impact of their products on the environment? What could they do to make their businesses more environmentally friendly?

Why would anyone queue for over 24 hours to buy an (arguably) over-priced phone? Especially when they could buy it from a shop around the corner for the same price and without queuing at all? Questions like these were puzzling passers-by on the day that the Apple iPhone went on sale in London for the first time.

The queues outside Apple's flagship store in Regent Street started two days before the iPhone's much pub-licised arrival. It was November. It was cold and wet. Even the people queuing seemed bemused as to why they were doing it. 'I'm a commercial director. This is ridiculous behaviour for someone like me', said one member of the queue, while a civil servant near the front offered at least a partial explanation for why he wanted to be one of the first to own the iPhone: 'Several of my colleagues have tried to arrange meetings with me on Monday just to have a look at it'.

The Apple iPhone combines a phone with a fully featured web browser, advanced camera and music player. Even at the time of its launch, it was by no means the only device on the market to do all of these things. There were a number of cheaper rivals but none of them inspired the adulation given to Apple's new product. Fans of the iPhone raved over the deceptive simplicity of the design and were especially enthusiastic about the minimalist touchscreen. The iPhone is beyond such restraints as a conventional keypad. Lucky iPhone owners just brush their fingertips over the sleek, full-colour display. *Time Magazine* called it 'the invention of the year'.

Over half a million iPhones were sold over the weekend of its launch in the USA. This extraordinary level of sales made the company's first-year sales target of 10 million devices look easily achievable. With that sales volume, Apple would achieve 1% global mobile market share which, while impressive for a new entrant in such a short space of time, would still be a long way short of market domination – in volume terms at least.

Apple has a reputation for leading-edge technology and attention to detail, particularly style detail. Very few other brands generate such interest and inspire the number of brand ambassadors that Apple does. Apple customers believe that the company really cares about the way they use the technology –and about the way people look while using the technology. As a web designer in the iPhone queue on that wet November morning in London said: 'the point is the attention to detail. I'm actually going to enjoy using my phone, and Apple are the only company that I know in most of consumer electronics who care about this stuff'.

The Apple Mac pioneered an icon-based operating system (the source of a long-running dispute with Microsoft over the Windows design) which was the starting point for Apple devotion. Mac users would not dream of trading in their computers for mere PCs and, years after the Mac revolution, Apple's entry into the MP3 market inspired a similar response. The iPod dominates that market, not least in terms of brand awareness and desired purchase. Apple products are recognised as style icons by a wide demographic: their appeal crosses divides of age, income, gender and taste – although approximately 93% of the queue for the new phone were male.

The phone's launch price was a hefty £269 (€399) but there was speculation that the price might come down. In the USA, Apple cut the original price of the iPhone by $200 (£100, €135) and then had to offer refunds to early customers who complained vociferously.

Price was not the only off-putting feature of the iPhone. In the UK, broadband Internet access was available through Edge but, at the time of the launch, Edge only covered 30% of Britain, so in most places iPhoners would not be able to use that feature. Additionally, in an attempt to maximise revenues, Apple had negoti-ated exclusive contracts with specific network providers. All iPhones bought in the UK were tied into the O2 network for 18 months. These network deals had already broken down in France and Germany, where local anti-competition laws had forced Apple to unbundle the iPhones and offer them with a free choice of network. This freedom of choice came at an even higher price, of course. In Germany, the unbundled iPhones were on sale at €999 (about £720), while it cost €399 (the same as in the UK) to buy an iPhone with a contract with Apple's German partner, T-Mobile.

Among all the Apple-inspired hype came a burst of bad publicity too. Green lobbyists took advantage of the interest in the iPhone's launch to make their own attack on the mobile phone market. Greenpeace claimed

(Continued)

(Continued)

that mobile phones were significant polluters and that mobile companies needed to do far more to minimise their impact on the environment. Zeina Alhajj, Campaign Coordinator for Greenpeace, said: 'Over the life cycle of a phone there is massive pollution. The phone companies are making big changes – transparency and reporting is far ahead of what it was four years ago, for example – but it is still far away from being a really green industry'.

A recent Greenpeace report claimed to have found evidence of widespread, hazardous chemical contamination of rivers and underground wells in countries where electronics goods are manufactured. Greenpeace also complains that consumers are wasteful, replacing phones more often than is necessary and so artificially inflating the demand for new phones. Western consumers in particular frequently replace working phones with the latest models, keeping phones on average for only 18 months when they are designed to last for 10 years.

Only a small proportion of these thousands of discarded phones are recycled. Nokia, the world's biggest mobile handset manufacturer, believes that about 48% of old handsets are abandoned or forgotten by their owners – many of them are just lying at the bottom of drawers.

Sources: Burkeman (2007); Judge (2007a, 2007b)

REFERENCES

Aaker, D.A. (2012) *Building Strong Brands*. London: Simon and Schuster.

Abraham, M. and Taylor, A. (2011) 'Brand housing', *Admap*, February 2011. London: WARC.

Anon (2003) 'Cosmo forced to scrap branded cafe project', *Marketing Week*, 7 August.

Burkeman, O. (2007) 'At 6.02pm the worshippers got their reward', *The Guardian*, 10 November, p. 3.

Burns, W. (2015) 'Disney proves that profitable marketing is about brand stories', *Forbes*, 9 June. Available at: www.forbes.com/sites/willburns/2015/06/09/disney-proves-that-profitable-marketing-is-about-brand-stories/#3d8082246c76 (accessed 27/10/16).

Caldieraro, F., Kao, L.-J. and Cunha Jr., M. (2015) 'Harmful upward line extensions: can the launch of premium products result in competitive disadvantages?', *Journal of Marketing*, 79 (6): 50–70.

Cleeren, K., van Heerde, H.J. and Dekimpe, M.G. (2013) 'Rising from the ashes: how brands and categories can overcome product-harm crises', *Journal of Marketing*, 77 (2): 58–77.

Czarnecki, S. (2016) 'Disney tops Cohn & Wolfe's inaugural Authentic 100 rankings', *PR Week*, 13 April. Available at: www.prweek.com/article/1390922/disney-tops-cohn-wolfes-inaugural-authentic-100-rankings (accessed 27/10/16).

Dahlen, M., Lange, F. and Smith, T. (2010) *Marketing Communications: A Brand Narrative Approach*. Chichester: Wiley.

The Economist (2015) 'It's the real thing', 14 November. Available at: www.economist.com/news/business/21678216-authenticity-being-peddled-cure-drooping-brands-its-real-thing (accessed 27/10/16).

Forbes (2016) 'The world's most valuable brands'. Available at: www.forbes.com/powerful-brands/list/#tab:rank (accessed 27/10/16).

Grönroos, C. (1997) 'From marketing mix to relationship marketing: towards a paradigm shift in marketing', *Management Decision*, 35 (4): 322–39.

Haig, M. (2003) *Brand Failures: The Truth about the 100 Biggest Branding Mistakes of All Time*. London: Kogan Page.

Hennig-Thurau, T., Houston, M. and Heitjans, T. (2009) 'Conceptualizing and measuring the monetary value of brand extensions: the case of motion pictures', *Journal of Marketing*, 73 (6): 167–83.

Holt, D.B. (2004) *How Brands Become Icons: The Principles of Cultural Branding*. Boston: Harvard Business Review Press.

Jones, P. and Vignali, C. (1994) 'Commercial education', *Journal of Retail Education*, cited in C. Vignali and B.J. Davies, 'The marketing mix redefined and mapped', *Management Decision*, 32 (8): 11–17.

Judge, E. (2007a) 'Green group shines light on safety of the Apple iPhone', *Times online*, 5 November. Available at: business.timesonline.co.uk/tol/business/industry_sectors/technology/article2806228.ece (accessed 27/11/07).

Judge, E. (2007b) 'Fresh blow for exclusive Apple iPhone strategy', *Times online*, 21 November. Available at: business.timesonline.co.uk/tol/business/industry_sectors/telecoms/article2914903.ece (accessed 27/11/07).

Kotler, P. (2003) *Marketing Insights from A to Z: 80 Concepts Every Manager Needs to Know*. New York: John Wiley & Sons.

Lauterborn, R. (1990) 'New marketing litany: four Ps passé; C-words take over', *Advertising Age*, 61 (41): 26.

Levitt, T. (1965) 'Exploit the product life cycle', *Harvard Business Review*, 43 (Nov/Dec): 81–94.

Levitt, T. (1983) 'The globalisation of markets', *Harvard Business Review*, 61 (May–June): 92–102.

Matzler, K., Pichler, E., Füller, J. and Mooradian, T.A. (2011) 'Personality, person–brand fit, and brand community: an investigation of individuals, brands, and brand communities', *Journal of Marketing Management*, 27 (9–10): 874–90.

Ohmae, K. (1989) 'Managing in a borderless world', *Harvard Business Review*, 67 (May–June): 152–61.

Peelen, E. (2005) *Customer Relationship Management*. Harlow: FT/Prentice Hall.

Pickton, D. and Broderick, A. (2004) *Integrated Marketing Communications* (2nd edn). Harlow: FT/Prentice Hall.

Reichfeld, F.F. (1994) 'Loyalty and the renaissance of marketing', *Journal of Marketing Management*, 2 (4): 10–21.

Smith, S. (2006) 'The evil that men do lives after them …', *Marketing Week*, 9 March.

WARC (2012) 'WARC briefing: brand architecture'. Available at: www.warc.com (accessed 02/01/13).

Whiteside, S. (2013) 'Rovio takes flight with Angry Birds: leveraging growth from a mobile gaming phenomenon', Event Reports: MMA (Mobile Marketing Association) Forum, May. Available at: www.warc.com (accessed 17/05/13).

Yoo, B., Donthu, N. and Lee, S. (2000) 'An examination of selected marketing mix elements and brand equity', *Academy of Marketing Science*, 28 (2): 195–211.

PART ONE	THIS IS MARKETING
PART TWO	MAKING SENSE OF MARKETS
PART THREE	THE MARKETING MIX
PART FOUR	MANAGING MARKETING

MARKETING PLANNING

MARKETING PLANNING CHALLENGES

The following are illustrations of the types of decision that marketers have to take or issues they face. *You aren't expected to know how to deal with the challenges now*; just bear them in mind as you read the chapter and see what you can find that helps.

- Your uncle runs a shoe factory that is struggling to compete with cheaper manufacturers from the developing world. He knows you've done a business course so he invites you to a management meeting to discuss the way forward. Do you have anything to contribute?

- A friend wants to start up her own company and needs a bank loan. The bank won't give her the loan without a marketing plan. She doesn't know how to write one. Can you help her?

- You run a medium-sized import/export agency. The international environment is turbulent and you are concerned that some of your markets and sources of supply will dry up. What should you be doing?

- You are the marketing director of a successful UK chain of restaurants. The company has money to put into expansion and you have been asked to present the options to the board.

- You work for a major British bank that is thinking of moving into the insurance market. You have to assess how well your bank is likely to be able to compete with the other insurance companies. How will you do this?

INTRODUCTION

Marketing decisions are key drivers to business success. Marketing has the power to influence every part of a business and affect how well organisations meet the needs of their customers, how they respond to competitors, deal with suppliers and financiers, as well as how they treat their employees. In turn, marketing outcomes and performance are influenced by a wide variety of individuals within the organisation and even many people outside the organisation who have associations with it. Marketing is not just the responsibility of the marketing department, other departments have significant influence over how well marketing is carried out.

How organisations manage their marketing activities is affected by many factors, including the extent to which they are market-orientated (see Chapter 1), what management style they adopt, what organisational structure they have and how they carry out their planning, for example is it a top-down approach or a bottom-up approach (see below)?

top-down approach

senior managers specify objectives, budgets, strategies and plans that are passed down to functions and departments to put into action

bottom-up approach

functions and departments recommend objectives, budgets, strategies and plans to senior management

This chapter will consider marketing's place in the company's overall plan and how marketing can help the organisation achieve its goals. It will cover the basic planning process and marketing analysis tools. It will introduce a wide variety of key strategic and managerial aspects of marketing. The chapter will consider some of the challenges faced in planning and implementing marketing: the approach to planning, barriers to planning, reasons for planning failure and organisational approaches to marketing. Having completed this overview, the rest of the chapter is structured in a way that mirrors the marketing planning process, taking each of the elements or stages in turn and introducing the more important concepts at each stage. The material covered in Chapters 6 and 11 is also relevant to marketing planning and these chapters should be read in conjunction with this chapter, especially the sections on branding, product development, the product life cycle and product portfolio management in Chapter 6 and varying the mix through the product's life and branding strategies in Chapter 11.

THE MARKETING PLANNING PROCESS

Marketing management and planning are parts of a wider activity that involves the whole organisation. The output of the total planning process is the production of a series of plans covering the various functional areas of the business. Such plans, while having a longer-term focus, usually cover a 12-month duration to coincide with the financial planning period.

At its highest level, the organisation has to set its corporate (business) mission and goals that act as an overall direction for the business. To achieve these goals, each of the functional areas within each of the strategic business units (SBUs) (if an organisation has them) needs to set their own plans, involving objectives, strategies and tactics. The plans for the SBUs come together to create the corporate plan for the organisation as a whole. For companies that do not have SBUs, the functional plans simply form the basis of the corporate plan, as illustrated in Exhibit 12.1. It is important to recognise that marketing planning does not take place in isolation from the rest of the organisation, but is an integral part of the corporate plan.

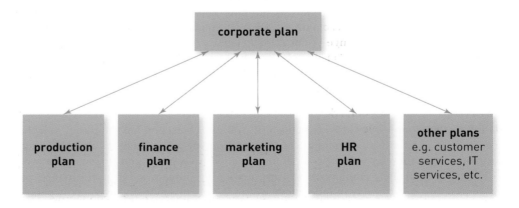

EXHIBIT 12.1 How functional plans combine into the corporate plan

The process for setting each plan within the overall corporate plan is similar but this book will concentrate solely on the marketing management and planning process.

Chapter 2 (Marketing environment) introduced the basic questions that need to be answered in marketing planning. Here that model is extended by adding extra questions to make a total of seven key planning questions. These extra two questions are important additions because by only asking 'where are we now?', we are only invited to consider the situation at a single moment in time. We need to know what we have done previously that has given rise to our current situation and also to consider if we continue to follow the same path of activities, where this will lead. Companies, unless just starting out, are continuing businesses that have a track record of performance in the marketplace that has to be recognised and understood in order to plan best for the future. A company's past, present and future form integral parts of the planning process.

Writing a marketing plan

The seven key planning questions, then, are:

1   Where are we now?

2   How did we get here?

3   Where will we be? (by the end of the planning period if we continue to do the same things)

4   Where do we want to be? (by the end of the planning period)

5   How are we going to get there?

6   Are we getting there?

7   Have we arrived?

The first three questions form a situation analysis which provides insights into the organisation's past and present.

The answers to the first four questions help with a strategic gap analysis. This is an important contribution to the marketing planning process. By evaluating what has been done in the past, the organisation can forecast what would happen if it continued on its current path (question 3). Armed with this understanding, and knowing where it wants to be by the end of the planning period (question 4), helps identify a course of action likely to achieve these new objectives (question 5). Those actions must be monitored continually though to make sure the organisation stays on course to meet its objectives – just as a boat might have to correct its course to ensure it reaches its destination, so might the organisation. The answer to question 6 shows if a change of course is needed within the current planning period while the strategic gap analysis helps identify changes required as the organisation moves from one planning period to the next. Exhibit 12.2 shows this process and the strategic gap that needs to be filled as the organisation moves into its new planning period.

strategic gap analysis
the difference between a desired outcome and an actual (or expected) outcome

While there are a variety of marketing planning process models, there is general agreement on the sequence and stages involved.

The first stage of the planning process is a situation analysis. Based on an understanding of the situation (past, present and future forecasts), new marketing objectives are set and strategies are determined to achieve them. The strategies, which are of a general nature indicating the direction that the marketing activities will take, are then made more detailed in terms of the tactics (operational activities) to be implemented. Exhibit 12.3 also illustrates how the evaluation and control of marketing activities feeds back into the rest of the planning process as a check that current plans are working as well as whether they have been achieved at the end of the planning period. These final evaluations provide a basis for the development of future plans. The feedback process allows plans to be modified throughout the planning period.

How to get your ideas to spread

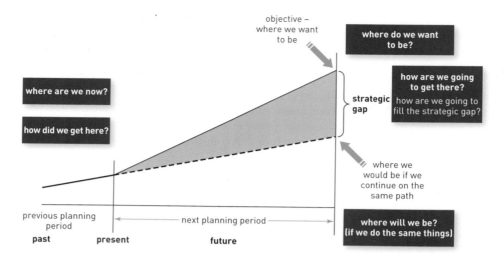

EXHIBIT 12.2 The strategic gap

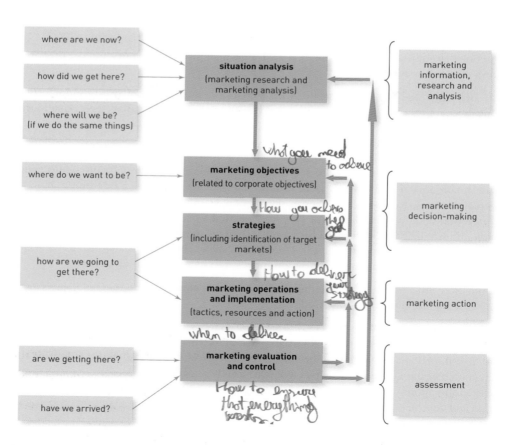

EXHIBIT 12.3 A model of the marketing planning process

SOSTAC

It is important to understand what works and why. If there have been changes in the marketing environment – perhaps competitor activity has increased – then the plans need to take account of these changes and the marketing activities need to be modified accordingly.

Within the overall framework of the planning process model, there are a number of marketing management tools that can be used at the different stages in order to aid analysis and managerial decision-making. They help achieve what is, basically, a systematic approach to identifying and analysing competitive advantage in the marketplace thus helping to achieve long-term benefits for companies. Examples of these tools are shown in Exhibit 12.4.

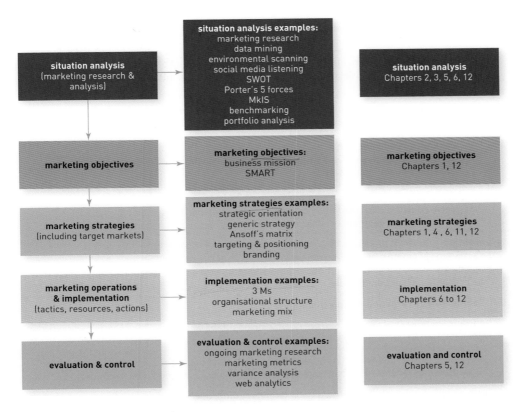

EXHIBIT 12.4 Developing the plan

What has been described above is a systematic, deliberate and prescriptive approach to planning and management. However, planning and management in practice tend to be a much less tidy business, in which ambiguity, inaccuracy, conflict and confusion can and do arise.

The main output from these planning activities is the marketing plan. The marketing plan is a document that summarises the plan and states the marketing activities to take place throughout the period of the plan. In reality, there may actually be a collection of marketing plans that together cover all products, markets and marketing functions rather than a single plan that covers everything. There may be separate plans for each brand or each main marketing function (e.g. advertising plan, sales plan, distribution plan, etc., covering all the elements of the marketing mix) or each target market or each market by area, region or country. It is vital that they all complement each other.

Marketing plans can appear in a range of different formats and structures but they should all contain some basic information (see Exhibit 12.5). The planning period must be specified as part of the plan. This may be over a total of three to five years in outline, but the detail is likely to be over a single year to coincide with the organisation's financial planning periods.

Section	Description
1 Executive summary	A brief overview of the main points of the plan highlighting the main objectives/intended outcomes, activities and resource requirements.
2 Current marketing situation	Summarises the environmental situation and trends: analysis of both internal and external factors including PRESTCOM and SWOT. Subheadings might include: 2.1 Key macro environmental influences (PREST factors) 2.2 Competitor analysis, e.g. industry structure, direct and indirect competitors and their activities, competing brands and distinctions between them (position map), expectations of competitive activity, assessment of competitors and their brands' strengths, weaknesses and positions 2.3 Organisation analysis, e.g. sales and profits, mission and objectives, strengths and weaknesses, online presence 2.4 Product analysis, e.g. product portfolio, branding issues, product market analysis (Ansoff's matrix), assessment of brand performances 2.5 Market analysis, e.g. marketing channel issues, customer/consumer analysis, e.g. identification of segments and targets, motivations, brand perceptions, buying habits, etc.
3 Objectives	What the plan should achieve. Objectives should be SMART (see later in this chapter). This section may contain a reiteration of the corporate objectives as well as the overall marketing objectives. Objectives are set for each of the elements of the marketing mix though these may be presented in section 6 below.
4 Target markets	Segmentation, targeting and positioning.
5 Marketing strategies	A broad statement of how the marketing objectives will be achieved. This section builds on the previous section on targeting, which itself is an aspect of the marketing strategy.
6 Marketing programmes	The details of marketing to be undertaken. These are specific activities, schedules, costings and responsibilities. There will be subheadings for each key marketing mix element, for example: 6.1 Product (e.g. details of product portfolio, branding issues, product development, new product launch, etc.) 6.2 Promotion/marketing communications: advertising, sales promotions, public relations, direct marketing, salesforce, other (such as events, merchandising). (Digital marketing may be shown under this subheading or separately – although it is important that all promotional activity is planned together.) These may be organised as push (aimed at trade customers) and pull (aimed at consumers or end users) promotional strategies (see Chapter 8) 6.3 Place: distribution channels, logistics, etc. (see Chapter 9) 6.4 Price: e.g. trade pricing, recommended retail pricing, discount arrangements, etc. (see Chapter 10) 6.5 Service: e.g. after-sales service, installation service; this might also include the remaining 3Ps of the 7Ps 6.6 Other elements might include issues of brand and corporate identity and image, social media activities.

Section	Description
7 Resources and financial aspects (budgets)	Statements of required financial budgets and human resources needed. These may have implications for recruitment, possibly upsizing or downsizing the marketing department or other related departments (e.g. customer services department) and salesforce, and for outsourcing, e.g. the use of promotional agencies, call centres, fulfilment companies, research agencies, etc.
8 Implementation controls	Evaluation and assessment of the plan on an ongoing basis and not just at the end of the plan. Contingencies may be identified at key points if the expected plan outcomes are not being achieved. Research and assessment to be carried out and the metrics (measurements) to be used.

EXHIBIT 12.5 Outline marketing plan

SITUATION ANALYSIS

Marketing analysis is about understanding of how the company is operating in its marketing environment. The marketing environment comprises a complex set of factors that affect marketing decisions and plans, and ultimately affect business performance. It is important that the company monitors itself and its environment in order to prepare for future activities and, particularly, to build and maintain competitive advantage. This type of analysis is not just a one-off, never to be repeated activity, but something that successful businesses do on an ongoing basis. Environmental analysis was covered in detail in Chapter 2 where situation analysis was also introduced. Some points are restated here to show how and why marketing analysis fits into the marketing management and planning process.

Measuring marketing

Marketing analysis case study

Thanks to sophisticated databases and extensive marketing research data, there is now a wealth of information available to marketers, who are increasingly being required to assess their performance and measure the effectiveness and efficiency of marketing activities. This assessment is known as marketing metrics. Marketing can be expensive so it is important that good measurement systems are in place to analyse its value to the organisation. Those same systems can also be used to improve marketing performance in the future. This information feeds into the marketing evaluation and control mechanisms that form part of the total marketing planning process.

DATA COLLECTION AND STORAGE

The phenomenal growth in cheap computing power has revolutionised the process of information gathering, storage and analysis. If anything, large organisations now have access to too much data and the challenge is to find uses for it all. Raw data can be classified as 'internal' or 'external', i.e. gathered from within the company or from outside. 'Internal continuous data', as the name suggests, is data that is gathered all the time, e.g. financial accounts and salesforce records. Customer transaction data is an important part of any marketing information system (MkIS). 'Internal ad hoc data' is gathered from activities undertaken for specific events within the business, e.g. to see how well a particular promotion has performed. Environmental scanning monitors the business environment (PRESTCOM factors) and 'marketing research', undertaken either continuously or as needed for particular purposes on an ad hoc basis, determines such things as customer attitudes to and opinions on product offerings.

marketing information system (MkIS) also known as a marketing intelligence system, the systematic gathering and dissemination of competitive and marketing information; this usually involves a computerised system

MARKETING INFORMATION SYSTEMS (MkIS)

Today's databases are very much more than simple customer listings. Computing power has created the ability to store and cross-analyse vast amounts of data, such as service and sales data, purchasing records, and attitudinal and behavioural data. There are many fields of data, covering millions of transactions and relationships. Without this information, it is unlikely that truly integrated marketing can exist. The database is the heart of a marketing information system.

The aim of an efficient and successful MkIS is to turn data into information that, in turn, can be turned into management knowledge from which decisions can be made and action taken. Exhibit 12.6 illustrates an overview of a marketing information system.

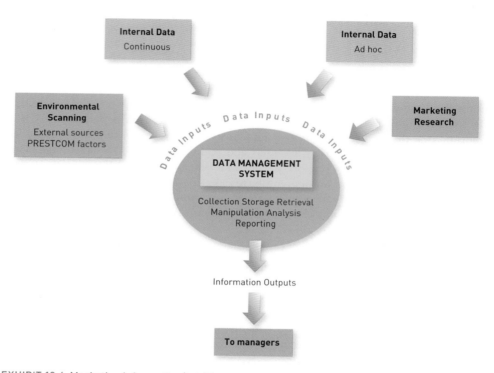

EXHIBIT 12.6 Marketing information/intelligence system

A fundamental function of the MkIS is to provide information when it is needed for decision-making. The information needs to be timely, accurate and trustworthy. The MkIS has three key components:

- data collection and storage
- analysis
- reporting.

Analysis

Companies gather huge amounts of data. Managers need to make sense of it and turn it into useful information upon which decisions can be made. Data analysis looks for patterns and trends in the data, e.g. a steady increase in sales of a type of product or a sudden drop in profit from a product line. Basic analysis often requires only fairly simple tools such as spreadsheets; however, the sheer amount of data now available (sometimes referred to as 'big data') has resulted in the development of more specialist data mining software, e.g. SAS Enterprise Miner (www.sas.com). Organisations may have millions of records. They could relatively easily establish how many people live in a particular city but with specialist data mining software they could also discover how many of those city dwellers earn above average incomes, live in large houses, have children and more than two cars. That helps them target better (for more on targeting see Chapter 4).

Unstructured text analysis software is a good way to analyse documents, web pages, etc. It is widely used in social media analysis, for example an analysis of individuals' interactions can help identify social leaders and build frighteningly detailed profiles of consumers.

Data mining with IBM SPSS

ethical focus: save the birds

Global bird populations are in decline. Nearly one fifth of species are at risk of extinction across the European Union. Intensive farming, climate change and over-exploitation of the oceans are affecting bird habitats and food supplies. Numerous government agencies and charities are working to save the birds – though it may be too little too late for some of the most at risk: those on the 'red list', i.e. in most urgent need of action, include puffins, lapwings and curlews.

The Royal Society for the Protection of Birds (RSPB) is the UK's largest nature conservation charity. As well as running bird sanctuaries and rescuing distressed birds, the charity conducts huge research projects designed to understand where the threats to bird populations come from and to save them from further decline. Past projects include: tracking the movements of kittiwakes and gannets as they forage at sea; correlating skylarks nesting success (or lack of it) with information on agricultural cropping patterns and pesticide usage; and analysing the foraging habits of albatrosses across the Southern Ocean in order to minimise death rates. RSPB researchers also test different conversation methods to determine which techniques are most effective for different species. All of this generates masses of data ('big data'), which needs careful analysis and interpretation if the conservation problems are to be clearly understood.

Source: released under the GNU Free Documentation Licence and the cc-by-sa-2.5 Licence by the photographer

The RSPB's other major role is as a lobbyist: they try to persuade governments and big businesses to take action – and they make their data freely available to further the birds' cause.

You would think that tagging birds or monitoring them as they fly possibly thousands of miles would be the hard bits, but the sheer volume of data generated presents a problem in itself. This 'big data' needs specialist data mining and advanced data analytics software to organise it and turn it into useful information – the kind of information that vital conservation plans can be built on.

Sources: *The Ecologist* (2015); RSPB (n.d.); SAS (n.d.)

Reporting

Based on the analysis conducted, reports meeting the needs of the different marketing managers should be produced from the MkIS on a regular basis. Sales force requirements differ from those of brand managers which differ from those of the marketing director, etc. The results of data analysis need to be distributed to the right people, at the right time, and in the right form so that they can make the best decisions. For example, a list of sales figures is of less use to a manager than a chart that shows which products are bestsellers; the information that 20,000 people took up an offer means more when that is presented in comparison to the take-up rate for other offers.

There are a variety of tools and approaches that can be used in marketing analysis. Some of the more important ones are outlined below.

digital focus: the social media plan

Digital marketing planning

Digital plans should be integrated into the overall marketing plan. However, sometimes it is helpful to consider aspects of an organisation's online presence separately to ensure that opportunities are not missed. This is particularly important given the rate of change in social media – companies that rely on updating sections from the previous plan could seriously miss out.

Take the environmental analysis, for example. A well thought through plan might include the following questions.

Internal environment:

- Which activities from the overall plan can be leveraged for social media marketing?
- Is the corporate culture supportive of the transparent and decentralised norms of social media?
- What resources do we have (e.g. skilled people, strong brands) that can help our social media presence?
- Do we have appropriate policies and procedures in place?

External environment:

- Are our customers social media users? Which sites?
- How are our competitors using social media? Is it succeeding?
- How might the key PRESTCOM trends already identified affect our decisions with regard to social media?

Most large companies already have a significant social media presence but some smaller, or newer, ones are playing catch-up. The early trial phase is all about listening and learning alongside your customers. They will show you what they want to talk about.

Source: Tuten and Solomon (2015)

PRESTCOM AND SWOT ANALYSIS

PRESTCOM was first introduced in Chapter 2 as a tool that can be systematically applied to analyse an organisation's internal and external environment. External factors are usually outside the control of an organisation, or they may have only limited control over them. Internal factors are under the control of the organisation. PRESTCOM is a mnemonic to remind us of the main areas that should be analysed by organisations. It stands for Political, Regulatory, Economic, Social, Technological, Competitor, Organisational and Market factors.

Once the key factors affecting an organisation have been identified, a SWOT analysis can then be undertaken to identify which of those internal factors are strengths of the organisation and which are weaknesses; which of the external factors are opportunities and which are threats. Opportunity and threat analysis can be made more meaningful by using opportunity and threat matrices in which the likelihood of the factor occurring and the potential impact it might have can be assessed. For example, if a threat is not likely to occur, or if it does and its impact is assessed as minimal, it can probably be ignored or relegated as being of low concern. If an opportunity has low cost implications, is within the capabilities of the organisation and is likely to be very profitable with limited competitive interference, then it might be a good opportunity to pursue. See Chapter 2 for more on PRESTCOM and SWOT.

COMPETITOR ANALYSIS

Marketers must understand how a company's products and brands compare with those of its competitors. Competitor analysis is important in determining whether or not the products marketed by a company have a sustainable advantage in the marketplace. This is not something that should be done just once at the launch of a new product, but should be undertaken on a continuous basis throughout the life of the brand.

competitor analysis
the process of obtaining an in-depth understanding of rival firms and their offerings

Competitor analysis involves an analysis of the strengths and weaknesses of competitive products/brands and of the basic capabilities of the competition. It may involve some form of benchmarking. This is where companies compare themselves to the best-in-class companies in their industry, typically the market leader, in order to identify areas for potential improvement. For example, the market leader might have better known brands but their products might be technologically less advanced. That is something a company could work with, using their technological advantage to strengthen their brand, perhaps through a communications campaign or with a change of distribution strategy. Companies use the elements of the marketing mix (the 4Ps or 7Ps) to compete with each other.

benchmarking
a process of systematic analysis and comparison of one company's performance, measured against another's (the industry leader's), in order to improve business performance

It is important to understand not only how competitors succeed in the market but also how they fail. It is so much better, and cheaper, to learn from someone else's mistakes than from your own. This sort of information is often gathered by talking to consumers and distributors. Other sources include commissioned market research; commercially available market information such as Mintel, Target Group Index and retail audits; the press; suppliers; or even other competitors. Very often, companies will attend conferences and trade exhibitions with a view to gathering competitive intelligence quite openly. Clearly, the better a company's market intelligence, the better its decisions are likely to be. Third- or fourth-hand data may be twisted out of all recognition and result in ineffective decision-making.

market leader
the company with the highest sales within a market (also sometimes used to refer to a groundbreaking firm that others follow)

competitive intelligence
information on rivals, their products and environments compared with one's own

Souhami (2003) has argued that in order to get the most out of their competitive intelligence, companies must stop just staring at the same old information they have always used, as 'competitive myopia' sets in when companies do not monitor their competitors systematically, i.e. by continuously gathering up-to-date information. Many companies use an MkIS for this purpose.

PORTER'S FIVE FORCES MODEL

Porter's five forces model (Porter, 1985) is a useful tool for analysing competitive activity by helping firms determine the strength of competitive threats. It assesses the intensity of competition, the threat of new entrants to the market, the threat of substitute products, and the relative bargaining powers of suppliers and customers (see Exhibit 12.7).

Porter's five forces model
a competitive environment analysis tool

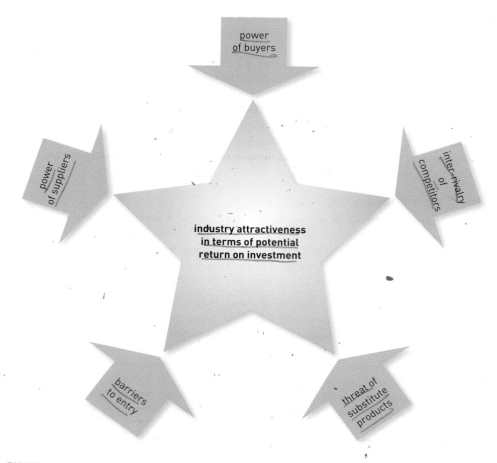

EXHIBIT 12.7 adapted from Porter's five forces model

Threat of new entrants

An organisation needs to monitor the activities of potential competitors as well as existing competitors. The lower the market's barriers to entry, the more likely it is that these potential rivals will become actual rivals.

Barriers to entry include:

- the costs of producing/providing for the marketplace; there may be the requirement for high capital outlay – perhaps to buy expensive production machinery, e.g. the nuclear power industry

- existing powerful brand names within the market, e.g. new entrants into the chocolate market would have to compete with Nestlé, Cadbury's, Mars, Suchard, etc.

- the size of the market – it may be too small to support any more competitors, e.g. a local high street may already have two good bakeries

- legal/regulatory barriers, e.g. a licence may be required to trade (selling alcohol, running a casino); in some countries foreign firms are banned from owning businesses in

barriers to entry

things that make it difficult, or impossible, for new competitors to enter a market, e.g. patents, high set-up costs

key sectors such as defence or the media. Patents are another means by which firms keep out potential rivals

- existing companies that control key resources, e.g. ownership or access to distribution chains or raw materials supplies

- existing companies that are large enough to benefit from economies of scale and therefore have lower cost bases than any new entrant would; this would mean that a new rival would be unable to match their prices without making a loss

- competitor reactions, e.g. fear or concern that competitors may react in ways either singularly or collectively that would make it difficult to enter a market successfully.

Threat of substitutes

The more alternative products there are, the harder it will be to maintain a competitive advantage and to make a good profit. For example, when crossing the channel, ferries and planes are substitutes for the Eurostar and Eurotunnel Le Shuttle. The threat of substitutes may be determined by:

Rolls Royce

- the pricing of substitute products and, therefore, the sensitivity of customers to pricing

- the costs of the customer switching to a competitive product – if these are low, the risk of substitution is higher

- whether customers have a high propensity to substitute or, in other words, customers have low loyalty levels.

Bargaining power of buyers (customers)

Customers will be powerful if, as individuals or buying groups, they are more important to the suppliers than the suppliers are to them. Major grocery retailers such as Tesco and Asda Wal-Mart are able to dictate terms to most of their suppliers because of the bulk of groceries that are sold through their stores. Manufacturers such as Kellogg's and Nestlé have to be seen on these supermarket giants' shelves. Smaller manufacturers actively compete for the supermarkets' shelf space. This has led to pressure on prices and, in some cases, insistence upon manufacturer-funded special offers such as BOGOFs (buy one get one free). Customers (buyers) are powerful when:

- there are few major buyers in the marketplace

- products are commoditised or standardised, i.e. there is little or no differentiation from the customer's perspective

- the company is not a key supplier to the customer and the customer holds the balance of power.

Bargaining power of suppliers

If raw materials or ingredients are scarce, then their suppliers can dictate terms. For example, after a bad coffee bean harvest, the price of coffee rose sharply in the shops (though little of this money went to the smaller coffee growers). Suppliers can redress the balance of power with retailers by developing strong brands. It would be a brave supermarket that refused to put Heinz baked beans on its UK shelves. Market leaders have a distinct advantage.

Suppliers are powerful when:

- there are few other sources of supply for the company
- the suppliers threaten to integrate along the supply chain, in effect becoming a direct competitor to the company
- the cost of switching to other suppliers is great; suppliers have been known to tie in their customers through financial pressure by extending credit terms so that companies they supply become dependent on such extended terms to help manage cash flow
- the company's business is not key to the supplier.

Intensity of rivalry of competitors

Just as some people are more competitive than others, so are some companies. Markets such as grocery retailing and fashion are highly competitive. In the first case, this is shown in price wars and intense below the line activity. In the second case, it is apparent in high advertising spend. Just how intensely firms compete with each other depends on a number of factors, one of which is the market growth rate. In a growing market, there is more business available for everyone and so firms do not need to steal each other's market share in order to make more sales. The intensity of rivalry between competitors may depend on:

below the line

non-commission-paying promotion, typically all forms except advertising

- the number of competitors in the market: the more there are, the more intense the competitive activity
- the cost structure: high capital investment may actually result in lower unit costs because management will want to ensure that its machinery operates at optimum capacity rather than laying idle, waiting for orders
- the differential advantages between products and brands, i.e. those brands perceived by customers to be differentiated are less likely to attract competitive activity
- the costs involved in customers switching to competing products: if these are high, then customers are less likely to switch, negating the need for such intense rivalry
- the strategic objectives being pursued by the competitors: if a competitor is holding or harvesting its products, then it is not as concerned with highly competitive behaviour
- the exit barriers, i.e. if these are high, then more competition will be encouraged to stay in the market, resulting in highly active competitive behaviour as they try to gain market share.

competitive advantage or competitive edge

something about an organisation or its products that is perceived as being better than rival offerings

If a company is to develop a competitive edge, then it must understand its competitors' strengths and weaknesses. An in-depth, up-to-date analysis of the competitive environment is the basis of any sound competitive strategy.

research focus: classic concept

Porter, M. (1980) 'Industry structure and competitive strategy: keys to profitability', *Financial Analysis*, **36 (4): 30–41.**
    Michael Porter's name is synonymous with competitive analysis and strategy. Here is an early paper in which he highlights the need to understand the competitive environment and outlines the key forces that drive industry competition.

BUSINESS MISSION

A business mission, or vision as it is sometimes called, is an explicit statement that captures the broad aims of the company. This is used to communicate those broad aims to all its stakeholders, both internal and external. Its purpose, ideally, is to provide an inspirational focus or strategic and operational direction for the whole company. Starbucks' mission statement is:

> To inspire and nurture the human spirit – one person, one cup and one neighborhood at a time.

Mission statements often have explicitly stated, underpinning values that help implement these broad, aspirations. Starbucks are:

> With our partners, our coffee and our customers at our core, we live these values:
>
> Creating a culture of warmth and belonging, where everyone is welcome.
>
> Acting with courage, challenging the status quo and finding new ways to grow our company and each other.
>
> Being present, connecting with transparency, dignity and respect.
>
> Delivering our very best in all we do, holding ourselves accountable for results.
>
> We are performance driven, through the lens of humanity. (Starbucks, 2016)

There are a number of general components to a good business mission statement. It should:

- identify the company's philosophy, i.e. its approach to business
- specify its product–market domain, i.e. where the company will operate in the marketplace
- communicate key values for those involved, i.e. how it will operate
- be closely linked to critical success factors, i.e. the things the company has to be good at to survive.

According to Levitt (1960), who created the concept of the business mission, when developing a mission statement a company's managers should ask themselves some basic questions: 'What business are we in?', 'What business should we be in?' and 'What business can we be in?' The answers should be given in terms of customer needs, rather than the products the company makes. See the examples in Exhibit 12.8.

This type of approach enables a company to identify much broader-based competition and think about how it could be more competitive and avoid 'marketing myopia' (Levitt, 1960). Marketing myopia is where a company forgets that a customer wants a product to solve a problem. The classic example highlighted by Levitt is a drill – he states that the customer actually wants the holes it makes. This can

business mission
the broad aims a business hopes to achieve

Kellogg's aims and objectives

critical success factors
things that the success of an organisation or activity depend upon; they must happen or the objectives will not be met

ACTIVITY

Search online for mission statements for companies you are familiar with.

Do the statements have all the content suggested above for a good business mission statement?

How well does the company measure up to its mission?

be taken further, however, because in fact customers do not usually want holes in walls, they want hooks for pictures or brackets for shelves.

Traditional definition of business	Customer need-based definition of business
Electricity	Power/Energy/Heat/Light
Train travel	Transportation
Cinema	Entertainment
Computers	Information processing
Telephones	Communications

EXHIBIT 12.8 Defining the business from the customer's perspective

Thinking about products in this way gives the company greater scope in its development of new products as well as highlighting the full range of products that may be competing for its customers. The process of identifying what business it is in, and could be in, will enable a company to develop an appropriate business mission. Having decided on a business mission, a company will use this to inform and develop its business and marketing objectives from which it will decide on specific strategies.

An organisation's objectives work in a hierarchy. At the top level are the corporate objectives. All other objectives, including marketing, should be designed to contribute to those overall, corporate objectives.

The objectives illustrated in Exhibit 12.9 are insufficiently detailed for the real world – they need to be more precise and further explained.

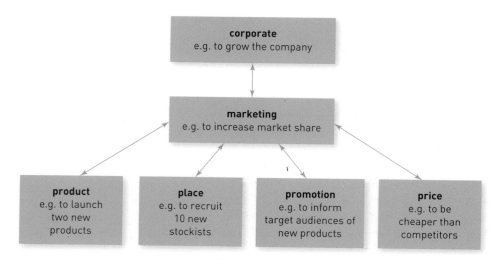

EXHIBIT 12.9 Hierarchy of objectives

The next section will look at setting strategies to achieve the organisation's objectives.

MARKETING OBJECTIVES

Different organisations are trying to achieve different things. However, there are some things that many hope to achieve:

- survival
- profits (however, not-for-profit organisations, such as charities or hospitals, might more usually refer to revenue and surpluses)
- a good reputation
- competitive edge.

Everyone within the organisation is expected to work together to meet these objectives and each business function (e.g. marketing) sets its own objectives which are designed to help meet the overall corporate ones.

Typical marketing objectives include:

- a move into a new market (perhaps another country or another market segment)
- launch a new product
- increase sales volume (i.e. quantity of goods sold)
- increase market share
- acquire another brand.

Objectives are things that the organisation wants. Businesses then organise their resources (money, people, machinery, etc.) to achieve or acquire those things that they want, i.e. to meet their objectives. Marketing objectives should be SMART:

Specific	clearly worded and directed at specific markets and/or audiences
Measurable	it must be clear that the objective really has been achieved; this normally means that it will be quantifiable, e.g. a percentage or absolute amount to be gained
Achievable	possible to do
Relevant	of value to the organisation and in keeping with other objectives; also objectives should always be challenging enough to act as motivators
Timed	with a deadline.

SMART

a mnemonic for the setting of objectives, which should be: specific, measurable, achievable, relevant and timed

So an example of a SMART objective might be to increase sales revenue from the pet food division (specific) by 10% (measurable) by 31 December 2012 (timed). This objective could be relevant if the company was seeking to grow, and achievable if it has the resources (money, people, facilities) to put behind the sales drive.

Overall marketing objectives are supported by objectives for each element of the marketing mix.

ACTIVITY

Do you have a career in mind? Develop SMART objectives for the next stage of it.

Porter's generic strategies

three main competitive strategies: cost leadership, differentiation and focus

Ansoff's matrix

comprises four possible growth strategies: market development, product development, market penetration/expansion and diversification

MARKETING STRATEGY

With a clear picture of the marketing environment and of the objectives it wishes to achieve, the company can now decide how it is going to take its business forward into the next trading period. It can think about this in terms of shorter or longer time periods. It is often much easier for managers to make decisions for the short term because they will have more detailed and accurate information about the marketplace but it is important to have medium- and long-term plans. There are a number of ways of thinking about possible strategies. Porter's generic strategies and Ansoff's matrix are discussed below. Branding strategies were introduced in Chapter 11 while Chapter 6 covered aspects of product portfolio management (the Boston Consulting Group matrix and the GE-McKinsey matrix), product development and the product life cycle.

Long-term decisions require managers to see into the future. Longer-term success is about being visionary, reading the market, knowing the business well and, sometimes, getting lucky. Even Marks & Spencer's experienced managers have not been able to do this with complete accuracy or total success in the past decade or so and have faced some very difficult times. From a peak in the late 1990s when M&S were reported to be the first British retailer to make pre-tax profits of over £1 billion from their combined international operations, they then immediately went through a period of major crisis from which they have still not fully recovered. The next sections look at how some marketing management tools can be utilised to develop strategic direction for the business. It is the choice of strategic direction that provides a focus for the company's longer-term continuation.

COMPETITIVE STRATEGY

One of the key elements of a marketing strategy is the decision on how the organisation will compete in the marketing place. The key strengths, weaknesses, opportunities and threats identified in the SWOT analysis can be used as the basis for decisions on how to compete, with whom and for which markets. There are a number of other tools to aid strategy development. One of the best known is Michael Porter's generic strategies model.

PORTER'S GENERIC STRATEGIES

Porter's generic strategies are a way of providing an overall strategic direction for the company (see Exhibit 12.10).

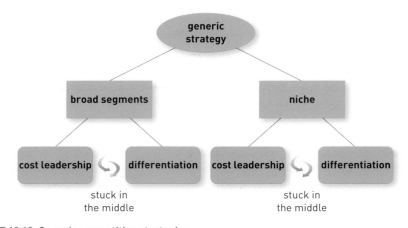

EXHIBIT 12.10 Generic competitive strategies

This model illustrates the main competitive strategic directions an organisation can take based on its identification of competitive forces and its view of the market:

- Mass (broad segments) or niche?
- Does the company concentrate on one segment or try to serve many?

Once that first decision is made, management continues to consideration of the following:

- differentiation, where the company chooses to differentiate itself based on some competitive advantage it has identified, e.g. a strong brand or customer service
- cost leadership, where the company is able to offer low prices thanks to its low production costs.

If the company ignores these choices, or attempts to pursue two simultaneously, Porter argues that it could be in danger of being 'stuck in the middle', i.e. where it has no clear direction and merely reacts to market conditions, therefore making it vulnerable to competitors.

b2b focus: a successful growth strategy

The Senator Group is one of the UK's biggest manufacturers of office furniture but it began as a family business in Blackburn in 1976 making affordable, basic furniture such as desks and filing cabinets. Over the years, the company has changed strategic direction and they now produce eye-catching, statement pieces that stand out from the competition: grand desks for multinational CEOs, funky sofas for PR companies and futuristic chairs (with footrests) for busy IT execs. The company employs about 1,100 people.

Their plan has been to grow the company steadily, focusing on the medium-to-long term. In 2016, turnover rose by 13% to £120 million with profits of more than £9 million. Overseas markets are seen as a key source of future growth: 35% of their turnover is already generated outside the UK. Their most important foreign market is the US where they have their own manufacturing facilities.

They are still a privately-owned family business and try to make sure that all their staff feel part of a worthwhile operation. Well-motivated staff are more likely to provide good customer service which is important to Senator as customer service is a vital part of their success. Their stated aim is to provide small business levels of excellent service while growing into a significant global supplier. They seem to be well on their way to achieving that objective.

Source: Burn-Callander (2016)

GROWTH STRATEGIES

Most commercial organisations wish to grow their businesses: to make more sales, more profit. The options available can be expressed quite simply: either sell more to existing customers or find new ones. Ansoff's matrix is a classic and invaluable tool for growth strategy development that expresses, and builds on, these basic options.

ANSOFF'S MATRIX

Ansoff's matrix (Ansoff, 1957) is another tool managers can use to help determine their strategic direction (see Exhibit 12.11). It is also known as the Ansoff growth matrix because it focuses on the ways companies can grow through increased sales opportunities. It looks at a product in relation to its market and helps managers to identify potential market opportunities. This matrix is one of the best-known strategic tools as, despite its simplicity, it is a very powerful way of looking at strategic options. The two-by-two matrix first defined by

Ansoff's matrix

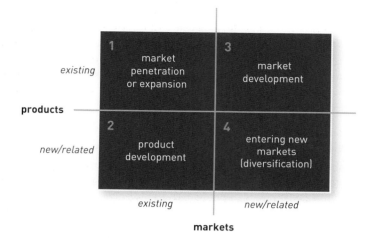

EXHIBIT 12.11 Ansoff's matrix

Ansoff can be made more sophisticated, and other authors have expanded the matrix into a three-by-three matrix that includes categories for modified products and modified markets.

The quadrants defined by Ansoff are identified as having different levels of business risk associated with them. As the top-left quadrant is best understood and experienced by the company, it is said to carry the least risk for growth. However, if this proves to be a highly competitive market that is stagnant or declining, and if the company has limited power in the market, this level of risk might become significantly higher and the company might be wise to move into other areas. The top-right and bottom-left quadrants are said to carry greater risk and the bottom-right quadrant carries the greatest risk to the company in that diversification with new products in new markets represents new and uncharted territory in which the company has the least or even no experience.

Quadrant 1: existing products in existing markets – market penetration strategy. This is about encouraging existing customers to use a current product more (more at each use, or more frequently, or to use competing products less). This quadrant emphasises strategies to develop sales from existing customers.

product development strategy

developing new products to sell in existing markets (part of Ansoff's growth matrix)

Quadrant 2: new or related products for existing markets – product development strategy. This involves some element of product development or improvement for existing customers. Car manufacturers are continually striving to improve their products, e.g. the Ford Escort has been replaced by the Ford Focus. This quadrant emphasises strategies to gain sales through product development or new products that are marketed to existing target customers (whether they are actual current customers or other potential customers in the target market(s) in which the company currently operates).

market development strategy

selling existing products to new markets (customers) (part of Ansoff's growth matrix)

Quadrant 3: existing products in new or related markets – market development strategy. This is about finding new uses for products or launching into new markets, e.g. different geographic areas of the world or different market segments. Lucozade was originally a drink for recuperating children, but when the company found that mothers were using it as a 'pick-me-up' during the day, it decided to relaunch the product. It is now firmly established as a 'sports' drink (albeit with a new formulation). This quadrant emphasises strategies related to marketing to newly defined target markets.

Quadrant 4: new or related products in new markets – diversification strategy. Taking new products into new markets is the hardest of the four directions from a company's perspective. This is because it involves moving into an area of business with which it is unfamiliar and, as a result, the risks of potential failure are high. The strategy works best when there is a close match with existing experiences. This quadrant emphasises strategies in which both product development and market development are combined and the consequential diversification can take many forms.

diversification strategy

developing new products to sell to new markets (customers) (part of Ansoff's growth matrix)

research focus: classic concept

Ansoff, I. (1957) 'Strategies for diversification', *Harvard Business Review*, **35 (5): 113–24.**
  Igor Ansoff has had a profound effect on our understanding of business strategies and was one of the early writers on the subject. In this article, he explores the strategies that relate to different diversification approaches.

digital focus: old news

Dramatic events such as the UK's referendum vote to leave the EU and Donald Trump's surprise US presidential campaign boosted newspaper circulations in the summer of 2016, however, this is an industry in overall decline. Even big news events such as these are unlikely to save the sector from its structural problems: the main one being a shift by readers – and consequently advertising budgets – from print to online disrupters of traditional media led by Facebook and Google.

  Newspapers have always relied heavily on technology. The invention of the printing press made the newssheets possible in the first place. Advances in printing technology made their large-scale production possible. Now the demise of printed paper in our Internet age is forcing another major change. Some people still read the printed version but national newspapers are now available in a number of formats. They can be read on PCs, tablets, e-readers and mobiles. The formats aren't perfect representations of the printed copy (for example, some of them can't cope with the crossword puzzle), but they have the advantages of being accessible on the move, preferred by most news consumers, and of being cheaper or free.

  How can newspapers keep going if their consumers expect to read them for free online? Sadly the answer is that they cannot, therefore a number of new strategies are emerging. Largely, it comes down to the newspapers being either funded by advertising or charging their readers a subscription. The outlook for print advertising is bleak. Print newspaper advertising spending in the UK, for instance, is likely to have fallen by £135 million to £866 million in 2016, an even steeper fall than the £112 million it dropped in 2015. Digital ad revenues have been hit even harder and the availability of ever more efficient ad blockers is not going to help.

  The Guardian has embraced the principles of crowdfunding and asked its loyal readers to become members in order to protect the paper's independence and support freedom of speech. *Guardian* supporters get benefits ranging from exclusive emails from *Guardian* journalists and an ad-free experience on the paper's mobile app to a welcome gift (a *Guardian* badged bag). *Guardian* readers may feel strongly enough about 'quality, independent journalism' and its role in a free society to spend £5 a month on top of the price of the paper to become a *Guardian* supporter but it is hard to imagine this approach working for all papers.

  Another approach is to expand into other areas; to find other services to sell to existing readers. Most newspapers' online sites now host video news stories – are they really papers anymore? Do they have to be printed at all?
  Source: Nicolaou (2016)

STRATEGIC ALLIANCES

How a company chooses to adopt any of Ansoff's alternative strategic directions depends on how much the company wishes to control the activities related to the marketing of its products. Growth can be achieved through internal development or by working with other companies through various types of strategic alliance, or through vertical or horizontal integration. Options include the following:

- *A network*: this is a loose association between a company and, for example, a series of distributors, e.g. many car manufacturers sell through a range of different types of outlet. It can also be a network of .agents, which is a strategy pursued by some companies when they enter an unfamiliar market or a new country. With a network, the company may have relatively little control over how the third party markets the products to end-users, or how end-users (consumers) are treated.

- *A contract or licence agreement*: here the company imposes conditions on the third party it uses to service its end-user needs. A contract or licence agreement may restrict the marketing operations to specifically those developed by the originating company. McDonald's use this strategy. As franchisor, they specify everything from outlet layout to the disposable packaging used by franchisees, and even the training received by counter and waiting staff.

- *A consortium or joint venture*: where two or more companies agree to develop joint operations on a contractual basis. This may be used by companies entering new markets or countries, and enables them to maximise their potential by taking on local working practices. This may also be a situation whereby companies remain focused on their core business but, through utilisation of each partner's specialisms, they develop a new or better product offering for the end-user.

- *An acquisition or merger*: this is the most likely way to gain complete control of the marketing channel, it does, however, mean that the company must be cash rich or, at least, able to raise sufficient capital. A number of companies have pursued this strategy in order to gain market share only to sell off their purchase at a later date when they have been unable to realise the expected returns. For example, in 2005 eBay bought Skype. The idea was that Skype would, among other things, allow eBay's buyers and sellers to communicate better and would thus drive business. Unfortunately, these synergies never materialised and they resold their holdings in 2009 (*The Economist*, 2009). In 2011, Microsoft bought Skype. A firm may only want part of another company to add to existing operations, such as a brand name, or the acquisition of other company's stores – something that Primark has done on several occasions, e.g. buying shops from Littlewoods and C&A.

INTERNATIONAL MARKETING STRATEGY

Why do firms trade internationally rather than stick with their familiar home markets? Most commonly, it is as part of a growth strategy. They want to increase sales.

The firm may want to market a wider range of products but has discovered that there is insufficient demand to support this in its home market, or it may be that the converse is true and the firm wishes to specialise in a narrower range of products. Either way, they will need a larger market for those products if they are to maintain sales revenue.

Apart from growth, there are a number of other good reasons for selling products internationally, including:

- as part of a competitive strategy
- risk spreading
- globalisation of markets
- excess capacity
- to extend the product life cycle.

Competitive strategy

Firms may trade abroad because competition has got too hot in their home market and they are looking for an easier market in which to trade. Alternatively, they may be trying to frighten off a new foreign competitor by keeping them busy back home. Internationalisation may be part of either a cost leadership or a focus strategy (see Porter's generic strategies above). Increasing sales is one way to increase profits, but the alternative (or complementary) way is through reducing costs. This can be achieved through the economies of scale that come from dealing in larger volumes of goods – volumes that the international marketplace can deliver. These cost savings can then be passed on to all customers as lower prices.

Risk spreading

Some firms trade in multiple markets in order to reduce risk through geographical diversification. The hope is that although some markets may suffer downturns, the others will make up for it. Unfortunately, as world trade becomes more and more globalised, and trading blocs such as the European Union grow larger, the economies of countries are more closely linked and they have a greater tendency to move together. It still remains the case, though, that risk may be spread by marketing a range of products in multiple markets.

Globalisation

One of the upsides of globalisation is that as markets become more similar, and more open to foreign products, it becomes easier to compete globally. It may even be necessary to trade internationally in order to maintain a reputation as a serious competitor.

Excess capacity

If demand is falling, or new technology has made a product easier to produce, or there have been significant productivity gains, then a company may have more products than it can sell. It will either have to downsize (produce less) or find new markets for its products – quite possibly overseas markets.

Extending the product life cycle

Moving to a new, foreign market, is a traditional method of extending a product's life cycle. Car manufacturers used to employ this strategy, selling their old models to third-world countries when their home markets no longer wanted them. With the increase in international communications, this has become harder to do. Consumers the world over see the latest products and styles on television and the Internet. It is harder to fob them off with old products.

ACTIVITY

Find three local businesses which do not trade internationally (they can be very small). What stops them from growing into international markets?

Market selection criteria

International marketing managers are constantly watching the international environment looking for threats and opportunities. They must select the most promising markets to trade in and reject the rest. They need to consider both the market generally and their own firm's potential within it. Management should set minimum acceptable levels for sales, profit, market share, and then analyse the potential of the new market to assess the likelihood of achieving those levels. This is called market screening. It requires managers to ask the following questions:

market screening

assessing the potential of a new market to achieve desired levels of sales, profit, market share and/or other objectives

- How does the market's potential for profit, sales, market share compare to the company's expectations from an overseas market?
- Does the country have an acceptable legal system (e.g. patent laws)?
- Is the market accessible?
- Is there a suitable marketing infrastructure (e.g. distributors, retailers, agencies)?
- Do existing competitors have too strong a hold on the market?
- Is the level of risk acceptable?

The assessment of political risk is especially important when considering whether to start trading in another country (or whether to stop). Some countries have unstable governments that may exercise powers that other governments would not, e.g. by nationalising an industry or demanding payments of various kinds to allow continued trading. Economic instability and changing exchange rates are also factors that introduce potential risk.

If the country passes the screening, then the company will want to assess its own chances of success in that market:

- How much experience does the company have in similar markets and how well has it done there?
- Are there matches in terms of language and other cultural factors?
- Are there opportunities for standardisation?

The answers to these questions, and others like them, will determine whether the new market is likely to be a success.

ethical focus: data theft worries US businesses

Many of us think about the problems of having our own personal data stolen but such worries are not confined to individuals, businesses are worried too. In a survey released at the end of March 2013, more than a quarter of American businesses reported that their propriety data or trade secrets were stolen from their China operations. More than 40% of the companies in the survey saw the risk of data breach in their China operations rising. Clearly, security is a major concern.

Source: Tejada (2013)

STANDARDISATION vs. ADAPTATION

A critical question in international marketing is whether to standardise your offerings worldwide or to adapt them to local needs. Remembering that the marketing philosophy is about satisfying customer needs and wants, it would seem that the best strategy would be to adapt to meet local needs. So if the Spanish want batter mix in smaller pack sizes, with less sugar and all the instructions in Spanish only – so be it. The main snag with this approach is that it is expensive.

This is not just about products themselves. It is almost always cheaper to do things the same way everywhere. Promotion is cheaper if you can make one advert for the world; use the same prize draw, the same media. Distribution can be handled more effectively if a company can use the same retailers, the same logistics.

Standardisation is not just about costs. It also fits with a strategy of marketing integration – the philosophy behind which is that if we standardise, then our offering sends the same message the world over, reinforcing the desired positioning and avoiding conflict and confusion. However, most product offerings are difficult to standardise across multiple countries and consequently very few truly global (i.e. standardised) products exist. There are, however, an increasing number of global brands.

Reasons to standardise internationally

- economies of scale
- the Internet and other technologies have bridged culture and language gaps
- globalised communications media mean that people across the world get the same information and are exposed to the same influences
- some products have no cultural sensitivity – the main barrier to standardisation is national culture but some products really have no cultural values associated with them, e.g. paper clips, raw materials, computer mice
- there are market segments that exist across international boundaries, e.g. the youth market
- members of trading blocs, such as ASEAN, are growing more similar. It would be a big mistake to assume that the citizens of such blocs are all the same though. EU countries, for example, are enormously culturally varied.

Reasons to adapt internationally

- different cultures
- different income levels – this affects product design (number of features, quality of materials) as well as pricing
- different market infrastructure – e.g. different competitors, different types of distribution systems
- different climate – think about clothing, for instance, or duvets
- different legal requirements and regulations
- availability and level of local skills – can a complex product be supported properly?
- differing uses – will a product be used every day or occasionally? By one person or by many? For example, bicycles may be everyday transport (in parts of South East Asia) or recreational (USA) or either (UK)
- brand history – sometimes a product is held dear by its customers and is hard to change, e.g. Coca-Cola still markets Thums Up in India though nowhere else. In Europe, Mars sells the Mars bar while in the USA this product is called a Milky Way. Milky Ways can also be bought in Europe, but they, of course, have a different recipe to the US ones.

India's bestselling cola.

Source: This file is licenced under the Creative Commons Attribution 2.0 Generic licence

The above lists are not exhaustive but present the most common arguments on both sides of the standardisation versus adaptation debate. Particular markets or products may have special reasons for choosing one strategy or the other.

global focus: what's in a name?

Increasingly, manufacturers are trying to use the same name for their products worldwide. In Britain, Jif cleaning cream became Cif to match the rest of Europe. Marathon bars became Snickers, and Oil of Ulay became Olay. The UK won on Twix, though; that used to be called Raider elsewhere, but now it's Twix to everyone.

Those name changes were made as part of global branding exercises. Having the same name helps to standardise brand positioning, promotes global recognition and, of course, it's cheaper in terms of packaging, support literature and promotion. Sometimes, though, the name changes because it has to. The existing name just will not do in other languages. For example, Vauxhall used to make a car called the Nova. Ask someone who speaks Spanish what 'no va' means and you'll see why they changed it. In China, Coca-Cola translated as 'bite the wax tadpole'. The Jolly Green Giant turned into 'Intimidating Green Ogre' in its Arabic translation.

Here are some products that never made it in English-speaking countries:

- Pocari Sweat and Mucos (soft drinks, Japan)
- Pipi (orangeade, Yugoslavia)
- Pschitt (soft drink, France)
- Skinababe (baby cleanser, Japan)
- Polio (detergent, Czechoslovakia)
- Shitto (hot pepper sauce, Ghana)
- Krapp (toilet paper, Sweden)

Sources: Paliwoda and Thomas (1999); Dennis (2010)

While the application of marketing management tools helps the company to develop its strategic focus, by providing the detail behind the business objectives and strategies, these strategies then need to be operationalised. The next section looks at marketing operations and implementation in more detail.

MARKETING OPERATIONS AND IMPLEMENTATION: TACTICS, RESOURCES AND ACTION

Once objectives are set and strategies decided upon, it is time to implement those strategies. That requires a detailed action plan. This is still part of the 'How are we going to get there?' question. The broad strategic decisions need to be turned into actual tactics and operational plans. The elements of the marketing mix form the basis of marketing tactics. Decisions have to be made about the specifics of pricing, marketing communications, distribution and the product.

It is important to set objectives before planning the marketing mix. If you just get into your car and drive, without first deciding where you want to go, then you will drive around aimlessly. To reach a destination, you have to know where you want to be and plan a route to get there. The marketing mix is the organisation's route to its marketing objectives.

A well-designed marketing mix will:

- achieve marketing objectives
- meet customers' needs

- create competitive advantage
- be well integrated (each element supporting the others)
- fit within the available marketing resources.

Resources and timing need to be carefully considered. One way of considering the resource requirements is the 3Ms approach that was first suggested by Smith, Berry and Pulford (1997). The 3Ms stand for:

- money
- men
- minutes.

MONEY

Money refers to budgeting for the plan – the financial requirements needed to put the marketing plan into action.

The budget is critical in determining what marketing activities can be afforded and also in assessing the overall contribution that marketing has made to the firm. Unless there are some particular and exceptional circumstances, companies expect the returns from marketing to exceed the expenditure so that marketing has made a positive financial contribution to the business. In practice, many related marketing costs may be hidden or placed in other budgets. For example, customer services may be part of a separate department and budgeted separately. Corporate branding, signage, livery and stationery may be a separate budget, PR and publicity may be separated from marketing, and so on. As a consequence, it is not necessarily easy to fully assess marketing contribution.

MEN

This element of the resources relates to the human resources (men *and women*) required by the plan, not only in terms of numbers of staff, but also their skills and experience and how they are to be organised. The marketing department may need extra staff, more sales staff may be required, the staffing may have to be restructured, a new call centre might need to be set up, new agencies appointed, and so on. Consideration has to be given to the extent to which in-house staffing will undertake the marketing activities versus outsourcing.

research focus

Ngo, L.V. and O'Cass, A. (2012) 'Performance implications of market orientation, marketing resources, and marketing capabilities', *Journal of Marketing Management*, 28 (1–2): 173–87.

This paper examines how market orientation, marketing resources and marketing capabilities contribute to a firm's performance. The results show that being market-orientated influences the level of marketing resources firms possess and the capability to deploy such resources. The findings show marketing resources and marketing capabilities are significant drivers of a firm's performance, and their impact is greater when they are complementary to each other.

extrapolate

use already established
data (or experience) to
predict the unknown, e.g.
using last year's sales
figures, adjusted for current
conditions, to forecast this
year's figures

market fragmentation

a market characterised by
a large number of relatively
small players, none of which
has significant competitive
advantage

market sensing

the need for an
understanding of the
market, rather than merely a
knowledge of it

MINUTES

Minutes are to do with the timescale of the plan, the scheduling of activities and the time for tasks to be completed.

CONTINGENCY PLANS

Analysing the market is not just a means to facilitate strategic choice; it also helps to plan for an uncertain future. The theory, of course, is that by analysing the past, one can extrapolate forward. Consider what happens if there is a recession, a war, a new unknown competitor, a new alliance between two firms that wish to steal your market share, a takeover bid for your main customer, further market fragmentation, Internet meltdown, an increase in average life expectancy to 145 years. Clearly, some of these are more likely to happen than others. Possible future events can be ranked by probability of their occurrence and their potential impact on the business. This can be part of the opportunities and threats analysis.

Although marketing research (see Chapter 5) provides good clues as to the nature of the problems that may arise in a market, there is always room for the unexpected. Piercy (2009) coined the term market sensing, which is the need for an understanding of the market rather than merely knowledge of it. Understanding is about synthesised knowledge – you may know a lot, but how well do you understand it? Piercy produced a framework to help managers categorise the potential series of events that may impact on their business (see Exhibit 12.12).

probability of event occurring

	high	medium	low
7			
6	utopia		field of dreams
5			
4		things to watch	
3			
2	danger		future risks
1			

effect of the event on the company

1 = disaster; 2 = very bad; 3 = bad; 4 = neutral; 5 = good; 6 = very good; 7 = ideal

EXHIBIT 12.12 Piercy's framework for market sensing

Source: Piercy (2009: 256)

The purpose, of course, in identifying potential problems is for the company to prepare itself to take some action. Then if the worst happens, the company is not left wondering what to do and can take an already agreed new course of action quickly (Plan B). It is, of course, not possible to develop masses of options as this could take as much time and effort as it did to develop Plan A, but it is prudent to have some rudimentary ideas that can be picked up quickly should things go wrong. Organisations must continuously scan their environment and monitor their original plans so that they see when a contingency plan needs to be put into action. This involves tracking of ongoing performance and evaluation of the outcomes at the end of the planned period. This is all part of the next stage of the marketing management and planning process – marketing evaluation and control.

MARKETING EVALUATION AND CONTROL

Evaluation and control of marketing activities provide an understanding of how well the decisions made by marketing managers are working. They address two of those strategic questions: 'Are we getting there?' and 'Have we arrived?' This involves ongoing tracking over the period of the implementation of the plan and a final evaluation at the end of the period. Tracking allows for modifications to the planned activities if required and, perhaps, the implementation of contingency plans, as described above. If necessary, objectives and strategies can be amended as can tactics and operations. The final evaluation is fed back into the next planning cycle. The process requires analysis of the variance between planned (target or budgeted) and actual performance across the range of activities that are affected by the decisions made (variance analysis). The evaluation process may also, and indeed often does, take into account how well the company has performed in comparison to its competitors, especially the industry leaders. Effective evaluation and control therefore result in successful adjustments to activities in order to achieve the intended objectives. Exhibit 12.13 provides a summary of the evaluation and control process.

variance analysis

measuring the difference between a desired (or expected) outcome and the actual outcome, e.g. sales objectives

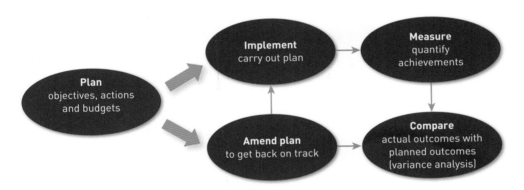

EXHIBIT 12.13 Marketing evaluation and control process

While it is clearly important to measure the extent to which the desired outcomes are being achieved, or have already been achieved, it is also necessary to assess the efficiency and effectiveness of the marketing effort. Marketing activities should always be carried out without wasting effort or resources. It is said that efficiency is about doing things right whereas effectiveness is about doing the right things, and both are important. The sort of questions that should be asked include:

- What was expected to happen?
- What did happen?
- What was the effect of each of the marketing elements as well as their collective effect? Can these effects be separated from other factors? That is, are we sure that the results were due to our specific marketing efforts?

- What were the reasons for success or failure?

- What was learned from the plan?

- What does this tell us that we can apply to the next planning period?

The range of evaluation and control mechanisms is vast. The following are just a few examples:

- profitability analysis

- production analysis

- sales analysis

- customer service analysis

- benchmarking and competitor analysis.

research focus

Wedel, M. and Kannan, P.K. (2016) 'Marketing analytics for data-rich environments', *Journal of Marketing,* **80 (6): 97–121.**

This paper is a critical examination of marketing analytics methods which traces their historical development, examining their applications to structured and unstructured data generated internally or externally to a firm, and reviewing their potential to support marketing decisions

All elements of the product offering and the marketing plan can, and should, be examined. Marketing metrics highlight the need to measure and assess all possible aspects of marketing that can be measured. The level and quantity of detail can be extensive. Measurements will include the following and a great deal more.

Product
- market share
- sales by segment and customer group
- performance of new products
- level of complaints.

Price
- profit margin
- discounts offered and level
- price analysis by customer segment
- comparisons to competing products
- level of contribution.

Place

- channel costs
- channel volume
- delivery time
- stock levels
- performance of individual channel members.

Promotion

- cost per contact made
- media coverage and levels of exposure to communications
- customer awareness levels; recognition and recall
- attitudes to, and perceptions of, the communication, brand, company
- customer enquiries generated.

Physical evidence

- customer awareness of, and attitudes towards, the physical aspects of service provision
- efficiency of store or outlet layout.

Processes

- length of time from beginning to end
- efficiency and effectiveness of the process
- how well the planning and management were carried out
- the systems and procedures to ensure customer satisfaction.

People

- number of people involved, agencies involved
- performance of the people, agencies involved
- skills and competencies
- training delivery
- qualifications
- rewards and incentives.

EXHIBIT 12.14 Elements of evaluation and control applied to the marketing mix

Having identified any areas of business that are underperforming, managers must decide how to address the shortfalls – either strategically or tactically – which is where contingency planning comes into force. The decisions, of course, will depend on the nature of the problem identified. For example, if there is a shortfall in sales, the company may decide to:

- target a new segment of the market (strategic)
- temporarily change prices (tactical)
- redirect the sales effort or send salespeople on a training programme (operational).

The speed and efficiency with which shortfalls are addressed are often crucial to the ongoing success of the business.

Failure to implement a strategic plan successfully may ultimately result in the failure of the company. The plan is likely to fail if there is a lack of support from employees or it may, quite simply, be the wrong strategic choice for the company at that time (see Exhibit 12.15 for possible reasons for failure).

<table>
<tr><td>Lack of chief executive officer (CEO) support or managerial conflict</td><td>Failure to take account of individuals and skills within the company</td></tr>
<tr><td>Too narrow an outlook (e.g. marketing myopia)</td><td>Using the wrong measures of success</td></tr>
<tr><td>Irreversible decline of the company or market</td><td>Failure to take account of changes in the marketing environment (e.g. technological advances)</td></tr>
<tr><td>Emphasis on where to complete, rather than how to compete</td><td>Lack of information, or incorrect information, or information withheld from key decision-makers</td></tr>
<tr><td>'Me-too' instinct</td><td>Failure to implement the plan as intended</td></tr>
</table>

EXHIBIT 12.15 Reasons for failure in strategic planning

ORGANISING FOR MARKETING

The structure of organisations may make it difficult to coordinate and manage different departments and specialisms. Management's response when faced with large, many-faceted tasks has been to divide them into sub-units (departments) in order to cope with the magnitude of operations and to outsource activities by commissioning specialists to undertake certain tasks (e.g. advertising and promotion agencies, market research agencies, call centres, etc.). While project teams and cross-functional assignments can help to improve working arrangements, organisational barriers remain that may impede the smooth implementation of marketing plans. Schultz (1993b) has identified these barriers as:

- hierarchical management structures
- vertical communications
- horizontal communications
- turf battles
- power struggles
- functional silos.

hierarchical management structure

each manager has a set place within a vertical chain of command

vertical communications

communications happen up and down the hierarchical organisation structure, e.g. sales manager to salesperson and vice versa

horizontal communications

sideways communications within an organisation, e.g. between workgroups or departments

turf battles

when individual managers or departments fight for their own interests at the expense of those of other managers or departments

functional silo

when departments or work groups act as independent entities rather than as components of a much larger system despite having many overlapping activities and information needs

When faced with these barriers, individuals and groups may conflict as they protect their own specialisation and interests. These stakeholders may be within the organisation or outside it, and their vested interests can vary significantly.

Shareholders will be looking for profits and returns on investment. Suppliers will be looking for continuity of custom. Employees will want security, a good working environment and good wages. They will be concerned with fulfilling their own departmental objectives, which will differ between departments even though they may share the same organisational objectives, and so on.

Somehow, the organisation as a whole needs to balance these interests to achieve a level of satisfaction for all. An added complexity is that marketing departments frequently make use of a wide variety of external agencies which may, in turn, experience barriers and conflict not only with the organisation itself but also between themselves. Where distribution channels are used, such as wholesaler, retailer and physical distributor companies, these channel members also add to the complexity of interrelationships. Thus, from a marketing point of view, the complete and extended marketing organisation is a family of interrelated departments and organisations, many of which lie outside the direct control of marketing managers but which nevertheless have to be managed.

research focus

Moorman, C. and Day, G.S. (2016) 'Organizing for marketing excellence', *Journal of Marketing,* **80 (6): 6–35.**
   This review of 25 years of scholarship on marketing organisation examines the individual and integrative roles of four elements of marketing organisation: capabilities, configuration (including structure, metrics and incentives), culture, and the human capital of marketing leadership and talent.

McKinsey's 7S framework helps with understanding the interaction between these different elements (both inside and outside the company) in implementing marketing strategies and programmes (see Exhibit 12.16).

A company uses the particular *skills* of many different *staff* who require organising (*structuring*) in a way that maximises their benefit to the company. The company uses different *systems* in order to operate, e.g. computer systems, decision-making systems, work processing systems. It adopts a distinct *style* based on its leaders and organisational culture, and all individuals must *share values* that are similar in order to meet the *strategic* goals.

Making strategy happen, however, presents a distinct set of problems to many managers as, by its nature, it involves change, which people have a tendency to resist. Change within the marketplace is to be expected and welcomed and the organisation has to respond appropriately. Change is also initiated within the organisation, not only as a response to market changes but also in a proactive way as managers seek to improve their performance, their effectiveness and efficiency, and plan for anticipated future events.

Addressing issues such as these requires internal marketing. The purpose of internal marketing is to address the concerns, and therefore needs, of different groups or segments of employees. For some, concerns may come from a lack of information on the changes, while others may not possess the know-how or skills to act upon the changes proposed. Others may have both the knowledge and the know-how but lack the willpower or may hold different vested interests.

Richard Branson: losing my virginity

internal marketing
also called internal PR, it addresses the needs (particularly information needs) of employees

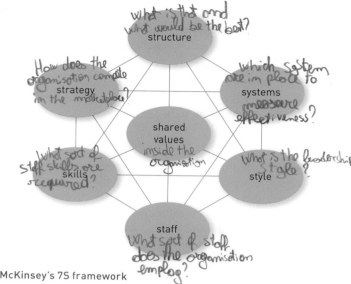

EXHIBIT 12.16 McKinsey's 7S framework

Source: Peters and Waterman (2004)

For each of these internal segments, management must inform, develop through appropriate training and incentivise appropriately. Internal marketing is an important activity that will enable a company to remain focused on the needs of its customers.

> Firms that do not or will not embrace the issues of internal marketing and incorporate those ingredients into their strategic marketing plan will see their market share and profit base erode. Internal promotion can create a positive and/or superior image of the firm and its products in the mind of the customer. (Greene et al., 1994: 10)

ORGANISATIONAL STRUCTURES

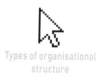

Types of organisational
structure

An organisation's structure gives clues as to how customer-focused it is and, therefore, its likely attitude towards marketing. Although many companies have a marketing department, roles within this department vary depending on the type of business conducted or types of customer it serves. For example, the marketing department in a b2b company, i.e. one that does not have direct contact with end-users or consumers, may primarily be a sales team, while a company managing a number of brands is likely to have product, brand and category managers.

The following are examples of different types of typical organisational structure:

- *functional*: based on the different management functions that run the business, e.g. marketing, human resources, finance, manufacturing

- *geographic*: based on the regions where the company operates, e.g. Europe

- *product*: based on the products, groups of products or brands the company manages

- *market/customer groups*: based on the markets or customer groupings in which the company operates, e.g. Dell operates in both customer and b2b markets, which include education, and small- and medium-sized businesses; particularly important customers, i.e. those that are strategically important to the company, may be dealt with as key accounts:

- *matrix*: a hybrid-type structure where the company incorporates all functions into teams supporting different products or brands
- *network*: a highly versatile and relatively new approach that is, in essence, a coalition between a number of independent specialist firms, coordinated by a 'control centre' organisation. Specialist firms may be product designers, component manufacturers or distributors.

A company may choose a mix of the structure types and structures may change over time. There is no single best solution. Exhibit 12.17 gives some examples of the different types of structure that can be adopted.

(a) Marketing organisation – functional management structure

(b) Marketing organisation – hybrid of product, geographical and functional

(Continued)

EXHIBIT 12.17 (Continued)

(c) Marketing organisation – product/brand management structure (FMCG)

(d) Marketing organisation – market/customer management structure

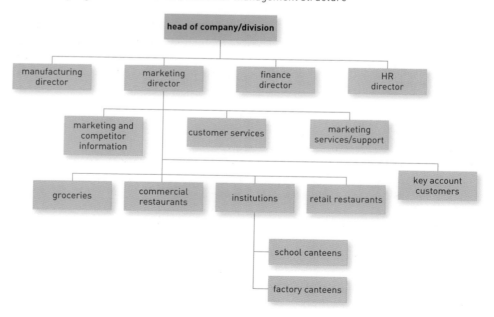

(e) Marketing organisation – matrix structure (product/market matrix)

| | | MARKET MANAGERS | | |
	Menswear	Womenswear	Furnishings	Industrial
Rayan				
Nylon				
Orlon				
Dacron				

PRODUCT MANAGERS

EXHIBIT 12.17 Illustration of organisational structures

The structure a company adopts depends on its core values and the strategies of the management team and should be in line with organisational aims and objectives. It is important to recognise that structure is evolutionary since companies operate in a dynamic environment and, in order to retain position, will evolve to ensure they remain at the forefront of their customers' minds. Such changes must be managed particularly well in order to ensure that the company's stakeholders are not alienated. It is why, yet again, we need to appreciate that internal marketing is an important part of the process in aligning the business to meet the needs of customers.

TOP-DOWN OR BOTTOM-UP PLANNING?

Top-down planning is when senior managers specify objectives, budgets, strategies and plans that are then passed down to operating functions to put into action. The bottom-up approach works in reverse. Objectives, budgets and plans are set at operational level and are passed up to senior management for approval and consolidation into the company's overall plans (see Exhibit 12.18). Both processes have their advantages and disadvantages but they do not need to be mutually exclusive. It is often advisable to use both approaches together. Involving more people in the planning process makes it more likely that they will agree with and adhere to the plans developed.

Some companies adopt an outside-in approach (Schultz, 1993a) to their management and planning, in contrast to an inside-out approach. An organisation with an outside-in approach looks outwards, focusing on the needs of the marketplace to determine appropriate courses of marketing action. Customer perspectives are adopted and so this approach corresponds with a strong marketing orientation (see Chapter 1). The inside-out approach is inner-directed and focuses on the needs of the organisation first, and customers and the marketplace second. Clearly, a balance of the two is required if the basic outcomes of marketing are to be achieved.

outside-in approach
the organisation looks outwards to focus on the needs of the marketplace to determine appropriate courses of marketing action

inside-out approach
focuses on the needs of the organisation first, and customers and the marketplace second

ACTIVITY

Find an organisation chart for your university, college or place of work.

Which of the structures covered in this chapter does it most closely resemble? Why do you think is has that structure and how well does it work?

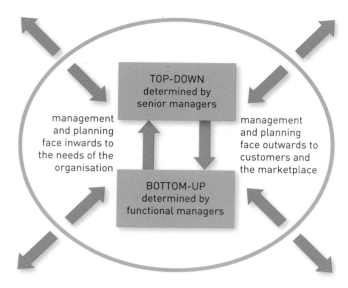

EXHIBIT 12.18 Focus of planning and management

SUMMARY

This chapter has reviewed the marketing management and planning process. Consideration has been given to the types of question that managers need to ask. A simple model of the planning process, which can be undertaken through a combination of top-down, bottom-up, outside-in and inside-out approaches, comprising five key stages that should be aligned to corporate mission, objectives and resources, was introduced. This was illustrated in Exhibit 12.3 and was used to provide the outline structure of this chapter.

CHALLENGES REVIEWED

Now that you have finished reading the chapter, look back at the challenges you were set at the beginning. Do you have a clearer idea of what's involved?

HINTS

- Porter's generic strategies and portfolio analysis.
- Marketing planning process model and marketing plan.
- Contingency planning and situational analysis and environmental scanning (see also Chapter 2).
- Ansoff's matrix.
- Marketing analysis, Porter's 'five forces' model, competitor capability analysis.

READING AROUND
JOURNAL ARTICLES

Darwar, N. (2016) 'Why localising marketing doesn't always work', *Harvard Business Review*, 1 September.

Gallo, A. (2016) 'A refresher on marketing myopia', *Harvard Business Review*, 22 August. Available at: https://hbr.org/2016/08/a-refresher-on-marketing-myopia (accessed 11/11/16).

Sweetwood, A.K. (2016) '4 roles every marketing organization needs now', *Harvard Business Review*, 5 October. Available at: https://hbr.org/2016/10/4-roles-every-marketing-organization-needs-now (accessed 11/11/16).

BOOKS AND BOOK CHAPTERS

Ambler, T. (2008) 'Marketing metrics', in M. Baker and S. Hart (eds), *The Marketing Book*. Oxford: Butterworth Heinemann, Chapter 21, pp. 414–27.

McDonald, M. and Wilson, H. (2011) *Marketing Plans: How to Prepare Them, How to Use Them* (7th edn). Chichester: John Wiley.

Tuten, T.L. and Solomon M.R. (2015) *Social Media Marketing* (2nd edn). London: Sage.

TEST YOURSELF

1   What are the main stages of the marketing planning process? (See p. 466)

2   What are SMART objectives? (See p. 479)

3   What are Porter's three generic strategies? (See p. 480)

4   Define the four growth strategies from Ansoff's matrix. (See p. 481)

5   What are the five competitive forces in Porter's model? (See p. 473)

6   Name and briefly explain four types of 'strategic alliance'. Why might a company enter into a strategic alliance? (See p. 484)

7   Why might a company want to trade internationally? (See p. 485)

8   When trading internationally, why might a company want to standardise its products – and why might it have to adapt them to local conditions? (See p. 486)

9   What is the difference between 'top-down' and 'bottom-up' planning? (See p. 499)

10 Why is marketing control important? (See p. 491)

REVISION TOOLS

Want to test yourself even more? Review what you have learnt by visiting
https://study.sagepub.com/masterson4e

- Practise for exams with **multiple choice questions**
- Revise key terms with **interactive flashcards**

MINI CASE STUDY: THE LOVELY, UGLY BUG

Read the questions, then the case material, and then answer the questions.

QUESTIONS

1   What were VW's objectives in launching the New Beetle? To what extent do you think they succeeded?

2   Applying Porter's generic strategies (see p. 480) how would you classify VW's strategy for the Beetle? Why? Did it change over the years?

(Continued)

(Continued)

3   Using Internet sources and market research reports such as Mintel, Euromonitor and Keynote, as well as the information below, write a PRESTCOM and a SWOT analysis for the VW Beetle.

4   Discuss the target markets for the Beetle and the Mini. How far do they overlap? Have they changed over the years?

5   Using your answers to questions 3 and 4 above, and drawing on the case material and this chapter, write an outline strategic plan for the VW Beetle for next year. You will have to make some decisions about the direction in which VW should go. Use the following headings:

- situation analysis (hint: be selective here, only include important factors)
- objectives
- target markets
- marketing strategies
- marketing mix objectives and strategies (hint: an overview of how each of the 4Ps will be used and what you hope to achieve through that)
- evaluation and control.

The VW Beetle has always been loved. Its original design dates back to the 1930s though it was first popularised as the 'People's car' in Germany in the 1940s. Its superior comfort and power made it the small car of choice in both Europe and the USA in the 1950s. Innovative advertising built brand awareness and fed its popular image. In the 1960s, it starred in movies like *The Love Bug* where, as Herbie, it raced to its owner's rescue and saved the day. This personification of the car added fun to its brand values. People just loved their VW Bugs.

© Robert Couse-Baker

In the 1970s, the story took a downturn. Sales declined as more advanced, comfortable and practical cars were launched. In 1974 the Beetle was superseded by the very first model of another VW winner: the Golf. The Beetle was not quite finished, however, as production moved to Mexico and the car became a favourite there until its much-lamented withdrawal in the mid-1980s.

In the 1990s, it was back! The New Beetle made its first appearance at the Geneva Motor Show in 1996. It was a sensation: streamlined design, slightly larger and much more comfortable than its predecessor and an updated engine, now more conventionally situated at the front of the car. As a nod to its hippy past, it sported a colourful daisy on the dashboard.

The New Beetle appealed to the young at heart: both those who'd loved it in the 1960s, and those who had never before had the chance. The timing of the launch was just about perfect. Fashion had gone retro as baby-boomers got nostalgic about their youth and the youth of the day were intrigued by what seemed to be a golden age. Unfortunately for VW, that sort of opportunity gets noticed by competitors too. In the late 1990s, another German car giant made a surprise investment in an outdated, long dead (but significantly not forgotten) British icon. In 2001, they were ready. The first BMW Mini burst onto a waiting market.

The Mini is quite possibly the most loved little car in the world. It is a piece of British history. A symbol of independence in the 1960s and 1970s, it had been the now defunct British Leyland's biggest hit.

The BMW Mini was a massive success story. It played on nostalgia and the driver's sense of fun. For the people who were old enough to have driven one before, it embodied youth and a carefree spirit. For the young, it was an unusual, quirky small car with a BMW engine. Clearly it was major competition for the Beetle.

Both these cars have an enviable heritage. The earlier models were undisputed design classics: the sort of thing that turns up in museums or is used in films to evoke an era. They are both quirky, fun, small and people tend to give them names. They were both film stars back in the day: Herbie was a Beetle and Minis were the cheeky getaway cars in *The Italian Job*. BMW Minis starred in the film's 2003 remake. They've both always been cool, so why did the Mini outsell the Beetle by such a huge margin?

Volkswagen revisited the design. In 2012, a new generation of Beetle with broader appeal hit the road. The 1990s New Beetle, with its Daisy in a vase on the dashboard, had been seen by many as a woman's car. In the twenty-first century this was a drawback. According to Mintel (2012a), most new car buyers are men in the upper income brackets. The 2012 Volkswagen Beetle was intended to appeal to design-conscious, nostalgic, cool men – as well as to women. A 2.0 litre diesel engine made it sportier in terms of performance as well as looks while also seeming greener. The starting price of just over £20,000 kept it relatively affordable – without actually being cheap.

What Car magazine's review of the Volkswagen Beetle concluded:

It isn't the greatest car to drive and there are other more practical and economical alternatives out there, but there's no doubt that the Beetle will turn heads as it goes past. For some buyers, that could be the clincher. (*What Car*, 2012)

It wasn't the easiest time to introduce a new car. Many of VW's key markets were (and still are) experiencing one of the longest recessions ever. Sales of new cars have fallen as people prefer to buy second-hand or just to make their old car keep going longer.

For many drivers, their car is hugely important to their self-image. Traditionally, cars are thought to confer status and say a lot about who you are and what you value. However, research conducted by Mintel (2012b) found that price is the most important consideration for today's car buyers (for both new and second-hand cars). Other important decision factors are reliability and fuel consumption.

Mintel reported a number of key trends in the car market:

- smaller and medium-sized vehicles are outselling larger ones with cars in the supermini, lower medium and upper medium categories accounting for around three-quarters of UK sales in 2011 (Mintel, 2012a)
- new car buyers in the UK are moving away from mass-market brands towards more individual and especially upmarket brands, leading to a rise in the popularity of German brands such as Audi, Volkswagen, BMW and Mercedes-Benz (Mintel, 2012a)
- value brands, such as Kia, Hyundai, Skoda and Seat, are also selling well (Mintel, 2012a).

BMW have continually innovated over the years and there are now a number of different ranges of Mini, with different price points. The recently introduced Mini Paceman is a cheaper competitor for cars such as the Range Rover Evoque. The Paceman is based on the Mini Countryman but has a re-designed, sloping roof to give it a sportier look. The Volkswagen Beetle will need to be really special, and well supported, if it is to compete.

REFERENCES

Ansoff, I. (1957) 'Strategies for diversification', *Harvard Business Review*, 35 (5): 113–24.

Burn-Callander R. (2016) 'Senator Group's innovation leads firm in funky, new direction', *The Telegraph*, Business, Private Equity Investment, 29 September. Available at: www.telegraph.co.uk/business/private-equity-investment/senator-group/ (accessed 24/02/17).

Chartered Institute of Marketing (n.d.) www.cim.co.uk (accessed 09/04/13).

Dennis (2010) 'Life's bloopers: foreign brand names', *True North Strong and Free*, Canada. Available at: http://tnsf.ca/bloopers/index.php?Page=FB (accessed 03/08/13).

The Ecologist (2015) 'One fifth of Europe's birds are in danger of extinction', 3 June. Available at: www.theecologist.org/News/news_round_up/2894658/one_fifth_of_europes_birds_are_in_danger_of_extinction.html (accessed 09/11/16).

The Economist (2009) 'Let's call the whole thing off', 2 September. Available at: www.economist.com/node/14349451 (accessed 4/11/16).

Greene, W., Walls, G. and Schrest, L. (1994) 'Internal marketing: the key to external marketing success', *Journal of Services Marketing*, 8 (4): 5–13.

Levitt, T. (1960) 'Marketing myopia', *Harvard Business Review*, 38 (Jul/Aug): 45–56.

Mintel (2012a) *Car Retailing – UK – July 2012*. London: Mintel.

Mintel (2012b) *Car Purchasing Process – UK – May 2012*. London: Mintel.

Moorman, C. and Day, G.S. (2016) 'Organizing for marketing excellence', *Journal of Marketing*, 80 (6): 6–35.

Ngo, L.V. and O'Cass, A. (2012) 'Performance implications of market orientation, marketing resources, and marketing capabilities', *Journal of Marketing Management*, 28 (1–2): 173–87.

Nicolaou, A. (2016) 'The future of newspapers: owners seek safety in numbers', *The Financial Times*, 31 October. Available at: www.ft.com/content/a212eb66-9125-11e6-a72e-b428cb934b78 (accessed 08/11/16).

Paliwoda, S.J. and Thomas, M.J. (1999) *International Marketing* (3rd edn). Oxford: Butterworth Heinemann.

Peters, T.J. and Waterman, R.H. (2004) *In Search of Excellence* (2nd edn). London: Profile Books.

Piercy, N. (2009) *Market-led Strategic Change* (4th edn). Oxford: Butterworth-Heinemann.

Porter, M. (1980) 'Industry structure and competitive strategy: keys to profitability', *Financial Analysis*, 36 (4): 30–41.

Porter, M.E. (1985) *Competitive Advantage: Creating and Sustaining Superior Performance*. Glencoe, IL: Free Press.

RSPB (n.d.) RSPB website. Available at: https://rspb.org.uk/ (accessed 09/11/16).

SAS (n.d.) 'Big data analytics is RSPB's secret weapon in saving endangered birds'. Available at: www.sas.com/en_gb/customers/rspb.html# (accessed 09/11/16).

Schultz, D.E. (1993a) 'Maybe we should start all over with an IMC organisation', *Marketing News*, 27 (22): 8.

Schultz, D.E. (1993b) 'How to overcome the barriers to integration', *Marketing News*, 27 (15): 16.

Smith, P., Berry, C. and Pulford, A. (1997) *Strategic Marketing Communications*. London: Kogan Page.

Souhami, S. (2003) 'Competitive myopia', *Marketing Business*, April: 32–4.

Starbucks (2016) 'Our mission'. Available at: www.starbucks.co.uk/about-us/company-information/mission-statement (accessed 02/11/16).

Tejada, C. (2013) 'Many US businesses in China cite data theft', *Wall Street Journal*, 29 March. Available at: http://online.wsj.com/article/SB10001424127887323501004578389433786413300.html (accessed 08/04/13).

Tuten, T.L. and Solomon M.R. (2015) *Social Media Marketing* (2nd edn). London: Sage.

Wedel, M. and Kannan, P.K. (2016) 'Marketing analytics for data-rich environments', *Journal of Marketing*, 80 (6): 97–121.

What Car (2012) 'New 2012 VW Beetle 2.0 TDI review', 17 September. Available at: www.whatcar.com/car-news/new-2012-vw-beetle-2-0-tdi-review/263895 (accessed 18/09/12).

GLOSSARY

4Ps a mnemonic (memory aid) for the marketing mix: product, promotion, place, price

7Ps a mnemonic (memory aid) for the services marketing mix: product, promotion, place, price, process, people, physical evidence

above the line advertising in commission-paying media, e.g. TV, posters, press, radio, cinema

adoption see product adoption process

advertising a persuasive communication paid for by an identifiable source and addressed to the whole of a target audience without personal identification

advertising proposition what the overall advert should say to the target audience, the impression that should be left in their minds (this is not the slogan; the whole of the advert should communicate the proposition)

advertisement see advertising

agent represents other businesses and sells products on their behalf; does not usually hold stock or take ownership of the goods, just takes orders and is paid a commission or fee

AIDA a sequential model showing the steps that marketing communications should lead potential buyers through: attention, interest, desire, action

ambient media unusual out-of-home (OOH) media, e.g. lasers, tickets, promotional clothing, tattoos, pavements

amplification sharing via social media networks that enhances the reach of digital content

Ansoff's matrix comprises four possible growth strategies: market development, product development, market penetration/expansion and diversification

area or cluster sampling the research population is divided into mutually exclusive groups (e.g. geographical region: perhaps by postcode) so that a random sample of the groups can be selected

aspirant (aspirational) groups to which an individual would like to belong, e.g. a professional football team or a particular club

asset-led see asset-led marketing

asset-led marketing basing marketing strategy on the organisation's strengths rather than on customer needs and wants, e.g. by developing products that can be made with existing equipment or through brand extension

attitude describes a person's consistently favourable or unfavourable evaluation, feelings and tendencies towards an object or idea

audience readers, listeners and/or viewers

audience profile a detailed description of audience characteristics used by marketing communicators to tailor their promotional efforts

awareness set a number of products or brands that may satisfy a customer/consumer need or solve a problem

b2b (business-to-business) business dealings with another business as opposed to a consumer

b2c (business-to-consumer) business dealings with consumers

barrier to communication anything that gets in the way of a message and prevents it from being received correctly

barriers to entry things that make it difficult, or impossible, for new competitors to enter a market, e.g. patents, high set-up costs

basic product a bundle of essential characteristics; a product described in terms of the features that deliver its core benefit (e.g. the ingredients of a soft drink – fizzy orange) without reference to service or other more sophisticated elements

behavioural segmentation dividing a market into subgroups (segments) of customers/ users according to how they buy, use and feel about products

belief how or what a person thinks about something, usually based on knowledge, opinion or faith

below the line non-commission-paying promotion, typically all forms except advertising

benchmarking a process of systematic analysis and comparison of one company's performance, measured against another's (the industry leader's), in order to improve business performance

benefits segmentation segmenting (splitting into groups) a market using the benefits people are looking for from the product, e.g. whiter teeth or healthier gums

biographical research an individual's story or experiences told to a researcher or found in other materials

blueprint the original, or master, plan for how to make or do something

BOGOF buy one get one free

boom when an economy experiences a rapid rise in spending, often accompanied by higher prices and raised investment levels

Boston Consulting Group (BCG) portfolio matrix a product portfolio analysis tool involving classifying products or SBUs (strategic business units) according to their relative market share and market growth rate, as stars, cash cows, problem children or dogs

bottom-up approach functions and departments recommend objectives, budgets, strategies and plans to senior management

brand used to differentiate between similar products by means of a set of visual cues (e.g. logos) that represent the brand's attributes and associations (e.g. history)

brand ambassador someone who is passionate and knowledgeable about a brand and recommends it to others; this may be an employee, a celebrity endorser, or a customer acting independently

brand architecture the structure of an organisation's brand portfolio which shows how their brands relate to one another; it typically includes master and sub-brands

brand community a group of people, usually consumers, formed on the basis of their shared admiration for a particular branded product or range of products, e.g. the BMW owners' group

branded entertainment leisure activities, most commonly television or radio programmes, paid for by an advertiser in order to draw attention to its products

branded house a form of brand architecture which uses a single master brand to span a set of products, known as sub-brands

brand equity the monetary value of a brand

brand extension offering further products under an existing brand name but in a new category within the same, broadly defined market, e.g. Mars ice cream built on the Mars bar brand

brand identity the distinguishing characteristics and ideas the company wants its customers to associate with the brand

brand image people's perception of the brand

brand leader the brand with the highest sales within its particular market

brand loyalty the attachment that a customer or consumer feels to a favourite product

brand manager responsible for marketing a particular set of branded products

brand map diagram of competing brand positions resulting from the perceptual mapping process; also called perceptual maps, position maps and space maps

brand name the product's, or product line's, given name

brand personality a set of human character traits associated with a brand, e.g. bubbly, elegant or friendly

brand portfolio see product portfolio

brand promise the way the brand sets out to fulfil a customer need, e.g. Pepsi might promise to be thirst quenching

brand stretching using an existing brand name on products in a different market

brand-switching buying an alternative brand

brand values how a brand is perceived by the market

break even see breakeven point

breakeven point the amount of goods a firm needs to sell in order to cover its costs

breaking down in distribution, unpacking goods (or putting them into smaller boxes) for easier handling

bricks and clicks an organisation, usually retail, that operates both online and offline, e.g. John Lewis, Tesco

business mission the broad aims a business hopes to achieve

buying centre comprises all the individuals that participate in the business buying decision process

c2c (consumer to consumer) business dealings between consumers, e.g. on eBay

capital goods (fixed assets) substantial purchases that are not used up in one go but are expected to be used multiple times

cartel a group of companies that get together and fix prices between them

case study contains in-depth information, built from multiple sources, that forms a detailed picture of a particular situation

cash and carry a wholesaler whose main customers are small retailers who visit the premises, pay for their goods and carry them away; cash and carries do not deliver

cash cows a category within the Boston Consulting Group portfolio matrix, products or SBUs (strategic business units) with relatively high market share in low-growth markets

categorical data also known as 'nominal' data, data that has no numerical value and so cannot be statistically analysed although each category may be counted, e.g. gender, star sign, hair colour

cause-related marketing a form of sponsorship whereby funds are raised for a worthy cause, often a charity (e.g. Tesco's Computers for Schools, Pizza Express's support of the National Trust through sales of its Neptune pizza)

census a survey that includes all members of a population

channel members the businesses that make up a distribution channel; intermediaries

classical conditioning the process of using an established relationship between a stimulus and a response, which can then be used to evoke the same response

classified advertising the small ads, usually placed into specific classifications, e.g. cars for sale, help wanted

closed questions questions that expect a one-word (usually yes or no) answer

co-branding when two companies' brand names appear together, e.g. Intel on IBM computers

cognitive dissonance when a person is troubled by conflicting thoughts; in marketing this is commonly with regard to a purchase decision: a customer may be unsure whether they made the right decision

cognitive learning active learning using complex mental processing of information

cold call when a salesperson calls on a prospect without an appointment

competitive advantage or **competitive edge** something about an organisation or its products that is perceived as being better than rival offerings

competitive advertising highlights and illustrates the uses, features and benefits that the advertised brand has and its rivals do not

competitive edge see competitive advantage

competitive intelligence information on rivals, their products and environments compared with one's own

competitor analysis the process of obtaining an in-depth understanding of rival firms and their offerings

complementary product   one that is required by another product, e.g. a printer needs paper, a DVD player needs DVDs

concentrated marketing   where only one market segment is chosen for targeting

conspicuous purchase   a product or service that is likely to stand out, perhaps because it has unusual or high status or will be consumed in public

consumer   the individual end-user of a product or service

consumer durables   products for use by individuals that can be expected to last for some time, e.g. a washing machine

consumer goods   goods that are bought/used by individuals rather than by companies

consumerism   the belief that increasing consumption is economically desirable

consumerist   someone who believes in consumerism

consumer models   representations of consumer buying behaviour, usually as diagrams

consumer panels   a primary research technique that seeks the views, attitudes, behaviour or buying habits of a group of consumers

content marketing   the creation and distribution of entertaining, helpful or informative material (usually online or mobile) in order to attract and engage a clearly defined audience

contribution   the amount of money remaining from the sale, when the variable costs have been paid

contribution pricing   a pricing method based on variable costs

controllables   events, issues, trends, etc. within the internal environment

convenience goods   products that customers buy frequently and think little about

convenience sample   a sample picked on the basis of convenience to the researcher, e.g. work colleagues

coopetition   when competitors cooperate with each other for mutual benefit, e.g. by sharing research costs

copy   text

copywriter   someone who writes the words for promotional materials, e.g. adverts

core benefit (core product)   the minimum benefits a product should confer, e.g. a pen must write, a car must go

corporate brand   a company brand name

corporate image   audiences' perception of an organisation

corporate social responsibility (CSR)   'the responsibility of enterprises for their impacts on society' (European Commission, 2011)

costs   what an organisation pays for the goods and services it receives; see also direct costs, indirect costs, variable costs and fixed costs

countertrade   exchanging goods for other goods rather than for money; there are various forms of countertrade, the best known of which is barter

creative execution   the way an advert is designed in order to put the message across

creative team   an art director and a copywriter; they work together to create ads

critical success factors   things that the success of an organisation or activity depend upon; they must happen or the objectives will not be met

CRM   see customer relationship management

cross-selling   persuading a customer to buy other products

crowdsourcing   where companies or individuals engage a large number of people (a crowd) to contribute to a specific project or cause often related to efficiency, innovation or problem-solving

CSR   see corporate social responsibility

culture   the set of basic values, perceptions, wants and behaviour learnt by a member of society from family and other institutions

customer   a buyer of a product or service

customer engagement   a customer's connection to a brand – this may have cognitive (thinking), affective (feeling) and/or behavioural (doing) aspects

customer journey   a customer's experience of the brand, incorporating all the customer's brand-related interactions and emotions; this journey can be mapped as an aid to planning

customer lifetime value   a calculation of the long-term worth of a customer using estimates of expected purchases

customer loyalty   a mutually supportive, long-term relationship between customer and supplier, which results in customers making multiple repeat purchases

customer orientation   the whole organisation is focused on the satisfaction of its customers' needs

customer profile   a description of the firm's customer base, used to target customers more accurately

customer relationship management (CRM)   attracting and keeping the right customers

customer value pricing   pricing a product or service according to the value placed on it by the customer

customised marketing   producing one-off products/services to match a specific customer's requirements, e.g. a made-to-measure suit or the organisation of a product launch party

DAGMAR   an acronym for Defining Advertising Goals for Measured Advertising Results; a hierarchy of effects model describing the stages individuals go through when making a purchase, or consumption, decision

database marketing   the use of computerised information used for targeted marketing activities

data mining   using specialist software to analyse large amounts of data (held in a database) to identify patterns or relationships in that data

data warehouse a large database holding copies of customer and environmental data taken from the organisation's other systems and designed specifically to make it easier to raise queries and produce reports

decision-making unit (DMU) all the individuals who participate in and influence the customer's purchase decision

demand the quantity of goods that customers buy at a certain price

demand-driven when a surplus, or potential surplus, of goods to be sold gives the buyers more power than the sellers

demographic segmentation markets segmented by population characteristics such as age, gender, occupation and income

depression when an economy experiences a severe fall-off in sales, usually accompanied by unemployment, lower prices and low levels of investment; sometimes called a slump

desk research (secondary research) the search for good-quality data that has been validated and is now published for use by others

destroyer pricing see predatory pricing

differentiated marketing differences between market segments are recognised and two or more target markets are selected, each receiving a different marketing programme

diffusion of innovations model (product adopters model) categorises product buyers/users according to their take-up rate of new products

digital start-up a newly opened online business

direct competitor a product that is similar to the company's own or the company that sells it. For example, Heineken is a direct competitor to Carlsberg, just as Coca-Cola is to Pepsi

direct costs costs that are clearly due to the making of a particular product, e.g. cocoa and sugar are direct costs of chocolate bars

direct export when a company makes products in its home country for sale abroad and then manages the overseas sales and marketing of them itself

direct mail promotional material delivered by post

direct marketing 'all activities that make it possible to offer goods or services or to transmit other messages to a segment of the population by post, telephone, email or other direct means' (Chartered Institute of Marketing)

direct marketing communications promotional material designed to prompt a direct response from the recipient to the sender

direct-response advertising 'advertising, or selling, through any medium inviting the consumer to respond to the advertiser' (*IDM Direct Marketing Guide*)

direct sales when a manufacturer deals directly with customers rather than through intermediaries in the supply chain

disassociative groups groups to which the individual does not want to belong or be seen to belong, e.g. an upmarket shopper may not wish to be seen in a discount store

discount a deduction from the price

disintermediation   reducing the number of intermediaries in a supply chain with the aim of increasing control and lowering costs

distortion   a barrier to communication; poor coding skills, e.g. a badly devised ad or a badly worded sales promotion, that prevent the message from being received correctly

distribution   the processes involved in moving goods from the supplier to the customer or user

distribution centres   large warehouses that repackage goods into smaller units and ship them to trade customers; they may be exclusive to one large retailer

distribution channel   a chain of organisations through which products pass on their way to a target market

diversification strategy   developing new products to sell to new markets (customers) (part of Ansoff's growth matrix)

dogs   a category within the Boston Consulting Group portfolio matrix, products or SBUs (strategic business units) with relatively low market share in low-growth markets

domestic market   a company's home market, i.e. markets in the same country as the company itself

duty   an import tax charged by the government

dyadic communication   a dialogue between two people or two groups

dynamic pricing   makes use of customer profile and web browsing data to adjust online prices on a user per user basis

early adopters   are amongst the first to try new products, following on from the innovators

early majority   a substantial group of customers who follow early adopters in buying a new product or service

earned media   channels of communication outside marketers' direct control that are used to talk about or report on brands, issues, organisations; traditionally PR media, e.g. newspaper columns/editorials (not advert space), an individual's blogs, individual social media pages

economies of scale   unit costs fall as larger quantities are produced; a cost advantage associated with large organisations

efficient market   a market in which prices adjust quickly, and frequently, in response to new information (in economic theory)

elasticity   a significant response to changes in a marketing variable, most commonly price; if the demand for a product is price elastic, sales volumes will change by a greater percentage than the percentage change in price, e.g. if the price goes up by 5%, sales fall by 7%; therefore if the price rises the sales revenue actually falls

embargo(es)   a ban on the trade of a particular category of goods (e.g. arms) or between certain areas (e.g. the USA and Iraq)

emergency goods   goods infrequently purchased but needed at short notice, e.g. rain capes, sun hats, plasters

end-user   the person who actually uses the product or service; this is not always the customer, e.g. a computer may be bought by a company's purchasing officer for use by the marketing manager (the end-user)

environmental scanning   monitoring the forces that influence the organisation in order to identify changes that may affect performance

environmental variables   factors within an organisation's environment that may change, i.e. PRESTCOM elements

EPOS (electronic point-of-sale)   a computerised system that collects sales data at a retail checkout

e-tailers   online retailers

ethnography   the description, or interpretation, of the patterns of behaviour in a social group or setting; the researcher will immerse himself or herself in a variety of ways into the culture of the group to be studied

evoked set   the products or brands from which a person will make their purchase choice

exchange   when two parties swap items perceived to be of approximately equal value

exclusive distribution   the distribution channel has only one or two specially selected outlets within a specified area

experiential marketing   provides customers with in-depth, personally relevant experiences with products to create a lasting impression either online, in the physical world or both

experimentation   a primary research technique that seeks to understand the behaviour of specified variables under controlled conditions, i.e. not real-world

exploratory (research)   initial research to see whether a more comprehensive study is needed

extension strategy   means of prolonging the product life cycle

external environment   organisations and influences that are not under the organisation's control, e.g. government, competitors, legislation

extinction pricing   see predatory pricing

extrapolate   use already established data (or experience) to predict the unknown, e.g. using last year's sales figures, adjusted for current conditions, to forecast this year's figures

family life cycle   a form of market segmentation based on the recognition that we pass through a series of quite distinct phases in our lives

feedback   a part of the two-way communications process whereby the receiver sends a message back to the original sender

field research (primary research)   carried out specifically for the research task in question

first mover advantage   the first significant company to move into a market often becomes the market leader and can be hard to dislodge from that position

fixed costs   costs that do not vary with production levels, e.g. insurance premiums

FLC   see family life cycle

flyer   a short brochure

FMCG (fast-moving consumer goods)   low-value items that are bought regularly (the shelves empty quickly), e.g. toothpaste

focus groups   a qualitative research technique using a group discussion overseen by a moderator, used to explore views, attitudes and behaviour with regard to a marketing issue; common in advertising research

fragmented industry   one in which there are a lot of players, few of whom have any significant power

franchise   a form of licence; the franchisee pays for the rights to run a business that has already been successful elsewhere, in a new territory and benefits from the expertise of the original owners (franchisors)

franchisee   a person or company who has bought a franchise

franchisor or **franchiser**   owner of a business idea or product who grants a licence to someone else to market or operate it

free trade   trade across international boundaries without government restrictions such as import duties and quotas

frequency   the number of times that an average member of the target audience is exposed to an advert during a campaign

full-cost pricing   prices are set by adding an amount (usually a percentage) to the full (i.e. total) costs of making and selling the product

functional silo   when departments or work groups act as independent entities rather than as components of a much larger system despite having many overlapping activities and information needs

GE-McKinsey matrix   a portfolio analysis tool developed by McKinsey & Co and GE involving classifying product lines or SBUs (strategic business units) according to their competitive position and market attractiveness

generic products   goods that have no discernible difference from each other; often used to mean unbranded goods

geo-demographic segmentation   markets are segmented by a combination of geographic and demographic approaches using house location and house type

geographic segmentation   markets segmented by countries, regions and areas

globalisation   the process of growing to a worldwide scale; it often involves the stand-ardisation of offerings and cultural convergence

goods   tangible products, i.e. those with physical substance

grey importing   when someone outside the official supply chain buys goods (usually very cheaply) in another country for sale in their home country

grey market   see grey importing

gross domestic product (GDP)   a way of measuring an economy; the total value of all goods and service purchased in a country

grounded theory   starts from the intention to generate, or to discover, a theory by studying how people interact in response to a particular phenomenon; theoretical propositions are developed from interview data and field research

hierarchical management structure   each manager has a set place within a vertical chain of command

hierarchy of effects models   describe the stages individuals go through when making a purchase or consumption decision

high-context culture   one where communication must be interpreted according to the situation; much of the message is in the context rather than being explicitly expressed in the words (*see also* low-context culture)

high-involvement purchases   purchases that customers expend time and effort on, usually high cost or high risk, e.g. cars, holidays, wedding dresses

high street multiples   chains of shops, such as WH Smith and Boots

horizontal communications   sideways communications within an organisation, e.g. between work groups or departments

horizontal integration   where a company owns a number of different businesses at the same level in the supply chain, e.g. Curry's and Dixons electrical retailers are part of the same company

hospitality   hosting clients (e.g. providing refreshments in a private room) at events

house of brands   a form of brand architecture which comprises a set of stand-alone brands with their own names and identities, although there may be a reference to the owning brand

hypothesis   a proposition put forward for testing

import duties   taxes paid when goods are brought into a country from outside

impressions   the number of times ad content is displayed

impulse goods   spur-of-the-moment purchases, i.e. not pre-planned, e.g. flowers bought at the station on the way home

impulse purchase   buying behaviour, made on the spur of the moment

incoterms   a set of rules governing the delivery terms for international sales

in-depth interviews   one-to-one research interviews; commonly used in qualitative research

indirect costs   costs that cannot be attributed to a particular product as they are not directly associated with its production or sale, e.g. the running costs of the chief executive's car

indirect export   using a third party (e.g. an export management company), based in the firm's home country, to sell products abroad

inelasticity   little response to changes in the marketing variable being measured (commonly price, advertising, competitive products, income); the percentage change in demand is less than the percentage change in price (or other variable), so if price rises, sales rise

infinite elasticity   the product can only be sold at one price; there is no demand at any other (this is really just a theoretical term)

inflation   when the prices of goods rise without a matching (or greater) increase in their actual value

information framing   the ways in which information is presented to people to ensure selective distortion does, or does not, happen

information search   identifying the various ways a need or problem can be satisfied

innovative product   a really new product, possibly a technological or medical breakthrough

innovators   people who are most receptive to new ideas and are first to try out new products

inside-out approach   focuses on the needs of the organisation first, and customers and the marketplace second

instrumental conditioning   another term for **operant conditioning;** learning a behaviour that produces a positive outcome (reward) or avoids a negative one

integrated marketing communications   the process of ensuring that all elements of the promotion mix are complementary in order to avoid mixed messages and strengthen the brand

intensive distribution   products are available at numerous outlets

inter-media decision   the choice of media class

intermediaries   businesses that form part of the distribution channel, passing goods on towards the end customer

internal environment   the organisation itself, its functions, departments and resources

internal marketing   also called internal PR, it addresses the needs (particularly information needs) of employees

international organisations   there is a head office in the home country which controls overseas sales

intra-media decision   the choice of media vehicle

judgemental sample   see quota sample

just-in-time (JIT)   a lean manufacturing and stocking approach where little or no stock is held

knowledge-based economy   one in which knowledge is the primary wealth creator

laggards   the last people to buy a new product, only purchasing when most other people already have it

late majority   a substantial group of purchasers of a specific product who wait until the product has been well tried out by others before purchase

learning   changes in an individual's behaviour arising from their experiences

legitimate power   influence over others conferred by law or regulations

level of confidence   the degree to which the researchers are sure that data are accurate

level of involvement   the extent to which the purchase is important to the purchaser

line extension   using the brand name on products within the same category

lobbying   a means of influencing those with power, particularly politicians and legislators

logistics   the flow of goods and services through the supply chain

logo   a graphical device associated with an organisation

loss leader   a product that is sold at a loss, usually to tempt shoppers to make other purchases

low-context culture   the information to be communicated is put into words explicitly; there is little need to take account of the surrounding circumstances (*see also* high-context culture)

low-involvement products   products that customers spend little time or effort in choosing, often low cost, low risk or regular purchases, e.g. toothpaste, washing-up liquid, jam

loyalty schemes   ways in which companies try to retain customers and encourage repeat purchases, often accomplished by awarding points (e.g. Tesco Clubcard, Air Miles)

macro-environment   the broad, external influences that affect all organisations in a market, e.g. the political situation in a country

mailing lists   any list of names and addresses to which mail is sent, often potential customers

marginal cost pricing   similar to contribution pricing, a margin is added to the marginal cost (the cost of making an additional product) to arrive at a price

market   a composite of individuals or organisations that have a willingness and ability to purchase products; a market can consist of single or multiple segments

market attractiveness   an assessment of how desirable a particular market or market segment is to an organisation

market challenger   a company that is trying to take over the market leader position

market development strategy   selling existing products to new markets (customers) (part of Ansoff's growth matrix)

market followers   take their lead from competitors and copy their successful ideas and strategies (*see also* market led)

market fragmentation   a market characterised by a large number of relatively small players, none of which has significant competitive advantage

market growth rate   the percentage increase in total sales within a category or market

marketing channel   another term for distribution channel

marketing communications   another name for promotion; communication designed and implemented to persuade others to do, think or feel something

marketing environment   the forces and organisations that impact on an organisation's marketing activities

marketing information system   (MkIS) also known as a marketing intelligence system, the systematic gathering and dissemination of competitive and marketing information; this usually involves a computerised system

marketing metrics   'measurements that help with the quantification of marketing performance, such as market share, advertising spend, and response rates elicited by advertising and direct marketing' (Chartered Institute of Marketing)

marketing mix (*see* 4Ps, 7Ps) the basics of marketing plan implementation, usually product, promotion, place and price, sometimes with the addition of packaging; the services marketing mix also includes people, physical evidence and process

marketing opportunity a chance to reach a particular group of customers with a product offer

market leader the company with the highest sales within a market (also sometimes used to refer to a groundbreaking firm that others follow)

market led companies take their lead from competitors and copy their successful ideas and strategies (they are also called market followers), i.e. they are more cautious and wait for more radical ideas to be tested by others first

market orientation provision of customer value determines an organisation's direction

market penetration pricing pricing a product lower than competitors in order to gain market share

market penetration strategy encouraging existing customers to buy more of a product in order to increase sales of existing products in existing markets (part of Ansoff's growth matrix)

market research the systematic gathering, recording and analysing of customer and other market-related data

market screening assessing the potential of a new market to achieve desired levels of sales, profit, market share and/or other objectives

market segment distinct part of a larger market; a group of buyers and users/consumers who share similar characteristics and who are distinct from the rest of the market for a product

market segmentation the process of dividing a total market into subgroups (segments) such that each segment consists of buyers and users who share similar characteristics but are different from those in other segments

market sensing the need for an understanding of the market, rather than merely a knowledge of it

market share a firm's sales expressed as a percentage of the total sales of that type of product in the defined market

market skimming setting a relatively high price to take advantage of limited competition

mark-up pricing the price is set by adding a percentage (a mark-up) to the direct cost

mass-customisation tailoring product offerings almost to meet individual needs

mass market a homogeneous market, i.e. there is no distinction between segments

mass marketing delivering the same marketing programme to everybody without making any significant distinction between people

mass media communications channels that reach a large, relatively undifferentiated audience, e.g. posters, the Internet, press; plural of mass medium

media class or **media category** type of media, e.g. television, press, posters, cinema

mediagraphic segmentation   markets segmented by reading and viewing habits

media vehicle   the TV programme, newspaper, magazine, poster site, film, etc. in which adverts appear

membership groups   groups an individual already belongs to and which therefore have a direct influence on his or her behaviour, e.g. students belong to a class

merchandise   see merchandising

merchandising   (1) selection and display of products within a retail environment; (2) a form of licensing spin-off products often inspired by entertainments (e.g. T-shirts at a concert)

message   the impression a promotion leaves on its audience

me-too product   a new product that is an imitation of an existing, competitive one

micro-environment   comprises an organisation's competitors, distributors, suppliers and its own internal resources

MkIS   (MarKeting Information System) also known as a marketing intelligence system, the systematic gathering and dissemination of competitive and marketing information; this usually involves a computerised system

modified re-buy   the buyer wants to modify an element of the re-buy, e.g. change colour, size, price or delivery time

monopoly   a market in which there is only one supplier

Multi-attribute Attitude Mapping (MAM)   a form of perceptual mapping comparing a product's key features (according to their importance to target customers) with features offered by competitive brands

multi-branding   a strategy employed by companies that have multiple products within the same category

multichannel distribution   the use of different types of channel to reach the same target market

Multidimensional Scaling (MDS)   a form of perceptual mapping that establishes similarities and differences between competing brands

multinational   see multinational organisation

multinational organisation   corporations with subsidiary companies in other countries which have significant power although they answer to the parent company

new media   makes use of modern technologies, e.g. the Internet, iTV, mobile phones, CD/DVD

new task   when someone buys a product for the first time

niche market   a market segment that can be treated as a target market; a small, well-defined market, often part of a larger market

niche marketing   a form of concentrated marketing in which the target market is relatively small, well defined and very focused

noise   a barrier to communication, usually from an external source, e.g. technological breakdown

not-for-profit organisations   organisations whose primary goal is something other than profit, e.g. government, charities, clubs, pressure groups

objective   a goal or target

observation   a primary research technique that involves watching how subjects behave in their normal environment

oligopoly   a situation where the market is dominated by a small number of very large companies

omnibus survey   a large questionnaire that provides data for multiple clients

on-pack promotion   a promotional offer printed on the product's packaging

open-ended questions   questions that invite the respondent to comment rather than just give a one-word answer

operant conditioning (instrumental conditioning)   learning a behaviour that produces a positive outcome (reward) or avoids a negative one

opinion formers   individuals with specialist skills or expertise who have influence over others, often through the media

opinion leaders   individuals who are often asked by people they know for advice or information

opportunities to see (OTS)   a measure of media effectiveness

opportunity cost   alternatives that could have been had/done instead, e.g. the opportunity cost of a lunchtime sandwich may be a pre-packed salad, and an evening at the cinema costs a night's study

organic search results   the natural consequence of a search engine applying its algorithm to find the most relevant answers to a user's query; they do not include advertisements

outside-in approach   the organisation looks outwards to focus on the needs of the marketplace to determine appropriate courses of marketing action

outsourcing   the subcontracting of a business process, e.g. delivery or maintenance, to another organisation

owned media   channels of communication which belong to or are controlled by the client company, e.g. an in-house newsletter, company website or brand Facebook page

own-label   products that bear a retailer's brand name, e.g. Tesco; sometimes called 'private brands'

pack shot   a picture of the product, in its packaging, used in an advert to aid recognition

paid media   channels of communication in which advertisers buy space, e.g. television, magazines, social media sites

parallel importing   when someone outside of the official supply chain sells goods that were bought abroad (usually more cheaply)

participant observation   a primary research technique in which the observer becomes involved with their subjects rather than remaining apart

patent   a legal protection for inventions that prohibits unauthorised copying

pattern adverts   partial standardisation of advertising, useful in international marketing; the adverts have the same look and feel although some images and the slogan may be written for a particular place or purpose

penetration pricing   see market penetration pricing

people   one of the elements of the marketing mix, concerned with distribution, delivery, supply chain management

perception   the process by which people select, organise and interpret sensory stimulation (sounds, visions, smell, touch) into a meaningful picture of the world

perceptual map   results from the perceptual mapping process and shows brands' relative positions (also called a brand map, position map or space map)

perceptual mapping   the process of visually representing target-market perceptions of competing brands in relation to each other

peripheral product   a secondary product often provided as part of a service, e.g. the complementary mints at the end of a meal, shampoo at the hairdressers

personality   a person's distinguishing psychological characteristics that lead them to respond in particular ways

personal selling   communication between a salesperson and one or more prospective purchasers

PEST   an acronym for the macro-environment (part of an organisation's external environment): political, economic, social, technological

phenomenological research   describes the experiences of individuals concerning some specific phenomena or occurrence

physical distribution   the process of moving goods and services between businesses and consumers

physical evidence   the tangible aspects of a service, e.g. a bus ticket, shampoo (at the hairdressers); one of the 7Ps of services marketing

piggybacking   when one company uses the distribution channels already established by another company, usually, but not always, in an overseas market

place   one of the elements of the marketing mix, concerned with distribution, delivery, supply chain management

PLC   most commonly, public limited company but often used in marketing to stand for the product life cycle

point-of-sale (POS)   the place where a product or service is bought

point-of-sale (POS) promotion   the general term for any type of promotion found where the sale takes place; most usually associated with retail outlets

POP (point-of-purchase)   see point-of-sale (POS)

population   a complete group of people, cases or objects which share similarities that can be studied in a survey

portal   a website that acts as a gateway to a number of other sites

Porter's five forces model   a competitive environment analysis tool

Porter's generic strategies   three main competitive strategies: cost leadership, differentiation and focus

portfolio analysis   the process of comparing SBUs (strategic business units) or products/services to see which are deserving of further investment and which should be discontinued

positioning   the place a product (brand) is perceived to occupy in the minds of customers/consumers of the relevant target market relative to other competing brands

position map   graphical representation of brand positions resulting from the perceptual mapping process; also called a brand map, perceptual map or space map

post-purchase dissonance   when a consumer is psychologically uncomfortable about a purchase

post-testing   evaluating the effectiveness of an aspect of a marketing campaign with its target audience after release

PR   see public relations (PR)

predatory pricing   also known as destroyer pricing or extinction pricing, it is when a dominant company sells products at a loss with the intention of driving a rival firm out of the market

pre-emptive pricing   setting prices relatively low in order to deter others from entering a market

premium price   a relatively high price

press   the types of media written by journalists, most commonly newspapers, and magazines and directories

press advertisements   adverts placed in printed media such as newspapers and magazines

press conference   a meeting at which journalists are briefed

press release   publicity material sent to editors and journalists

PRESTCOM   an acronym for the marketing environment: political, regulatory, economic, social, technological, competitive, organisational, market

prestige goods   high-status goods, e.g. Rolls-Royce, Rolex

prestige pricing   pricing a product high in order to enhance its status

pre-testing   evaluating the effectiveness of an aspect of a marketing campaign with its target audience before release

price   how much each product is sold for

price discrimination   charging different prices for the same products/services to different market segments, e.g. off-peak fares

price elastic   when the demand for a good changes significantly after a price change, e.g. price goes up by 10%, demand falls by 20%

price elasticity of demand a measure of the degree to which demand for a good changes when its price is changed

price followers firms that set their prices in accordance with others in the market, notably a price leader

price inelastic the percentage change in demand is less than the percentage change in price, e.g. price goes up by 10%, but the demand is unaffected or is effected to a lesser extent

price inelastic demand product sales are not very sensitive to price changes (*see also* inelasticity)

price leaders set prices for a market; other firms follow their lead

price makers another term for price leaders

price premium a high price charged to give the impression of superior quality

price takers another name for price followers

price war two or more firms keep undercutting each other in an attempt to build market share until one or the other backs off or goes out of business

primary data first-hand data gathered to solve a particular problem or to exploit a current opportunity

primary research (field research) research carried out specifically for the research task in question

problem children a category within the Boston Consulting Group portfolio matrix; products or SBUs (strategic business units) with relatively low market share in high-growth markets

process one of the 7Ps of the services marketing mix; the way in which a service is provided

product adopters model (product diffusion model) categorises product buyers/users according to their take-up rate of new products

product adoption process the stages a buyer goes through before purchasing a product

product breadth the number of product lines a company supports

product depth the number of items within a product line

product development strategy developing new products to sell in existing markets (part of Ansoff's growth matrix)

product life cycle a product analysis tool based on the idea that a product has life stages: introduction, growth, maturity, decline, deletion

product line a product and all its variants (models, colours, styles, sizes, etc.)

product line pricing coordinated pricing for a group of related products

product manager the person responsible for the marketing of a specific product or product line

product orientation the philosophy of an organisation that focuses on making the best possible product rather than on its customers' needs

product placement   arranging for products to be seen, or referred to, in entertainment media, e.g. during TV or radio programmes, films, plays, video games

product portfolio   all a company's or strategic business unit's products

product portfolio analysis   the process of comparing products/services to see which are deserving of further investment and which should be discontinued

product range the products sold by a particular company or, more commonly, brand

production orientation   the philosophy of an organisation that focuses on production rather than marketing

profit   the difference between what something costs to make and the price for which it is sold

profit margin   the difference between cost and price, expressed as a percentage

promotion   another name for marketing communications (one of the 4Ps); communication designed and implemented to persuade others to do, think or feel something

promotion mix   traditionally, advertising, PR, sales promotion and personal selling

prospect   prospective (i.e. possible future) customer

prospecting   looking for prospective customers

psychographic segmentation   using lifestyles, values, personalities and/or psychological characteristics to split up markets

psychological price barrier   the top price a customer is prepared to pay

psychological pricing   the idea that prices ending in certain numbers (usually 9s) appear to be considerably cheaper than slightly higher ones, e.g. £9.99 seems more than 1p less than £10.00

publicity   the stimulation of demand for goods or services by generating news about them in the mass media

publicity stunt   an event designed to capture the attention of the media or other publics

public relations (PR)   planned activities designed to build good relationships and enhance an organisation's or an individual's reputation

publics   PR term for target audiences, the groups of people with whom the organisation communicates

public sector   government-owned organisations

pull   common usage descriptor for part of a pull strategy

pull strategy   a promotional strategy aimed at end customers or consumers

purchase consideration set   the mental shortlist of products or brands from which a person will make their final purchase choice

purchase decision   the selection of the preferred product to buy

pure play   an organisation that only sells online, e.g. Amazon, eBay

purposive sampling   a non-probability sampling method, which means that every member of the research population does *not* have an equal chance of being picked; the researcher uses their judgement to choose the units to be studied

push   common usage descriptor for part of a push strategy

push strategy   a promotional strategy aimed at distribution channels

qualitative research   investigates people's feelings, opinions and attitudes, often using unstructured, in-depth methods

quantitative research   seeks numerical answers, e.g. how many people have similar characteristics and views

question marks   an alternative name for problem children; also sometimes called wild cats

questionnaire   a set of questions for use during a survey

quota sample   picks respondents in proportion to the population's profile, e.g. if 25% of the population are under 25 and female, then researchers set a quota of 25% females under 25 for the sample

random sample   a probability sample (*see also* simple random sample)

reach   the number (or percentage) of the target audience exposed to an advert or other promotion during a campaign; also referred to as coverage or penetration

recall   remembering things (e.g. products, brands, adverts); may be prompted (i.e. aided by stimulus material such as part of an advert) or unprompted (i.e. unaided)

recession   when an economy experiences reducing sales and investment; if this continues, it may go into a depression

recognition   being aware of something, e.g. a product or an advert, when shown

reference groups   the groups to which an individual belongs or aspires to belong

referent power   influence over others gained through superior knowledge or expertise

reintermediation   when a firm seeks to gain competitive advantage by reintroducing or adding a supply chain intermediary

relationship marketing   a long-term approach that nurtures customers, employees and business partners

repositioning   involves moving existing perceptions to new perceptions relative to competing brands

reseller   a business that buys products in order to sell them on to another business further down the marketing channel

response   a reaction to a stimulus

retail   selling goods to customers for their own use, i.e. not for resale

retail audit   a research implement that provides information on retail product sales, e.g. value, volume, market/brand share

retailer   a sales outlet that deals with end customers, e.g. a shop

return on investment (ROI)   profit expressed as a percentage of the capital invested

revenue (sales revenue)   the income a firm receives from the sale of goods and services

reward cards   similar in appearance to credit cards, used to register points given away with purchases (e.g. Nectar card, Tesco Clubcard)

sales orientation   strategic view that focuses on short-term sales

sales promotion   short-term special offers and other added-value activities, e.g. two for the price of one

sales quota   target number (or value) of sales set for a salesperson

sales revenue   the income a firm receives from the sale of goods and services

sales value   the revenue derived from items sold

sales volume   the quantity of goods sold, expressed in units, e.g. 2 million apples

sample   a smaller number of people, or cases, drawn from a population that should be representative of it in every significant characteristic

sampling frame   a list of the actual members of a population from which a sample is then chosen

SBU   see strategic business unit (SBU)

search algorithm   the often complex sets of rules that a search engine applies in order to filter and prioritise web pages

search engine optimisation   a range of techniques employed to improve visibility of websites as high as possible in the list of search results

secondary data   data previously collected for other purposes that can be used in the current research task

secondary research (desk research)   the search for good-quality data that has been validated and is now published for use by others

segmentation   see market segmentation

segmentation variables   the characteristics used to divide a market into distinct groups (segments) and to differentiate between members of those groups, e.g. income, education, gender.

segment   the process of dividing a market into groups; see also market segment

selective attention   the process by which stimuli are assessed and non-meaningful stimuli, or those that are inconsistent with our beliefs or experiences, are screened out

selective distortion   occurs when consumers distort or change the information they receive to suit their beliefs and attitude

selective distribution   the distribution channel is restricted to a few outlets

selective retention   the way consumers retain only a small number of messages in their memory

self-liquidating special offer   a sales promotion that pays for itself (usually because the company making the offer has bought the promotional items in vast quantities and so obtained a substantial discount)

sentiment analysis   aims to identify the feelings (i.e. attitudes, emotions and opinions) underlying user-generated content

service convenience   a measure of how much time and effort consumers need to expend to use the service offered

service-dominant logic (S-D logic)   the idea that all organisations are primarily concerned with the exchange of services rather than physical products

service encounter   the time during which a customer is the recipient of a service, e.g. the duration of a meal in a restaurant

service recovery   trying to retrieve a situation caused by a bad product or poor service encounter

services   intangible products

servicescape   the total environment in which a service is experienced

shopping agents   programs which search the Internet and then display a table of comparative prices for a specified item

shopping goods   carry a relatively high risk, perhaps because they are a high price or it may be that the cost of product failure is high

SIC (Standard Industrial Classification)   a system of classifying products by allocating numbers (codes) to every product category, industry or business sector

simple random sample   the Rolls-Royce of sampling methods, every member of the population has an equal chance of being selected; this can be expensive and often difficult

situation analysis   an investigation into an organisation's or brand's current circumstances to identify significant influencing factors and trends; the most common framework used is SWOT (Strengths, Weaknesses, Opportunities, Threats)

slump   when an economy experiences a severe fall-off in sales, usually accompanied by unemployment, lower prices and low levels of investment, sometimes called a depression

SMART   a mnemonic for the setting of objectives, which should be: specific, measurable, achievable, relevant and timed

social costs   the costs incurred by society generally as a result of business processes or decisions, e.g. the clearing up of pollution, the provision of transport infrastructure

social grading   segmentation by occupation of head of household; the typical classifications used are A, B, C1, C2, D and E groups

social media listening monitoring social media conversations around specific words, phrases and hashtags

social responsibility   a sense of duty towards all organisational stakeholders

societal marketing   meeting customers' needs and wants in a way that enhances the long-term well-being of consumers and the society in which they live

space map   see position map

speciality goods   unusual, probably quite pricey, products

sponsorship   giving financial aid, or other resources, to an individual, organisation or event in return for a positive association with them, e.g. the Coca-Cola Cup

SPSS (Statistical Package for the Social Sciences)   a software program for statistical analysis

stakeholders   individuals or groups who are involved in, or affected by, the organisation's actions and/or performance

staple goods   essential goods, regularly purchased, perhaps always kept in the cupboard, e.g. coffee, milk, shampoo

stars   a category within the Boston Consulting Group portfolio matrix; products or SBUs (strategic business units) with high market share in a high-growth market

stimulus   something that provokes a reaction, activity, interest or enthusiasm

stock-out   when a supplier runs out of a particular product

stock turnover   a measure of the frequency with which items for sale need to be replenished

straight re-buy   where the buyer routinely reorders a product or service without any change to the order whatsoever; it may even be an automatic process

strap line   a subheading in a press article or advertisement

strategic alliance   a form of joint venture in which two organisations work together to achieve their goals

strategic business unit (SBU)   a distinct part of an organisation that has an external market for its products and services

strategic gap analysis   the difference between a desired outcome and an actual (or expected) outcome

stratified random sampling   the research population is divided into mutually exclusive groups and random samples are drawn from each group

subscription   regular purchase payment, usually as part of an ongoing contract to buy something, e.g. a monthly magazine

substitutes   other products that might be bought as alternatives; they satisfy the same or similar needs

supply   the quantity of goods that sellers are prepared to put on the market at a certain price

supply chain   the network of businesses and organisations involved in distributing goods and services to their final destination

supply-led   when a shortage, or potential shortage, of products to be sold gives the sellers more power than the buyers

survey   direct questioning of market research subjects

SWOT analysis   a situational analysis tool that assesses the organisation's strengths and weaknesses (internal) and opportunities and threats (external)

syndicated data services   combine data from responses to questions on various topics, e.g. the British Market Research Bureau's (BMRB) Target Group Index's (TGI) questionnaire

syndicated research   data consolidated information from various studies

systematic random sampling   uses the whole population as a sampling frame but draws subjects from it at regular intervals, e.g. every 10th name on the list

target audience   the people, or organisations, that are selected to receive communications

targeting strategies   used to select a single target market or group of target markets

target market   a group of buyers and consumers who share common needs/wants or characteristics, and on whom the organisation focuses

target marketing (targeting)   the selection of one or more market segments towards which marketing efforts can be directed; sometimes called market targeting

tariffs   import taxes charged by governments

telesales   making sales calls by telephone

tender (tendering)   where firms bid for a contract and, usually, the lowest priced bid wins

test market   a subset of a market in which a product offering can be sold for a short period of time in order to predict demand and to try out and refine the marketing mix

top-down approach   senior managers specify objectives, budgets, strategies and plans that are passed down to functions and departments to put into action

total costs   all product costs, i.e. direct + indirect, or fixed + variable

total product offering   the total package that makes up, and surrounds, the product, including all supporting features such as branding, packaging, servicing and warranties

touchpoints   all a customer, user or consumer's contacts or interactions with a brand including communications and actual use

tracking   marketing effects are monitored over time

trade cycle   patterns of economic activity consisting of boom, downturn (recession), slump (depression), upturn (recovery); also known as the 'business cycle'

trade trial promotions   sales promotions aimed at members of the supply chain, e.g. a prize for selling 100 cases of wine

trading bloc   a group of countries that work together to promote trade with each other and present a common front to outside nations, e.g. the European Union (EU), NAFTA (North American Free Trade Association)

transactional exchange   a one-off sale or a sale that is conducted as if it were a one-off

transactional marketing   focuses on the immediate sale

triadic comparisons   technique used in perceptual mapping in which three products are compared to each other at a time

turf battles   when individual managers or departments fight for their own interests at the expense of those of other managers or departments

turnover   the monetary value of sales; also called revenue or sales revenue

uncontrollables events, issues, trends, etc., within the external environment that are outside the firm's control

unconvertible currency cannot be exchanged for another currency

undifferentiated marketing where the market is believed to be composed of customers/consumers whose needs and wants from the product are fundamentally the same; in undifferentiated or mass marketing, the same marketing programme is used for all

unique selling proposition (USP) a clear point of differentiation for a product/service

unit costs how much it costs to make a single item (usually worked out on average)

unit elasticity price and quantity demanded change at exactly the same rate; as a result, whatever you do to the price, there is no increase in the company's revenue

up-selling persuading a customer to trade up to a more expensive product

value proposition a promise of value to be delivered by an innovation or feature designed to make a company or product attractive to customers

variable costs costs that go up as production increases and down when it decreases, e.g. electricity bills

variance analysis measuring the difference between a desired (or expected) outcome and the actual outcome, e.g. sales objectives

vendor rating a vetting process to help buyers identify where there may be potential benefits or difficulties associated with a particular supplier

vertical communications communications happen up and down the hierarchical organisation structure, e.g. sales manager to salesperson, and vice versa

vertical integration where a company owns a number of different businesses above or below it in the supply chain

viral marketing an electronic form of word-of-mouth marketing that spreads rapidly (like a virus) within the population

visual identity all the outward trappings of the brand, e.g. logo, name, colours and packaging

white goods large electrical appliances for domestic use, e.g. fridges, washing machines (traditionally coloured white)

wholesaler a reseller, buying products in bulk to sell on to other businesses in smaller quantities

wild cats an alternative name for problem children; also sometimes called question marks

word of mouth individuals passing on information, experiences or promotional messages to each other; *see also* viral marketing

working capital net current assets, i.e. available cash and anything that can raise cash in the short term (e.g. stock)

World Wide Web the graphical user interface to the Internet

zero elasticity completely inelastic; you can do whatever you like to the price (or other marketing variable), as there will be no change in the quantity demanded

INDEX